The Holiday Which?
Guide to France

The Holiday Which? Guide to France

ADAM RUCK

Edited by
INGRID MORGAN

Published by Consumers' Association
and Hodder & Stoughton

The Holiday Which? Guide to France is published by
Consumers' Association, 14 Buckingham Street,
London WC2N 6DS and Hodder & Stoughton, 47 Bedford Square,
London WC1B 3DP

Text copyright © 1987 Consumers' Association

Illustrations copyright © 1982 and 1985 Peter Byatt, Spectron Artists

Maps © 1987 Consumers' Association

First edition 1982
Second edition 1985
Third edition 1987

Design: **Bridget Morley**
Illustrations: **Peter Byatt**
Cover illustration: **Ray Evans**
Cover design: **Tim Higgins**
Maps: **David Perrott**, Machynlleth; **Cartographic Services (Cirencester) Ltd**

Contributions: **Val Campbell**
Research: **Martin Hitchcock, Lindsay Hunt**

Filmset by Servis Filmsetting Ltd, Manchester

Printed and bound in Great Britain by Hazell, Watson & Viney Limited,
Member of the BPCC Group
Aylesbury, Bucks

ISBN 0 340 39965 1

Contents

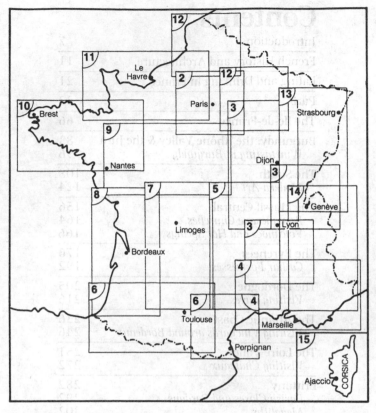

Regional maps of France, designed to help situate most of the places mentioned in the text, are included at the beginning of each chapter. Some chapters cover areas for which there are two or three regional maps (The North, for instance); one map serves part of two chapters (The South and The Pyrenees). The numerical sequence follows the order of the regional chapters after Paris (map on page 34):–

Introduction

Less than an hour from the white cliffs of Dover lies the other world we call the Continent. For the British, France is the closest foreign holiday destination and the closest to the heart. Like the Grand Tourists of the past, you may simply pass through on the way to more exotic climes; but you may look no further, confident that there are few countries which have so much to offer the holidaymaker. The French have long recognised that there is no justification for foreign travel for annual recuperation, and for once this is not chauvinism: France can satisfy every taste in climate, scenery, and holiday activity. You can camp rough in a field, or in the grounds of a château on a luxuriously appointed site with dishwashers and televisions; you can stay in lavishly converted fortresses and watermills, or simple family-run hotels at the centre of any village; you can take a barge on a canal, canoe through white-water rapids, or hire a cruiser to park outside your marina resort apartment; you can meander through vineyards, wine-tasting as you go, or marvel at the most gracious Renaissance châteaux and the most vertiginous Gothic cathedrals; you can risk your neck on an Alpine rock-face, or hike for days through empty hills; you can go to a custom-built sports resort, or potter along country lanes on a hired bicycle.

In southern France, the winter sun ripens citrus fruit and only two hours' drive away shines on the finest of snow fields, while England snuffles in the fog, frost and rain. In summer, you can choose your climate, not with certainty, but with much less risk of soaking disappointment than the holidaymaker in Britain.

There is every possible scenic variation. The Atlantic coast has rugged capes to rival Britain's Celtic fringes, and miles of almost deserted dunes beloved by surfers and naturists; the Channel coast has sandy beaches and quiet coves sheltering long-established family resorts; in the south, the Alps and Pyrenees drop into the Mediterranean producing some of the most dramatic of all European coastal scenery.

Inland there are tamed mountain pastures beneath rocky peaks of breathtaking altitude; there are deserted and windswept limestone plateaux split by wild gorges and pitted with caverns; there are gentle poplar-lined river valleys; there are arid stony hillsides, punctuated by olive trees, striped with lavender and vines. For the homesick, there are well-watered pastoral regions whose orchards are fruitful and whose grass is as restfully green as lushest England.

For the serious or not so serious tourist, France has an exceptional cultural heritage, which can easily be enjoyed as a greater or lesser part of a touring holiday. Paris overflows with art treasures, and is a living work of art in itself—an absorbing place to visit for a few days or a few weeks; but it has no monopoly of cultural interest—the most beautiful churches and châteaux are to be found not only in towns, but throughout the length and breadth of rural France. Provincial museums do not rival the range and wealth of those in Paris but have more than enough treasures to satisfy the most discriminating art lover, and to turn rainy afternoons into a pleasure—even for those with no more than a casual cultural interest.

The French take holidays seriously. One family in nine has a second home (in Britain it's one in 200), and at *le weekend* there is a mass urban exodus to dilapidated rural retreats and to apartments in resort new-towns, such as those which are springing up all along previously deserted coastal regions which Parisian planners have earmarked as the recreation areas of the future. Purpose-built marinas, naturist centres and ski resorts, with quick and easy access to yacht, supermarket and piste, answer the need for convenience tourism. In all the new resorts and rural conversions, French holidaymakers cater for themselves, and more and more British visitors do the same.

The Mediterranean coast has become the epitome of the French holiday experience: steaming, polluted, humanity-packed beaches, the most exclusive and the most action-packed resorts, the finest and the worst value restaurants. Because of the French penchant for doing everything *en masse*, the south coast experience during the holiday months of July and August includes phenomenal crowding, monumental traffic jams and a frenzied atmosphere, while many of the most beautiful inland areas—some of them within easy range of the coast—provide ample opportunity for peace and quiet off the beaten track.

For the British, the lifestyle of the French—preferably when they are not on holiday—is a major part of the attraction of a holiday in France. Everyday life means riotously colourful vegetable markets; shops and stalls with innumerable luscious cheeses and take-away banquets as artfully delightful to the eye as to the palate; and boulevard cafés for idling away an hour or more. Eating and drinking is a serious business, which takes up a greater proportion of French life and income than would be considered decent on this side of the Channel; produce is richly varied, and French wines range from the world's best to those which cost less than water. A new generation of publicity-conscious chefs enjoys super-star status, and they have done themselves and French cooking nothing but good by stirring up gastronomic controversy to stimulate public interest, which has not decreased despite the growing reliance on convenience foods in the home. Eating out, critically and well, is part of life. It explains why French standards are so high, which makes eating out such a special element of holidays in France for British tourists. Highly priced restaurants, which would be exclusive in England, thrive on the custom of great and small who are united in their enjoyment of a speciality creation and in their willingness to pay for good food. The French feel no need to dress up for eating out, and the best classical restaurants feel no need to dress up their dining rooms nor to cast subtle shadows over the food. As far as eating and drinking are concerned having children in tow is much less of a constraint than in England. They are not considered an embarrassment—even for dinner—and are an essential part of the statutory four-hour Sunday lunch with granny that takes place in every rural or small-town restaurant. Thanks to relaxed licensing laws and the nature of the French café, thirsty parents and hungry children need neither be denied nor parted from dawn till dark.

Have the French as friends, not as neighbours was the advice of one punch-drunk ruler who had to negotiate with mighty Charlemagne. For centuries we have had the French as neighbours, but not as friends; indeed the French are still to many closed minds the single greatest drawback of France. The French may be unfriendly to certain visitors from perfidious Albion—the ones who demand ketchup (or still worse mint sauce) with *gigot d'agneau* and who adamantly expect all foreigners to speak English. Any visitor prepared to make an effort, to don a mental beret, will find the French as hospitable and generous as any nation, and will agree with Sir Philip Sidney that France is "that sweet enemy".

This book is the indirect result of research carried out by Holiday Which? over a period of more than ten years, aided by the recommendations of 2,000 Consumers' Association members. Our inspectors have travelled throughout mainland France, visiting cities, towns, villages and resorts. We have inspected museums, art galleries, châteaux and beaches. We have sought out the attractive areas, towns and villages to stay in, and have discovered those which are less attractive. We have inspected, and stayed in, hundreds of hotels. In direct preparation for this edition, a renewed campaign of inspection over the last year covered every area of the country and every hotel selected for inclusion.

France is full of simple, reasonable, peaceful, family-run hotels in town, village and country, where you will be well received and well fed. The hotels we have selected are more than this: whether it be in their setting, their character, their value for money or the quality of their food, they are above even the high average of French family hotels. Many of them are simple country inns, or modest village hotels; some are luxurious hotels, with which France is no less well endowed. Of all the converted medieval fortresses, Renaissance châteaux, watermills and winter palaces, some have style and facilities to match their pretensions, many merely charge high prices. In those we have selected, you are unlikely to be disappointed.

The most frequent requests addressed to the Holiday Which? team are for hotel recommendations. Everyone has different priorities—about food, situation, atmosphere and price. We have not tried to please everyone with every hotel recommendation; we have tried to include only those that we would recommend to friends, and not to exclude any that we wanted to keep secret. The factor that all the hotels selected have in common is the excellence of their food, even in the simplest establishments. Contrary to some reports, it is not rare to encounter bad value and disappointing food in French dining rooms. Many of the hotels which met our criteria in many other respects failed in this vital one. We have, however, included (indicating our reservations) a few hotels which did not feed us exceptionally well, but which are outstanding in other ways—in some cases because there was little else in the area. In city centres, we have not sought out hotels with restaurants. In all but large cities, French hotels are where locals and tourists alike go out to eat. Rural restaurants which do not offer accommodation are rare. Holidaymakers tired of self-catering in a cottage or on a campsite are encouraged to make use of our hotels as a restaurant list.

Hotel Sections: explanation of symbols

All hotels have a restaurant and lift unless we say so. Accommodation prices are the cost of a double or twin-bedded room, and do not include meals. Because we have chosen hotels with a particularly high standard of cooking, there is less variation in restaurant prices than room prices; in nearly all establishments included you could find a set menu for about £15. Some of the prestige restaurants we have included have simple bedroom accommodation; in these, prices are likely to be relatively higher per person for the food than the room.

£	You can expect to find a room for under £15
££	You can expect to find a room for £15 to £25
£££	You can expect to find a room for £25 to £35
££££	You can expect to find a room for £35 to £45
£££££	You should expect to pay over £45 for a room

French History and Architecture

History

Celts, Gauls and Franks France during the last thousand years before Christ was gradually occupied by tribes of Celts from the east. In the 6th century BC Greek traders established themselves in Mediterranean sea ports and, in the 2nd, the Romans arrived. Southern France became the Provincia Romana, three-quarters of a century before Caesar conquered all Gaul in 7 years (58–51 BC). Even when Gaul was Roman, the old southern Provincia was much more thoroughly colonised and the influence of Romans, Roman law and Roman buildings has survived in the language, customs, way of life and the style of architecture of southern France.

Several centuries of Roman peace were brought to a bloody end in the 4th and 5th centuries AD by another succession of invaders from the east, the most destructive among them being the Huns. In the late 5th century the originally German tribe of Franks established control over what is now roughly France, and later rulers extended their control over most of Europe; Charlemagne was crowned Holy Roman Emperor by the Pope in Rome on Christmas Day 800.

These empires were personal ones and did not survive the conqueror, for inheritance was divided. What did survive was the concept of united throne and altar, symbolised in the coronation ceremony at Reims, which went back to 496 when king Clovis was baptised by saint Remi. The moral and material support of the church was of great importance to the later medieval monarchs of France in their struggle to establish true control of the lands and minds of the French people. The story of this struggle, long and bloody, is the political history of France throughout the Middle Ages and beyond, not really concluded until the time of Louis XIV.

Feudalism and war The feudal system has been described as everybody belonging to somebody else and everyone else belonging to the king. In practice, royal control over lands outside the royal domain around Paris was negligible, and resisted by local lords who behaved like kings in their own realms. As long as it worked, the social contract—the lord's protection in return for the subject's economic and military support—bred no particular enthusiasm for the monarchy, whose main interest was revenue.

In the king's favour was time, and the weariness engendered by long periods of fighting. In the 14th and 15th centuries one particular feudal conflict took on national dimensions and did much to awaken national spirit in France. The warring parties were the kings of France, and the kings of England in their capacity as French landowners—English kings up to and including Edward III spoke no English. In the 12th century the Plantagenet kings of England had built up a mighty empire in France and lost most of it thanks mainly to the weakness (always called pusillanimity) of king John. In the 14th century the renewed power struggle was given a new dimension by the extinction of the ruling dynasty of France. Edward III's claim to the French throne and Philippe de Valois' resistance to his claim began the Hundred Years' War, wherein the French and English sides were repeatedly swollen and depleted by other French factions (notably Brittany, Burgundy and Orléans) whose main interest was to ensure that neither side could win. The English seemed to have won in 1418 when, in an alliance with the Burgundians, they forced the dauphin Charles to flee Paris; in 1420 Henry V of England married the French king's daughter and was recognised as regent and heir to the throne of France. Then the almost contemporaneous deaths of the kings of England and France were followed by the appearance of saints to a peasant girl in Lorraine, conveying a divine mission to rid France of the English, which she did. Saint Joan is the patroness of France, the outward and visible sign of an inward and spiritual birth of French national consciousness.

Crusade and pilgrimage The Middle Ages were ages of faith as much as ages of warring nobles and land disputes. A majority of the nobility had no land, for shared inheritance had been discarded in favour of primogeniture (leaving everything to the eldest son). Younger sons could join the church, they could fight for land or a cause far from home, or they could do both by going on a crusade. Crusading is a leitmotif of medieval Europe, begun in defence against invading Saracens in 8th-century Spain, and in the late 11th century becoming a Holy War to recapture Jerusalem and then defend it against the infidel. In the early 13th century, a crusade was launched to stamp out heresy in south-western France. The religious issue cloaked nothing more edifying than a lust for blood and land, and the war which destroyed the power and civilisation of Toulouse to the benefit of the crown illustrates how the church helped the monarchy.

The peaceful version of the crusade was the pilgrimage. In the Middle Ages people travelled far and often: throughout the land there were miracle-working relics and venerated tombs which brought pilgrims and prosperity to a religious community. The pilgrims were not content to pay their respects and make their requests simply at the nearest shrine. The great journeys were to Jerusalem, to Rome and to the tomb of saint James at Compostela in the north-western corner of Spain. Four major pilgrimage routes led across France to converge in the Atlantic Pyrenees on the way to Compostela, and were marked by important secondary pilgrimage churches on the way and by monasteries and hostelries for the accommodation of pilgrims. The international security of the pilgrim was in the hands of two orders of knights which were founded to defend the Christian kingdom in the Holy Land and which were granted lands all over Europe (the Knights Templar and Hospitaller).

Consolidation and Reform The Messianic appearance of Joan of Arc was one sign of a new France: there were many more practical ones in the late 15th century. Charles VII was the first king to have a permanent or standing army, and he had recourse for his war-waging to the funds of a brilliant merchant banker, the bourgeois Jacques Cœur, who made his fortunes from the spice trade with the Orient. Louis XI saw the sense of surrounding himself not with his peers, as feudal monarchs had to do, but with men who owed all their success to the king's pleasure—civil servants. By subtle manoeuvring (he was often called the spider), bribery and alliance with the Swiss, Louis overcame the last of the great representatives of the age of chivalry, Charles the Rash of the noble house of Burgundy.

The 16th century throughout Europe was the century of religious reform, an issue which in France gave the nobility a chance to stand and assert itself again. Religion became a pretext for civil war, involving the crown, the nobility and the towns, both of the last trying to recover some of their lost freedom. On St Bartholomew's Eve 1572 2,000 Huguenots (Protestants) were massacred in Paris, setting the tone of the religious wars which were bloody and unprincipled, as only religious wars can be, and having a similar effect on the countryside and population of France as the endemic warfare of the Middle Ages. In 1589 the crown fell to Henri IV, but the gates of Paris would not open to him because he was a Protestant. Having weighed the moral and political considerations carefully, he renounced his faith in 1593 with one of the most famous throw-away lines in the history of Catholicism: "Paris is well worth a mass".

Royal supremacy The 17th century saw the great consolidation of royal power. By the Edict of Nantes, the far-sighted and tolerant Henri IV attempted to enforce religious compromise by guaranteeing Huguenots freedom of religious practice—allocating them several towns in the south-west—and the wars subsided. Religious wars of a different complexion, but similar savagery, so devastated 17th-century Alsace that the province looked to the French king Louis XIV for protection.

The most glorious period of the French monarchy, the *Ancien Régime*, is the century and a half when the throne was occupied by three Bourbon kings, Louis XIII (1610–1643), Louis XIV (1643–1715) and Louis XV (1715–1774). It is the period of the great civil servants—after Henri IV's Sully came cardinals Richelieu and Mazarin under Louis XIII, and Colbert among others under Louis XIV; of the destruction of medieval fortresses; and of the installation of provincial governors and *intendants* to strip the nobility of their local power.

Louis XIV's accession at the age of five gave the nobility the chance once again to attempt to win back lost influence over the crown. This meant civil war (the *Fronde*) between noble factions, and the king grew up in a humiliating climate of being a refugee in his own kingdom—an experience which made him determined when he finally took full possession of his powers in 1661 to establish the absolute nature of royal authority. Versailles was the appropriate context for king worship and the place where the aristocracy of France could be kept under control—and under-employed except with questions of courtly protocol. The provinces becoming merely the place for disgrace, exile or poverty; as a result, rural France suffered neglect and economic stagnation.

Louis' own comparison between himself and the sun is irresistible. It was a brilliant, heroic period for the arts and philosophy and thanks to the administrative achievements of the civil servants Louis was able to take war abroad and extend the frontiers of France to the east and north-east. But it is in the nature of the sun not to remain at its zenith; the evening of Louis' reign is more notable for lengthening shadows than glorious sunset. After the revocation in 1685 of Henri IV's Edict of Nantes, over 400,000 Protestants took their skills to other countries—the decline of the Aubusson tapestry manufacture is just one example of the effect of emigration. The wars of the early years of the 18th century against a network of European allies were disastrous for France and Louis left his realm in much more of a mess financially than he had found it.

Royal decline Like his great-grandfather, Louis XV came to the throne at the age of five; unlike him he was never strong enough to take for himself full kingly control. The reign of Louis XV was a period of *distractions*, to keep courtiers deprived of political utility and amused. A special Ministry of Lesser Pleasures for Versailles entertainment was the recipient of a lavish endowment of state funds. The nobility's lack of power in the realm was exceeded only by the extent of its privilege, for aristocratic acquiescence in the robbery of its power had been dearly bought in terms of tax exemption. In such a climate it may seem surprising that a revolution took so long to come. It was only in the reign of Louis XVI, when attempts were at last made to improve the lot of the mass of French society, that serious objection to the *Ancien Régime* was articulated in line with the enlightened ideas of 18th-century philosophers. Demands for social and constitutional reform came to a head all over France. Meetings of the three estates (nobles, clergy and commons) were followed by the first meeting for nearly two centuries of the Estates General of the realm. At Versailles, with the famous tennis court oath, the third estate declared itself a national assembly and swore not to disband until France had a constitution. On 14th July 1789 a Paris mob in search of arms went to the Bastille—a once notorious prison for political subversives—stormed it, and liberated the seven remaining prisoners. Bastille Day is celebrated with fireworks all over France.

Republic and Empire The idealism of the Revolution—a longing for freedom—was greeted in intellectual circles throughout Europe and especially in England with the same ecstatic euphoria as it was in France, but soon revealed itself to be above all destructive. Religion and the established church was the main target; churches all over France were sacked. The Revolutionaries even changed the calendar, starting history again at the year 0 and giving the months of the year naturally inspired names—Thermidor for the hot period, Ventose for the windy one and so on. The old order was replaced not by liberty (nor equality and fraternity) but by savage mob rule (the Terror), of which two inevitable victims were the king and queen, guillotined within a few months of each other in 1793. The French soon longed for servitude under an absolute order again.

The architect of the new order was to be Napoleon Bonaparte, a brilliant and daring commander who led the forces of Revolutionary France to conquest all over continental Europe, and met even less resistance in his adoption of imperial powers and status in France. Consciously attaching himself to the tradition of Charlemagne and Christian monarchs of medieval France, in 1804 Napoleon made a humiliated Pope watch him place the crown on his own head. Napoleon's ambitions were not just military. Under his rule, and after it under his influence, France was subjected to more social, administrative and legal reforms than ever before. He confirmed the peasants in their land and freedom, restored the Catholic state, created authoritarian government and established a new system of civil, criminal and rural law—the civil code was known as the Code Napoleon. The Anglo–Austrian alliance finally broke Napoleon's power in 1814 (and again in 1815 when an attempted comeback failed at Waterloo). Several attempts to revive the monarchy all proved unsatisfactory; a Second Republic was even more short-lived than the first and was followed in 1851 by another Empire and another Bonaparte, Napoleon III. France grew fat and industrial as nephew followed uncle's social and economic reforms, but not his military exploits. After a series of defeats the bourgeois Second Empire finally succumbed to Prussian might at Sedan in 1870. Paris spent a winter under seige and Alsace and much of Lorraine were ceded to Germany. The Third Republic, proclaimed after the débâcle at Sedan and confirmed by one vote after the *communard* uprising in the capital had been suppressed, was to last until the Second World War.

The World Wars By the turn of the century, the balance of power in Europe had unmistakably changed in favour of Germany. France allied herself with England and Russia. When Russia resolved to risk a European war in the name of the Serbian cause, France was dragged into the First World War by her obligations, as Britain was by hers to France. By November 1918 France was an exhausted victor, her richest departments had been devastated, her most valuable industries ruined and almost 1,400,000 men lost. The feeling of relief that the war was over—and the need to believe that it must have been worthwhile—was naturally greater in France than anywhere else; it helps to explain the fervent pacifism of French government policy in the inter-war years. When in May 1936 Hitler tested the temperature of the water by occupying the Rhineland, France, to his great surprise, made only token protests. Despite belated rearmament, France was inadequately equipped to resist the German invasion of 1939. After only a few months, Marshal Pétain, something of a folk hero from the First World War and the head of government, asked for an armistice which was granted on terms which included surrender of two-thirds of France. France withdrew from the War and the government adjourned to Vichy, which became the capital of non-occupied France. From November 1942, however, the Germans occupied the whole country. A resistance movement, known as the Maquis, was gradually organised to fight the occupiers and given a lead by Charles de Gaulle. From his base in England, de Gaulle recruited for the Forces of Free France and sent them with the British and Americans to land on the Normandy beaches on D-Day, June 6th 1944. Shortly less than a year later, the last German outpost (Bordeaux) was liberated. General de Gaulle was recognised as the head of provisional government of the French Republic.

Post-war politics After disengaging herself from war in Indo-China France had to face the civil problem of Algerian nationalism (the country was constitutionally part of France), which took on the status of a war of independence after a coup d'état in 1958; de Gaulle was called back from retirement to deal with the crisis. With popular approval for a new constitution (the Fifth Republic) de Gaulle became president with virtually dictatorial power and led France through a decade of renewed confidence and economic boom. The growing complacency, and de Gaulle himself, were broken in 1968, when student riots in Paris and other towns escalated to a general strike.

The influence of the Second World War on French political loyalties has been a lasting one. Such was the bitterness of the years of occupation, when resistance Frenchmen hated collaborating Frenchmen more even than occupying Germans, that a politician's war record is still an important part of his manifesto. Valéry Giscard d'Estaing was the leader of a new generation of technocrat politicians; his record was a financial rather than a military one. Repeatedly Giscard and the Gaullistes called on the French bourgeois fear of communism to keep socialists out of power (socialists and communists have been formally allied since 1972), and it was assumed that as long as the alliance lasted that fear would keep it out of power. In the 1981 Presidential Election the French showed, contrary to all expectations, that they wanted a change not from the old order, but from the new. President Mitterrand is one of the last of the resistance heroes in French politics.

Architecture

Prehistory The earliest evidence of man's architectural impulse in France is the wealth of large stones or megaliths that he raised all over the country but nowhere in such numbers and in such arrangements as in Brittany (see also page 292). These alignments appear to have had mystical significance, oriented like embryonic temples according to the sun's axis.

Roman Gaul There are marvellous Roman amphitheatres, theatres and other civil monuments: Nîmes has one of the most perfectly preserved Roman temples anywhere, built according to pure classical principles. Provence is the fortunate possessor of most of the surviving Roman remains; here invaders from the east penetrated less thoroughly and used Roman amphitheatres for their own fortifications, and old Roman cities were developed much less in later centuries. In other areas Roman buildings were used unscrupulously as quarries by later builders: in Le Puy cathedral you can see Gallo-Roman relief carvings incorporated at random in the fabric of the medieval walls.

Medieval churches There are treats for the lover of churches in almost every area of France. The south is mostly Romanesque (11th to 13th centuries), the north mostly Gothic (13th to 15th centuries). The five centuries preceding the year 1000 were troubled and dangerous times of barbarian rampage and arson; most early Christian buildings were replaced in the new wave of church building which followed. The new era was one of relative order; travel by pilgrims, crusaders, merchants, kings and masons led to the exchange of ideas and artistic influence. It was also an age of faith and economic growth, and powerful monastic orders played a major role. The most important was the Benedictine order of Cluny, which spread from Burgundy all over Europe, pushing back forests and putting up churches.

The style of these churches has since the last century been termed **Romanesque** (*Roman*) to express its derivation from the Latin style, in the use, for example, of the round arch. Compared with classical architects, Romanesque church builders were free from the shackles of theory; styles evolved from the nature of materials, the tastes of patrons and the functional requirements of buildings—abbey, pilgrimage or parish church. As a result Romanesque churches are fascinating in their local variety, their liveliness and their personality. In the north the warlike Normans evolved a powerful and undecorative version of the Romanesque which they exported to England. Because of its sobriety, a familiarity with Norman architecture in England gives no hint of the richness of French Romanesque south of the Loire, where influences from further south and east penetrated along trade and pilgrim routes. North Italian masons took their style and their elegant arcaded belfries to the cosmopolitan and economically precocious Mediterranean area of Catalonia, where monastic builders also drew inspiration from Islamic and Byzantine *objets d'art* and manuscripts to produce marvellously decorative carving in local marble to adorn their churches. The sculptural style spread, not without modification, throughout south-western France; its examples remain the greatest artistic heritage of the area. In Poitou, fresco painting in a similar style was particularly popular; in Provence, Roman remains were the inspiration for a very classical local style of sculpture and architecture. Arab influence is to be observed in architectural features of the Massif Central, and—with less certainty— in the domes which proliferate in a limited area around the Dordogne.

No better reason for the existence of these churches in this area has been found than human contacts; for example, the bishop of Cahors went to Constantinople and when he returned ordered domes like those of Constantinople's church of the Apostles for his new cathedral.

Other developments were practical. The system of a passage or ambulatory around a central shrine, with subsidiary radiating chapels for little shrines, was first hit upon to cope with the crowds at the great pilgrimage church of St-Martin-de-Tours—the victim, like so many churches, of the Revolution. Another victim was Cluny, the greatest Romanesque church of all, whose builders were highly adventurous with vaulting to achieve optimum acoustics for their chant.

The **Gothic** style, which dominated Christian church building from the late 12th until the 16th century, was an engineering revolution; still more it was a spiritual, intellectual and even a political one. It spread across France from Paris and the north in step with royal control and influence—the style for a new era of monarchy. In contrast with the charm and invention and sheer decorative exuberance of Romanesque architects and stone carvers, the Gothic cathedral is programmatic and intellectual. The cathedral as a whole represents heaven, so lofty that it seems to exist as much in the sky as on the ground, and bathed in an unearthly coloured radiance by stained glass. The main doorway or gateway to heaven reminds the visitor of the requirements of entry with a representation of the Last Judgement. The Virgin also features prominently as the period's favourite intermediary between man and a remote God. Stained glass illustrates the scriptures, not just as a picture book for the illiterate but for symbolic reasons—the light of heaven shines through the scriptures to illuminate the faithful.

The new style was made possible by the development of the pointed arch, reducing the outward thrust of round vaults which had a tendency to make walls collapse. The use of ribs in a vault conducted weight to specific points instead of all along the wall, and the flying buttress enabled the vault to be supported not by reinforcing the wall itself, but by using pillars isolated from it. With these techniques, it was possible to build enormously high vaults above slender pillars. Instead of vast areas of masonry requiring frescoes and carvings for decoration, with small openings in the thick fabric for light, the stonework became a mere skeleton for the enormous expanse of stained glass.

The Gothic cathedrals of northern France produce a phenomenal impression of verticality. Architects and patrons often overreached themselves—it was standard practice before the scaffolding was removed to say a mass imploring divine support for the building. The vertiginous isolation of the choir of Beauvais, to which no nave could successfully be attached, is the most striking example of the hubris of daring Gothic architects and vain episcopal patrons.

The great Gothic century was the 13th. In the 14th century everything went wrong—France was torn apart by the Hundred Years' War, the monarchy was humiliated at Crécy and Poitiers, and plague reduced the population of Europe by a third. Confidence was not unreasonably shaken, church building interrupted, and people looked to their faults and those of the church: religious feeling turned inward. Artistic achievements became those of individual works of painting and sculpture; one admires not the *élan* of the whole, but the fineness of the decorative detail. General pessimism seems to be expressed by the flame form of stonework which has given the name *flamboyant* to the late Gothic style.

Medieval secular architecture From the Romanesque age of faith, few non-religious buildings of distinction survive: all aesthetic architectural effort seems to have gone into church building. Later centuries brought prosperity, and town houses began to be built with pride, as at Cordes near Albi. In the wealthy north, town councils spent large sums on the building of magnificent town halls and belfries, monuments of civic spirit.

Most non-religious Gothic buildings are fortified. Such was the war-torn tenor of medieval French life, and the remote nature of royal control in many areas, that castles, fortified churches and monasteries, and complete fortified towns covered France; their ruins remain. Almost every area was strategically important for somebody, from the kings of France and England to local lords who defied anybody from rocky strongholds. In the border zones of English and French territory in south-western France, rival powers tried to secure footholds in an under-populated landscape by founding new fortified towns called *bastides* and attracting loyal subjects to inhabit them. The popes fortified themselves on the edge of their territory in Avignon; the kings of France responded by fortifying a hill on the other side of the Rhône. As royal power was extended, fortresses were frequently maintained to buttress the central authority, or (if appropriately situated) to defend France. Development of artillery forced a major revision of the style of fort building, from the high and dominant to the low and massive. Many other refinements to the style of military architecture (including the use of round towers and concentric plans) had been learnt from crusading experience.

Medieval architecture—destruction and restoration Many medieval fortifications presented a threat to law and order and were destroyed, notably by cardinal Richelieu in the 17th century. Some fortifications have survived because places lost their importance: one example is the old crusading port of Aigues-Mortes where the sea retreated, and the town never grew. In other places, what remain are not survivals but restorations, after centuries of destruction in the religious wars when puritanical Protestants stripped statues—idols—down from niches in façades, and during the Revolution.

The Middle Ages came into fashion in the 19th century. There was a rapid Catholic reaction after the Revolution: in a climate of romantic nostalgia for mossy, overgrown and tenebrous medievalism, Prosper Mérimée was appointed Inspector General of Historic Monuments in 1833. He engaged the young and brilliant architect Viollet-le-Duc to restore churches and fortresses, Romanesque and Gothic, all over France. Without these two, scores of France's greatest medieval monuments would not have survived. Much of Viollet-le-Duc's work has been criticised partly because, as at Carcassone, he imposed a strictly regulated uniformity of style. Carcassonne, having evolved over many centuries, had never had this; what we see today has been described as a puristic concoction. At St-Sernin in Toulouse, Viollet-le-Duc took out all post-Renaissance works of art from the pilgrimage church—where they have lately been reinstated. Another aspect of many restored churches which tends to shock the visitor is the garish re-painting of pillars and capitals and vaults; it is clear that in some areas at least a taste for the gaudy painting of church interiors accompanied the taste for frescoes. What to do about restoring the work of the restorers is still an open question in France.

Architecture

Renaissance to Revolution The 16th century was a period of relative peace. Together with the spread of royal power and refinements in the technique of war-making, this produced a change from fortress to château. From their military campaigns in northern Italy in the late 15th and early 16th centuries the French brought back a taste for extravagant, classically inspired ornamental detail applied to Gothic architectural forms. In the Loire valley, where the kings of France hunted and held court, châteaux were built with many of the characteristics of medieval fortresses—such as machicolations and round towers—preserved and transformed for their decorative value, giving the buildings a quality of playful fantasy. Later in the century architects became more serious students of theory, and directed the French Renaissance into a more classical phase.

At Fontainebleau, François I built the first great royal palace of the Ile-de-France, importing Florentine artists to take charge and give his royal palace the grandeur and Italian pedigree appropriate to his imperial pretensions. In the same way that François' image and ideas are thus reflected in the "Fontainebleau" style, later trends in French architecture throughout the 17th, 18th and even most of the 19th centuries reflect the personal style of the ruler as well as the trend of taste throughout Europe (Baroque, Rococo, neo-Classical). It is not merely convenient abbreviation that has led to the different styles (which do not exactly coincide with the individual reigns) being called after kings Louis XIII, Louis XIV, Louis XV and Louis XVI. "Louis XIII" is a style of sobriety and restraint, in contrast with the excesses of the Fontainebleau school.

The long reign of Louis XIV, the Sun King, was marked by military conquest abroad, and at home by the extension of autocratic royal control over an anarchic and constantly bickering nobility. For such a period, the imposing, rich but ordered grandeur of the Louis XIV style was made to measure—exemplified by the architecture, to an even greater extent by the interior decoration, and even by the regulated order of the park, at Versailles. Characteristic of French might at this time are the fortresses built in an uncompromising geometric way all along France's frontiers by Louis XIV's military architect and engineer Vauban.

The 18th-century age of the Rococo and Louis XV was one of elegance and refinement of manners. It was accompanied by a taste for less formal gardens, more intimate rooms on a smaller scale, and an architectural and decorative style where emphasis was placed on delicacy of detail rather than on the grandeur of the whole.

The second half of the 18th century saw the development of a new moral climate. At first it was a sentimental kind of morality, exemplified by romantic ideas of nature and the noble savage; later, a heroic republican consciousness that built up to the Revolution was accompanied by a return to the strictest classical principles in art and a new interest in the Greeks and the Romans, leading on in turn to the Empire style of the Napoleonic age. The spirit of revolution inspired radical projects from the neo-classical architects but few of the plans for new Utopian cities—built for a new society glorifying neither God nor king—were ever put into practice. In general, the Revolution was a period of destruction on a far greater scale than construction.

The 19th century Napoleon stepped into the ruins of the Republic and replaced it with Empire; Republican classical art became Imperial classical art. Napoleon did not build new royal palaces, but redecorated

Architecture

old ones in what is now known as the Empire style, drawing heavily (and ponderously) on ancient Egypt for inspiration as well as Rome. Napoleon's monumental ambitions were not confined to individual buildings. He wanted to fashion Paris in his image, and did so, thanks to later rulers who carried out his plans. It is to Napoleon that we owe the great perspectives of Paris—including the Champs-Elysées with a triumphal arch at each end.

Napoleon's urban planning for Paris was completed and extended under his nephew Napoleon III in the style known as Second Empire. All the restraints of classicism were abandoned in the new taste for an overload of luxury and display—the tastes of a bourgeois age of money-grabbing and materialism. Baron Haussmann ploughed up insanitary old Paris, drained it and laid 85 miles of new streets lined with façades whose architecture was dictated with no less rigour than Versailles 200 years before, but with considerably less aesthetic success.

The deluxe style of the Second Empire was well suited to the casinos and Riviera resorts which sprang up at the end of the century; since this was the age of the railway, it was also the style of the railway station façade. In other fields the late 19th century was merely eclectic—churches were built by antiquarians in more or less faithful Romanesque and Gothic styles, thermal baths were built in the exotic Oriental manner. Restoration of medieval buildings was undertaken on an unprecedented scale.

The builders of railway stations and department stores exploited steel, and soon learnt not to hide its use. Gustave Eiffel engineered prodigious bridges of cast iron, and for the Paris Exhibition of 1889 designed the 984ft tower which dominates Paris. The Eiffel Tower—like Beauvais Cathedral—has an enormous element of sheer virtuosity, but as well as being a feat of engineering it has many decorative elements which foreshadow the development of Art Nouveau, or modern style as the French called it, in the 1890's. This style, which owes much to a taste for Japanese art and English ideas (William Morris) is essentially one of interior decoration. Its profusion of arabesque and vegetable forms, in paint or more characteristically in metal, can transform a simple staircase into an exotic hothouse dream world. Paris is full of splendid examples of this the *fin de siècle* style; a few of the original Metro signs still stand, as does Maxim's restaurant and the Petit and Grand Palais exhibition halls.

Modern France Even before the First World War architectural fashion was swinging back to economy, extreme simplicity of form, and emphasis on structural features. The most influential architect of 20th-century France, Le Corbusier, described his work in the 1920s as the construction of *machines à habiter*; and this is the impression, cheerless and functional, made by most of the urban reconstruction after the enormous damage inflicted by two World Wars. But Le Corbusier's commemorative chapel of Notre-Dame-du-Haut at Ronchamp, built in the 1950s, is a work which points in a completely different direction—anti-rational and expressive, like an abstract sculpture yet inspired partly by its surrounding landscape. The concern to fit into a context rather than express a general stylistic ideal has characterised much of the most ambitious recent development—in many cases new holiday villages in severe natural settings of high mountains or flat coastal sands. There has been no lack of daring in these projects; nor a shortage of failures.

Eating and Drinking in France

Eating and drinking in France means eating and drinking well. Raw materials are of the highest quality, and varied regional styles of cooking make the most of them. French food is equally suitable for appreciation in restaurants and around picnic tables. The traveller who crawls around from restaurant to restaurant misses food shopping, hardly less enjoyable than eating. The ideal balance is one meal a day in a restaurant; another, more simple, in a field, campsite, flat or gîte.

Food shopping

French food markets are a delight to the eye and nose. There are nearly always good cheese, fruit and vegetable stalls; and, depending on location, shellfish, fish, poultry or game (sometimes brought live to market). *Boulangeries* (bakeries) offer a wide variety of long French loaves, from the tiny *ficelle* to the regular *baguette* and the larger *gros pain*. Smaller loaves go stale quickly; there are several bakings daily, so bread purchases should be delayed to the last possible moment. Longer-lasting loaves include the large *pain de campagne*, brown *pain complet*, or *pain de seigle* (rye bread). Bakers sell *croissants*, *brioches*, and *pain au chocolat* (buns with a chocolate heart). *Pâtisseries* also sell these and more exotic cakes, fruit tarts, and usually speciality sweets.

Charcuteries sell a much wider range of food than the pork-based products which are at the origin of the name. As well as cooked meats and pâtés, there is a variety of salads and cooked dishes: vol-au-vents, quiches, pies, pizzas, sausage, cooked chicken and fish, and delicacies in tins and jars. These are among the most enticing of food shops, their produce often expensive.

There are relatively few specialist cheese shops. Dairy products are most often sold in *épiceries* (grocers), *alimentations* (general food stores), and in supermarkets and hypermarkets, which have far more to offer in terms of variety and quality than the average UK supermarket.

Poissonneries (fishmongers) often sell cooked as well as fresh fish. If you are not equipped to open oysters, ask the fishmonger to do it for you.

Boucheries (butchers) usually sell poultry, game, and *abats* (offal), as well as meat. The cheapest mince is not usually intended for human consumption.

Cafés

Snacks are not part of French life. In most cafés it is possible to eat something, but rarely anything imaginatively or carefully prepared, or good value. A *sandwich* consists of a lot of French bread, and a little pâté, cheese or ham, usually without butter. *Croque monsieur* (grilled ham and cheese sandwich) is a staple but very variable. Cafés are for passing the time of day over a drink. *Un café* is small, black and strong, *un café crème* is the same with a little hot milk, *un grand crème* is larger:

café au lait is very milky. Tea comes without milk or lemon unless specified. Beer comes in bottles or *à la pression* (draught); the usual measure is *un demi* (about half a pint). Cafés serve wine (occasionally a selection) by the glass, all sorts of alcohols, fruit juices, *syrops* (fruit flavoured syrups), fizzy drinks and mineral water. Drinks taken at the bar are cheaper. Payment is made on departure, not after every drink. Some cafés are *tabacs* (tobacconists), and sell not only a wide range of tobacco, cigarettes and cigars, but also stamps. French cigarettes are much cheaper than foreign ones.

Restaurants

Nearly all restaurants, except the most humble and the most pretentious, offer *à la carte* and fixed price meals. *La carte* is the menu, *le menu* is a fixed price meal. The simplest *menu* usually consists of three or four courses—a starter, a meat dish of the day accompanied by *frites* and perhaps a green salad, cheese and/or a dessert. In simple restaurants, little more is to be expected than *crudités* (raw vegetable salad) or soup to start with; ice cream, tart or fruit for dessert. Very often the menu includes a quarter litre of house wine (*boisson compris*). Nearly all restaurants have a range of different *menus*, usually offering better value than *à la carte*. The cheapest menu cannot be relied upon to provide the best value; *menus touristiques* and restaurants which advertise them are generally to be avoided. Prestige restaurants often have a *menu* described as *gastronomique* or *dégustation*, which includes some of the great specialities of the house. The first usually means a huge blow-out, the second a long sequence of small portions designed to show off the chef's expertise. In all but the most expensive restaurants you can eat for well under £20 including the additional cost of a modest wine. Food but not wine prices are displayed outside restaurants.

Many French eating customs differ from ours: table-cloths are often disposable paper; bread is provided, but rarely butter or side plates; vegetables are often served separately from the main course (and salad always is); cheese is eaten before the dessert. Meat is usually served rarer than here (fish, too, in some restaurants). If you like 'medium' steak, ask for *bien cuit*; if you like 'rare' meat, ask for *à point*. 'Rare' for the French is *saignant* (bleeding), or still rarer *bleu*.

For most French (especially outside the large cities), lunch is the main meal of the day. This starts at around noon, and popular restaurants fill up by 12.30. If you arrive after 1.45 pm, you may be turned away, even if there is room. Sundays and holidays are days for large family lunches, so booking is advisable. Dinner is eaten at about 7.30 in most family hotels and resorts (later in the south and in big towns). Few people eat out on Sunday evenings.

Nouvelle cuisine

This new style of cooking was started in the '50s by the great chef Fernand Point, and continued by his students Pierre Troisgros, Paul Bocuse and Alain Chapel. It is considered to be the first major development in French cooking since Escoffier, a revolution in *haute cuisine*. Point's idea was to reject the rigidity of classic dishes and to avoid unnecessary complication, in favour of simple techniques. He stressed the need for excellent ingredients and shorter cooking times, and made greater use of poaching, baking, and above all steaming. Food is cooked in its own juices, and avoids rich roux-based sauces which mask or disguise its natural flavour. Vegetables assume a greater importance than in classic French dishes, and are also used to thicken sauces. Flavours are daringly inventive, and the presentation of dishes becomes a work of art (the influence of Japanese and Chinese cuisine has been important).

Nouvelle cuisine has made a positive contribution to French cooking; it has also become very fashionable, enabling large numbers of unworthy restaurateurs to jump on the bandwagon and serve up small and expensive portions of cuisine which is only *nouvelle* in the sense of being anti-classical—bizarre concoctions with no gastronomic logic.

Regional specialities

No less a characteristic of French food than its general excellence is the regional variety of food produce and styles of cooking. Norman cooking is based on the excellence of its dairy products, Provençal on its olives and herbs. Local styles and a few of the most important specialities are listed in the sections below. Inevitably the selection misses out as much, more even, than it includes, because such is the local gastronomic pride that every town has its specialities—often sweetmeats such as Toulouse's candied violets and Agen's stuffed prunes. Nor can this selection include all the local names applied to dishes like *coq au vin* or fish stew (there are at least 14 different varieties, from *bouillabaisse* in the south, to *marmite Dieppoise* in the north).

Nowhere perhaps is French regionalism more obvious than its cheese. Nearly all French cheeses are the products of very small areas, and nobody, as de Gaulle observed, can unite a country which has 265 speciality cheeses. Some cheeses travel, and these are the ones we know at least by name—Bleu de Bresse, Roquefort, Munster, Camembert. Even the most familiar can be rediscovered in the locality of their production, and in speciality cheese shops which offer only the very best. Other cheeses, such as the little Azay-le-Rideau of the Loire or the infinite different goats' cheeses of Poitou, travel hardly at all, and discovery of them is one of the great joys of travelling in any area in France. Many French believe that the cheeseboard is the best sign of whether a restaurateur is serious about his business or not; if it looks good, be sure to ask not just for names, for they will surely baffle, but for advice.

Burgundy, the Rhône Valley and the Jura

Beef from the Charolais region; *boeuf bourguignonne*, beef stew with red wine, onions and mushrooms; mountain ham from the Morvan, often with a cream sauce; *jambon persillé*, jellied ham flavoured with parsley; *pochouse*, a fish stew; corn-fed chicken from Bresse; *escargots*, snails; sauces based on Dijon mustard; *oeufs meurettes*, eggs poached in red wine with bacon and mushrooms; onion soup in Lyon; *quenelles de brochet*, pike dumplings, classically from Nantua; Brie, Coulommiers, Chaource, Epoisses and Bleu de Bresse cheeses; blackcurrants in sorbets, or used for *cassis* liqueur.

The South

Provence Olive oil is used in all dishes which require fat; *bouillabaisse*, fish stew: the classic version contains *rascasse*, scorpion fish, red gurnet and conger eel, seasoned with (among other things) saffron, fennel and orange peel, usually served with *rouille*, a paste of peppers; *bourride*, a

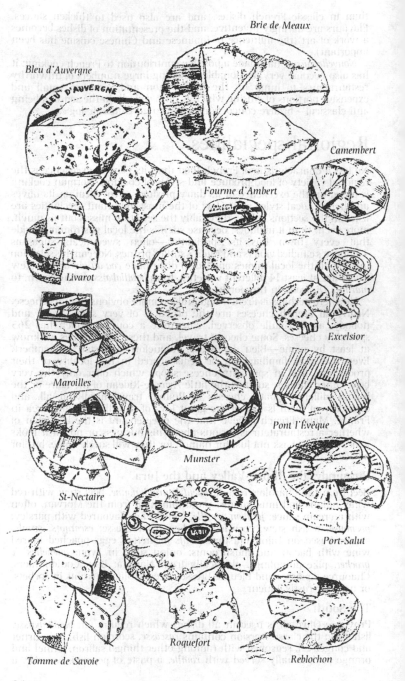

Bleu d'Auvergne

BLEU D'AUVERGNE

Brie de Meaux

Camembert

Fourme d'Ambert

Livarot

Excelsior

Maroilles

Pont l'Évêque

St-Nectaire

Munster

Port-Salut

CAVE INDÉPENDANTE ROQUFORT

Tomme de Savoie

Roquefort

Reblochon

creamy fish soup; *aïoli*, a garlic mayonnaise; fish including *rouget*, red mullet and *loup*, sea bass—often grilled with fennel; *brandade de morue*, creamed salt cod with olive oil and garlic from Nîmes; lamb grilled with herbs and garlic; *pissaladière*, anchovy tart; rice dishes in the Camargue; *ratatouille*, vegetable stew; olives (from Nyons); herbs including rosemary, thyme and basil; *soupe au pistou*, a garlic-flavoured soup, *ravioli* in Nice; *salade Niçoise*, with French beans, olives, egg, and sometimes tuna; *pan bagna*, a salad and anchovy roll; *pieds-et-pacquets*, a kind of tripe, from around Marseille; almond sweetmeats; fruit and glacé fruits.

The Languedoc *Cargolade*, snails stewed in wine; *bouillinade*, a variant of *bouillabaisse*; fish including sardines, tuna, mackerel and squid; pickled anchovies from Collioure; *langouste à la Sètoise*, spiny lobster in tomato and wine sauce.

The Massif Central

Tripoux, mutton tripe with stuffed sheeps' feet; cured mountain ham; dry sausage; trout; salmon from the Allier; *aligot* or *truffade*, a potato and cheese dish; green lentils from Le Puy; Cantal, St-Nectaire and several blue cheeses including Roquefort, Bleu d'Auvergne, Bleu des Causses and Fourme d'Ambert; *clafoutis*, a sort of cherry flan.

The Pyrenees

River fish including trout; mountain ham; snails; ewes' milk cheeses (*fromage de brebis*); Basque dishes (see Atlantic Coast) and Mediterranean (see the South) in the west and east respectively; *cassoulet*, stew of haricot beans and mixed meats (sometimes including potted duck or goose) in the area around Carcassonne.

The Dordogne

Foie gras, goose liver (sometimes made into a pâté or terrine); *confit*, potted and preserved meat (usually duck, or goose); *magret* or *maigret de canard*, fillet of duck served rare; truffles; mushrooms (especially the large *cèpes*); *pommes sarladaises*, potatoes with goose fat and truffles; prunes from Agen; walnuts (used in walnut oil for salad).

The Atlantic Coast

The North Fish and shellfish, particularly mussels (used in *mouclade*, mussel stew with white wine and cream) and oysters; sardines from Royan; *chabichou*, and many other goats' cheeses, from Poitou; melons from the Charentes.

Bordeaux and the Landes *Agneau de pré-salé*, salt-marsh lamb, from Pauillac; *lamproie*, lamprey eel, in Bordeaux; ortolans and *palombes*, wood pigeons; oysters from Arcachon; cured ham from Bayonne; sauce *à la bordelaise*, with bone marrow, shallots, tarragon and red wine.

Basque Country Tuna from St-Jean-de-Luz; sauce *à la basquaise*, with garlic and onion; *ttoro*, Basque fish stew; *chipirones*, little squid usually cooked in their own ink (*à l'encre*); sardines; *pipérade*, scrambled eggs with tomatoes, peppers and onions.

The Loire Valley

River fish (carp and salmon; *brochet*, pike; *alose*, shad) with *beurre blanc*—sauce of butter, shallots and vinegar—or *à l'oseille*, with a sorrel sauce; *rillettes de porc*, potted pork; *rillons*, braised breast of pork; pork with prunes; game and wildfowl from the Sologne; mushrooms; *crémets*, fresh cream cheeses; goat cheeses; mushrooms; asparagus; fruit.

Brittany

Fish and shellfish of all kinds, particularly *homard*, lobster, *langoustes*, crayfish, and *langoustines*, scampi; *araignée*, spider crab; *palourdes*, clams (*gratinées* or *farcies* means in half-shells, buttered, breadcrumbed, grilled, and usually with garlic); *coquilles*, scallops; oysters (the best from the Belon river); *moules*, mussels; *cotriade*, fish stew; salmon from the Aulne and Elorn; trout; *agneau de pré-salé*, salt-marsh lamb; strawberries from Plougastel and artichokes from Roscoff; *crêpes* or *galettes*, pancakes (wheat or buckwheat, sweet and savoury); cakes (*Kouign-aman* and *gâteau breton*) and biscuits (especially *crêpes dentelles* from Quimper).

Normandy

Sauces using butter, cream, apples and *calvados*, apply brandy (dishes usually described as *Vallée d'Auge*); tripe, especially *à la mode de Caen*, stewed in a spicy sauce; sole in various sauces (the most famous is Dieppoise, with white wine, cream and shellfish); mussels; mackerel from around Dieppe; oysters from Courseulles and the eastern Cotentin; *andouille*, tripe sausage from Vire; Camembert, Livarot and Pont L'Evêque cheeses.

The North

Picardy and Artois Soups (particularly vegetable) and stews (*hochepot*, mixed meats with vegetables; *potée*, with cabbage); vegetables (artichokes, leeks, haricot beans, cauliflowers); *flamiche*, leek tart; *pâtés* (duck, woodcock, eel); herring (particularly pickled herring in Boulogne), mackerel, sole, turbot, shellfish (particularly mussels); Maroilles cheese and *flamiche* (tart) *au Maroilles*.

Ardennes Game (venison, wild boar) as main dish or made into pâtés; river fish including trout and pike; ham.

Champagne *Andouillettes*, tripe sausage; *tarte aux raisins* (with grapes).

Alsace, Lorraine and the Vosges

Alsace and Vosges *Foie gras*, poultry and river fish *au riesling* (with white wine sauce); pork (smoked or in sausages); *choucroute*, sauerkraut; game (venison, wild boar, hare, partridge); *baeckeoffe*, hotpot of mixed meats; fruit tarts, onion tart and *tarte aux vigneronnes*, potato pie; *kugelhopf*, brioche cake; Munster cheese.

Lorraine *Quiche Lorraine*; *potage Lorraine*, potato and leek soup; *potée*, cabbage and pork soup; *charcuteries*.

The Alps

Lake fish such as *omble-chevalier*—like salmon trout or char—*féra* and *lavarat*, also like salmon; trout, *gratin dauphinois/savoyard*, potatoes cooked with local cheese and cream; *fondue savoyarde*, melted local cheese with wine, kirsch and garlic, eaten with cubes of stale bread; *raclette*, grilled cheese scraped onto hot potatoes with garnish of mountain ham and gherkin; French Gruyère, Emmenthal, Beaufort and Reblochon cheeses.

Corsica

Charcuterie from chestnut-fed pigs—*lonza*, *coppa*, *figatelli*; pâtés from game of the *maquis* including blackbirds; seafood especially lobster and spicy fish soups; meat stews of pork, mutton, kid, wild boar; pasta, often eaten with *brocciu*, the most versatile of many goat and sheep cheeses; chestnut-flavoured biscuits and puddings; honey, fruit preserves.

Wine

Reading a French wine label

There are three main **categories of wine**: Appellation Contrôlée (AC), the highest; Vin Délimité de Qualité Supérieur (VDQS); and Vin de Table. AC on a label guarantees not only the origin but also the method of production and grape variety. An AC may apply to a single vineyard or to a large district. For instance, if a wine carries an AC Bordeaux label, it can come from anywhere in the large Bordeaux wine-producing region. There are *appellations* within *appellations*, such as Médoc within Bordeaux, Haut-Médoc within Médoc, and St-Julien within Haut-Médoc. In general, the more specific the region designated by the *appellation*, the better the wine. Unlike the other wine producing areas, Alsace is not divided into a large number of greater and lesser *appellations*; champagne, although regulated like other AC wines, does not have to have AC displayed on its labels. Like AC wine, VDQS is produced within a framework of regulations; it is generally less expensive, and often very good value. *Vin de Table* is by far the largest category in volume; much of this *vin ordinaire* is blended and foreign. *Vin de Pays* is a recently-introduced sub-category which does guarantee origin; many are robust good-value reds from the large wine-producing areas of the Midi.

Classed growths (*crus classés*) are wines that come from a vineyard which has been officially classified. The hierarchy of *crus* can be confusing, and each area varies in its terminology. In the Bordeaux region, the top Médoc vineyards have been classified into five categories, starting with *Premier Cru Classé* at the top, to *Cinquième Cru Classé*, then followed by *Cru Exceptionnel*, *Cru Grand Bourgeois*, *Cru Bourgeois Supérieur*, and *Cru Bourgeois*. In St-Emilion, at the top of the pecking order is *Premier Grand Cru Classé*, followed by *Cru Classé*. In Burgundy, the highest category is called *Grand Cru*, followed by *Premier Cru*.

Many classed growths are named after individual chateaux. However, the fact that a bottle carries the word **château** is not in itself any indication of quality. Château N can simply be the name of a small estate, or even a brand name, and there may be nothing resembling a château on or near the vineyard.

Good wine proclaims its **vintage** on the label. The best wines—particularly the reds of Bordeaux, Burgundy and the Rhône—improve with age (in general, the better the wine, the further it is from its peak when young). It does not, however, follow that the oldest wines are the best, because wine does not improve indefinitely, and because some vintages are better than others. A bottle of wine made in a good year (that is, when the weather, condition of the soil and a host of other factors are just right) costs much more than one of a poor year. In general, the finer the wine, the more variation between vintages. Vintage charts state the best years for the different wine-producing areas, but can only be used as a general guideline; there are so many factors which may affect the flavour of a wine that, in a certain year, one vineyard may produce a superlative wine, while another vineyard down the road may produce a mediocre one. Everyday wine can be made from most vintages, however, and a good winemaker will in part be able to compensate for the weather.

All but the very best wine should be drunk quite young (about two to three years after the vintage). A few should be drunk within a year (Beaujolais Nouveau, released in November, within six months).

Labels on bottles of sparkling wine give clues as to the degree of **sweetness** and **sparkle**. Champagne must come from the Champagne *appellation* and made sparkling by the *méthode champenoise* (see page

348). Other regions produce sparkling wine, either by the same means or by other methods generally considered to give less good results. A wine that is *mousseux* is more fizzy than one which is *crémant*; still less sparkling are those described as *pétillant* or *perlant*. *Brut* is very dry; *sec* dry; *demi-sec* or *moelleux* semi sweet; *doux* sweet.

Drinking wine in restaurants

Thoughts about sampling the finest French wines in restaurants are likely to be dispelled by the first glance at a wine list. The mark-up in French restaurants is very high (sometimes as much as 300%), particularly for the best burgundies and clarets. However, you can expect to drink good, even fine, wines in the simplest of restaurants, nearly all of which have a selection of AC wines at reasonable prices. Crowning the list you can expect to find a few prestige names which would command higher prices at the lower end of a list in a more exalted establishment. For economy, the safest policy is to order the house wine, variously known as *cuvée/réserve de la maison/du patron*, or simply *réserve*, served either by the bottle or by carafe of half or quarter litre. The *réserve* is much less likely to be a poor wine than the cheapest bottles on the wine list, for it is the restaurateur's personal selection of a budget wine. The large majority of French wine is consumed locally, so few names at the lower end of wine lists are familiar from UK wine merchants' selections. This should be no deterrent from sampling local wines.

Tasting and buying wine

At the top end of the market, buying wine (particularly choice clarets) in France may be more expensive than buying it in Britain. At the other end of the scale, it comes as a surprise to many holidaymakers to find how cheap the cheapest wine can be—under 50p a litre for basic *vin ordinaire*, bought in plastic bottles in a supermarket, or *en vrac*—on tap direct from a vineyard. In between these two extremes lies a whole gamut of exciting vinous discoveries.

Price is not a reliable guide. There are very expensive wines which are no more than good; and there are some cheap wines which are very pleasant, others as unpleasant as any in the world. The best way to find out whether you like a wine is to taste it. Fortunately, France is an excellent country in which to do just that, for the vineyard areas, without exception, are usually happy to let you sample their bounty.

For the tourist interested in wine tasting, there is a variety of possible approaches. Local tourist offices have information on properties which offer tours and tastings, and those where you can buy wine. In some vineyard villages there are *maisons du vin* where you can taste and often buy the produce of several vineyards. If it is a collective growers' outlet, rather than a commercially-run shop, prices are similar to those you would pay at the vineyard itself. A *cave co-opérative* which makes and markets wines from the blended produce of several small vineyards is a good place to buy cheap wine; do not expect wine bought straight from the barrel to last or travel well.

In vineyard areas there are usually signposted *routes du vin*, tourist routes which lead through the heart of the vineyards. Some of the grandest vineyards, including many Bordeaux châteaux, only admit visitors who have made an appointment, or have brought a letter of introduction from a wine merchant. Others, including some of the most prestigious, offer regular guided tours with tastings for which no appointment and no expertise is necessary. The majority of vineyards have no set policy for tourists, and whether or not they welcome the unannounced visitor for an informal tour depends on how busy they are and how interested and communicative the visitor is. *Vignerons* in general like nothing better than the chance to share their enthusiasm, and the better informed your questions, the more likely they are to down tools and expatiate on their favourite subject, and to give you the chance to sample the maturing wine from the barrel. During the autumn wine harvest time (*vendange*), few *vignerons* have any time for visitors.

The roadside sign *dégustation* is an invitation to taste wine. There is usually no charge, nor any strict obligation to buy, although you may feel honour-bound to do so after half an hour spent with a small producer sampling several vintages and discussing the relative merits of a 1984 and a 1985. It may come as a relief in other places to pay what is usually a modest charge, to acquit yourself of all obligation. Even an entrance charge which at first seems extortionate may well turn out to be exceptionally good value to the tourist who has a genuine interest, time to spare, and no immediate need to drive.

You are allowed to bring home 8 litres of wine bought in France free of duty (which means just under 11 standard 75cl bottles). If you bring home more, you will be charged excise duty (a standard amount of under £1 on a bottle, whatever its original cost) plus VAT of 15% on the purchase price. There are no formalities to be observed: just go through the Red Channel at customs and declare what you have bought.

The wine areas

Lists of the most prestigious vineyards in each wine area, and information on opportunities for visits, should be sought from tourist offices, *maisons du vin* or *syndicats viticoles* locally. In this section we indicate the general characteristics of the major French wine areas, and give some suggestions of less prestigious and expensive wines which you are likely to encounter on wine lists and in shops.

Bordeaux

The most important quality wine region, producing some of the world's finest reds and sweet whites. At the top end of the market, you can often buy more cheaply at home than in France.

There are four main fine wine districts: Médoc (red) which divides into Haut-Médoc and the lesser Bas-Médoc; Graves (white); St-Emilion and Pomerol (red); and Sauternes (sweet white). The red (known to us as claret) is dry, elegant and rather austere, almost always drunk with meals.

The wine areas of Premières Côtes de Blaye and Côtes de Bourg, Côtes de Castillon, Canon Fronsac and Fronsac, and the satellite villages of St-Emilion—such as Montagne and Puisseguin—and villages in the St-Emilion and Pomerol area—such as Néac and Lalande—are good hunting grounds for good value red wines. The Loupiac and Ste-Croix-du-Mont areas produce cheaper sweet white wines than those of Sauternes.

The South-west

There is no shortage of cheaper local alternatives to Bordeaux wines in south-western France. Some of the best of them are to be found on restaurant lists in other areas.

Bergerac The best red (similar to lesser St-Emilion) comes from the village of Pécharmant; Château de Monbazillac (a co-operative) produces a fine sweet white; Rosette produces better than average sweetish whites.

Cahors Mainly fruity and tannic red—much of it handled by the co-operative Les Caves d'Olt at Parnac.

Gaillac Beaujolais-style reds (a good value one from Cunac co-operative), and lively whites.

Côtes de Duras Similar to Bergerac reds, and some good value whites.

Côtes du Marmandais Light reds, and plain whites.

Côtes de Buzet Bordeaux-like reds, from the co-operative.

Côtes de Fronton Good value light red.

Béarn Lightweight red, white and rosé.

Madiran Vigorous red; also sweet and dry white from Pacherenc-du-Vic-Bilh.

Jurançon Unusual dry and sweetish whites.

Tursan Reds resemble Madiran, whites Jurançon.

Irouléguy Red, white and rosé.

Burgundy

Produces less than one-tenth of the volume of the Bordeaux AC area, and has 100 or so different *appellations*. Superlative reds (generally higher in alcohol, and sweeter than claret) and whites.

There are four main areas: the best of all is the Côte d'Or (red and white) which divides into Côte de Nuits and Côte de Beaune; Chablis (white); Mâconnais (red and white); and Beaujolais (red).

More accessibly priced red wines than the world famous burgundies are produced at the villages of Givry and Mercurey on the Côte Chalonnais, and in the vineyard areas of Hautes Côtes de Beaune and Hautes Côtes de Nuits, and Côtes de Beaune Villages and Côtes de Nuits Villages.

For white wines, good villages for cheaper alternatives to the top burgundies are Montagny and Rully on the Côte Chalonnais, Mâcon-Viré (which has a good co-operative), and Mâcon-Lugny. The villages of Pouilly-Vinzelles, Pouilly-Loché and St-Véran produce similar whites to the more highly priced Pouilly-Fuissé. In general, simple AC Macon Blanc, made from the noble Chardonnay grape, is better than its red counterpart made from the less classy Gamay grape.

All the Beaujolais wines, including the 9 *grands crus*, are reasonably priced.

The Loire Valley

Abundant generally good value wines. There are good dry whites; rosé, red, sweet white, and sparkling.

The best-known Loire wine is Muscadet—the best from the Sèvre-et-Maine district, or Muscadet des Côteaux de la Loire. *Sur lie* means it's been bottled straight off the lees and has more flavour and freshness than average, plus a slight prickle on the tongue. Gros Plant is a less interesting wine.

There are several wines, dry and sweet, made from the Chenin Blanc grape. One of the best dry whites is that from Savennières—La Roche aux Moines and La Coulée de Serrant vineyards. Vouvray and Montlouis produce dry, sweet and sparkling whites (some are superb) using the champagne method. Vouvray has a good co-operative.

Sancerre and Pouilly produce excellent dry white wines (made from the Sauvignon grape). Those from the villages of Quincy, Reuilly and Menetou-Salon are similar but less distinguished. Other Loire wines are known simply by their grape type rather than by a vineyard (Sauvignon, and Chardonnay). Wines known as Pouilly-sur-Loire made from the very commonplace Chasselas grape and are quite unlike the pricey Pouilly-Fumé from the same village.

Rosé d'Anjou is another well-known Loire product, which can vary from refreshingly fruity to rather sweet. Cabernet d'Anjou rosé is a finer wine.

Reds from St-Nicolas-de-Bourgueil and Chinon should be drunk young and slightly chilled. A good one is not unlike Beaujolais.

Alsace

Good value wines, mostly bone dry, full-bodied and perfumed, and of a consistently high quality (to drink with food, unlike the similar and sweeter German ones which can more easily be drunk on their own). Alsace wines are sold by the name of their grape variety; there's only one AC (and a relatively new system of *Grands Crus* for designated vineyards. The top Alsace grape is the Riesling; the Gewürztraminer (an unusual, fruity, spicy, and scented wine), the Pinot Gris and the Muscat (which makes an apéritif wine) are all termed *grands vins*. Edelzwicker is a blend of less than noble grapes. The words Grand or Réserve indicate a higher degree of alcohol than others. *Vendange tardive* (or *spätlese*) means late-picked grapes, implying more strength and usually sweetness.

Alsace co-operatives generally have high standards, and are good places to taste and buy wine.

The Rhône Valley

Produces some of the best-value red wines in France, slow-maturing and full-bodied from the northern Rhône, softer from the southern. In the north, Hermitage is the classic red, Crozes-Hermitage a paler version (both also produce some white wine). In the south, wines are modelled on the well-known Châteauneuf-du-Pape, with alternatives from the nearby ACs of Côtes du Ventoux, Côteaux de Tricastin, and from the villages of the Côtes du Rhône Villages (a step up from the Côtes du Rhône). The co-operatives in these villages are good, too, particularly Cairanne, Chusclan, Tulette, Ste-Cécile, Puymera, and Gigondas (which now has its own AC).

Tavel is renowned for its rosé; Lirac produces a slightly lesser version and also red and white. Rasteau and Beaumes-de-Venise produce sweet dessert wines, the latter one of the best sweet muscats in France.

The South

Provence Reds, whites and rosés are produced; rosés have most appeal (the reds are usually unexciting, the whites often dry but lacking in acidity). Exceptions are from the ACs of Bandol (red), Cassis (white—not to be confused with the blackcurrant liqueur), Bellet (red, white and rosé). The VDQS areas of Côtes de Provence, the more important Côteaux d'Aix en Provence—notably Château Vignelaure—and Côtes du Luberon can produce some sound red, white and rosé.

Languedoc-Roussillon Produces vast quantities of mostly ordinary reds. Exceptions are the ACs of Fitou, in the Corbières, and Collioure. Areas of most potential are St-Chinian, Minervois, Corbières and Roussillon (and the Côtes du Roussillon AC). The Costières du Gard has characteristics of the Rhône Valley; in addition to red, it produces some surprisingly fresh whites.

Vins de Pays, mainly from the departments of Aude, Herault, and Gard, are cheaper (and usually lesser) wines.

The sparkling Blanquette de Limoux is a white wine of some distinction. Banyuls, Rivesaltes, Côtes d'Agly and Maury produce sweet dessert wines.

The Alps and the Jura

Almost all white, and light—some sparkling. Ayze produces sparkling, Crépy and the communes of Apremont and Abymes still white, Seyssel still and sparkling wines.

The Jura produces some very fine wines with some of the best being rosés (called *vin gris* here) from Arbois and the villages around it, and whites from L'Etoile. There's also a rare, very dry, *vin jaune* from AC Château-Châlon, not unlike a fino sherry in taste.

Other regional drinks

North and west of a line which runs roughly from the mouth of the Loire through Paris to the Ardennes, wine is imported. In the north and north east, the local brew is beer. Surprising though it may seem, Mutzig and Carling are in France. Most French beer is *blonde* (lager).

In Normandy and Brittany the local drink is cider. French cider varies greatly, but is rarely to be found as rough and bitter as English country cider. It is bottled like champagne, and drunk alone or with a meal.

The Normans use their apples to produce apple brandy—Calvados—one of the best known of French fruit-based alcohols. There are many others to be discovered all over the country, particularly in Alsace (*quetsch* and *mirabelle* from plums and *kirsch* from cherries), and around the Dordogne (*eau de noix* from walnuts) where fruit such as luscious Agen plums steeped in brandy are a special favourite. Some of the fruit alcohols (such as *poire* and *fraise*) are colourless and piercing in taste, others sweet and sticky. A catching habit is the Burgundian one of putting a splash of syrupy blackcurrant liqueur (*cassis*) into an ordinary white wine to turn it into an apéritif (called *Kir* after a mayor of Dijon). Variants include the use of champagne or vermouth instead of wine.

Particularly in mountain areas, flowers and herbs are used as a base for fortified wines and distilled alcohols. Vermouth comes from the Alpine region and Chambéry produces a delicate herby version. Monks are traditional distillers throughout the country—responsible for the famous Bénédictine from Fécamp in Normandy, and for the strong green Chartreuse made in secrecy from over 100 Alpine herbs.

Pastis, the aniseed alcohol which is the colour of amber until brought into contact with water which renders it opaque, is southern in origin—it is drunk on the rocks, just with water, or with a fruit syrup.

Cognac and Armagnac are both distillations from the grape which vary in quality as much as wine, from the rough warming nip to the antique after-dinner luxury which commands £20 a glass. Marc is a clear alcohol made from grape skins, usually very rough and strong.

Paris

Pompidou Centre

"Fickle in everything else, the French have been faithful in one thing only—their love of change" (Sir Archibald Alison)

Paris

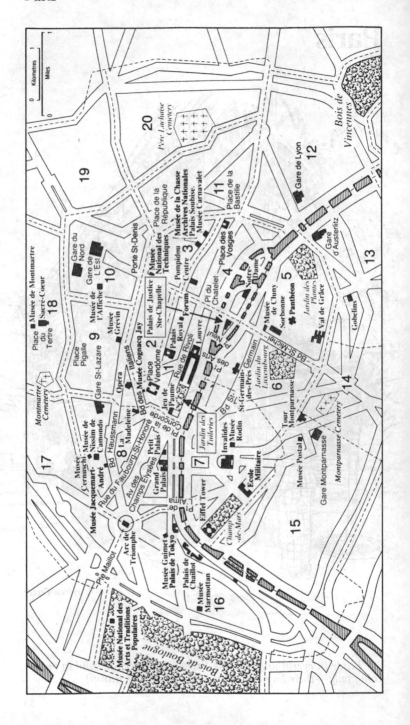

The heart of France pulsates with life and pumps life—economic, political and cultural—to the rest of one of the world's most centralised nations. The capital, where every aspect of French life except its essentially regional culinary excellence is concentrated, distils many of the qualities of the French people: their exhibitionism, their excitability, their charm, and their sense of their own importance—and especially their importance in civilising the world. Victor Hugo said Paris was the synonym of cosmos.

Paris is a notoriously trying place to inhabit but a marvellous place to visit—as full of modern life and as pacy as New York, as full of historical and cultural interest as Rome, as compact and picturesque as Oxford. It is a city which earns a special place in the heart of every visitor not because of its art treasures but because of its atmosphere, its smells, its noises, its inhabitants and its landmarks, shown off as skilfully as a woman's most seductive features.

First on the list of natural advantages is the curvaceous Seine, which carves a gracious sweep through most of central Paris. It was the Seine, flowing past an island or three, which defined the original settlement of Lutetia (meaning marsh) which, as Caesar reported, was inhabited by the Parisii and joined to the boggy terra firma by a couple of wooden bridges. Today the Seine—still the heart of the city—has banks planted with chestnut groves where it is so delicious and fragrant to idle in Paris' famous spring; the embankment pavements are lined with stalls of salacious old books and prints; and artists plant their easels by the most picturesque of Parisian scenes.

Paris shows off nearly all its great monuments along the river, so a stroll along the *quais* (embankments) or a boat trip along the river are the best and most delightful ways to get a first feel for the layout of the city, and by following the river you cannot get lost. The styles of the two banks are different, but the Seine does not divide Paris as the Thames divides London. Bridges are numerous, in many cases very decorative, and crossing them on foot is no more of an expedition than crossing a main road.

Many of the city's monumental perspectives span the Seine: the colonnades of the Madeleine and the Chambre des Députés deliberately echo each other across the river on either side of the Place de la Concorde; and Notre-Dame enjoys the most picturesque setting of any French cathedral, on an island in the river, beautifully shown off and reflected in its waters.

Although long vistas are one of its great visual characteristics, Paris did not grow according to a plan but spread naturally in all directions from the Ile de la Cité, and had a semblance of order imposed upon it only by demolition and reconstruction in later periods. Not content with nature's thoroughfare, Napoleon created another through central Paris—arrow-straight and running just to the north of the river: from the Bastille in the east through the Louvre, the Tuileries Gardens and the Place de la Concorde, along the Champs-Elysées to the Arc de Triomphe. For most of its course it is an imposing axis and, like the river, very convenient for purposes of orientation. Its arrangement changed the balance of the city westwards: until the 19th century the Ile de la Cité and the Louvre were the centre of town, and today's Champs-Elysées fields on its western outskirts; now the Place de la Concorde is the centre. Later in the century many miles of long wide boulevards were laid down with Germanic thoroughness and uniformity by the prefectorial Alsatian baron Haussmann, who moved bridges so that roads could go geometrically straight across the Ile de la Cité. Haussmann's façades, regulated in architectural style and size, are among the most characteristic and least attractive aspects of the capital; but although much was destroyed to make way for them, much was left standing in between—including labyrinthine *quartiers* and the monuments with which earlier monarchs had embellished the city.

In contrast to Haussmann's heavy-handed approach, the turn-of-the-century monuments, which rarely win much applause for architectural merit, are light and ornamental, in tune with the not too serious spirit of the time, and of Paris. The Pont Alexandre III, with its gilt metal statuettes, and the greenhouse-style Petit and Grand Palais lighten the grandeur of Louis XIV's Invalides in a way which should, no doubt, be deplored but which is rather fun and very Parisian. The Eiffel Tower was put up as a feat of virtuosity—a 300-metre flagpole for the World Exhibition of 1889—and was greeted with howls of horror from all remotely serious Parisians, but it has become the defiantly cheeky symbol of Paris, looking down on the Louis XV elegance of the Ecole Militaire. From the hill of Montmartre, all Paris is overlooked by the no less derided mock-oriental white domes of the pilgrimage basilica of Sacré-Coeur, now an accepted and essential part of the city skyline.

The second half of the 19th century did as much to fashion Paris' image as it did to change its physical appearance. It was at this time of accumulation of wealth that Paris became the frolicsome fun city of Europe—"gay Paree". City dwellers acquired a taste for pleasures: they rode out to play in the Bois de Boulogne—newly laid out under the inspiration of Hyde Park—or to socialise at the Longchamp races. The musical note of the age was the light comedy of Offenbach, and the new, sumptuously over-decorated Opera House was adorned with wonderfully lively sculptures called La Danse. Parisians danced in the Tuileries, and they flocked to watch the high-kicking dancing girls of the Moulin Rouge at the foot of Montmartre, the picturesque hill village of windmills and Bohemians—the hard-up artists and poets of Puccini's opera. The turn of the century was the "Belle Epoque"—the high life of *haute couture* and high spirits, of cafés filled with the noise of popping corks and clinking glasses. It was also the time of the low life reality behind the façade—the heavy make up, the premature lines shown up in the mirror under the harsh artificial lights, the humourless smiles that scowl, the absinthe drinkers staring sightless—as recorded for ever by Manet, Degas and Toulouse-Lautrec. The visitor seeking the image conjured up in the painting and literature of the era is bound to be disappointed. The Moulin Rouge and other traditional cabarets are still there, with dancing girls still going through the ritual can-can, but the audience is no longer Parisian, and the show has lost its earthy vitality. Now nocturnal Parisians are to be found in throbbing discothèques all over town, and for those who want to do more than just dance, there are places to cater for all tastes and proclivities.

Another traditional part of Paris' image is the café where, once upon a time, intellectuals discussed the human condition in a fog of *caporal* tobacco over coffee in St-Germain-des-Prés, and idly rich Parisiennes discussed their extramarital affairs in a haze of Virginia cigarettes, also over coffee, on the Boulevard des Italiens. The cafés are still there, seats facing the street so that the consumer can watch the world go by and be watched by the bypassing world, and the coffee is still the same—strong and sharp and taken in after-dinner quantities. But Parisians don't seem to have the time to sit around in cafés any more, and even in the

36

university quarter students have adopted a hard-working, library-bound realism instead of the lazy radicalism which filled the cafés of the Boulevard St-Michel in the '60s. Now the cafés are of greater assistance to footsore and nostalgic pedestrian tourists.

The *cuisine* that is *nouvelle* or at least *actuelle* in Paris today is fast food. More and more cafés have become burger bars, luxury ice-cream parlours and *"le drugstore"*—a complex of chemist/bookshop/news-agent/record shop and snack bar open late into the night. Not many Parisians buy a *croque monsieur*, or a *crêpe au Grand Marnier* from one of the pancake friers on the Place St-Michel, but they are still there—typically Parisian for the visitor hungry for a taste of Paris.

The Grands Boulevards—traditional avenues for crinolined ladies and their beaux to promenade—are now distinguished by a succession of cinemas showing mostly American films, dance palaces for urban cowboys, fast-food counters, and sex shops. They are noisy, crammed with traffic, and no longer suitable for strolling—for which the Parisians have no time anyway.

In other ways Paris remains less deniably Paris. For contemporary art it still has the most adventurous and varied selection of private galleries, even though the throughput of today cannot compare with that of the half century between 1870 and 1920 when Paris hosted Impressionist and Cubist revolutions. There is still a willingness to brave controversy by adding to the city's surprising architectural contrasts. President Pompidou in particular was concerned that Paris should not become a museum city, and was in a position to ensure that what he wanted came about. After decades of strict control of the maximum height of new buildings the 56-storey Montparnasse Tower was given the go-ahead in the '60s; and the very colourful and tubular Centre Georges Pompidou—"Museum and Centre for Cultural Creation"—was opened in 1977 in the middle of the old heart of Paris, as part of a major redevelopment of the area. No less controversially, the great perspective from the Tuileries up to the Arc de Triomphe has been changed by a dark, looming silhouette in the distance: the skyscrapers of the commercial complex of La Défense.

Many areas (even central ones) still retain a village atmosphere with wonderfully colourful and lively street markets, full of the largest array of cheeses to be seen anywhere in the world. In centralised France, Paris is assured the finest produce from its regions—early vegetables from the Loire, exotic fruits from Provence, winter truffles from the Périgord, and Brittany oysters all the year round. There are still homely family-run *bistrots*, and also the finest and most costly gastronomic temples in the land.

For fashion, too, Paris is most of what it ever was, with streets of fabulous *couturiers* and bootmakers whose standards and whose prices have remained unshakeably high despite all pressures for economy and standardisation. The presentations of the annual collections are still the biggest events in the world fashion calendar and the shop windows make mouth-watering sightseeing. Parisians too remain Parisians: extrovert, demonstrative and short-tempered, closer to a Mediterranean temperament than Paris' geographical position would suggest, always in a hurry to work or play hard; the streets of the city stay busy late into the night—much later than London and anywhere in provincial France.

Perhaps the most important contribution to the city's vitality, and to its problems, has been the fact that until very recently Parisians have preferred to live an urban rather than a suburban existence. The city has for centuries been the most densely populated in Europe and has twice as many people per acre as London. Most people live in apartment blocks, there are few private or public gardens (mainly dusty gravel with trees) and hardly any parks—except the Bois de Boulogne and the Bois de Vincennes which are both on the periphery and do nothing to ventilate the centre. The density of cars is no less a problem than that of humanity. The complete circular motorway around Paris helps keep juggernauts out of the city, but at rush hours it seems only to ensure that all traffic going in or out of Paris is travelling in the same direction. Weekend exits and re-entries are horrific, and solid traffic jams in the Champs-Elysées and around the Opéra at midnight are common. In cramped Paris, which outgrew a series of confining town walls, there is no more room for any new roads. One bank of the Seine has been turned into an expressway, and President Pompidou planned to do the same for the left bank before his successor, environmentally more respectful, squashed the project. The result of all this has been that an aesthetic reluctance to contemplate the building of skyscrapers has had to give way to the practicalities of land shortage, and Parisians have been seduced from the centre to greener grass on the other side of the Boulevard Périphérique. The Métro system has been extended to reach American-style suburban new towns at the gates of the city.

Parisians, who barricaded their streets in so many revolutions and welcomed with equal unanimity so many dictatorial rulers, still love to do things *en masse*. They know it doesn't make sense, but with a Gallic shrug they accept city life, with all its stresses, as being preferable to a more sensible but oh, how boring provincial existence—as long as they can escape to the country. As well as a mass movement at weekends, there is an even greater exodus from the city in July and August. It may sound attractive to be able to enjoy the picturesque townscape and museums without all the traffic jams and the horn blowing, but it isn't. Paris without the Parisians seems pointless. Large numbers of shops, restaurants and even some museums are closed. It is the same at Easter weekend, when thousands of tourists ready to be thrilled by the romantic charm of Paris in the spring queue up for hours for the few rooms of the few museums and the few cafés that stay open. To visit at these times is to learn that Paris is not what you see on postcards but a living city where, as Balzac wrote, "*tout fume, tout brûle, tout brille, tout bouillonne.*"

Getting around

It is easy and inexpensive to get to Paris by plane, train or bus, so there is no need to attempt to see Paris by car. Parking is usually a major problem, and driving habits take some getting used to: Parisians believe that bumpers, no less than horns, are made to be used—in spite of the fact that the law forbids the use of the horn throughout Paris.

From a fairly central hotel you will find most essential places from the tourist point of view within manageable walking distance. It is much the most enjoyable and indeed the most relaxing way to get around, although dodging traffic often calls for some agility—pedestrians are not respected by drivers and if you try the favourite tourist game of reaching the Arc de Triomphe on foot overground you have only yourself to blame for the consequences.

When the feet give out, you are never more than a few hundred yards from a Métro (underground, mostly) station. The Métro system looks very complicated on a map because there are so many different lines, but it is generally efficient and easy to use. Many stations have maps which light up to indicate the route you should take to a given station. The trick is to remember the name of the station at the end of the line you need, in the direction you need, and follow signs to it, either headed *Direction* or *Correspondances* (connections). Lines close at 12.30 am. Some trains are modernised and smoothly cushioned on rubber tyres, others more attractively old, rattling and much slower. Doors have to be opened by releasing a catch. There are two classes, the only advantage of First Class being extra space in the rush hour. There is no smoking, no spitting and some seats have to be given up to pregnant women and wounded war heroes. You can go anywhere on the Métro for one standard price ticket which when bought individually is nearly double its price as part of a book (*carnet*) of 10. Métro tickets are valid on Paris buses, and 2, 4 and 7-day tourist passes for unlimited use of both systems are also available from major Métro stations.

In recent years the RER (Réseau Express Régional) has been grafted onto the Métro system, initially extending it into the suburbs and beyond, now crossing Paris. It has a ticket system of its own and is only of relevance to tourists who want to get out of the city—to St-Germain-en-Laye, for example, or to Charles de Gaulle Airport (from the Gare du Nord).

Paris buses are more expensive than the Métro (journeys of more than a few stops require two tickets and if you change you pay again) and less comprehensive in coverage especially on Sundays and public holidays when many bus routes are closed; it is however a much more attractive way of travelling around town. Because of the one-way systems, buses often take different routes back and forth. Books of tickets cannot normally be bought on buses.

There is nothing strange about Paris taxi drivers except that they are taciturn by comparison with those of London or New York. They wait in ranks with telephones, they display fares on the meter, they expect a tip and they charge extra at night.

One of the nicest ways of seeing central Paris is to take a boat (*bateau mouche* or *vedette*) from the Pont de l'Alma, Pont d'Iéna, or the Pont Neuf. There are covered sections for rainy days, and commentaries in English. At night, some boat trips include a meal.

Another good way of getting your bearings is to take a bus tour around town by day and/or night (particularly recommended for illuminations); some night tours include cabaret stops and a meal. Be prepared for over-diligent translations—the Elysian fields, Peace Street and so on. You can obtain information from your hotel or a tourist office (the main one is at 127 Avenue des Champs-Elysées). They will also have information on coach excursions out of Paris—a great variety, from half a day to a château in the Ile-de-France to several days in the Loire valley.

The map on page 34 shows the major sights and landmarks, and the different districts (*arrondissements*) numbered 1 to 20.

Michelin produces a Paris atlas with street maps in book form, and some useful information including bus and Métro maps. The Green Michelin Guide to Paris (available in English) has adequate maps for most tourist purposes.

Paris area by area

Paris is divided into administrative districts (*arrondissements*) which spiral clockwise from the centre (the Louvre) from numbers 1 to 20. The inner twist of the spiral from the 1st to the 8th *arrondissements* contains most of the museums, the sightseeing and the shopping.

The Right Bank

The Arc de Triomphe crowns Paris' most famous processional perspective, the gentle climb of the **Avenue des Champs-Elysées** from the **Place de la Concorde** to the starfish **Place Charles de Gaulle** (ex Etoile), its course interrupted in the middle by the fountains of the Rond-Point des Champs-Elysées. On the Concorde side, the Champs-Elysées has kept its gardens, with theatres, exhibition halls and the presidential palace. On the Etoile side it is broad, commercial (car showrooms, travel agents, and department stores) and cinematic. The area to the south and west between the Champs-Elysées and the **Avenue George V**, particularly the **Avenue Montaigne**, is a select one for hotels, *couturiers*, food shops, embassies and cabaret. The further you penetrate westwards into the 16th *arrondissement* the more drearily residential Paris becomes. To the north and east of the Rond-Point, the best streets for well-established art galleries (**Avenue Matignon**) and *haute couture* (**Rue du Faubourg St-Honoré**) lead towards the Palais du Louvre.

The central area around the **Louvre** and the **Place de la Concorde** is the least residential in Paris. It has most of the luxury hotels (the occupying German commander in the Second World War had his headquarters in the Meurice) along the arcaded **Rue de Rivoli**, and set quietly back from it, like the Ritz on the **Place Vendôme**—the 17th-century square which is probably the most beautiful in Paris, spoilt only by the outrageously oversized column of Napoleon as Caesar. Shops and restaurants vary from the most exclusive (the **Rue du Faubourg-St-Honoré**, the **Rue de la Paix** and Maxim's restaurant) to the merely expensive (the Rue de Rivoli itself which specialises in clothes for export and also has an English bookshop and tea-shop). It is an area for the theatre and opera, museums (the Louvre and the Jeu de Paume), and for perspectives—up the Tuileries to the Arc de Triomphe, up the Rue Royale to the Madeleine, up the Avenue de l'Opéra, now lined with travel agents, to the Opéra itself—the most extravagantly brassy of all the buildings of the Second Empire. It is also an area where resting your feet in a café will cost you dearly, so it's better to pause in the **Tuileries** gardens, partly dusty with a few feeble fountains and ponds popular with model boat enthusiasts, partly arranged with lawns and statues and the diminutive pink marble Arc de Triomphe du Carrousel. To avoid being pestered by eternally hopeful polaroid camera touts, you could repair to the quieter and more elegant central backwater of the **Palais-Royal** gardens surrounded by 18th-century arcades with fascinating off-beat shops.

The *quais* (embankments) are particularly attractive and amusing to the east of the Louvre: booksellers' stalls on the river side, noisy petshops on the land side, and delightful views. The famous pedestrian **Pont des Arts** used to give the most picturesque views of all, but is now truncated and closed.

To the east of the Palais-Royal is the huge building site which used to be **Les Halles**—the central food market, the stomach of Paris according to Zola's celebrated formula. The market has for practical reasons been removed to the suburbs, and in its place came only indecision and

Place des Vosges

finally an underground commercial complex—the **Forum**. In the old days Les Halles was the place for all-night restaurants and the tradition lives on. The famous Pied de Cochon is open 24 hours a day, 365 days a year and nobody can remember when it last closed. Between Les Halles and the other major development scheme of modern Paris, Beaubourg, the **Rue St-Denis** runs north/south up to the Porte St-Denis. The Rue St-Denis has become synonymous with porno entertainment and shops, and you do not have to wait until nightfall to see what is for sale around here. Thousands of tourists and Paris-By-Night coachloads crowd the area, too; the atmosphere is not particularly threatening, although hardly refined, and spectating is a popular pastime.

Beaubourg is the name of the area redeveloped in the early '70s which includes the Pompidou Centre. The idea, as President Pompidou conceived it, was to provide not only a museum for modern art but also a focus for contemporary French culture. Inside the building, extraordinary and controversial in itself, there is lots to see and do. The plaza in front is a bit bleak but usually animated by all sorts of pavement artists. The whole area has benefited from the development, commercially at least; some seven million people a year visit, and new arty shops and restaurants are springing up all the time in what used to be an unsavoury part of town.

Between Beaubourg and the river, the seedy end of the **Rue de Rivoli** is the place for the most inexpensive department stores, and the **Place du Châtelet** for popular theatre. The Hôtel de Ville, on the old executionary Place de Grève, was rebuilt completely in the late 19th century in imitation Renaissance style, and is a building of no aesthetic distinction. Along the north of the central area from the Madeleine to the Bastille, the so-called **Grands Boulevards** (the only wide ones there were in Paris before Haussmann's time) occupy the site of the city walls knocked down by Louis XIV in the 17th century (Paris fortifications were thought to be more likely to be used against him than by him). Louis also put up a couple of handsome arched gateways—the Portes St-Denis and St-Martin—at what is now very much the popular end of the boulevards. Around the Opéra there are still some reminders of a grander and even more fashion-conscious style of living when dandies, beaux and many others paraded along the **Boulevard des Italiens**—the centre of Parisian elegance throughout the 19th century. Many of the succession of famous cafés and restaurants have now disappeared. The **Boulevard Haussmann**, which joins the Grands Boulevards behind the Opéra, has many of the bank headquarters and the biggest and best-known of Parisian department stores (Galeries Lafayette, Au Printemps).

To the east of the Hôtel de Ville—between the river, the Bastille and the easternmost Grands Boulevards—the area called the **Marais** (like Lutetia meaning marsh) is the former 17th-century heart of the city. It was later abandoned by fashionable residents and left to crumble, until a major campaign of restoration was started in the '60s. Now the old palaces, from the medieval Hôtel de Sens to the 18th-century Palais Soubise, and the delightful 17th-century **Place des Vosges** (formerly Place Royale), have been cleaned and restored to all their former resplendence; the area has come to life in an attractive way, with galleries, restaurants and a number of quiet and comfortable hotels. It is a fascinating area to explore—the only part of central Paris which does not bear the scars of botched 19th-century architectural surgery. The **Place de la Bastille** has no more prison, just a column commemorating a second generation of July revolutionaries (of 1830). It would be a more interesting place if Napoleon's plan to install a huge bronze elephant had been carried out.

The islands in the Seine—once three, but since the 17th century only two—are joined by a footbridge; they come into the 4th and 1st *arrondissements* and so are more "right" than "left" for administrative purposes, but fall between the two in style. They are moored to the banks by no fewer than 13 bridges; the **Pont Neuf**, despite its name, is the oldest (16th-century) and finest of Parisian bridges. The **Ile de la Cité**—the oldest part of Paris—is dominated by Notre-Dame, one of the finest Gothic cathedrals in France and one of the minority of Parisian landmarks which are more than merely picturesque. The imposing Palais de Justice hides most of the Sainte-Chapelle—saint Louis' royal chapel in what used to be his royal palace. One splendid part of the palace, complete with medieval round turrets, has not been destroyed—the Conciergerie, an infamous Revolutionary waiting room for condemned prisoners, including Marie Antoinette. Between Notre-Dame and the Palais de Justice is a flower market and in the angle of the bow of the ship (a comparison to which the *cité* lends itself irresistibly) the secluded, elegant **Place Dauphine** is one of the best addresses in Paris. There are interesting antiquarian shops all around the island's *quais* and very good views from both main banks of the river.

The **Ile St-Louis** was not inhabited until the 17th century; since then it has been endowed with some of Paris's most magnificent *hôtels*, which you cannot easily visit. It is still quiet, although hardly the residential backwater it once was—there are restaurants and hotels all along its main street—and it is one of the best places of all to stay as long as you don't have a car to park.

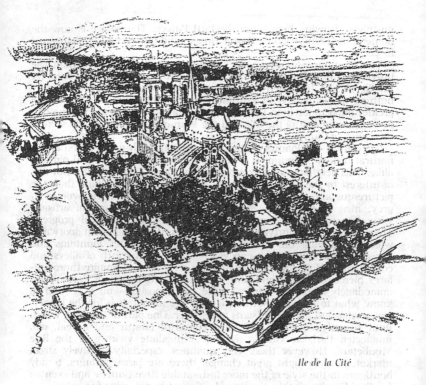

Ile de la Cité

The Left Bank

The Ile de la Cité and Ile St-Louis are moored to the Left Bank and the **Quartier Latin**, so called because of the common language of medieval Europe's most excellent and international university. The **Montagne Ste-Geneviève**, which climbs from the *quai* giving the best views of Notre-Dame to the domed churches of the Sorbonne and the Panthéon, is a genuine student quarter with academic bookshops, cheap oriental restaurants, cheap accommodation and cinemas for *cinéphiles*. The two main axes—the **Boulevard St-Germain** and especially the **Boulevard St-Michel**—have lately become anonymously commercial with Watney's pubs, Macdonalds and knick-knack stalls. The dominant Panthéon, a ponderous, domed neo-classical temple dedicated to the heroes of republican liberty, stands on top of the hill on the site of the former abbey of Ste-Geneviève, patron saint of Paris and its protectress against 700,000 Huns in the 5th century—as illustrated on the inside walls of the Panthéon. Its dome is best seen from down a sandy avenue in the **Luxembourg Gardens**, a traditional and very attractive context for student idleness. The Luxembourg is a mixture of formal and informal gardens: there are terraces, lawns, statues, a puppet theatre, tennis courts, and fountains—one of which, the 17th-century Fontaine de Médicis, is beautifully shaded and impressively monumental in proportions, with the sculpture of a cyclops about to squash some unlucky victims. The gardens originally belonged to the massive Luxembourg Palace, built for Marie de' Medici in a style to cater for her Florentine

43

nostalgia, drawing heavily on the Pitti Palace. The palace is now the home of the French Senate (Upper House) and only occasionally opened to visitors.

The Montagne Ste-Geneviève's history goes further back than the university: the hill was the main Roman settlement (the Gauls were on the Ile de la Cité). There isn't much left of Rome in Paris—certainly nothing to compare with Provençal remains of towns which were of greater importance than Lutetia—but remains of the Roman arena can be seen to the east of the hill, and the Roman baths can still be seen in the Hôtel de Cluny.

The **Jardin des Plantes** (botanical gardens), with a small zoo and a natural history museum, is a favourite park for children and old folk alike. This neighbourhood is a corner few tourists bother with. But it is of interest to the tourist who realises there is more to Paris than the picturesque and the exclusive central areas: old, poor Paris, women in grey, men in berets, Algerian immigrants and all sorts of artisans struggling against the overwhelming tide of technological progress. There are cobbled courtyards and mysterious dingy half-open doorways, washing hanging out of windows, communal water fountains and Paris' mosque (which you can visit)—all in a labyrinth of alleys and courtyards and peeling façades that the wide Second Empire thorough-fares pierced, crossed, but failed to reach. This aspect of Paris is not immediately attractive—indeed quite the opposite—and it is hard to know what to look for. Rather than for the tourist, it is for the longer-stay visitor and native Parisians to discover. One part of this area which until recently combined the most colourful charm and a real, old, unaffected Parisian vitality was the immediate vicinity of the **Rue Mouffetard**. However these very qualities, especially its lively street market, have brought great change: there are pizza parlours, trendy boutiques in the style of the more fashionable Rive Gauche and even *un bowling*. Despite all this, the Rue Mouffetard is still great fun.

Fashionable Rive Gauche means **St-Germain-des-Prés**, named after the most important of the abbeys of the Left Bank, whose noble church still stands at the heart of the *quartier*, looking down over the Cafés de Flore and des Deux Magots, the two melting pots for radical artistic and philosophical ideas of the first half of this century. Nowadays the cafés are expensive, and fuller of expectant tourists than intellectuals, and the tone of the area is set more accurately by the modern Drugstore across the road. All the same, the areas either side of the **Boulevard St-Germain** are full of very atractive, trendy and youthful shops, restaurants and art galleries. Leading down to the Ecole des Beaux-Arts by the river, the **Rue Bonaparte** is full of fascinating antique and antiquarian shops and there is a colourful market in the **Rue de Buci**. St-Germain-des-Prés is perhaps the most fun of all areas to stay in, and there is a wide selection of reasonably quiet hotels.

Between St-Germain-des-Prés and the Invalides, the **Faubourg St-Germain** was the favoured aristocratic residential area of the 18th century, and although ministries occupy much of it now, it is still an area of some elegance and little excitement. One *hôtel* to visit is the Hôtel Biron, now the beautiful setting for the Rodin museum. The Hôtel des Invalides, the majestic architectural complex that was Louis XIV's greatest legacy to Paris, was originally built to lodge war veterans, and now houses the Musée de l'Armée; the neighbouring Ecole Militaire is another of the finest examples of French 18th-century architecture. The approaches to these great military institutions from the river enclose another area much favoured as a place to live, quiet and well situated but without particular attractions for tourists.

Facing the Ecole Militaire, the **Champ-de-Mars** and the Eiffel Tower are about as far as most tourists will want to go downstream on the Left Bank.

To the south of the Invalides, **Montparnasse** was the Bohemian quarter of the early 20th century. Now it is no longer even particularly squalid, just lively and popular as a nightlife area, whose atmosphere (or lack of it) fits in with the bare modernism of the great Montparnasse tower.

Out of the centre

Of the outlying inner-city areas, the hill or *butte* of **Montmartre** is the one that all tourists want to visit, to admire at close quarters the basilica of Sacré-Coeur, whose domes pop up at the end of street perspectives all over the capital (even irreverently crowning the Madeleine from the Concorde). The Butte's other attraction is its past as the Bohemian village of the 19th century, with its narrow, steep cobbled streets and staircases. Utrillo's Montmartre is still a picturesque place to explore, and a couple of windmills have been preserved. Among the trees beneath the silhouette of the basilica, the **Place du Tertre** is the dense forum of snap-happy tourists and aspiring artists, who prop up their canvases but never seem to do much painting. It is a place to watch your pockets, and very lively at night, with crowds of young people around guitarists, and boisterous cafés and restaurants. Away from the small over-run area immediately around Sacré-Coeur, the slopes of Montmartre live up to their reputation as a good place for traditional bistros.

Clichy/Pigalle, at the foot of the Butte, lives off its reputation for traditional Parisian nightlife. Coaches still tip their loads into the eager portals of Clichy cabarets for music-hall *diner-spectacles*. By day, the area teems with popular Parisian life, with lots of cheap markets on the main boulevards.

On the western edge of the city, the **Bois de Boulogne** was laid out like Hyde Park when Anglomania was at its height. The Bois became the place to be seen horse-drawn, and still has style, with lakes for boating, paths for jogging or sporting a saluki, elegant open-air restaurants, race courses and *the* Paris sports club. There is also a less salubrious aspect to the Bois, and it is traditionally the place where Parisians abandon their pets before leaving the capital for a month's sunbathing in the traffic jams of the Autoroute du Soleil.

The **Bois de Vincennes**, like that of Boulogne, was made into a park in the late 19th century, and included within city limits half a century ago. You can visit the very impressive keep of a medieval royal fortress, France's largest zoo, exotic gardens, and several museums, including a good one devoted to the arts of ex-colonial Africa.

Sightseeing

So many of Paris' great monuments border the river, or like Notre-Dame float on it (*fluctuat nec mergitur*—she is tossed but not submerged—is the town's watery motto) that to walk along the banks of the Seine and over the bridges is the most agreeable introduction to Parisian sightseeing.

Viewpoints

Arc de Triomphe Massive triumphal arch planned by Napoleon but not finished for many decades (Napoleon put up a canvas version for a triumphal procession), crowning the view from the Louvre. Of the sculptures, one of those facing the Champs-Elysées is Rude's masterpiece of Republican ardour (the Marseillaise). Tomb of the unknown soldier beneath; splendid view of radiating avenues (commemorating Napoleonic victories) and most of Paris from upper platform. Closed Tues.

Eiffel Tower The appropriate symbol of Parisian lightness and exhibitionism (its 7,000 tons are only the equivalent of 57 lbs per square inch dead weight, and it was built for the 1889 World Exhibition) gives the highest (nearly 1,000ft) view—which does not mean the finest, to most eyes—of the capital and beyond. Lifts or, if your legs and stomach are up to it, 1,652 stairs. Top stage no longer closed in winter since four new electric lifts have been installed. Restaurants at stages one and two.

Montparnasse Tower Very big views; on the 56th floor an observatory with orientation frieze, and a bar and restaurant.

Notre-Dame Climb the towers for very good views, not least over the spine, statues and gargoyles of the cathedral herself.

Sacré-Coeur Good views of Paris from the terrace in front of the basilica, and from the walkways around the domes.

Samaritaine Department Store Free and beautiful, although modestly elevated, view over the *cité* from the roof terrace.

Museums

From cigarettes to meteorites, there is a museum for it in Paris. For art lovers there are the museums of world-wide celebrity—the Louvre and the Jeu de Paume—and also private collections bequeathed to the nation, less exhausting and in some ways more satisfying. Everyone can enjoyably sample a few of the less obvious Paris museums: the Musée Guimet for Oriental Art, or the Museum of Posters; and those with some knowledge of French history and literature may enjoy a visit to famous Paris cemeteries. Some museums are of specialist interest, notably those devoted to particular artists—Moreau, Delacroix, Balzac. All those we have chosen offer exceptional collections of their kind; some are better displayed than others.

Most national museums in Paris close on Tuesday, and some are either cheaper or free on Sunday or Wednesday. Those run by the Municipality of Paris generally stay open on Tuesday, and outside the capital Versailles too is open then.

Musée de l'Affiche The poster as art, and the history of advertising and thereby society—fascinating stuff. Closed Tuesday.

National Archives (Bibliothèque Nationale) Not just dusty shelves, but a museum of national history. Particularly fascinating section on the Revolution—Louis XVI's diary of July 1789 with an entry for July 14th: "Rien". Well worth a visit just to admire the decorations of the rooms which house the museum: the Palais Soubise and the nearby Hôtel de Rohan are the best examples of Rococo refinement in France.

Musée de l'Armée In the Hôtel des Invalides, one of the finest military museums in the world, with splendid collections of arms and armour, Napoleon's greatcoat, battle models and film shows. The superb domed church, France's masterpiece of Baroque church architecture, seems made to measure for the huge porphyry tomb of France's greatest soldier, surrounded by symbolic victory figures. In the upper part of the church there are more tombs of French martial heroes (Foch, Turenne).

Musée d'Art Moderne de La Ville de Paris Near the Palais de Chaillot, this is the municipal modern art museum, with choice works from Paris' great arty period at the beginning of the century. Free Sunday; closed Monday.

Musée des Arts Décoratifs In the Louvre Palace (entrance Rue de Rivoli), the evolution of French taste in applied art down the ages. Fascinatingly displayed; reopened 1985 after a number of years of large-scale reorganisation. Closed Monday and Tuesday.

Musée National des Arts et Traditions Populaires On the edge of a children's amusement park in the Bois de Boulogne; rural French life and folklore past and present, attractively displayed. Closed Tuesday.

Musée Carnavalet A beautiful partly Renaissance *hôtel* with formal gardens in the heart of the Marais, containing a municipal museum mainly devoted to the history of Paris: old prints and paintings, models, a collection of inn and shop signs and a series of reception rooms decorated as in the days of Madame de Sévigné, who held her famous salon here. Free Sunday; closed Monday.

Palais de Chaillot Four museums and a theatre, in the curved wings with gardens and fountains which were built on the the Trocadéro Hill for the 1937 Exhibition, to crown the monumental perspective that stretches from the Ecole Militaire up the Champ de Mars to the Eiffel Tower. The **Musée de la Marine** has model ships, old maps and navigational instruments; maritime history from Christopher Columbus to Jacques Cousteau. Children love it. Closed Tuesday. The **Musée des Monuments Français** was based on Viollet-le-Duc's scholarly initiative: plaster-cast highlights of French architecture and sculpture and repro-duced frescoes, often very much more easily admired than in dingy country churches. A fascinating place if you like that kind of thing (children usually don't). Closed Tuesday. The **Musée de l'Homme** (ethnography and anthropology) has displays of art and artefacts from civilisations all over the world—Easter Islands to Greenland—and of the evolution of man. Half-price Sunday; closed Tuesday. In the basement is the **Musée du Cinéma**—closed Tuesday.

Musée de la Chasse Hunting museum including animal paintings, in the splendid 17th-century Hôtel Guénégaud; a favourite with children. Closed Tuesday.

Musée de Cernuschi A private collection of oriental art, including terracotta funerary statues of great antiquity. Closed Monday.

Musée de Cluny Housed in one of the few surviving medieval *hôtels* in Paris. An exceptionally fine collection of medieval works of art, including the famous series of tapestries The Lady and the Unicorn; and remains of Roman baths dating from the 3rd century AD. Half-price Sunday; closed Tuesday.

Musée Cognacq-Jay Another private collection, of mainly 18th-century works of art. Free Sunday; closed Monday.

Conciergerie The Law Courts' prison dates from the 14th century, but its historical interest is of the time of the Revolution when it was the antechamber to the guillotine. You can visit the Prisoners' Gallery, the Women's Court, Marie Antoinette's cell and mementoes of her kept in the Girondins' Chapel museum. Half-price Sunday.

Les Gobelins A chance to see tapestries being woven in the old-fashioned way, in the state factory by royal appointment to Louis XIV. Visits afternoons only, Tuesday, Wednesday and Thursday.

Grand Palais The principal location for temporary art exhibitions, near the Place de la Concorde. The Grand Palais also houses the **Musée de la Découverte**—science museum with films, lectures, and working models which you can operate yourself—and the **Planetarium**, both popular with children. Other sites for temporary exhibitions are the **Orangerie**, the twin of the Jeu de Paume at the end of the Tuileries, with a room full of waterlilies by Monet, and a recently opened extension of the **Palais du Luxembourg**.

Paris

Musée Grévin A Madame Tussaud's of France: disappointing compared with the London version, but always popular and open every day. Further exhibits (illustrating the Belle Epoque) are displayed in an annexe in the Forum des Halles centre.

Musée Guimet A national collection of arts from the Orient, from India to Japan. Half-price Sunday; closed Tuesday.

Musée Jacquemart-André A very fine private collection, with many beautiful French 18th-century paintings, and some from the Italian Renaissance. Closed Monday and Tuesday.

Musée du Jeu de Paume In a former tennis court in the Tuileries Gardens beside the Place de la Concorde. Closed August 1986: reopening (for temporary exhibitions only) as the Galérie de Jeu de Paume. The Impressionists are now in the Musée d'Orsay.

Musée du Louvre Speculation as to the world's richest museum usually ends at the Louvre: there can be few rooms in the world to beat the Salle des Etats, where the Mona Lisa is just one among many master works of the Italian Renaissance. The Louvre is a vast and magnificent royal palace beside the Seine, built first as a fortress by Philippe Auguste in the late 12th century and not finished until the late 19th century in the stodgy architectural style of the Second Empire. The oldest and most distinguished part of the exterior is a section of the closed court (Cour Carrée) dating from the late 16th century, and the colonnade of the east end designed by Perrault for Louis XIV. The museum itself is of daunting size, even though it fills only a part of the huge palace. It cannot possibly be visited all at once (imagine trying to do the National Gallery, British Museum and V & A in a day), and you should plan the route carefully to satisfy particular interests. If you just want to see the world-famous masterpieces, make sure that you do not get side-tracked and exhausted on the way.

Because François I persuaded Leonardo da Vinci to spend his last years in France, the Louvre is richer than anywhere else in the world in the works of one of the greatest and least prolific of painters. You can follow the Louvre's supremacy in French painting from the 14th century to the middle of the 19th, with two particularly good rooms containing many 19th-century masterpieces. Other countries, with the notable exception of Britain, are also very well represented. There are also large and very distinguished collections of Oriental, Egyptian and classical antiquities (stars in the last category being the Venus de Milo and the Winged Victory of Samothrace), European sculpture (Michelangelo's Slaves) and *objets d'art*, including the French crown jewels displayed in the magnificent Apollo Gallery, designed by Le Brun. There are lecture tours twice daily, except Sundays. Entrance is free on Sunday, but some rooms are liable to be closed. Closed Tuesday.

Musée Marmottan In a sedate residential quarter on the edge of the Bois de Boulogne, a connoisseur's private collection (furniture and works of art from various periods) has been given much wider appeal by two important bequests of works by Monet, including the "Impression—Sunrise" which christened the Impressionist school, and endless water-lilies painted at Giverny. Relatively expensive but uncrowded; closed Monday.

Musée de Montmartre A small museum of the history of the hilltop village and its Bohemian villagers, among Paris' only vines. Open each afternoon and from 11.00 on Sunday.

Musée Nissim-de-Camondo Next door to the Cernuschi, in the patrician residential area on the edge of the Parc Monceau; an outstanding collection of 18th-century furniture in an elegant and period context. Closed Monday and Tuesday.

Musée d'Orsay Comprehensive new national collection of art between 1848 and 1914 including the Impressionists from the Jeu de Paume. Splendidly housed in the restored Gare d'Orsay—its former hotel still extravagantly *fin-de-siècle*, its vast nave full of multi-level modern galleries.

Petit Palais Another of the municipal museums which come into their own when national ones close. This is a fun art-nouveau palace in itself, and its art collections are varied, beautiful and not too big. Paintings, especially of the 19th and early 20th centuries; tapestries, *objets d'art*, furniture, some temporary exhibitions. Closed Monday.

Musée Picasso In a 17th-century Marais *hôtel*, opened September 1985, the artist's own very extensive collection of his and other contemporary artists' works. Closed Tuesday.

Centre Georges Pompidou (Beaubourg) Among many other cultural workshops, libraries and reading rooms (which it was hoped would make Beaubourg into the engine-room of living French culture) is the **National Museum of Modern Art**, which is as good as it should be here in the most important centre of early 20th-century art. Free Sunday; closed Tuesday. Opposite, in a basement in the Rue Beaubourg, is the small **Musée Français de l'Holographie**, where three-dimensional images are created from patterns of diffracted light. Fascinating for children.

Musée de la Poste History of communication and rare stamps. Closed Sunday.

Musée Rodin A great favourite among the lesser known and less visited museums, and the best endowed of those museums in Paris devoted to individual artists. The works of this 19th-century sculptor are displayed inside and around a beautiful *hôtel* near the Invalides. Half-price Sunday; closed Tuesday.

Musée National des Techniques France's national science museum; very interesting and enhanced by the setting in the old abbey of St-Martins-des-Champs, with a magnificent 13th-century refectory, and very early Gothic church housing old planes and cars. Free Sunday; closed Monday, and mornings Tuesday to Saturday.

Churches

With a few notable exceptions, Paris is not a city that you remember for its churches—as you do Rome or Florence. Most visitors will want to see Notre-Dame—you can hardly avoid it—and the Sainte-Chapelle; and Paris has the best examples in France of church building after the

Renaissance—which means little more than a few splendid domes, the most splendid of them all sheltering Napoleon's tomb. Several of the churches listed below close at lunchtime, and on certain days of the week; some are undergoing restoration. Enquire at the tourist office for up-to-date information.

Madeleine Built like a Greek temple with the Last Judgement on the pediment. According to the grand design of Napoleon, the Madeleine's colonnade is an admirable finish to the perspective which crosses the Place de la Concorde to the similar colonnade of the Chambre des Députés across the river. The domed interior is sumptuously decorated.

Notre-Dame A great Parisian landmark, and one of the great Gothic cathedrals in France. Superlative early Gothic sculpture around front and side doorways, atmospheric warm lighting within. It's well worth admiring the east end from the gardens behind. Frequent organ recitals.

Sainte-Chapelle After Notre Dame, the church in Paris which everyone wants to visit. It's a Gothic chapel on the site of an old royal palace, now in the middle of the law courts; very small and often extremely crowded. The crypt-like lower floor for servants is distinguished by 19th-century repainting of glistering unpleasantness; the upper chapel is slender and uncomplicated, just a framework for stained glass of exceptional beauty (undergoing restoration). Entrance charge.

St-Denys-du-St-Sacrement Not a very beautiful early 19th-century church in the Marais, but Delacroix' very powerful altar-piece of the *Pietà* is well displayed.

St-Etienne-du-Mont A very unusual church with a jumbled classical façade dating from the early 17th century, and inside an exceptionally delicate Renaissance rood screen with spiral stairways around its pillars.

St-Eustache On the edge of the old Les Halles market, renamed the Temple of Agriculture in the Revolution. One of Paris's most impressive churches, a 16th- and 17th-century giant, built in the conventional Gothic way—with rose windows and flying buttresses—long after the style breathed its last vital gasp. Very good recitals.

St-Germain-l'Auxerrois Gracious Gothic and Renaissance royal parish church opposite the classical façade of the Louvre. Unwittingly, St-Germain bell ringers triggered off the massacre of St Bartholomew's Day (August 24th, 1572) which started the wars of religion. The interior is much damaged and diminished in works of art but still of interest. Lovely Flemish altar-piece in the chapel on the left-hand side.

St-Germain-des-Prés Paris's oldest surviving church, once part of a large abbey in the fields, now at the heart of one of the most colourful and attractive areas of the city. Romanesque tower and parts of the nave; varied works of art inside.

St-Gervais-St-Protais A late Gothic church built mostly in the 16th century with the first systematic classical façade in France. It was hit by a shell on Good Friday 1918 by a long-range German gun (Big Bertha); 50 people were killed. Very varied works of art inside. Recitals.

St-Julian-le-Pauvre Tiny, very old and charming, with an appropriately small garden giving a favourite view over Notre-Dame.

St-Louis-en-L'Ile A beautiful and harmonious late 17th-century gilt interior adorned with contemporary sculpture. Older works of art around the chapels.

St-Paul-St-Louis Built in the domed Jesuit style in the mid-17th century, a tall and imposing classical façade and some beautiful works of art inside including a 16th-century marble Virgin by Pilon.

St-Séverin A very Parisian Gothic church in that it grew in width because there was no land available for lengthy extension. There is an unusual, very pleasing double ambulatory, and a famous organ.

St-Sulpice Large and somewhat ponderous classical church containing exceptionally fine mural paintings by Delacroix in the first chapel on the right. Beautifully decorated Lady Chapel at the east end, and another famous organ.

Val-de-Grâce Architecturally distinguished domed mid-17th-century church built for Anne of Austria in thanksgiving for the birth of Louis XIV after 23 years of waiting. Inside, a museum of military medical history—the former abbey became a military hospital at the time of the Revolution.

Cemeteries A favourite and moody place for reflective Parisian perambulation, in a particularly gloomy part of town, is **Père-Lachaise**: lots of famous tombs (Abelard and Heloïse, Oscar Wilde, Edith Piaf) and a common one for 147 anonymous defenders of the Commune, whose resistance came to an end in the cemetery on May 28th 1871. The **Montparnasse** and **Montmartre** cemeteries have other famous artists' and poets' tombs.

Shopping

Haute couture The most famous names are in the 8th arrondissement, around the Champs-Elysées—Avenues Marigny, Montaigne, George V, Victor Hugo, and Faubourg St-Honoré. Don't assume that they're all inhospitable to the casual shopper—small items and accessories are sold too, and perfume may be as cheap as duty-free.

Prêt-à-porter Famous names (but slightly more accessible to the average consumer) are scattered throughout Paris, but several (Cacharel, Benetton, Ted Lapidus, Micmac) have boutiques in the new Forum des Halles centre, or in the Claridge centre in the Champs-Elysées. Another good hunting ground is the Boulevard St-Germain.

Jewellery The famous names are mainly around the Place Vendôme, Rue de la Paix and Faubourg St-Honoré; also Forum des Halles.

Boots and shoes Several good shops in Rue François Ier; also Forum des Halles, Boulevard St-Germain, and Rue du Faubourg St-Honoré.

Books Particularly numerous bookshops (of all sorts) in the 6th *arrondissement* (around the Boulevard St-Michel and Boulevard St-Germain).

Antiques Many in the 6th and 7th arrondissements, including Rue du Bac and Rue Bonaparte.

China, porcelain and glass The big names—including Christofle, and Lalique—can be found in the 8th *arrondissement* (Rue Royale); and the Rue de Paradis (10th) has no fewer than five good shops, including Baccarat for crystal.

Department stores Two of the largest and best are in the Boulevard Haussmann: Galeries Lafayette, and Au Printemps. La Samaritaine is by the Pont Neuf.

Food and wine The big names—including Fauchon, Fouquet, Hédiard and Michel Guérard's Comptoir Gourmand—are treasure troves of goodies, selling almost anything including *foie gras*, honey, cakes, chocolates, mustard, wine; they are concentrated in and near the Place de la Madeleine (8th *arrondissement*), where you will also find La Maison de la Truffe, and specialist cheese and wine shops. The Rue St-Louis-en-l'Ile has a good cheese shop, and one of Paris best ice-cream makers, Berthillon. L'Herbier de Provence has several branches of its herb shops, including one in the Forum des Halles. For year-round (and daily) oysters, try Boutique Layrac in the Rue de Buci, which also has produce from several French regions.

Markets Eight different flea markets in the St-Ouen area around the Porte de Clignancourt (open Saturday, Sunday and Monday); others at the Porte de Montreuil, Porte de Vanves, Porte de Lilas, and Porte de Pantin. Popular and colourful food markets in the Rue Mouffetard (5th *arrondissment*) and the Rue de Buci (6th), and a large flower market on the Ile de la Cité.

Information

The main tourist office, Office de Tourisme, is at 127 Avenue des Champs-Elysées, tel (1) 47.23.61.72.

Hotels

The Office de Tourisme can help with hotel bookings, and can give information on accommodation. It is very important to book accommodation well in advance, even during the quieter months. Hotels in Paris are more expensive than those of equivalent standard outside the capital; in general (with the exception of the luxury hotels) their bedrooms are small, they have no restaurant (though breakfast is almost always available), and they have quite a wide range of prices depending on the exact facilities of the bedroom (private bathroom, or basin and bidet). In the simpler hotels there are usually few facilities: very often no porter, or lift, for instance. There are many more hotels of character in Paris than in London; but some hoteliers share Parisians' abruptness. It is often worth asking for a room at the back, or on the courtyard side.

The following is our selection of Paris hotels, covering all but the cheapest categories. Most are central, and within easy reach of a Métro station; many are charming. Most have no restaurant; where they do, there is no obligation to eat there. We haven't inspected any of the restaurants in the hotels in this section.

The price categories in this section differ from those in the other area chapters, reflecting the larger range.

£ = You are likely to find a bedroom for under £30.
££ = Most bedrooms cost between £30 and £45.
£££ = Most bedrooms cost between £45 and £75.
££££ = Most bedrooms cost between £75 and £100.
£££££ = Bedrooms cost over £100.

These prices are for a double or twin room and do not include breakfast.

ABBAYE ST-GERMAIN £££
10 rue Cassette, 75006, 6e   Tel: (1) 45.44.38.11

Set back from a street of small shops, this was a 17th-century town house; occasional touches remind you, but the interior is otherwise stylishly modernised. There are two salons, one opening onto the charming central courtyard, used in summer for drinks and breakfast. No restaurant, but a cosy breakfast room and an attractive bar. The bedrooms (and bathrooms) are fresh and pretty, excellent quality throughout. It's an exceptionally comfortable hotel, with friendly staff, central and peaceful—not surprisingly, it's usually booked up very early.

45 bedrooms; no rest; parking. *Métro:* St-Sulpice

ANGLETERRE £££
44 rue Jacob, 75006, 6e   Tel: (1) 42.60.34.72

Cream-coloured 19th-century building (once the British Embassy) in an attractive street of shops and galleries between the Seine and the Boulevard St-Germain. There's an elegant lounge with velvet sofas and a piano, and a pretty breakfast room; the slight formality of the public areas is lightened by a cheerful glassed-in garden overlooked by a small pleasant bar. Bedrooms vary in size and style— mostly traditional. Excellent value for a comfortable central hotel.

31 bedrooms; no rest. *Métro:* St-Germain-des-Prés

BALZAC   £££££
6 rue Balzac, 75008, 8e   Tel: (1) 45.61.97.22

Dignified 1910 street-corner building (formerly the Hotel Celtic) near the Champs
Elysées, recently converted into a very stylish luxury hotel. Art deco mixes with
ultra modern, thoroughly comfortable. Bedrooms are well equipped (and air-
conditioned), spacious and elegant; the bar and restaurant atmospheric with
subtle lighting, domed ceiling and boxed trees. Cheaper than the other hotels in its
class.

70 bedrooms. *Métro:* Etoile.

BRADFORD   ££
10 rue St-Philippe-du-Roule, 75008, 8e   Tel: (1) 43.59.24.20

On a minor crossroads in a central area of bars and restaurants near the Champs-
Elysées, the Bradford is a comfortable hotel with classical décor—there's a
civilised and quite formal salon, and a smaller plainer breakfast room. Bedrooms
vary considerably in size but are well furnished in similar traditional style;
bathrooms are old-style and slightly disappointing by comparison. The
quieter rooms are those overlooking the inner courtyard.

48 bedrooms; no rest. *Métro:* St-Philippe-du-Roule

BRETONNERIE   ££
22 rue Ste-Croix de la Bretonnerie, 75004, 4e   Tel: (1) 48.87.77.63

This 17th-century house in the Marais, picturesque old heart of Paris, has been
skilfully transformed into a hotel of charm and character. Sturdy old beams and
some rough-stone walls set the style; solid period furniture and gentle lighting add
to the atmosphere. Your bedroom may be split-level, or tucked under sloping
eaves. Even the more ordinary rooms are prettily decorated, and there's nothing
antique about the bathrooms.

30 bedrooms; no rest. *Métro:* Hôtel de Ville

BRISTOL   £££££
112 rue du Faubourg Saint-Honoré, 75008, 8e   Tel: (1) 42.66.91.45

One of the grandest luxury hotels, in one of the most expensive streets, the
Bristol—convenient for the Elysée Palace—is patronised by diplomats and heads
of state. Its splendours include signed period furniture, Gobelin tapestries, vast
expanses of oriental carpet, marble pillars, old masters. . . it also has a swimming
pool on a 6th-floor terrace. The salons and the superb restaurant surround a
formal French garden. Bedrooms are coolly classical, bathrooms voluptuous; a
new wing has more modern elegance.

191 bedrooms; parking. *Métro:* Miromesnil

DES CÉLESTINS   £
1 rue Charles V, 75004, 4e   Tel: (1) 48.87.87.04

Set on a quiet corner in the Marais district, this small hotel feels personally
welcoming. There's no lounge, but you can relax with a magazine among the
paintings, plants and antiques of the attractive reception area. Bedrooms are
individual and charming, with old beams (the house dates from 1623), tiled floors
and pretty chintzes; bath or shower rooms, equally appealing, are well-planned.
It's also good value—as British visitors have already discovered.

15 bedrooms; no rest; no lift. *Métro:* Sully-Morland/Bastille

Hotels

COLBERT   £££
7 rue de l'Hôtel Colbert, 75005, 5e   Tel: (1) 43.25.85.65

Elegant modern cream building on three sides of a small front courtyard, in a street of restaurants between the Seine and the Boulevard St-Germain. It's formal and heavily traditional, with a restful bar-lounge and reception area; bedrooms are soft blues and greys, fairly small but prettily furnished. Very little street noise considering its location.

40 bedrooms; no rest. *Métro:* Maubert-Mutualité

COLISÉE   £££
6 rue du Colisée, 75008, 8e   Tel: (1) 43.59.95.25

In a relatively quiet street off the Champs-Elysées, this modernised hotel exudes traditional comfort. Substantial buttoned chairs and chesterfields (and brown-windsor tones) make the lounge and bar a clubby retreat; bedrooms are lighter, in pleasant co-ordinated colours. Good traditional-style furniture, convenient modern gadgets and pretty bathrooms provide an atmosphere of well-planned tranquillity.

45 bedrooms; no rest; parking nearby. *Métro:* Franklin D. Roosevelt

CRILLON   £££££
10 Place de la Concorde, 75008, 8e   Tel: (1) 42.65.24.24

The Crillon's 18th-century façade is a landmark: soundproofed windows overlook the roaring concourse of Right Bank traffic. One of the world's great hotels, it's pride is to remain authentically French—all renovations retain or recall the Classical elegance of Louis XV. The building itself is beautiful; a stately sequence of salons, a graceful inner courtyard, a grand staircase; however rich the décor, tranquil dignity prevails. Only the famous restaurant is unrestrainedly sumptuous. Bedrooms and apartments are vast, peaceful, exquisite.

190 bedrooms; parking nearby. *Métro:* Concorde

DANUBE   £££
58 rue Jacob, 75006, 6e   Tel: (1) 42.60.94.07

In a fairly busy St-Germain street, a pleasant old house decorated throughout with care and charm. The public rooms are fresh and light, a summery blend of flowery walls, trailing greenery and white chairs. In the ample bedrooms matching fabrics set the style—"very Sanderson"—and colour schemes are restful. Some are a little faded now, though, and bathrooms are small.

45 bedrooms; no rest; parking nearby. *Métro:* St-Germain-des-Prés

DES DEUX CONTINENTS   ££
25 rue Jacob, 75006, 6e   Tel: (1) 43.26.72.46

Another of the several hotels in this attractive shopping street, with bedrooms in two of its three buildings overlooking the rear courtyard away from traffic noise (though without lift access, and therefore cheaper). This is an inexpensive central hotel, with a warm atmosphere; antiques in the friendly lounge, cane in the green and white breakfast room; bedrooms neat and pretty at the back, more traditional at the front.

40 bedrooms; no rest; no lift at rear. *Métro:* St-Germain-des-Prés

DEUX ÎLES £££
59 rue St-Louis-en-l'Ile, 75004, 4e Tel: (1) 43.26.13.35

In the middle of the island on a narrow street of boutiques and restaurants, this is
a 17th-century building with balconies whose imaginative conversion into a
hotel a few years ago retained the personality of a private house. The combined
reception and lounge area is most appealing, and there's a glass-sided central
garden well. The basement bar (not open in high season) is a rustic-style
"tavern". Bedrooms are not large, but charming and comfortable with a
frequency of blue and white, repeated in the particularly nice bathrooms,
decoratively tiled. It's central, quiet and altogether pleasing.

17 bedrooms; no rest. *Métro:* Pont Marie

DUCS DE BOURGOGNE ££
19 rue Pont Neuf, 75001, 1er Tel: (1) 42.33.95.64

This modern hotel is in a wide street just off the rue de Rivoli near the Louvre. It
was renovated recently and the public rooms—the lounge, and the basement
breakfast room—are comfortable. Bedrooms are simple, with modern décor, and
pretty bathrooms. Modest, friendly, noisy at the front.

49 bedrooms; no rest. *Métro:* Pont Neuf

ESMERALDA £
4 rue St-Julien-le-Pauvre, 75005, 5e Tel: (1) 43.54.19.20

Small Left Bank hotel opposite a green square near Notre-Dame, dating from the
17th century but smartly renovated outside. The interior is slightly eccentric, like
its friendly lady owner—her reception area is a delightful cluster of antiques,
worn velvet and riotous plants. There's no lounge, but a small light breakfast
room. Bedrooms have an old-fashioned *boudoir* flavour—low-hanging lamps and
plush velvet—but they're rather small and dark. Bathrooms vary from good
modern to *tiny*. Some street noise filters up.

19 bedrooms; no rest; no lift. *Métro:* St-Michel

FRÉMIET £££
6 Av Frémiet, 75016, 16e Tel: (1) 45.24.52.06

In a peaceful side street not far from the Palais de Chaillot and (across the river)
the Eiffel Tower, this is an attractive and well-appointed hotel. With the exception
of the striking modern breakfast room—stone-walled, lamp-lit, black bamboo
with flowery cushions—the house style is traditional French. Bedrooms are light
and spacious, individually planned and well-furnished, with modern bathrooms.

36 bedrooms; no rest; garage nearby. *Métro:* Passy

GAILLON OPÉRA £££
9 rue Gaillon, 75002, 2e Tel: (1) 47.42.47.74

Slim 7-storey building in a side-street near the Opéra, built around a small
glassed-in courtyard garden. Bedrooms (some fairly small) are attractive and
comfortable, individually decorated, with good bathrooms; the salon is cosy, with
beams, stone walls and velvet chairs. Not cheap, but centrally situated.

26 bedrooms; no rest. *Métro:* Pyramides

Hotels

GRANDS ÉCOLES £
75 rue de Cardinal Lemoine, 75005, 5e   Tel: (1) 43.26.79.23

Set well back from an undistinguished street in the Latin quarter, this hotel resembles a Provençal house—cream walls, blue shutters and creepers, surrounded by rampant garden and shady trees. It's fairly basic; there's a cheerful homely reception area but no other public rooms. The bedrooms are simply furnished, rustic-style with pretty prints, some with shower and some limited to a basin: garden views—the trees so close that they darken some of the windows— and a fair amount of space. *Not* luxury, but an enjoyable rural atmosphere.

36 bedrooms; no rest; no lift. *Métro:* Cardinal Lemoine/Monge

DES GRANDS HOMMES/PANTHÉON £££
17 and 19 Place du Panthéon, 75005, 5e   Tel: (1) 46.34.19.60
                                                and (1) 43.54.32.95

Neighbouring elegant 18th-century buildings which have been well renovated in varying styles. Both have glassed-in gardens; you breakfast on tapestry chairs under vaults of roughcast stone. Bedrooms retain their beamed ceilings, and are attractively and individually furnished; bathrooms are glossily modern. Two civilised hotels, on a square that's quiet by night.

32 bedrooms; no rest; parking easy. *Métro:* St-Michel/RER Luxembourg

L'HÔTEL £££££
13 rue des Beaux-Arts, 75006, 6e   Tel: (1) 43.25.27.22

Ultra-sophisticated hotel with unique atmosphere and outrageous prices; it's in a street once the home of artists and academics, and has been a hotel in various guises since the 18th century. The building's not conspicuous, but bears a plaque commemorating Oscar Wilde—here in 1900 he "died beyond his means"—and the theme is played up; his room is recreated, and the receptionist sports a bow tie and centre parting. The whole place is exclusive, eccentric and full of flair. Décor is mostly 18th and 19th century, both reproduction and real (Mistinguett's furniture)—with excursions into cocktail modernity. Bedrooms are plush and padded with sumptuous bathrooms but small except at the top of the price range. A fascinating place, frequented by Paris society and famous names.

27 bedrooms. *Métro:* St-Germain-des-Prés

D'ISLY ££
29 rue Jacob, 75006, 6e   Tel: (1) 43.26.32.39

Grey 18th-century building next door to the *Deux Continents*; it's modernised inside, with an air of helpful efficiency. The open-plan reception and lounge has comfortable sofas and a small breakfast area; bedrooms are well decorated but lack charm. Not a specially French hotel, but good value.

37 bedrooms; no rest. *Métro:* St-Germain-des-Prés

LANCASTER £££££
7 rue de Berri, 75008, 8e   Tel: (1) 43.59.90.43

One of the smaller grand hotels of Paris, with copious courteous staff and the sort of service that would undoubtedly include babysitting. Its traditional elegance is attractively warm and varied—original Impressionists in one salon, a "club" atmosphere in another, flowers everywhere, no two sumptuous bedrooms alike. Many rooms open onto the delightful central courtyard-garden where drinks and meals are served in summer; street-facing rooms are insulated from noise.

58 bedrooms; parking. *Métro:* Etoile

LENOX ££
9 rue de l'Université, 75007, 7e Tel: (1) 42.96.10.95

Among book and antique shops in this not too noisy street in the Faubourg St-Germain, the Lenox was totally renovated a few years ago. Its marble salon has a drawing-room atmosphere, with chintz and velvet, and there's a bright and stylish bar. Bedrooms are warm and beautifully decorated, compensating in charm for their smallish dimensions. A very civilised hotel—comfortable and traditional without being stuffy.

34 bedrooms; no rest. *Métro:* Rue du Bac

LUTÈCE £££
65 rue St-Louis-en-l'Ile, 75004, 4e Tel: (1) 43.62.23.52

Near its sister hotel the *Deux Iles* in the same street, the Lutèce has a similar façade, and inside considerable charm but less class. Its reception-and-lounge area feels like a spacious country house, with the original beamed ceiling, tiled floor and stone fireplace. In the bedrooms modern fabrics mix with antiques; they're on the small side but comfortable and individual, with good bathrooms.

23 bedrooms; no rest. *Métro:* Pont Marie

DES MARRONNIERS ££
21 rue Jacob, 75006, 6e Tel: (1) 43.25.30.60

This tall old hotel is peacefully set between a courtyard and a garden, complete with the chestnut trees, overlooked by a graceful glazed veranda. In the spacious old stone-vaulted cellars, the breakfast room and lounge are comfortably furnished with antiques, rugs and real flowers in profusion. Bedrooms too have antiques and fine old beamed ceilings; some are light and airy, some smaller and vivid; all very pretty. Bathrooms, even when small, are well-equipped. A soothing and delightful place, understandably very popular.

37 bedrooms; no rest. *Métro:* St-Germain-des-Prés

MAYFAIR ££££
3 rue Rouget de Lisle, 75001, 1er Tel: (1) 42.60.38.14

In a side street off the rue de Rivoli, this very central hotel is peaceful and civilised, a blend of 19th-century proportions and modern convenience. The lounge and reception area is elegantly traditional, but provides pleasantly squashy seating for weary sightseers and a piano; the bar is comfortable and subdued with panelling and velvet. Spacious bedrooms with quiet colour schemes incorporate TV and minibars in their uncluttered comfort, and bathrooms are impeccable.

53 bedrooms; no rest. *Métro:* Concorde

MAYFLOWER ££
3 rue de Châteaubriand, 75008, 8e Tel: (1) 45.62.57.46

Next door to the *Résidence Lord Byron* and now under the same ownership, this is a pleasant and well-run hotel. The lounge (doubling as breakfast room) has attractive chairs and sofas, warm colours and low lamps. Bedrooms are light and modern, restful and quite pretty, with good-sized bathrooms. Conventional, comfortable, relaxed.

24 bedrooms; no rest; garage nearby. *Métro:* Georges V

Hotels

MOLIÈRE ££
21 rue Molière, 75001, 1er · Tel: (1) 42.96.22.01

In a historic little street, this, they say, is the oldest hotel in Paris; the house goes back 380 years and was occupied by Voltaire and used as a private theatre. It's very traditional and very French. Public rooms are simple, comfortable and old-fashioned: lounge rather formal, bar club-style in leather. The bedrooms are quiet at the back, noisy at the front, some rather small and some rather dark but all cosy. It's a welcoming place, of considerable charm.

32 bedrooms; no rest. *Métro:* Pyramides

PANORAMA ££
9 rue des Messageries, 75010, 10e · Tel: (1) 47.70.44.02

Should you require a quiet hotel convenient for the Gare du Nord or the Gare de l'Est, the Panorama is comfortable. Behind its bland modern façade it has a pleasantly traditional lounge and reception area with fat velvet sofas, a pine-panelled breakfast room, and spruce well-furnished bedrooms with particularly attractive bathrooms.

48 bedrooms; no rest. *Métro:* Poissonnière

LE PAVILLON £
54 rue St-Dominique, 75007, 7e · Tel: (1) 45.51.42.87

This captivating little hotel is set back from a small shopping street near the Eiffel Tower. It's an 18th-century former convent, a white-painted building with flowery window boxes; in front there's a cheerful patio. Very little public space inside; just the reception room. Bedrooms are fresh and quiet, their flowery charm compensating for their smallness. It's altogether homely and modest, with a delightful atmosphere.

19 bedrooms; no rest; no lift; parking nearby. *Métro:* Invalides

PLACE DES VOSGES £
12 rue de Birague, 75004, 4e · Tel: (1) 42.72.60.46

An old and pretty building on a quiet street in the Marais district, this hotel has been thoroughly converted inside. Downstairs the décor is pleasantly French-traditional; rather rustic in the reception and breakfast area, with stone walls and ornate chairs. Upstairs is more neutrally modern—neat, bland and small bedrooms and efficient bathrooms, all in excellent order. Good value in an attractive location.

16 bedrooms; lift from first floor only. *Métro:* St-Paul

PRIMA-LEPIC £
29 rue Lepic, 75018, 8e · Tel: (1) 46.06.44.64

An unusual hotel in busy Montmartre, its ground floor conceived as an indoor patio. In both lounge and breakfast room, white garden furniture provides hard but decorative seating among a great many plants and flowers (some real, some not); there's a new, beamed TV area. Bedrooms are cosier—individual, small and prettily decorated, with careful colour schemes and mostly traditional furniture. Bathrooms are modern. Bedrooms at the front of the hotel are now double glazed and quiet.

38 bedrooms; no rest. *Métro:* Blanche

PRINCE ALBERT ££
5 rue St-Hyacinthe, 75001, 1er Tel: (1) 42.61.58.36

A thoroughly traditional hotel in a 200-year-old building, right in the centre of Paris. Its public rooms are pretty and welcoming; comfortable chairs under the chandelier and elaborate cornice of the lounge, a small panelled breakfast room. Upstairs, rather dim corridors lead to bedrooms which vary considerably in appeal; but all are very well-kept, and bathrooms are spacious. Distinctly good value in the area.

33 bedrooms; no rest; garage nearby. *Métro:* Tuileries

RAPHAEL ££££
17 Av Kléber, 75016, 16e Tel: (1) 45.02.16.00

Built in the 1930s, set on a busy street near the Arc de Triomphe, this is the smallest of the Parisian grand hotels. Its period style (Louis XVI, Empire) is both restful and fascinating; wood panelling everywhere, glowingly dark or gracefully light, is the background for vast mirrors and dim paintings. Contemplation of rich detail is positively invited by the old-fashioned comfort of the elegant public spaces. Enormous bedrooms with splendid bathrooms are sumptuously appealing—panelled, mirrored, draped and beautifully furnished. The whole hotel is a magnificent retreat from the traffic, the weather or just the modern world.

87 bedrooms; carpark nearby; *Métro:* Kléber

RÉCAMIER £
3bis, Place St-Sulpice, 75006, 6e Tel: (1) 43.26.04.89

Small friendly hotel tucked away on a shady square opposite the church—very central (St-Germain-des-Prés), yet quiet. It's a tall narrow Victorian-style building, severe from outside but cheerful within; there's a homely little lounge and breakfast room, no bar or restaurant. Bedrooms are modern and bright, on the small side but quiet and with a pleasant outlook; bathrooms adequate. Convenient and popular.

30 bedrooms; no rest. *Métro:* St-Sulpice

RÉGENCE-ÉTOILE ££
24 Av Carnot, 75017, 17e Tel: (1) 43.80.75.60

A Regency-style hotel on an attractive but busy tree-lined boulevard, comfortably traditional throughout. The lounge is divided into three, with areas for breakfast and television off the main salon. Bedrooms are pleasantly old-fashioned with some feminine touches; most are a good size with modern bathrooms; those at the back darker and quieter. Good value.

38 bedrooms; no rest. *Métro:* Étoile

REGENT'S GARDEN £££
6 rue Pierre Demours, 75017, 17e Tel: (1) 45.74.07.30

Set back from a quiet residential street a few minutes' walk from the Arc de Triomphe, this fine 19th-century townhouse was built for Napoleon III's physician. Rear windows open onto its urban garden; lawn and flowers, tall trees and small statues, scattered tables for summer breakfasts. Indoors the handsome public spaces are furnished in period. Bedrooms too are traditional; they vary in size (some enormous) but all are pretty and solidly comfortable, with excellent modern bathrooms.

40 bedrooms; no rest; small carpark. *Métro:* Ternes/Étoile

Hotels

RELAIS CHRISTINE ££££
3 rue Christine, 75006, 6e Tel: (1) 43.26.71.80

This hotel, opened in 1979, is a luxurious conversion on the site of a 16th-century abbey, in a relatively peaceful little street of old houses in St-Germain-des-Prés. There's a courtyard and a green garden (not for use, only to look at); rooms overlook one or the other. The whole interior is calm and spacious, a blend of rustic and rich modern design. There's no bar or restaurant, but there's an imposing breakfast room in a vaulted cellar and a clubby, panelled salon. The bedrooms have the same plain warm tones and handsome design; some are split-level, all have excellent bathrooms, minibars and other conveniences. Comfort of high degree.

51 bedrooms; no rest; parking in basement. *Métro:* Odéon

RÉSIDENCE DU BOIS ££££
16 rue Chalgrin, 75116, 16e Tel: (1) 45.00.50.59

Delightful exclusive small hotel in a minor road close to the Arc de Triomphe; it's a Napoleon III mansion, restored in period throughout with antiques, tapestries, paintings and murals. Two glowing little salons; a small clubby bar; beautiful silk and velvet bedrooms, elegant and very quiet; luxurious bathrooms. Drinks and light meals are served in the charming leafy garden.

19 bedrooms; no rest; no lift. *Métro:* Étoile

RÉSIDENCE DU GLOBE £
15 rue des Quatre-Vents, 75006, 6e Tel: (1) 43.26.35.50

A 17th-century St-Germain house, where all the rooms are small, personal and completely charming. Past the discreet reception desk the ground-floor lounge is adorned with antiques, massed paintings and a suit of armour; the tiny bedrooms and bathrooms under the old beams have rugs and hangings, assorted pretty furniture and more paintings. Breakfast and drinks are served in your room, and a thoroughly intimate atmosphere prevails.

Closed 3 weeks Aug; 15 bedrooms; no rest; no lift; parking nearby. *Métro:* Odéon

RÉSIDENCE LORD BYRON ££
5 rue de Châteaubriand, 75008, 8e Tel: (1) 43.59.89.98

On a narrow street near the Champs-Elysées, this is a square 19th-century building with an imposing entrance and a very elegant reception lobby. Glass doors lead through to a patio. The lounge is more relaxed and modern in shades of blue with comfortable cushioned seating and T.V. Bedrooms, some rather small, are well modernised with occasional Victorian touches, quieter at the back. No bar, but drinks are available and the bigger "apartments" have minibars; service and atmosphere pleasantly personal.

30 bedrooms; no rest; garage nearby. *Métro:* Georges V

RIBOUTTÉ LAFAYETTE £
5 rue Riboutté, 75009, 9e Tel: (1) 47.70.62.36

Off the rue Lafayétte in an area convenient for department stores, nightlife and the main railway stations, this hotel has been recently refurbished inside. The small reception and lounge area is light and bright. Bedrooms too are small, friendly and colourful, with new modern bathrooms. Quiet and good value.

24 bedrooms; no rest; car park nearby. *Métro:* Cadet

RITZ   £££££
15 Place Vendôme, 75041, 1er   Tel: (1) 42.60.38.30

Opened in 1898 and patronised by the *haut-monde* ever since, the Ritz was
revamped in 1972 losing none of its sumptuous grandeur. Public rooms range
from Louis XV salons, ornate and dignified, to comfortable modern bars; the
restaurant is exquisitely elegant; summer eating and drinking also takes place
in the flowery gardens. A Ritz bedroom is the height of rococo splendour, draped
and gilded; a Ritz bathroom is a classic in marble. Here—for those who can afford
it—is the ultimate in formal French luxury, in the most exclusive part of Paris.

163 bedrooms; parking. *Métro:* Concorde

ROBLIN   £££
6 rue Chauveau-Lagarde, 75008, 8e   Tel: (1) 42.65.57.00

Fin de siècle hotel on a busy street near the Madeleine, with a sheltered inner
courtyard. Its unchanging old-fashioned comfort can seem faded and lifeless or
elegantly atmospheric, depending on your taste. The public rooms are spacious
and formal; the bar and breakfast room are more modern, relaxed but rather
dark; the restaurant is attractive in white and gold. All the bedrooms have high-
ceilinged proportions and a spacious air, while they in fact vary in size—the
biggest and grandest overlook the noisy street; others, in the same house style,
have tall windows opening onto the courtyard. They're solidly comfortable, with
good bathrooms.

70 bedrooms (lots of singles). *Métro:* Madeleine

SAINT-DOMINIQUE   £
62 rue St-Dominique, 75007, 7e   Tel: (1) 47.05.51.44

The street is busy, but most rooms of this 18th-century building overlook a quiet
courtyard at the back. The hotel has been renovated quite simply, in varying
styles. Most traditionally attractive is the lounge and reception area: beams and
white walls, antiques and plants, red velvet cushions and a friendly welcome.
There's a little breakfast room, rustic-style. Bedrooms (and bathrooms) are
disappointingly cramped; they're prettily papered, with modern fittings. A good-
value sightseeing base.

32 bedrooms; no rest. *Métro:* Latour-Maubourg

ST-GERMAIN-DES-PRÉS   £££
36 rue Bonaparte, 75006, 6e   Tel: (1) 43.26.00.19

A well-kept traditionally French hotel; shuttered front windows overlook a fairly
busy street, but it's peacefully secluded within. The public area is a single large
room, comfortably spread with traditional furniture and lots of plants. Bedrooms
feel intimate rather than small—they're well fitted and discreetly lit; bathrooms
are modern.

30 bedrooms; no rest. *Métro:* St-Germain-des-Prés

SAINT-LOUIS   ££
75 rue St-Louis-en-l'Ile, 75004, 4e   Tel: (1) 46.34.04.08

The third of the sister hotels in this very central street (guests can use the bar of
the *Deux Iles*), this is rather the poor relation—five storeys with no lift, smaller
and plainer bedrooms in modern style, some cramped bathrooms. But though less
comfortable, it too has charm and character and the public area is attractive.

21 bedrooms; no rest; no lift. *Métro:* Pont Marie

Hotels

SAINT-SIMON £££
14 rue de St-Simon, 75007, 7e   Tel: (1) 45.48.35.66

Very pretty white 18th-century house on a stylish little street of restaurants and
wine bars off the Boulevard St-Germain—it's bigger than it looks, with a second
19th-century building behind, and a flowery patio. The salon is charming,
elegant and very lived-in, full of antiques and personal treasures. The bedrooms
(most face away from the street) have character, and individual appeal; double
rooms rather small but twins a good size. Altogether a quiet and very welcoming
hotel.

34 bedrooms; no rest. *Métro:* Rue du Bac

SCANDINAVIA ££
27 rue de Tournon, 75006, 6e   Tel: (1) 43.29.67.20

Unique and extraordinary little 15th-century *hôtel*, outwardly inconspicuous
among bookshops and boutiques near the Luxembourg Gardens. The interior has
been restored throughout to Louis XIII period, with an abundance of portraits,
armour and antiques. There's no restaurant, no bar and no alcoholic drinks
available but it still feels welcoming. The bedrooms are ornate and astonishing,
each with a different handsome blend of antiques, mirrors, candelabras, rich
velvets and elaborately carved beds. They're so warmly interesting that it seems
almost irrelevant to mention that they're fairly small, and slightly noisy on the
street side.

Closed Aug; 22 bedrooms; no rest; no lift. *Métro:* Odéon

SOLFÉRINO ££
91 rue de Lille, 75007, 7e   Tel: (1) 47.05.85.54

On a relatively quiet street near the Seine and Concorde, the Solférino is within
easy walking distance of attractions on both sides of the river. It's a white, early
19th-century building, with a particularly fresh and inviting interior. The lounge
area has a touch of grandeur—lofty ceiling, large classical oil-painting, handsome
carpets and furniture—while the little breakfast room is simple and summery.
Bedrooms are small, but mostly bright and pretty; there's very little noise. It's a
hotel with a lot of charm and a very welcoming atmosphere.

Closed 2 weeks Dec; 33 bedrooms; no rest. *Métro:* Solférino

SUÈDE ££
31 rue Vaneau, 75007, 7e   Tel: (1) 47.05.00.08

An attractive *Directoire* building in a rather dull street of embassies near the
Invalides, this hotel has only a small gravel patio of its own but overlooks gardens
at the back—including the Prime Minister's. Inside it is suitably *Directoire* in style;
the comfortable panelled lounge is spacious and sophisticated. Bedrooms vary
only in size—each has a restful colour scheme, a good bathroom, and elegant
furniture including a desk. There's a little traffic noise at the front, but many
rooms have a peaceful leafy rear view.

41 bedrooms; no rest. *Métro:* Sèvres-Babylone

THOUMIEUX
£££
79 rue St-Dominique, 75007, 7e   Tel: (1) 47.05.49.75

Jolly, popular and very Parisian restaurant with rooms in a small shopping street
near the Eiffel tower. Bedrooms are well decorated and stylish, with good
bathrooms. There's a comfortable salon and breakfast area, and good
straightforward country cooking in the restaurant. A thoroughly friendly place.

10 bedrooms. *Métro:* Tuileries.

LES TUILERIES
£££
10 rue St-Hyacinthe, 75001, 1er   Tel: (1) 42.61.04.17

Late 18th-century house, very centrally located in a small quiet street near the
Place Vendôme. Recently renovated, it's elegant throughout in Regency style.
Public space is very limited; hallway and tiny pretty salon which doubles as
breakfast room. Bedrooms are either quiet spacious and elegant at the front, or
smaller and darker at the back; all have pleasant compact bathrooms.

28 bedrooms; no rest. *Métro:* Tuileries

UNIVERSITÉ
££
22 rue de l'Université, 75007, 7e   Tel: (1) 42.61.09.39

In a narrow street in the Faubourg St-Germain, this old town house keeps its
original stone walls and beams and has a fine collection of antiques. A glassed-in
garden softens the handsome reception area; the lounge is split-level and relaxed.
Bedrooms vary considerably (reflected in the tariff); all have antiques and charm,
but some are showpieces complete with marble bathrooms.

28 bedrooms; no rest. *Métro:* Rue du Bac

DE VARENNE
££
44 rue de Bourgogne, 75007, 7e   Tel: (1) 45.51.45.55

From its narrow street this hotel looks unpromising, but through the arched
entrance you're welcomed by a pretty breakfast patio with pots of flowers and
high creeper-covered walls. Inside the décor is sober, but the atmosphere very
friendly. The small reception area is open-plan with the dim but comfortable
lounge (serious wallpaper and velvet armchairs). Bedrooms are modern,
inexpensively but prettily furnished, with new bathrooms; most are quiet.

24 bedrooms; no rest. *Métro:* Varenne

WELCOME
£
66 rue de Seine, 75006, 6e   Tel: (1) 46.34.24.80

Small, attractively renovated hotel in a lively street of food shops and stalls, on a
corner of the noisy Boulevard St-Germain. Some rooms are triangular—including
the first floor lounge with its beams and rough plaster walls. Bedrooms are small
but new and bright with pretty colours and fabrics, bathrooms equally small but
well modernised. It does live up to its name, with a warm and friendly
atmosphere.

30 bedrooms; no rest. *Métro:* St-Germain-des-Prés

The Ile-de-France

Château de Versailles

"*La gloire est le soleil des morts*" (Balzac)

The Ile-de-France

The Ile-de-France, original land of the Franks and cradle of the monarchy, is one of the sightseeing treasure grounds of France; yet few visitors to Paris bother to venture beyond the gates of the capital which it surrounds. From the point of view of the tourist, the Ile-de-France may be compared with the Loire valley. It may not have the river, nor the wine, nor the regional identity; but it does have châteaux great and small. Although these don't look like illustrations in a book of fairy stories, they're more rewarding to visit, for in general their contents are more lavish and their historical interest more varied.

After a short half-century of royal château building in the Loire (something of a playful period of recuperation after the long suffering of the Hundred Years' War) the kings of France inevitably moved back to the Ile-de-France, whence they had been banished by the English and Burgundians. At Fontainebleau, François I created a court for himself in a new style, and later kings added St-Germain-en-Laye and eventually Versailles, Compiègne and Rambouillet to the list—all royal palaces within range of and not too close to Paris, a compromise between hunting pursuits and administrative convenience. In these royal châteaux and in the no less interesting ones built by royal servants and the nobility, the full development of French history, architecture, painting, furniture, garden and park design—in short, taste—from the middle of the 16th century until the late 19th century, is on display as nowhere else. In addition to this wealth of châteaux, the Ile-de-France has some of the finest examples of the Gothic style of architecture, first convincingly put into stone and glass by Louis VI's versatile advisor, abbot Suger, in the church of St-Denis. Chartres and Beauvais can claim perhaps the most beautiful and certainly the most extreme realisations of the style.

The countryside of the Ile-de-France is attractive, and to the beauty of the landscape is added the pleasure of seeing it through the eyes of 19th-century painters. It was then that landscape painting became fashionable, and artists abandoning Paris found the rivers, poplars and forests of the Ile-de-France waiting for them. Impressionists loved to paint Parisians at leisure in the then countrified surroundings of the Seine (now swamped by the westward growth of Paris). Monet—who was more interested in pure landscape—went to the Epte, others to the Oise. The Barbizon school has even stronger links with a particular area: the Fontainebleau forest. More than the Impressionists who came after them, Fontainebleau artists were landscape painters in the tradition of the Dutch 17th-century masters, relishing the chiaroscuro light effects of the forests and the images of everyday peasant life. The forests of Chantilly, Fontainebleau, Compiègne, and Rambouillet—which attracted the French kings (and more recent rulers) as the forest of Chambord did in the Loire—have now been preserved from destruction, and count among the Ile-de-France's greatest attractions.

The Ile-de-France has changed, of course; some would say it is becoming Greater Paris. But by comparison with London at least, it does not give this impression. The city of Paris is very densely populated, and commuting from the Ile-de-France happens on only a relatively small scale. Recent decentralisation has resulted in a few industrial new towns

The Ile-de-France

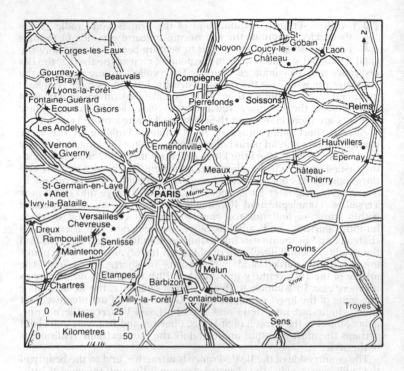

on the edge of Pontoise and Meaux, for example, and the extension of the Métro (the Réseau Express Régional) has been accompanied by the growth of a few new residential communities in the countryside; but these remain fairly isolated and the Ile-de-France is—apart from week-end tourism—remarkably little affected by Paris. By Parisians however the area is in no way neglected, now that nature, fresh air and healthy outdoor pursuits as an antidote to the stresses of modern city life, and especially Parisian life, have become such a serious and indeed worrisome preoccupation of the city dwellers. The gates of Paris on Friday evenings, Saturday mornings and Sunday evenings are the scenes of such horrific traffic jams that Parisians on their way to week-ends in the country must wonder whether a week-end in Paris would not after all be more relaxing. At week-ends the woods, rivers and châteaux are packed with day-trippers. But during the week the area is comparatively empty, and you can visit the sights—including the great royal palace of Fontainebleau—without having your enjoyment spoilt by an uncomfortable degree of crowding.

Our description of the Ile-de-France divides the area into sectors which can be visited in separate excursions from Paris, although a number of them cannot reasonably be attempted in a single day. Many of the sights feature in organised coach excursions from Paris, and most of the towns and some of the villages can easily be reached by train or by underground. But the Ile-de-France is certainly not to be discounted as a region to tour, and in which to stay—there is plenty of accommodation, mainly catering for the needs of Parisians (prices are relatively high as a consequence). Barbizon is outstanding for the quantity and variety of its hotels; here, as elsewhere in the region, most are comfortable but may seem rather artificial with their studiously rustic style.

South-west and west of Paris

The **Château de Versailles** is France's most popular tourist attraction, visited by some 3 million tourists every year. You will get your wings burnt if you pay less than a full day's homage to its creator, Louis XIV, the Sun King; and a full day will leave you, though not Versailles, exhausted. For this is not just another château where you do the interior, perambulate briefly in the surrounding gardens and continue on your way. There are various guided tours around different sections of the palace as well as a large part of it where your visit is described as "libre"—unguided but not free. The park and gardens are large (although only one-tenth of their original size) and varied and even contain a couple of out-châteaux to visit.

Louis said "L'état c'est moi"; but he might with no less truth have said "L'état c'est Versailles". Versailles was the *Ancien Régime*, the gilded prison which kept the most important element of the French nobility busy with petty intrigues far from their provincial power bases. It also provided the appropriately magnificent and rigorously ordered image of Louis' monarchy for public consumption. The personality which is expressed by the place is not that of the artists that created it but of Louis XIV; the great triumvirate achievement (Le Vau succeeded by Mansart for the architecture, Le Brun for the interiors and garden sculptures, and Le Nôtre for the gardens) is a team effort of individual talent subordinated to the effect of the whole. Louis' own role he likened to that of the sun—his bed was sited at the exact centre of the château, on the east-west solar axis.

But Louis did not create his egocentric universe in seven days. The marshy land on which his father's small brick and stone château stood had to be drained (and paradoxically water had to be supplied to feed 1,400 fountains). The vast palace and gardens themselves had to be constructed in several campaigns spanning decades. Eventually over a thousand members of the French nobility and their servants lodged in the palace itself—in notoriously insanitary conditions. Louis also saw to it that Versailles town, which had to grow rapidly to accommodate all the courtiers, did so in appropriate style. He granted land for nothing except a promise to follow strict architectural guidelines, to ensure that the town should not rival the château but show it off with a degree of architectural unity. The town retains this severe classical unity today despite its growth into an important residential suburb, with the N10 passing right round the spacious Place d'Armes in front of the château.

To the west of the palace terraced gardens and park represent the strict order Louis XIV imposed on Nature as he did on his country. There is a formal section with crisp gravel, pools with splendid river gods, and an orangery; and there is a spacious area with imposing avenues, intimate arbours, a beautiful marble colonnade where Marie-Antoinette listened to concerts, and fountains and sculptures rising from the waters of their basins. In the park beyond there are more waters and an artificial Grand Canal, where Louis XIV had a troop of Venetian gondoliers running a fleet of boats (you can still hire boats). From here there is a splendid view of the palace from a distance of nearly two

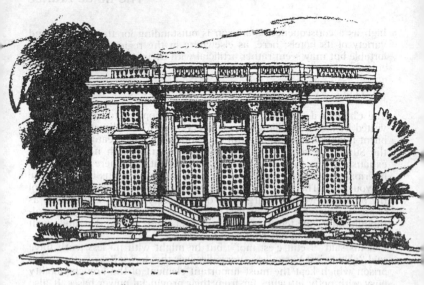

Petit Trianon, Versailles

miles. The great event in the gardens is the so-called Grandes Eaux, when all the remaining fountains are activated for an hour or so in the afternoon of the first and third Sundays of summer months. It is crowded of course, but memorable.

The interior of the château has been changed even more than the exterior, much of it having been transformed in the 19th century into an historical museum dedicated "to all the glories of France". But the central section of the building has kept many of its original Louis XIV decorative schemes and these are being restored, slowly but to magnificent effect. After the superb chapel, you visit the most impressive rooms, the Grands Appartements. Although not all furnished (many of them never were, being reception rooms) they are sumptuously decorated, with paintings and stucco-work, all with predictable themes related to Louis, triumph, and the sun. You visit too the apartments of king and queen—the Queen's Bedroom, where royal births were watched by crowds, has been the object of particularly beautiful restoration. The fabulous 75-metre Galerie des Glaces (mirrors not ice-creams) which looks out over the gardens was where most important festivities and receptions took place, as did the signing of the Treaty of Versailles in 1919. To the south of the Queen's Apartments is the even longer but architecturally uninteresting Galerie des Batailles, constructed in the 19th century to house dozens of huge paintings of French victories. Other parts of the museum are devoted to French history from the 16th to the 19th centuries. Most visitors find the Grands Appartements quite enough. Those who want to see more can visit the Petits Appartements of king and queen with a guide. Not surprisingly, they are smaller and more intimate. Louis XV preferred this style and a certain amount of privacy, and took up residence in the king's Petit Appartement which is now a marvellous example of the decorative style of his reign, a delicate contrast to the monumental grandeur of the Louis XIV style.

The Ile-de-France

Another masterpiece of restoration is the opera house, which was built at the end of Louis XV's reign to celebrate the marriage of Louis the Dauphin with Marie-Antoinette of Austria. It was here, in the alcoholic and smoky aftermath of a banquet where Versailles bodyguards entertained Flemish officers on October 1st 1789, that a toast to the nation was refused and tricolour rosettes trampled underfoot. When the news of this insult reached Paris the queen was blamed—as she was for everything else—and the great march on Versailles followed.

On the north-west edge of the palace, on land bought from the monks of the parish of Trianon, Louis XIV commissioned a small pavilion, called the Porcelain Trianon after its Oriental-style décor. In 1687 Mansart built in its place the much more magnificent Grand or Marble Trianon. Its manageable size affords a pleasant contrast with the main palace, but it is no less sumptuous inside; now it is used for the most prestigious of state visitors. Most of the furniture is in the Empire style of the early 19th century. Nearby there is a carriage museum and the sober classical Petit Trianon, like an elegant town house, built by Louis XV for madame de Pompadour. Marie-Antoinette, who couldn't stomach the minutely regulated etiquette of court life, spent weeks on end here in what were construed by the poisoned tongues of jealous courtiers to be extravagant orgies. But there is no evidence that the Queen indulged in anything more shocking than amateur drama at the Petit Trianon, which has also been recently restored and contains some late 18th-century furniture and *objets d'art*. The gardens are appropriately informal, a Rousseau-inspired idyll with a curious pseudo-rustic hamlet around a lake where Marie-Antoinette and her friends liked nothing more than to play at being peasants, until the peasants decided to play at being royalty.

The area south-west of Paris cannot, even excluding Versailles, be seen in a day. If no more time is available, one of the châteaux in the **Chevreuse** area may reasonably be combined with the town of Chartres. Dampierre is the most beautiful of them, but Breteuil and Rambouillet of more varied interest.

This a particularly green and intimate region of river valleys and sandy woods (**Les Vaux de Cernay**), good for picnics and walks, and frequented at week-ends. **Chevreuse** lies on the river below feudal ruins, but has no particular charm. **Senlisse** has a choice of restful accommodation. The **Château de Dampierre** is a moated brick and stone building of impressive and sober elegance, mostly built in the late 17th century. The interior (with guided tour) contains some beautifully furnished and decorated rooms in the styles of Louis XIV and XV, as well as much from the 19th century in a more ponderous vein—nowhere more ambitious and less successful than in the remarkable Salle des Fêtes upstairs, where the ageing Ingres tried to do for Dampierre what Raphael did for Rome. There is a large and well-maintained park with swans.

Realising that their château is not going to pull crowds for reasons of architectural or decorative distinction, the enterprising proprietors of the **Château de Breteuil** have filled its rooms with well-dressed wax models of those prominent people whose paths members of the distinguished Breteuil family have crossed. A gouty Louis XVIII sits in his very own chair, Marcel Proust reclines in a lacquer bed, and the prince of Wales (Edward VII) and French prime minister discuss the Entente Cordiale over a drink with cigars. There are temporary exhibitions in the old kitchens, concerts in summer, and a snack bar which is open at week-ends.

The **Château de Rambouillet** has been a presidential residence for the last 85 years. The building itself (with guided tours) is no beauty outside or in but the park is of interest. Here as at Versailles Marie-Antoinette is thought to have employed the landscape painter Hubert Robert to create gardens in the English style, with rare trees and rhododendrons. Her pastoral tastes are commemorated by a classical temple-like dairy which was built so that she could escape from the château which she hated and drink milk, which is about as far as her involvement with the dairy process ever went. Nearby there is a thatched cottage whose round main room is entirely decorated with sea shells and mother of pearl. Louis XVI's agricultural interests were more serious than those of his wife: to improve the quality of French cloth he bought a flock of merino sheep from the king of Spain, and had them shepherded on an epic journey. On June 15th 1786, 334 ewes, 42 rams and 7 leading sheep left Segovia, crossed the Pyrenees at St-Jean-Pied-de-Port, and all but 16 ewes and one ram safely reached Rambouillet on October 12th. The National Sheep Farm is still flourishing, and you may be guided around it by one of the young and enthusiastic students of ovine genetic engineering and other related topics. If you've never thought of sheep as magnificent beasts, you may be in for a surprise.

At the northern end of Rambouillet forest (which has lakes, cycle and walking trails), **Montfort l'Amaury** is a delightful old village at the foot of a ruined fortress. The ruins themselves are less interesting than the elegant Gothic-Renaissance church which has a beautiful series of 16th-century windows.

Between Rambouillet and Chartres you may pause at **Maintenon** to admire the unfinished aqueduct whereby Louis XIV hoped to feed Versailles with water for its fountains. To divert the river Eure a three-tiered aqueduct of nearly three miles in length was planned, but unfortunately Louis' funds were diverted instead of the river, human resources were eroded by malaria, and after over 100,000 man-years of work—by which time the short bottom register of arches had alone been accomplished—the project was abandoned. The **Château de Maintenon** is a composite building of medieval, Renaissance and 17th-century elements. It was bought by Louis XIV in 1674 for the young and beautiful Françoise d'Aubigné, later madame de Maintenon, who took charge of the king's children by madame de Montespan and gradually supplanted their mother in the king's affections. Soon after the death of the queen in 1683 Louis XIV secretly married madame de Maintenon, who became a major force beside the throne for the last 30 years of the king's reign occupying the difficult position of king's wife (but not queen) with great humility and tact. The guided tour around the château reveals many souvenirs of the good if disingenuous woman, but little of great beauty. Most of the gardens are out of bounds, for the château is still inhabited by madame de Maintenon's descendants.

Chartres is the principal market-town of the flat cereal-growing Beauce Plain—not really part of the Ile-de-France, and different from it in its spaciousness. The town is well situated by the Eure, from whose banks and hump-backed old bridges there are beautiful views of the cathedral, one of the great treasures of France and perhaps her best-loved church. Chartres is well worth the journey from Paris, and is also well placed beside the motorway for visits in transit. Its accommodation is however not very attractively situated—around the station or on the busy ring-road.

The Ile-de-France

✳ *Cathedral* The glorious pale golden church is world famous thanks to its
stained glass and its asymmetrical western façade whose twin towers dominate
the surrounding cornfields. Apart from the elaborately carved Gothic spire
which crowns the north tower, the façade dates from the 12th century, and
the famous south tower is the tallest of the Romanesque period in France,
sober, solid and elegant. Around the west doorways there are marvellous
examples of the elongated figure sculpture of the period, contrasting sharply
with the more realistic later sculptures—hardly lesser masterpieces of their
period—around the south and north doorways. Once inside the widest nave in
France, you may be dazzled by the 13th-century stained glass, whose famous
blue is so brilliant that sun seems to be pouring through it on the dullest days.
The screen around the choir is decorated with a wealth of remarkable carving,

*From the cathedral's west door a carving
of Aristotle, Greek philosopher whose
logical writings formed one of the pillars of
medieval scholarship; cathedral schools like
the one at Chartres played a major role in
the education of the period*

73

most of which dates from the last days of the Gothic style and is full of fascinating detail and great vitality. There is an abrupt change to vapid posturing and fluttering draperies in the scenes executed in the 18th century to finish the series (Lives of Christ and the Virgin). On the floor of the nave there is a rare labyrinth, a spiral pattern of black and white stone (usually obscured by chairs) around which pilgrims advanced on all fours. Those interested in giving the cathedral more than a cursory glance will find the daily guided tours in English rewarding. There are also official guided tours, in French, around the 11th-century crypt, the largest in France, which has some interesting frescoes.

✷ *Fine Arts Museum* An interesting collection of glass, furniture, tapestries, paintings, and an exceptional series of Limoges enamels, all housed in the elegant 18th-century archbishop's palace in gardens behind the cathedral.

✷ *St-Pierre* A large Gothic church in the lower town beside the Eure near the best viewpoints for the cathedral. The church itself has a splendid array of flying buttresses and its own distinguished stained glass from the 14th and 16th centuries.

At the **Château d'Anet** just about enough remains to give you an idea of the architectural beauty of what was once the finest of all French Renaissance châteaux, built by the highly original Philibert de l'Orme for Diane de Poitiers around 1550; very little is left of the splendour of its decoration which included the enamels now at Chartres. The most interesting surviving elements are the circular domed chapel and the entrance gateway, featuring a cast of Cellini's famous bronze of Diana. South of Anet, **Dreux** is an important old frontier town (between France and Normandy) on the edge of a magnificent forest. Its best known monument is a fine belfry—part Gothic, part Renaissance.

The châteaux of Malmaison and St-Germain-en-Laye are both accessible by Paris public transport and can be visited together in a suburban excursion. In the ugly suburb of Rueil-Malmaison, the **Château de Malmaison** is externally unexceptional and very little of the gardens remains. The inside however is a rich and fascinating Napoleon museum. Malmaison was bought by Josephine Bonaparte in 1799 and became Napoleon's favourite resort in pre-Imperial days. Although the château was emptied of its contents in the 19th century it has been thoroughly restored, and now contains many more interesting and beautiful works of art and pieces of furniture than it did when the Bonapartes were in residence. There are many personal mementoes of interest, something of the atmosphere of a residence if not a home—the decorative schemes of the rooms, in many cases characteristically pretentious and eccentric, have also been restored—and an ensemble of decoration, furniture and works of art which forms one of the finest collections of the Empire style.

The old royal **Château de St-Germain-en-Laye** is situated in a more attractive suburb and stands on a hill above the Seine with what must once have been a splendid view as far as the Arc de Triomphe nearly 15 miles away. The château is a sombre red-brick pile built for François I. but incorporating some elements of an older fortress (notably the early 13th-century chapel which is rather like the Sainte-Chapelle in Paris without the stained glass). Building works going on all round the château do not help the general effect. Until Louis XIV moved to Versailles, St-Germain was the most important residence of king and court, though it shows little sign of its royal past. Since the 19th century the château has been occupied by the National Museum of Antiquities which has recently been modernised. The large and important archaeological collection illustrates the history of homo sapiens and France from the earliest times up to the 8th century AD. Although the gardens are not what they were in St-Germain's 17th-century heyday, it is worth wandering as far as Le Nôtre's famous terrace, whence the view reminded the exiled James II of Richmond.

Just outside the western edge of the forest of St-Germain—but sadly robbed of all its park and gardens—the **Château de Maisons** in Maisons-Laffitte is one of the masterpieces of French classical architecture, built in the 1640s by François Mansart, and intact apart from the grounds. There are a few guided tours each week (take counsel before setting off) around the richly decorated but unfurnished interior.

North and north-east of Paris

Most of the interest in the wide area between the right banks of the Seine and the Marne falls along or near the valley of the Oise. There is too much to see for one day; the two main centres of interest, Chantilly and Compiègne, deserve separate excursions.

Isolated in the north of the region **Beauvais** is like Chartres best situated for transit visits, on the road from Boulogne to Paris. Like Chartres too it is the large centre of a wide agricultural area which is dominated by the soaring silhouette of an astonishing cathedral. From 1664 to 1940 Beauvais was one of the greatest centres of French tapestry making, but bombs destroyed the tapestry manufacture and most of the old town.

* *Cathedral* Architects and their patrons in the early days of the Gothic style strove to outdo each other in terms of sheer height. The trend reached its dizzy climax at Beauvais where an early 13th-century bishop and chapter commissioned a new church to rival Amiens, Paris and the rest. The vaults of the choir were built over 150ft from the ground, but had inadequate foundations and collapsed twelve years after completion. Today the reconstructed choir is the highest Gothic vault in existence. The transept was built in the very elaborate style of the early 16th century, and an ambitious attempt to erect a 450ft spire over the crossing caused another collapse. The project of adding a nave was eventually abandoned leaving just a part of the 10th-century cathedral (a very rare example of the period) dwarfed by the immense Gothic greenhouse to which it is attached. Despite the damage the building has suffered, the south and north transept doorways (Renaissance and Gothic respectively) are full of delightful carvings. As well as being architecturally remarkable, the interior has some very fine tapestries and stained glass in the transept. Near the north door there is a 19th-century astronomical clock of great complexity.

* *St-Etienne* A very interesting church with a late Gothic choir, and a late Romanesque nave and transept. There are very beautiful 16th-century windows around the choir, including a celebrated one depicting the Tree of Jesse.

* *Tapestry Museum* Next to the cathedral. Tapestry-making explained and demonstrated, with some beautiful finished works on display.

The **Château de Compiègne** has been an important place in the history of France and a royal residence from the days of Pépin the Short to those of Napoleon III, with whom the château is mainly associated.

Its magnificent forest which attracted hunting monarchs is still the finest natural feature of the area, and a restful place to stay—there are a number of simple hotels deep in the forest.

The interior of the château (with guided tours) is mainly decorated and furnished in the styles of Louis XVI, and Napoleon I and III. The best that can be said for it is that it may help you to answer the interesting question posed by the historian Alfred Cobban: "whether the official art of the Second Empire was, or was not, more boring, pretentious and vapid than that of the First". Many visitors will find more entertaining the magnificent collection of old cars, bicycles and historic carriages housed in another part of the château.

Other buildings of interest in **Compiègne** include the early 16th-century town-hall, where wooden soldiers are set in motion on the striking of the quarter hours, and the Vivenel Museum, which has a very distinguished collection of Greek vases as well as a variety of medieval *objets d'art*.

Near the left bank of the Aisne to the east of Compiègne a railway carriage stands in a clearing; it is not the one which hosted the signature of two armistices, on November 11th 1918 and on June 22nd 1940, but a commemorative replica. Inside, more is understandably made of the earlier of the two occasions.

Napoleon III and Eugénie liked nothing better than to take their guests through the forest to the village of **Pierrefonds**, which became something of a spa and resort, romantically overlooked by the ruins of a

Pierrefonds

once magnificent medieval fortress which had been bought very cheaply by Napoleon I. In 1858 the emperor instructed Viollet-le-Duc to restore the fortress to its original condition. The result of over 20 years' work is the fortress you can visit today, a massive quadrangular building with solid round towers and conical roofs. However vulnerable to criticism some of the details of reconstruction may be it's tremendously impressive as a whole.

South of Pierrefonds, the hamlet of **Morienval** has a large and very splendid church dating from the 11th and 12th centuries, also much restored in the 19th.

The area around Chantilly is one of the best for excursions from Paris, offering a variety of fascinating monuments, a wealth of historical and literary asssociations, and very pleasant countryside (although the Oise valley is rather industrial around Creil).

Chantilly is a smart little town famous for lace, aerated cream and some of the classiest race meetings in France (the Prix de Diane and the Prix du Jockey-Club) which take place in a magnificent setting every

June. Spacious turf is bordered by what must be the most noble stables in the world (they're often open to the public). Next to the race course is a château which completes the scene perfectly with its fairy-tale pinnacles and domes and swans idling on the water. The château is in no sense an architectural masterpiece; of its two sections the smaller (Petit Château) dates externally from the 16th century, the rest is no more than about a hundred years old. The magnificent 17th-century Grand Château was destroyed during the Revolutionary period. Inside the extremely precious Condé collection of works of art is presented not museum-style but as a private collection, arranged by its great accumulator, the duc d'Aumâle. There are magnificent medieval manuscripts including the *Très Riches Heures du duc de Berry*—too fragile to display in the original; Renaissance portrait drawings; and old master paintings from Raphael to Ingres. From the decorative point of view the old section of the château is the most interesting; it was redecorated at the end of the 17th century to commemorate the Great Condé, a towering hero and villain of 17th-century France. He distinguished himself on the battlefields of northern France and the Low Countries and even the streets of Paris both for and against France with devastating energy and boldness, and eventually retired to Chantilly which he embellished and where he surrounded himself with the foremost intellects and writers of his day. Condé entertained on a lavish scale; in April 1671 the king and thousands of courtiers descended on Chantilly and such was the strain on the catering corps that its commander-in-chief, the great Vatel, veteran of many such campaigns and hardly less of a key figure in the creative aspect of Louis' court than Le Nôtre or Le Brun, slept not a wink for days. When the fish failed to arrive one morning Vatel preferred to end it all rather than face his master's wrath.

Senlis is an attractive old town on the edge of the forest near Chantilly, one of the best preserved in the Ile-de-France. It has a very fine, weatherbeaten, lichen-encrusted cathedral of mixed Gothic styles with particularly fine examples of the styles of architecture and carving of the 12th and 16th centuries (west and south façades) and a beautiful 13th-century steeple. Near the cathedral within the substantially surviving Gallo-Roman walls there is an interesting hunting museum.

The only reason to visit the large village of **St-Leu-d'Esserent**—whose quarries provided the stone for Versailles—is its disproportionately large and very elegant church which looks out from a dominating position over the wide Oise valley. As in so many cases the oldest and most curious part of the church is the west end (mid-12th-century tower and porch). The interior is bright and uncluttered—a beautiful and pure example of the early Gothic style, with modern stained glass. Very little remains of the cloisters.

The **Abbaye de Royaumont** is one of those abbeys which may not feature in text-books on the history of architecture, but is much more rewarding to visit than many churches which do. There are delightful shady gardens, and an interesting series of monastic buildings to visit, including a very beautiful cloister and refectory. Of the church itself very little escaped revolutionary demolition. The monastery (guided tours) is now occupied by a cultural foundation which lays on occasional concerts and exhibitions.

The **Abbaye de Chaalis**, though less interesting than Royaumont, enjoys an even more privileged position deep in the forest of Ermenonville. There are a few attractively overgrown abbey ruins in the grounds, but the main part of the visit is a guided tour around the sober

18th-century abbey building turned into a private château in the 19th century and left to the nation as an art museum by the last owner. The works of art displayed are diverse and uneven in quality. Just at the gates of Chaalis, one of the natural curiosities of Ermenonville Forest, the so-called Sea of Sand—which is indeed a surprising expanse of bright white sand in the middle of the woods—has been much commercialised with train rides, camel rides and other attractions including a small zoo. **Ermenonville** itself is proud of its associations with Jean-Jacques Rousseau, the radical and sentimental philosopher whose feelings were of paramount importance in the development of European taste (and thus art, fashion, literature, social behaviour) and whose thoughts, at least according to Napoleon, were the single greatest cause of the Revolution. Rousseau died at Ermenonville in 1778 when living as a guest in a pavilion in the marquis de Girardin's park which was, and remains, a splendid example of Rousseau's principles in landscape put into practice, with numerous thought-provoking symbolic monuments and inscriptions dotted around. Rousseau's empty tomb, classical in style and inscribed "Man of Truth and Nature" stands on an island in the lake.

Ecouen and St-Denis lie on the main road from Paris to Chantilly and can be included in a excursion there. **St-Denis**, which lies beneath a splay of motorway junctions at the busiest northern gates of Paris, is accessible by Métro. It is a seedy suburb whose basilica, necropolis of the kings of France, is about as congruous as Westminster Abbey would be in Wapping. The basilica itself is neither enormous, nor architecturally very interesting except as being in part one of the earliest systematic applications of the Gothic style (porch and apse date from about 1140). Its contents are however of the greatest interest although not always easy to appreciate under the régime of guided tours which applies. All but a very few French kings since the 10th century are buried here. The remains of most of them were scattered to the winds during the Revolution, but the tomb sculptures were saved and many of them are superb, from the simple 12th- and 13th-century statues to the elaborate Renaissance monuments for Louis XII, François I and Henry II and their queens.

The imposing **Château d'Ecouen** is a thoroughbred building of the classical phase of the Renaissance in France, contrasting with the decorative, still Gothic fantasy of Loire château architecture; it is an appropriate place for a museum devoted to the interior decorative style of the Renaissance. As well as collections of furniture from the period there are some Brussels tapestries of the highest quality and elaborate painted and carved chimney-pieces. The nearby church of **St-Acceul** has a notable series of Renaissance windows.

The Oise curves pleasantly between some wooded and other merely green hillsides from near Chantilly to Pontoise and its junction with the Seine. This is Impressionist country—not what it was, of course, but less spoiled than other of the painters' haunts nearer the capital Argenteuil. When Seurat painted at **Asnières** there was a factory in the background, which didn't stop the summer week-end exodus from the metropolis. It still doesn't, at least to **Boran-sur-Oise** and **L'Isle-Adam** which are lively and attractive little river-side resorts. Apart from Asnières the painters frequented **Auvers**, where Van Gogh committed suicide in 1890, and the old capital of the area, **Pontoise**—now with a new industrial neighbour, **Cergy-Pontoise**—which is well situated beside the river but without any monuments of outstanding interest.

East and south-east of Paris

The wide open area around the Marne valley east of Paris is more distinguished for creamy cheese (Brie, classically from Meaux, and the variant Coulommiers which, when just so, runs as well but travels less) than for sightseeing interest. **Meaux** itself has an interesting Gothic cathedral (though it is hardly exceptional by the standards of northern France) and attractive old precincts (gardens designed by Le Nôtre, old chapter house and bishop's palace). One of the more interesting towns east of Paris on the borders of the Ile-de-France and Champagne—more importantly situated for trade in the Middle Ages than for tourists now—is **Provins**, whose upper town is well preserved and surrounded by massive medieval ramparts on two sides. The great landmark of the town crowning it like a 12th-century warhead is the splendid Tower of Caesar.

The **Château de Champs** is one of the great examples of the Louis XV style, still very much of a piece architecturally and decoratively (there are guided tours). It was built in the first years of the 18th century with a new concern for comfort in the design, and lightness and gaiety in the decoration; it later belonged to Louis XV's mistress Madame de Pompadour. There is a particularly fine room decorated in the Chinese style, and beautiful formal gardens. The **Château de Gros Bois** (which is accessible from Paris by Métro—to Boissy-St-Léger, and then on foot) is a century older and presents inside some rare decorative schemes from the early 17th century, with ceilings of painted beams. Other rooms contrast with a lavish collection of Napoleonic Empire furniture.

A day's outing to Fontainebleau and around is perhaps the most satisfying of all to be made from Paris, a perfectly balanced diet of châteaux royal and private, forested landscapes of exceptionally varied beauty and interest, and charming forest villages made famous by 19th-century landscape painters.

The **Château de Vaux-le-Vicomte** lies a few miles north-east of the large and not very interesting market town of Melun. It is a magnificent château which quite literally prepared the way for the building of Versailles, and which is in no way except sheer size overshadowed by it. The glory of Vaux is not architecture alone but the whole effect of moated château and gardens, by no means small but appreciable in one superb vista. Little wonder that it is a favourite subject for tourist office posters. This harmonious ensemble was created with astonishing rapidity and at enormous expense between 1657 and 1661 for Louis XIV's superintendent of finances Nicolas Fouquet; there have hardly been any additions or alterations subsequently. The house and gardens have been beautifully restored by the family who bought Vaux some 100 years ago—which makes it perhaps unreasonable to moan about the relatively high cost of entry and the use inside of unnecessary gimmickry.

Before the château was quite finished (the oval salon still lacks its ceiling paintings) Fouquet entertained the young king and his court at Vaux on August 17th 1661. A magnificent repast was served on 36 dozen gold platters (Louis had had to melt his gold down to pay for war) and an alfresco musical entertainment was laid on by Molière. Louis could hardly fail to be provoked to jealousy and anger by the splendour of the occasion, which far outshone events at Fontainebleau and St-Germain-en-Laye; by Fouquet's style—his motto "Quo non ascendam?" (what heights will I not reach?) and his emblem the squirrel were evident all over the decoration of the château—and by this example of the hugely extravagant use of public funds. The story goes that Louis was so incensed that he had to be restrained from arresting the

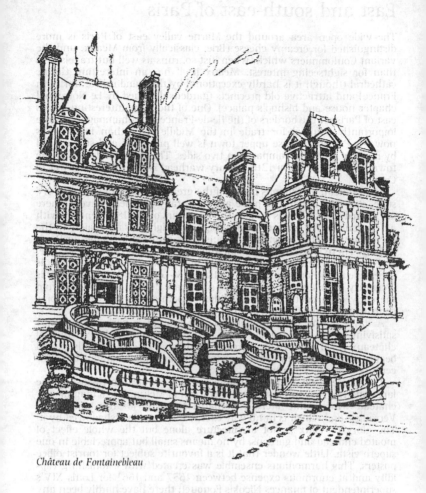

Château de Fontainebleau

superintendent that very night. Although the king and his prime minister Colbert had certainly been plotting Fouquet's downfall for some time, the fact remains that he was arrested 19 days later; Louis and Colbert then appropriated for Versailles Fouquet's entire team—not only Le Vaux, Le Nôtre and Le Brun, but also the tapestry factory, the poets, composers, caterers, and even the pick of Fouquet's statues and rare trees. Inside the château (notes in English available) the rooms open to the public are not great in number but magnificently decorated.

Fontainebleau is a smart and busy international town with one of the most important and interesting of royal châteaux. The forest was a favourite hunting resort for French kings but it was not until the mid-16th century that the hunting lodge became a palace for François I. For the **Château de Fontainebleau**, the king imported Florentine artists to create a new style appropriate to his grand ideas of himself. Rosso's richly complex Michelangelesque decoration of the François I gallery and Primaticcio's painting of the splendid ballroom represent the greatest achievement of what became known as the Fontainebleau style. Here at its best, it is dense and wonderful art, far removed from the usual French château decoration in the styles of Louis XIII to XVI. There's much more to the château than this, for subsequent kings added and altered. The interior takes you swiftly and superbly through the evolution of French decorative style from the Renaissance to the Empire: there are some rare painted ceilings from the late 16th-century; the gracious and famous snaking double staircase at the entrance to the château dates from the early 17th; Louis XIV redecorated some apartments including the imposing Throne Room; the Council Chamber is a beautiful example of the Louis XV style; Marie-Antoinette's boudoir is decorated in the neo-classical style; and inevitably there is much that is the work of Napoleon who was at Fontainebleau when he decided to abdicate in 1814. For most people the unguided tour round the major apartments will suffice, though other sets of rooms of lesser interest can be visited with a guide. There are some delightful gardens and a fine forest with marked trails for walkers and riders (horses are for hire at various places). Near the village of Barbizon on its north-west edge are some of the remarkable and desolate hills and valleys with piles of huge and often grotesquely shaped grey boulders which have made the forest famous (the **Gorges de Franchard** and **Gorges d'Apremont**); some of the rocks are challenging and large enough for real climbers.

Barbizon itself is a delightful and peaceful village, which exploits its mid-19th century luck: it attracted landscape artists and gave its name to their school of painting. This might reasonably be called the Fontainebleau forest school but for the role of Jean-François Millet, who was more interested in the peasants labouring in the fields around Barbizon and Chailly than in the broken light effects of the forest itself. Like Pont-Aven in Brittany and St-Paul-de-Vence in the south, Barbizon's popularity with the painters had much to do with the presence of an enlightened and sympathetic and no doubt non-profit-making inn-keeper, in this case the Père Ganne. Nowadays the village is full of hostelries; they're run on less charitable lines but nevertheless make it a good place to stay. There are several galleries and you can also visit the studios of Théodore Rousseau (the master of the forest painting) and Millet, which both contain a few minor works. Their tombs are at Chailly where Millet painted his famous Angélus, the painting of rural piety that hangs at the head of countless French beds.

Another very attractive and less commercialised village on the western edge of the forest is **Milly-la-Forêt**, with waterways and many old buildings including a splendid 15th-century market hall. The poet and artist Jean Cocteau decorated the interior of the 12th-century chapel of St-Blaise in 1959. Nearby **Courances** has a majestic Louis XIII château visible from the road; only the park is open, and that only occasionally.

On the south-east of the forest **Moret-sur-Loing** is beautifully situated on a wide stretch of the river shortly before it joins the Seine: there is an old bridge, a number of little islands overlooked by a fine Gothic church, and the single tower remaining from the old royal fortress. The English Impressionist Alfred Sisley lived and painted here for twenty years and died, as he had lived, in extreme penury.

Between Milly-La-Forêt and Paris the quiet rural village of **St-Sulpice-de-Favières** has an important late 13th-century Gothic pilgrimage church sometimes referred to as the most beautiful village church in France. It has damaged sculptures round the doorway, some interesting stained glass, and amusingly carved choir stalls.

Hotels

Barbizon, 77630 Seine-et-Marne   ££

LA CLÉ D'OR   Tel: (1) 60.66.40.96

An old stone inn on the main street of this historic painters' village, now a restaurant with rooms—a few on the first floor but most in the single-storey annexe opening onto the pretty garden. Situation is their chief charm; though spacious they're simply furnished (but with good bathrooms). The public area in the main building is dominated by the big modern bar. The restaurant is small, pleasant and unpretentious; in summer you can enjoy a table outside, under the chestnut trees. Service is friendly and the food reasonably priced—go with an appetite; the helpings are generous. Sadly, we've received a report of an incident which revealed less-than-helpful management; is this an isolated case? More reports, please.

Closed Sun dinner and Mon; 15 bedrooms; no lift.

Chartres, 28000 Eure-et-Loir   £££

LE GRAND MONARQUE   Tel: 37.21.00.72

Le Grand Monarque is the only noteworthy establishment of its kind in Chartres—a large, elegant building (slightly spoilt by the automatic sliding glass portal bearing the Mapotel insignia) on the inner ring road round the town centre. It is a much better situation than it sounds, within easy walking distance of the station and the cathedral, but not uncomfortably close to either. Apart from the cost of drinks in the plush bar, the milling, lobby-like atmosphere of the entry hall, and the absence of any relaxed sitting room for residents, the hotel has none of the unpleasantness you might expect of a chain hotel for business people. Bedrooms are bright and comfortable and not too expensive; many of them enjoy cathedral views (what building within a ten-mile radius of Chartres doesn't?) The service we enjoyed in the spacious and attractive dining room was friendly, attentive and polished, and the food on the good-value *menu dégustation* (*salade de légumes frais, petite fricassé d'écrevisses aux deux juliennes, dos de bar braisé au vin de Touraine, pigeon farci en habit vert, gratin de fruits rouges aux pistaches*, followed by *mignardises* and preceded by *amuse-gueules*) was excellent; there's a less daunting cheaper fixed-price menu, too. The wine list is vast. Chefs come and go here, but the standard seems to have been maintained.

Rest closed Christmas; 46 bedrooms; garage.

Flagy (near Montereau), 77156 Seine-et-Marne   ££

LE MOULIN   Tel: (1) 60.96.67.89

A skilfully converted 13th-century mill by its stream in a hamlet of unspoilt rural charm. The lounge, created around the mill-wheel, has squashy sofas, quiet classical music and magazines galore. The dining room has large picture windows looking out over the garden and water, and there's a terrace for drinks. Bedrooms are on the small side, but cosy, in a rustic style in keeping with the place. An enchanting place to stay, with lowish prices and a more-than-competent chef; it has become popular with British visitors, who appreciate the very warm welcome from the friendly owners, and to whom dishes such as '*salade* Gentleman Farmer' are dedicated.

Closed mid-Sept, mid-Dec to mid-Jan, Sun dinner and Mon; 10 bedrooms; no lift.

Burgundy, the Rhône Valley and the Jura

Aloxe-Corton

"*To happy convents, bosomed deep in vines,*
Where slumber abbots, purple as their wines" (Pope)

Burgundy, the Rhône Valley and the Jura

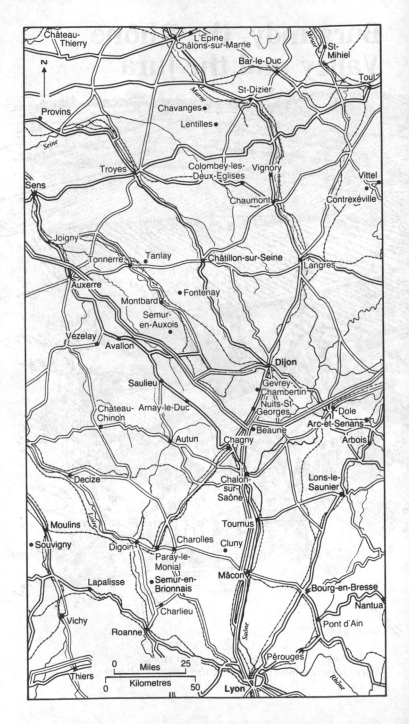

Burgundy, the Rhône Valley and the Jura

Not one landscape but many, among whose changing colours the greenest green in France plays harmonies with fields of brilliant mustard, villages of warm ochre and roofs of red and geometrically multi-coloured tiles. Burgundy, wedged heart-shaped between the unlovely Saône and the transitional Loire, has many of the ingredients of the Dordogne's rural charm. Although it has no river to match the beauty of the Dordogne, there is a network of canals, some still used for commercial communication, others reserved for non-commercial traffic; Burgundy, where a leisurely water-borne pace is most appropriate for savouring the beauty of the countryside, is a favourite place for canal holidays.

The Burgundian table is one of the best in France; the finest beef comes from the white Charollais cattle which are such an attractive component of the landscape throughout western Burgundy. To the east the vineyards of the Côte d'Or, the most expensive agricultural land in France, produce the world's most expensive wines which have given the word burgundy its association with blood-red velvet luxury. The wine is the single most potent reason for breaking a journey south, and the vineyard capital Beaune is the perfect place to admire, taste, learn and inwardly digest. Along the different *routes du vin* you can roll the great names sonorously round the palate, sample humble wines more liberally, and stay in attractive vineyard villages.

There is great splendour and ceremony to the Burgundy wine industry; because of the quality of the produce and the sums of money involved—around Vougeot land changes hands in units of one-tenth of an acre—*vignerons* are no mere labourers of the earth, but citizens of standing. They are also likely to be *chevaliers* of the noble confraternity of Tastevins, whose year reaches a climax every November with the celebration of the *Trois Glorieuses*. There are banquets at Clos de Vougeot and Meursault, and another at Beaune after the world's most famous and influential wine sale, the annual Hospices de Beaune auction which takes place in the town's splendid medieval market building, decorated with ancient tapestries for the occasion.

All the ritual, the sumptuous costumes, the banqueting and the medieval halls set the Burgundy wine trade firmly in the glorious past of the province, whose power and brilliance in the late Middle Ages are of much more than merely academic interest. Burgundy's great period started when the French king awarded the duchy of Burgundy to his son Philip, known as the Bold, in 1363. By a bold and brilliant marriage policy, Philip gained control (in principle for France but, as it later turned out, for Burgundy) of large areas of the industrially powerful Low Countries, and made diplomatic alliances all over Europe. He was the most powerful nobleman in France. His successor John the Fearless disputed, and mostly achieved, control of mad king Charles VI and his revenues, and did very little to advance the French cause against the English in the Hundred Years' War (he was absent from the field of Agincourt). His assassination in 1419 by agents of the dauphin Charles threw young Philip the Good firmly into the arms of the English.

85

Together. English and Burgundians (who controlled Paris) forced the king to recognise Henry V as his son and heir, and Henry and Philip as co-regents. Philip captured Joan of Arc and sold her to the English; then when England sank into the depths of civil war, he neatly abandoned those whom he no longer needed (and no longer needed to fear) and dictated his terms for support of Charles VII, which included even greater—virtually sovereign—authority. At this time, Burgundy was a power unrivalled in Europe, its ruler—self-styled Grand Duke of Occident—lacking only a royal crown.

The wealth of 15th-century Burgundy was the envy of all Europe, and the taste of the dukes for surroundings of dazzling luxury was part of a deliberate policy to outshine. Philip the Good was in the habit of wearing a sash, decorated with balas rubies and pearls, worth a hundred thousand crowns. The Order of Tastevins recalls his foundation of the chivalrous Order of the Golden Fleece, which survived in the noble houses of Austria and Spain until the 1930s. Greatest among the surviving buildings of this period is the Hôtel-Dieu in Beaune, the hospital founded in the 1440s by chancellor Rolin for the benefit of the poor on earth, and of himself on the Day of Judgement. Van der Weyden's Last Judgement polyptych inside the Hôtel-Dieu is one of the greatest masterpieces of 15th-century Flemish art, which in its golden age was Burgundian court art. Philip the Bold brought artists from the Low Countries to embellish his capital Dijon; in the Dijon museum there are marvellous ducal tombs, and at the Chartreuse outside the town some of the most monumental and vigorous of medieval sculptures.

The mid-15th century ascendancy was not to last, though; king Louis XI set his mind on the destruction of Burgundian power, and although Charles the Bold, the fighting Téméraire, pulled off a few military successes, he had not, in the words of the historian Comines, "enough sense or malice", and he behaved more and more wildly as Louis wove a spider's web of bribed alliances against him. Trying to unite Burgundian dominions north and south, Charles met his death outside Nancy on January 5th 1477.

Earlier Burgundy had been the cradle of medieval monasticism. In 910 duke William of Aquitaine founded a Benedictine abbey at Cluny. Under the leadership of a distinguished series of abbots, Cluny established order in monastic Europe, and hundreds of dependent priories sprang up. At Cluny itself abbot Hugh started, and his successor Peter the Venerable completed, the greatest Romanesque church in Christendom—so beautiful, it was said, that if it were possible for the inhabitants of heaven to be happy in a building constructed by man, it would be the ambulatory of angels. Of the enormous abbey church all but a tower of the south transept has been destroyed; but all over Burgundy there are superb examples of the Romanesque style, from the great pilgrimage church of Vézelay, where kings of France and England took the cross in 1187, to the most humble village church.

The Cluniac order was never particularly rigorous in its discipline. Its churches were magnificent, and it grew ever more prosperous. Criticism of the order and its lifestyle was vigorously expressed by one of the great orators and church politicians of the Middle Ages, saint Bernard of Clairvaux, who sneered that the welfare of the order was held to consist in the magnificence of its feasts and its buildings. Speaking of the carved Romanesque capitals, Bernard asked "what are these monsters doing in cloisters under the eyes of monks occupied with their reading? What are these filthy apes, monstrous centaurs doing here? If not ashamed, one

Burgundy, the Rhône Valley and the Jura

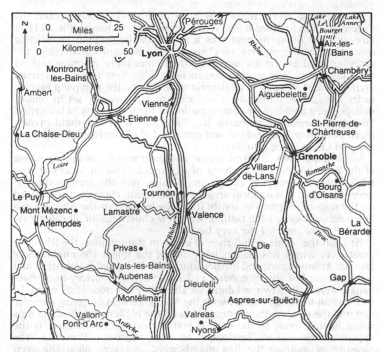

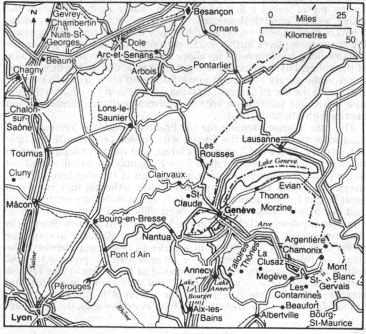

should at least regret the expenditure of money". A new order, the Cistercian, was founded a few years before Bernard joined it in 1111 at Cîteaux near Dijon; its goal was a return to the original Benedictine spirit sharing the poverty of Christ. Under Bernard's leadership, the order enjoyed enormous success, which inevitably compromised its founding principle of worldly renunciation. Needless to say, Cistercian architecture is stripped of all decorative elements; the surviving monasteries are simple, harmonious and elegant, and usually set in remote valleys. They are ideal for contemplation of the tranquillity of both rural French and medieval monastic life. Fontenay, near Montbard in northern Burgundy, is one of the best preserved of all the representations in stone of Cistercian spirituality.

In its many ways, cultural, scenic and gastronomic, Burgundy is one of the most completely satisfying of all French areas. It lacks only the sea—which means that except for Beaune, and the motorway, it is never crowded. It is an ideal area for a short visit, conveniently situated on the way to or from the south, Italy, Switzerland or the Alps. Have a few meals, do some wine tasting, see a few churches—in all categories, you will have sampled the very best.

At Lyon the Saône, a dull river of medium stature, joins the Rhône, a great river which has always been one of the major thoroughfares of Europe. Around Lyon, and further south, the river itself is industrial and unattractive; but the motorway at least avoids the factory-lined river banks, so travellers by road don't see the Rhône corridor at its worst. In fact it is an impressive drive, with the Massif Central dropping abruptly down to the river on the western side and the higher massifs of the Alps rising further away to the east. If you are driving south there is the appetising change of landscape as you approach Provence—the pleasure of spotting the first poppy-fields, and very often the even greater joy of seeing a first break in the clouds south of Lyon as the valley widens around Montélimar. Along the Rhône there are some towns of very ancient importance, but they do not compare in sightseeing terms with places further north or south. You can take panoramic detours along winding roads up above the vineyards on the western side of the valley, but these routes are not as spectacular as the drive along the Ardèche gorges—the most powerful reason for a diversion (see the chapter on the Massif Central). Another good reason for a halt is the fact that the Rhône valley is an area of renowned culinary excellence, and bristles with Michelin rosettes.

The Jura is approximately the old Franche-Comté, or free county of Burgundy which, unlike the duchy, was outside France until the time of Louis XIV. The word Jura means forest, and the mountainous region has a very different kind of appeal from Burgundy. In complete contrast to the civilised thoroughfare area, it is an out of the way land of lakes, rivers, farms, and wooded mountains which, although they rise to no great height by continental standards (1,723 metres), are so structured that communications have always been difficult. The mountain range drops steeply down to Lake Geneva, whose crescent shape it echoes. On the French side, the mountains descend like a staircase towards the plains of Burgundy and Belfort in a series of ridges and plateaux. The ridges are thickly and monotonously covered with evergreen at the top, with a more interesting variety of woodland lower down. The highest part of the Jura near Geneva is bleak and very snowy in winter, and popular for cross-country skiing— for which it is the best area in France. In summer it attracts tourists who like the woods, the lakes, and the uncommercialised rural mountain life which is still based, as it has been for centuries, on the cutting of wood and the making of cheese. On its lower slopes, the Jura has more of the wealth and variety of the Burgundian landscape; there are orchards and golden stone villages, and vineyards producing small quantities of a little-known golden wine (*vin jaune*) which commands respect and high prices.

One of the great admirers of the landscape of his native Jura was the 19th-century painter Gustave Courbet, of Ornans. The shady river valleys, waterfalls and the grassy escarpments all around Ornans are an enormous Courbet gallery. He was a character larger than life, stubborn, iconoclastic but very canny, fully aware of the publicity value of posing as a rough-cut peasant when everyone else was posing as an intellectual, and loving nothing better than doing exactly the opposite of what was expected of him. In all this he was a typical product of a region which, until the 17th century, was independent of the French monarchy and, for all practical purposes, of any outside control; and which fiercely defended its independence against campaigns of French devastation for nearly 200 years after the death of Charles the Bold of Burgundy.

Northern Burgundy

Sens and Auxerre are two northern gateway towns to Burgundy. Somewhere between the two, near Joigny, the southbound traveller goes over the brow of a hill and looks down over a wide and pleasant, swollen landscape chequered with brilliant yellow mustard fields; this is the **Auxerrois**, and it is Burgundy—warm and welcoming. Of the two towns beside the Yonne, **Sens** has a less attractive old centre, but a more distinguished cathedral; St-Etienne is the oldest of all French Gothic cathedrals, and his statue on the pillar of the central doorway of the west façade is particularly beautiful. Inside there is a splendid array of medieval stained glass; one of the 12th-century windows on the north side of the choir tells the story of the murder of Thomas à Becket, who had spent years of exile at nearby Pontigny. The north and south transept doorways are very fine examples of intricate Flamboyant decoration, and the treasury has an exceptional wealth of precious vestments, goblets and reliquaries.

Auxerre should be admired from the east bank of the river Yonne. The *quais* are planted with trees, and above them three great churches on the hill turn their shapely backs to the river. The centre of town has cobbled streets, a Gothic clock tower, and timbered houses.

✱ *Cathedral* Damaged but richly decorated façade with a wealth of story-telling around the doorways; exceptional 13th-century stained glass.
✱ *St-Germain* The abbey church of this once celebrated Carolingian monastery is of no particular interest, but there is a series of underground sanctuaries of great age beneath it, with 9th-century frescoes.
✱ *St-Pierre-en-Vallée* Not much to admire inside, but a rich mixture of an exterior, with a late Gothic tower and a laden 17th-century façade.

Auxerre is where Burgundian exploration most coveniently begins, whether by canal or by road. The motorist heading in the direction of Beaune has two main choices: to the east of the motorway lie beautiful Renaissance châteaux, perhaps the most satisfying Cistercian monastery of all, the provincial capital Dijon, and the great vineyard *côte*. To the west lie the wilder wooded mountains of the Morvan, and just a couple, but among the very finest, of Romanesque churches.

Starting clockwise, the northernmost Burgundian vineyards produce wines of distinction, best-known amongst them from **Chablis**, which is not as attractive as little **Irancy** on the Yonne, whose very good red and rosé enjoy less widespread fame. Like Chablis, the Cistercian **Abbaye de Pontigny** grew up beside the river Serein. Of the monastery only the church survives—vast, sober and very impressive. All around Auxerre, the Yonne is delightful, still as Walter Pater described it in the last century: "bending gracefully link after link through a never-ending rustle of poplar trees, through lovely vine-clad hills . . . the child's fancy of a river like the rivers of the old miniature painters, blue and full to a fair green margin".

Beyond the small market town of **Tonnerre**, Tanlay and Ancy-le-Franc (both 16th-century) are the two finest châteaux in Burgundy. The sober classical Renaissance **Château d'Ancy-le-Franc** is built around a richly decorated closed courtyard. Inside there is a magnificent ensemble of Italian Renaissance furniture and decoration, the work of Fontaine-bleau artists. Sadly, it's in sore need of restoration. The **Château de Tanlay** is more interesting from the outside. With its round towers and bell-shaped domes, and the wide, flattering mirror of its moat, it has the charm of a Loire château. There are many treasures inside, and there is the added appeal that the château is still inhabited.

Châtillon-sur-Seine is a small town with lawns and avenues of chestnuts and limes beside the young river. The only reason for a visit is the museum, which among many Gallo-Roman finds has the huge and magnificent 6th-century BC Greek bronze vase ("crater") and other treasures found in a princess's sepulchre at Vix, marvels of the art of their time.

The **Abbaye de Fontenay**, founded by saint Bernard in a softly wooded vale among well-kept and well-watered gardens, is the most perfect and expressive surviving example of a Cistercian monastery. In the 19th century, the abbey was used as a paper factory by the ballooning Montgolfiers, and the 12th-century church now stands beside the cloister and abbey buildings, intact but completely stripped of its fixtures and fittings—even its stone floor.

Near Fontenay, there are a number of minor but rewarding visits for the unhurried tourist. The **Château de Bussy-Rabutin** was mostly built and entirely decorated by its 17th-century lord Roger de Rabutin, a general who wielded the pen with such witty, penetrating and tactless facility that he was exiled from court and spent years of nostalgia adorning his rooms with portraits and allegorical scenes about Versailles. **Alise-Ste-Reine** is a small village on the flank of the natural fortress of Alésia, where Vercingetorix failed (but only just) to resist a Roman siege in 52 BC. You can visit the excavations of a Gallo-Roman town and a small museum.

Semur-en-Auxois is old and picturesquely set, with roofs of mottled tiles beneath the round towers of its castle which surveys a bend in the river Armançon. The fine Gothic church has Burgundian snails carved on the façade. **Flavigny-sur-Ozerain**, famous for its aniseed sweets, is a smaller and thoroughly charming fortress village hundreds of feet above its almost encircling rivers, with well preserved and restored houses.

Dijon, Burgundian capital medieval and modern, is a railway junction city of heavy industry though it is best known for its mustard and

Burgundy, the Rhône Valley and the Jura

cassis. After the decline of Burgundian power Dijon remained an important regional capital and most of the public buildings date from 17th and 18th centuries: the semi-circular Place de la Libération and façade of the old Grand Dukes' palace form a splendid late 17th-century ensemble. There are, however, a few medieval parts of the palace left, and behind it some attractive medieval streets and squares.

✻ *Musée des Beaux-Arts* In the ducal palace, a very rich and varied collection of sculptures and paintings of many periods, of which the masterpieces are grouped in the 15th-century Salle des Gardes. The tombs of dukes Philip the Bold and John the Fearless, their recumbent statues supported by wonderfully lively cortèges of grieving mourners, are among the most beautiful works of art to be seen in Burgundy.

✻ *St-Michel* An imposing and richly decorated façade, Gothic in plan, but Renaissance in style.

✻ *St-Bénigne* Once one of the greatest Romanesque churches in France, with a circular choir. The cathedral is now Gothic, but its original crypt, also circular, has been excavated.

✻ *Notre-Dame* A beautiful early Gothic church, with rows of gaping gargoyles on the west façade.

✻ *Chartreuse de Champmol* Now an unlovely suburban asylum, the dukes' purpose-built necropolis has kept two masterpieces of late 14th-century sculpture which will be shown on request: the hexagonal base for a calvary, surrounded by six magnificent prophets, and the group of statues around the chapel doorway.

To the south and west of the motorway lie the **Morvan** hills—a land of woods, rivers and reservoirs, with little cultivation and few inhabitants. It has become popular for watersports (the river Cure is good for canoeing), riding (marked rides and a number of equestrian centres around the periphery of the **Morvan Regional Park**), and walking. A hiking trail crosses the Morvan from top (Vézelay) to toe (Autun). Other bases around the park are **Château-Chinon**, which has little character; and **Saulieu**, a main road town with a long-established gastronomic reputation and a Romanesque basilica with beautifully carved capitals.

French motorway builders take a teasing delight in putting notices beside the carriageway telling you what you are paying to avoid. One pointing upwards and westwards at nothing very obvious says simply *"Vézelay, colline éternelle"*. The description is hardly adequate, but does express the fact that **Vézelay** is not just a most beautiful and beloved Romanesque church; it is also a place, a pilgrimage village on a hill, looking out over the most opulent Burgundian countryside. The village is often packed with coaches; it is worth staying nearby (the choice of good places at Vézelay, Avallon, and the leafy Cousin valley is extensive) and waiting to make the pilgrim's climb in the evening or early morning.

The abbey of Vézelay was a starting point of one of the medieval routes to Compostela. The mainly 12th-century church has a beauty to which few are insensitive; its glories are the majestic relief sculptures above the inner doorways (there is an antechamber or narthex), the chocolate and ochre bands of the arches supporting the main vault, and the capitals all around the nave. You can spend hours studying details of the stories and fantastic monsters depicted for the edification and more obviously the amusement of queueing pilgrims. A detailed guide is recommended.

Vézelay

The nearby village of **St-Père** also has a beautiful Gothic church, with the tomb of its founders in the porch. **Avallon** is more than just a town for good hotels near Vézelay; the old centre has cobbled streets and ramparts above attractive terraces leading down to the wooded Cousin valley.

At the southern edge of the Morvan, **Autun**, as Roman Augustodunum, was capital of Burgundy and one of the most important Gallo-Roman cities; it has kept two splendid town gateways, and fragmentary remains of the largest theatre in Gaul. The Romanesque cathedral of St-Lazare is surmounted by an elegant Gothic spire; the carving of the main tympanum is a Last Judgement of grimacing devils, howling damned souls and trumpeting angels. Like Vézelay's tympanum, it is one of the great masterpieces of the period. Many of the most beautiful capitals inside are grouped together in the chapter room. In the Musée Rolin, there is Gallo-Roman archaeology, and medieval works of art including a very beautiful Nativity by the Maître de Moulins. Between Autun and Beaune, you can admire only the outside of the splendid moated Renaissance **Château de Sully**. Madame de Sévigné said its walls enclosed the most beautiful courtyard of any château in France.

The Nivernais Loire divides Burgundy from the Berry; south of the best Loire vineyards (Sancerre and Pouilly-sur-Loire), the Burgundian bank is overlooked by the old abbey church of **La Charité-sur-Loire**, once the second largest church in France after Cluny. The church has suffered much damage from the town's importance as a Loire bridge-head (the handsome 16th-century bridge has weathered better) but although some of the nave has been destroyed, leaving a single tower of the original façade, the beautiful choir and transept have survived more or less intact. Little is left of the old abbey buildings, but a gallery of the old cloister leads around behind the church, giving a splendid view.

Nevers is a large through town, famous for glass and porcelain since the 16th century when a Gonzaga prince took over the Nivernais duchy and imported talented Italian artists. The manufacture of Nevers faience flourished until the Revolution, and there is a good collection of it in the town museum. There is a variety of other monuments—the Renaissance ducal palace in its gardens, a very picturesque 14th-century town gate (Porte du Croux), and two contrasting churches—the cathedral with an interesting variety of architectural styles and works of art, and St-Etienne, a very pure late 11th-century church of surprising interior grandeur.

Southern Burgundy

Beaune is the centre of the local wine industry, at the heart of the most prestigious vineyards. It is a beautiful historic town, full of art treasures and a very good place to use as a base for the region. The centre of the town is still surrounded by old ramparts and plane trees, and there are many fine 17th-century buildings, now the offices of the wine trade establishment. For most tourists the first priority will be a visit to one or more of the many wine cellars (see page 96).

✴ *Hôtel-Dieu* Medieval hospital, founded in the 15th century by the Burgundian chancellor Rolin, run as a charitable hospital until a decade ago and still functioning as a home for the aged. It is staffed by nuns, and funded by the proceeds of the annual auction of wines produced by the 52 hectares of vineyards it owns. The auction, which takes place with great pomp and circumstance, no longer in the Hôtel-Dieu itself, is the central event of the Trois Glorieuses (3rd Sunday in November) and sets the trend for burgundy prices. The sombre grey exterior conceals a cobbled courtyard with wooden galleries and the most brilliantly colourful of Burgundian roofs. The guided tour of the interior reveals a medieval ward with double beds curtained off from the chapel, medieval kitchens still in use, an old pharmacy with jars for herbal and more exotic medicaments, and a museum with beautiful tapestries and Van der Weyden's superlative Last Judgement polyptych which is displayed behind a mobile magnifying glass for the study of individual detail.

✴ *Notre-Dame* A mostly Romanesque church, with a series of 15th-century tapestries depicting the Life of the Virgin—not on show in winter.

✴ *Musée du Vin* Set in a handsome old *hôtel* near Notre-Dame, a very informative and attractive display of things viticultural.

The greatest Burgundian vineyards extend a short way south of Beaune, but principally north to Dijon, along the lower slopes of a continuous hillside which looks south-eastwards over the main road and the motorway. This is the **Côte d'Or**, 40 miles long by less than a mile wide from Dijon to Chagny, covering only 4,000 hectares, not very much more than a large farm. It is split up into the **Côte de Beaune** in the immediate neighbourhood of the town, and to the north the **Côte de Nuits** which produces what are considered by most fortunate consumers to be the greatest of all burgundies, and by many of those who carry their taste for hierarchy even further to be the greatest of all wines. Certainly, they are among the most expensive. The vineyard drive is not perhaps the most attractive in France, but the villages have their golden

Hôtel-Dieu, Beaune

Burgundian beauty. Along the Côte de Nuits (not on the main road), the village signposts read like an exclusive wine list—**Gevrey-Chambertin, Vougeot, Chambolle-Musigny, Vosne-Romanée**, and **Nuits-St-Georges**. There are wine cellars all along tempting you indoors, but do not expect free gulps of a great and aged burgundy (the finest do not reach their prime until they are over ten years old). **Clos de Vougeot** is one of the most picturesque wine châteaux, and one of the few to visit. Vast expanses of rust-coloured tiles drop almost to the famous vines of the walled Clos, now the property of the confraternity of Tastevins, who hold a famous banquet in the château on the day before the Hospices de Beaune sales. There are guided tours, revealing splendid vaulted chambers and some magnificent old wine presses. On the Côte de Beaune, **Aloxe-Corton** produces a white wine of great distinction (Corton Charlemagne); so too does **Meursault**, to the south of Beaune. Its château (see page 96) is the setting of the third of the *Trois Glorieuses*.

The area south of Chagny produces wines of lesser distinction than the Côte d'Or, but the vineyard landscapes—where land and produce is less expensive—have in many ways a more attractively rural charm, and not surprisingly *vignerons* are much more liberal in the dispensation of their wine. As well as the vineyards, there is a wealth of beautiful churches, a few major ones, but mostly small and simple parish churches in small and simple country communities which, perhaps more than anywhere else, live up to the ideal image of rural French life evoked by the name *Clochemerle*.

Chalon-sur-Saône is no Clochemerle: a commercial and industrial river port without appeal, unlike the nearby vineyard villages of **Rully** and **Mercurey**, which produce very good wine and offer accommodation. **Tournus**, hemmed in between motorway and river, is an old town in the shadow of its fortress-like 10th- and 12th-century basilica of St-Philibert—one of the finest churches in the region. It was built in a massive and uncomplicated style, beautifully enhanced by its soft pinkish stone. The nave is vaulted by a series of transverse barrels.

Burgundy, the Rhône Valley and the Jura

At **Cluny**, high point of medieval monasticism and post-Revolutionary vandalism, little remains (just one lonely transept tower) of the greatest Romanesque church of all—nearly 200 yards long, with two transepts and five naves. You can find out all about it from informative displays and models and unearthed capitals in the surviving buildings, mostly dating from the 18th century; there is also a small museum.

Throughout the Mâconnais and the green pastures of the Brionnais (west of the vineyards) Cluny's influence has left countless Romanesque churches. There is a marked tourist route in the **Brionnais** which includes some of the following selection, which is not exhaustive. **Brancion** is a very picturesque rampart-encased village on a rocky spur, with a fortress, overgrown houses, streets of earth, and a squat, harmonious 12th-century church with later medieval wall paintings inside. **Chapaize** has a very old (11th-century) church with a splendid, disproportionately large bell-tower. **Berzé-la-Ville**, near Cluny, has a small chapel which was part of abbot Hugh's summer retreat; frescoes originally covered the whole of the interior. Only the apse paintings survive, with a Christ in Majesty (of Byzantine inspiration) which is indeed majestic, and beautifully preserved, having been protected by whitewash for centuries.

At **Paray-le-Monial**, well situated by the waters of the Bourbince, the basilica of Sacré-Coeur is the closest approximation on a smaller scale to what the church of Cluny must have been, with a splay of chapels around the east end, a trio of pointed towers, and an interior of sober elegance. In many ways, the Romanesque style of architecture is better suited to smaller churches, like the one at charming **Semur-en-Brionnais**, with lively relief carvings. At **Anzy-le-Duc** there is another early Romanesque church, built of a stone which is exceptionally golden even by Burgundian standards, with an octagonal belfry, amusingly primitive carvings, and some ill-preserved frescoes.

The small market town of **Charlieu**, in the **Charolais**—another area of golden villages, green pastures and white cows—had an important abbey; enough remains of it to reward a visit. There are guided tours around the surrounding buildings, many of them like the elegant cloister dating from the 15th century; but the glory of Charlieu is the very densely decorative carved doorway (12th-century) which can be seen from outside.

The **Mâconnais** is an attractive hilly vineyard and farming region, whose finest wines—dry, fruity and white—come from the neighbouring villages of **Pouilly** and **Fuissé**. **Solutré** too makes good wine, but is better known in a prehistoric context: at the foot of the great rocky cliff which flanks the village like a petrified wave, some 100,000 skeletons of horses were discovered, and the place is thought to have been a kind of prehistoric abattoir. Finds (not only equine) are displayed in the museum at **Mâcon**. Apart from this, and omnipresent reminders of the Mâconnais origins of the Romantic poet Lamartine, there is nothing memorable about Mâcon, a busy wine trading town on the Saône; but it is animated, and not unattractive by comparison with Chalon to the north and Villefranche to the south.

The north of the **Beaujolais** vineyards adjoins the south of the Mâconnais, but the Beaujolais is usually considered to be outside Burgundy. Its wine, unlike Burgundy, should be drunk cool and young. Indeed, so young has it become fashionable to drink Beaujolais that every autumn Beaujolais Nouveau is flown to eager imbibers in London wine bars within hours of the season being declared legally ▷ p97

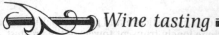 *Wine tasting*

One of the most convenient places for sampling burgundy is Beaune, where most of the big wine merchants have their headquarters. The tourist office has a list of houses which offer tours with wine tasting, including those which have an English commentary; but the ones on their list are not necessarily those which are the best to visit. Some offer free tastings of small quantities of decidedly uninteresting wines, followed by a hard selling exercise; others are geared to French tourists, with amusing anecdotes in colloquial French. The tourist office also has a list of vineyards in the surrounding area that are open to visitors, but you may find it just as easy to find places yourself by following the signposted *routes du vin* in the various areas, and by enquiring locally or looking out for signs announcing *dégustation*. The following is a selection of good places for tasting wine, and in most cases for buying as well.

Marché aux Vins, Beaune The best place to give yourself a taste of what burgundy is all about: for a modest fee, you have an opportunity to taste over 30 wines, ranging from Bourgogne Ordinaire and Beaujolais to the big names. You are left to yourself, with help and advice offered by sales staff if you want it. If you intend to appreciate the more prestigious wines, you'll need to be circumspect at the start.

Château de Meursault A similar system to the Marché aux Vins (with entrance charge), though with fewer wines. The château itself (16th-century) is attractive, as are the cellars; there is a small museum of modern art in the former orangery.

Cave Co-opérative, Mâcon-Viré Good village co-operative where you can taste (small fee) and buy the excellent and reasonably priced white Mâcon-Viré.

Cave du Val d'Or, Mercurey Has a good range of Mercurey and other burgundies which you can taste (free) and buy.

Union des Producteurs, Solutré Not a co-operative, but a place where you can taste (small fee) and buy the produce of several vineyards of Pouilly-Fuissé. Selections are anonymous.

open, amid fanfares of publicity, and with unparalleled (and to many minds undesirable) speed. The Beaujolais landscape is inviting, with hills rising to over 1,000 metres, pine forests above and behind the vineyards, attractive villages with simple accommodation and excellent restaurants, and plentiful wine tasting opportunities at the village co-operatives. **Oingt** and **Ternand** are among the most attractive old villages.

To the east of the Saône, the flat **Bresse** plains were in the past divided between France and Empire. As a whole, it feels neither Burgundian nor part of the Jura. To the French, the Bresse means the tastiest of chickens, a local speciality. Visual treats for the tourist are two architectural features which could not form a greater contrast—brick farmhouses with outside staircases and wooden galleries supporting huge overhanging (occasionally thatched) roofs, and on the edge of the market town of **Bourg-en-Bresse**, the monastery church at **Brou**—one of the most brilliant and extreme examples of the luxuriant virtuosity of late Gothic art. The building was carried out in the first decades of the 16th century by Margaret of Austria, duchess of Savoie, ruler of the Franche-Comté and the Low Countries; it is, like so much in Burgundy, the work of artists brought in from the north. The main doorway is a richly decorated hint, no more, of what is inside, enclosed by a stone screen of great beauty: the tombs of Margaret of Austria, her husband Philibert and her mother-in-law Marguerite de Bourbon; carved oak choir stalls; and stained glass windows—all miraculously preserved, perfect.

The Rhône Valley

The Rhône runs west from Lake Geneva to Lyon, then, like most tourists, it charts a purposeful southward course. It is an area of greatest interest to the tourist whose itinerary is planned around visits to prestigious restaurants. The memory of Point, pharoah of changeless gastronomic tradition, is perpetuated by Madame Point at Pyramide in Vienne. The new generation of super-star chefs, who have brought to the traditional skills the more modern ones of public relations and advertising, are to be found in force as well: Bocuse at Collonges, Chapel at Mionnay, and Blanc at Vonnas, and many others who thrill the taste buds no less surely than they lighten the pecuniary load. The area around the source of the Loire, and the Ardèche gorges, both within easy range, rank among the most beautiful parts of the Massif Central (and are described in the chapter on that region).

Lyon has grown up economically powerful, thanks to the natural passage of international trade and to the favours granted in the late Middle Ages to encourage trade fairs. Merchants were given a monopoly of the silk trade, originally imported from Italy, and its manufacture became the great speciality of the city. Lyon occupies both sides of the confluence of Rhône and Saône, and the long peninsula between the two. The meeting of the two broad rivers gives Lyon an impressive setting, with terraces of houses stacked above the waters, but it is not as a whole a very charming place; Lamartine called it a "sombre, austere, monastic town", and it is almost as famous for its fog as London. Few tourists will feel the urge to do more than pay cursory homage to its major sights.

* *Fourvière* You can drive, walk, or catch a funicular up the steep hill on the west of town, crowned by a great 19th-century pilgrimage basilica, with no more aesthetic distinction and considerably less charm than Montmartre in Paris. Nearby, there are substantial but nevertheless fragmentary remains of two Roman theatres and a museum devoted to Gallo-Roman Lyon.

* *Old town* A mostly Renaissance area at the foot of Fourvière, currently undergoing cleaning and restoration. Many beautiful *hôtels* (one of the finest, the Hôtel Gadagne, houses an international puppet museum) and the only church in Lyon of any particular distinction, St-Jean—mostly Gothic, but with a beautiful Romanesque choir and particularly fine carving around the doorways of the main façade.

* *Musée Historique des Tissus* Not just Lyon silk and its history, but stuffs from all over the world; a museum of exceptional interest.

* *Musée des Arts Décoratifs* A rich collection of furniture, tapestries and faience, from many periods.

* *Musée des Beaux-Arts* More like a national than a regional museum, large and extensive in its coverage of different styles, periods and places of origin. Housed in the old nunnery beside the Place des Terreaux. The only local artist particularly well represented is Puvis de Chavannes.

To the east of Lyon, either side of the Rhône, two very different medieval perched towns are well worth seeing: **Crémieu**, with its old gateways and towers, and its 14th-century market buildings, is crumbling, little cared for, and little visited; **Pérouges**, originally colonised by immigrants from Perugia, is much more picturesque, having been identified long ago as special, preserved from spoiling, brought to the notice of tourists, and restored. Many a film maker has resorted to Pérouges for his local colour—ramparts, cobbled streets, late-medieval houses, and a central square with a single bicentennial lime tree.

South of Lyon the Rhône is at its most industrially ugly. **Vienne** is a riverside town of no particular beauty, but it has the greatest concentration of sightseeing interest of the whole Rhône valley. From the early days of the Roman conquest until the early Middle Ages, it was a more important city than Lyon. Today, it is attractively busy, without being oppressively urban like its northern neighbour.

* *Roman remains* A Corinthian temple, less perfect than the Maison Carrée in Nimes, but very like it; a huge theatre often used for summer drama; and an elegantly decorated archway. On the southern edge of town, there's an isolated pyramid, once the centrepiece of the chariot race track.

* *Churches* Two very early Christian churches, with later Romanesque additions (St-Pierre, now a museum of Gallo-Roman statuary; St-André-le-Bas, with a beautiful cloister), and a large and handsome cathedral, part Gothic, part Romanesque, with beautiful carving on the façade and inside. Across the river you can visit Gallo-Roman excavations.

The main roads follow the east, or Dauphinois, side of the Rhône. From Vienne, tourists in no hurry can take minor roads through the vineyard hills on the Massif Central side of the river. The most impressive drive climbs from behind Tournon to St-Romain-de-Lerps, giving extensive views down over the river valley and down to Valence past the ruins of the **Château de Crussol. Tournon** shows an attractive aspect to the river, with a castle on granite rocks, and a gracious promenade of plane trees. **Tain-l'Hermitage** is dominated by the steep slopes which produce the virile Hermitage, finest of all Côtes du Rhône wines.

Valence is a large thriving commercial town, with something of an old centre around the Place des Clercs, including a few Renaissance *hôtels*. The museum in the archbishop's palace has a collection of late 18th-century chalk drawings of Rome by Hubert Robert, a reminder of how the Rhône once carried Grand Tourists towards the treasures of classical antiquity. The artists were impatient to hurry on, and Valence does not delay many tourists now; neither does **Montélimar**, the world nougat capital. South of Valence, the Rhône, despite the occasional embellishment of a ruined fortress on its western wall, becomes characterised chiefly by hydro-electric and even atomic power stations.

The Jura

The southern Jura mountains have none of the gentle gradations of the centre. Relatively high peaks, like the Grand Colombier, are crowded together and drop abruptly down to the Rhône. Villages along the river produce cheerful sparkling wines (Seyssel), but have no great charm, and there is little except the hills themselves to tempt you up into the **Bugey**, as this region is known.

The highest mountains are to the north of Geneva, and attract most of the active summer tourists. Unpretentious **Les Rousses** is the region's liveliest resort, with riding and board-sailing; it is a good place to stay, with a variety of hotels; the dairy is well worth a visit. From the **Col de la Faucille**, there are ski lifts up to the Mont Rond for impressive views across Lake Geneva to the Swiss and French Alps. You can drive down from the mountains to the wholly Swiss-seeming lakeside spa of **Divonne-les-Bains**, with its casino and very clean streets, without leaving France. Further north, the Franco-Swiss border cuts into the heart of the mountains, so there is a large area (above Lake Neuchâtel) of Swiss Jura. **St-Claude** is a real town, not particularly beautiful, but dramatically situated—cramped high above two rivers in a bowl of mountains—and a convenient base for excursions. Its cathedral is austere, but curiously fortified and amusingly decorated with 15th-century choirstalls; in front of it an elaborately-wrought pipe made of flowers indicates St-Claude's traditional industry of pipe making. The **Gorges du Flumen** to the south of town offer a particularly impressive excursion for motorists.

To the north of St-Claude, the **Ain** valley has been dammed to create long, sinuous reservoirs banked with pines; it is a favourite area for camping and nautical sports. So too are the natural lakes around the attractive villages of **Clairvaux-les-Lacs** and **Doucier**, which offer simple accommodation. For walkers, the best excursion is the shaded woodland trail beside the Hérisson, which drops through a series of magnificent waterfalls accessible from Bonlieu, Ilay, or Doucier. Between Lons-le-Saunier and Arbois, the lower and very attractive vineyard slopes of the Jura are broken up by a series of beautifully symmetrical dead-end valleys, eroded from the plateaux, flanked and abruptly terminated by steep rocky escarpments. The most impressive and shapely of these *reculées* is the **Cirque de Baume** near Lons-le-Saunier; the valley floor has grottoes, cascades, and (at the open end) the old **Abbaye de Baume-les-Messieurs** (the title added by noble canons in the 16th century) whence 12 monks set out in 910 for Cluny. The golden abbey buildings are mostly ruined but the church remains—powerful, simple, and harmonious. Other *reculées* are the **Cirque de Ladoye**, the **Culée de Vaux**, the **Reculée des Planches**, and the **Cirque du Fer à Cheval**; and far to the north-east, the **Cirque de Consolation**.

The small town of **Arbois** is one of the most attractive holiday bases in the Jura; the golden stone of its domed church belfry and the russet tiles of its roofs are beautifully set off against the surrounding greenery; there is good fishing all around. It lies at the heart of the finest Jura vineyards, which produce the unusual *vin jaune*, of which the best—and this is very good—comes from **Château-Chalon**. The origins of the Savagnin grape are obscure; the wine-making process is eccentric. The end product tastes like nuts, prunes, fino sherry or what you will, but in fact like nothing else; with a bottle life of centuries—and months even when opened—and an aftertaste on your palate which has been timed by experts at well over a minute, its characteristics are unique and cannot be guaranteed. The liquorous and very strong (17°) *vin de paille*, made by keeping grapes for months before pressing and not bottling the wine for over a decade, is even more unusual.

The Jura's salt-rich springs have been exploited since prehistoric times. **Lons-le-Saunier** and **Salins-les-Bains** were both salt towns, and at Salins you can visit the mines where salt is still extracted. Quite apart from this, Salins is an attractive place, with casino and gardens beside the river Furieuse, and a very handsome 18th-century Hôtel de Ville and domed chapel. The salt-mining establishment of **Arc-et-Senans** is of even greater interest. It was planned and built in the 1770s as part of a complete Utopian city by the visionary architect Ledoux. Monumental temples stand to the glory not of God or king, but industry. Today the buildings house a wealth of information about Ledoux and his ideas (more interesting, it must be said, than his achievements) and temporary exhibitions on appropriately futuristic philosophical and aesthetic subjects.

To the north of Arc-et-Senans, **Besançon**, the main town of the Franche-Comté, fills a deep bend in the river Doubs and is dominated by one of the largest, most imposing and best preserved citadels left by Vauban—having expended so much effort to establish control of the Franche-Comté, Louis XIV was clearly anxious not to lose it. There are no less than four museums inside the citadel, two of them devoted to local traditions and crafts. At the foot of the citadel, there is a very dirty Roman gateway, and beside it the cathedral which contains beautiful works of art including a very well-displayed masterpiece by the Renaissance Florentine artist Fra Bartolommeo. The good fine arts museum, housed in one of the finest *hôtels*, includes several works by Courbet.

Rather than go into the city, many tourists will prefer to trace the river Loue from Arc-et-Senans through beautiful wooded hills and valleys to the ramshackle town of **Ornans**. Old houses hang over the shallow, swift-running river, and rocky cliffs provide a splendid backdrop to Courbet's home town. There is a very good museum devoted to the artist. The rivers Loue and Lison and the cascading springs at their sources, both deeply sheltered beneath a canopy of lush vegetation, were beloved by the artist, and have lost none of their beauty.

The most attractive feature of the northern part of the French Jura is the **Doubs** valley. Near its source, **Malbuisson** is a quiet resort beside the Jura's largest but scenically rather dull lake, good for fishing and boating. Below the market town of **Pontarlier**, the river follows a peaceful meandering course, which may be abandoned to visit the old **Abbaye de Montbenoît**, with its humorous Renaissance choir stalls.

Downstream the Doubs enters a more dramatic phase, as tight gorges alternate with broad natural reservoirs; boats can be taken from **Villers-le-Lac** offering the best opportunity to admire the river. The Saut du Doubs is a particularly impressive tumultuous waterfall, below the Barrage du Chatelot. The Doubs is the national frontier, and runs between thickly evergreen gorges, which if you are carbound can best be seen around **Goumois**, a good and extremely quiet base for walking, fishing, and doing nothing.

Hotels

Aloxe-Corton, 21200 Côte-d'Or   £££££

CLARION   Tel: 80.26.46.70

Beautifully converted 17th-century house in the heart of one of the most prestigious wine villages of the Côte de Beaune, next to a delicious tiled-roof château depicted on countless tourist brochures. It's been modernised tastefully. Bedrooms are stylish in subtle pastel shades, with excellent marble bathrooms; there's a comfortable salon with open fire and beams, and a garden overlooking the vineyards. Babysitting (and feeding) offered. An excellent base for Burgundian expeditions.

10 bedrooms; no rest; no lift.

Arbois, 39600 Jura   £££

DE PARIS   Tel: 84.66.05.67

The Jeunets, father and son, run an excellent restaurant in the centre of Arbois, with a few varied, mostly no more than adequate bedrooms. Jeunet *père* specialises in classical dishes (*poularde au vin jaune*), Jeunet *fils* has new ideas which feature increasingly on the menu; the collaboration is a great success, and the dining room décor—stags' heads, stuffed birds, cowbells and hunting horns—is amusingly eclectic. Splendid local and far-reaching wine list.

Closed mid-Nov to mid-Mar (rest Mon dinner and Tues out of season); 18 bedrooms; no lift.

Arnay-le-Duc, 21230 Côte-d'Or   £££

CHEZ CAMILLE   Tel: 80.90.01.38

A main-road restaurant-with-rooms in the town centre, with a very pretty summery courtyard restaurant (glassed-in roof) filled with wicker, trellis and greenery, and equally pretty bedrooms, newly done up and soundproofed. There's a small salon with open fire, and a small sauna; the Poinsots have plans to extend by providing a couple of family rooms in their home, about 5km away, where they now house the odd last-minute guest, or perhaps those whose bookings haven't been confirmed. The food is very good; there are a few good-value fixed-price menus (the cheapest including a light and very local wine), including a 'surprise' one. An inexpensive and pleasant halt, ten miles from the Autoroute du Soleil.

Closed 3 weeks Jan; 15 bedrooms; no lift.

Hotels

Beaune, 21200 Côte-d'Or   ££££

LE CEP   Tel: 80.22.35.48

A fine 17th-century town house in the heart of old Beaune. The décor is largely *style Louis XV* (and XVI), heavy in parts with plush red and gold velour, large stone fireplaces, polished wood floors and tapestries. It's all well cared for, and the traditional bedrooms have good bathrooms; there's a barrel-vaulted breakfast room in the basement, and a salon. A further 29 rooms are to be added this year, when the conversion of the neighbouring house has been finished; given Beaune's popularity with southbound tourists, there should be no difficulty filling them. A good base without restaurant.

Closed Dec to mid-Mar; 21 bedrooms; no rest; no lift; garage.

Beaune (Levernois), 21200 Côte-d'Or   ££

PARC   Tel: 80.22.22.51

On the edge of a quiet village off the motorway 5 km from Beaune, the Parc is a pleasant old stone house, flowery and inviting, with a small courtyard beside it and countryside beyond. There's a breakfast room and a rustic bar, spruce and simple; no lounge or restaurant. Bedrooms are spacious, fresh, traditionally neat. It's a peaceful little hotel of some character, offering excellent value and very popular.

Closed mid-Nov to early Dec, and Mar 1 to 17; 20 bedrooms; no rest; no lift.

Bouilland, 21420 Côte-d'Or   ££££

LE VIEUX MOULIN   Tel: 80.21.51.16

This attractive restaurant with rooms, stone-built with an old granary above, is peacefully set on the edge of the village; on the road the only traffic noise is cowbells. There's a shady terrace, a garden and two small salons. All is rural simplicity, or so it appears at first glance. However, M. Silva has ambitious plans, as befits one of the finest chefs in the region—still a little behind the big five in the local pecking order, but doing his best. His restaurant is formal and serious, with garden views through the large windows; and the few rather simple and cheerful bedrooms are shortly to be converted into (fewer) larger and better bedrooms, to join those newly added last year—with a higher standard of comfort, at higher prices. Excellent (and excellent-value) fixed-price menus, wonderfully inventive.

Closed 5 weeks in Dec and Jan (rest Wed, and Thurs lunch); 13 bedrooms; no lift.

La Celle-Saint-Cyr, 89970 Yonne   ££

LA FONTAINE AUX MUSES   Tel: 86.73.40.22

Pretty creeper-covered farmhouse dating from the 17th century, near a sleepy village in the heart of the Auxerrois and only 7 km from the A6 (Joigny exit). It has been converted into a simple, rustic-style hotel, and has a swimming pool, tennis and pretty garden. The bedrooms vary in style, some with tiled floor and beams, another with bamboo; not all bathrooms are ultra-modern. There's a small and atmospheric bar/salon, an attractive restaurant, and a music room which M. Langevin allows guests to use when he isn't composing. Cooking is homely and hearty—*soupe, terrine, confit, tarte*—at reasonable prices, à la carte only.

Closed Mon (rest Mon dinner and Tues lunch); 14 bedrooms; no lift; swimming pool.

Burgundy, the Rhône Valley and the Jura

Chagny, 71150 Saône-et-Loire   £££££

LAMELOISE   Tel: 85.87.08.85

This isn't the best setting imaginable for indulging in sampling the fare of one of Burgundy's top chefs, which means one of France's, for it's a street-side house (ancient, admittedly) in the town centre, without garden or terrace. Of course, it is hardly uncomfortable—bedrooms are reasonably spacious and very well furnished, there's a small modern bar, and a small traditional salon by the reception. But it's the food that counts, and there need be few complaints here, as long as the reasonable fixed-price *menu affaire* meets with your approval, or you can manage the *menu dégustation*, more costly and exciting. Desserts on even the cheapest menu are accompanied by exquisite *petits fours* and *mignardises* and rounded off by sorbets—there is no question of leaving hungry.

Closed mid-Dec to mid-Jan (rest Wed, and Thurs lunch); 21 bedrooms.

Charolles, 71120 Saône-et-Loire   ££

DE LA POSTE   Tel: 85.24.11.32

The Doucets take great pride in their little post house, just by the church and the municipal carpark in the centre of this little town in prime cattle country. So traditional provincial décor is giving way to a rather more formal style in the restaurant to reflect M. Doucet's ambitions in the cooking line. There is no better place to sample a fine *entrecôte charolaise*, vast and very tasty, accompanied by a fine *gratin dauphinoise*, or for finding better value—in the fixed-price menus and in the wine list, with its excellent selection of beaujolais. Bedrooms are solidly traditional and comfortable. An excellent simple hotel.

Closed first week June and Nov (rest Sun dinner and Mon out of season); 9 bedrooms; no lift.

Chonas-l'Amballan, 38121 Isère   £££

LE MARAIS SAINT-JEAN   Tel: 74.58.83.28

This former old farmhouse, now utterly spruced up and looking almost new outside, is set in a quiet spot near a quiet village 9 km from Vienne. Inside it's very spruce, too, and very comfortable; beams, quarry tiles and rustic furniture give it a cosy ambience. There's a terrace and garden, bar and salon; the cooking is well above average, and both the *carte* and fixed-price menus are good value (*ris de veau au poivron, panaché de poissons en soupe, chevre grillée aux herbes* and a superb *gratin de framboises* formed one of the cheaper ones). A peaceful stop-over.

Closed Feb (rest Tues dinner and Wed); 10 bedrooms; no lift.

Cluny, 71250 Saône-et-Loire   £££

DE BOURGOGNE   Tel: 85.59.00.58

Weathered old creeper-covered hotel in the abbey square, built round a small central garden and courtyard. The lounge has something of the atmosphere of an elegant country house; the simple homely bar doubles as a breakfast room—with classical music still playing. It's more appropriate at dinner, in the spacious white restaurant with its old stone fireplace, where the food is traditional yet light. Bedrooms are spacious and traditional, three with wood floors. A pleasant family-run establishment.

Closed mid-Nov to mid-Mar (rest Tues lunch and Wed lunch, and Tues dinner out of season); 18 bedrooms; no lift.

Hotels

Dijon, 21000 Côte-d'Or   £££££
DE LA CLOCHE   Tel: 80.30.12.32

On the edge of the old town (near the archaeological museum), a hotel has been
on this site since 1424. The present one dates from the 1870's, a fine dignified
stone building, recently entirely rebuilt inside its classified façade. The new style
incorporates fine wood and marble floors, and ultra-refined modern furniture.
Bedrooms are spacious and very comfortable, if a trifle anonymous (some in
duplex arrangements); there's a bar, small garden and terrace, and two dining
rooms—one an airy conservatory, one in the barrel-vaulted cellar. The
restaurant is run by M. Billoux, who has recently lef his acclaimed Hôtel de la
Gare in Digoin. It would be in order to expect great things from him here, too.
Comfort of a high degree, at prices not unreasonable for a city hotel of this
stature.

Closed Feb (rest Sun dinner and Mon); 80 bedrooms; garage.

Gevrey Chambertin, 21220 Côte-d'Or   £££
LES GRANDS CRUS   Tel: 80.34.34.15

In the very heart of the finest vineyards, this pleasant modern house, built in local
style with steep tiled roof—and complete with beams, monumental fireplace,
quarry tiles and old polished oak—offers solid bourgeois comfort, without great
style. There's a pretty little garden, and a small salon/breakfast room; it's very
peaceful, and well situated for a crawl along the Route des Grands Crus.

Closed mid-Dec to mid-Feb; 24 bedrooms; no rest; no lift.

Goumois, 25470 Doubs   ££
TAILLARD   Tel: 81.44.20.75

This solid 19th-century chalet looks out across the deeply green Doubs valley
to Switzerland: so unbendingly traditional is the style of the establishment and its
cooking that you might imagine yourself on the other side. The river is a paradise
for fishermen with a taste for restful scenic beauty, and the restaurant is the
perfect place to sample the fruits of the Doubs. Bedrooms are comfortable and
good value; there's a splendid terrace, and a comfortably neo-rustic salon/TV
room for rainy days, which are not infrequent around here. The welcome is
warm, and advice about excursions plentiful.

Closed Nov to Feb (rest Wed in Oct and Mar); 17 bedrooms; no lift.

Joigny, 89300 Yonne   ££££ and £££££
LA CÔTE SAINT-JACQUES   Tel: 86.62.09.70

Less than two hours from Paris by motorway, Joigny is a convenient halt for
southbound travellers who have caught a morning ferry and do not feel an
inclination to reach Burgundian vineyards by nightfall. The hotel, on the edge of
town, straddles the RN6—on one side the subdued and formal restaurants and
older, cheaper, bedrooms; on the other a bar, indoor pool, 15 new, ultra-
luxurious bedrooms and a terrace overlooking the River Yonne (all linked by a
rather exquisite underground passage). This is no roadhouse, and les Lorains are
anxious to make you linger; only your pocket will suffer. Michel Lorain and his
son Jean-Michel (recently back from Girardet in Switzerland) work brilliantly
together, and the result is one of the finest eating experiences in France, best
sampled on the fixed- and high-priced *menu gourmand*.

Closed 3 weeks Jan; 18 bedrooms, 15 apartments; swimming pool.

104

Burgundy, the Rhône Valley and the Jura

Mailly-le-Château, 89660 Yonne   ££

LE CASTEL   Tel: 86.40.43.06

In the church square, high up in this sleepy village with views over the River Yonne, a simple beige shuttered building with lawns and terrace to the front. Inside, much is Empire-style—traditional and rather faded in parts. But there's a good atmosphere, a friendly welcome from the English-speaking owners, and very reasonable food—both in quality and price. A pleasant and peaceful halt.

Closed mid-Nov to mid-Mar (rest Wed); 12 bedrooms; no lift.

Mercurey, 71640 Saône-et-Loire   ££

LE VAL D'OR   Tel: 85.47.13.70

A roadside restaurant-with-rooms in a rather dull wine village, with a tiny gravel terrace next to the parking area behind, and a rustic-style bar. The bedrooms are small, and solidly traditional, with floral drapes and rustic-style furniture. Without doubt, the main reason that its many British devotees come here again and again is the excellent cooking, both inventive and good value. *Persillé de homard et ris de veau aux herbes, feuilleté de lapin et d'escargots à l'estragon, saumon rôti au Mercurey rouge*—and splendid desserts—will not cost an arm and a leg, and neither will the accommodation.

Closed 4 weeks from 8 Dec and 10 days at end of Aug (rest Mon; Tues lunch in summer; Sun dinner in winter); 12 bedrooms; no lift.

Meximieux, 01800 Ain   £££

CLAUDE LUTZ   Tel: 74.61.06.78

Not far from Lyon, and near enough to picture-book perched Pérouges for you to be able to enjoy an aperitif or a renowned *galette* in front of the considerably more expensive establishment there, before repairing to the lesser comforts, but not to a lesser repast, chez Lutz. The ambiance is relaxing, menus are interesting and very good value, and the wine list has a reasonable selection. Bedrooms (many family size, and also very good value) face the street and have some traffic noise in the morning, so you're sure of an early start. An excellent stop-off hotel.

Closed mid-Oct to mid-Nov and 10 days in July (rest Sun dinner and Mon); 16 bedrooms; no lift.

Les Rousses, 39220 Jura   £££

FRANCE   Tel: 84.60.01.45

It's a shame to be right in the middle of this small but tightly packed resort in summer (cheaper bedrooms have views only of wallscapes), but the Hôtel de France is comfortably done up in a simple rough-stone way that suits the region. There is an attractive bar and a comfortable sitting area, and a plush modern TV room upstairs. The dining room is functional and a bit cramped, but the food, and especially the fish, is surprisingly good and could not be less institutional.

Closed mid-Nov to mid-Dec, and end May; 34 bedrooms; no lift.

Hotels

Saulieu, 21210 Côte-d'Or   ££-£££££

LA CÔTE D'OR   Tel: 80.64.07.66

This isn't the most exciting hotel in which to sample the creations of one of
France's foremost chefs, but Bernard and Chantal Loiseau are, bit by bit, bringing
their main-road lodging house (on the RN6) up to the standard of their
restaurant. Last year saw the addition of nine splendid new bedrooms—some
duplex, some ground floor—and plans are afoot to refurbish the older, smaller
and much cheaper bedrooms. Meanwhile, there's a cosy small salon, a breakfast
room and a pleasant garden, and the restaurant—atmospheric and comfortable.
If the décor is less stylish than the other greats, the cooking isn't. There's a
reasonable fixed-priced four-course menu, an equally reasonable vegetarian
menu, rare indeed in France, and a surprise *menu dégustation*—expensive, but
perfectly in line with others in the same class.

Closed 3 week in Nov (rest Tues and Wed lunch in winter); 24 bedrooms; no lift.

St-Florentin, 89600 Yonne   £££

LA GRANDE CHAUMIÈRE   Tel: 86.35.15.12

Pretty little town-centre hotel, next to the old market square, with an attractive
light and modern pink restaurant, clubby lounge, and garden. The bedrooms are
a reasonable size, vividly decorated and with good bathrooms. Cooking is good,
without being very exciting; there are a couple of good-value fixed-price menus,
and a *carte* that is not expensive. Your meal may be accompanied by modern or
classical music; service is efficient. A pleasant and simple halt, not too far (162
km) from Paris, and between Auxerre and Troyes.

Closed mid-Dec to mid-Jan (rest Wed out of season); 10 bedrooms; no lift.

St-Père-sous-Vézelay, 89450 Yonne   £££££

L'ESPÉRANCE   Tel: 86.33.20.45

Elegant white-shuttered building, set back from the main road through the
village; the idyllic green garden has two streams complete with ducks. The
interior is equally inviting—full of light and colour. Bedrooms are extremely
luxurious and stylish; some are up the road in a converted mill, more rustic in
style and more spacious. Marc Meneau's cuisine is of great distinction; he is now
agreed to be one of the noble band of France's top chefs, and offers some of the
best-value fixed-price menus of any restaurant in its class.

Closed Jan (rest Tues, and Wed lunch); 21 bedrooms; no lift.

Sens, 89100 Yonne   £££

PARIS ET POSTE   Tel: 86.65.17.43

Fine 19th-century *hostellerie* in the heart of Sens, right by the splendid cathedral.
Inside, it remains the epitome of a traditional French provincial—and fairly
grand—hotel; there are heavy floral patterns, panelled walls, stags' heads, and
crisp white tablecloths in the restaurant; and the bedrooms are spacious and
similarly trad (even the newly redecorated ones, some of which have wood floors).
Standards remain high, too—excellent service and cooking, with a couple of
reasonable fixed-price menus, and a more expensive gourmet one if you're feeling
hungry. *Carte* specialities are *escargots, boudin noir senonais aux pommes*, and a
two-course *demi caneton*.

30 bedrooms; no lift; garage.

Burgundy, the Rhône Valley and the Jura

Val-Suzon, 21121 Côte-d'Or ££

HOSTELLERIE DU VAL-SUZON   Tel: 80.35.60.15

Once an old mill, now a simple and peaceful little hotel in a tiny hamlet in a green valley some 10 miles north-west of Dijon. The gardens have views and shady limes and willows; bedrooms are beamed and pretty; the dining room has candles and log fire, and you can eat in the gardens in summer. Yves Perreau uses traditional local produce, including plenty of fish, and is becoming a good and inventive chef. There's a small chalet annexe at the end of the garden.

Closed Jan and Wed; 17 bedrooms; no lift.

Verdun-sur-le-Doubs, 71350 Saône-et-Loire £££

HOSTELLERIE BOURGUIGNONNE   Tel: 95.91.51.45

A rather ugly 19th-century *auberge* on the edge of the village, set back from the road behind a terrace, garden and childrens' play area. Inside, there's a small salon area and bar, and a large and welcoming restaurant with traditional rustic décor. Cooking is traditional, too; specialities, which feature both on the good-value fixed-price menus and on the *carte* are *pochouse Verdunoise* (a stew of eel and river fish), *jambonnette de poulet de Bresse* and *blanquette de ris de veau*. Some bedrooms are small, some have old-fashioned bathrooms or small baths.

Closed Jan and Feb (rest Tues dinner and Wed); 13 bedrooms; no lift.

Vézelay, 89450 Yonne ££££

POSTE ET LION D'OR   Tel: 86.33.21.23

If you want to visit the glorious 12th-century hilltop church of Vézelay in the evening or early morning, before the onslaught of tourists can mar your enjoyment, there is no more convenient place to stay. This fine 18th-century post house sits at the foot of the hill, with fine countryside views, and offers solid traditional comforts of a high standard. Bedrooms, well furnished in rather heavy styles (and with very good bed linen) generally have large old-fashioned and well-equipped bathrooms. In the brightly-lit and slightly formal restaurant, the food is good, though not very exciting and not cheap; but the short and rather dull wine list at least offers more bottles under 100FF than over, and many half-bottles.

Closed Nov to Mar; 48 bedrooms; no lift.

Vonnas, 01540 Ain £££££

GEORGES BLANC   Tel: 74.50.00.10

It is hard to find anyone to disagree with the fact that Georges Blanc is one of the greatest chefs in France. And it is almost impossible to find fault with any aspect of his refurbished and elegant hotel right on the banks of the little river Veyle, which is now in keeping with his three-star status. There's a fine swimming pool, tennis and helipad, lots of comfortable sitting areas and a very fine restaurant indeed. Blanc, the fourth generation of patron/chefs (a fifth is up-and-coming), is one of the foremost proponents of *nouvelle cuisine* at its very best, and it would be a shame not to try his six-course *menu découverte*—which, for around £40, shows off his skills superbly. If you are content with a mere four courses and no choice, there's a cheaper menu (but there's little chance of ending up hungry, as everything is of course rounded off with *petits fours et mignardises*).

Closed Jan to mid-Feb (rest Wed, Thurs lunch, also Thurs dinner out of season); 30 bedrooms; swimming pool.

The South

Promenade des Anglais, Nice

"There was sun enough for lazing upon beaches,
There was fun enough for far into the night" (Sir John Betjeman)

The "South of France" has a distinctive ring. To announce you're off to the centre or the west, still less the east or the north, just won't impress your friends in the same way. The image is one of holidays in style on the coast, where others spend whole seasons, lives even, of millions won and more often lost at the wheel of gambling fortune, of shoulders rubbed with film. stars, rock stars, writers, painters and royalty. Fifty years ago the South of France conformed to this image: the Riviera—a small section of the Mediterranean coast between Cannes and Menton—was the playground of the predominantly British rich. Now it is only a small part of what the South of France means to tourists, and irrelevant to many. As the British have lost their wealth the Riviera has lost the British, or at least the atmosphere of a decadent imperial colony. The mild winter climate which brought the first visitors to the most sheltered parts of the south coast has lost its importance as an attraction compared with the midsummer sun about which there is nothing mild, and which beats down on the whole coast. For in the Midi (as the French call the south), the sun is king. Its light, so harsh at midday that you repair to the shade of a eucalyptus to drink, talk and sleep, so luminous at each end of the day that it seems to paint the landscape in colours of a new intensity, alone gives unity to the area we call the South of France.

The original Provincia Romana covered most of southern France. In the Middle Ages the region became known as the Languedoc, an area characterised by the Provençal language of the medieval troubadour poets of the court of Toulouse, which is closer to Latin than is the French of northern France. In the Languedoc they said "oc" for "yes" whereas in the north, the Languedoïl, they said "oil" for "oui". The heart of the Provincia was the area around the Rhône delta, now known as Lower Provence. The Roman influence on the area is profound and provides the main attraction to tourists. Though perhaps not uniquely endowed with great buildings, its monuments remain intact as nowhere else in France—particularly in Arles and Nîmes; many are still used.

However, sightseeing need not be confined to Roman remains, for there is far more to see in Lower Provence. Aigues-Mortes and Les Baux are two of the most extraordinary old towns in France, the one intact within its walls on the salt flats, the other partly ruined on one of the sudden lonely rocky outcrops that characterise Provence. Avignon has the magnificent palace where the popes resided under the protection and control of the kings of France for 150 years. Arles—the capital of Roman Gaul—is a beautiful town with monuments from all periods and like nearby St-Rémy rich in artistic associations, notably with Van Gogh. Aix is the glory of the post-Renaissance classical period, a mellow and harmonious town seemingly rebuilt all of a piece in the 17th and 18th centuries. South-west of Arles in the Rhône delta lies the Camargue, land of shifting coastline, salt marshes, wild horses and bulls, leather-clad cowboys and flamingoes.

With the exception of a few rocky and dramatic crags and peaks, the landscape of Lower Provence is relatively flat, and swept by the *mistral* wind which howls dry and cold down the Rhône valley. Much of its

The South

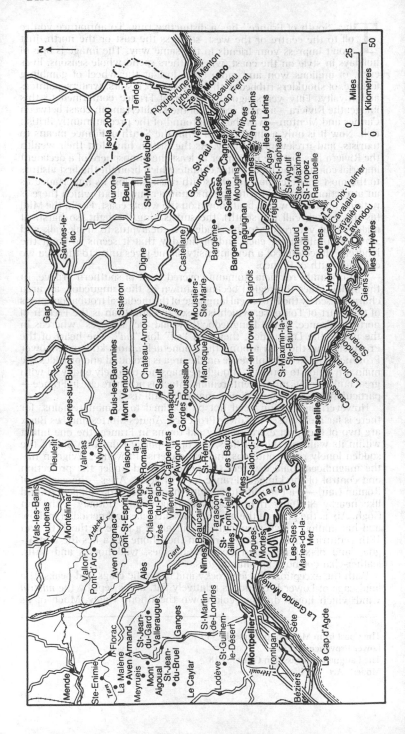

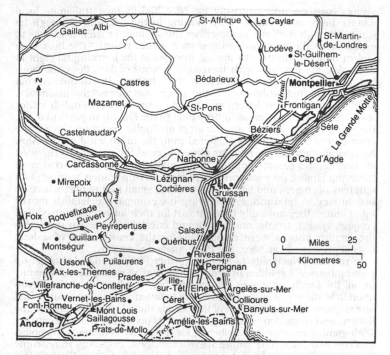

natural scrubland has been turned to profit, with olive and almond groves, cherry orchards, vineyards and lavender beds. Although the fertility of Provence is no grassy lushness, it is a fruitful land—Provence produces two-thirds of France's almonds, half of her olives, half of her table grapes, three-quarters of her melons and tomatoes.

Behind the Côte d'Azur—the stretch of coast between Marseille and Menton—lies Upper Provence, a mountainous region of great natural beauty, still little frequented by tourists. On almost every one of its hills there seems to perch a village. Some of the most strikingly situated, especially those looking down over the coast, have become tourist traps—which doesn't detract from the beauty of their situation but will disappoint many visitors. In general the perched villages further inland are much less frequented and even though the views they command may be less dramatic they more greatly reward a thirst for authenticity. At the foot of the hills and mountains, the coast has grown apart from the interior because of tourism. Nearly all those who go to the coast go for the coast, and venture very little inland (in high season the density of traffic makes it very difficult to venture anywhere). Those who go to visit Roman Gaul or just to relax in a sleepy inland hideaway turn back in horror if they set out for a day on the beach, and sink gratefully back into the quiet shade of their village plane trees or into contemplation of a classical pediment.

The Riviera began with the British. The writer Tobias Smollett spent 18 months in Nice in the early 1760s because of his asthma; in many ways his experience is typical of the Riviera as it was to develop in the 19th century. In all his time in Nice he hardly associated with any non-

111

visitors (perhaps not surprising for Nice had its own Italianate local patois); he aroused curiosity by bathing in the sea; and although he stayed through the year he describes the summer in such a way as to explain why the Riviera developed as a winter resort: "The heat is so violent that you cannot stir abroad from six in the morning till eight at night. We are pestered with incredible swarms of flies, fleas and bugs but the gnats are more intolerable than all the rest". It was not just that the sun was not fashionable—the place was downright insanitary. Smollett published his letters and twenty years later an English visitor was "disgusted by the gross flattery paid to the English in particular . . . the whole neighbourhood has the air of an English watering place". The coast east of Nice, which is sheltered from the north wind by the Alps, became an increasingly popular place to spend the winter. To the west of Nice, Cannes became popular in the mid-19th century by accident: a travelling English peer was prevented from leaving France because of an outbreak of cholera and fell in love with the small fishing port where he had to stay in quarantine. Following his example the English moved into Cannes; they annually brought turf for their lawns, and introduced croquet, cricket, tennis, and acacia and eucalyptus trees. In the 1820s the English visitors were responsible for the construction of a long coastal promenade at Nice, the Promenade des Anglais.

In the tiny principality of Monaco, prince Florestan decided to set up gaming houses (forbidden in France) as a way of raising some revenue, for all the family estates in France had been confiscated at the Revolution, and the expedient of extra heavy taxation and customs duties had already been tried. By the end of the decade the railway had reached the Riviera, and so sudden was the growth of its popularity that in February 1869 gaming revenue was sufficient for the prince of Monaco to abolish all taxes and rates. The young traveller of 1861, Augustus Hare, came back over 30 years later to write a guidebook to the Riviera and described what had happened in the intervening period: "Up to 1860 Menton was a picturesque town with a few scattered villas let to strangers in neighbouring olive groves; now much of its lovely bays is filled with hideous and stuccoed villas in the worst taste . . . pretentious paved promenades have taken the place of the beautiful walks under tamarisk groves by the seashore. Menton is vulgarised and ruined but its climate is delicious, its flowers exquisite and its excursions for good walkers inexhaustible and full of interest". Monte Carlo, "a wild spot covered with heath and rosemary until the 1860s" he now found to be "a snare, never more plainly set". Exotic gardens, the finest orchestras, and lavish reading rooms were all laid on free, but "*faites le jeu, messieurs* is heard from noon till midnight and the faster people ruin themselves and send a pistol shot through their heads before the faster others take their place". Queen Victoria came to Cimiez, and Edward prince of Wales came to Cannes. Luxury trains came from Calais, St Petersburg and other European capitals, and an English newspaper announced the new arrivals, as if the winter Riviera was one enormous ball, which it was. Nice is estimated to have received 25,000 winter visitors in the 1880s, but only one hotel of standing stayed open in the summer.

The Riviera was aristocratic (British and Russian) but even more than that it was rich, and whereas there may originally have been a coincidence between riches and titles, by the 1920s there was not. Katherine Mansfield, one of the many tubercular visitors to the Riviera described Nice (in 1920), as a bourgeois paradise and life on the Riviera as "ignoble. It all turns on money". Americans played an ever larger part in the seaside society and being used to the heat started the fashion for summers on the Riviera; in the '20s they launched the summer resort of Juan-les-Pins. Perhaps the last great representative of the Riviera's golden age was Edward VIII; when the war was over Edward and Mrs Simpson did not go back to the Riviera for long, for it was becoming a mass destination for French summer tourists. Its winter attractions remain, and have even been increased by the development of well-equipped ski resorts very close to Nice; but those with the means and the inclination to winter on the Riviera are a select few.

Considering the tourist revolution that has taken place, the look of the Riviera is remarkably little changed. Everything still turns on money, and the principality of Monaco's crop of high-rise tax-free international banks are quite in keeping with the atmosphere of gambling Monte Carlo. Architecturally the Riviera is still dominated by exotic villas and overblown neo-baroque palaces—although many of these have been institutionalised. Along the Riviera there has simply been very little space for development: the seafront from Menton to Nice was heavily built up before 1900 and the mountains come right down to the sea. To the west of the Var river there is a little more space and some striking modern architecture in the new beach and marina resorts that continue to be built to accommodate the crowds.

The coast is hardly a relaxing place for a midsummer holiday; it is Paris-on-Sea with many of the qualities of the capital—flashy, self-conscious, exciting, an absorbing spectacle, where people come to see and be seen. The season reaches a peak of intense crowds in July and August, when the coast roads come to a standstill (as does the motorway south from Paris on peak weekends). At no time of the year is it empty, as a ski resort can be in summer or a pure beach resort in winter, but somehow when it isn't full it seems rather sad—like a fast car being driven at 30. You may enjoy the landscape more, but that isn't the point.

When the Parisians took over the coast they did not confine themselves to the Riviera—strictly the stretch of coast east of Cannes. Now the coastline between Cannes and Marseille, which had been more or less ignored by visitors and in parts bypassed by the railway, is hardly less frequented than the eastern stretch, and although the resorts press less closely one against the other the crowd factor is no less marked. The obvious difference between the two parts is the absence on the western stretch of Riviera-style architecture, which barely extends beyond Cannes and finally expires at St-Raphaël with a few cheap and nasty imitations of what is at its best an imitative style. Another difference is the landscape: the west lacks the distant snowy backdrop of the Alps but instead has red rocky mountains—which are related not to continental France but to Corsica and the Balearics—and long beaches with pines. But the most important difference is harder to express clinically; it is a difference of style. It is not simply a question of wealth: there are infinite gradations of atmosphere. Just as a Cap Ferrat person would not be confused with a Cannes person, still less with a Menton person, a Ste-Maxime person would not be seen dead in Le Lavandou, still less St-Raphaël or Hyères-Plage. Paris-on-Sea is as class-ridden as Paris, and on the coast the different ingredients of the metropolitan social mix have separated. The exception is St-Tropez, no less potent in its image-conjuring power than Monte Carlo, and classless. The arty bohemian resort where topless sunbathing started in the 1960s, St-Trop' has retained its hold on the public imagination, and its own inimitably laid-back exclusiveness. It is the radical chic (still chic in France) of denim and leather and Harley Davidson, of the Left Bank and the ever-youthful pop star Johnny Hallyday. At St-Tropez, in complete contrast to the Riviera, you can recognize the smartest people by the scruffiness of their clothes.

West of the bay of St-Tropez are small family resorts—with holiday homes rather than hotels and more emphasis on practicality than style. These resorts have grown to receive tourists where barely a community existed before; few of them are large or exciting or hideous or noisy, and most of the coast is very beautiful. Around the important ports of Toulon and Marseille, the landscape is rather spoilt by industry and ill-thought-out development.

Between the Rhône delta and the Pyrenees the coast of Languedoc and Roussillon (Catalonia in France, centred on Perpignan), is characterised by two things: red wine, produced in greater quantity than anywhere else in France, dark and strong and usually described as unpretentious; and a flat, straight, sandy coast broken up by lagoons and marshes, only recently drained for development. Except at the extreme south there are no hills immediately behind the beaches. Until the 1960s there were few people except Sunday sunbathers from Montpellier, Béziers, Narbonne and Perpignan—cities of France's greatest rugby players and bullfighters. Now the Languedoc/Roussillon coast bristles with what were heralded in the '60s as the resorts of the future. Here the architects and the planners have asserted themselves, working hard to build with themes and styles, more often around marinas than beaches. Naturism flourishes in many. Just as in the modern Alpine ski resort holidaymakers can walk out to a lift and ski back to the door, here they can sail to and from their backyard; and just as in the ski resorts the hotel plays very little part, here everyone owns or rents flats and yachts. The style varies from the futuristic geometry of La Grande Motte, the first and most ambitious of the new resorts, to the subsequently more fashionable borrowing of inspiration from the simple rustic architecture of southern France. In contrast to the Riviera these resorts are almost devoid of life outside the midsummer months.

The Coast from Menton to Marseille

Between Nice and the Italian border just east of Menton the Maritime Alps descend steeply into the Mediterranean, giving some of the most beautiful coastal scenery in Europe, and sheltering the shore from the north wind. This is the area for summer flowers and lemons in winter, and is the original winter resort for those too fragile to withstand the northern cold. Very little of the coast is much built up.

There are three roads along the coast. The **Corniche Inférieure** runs right along the coast serving all the resorts, inadequately. The **Grande Corniche** is the most exciting; it's the far from straight old Roman road from Nice to Genoa, reaching a height of nearly 450 metres above the sea. It passes behind some of the coastal peaks and gives a mixture of views down over the bays of the Riviera and up into the barren Alps, snow-covered for most of the year. One of the few villages the road passes is **La Turbie** which was the point of division between the Roman Empire this and that side of the Alps. The great monument (Alpine Trophy) which was erected on the site in 6 BC to commemorate the conquest of the Alpine regions, which united the Empire and heralded three centuries of *Pax Romana*, must have been very impressive, to judge from the model in the museum. Even the fragment that remains is arresting.

The **Moyenne Corniche** gives the most consistent sea views and access to **Eze**, the most astonishingly perched village of all. The view from it is one of the classics of the Riviera. Eze is one of the most popular excursions from the coast, so do not expect an unspoilt old village. At the top, on the site of the old castle, there is an exotic garden with cacti.

Menton has a reputation of being the best resort for health, and the new town on the western bay has something of the atmosphere of a spa as many of the imposing old winter palace hotels have been taken over by French institutions for holiday colonies. The mostly 17th-century town between the two bays is still attractively Italianate with ochre painted houses and dripping laundry strung across the narrow streets beneath the baroque belfry of St-Michel, whose little square is a delightful setting for summer evening concerts. Like many of the Riviera resorts, Menton has its winter carnival—here celebrating the lemons and oranges for which it is most famous. Above Menton and its adjacent resort of Roquebrune-Cap-Martin, the village of **Roquebrune** remains intact, medieval and perched, or rather clinging to the side of the hill. Its narrow and in many cases covered streets are all confined within the precincts of a 10th-century fortress built for defence against the Saracens.

Between Menton and Roquebrune, roads lead back up the hillsides to the finely situated villages of **Gorbio** and **Ste-Agnès** both of which are old and panoramic. Ste-Agnès, the highest of the villages immediately behind the coast, occupies such a commanding position that it was endowed by German occupiers with blockhouses, which remain.

You don't need a sign to announce the tiny **Principality of Monaco**, which occupies less than a square mile of ground, but the surface area of whose buildings must be many hundreds of times larger. On the French side of an imaginary line down the hillside there are old houses and small villas, on the other side soaring tax-free international banks. The Principality, unable to grow on land, has grown upwards, down into the ground (underground carparks) and even into the sea where there are several new tourist developments. **Monte Carlo** is the new town of banks, some occupying modern skyscrapers, others in the old, that is to say late 19th-century, villas which have all the grace and beauty of elephants dripping with diamonds. The neo-baroque style surpasses itself in the sumptuously plush Hôtel de Paris and the adjacent casino, the work (it is no surprise to learn) of the architect of the Paris Opera House. You can visit the casino, archetype of the French casino style and setting for so many bank-breaking exploits, without risking a fortune. Standing at the end of an exotic garden of palms it is much more than just a series of gambling rooms, having a night club, theatre, and of course a tearoom. Just wandering around, it is impossible not to be affected by the charged atmosphere.

The modern development of the resort is still going on down below the casino along the water, around the famous summer Sporting Club. There is a beach, with a lift down from the centre of Monte Carlo. Beyond **La Condamine**, the antique port of Hercules, the old settlement of **Monaco** stands on a natural fortress, with 150ft cliffs down to the water on three sides. The small town (tourist access on foot or by bus only) is old and painted, and has only one building of substance, the princely palace of the Grimaldis, very heavily restored when wealth came to Monaco and architecturally uninteresting. It is open in summer months when the family is away, and contains a surprisingly impressive mostly 17th-century courtyard of honour with distinguished frescoes and a marble staircase. As well as the stagey square in front of the palace with its crenellations and cannons, Monaco has a 19th-century cathedral with two beautiful altar-pieces of Nice's Bréa school, and a celebrated aquarium in its oceanographic museum.

Grimaldi Palace

Though many interests are now vested in its continued existence, the tiny principality owes its survival largely to luck and the tenacity of the Grimaldis. The family probably came from Genoa to defend the harbour against the Saracens and bought control of Monaco in the 14th century, later adding Menton and Roquebrune. Napoleon incorporated the principality into the Alpes Maritimes, but surprisingly the Allied Powers gave it back to the Grimaldis in 1814. The sporting British started a number of famous competitions, of which the most celebrated are the Monte Carlo rally, the Grand Prix, and the tennis tournament, the first of the international season.

Back in France, **Beaulieu** is a very sheltered resort, not unlike Menton in character. The **Cap Ferrat** peninsula remains one of the most exclusive villa communities on the Riviera, which makes it one of the most exclusive places anywhere. At the little port of **St-Jean-Cap-Ferrat** there is a large marina which is good for yacht spotting. Near St-Jean you can visit the delicious villa and gardens built round the very precious art collection of the early 20th-century Rothschild heiress Madame Ephrussi (the Ile-de-France Museum). The French 18th century is particularly well represented. On the western side of the Cap, **Villefranche** guards one of the finest, most enclosed bays of the Riviera, however, its beach is rather narrow. The old town of tall houses, narrow streets and stairways climbs up from the fishing port and 16th-century citadel and is pleasantly unspoilt. Beside the quay the small chapel is decorated by Jean Cocteau. The next twist in the coast leads round to the sweeping Baie des Anges at whose head stands Nice with its long, wide and graceful Promenade des Anglais.

The South

Nice is the big city of the Riviera and one of the most important in southern France. Its inhabitants go quite mad for a fortnight before Lent at carnival time. With its long beach of shingle backed by a six-lane promenade highway with palm trees and ornate hotel façades, it looks like an enormous resort; but there is more to Nice than its seafront. The old town behind the pink classical buildings of the working port is still very much a living part of the city, with colourful flower and vegetable markets and pungent smells. There are several baroque churches, the most interesting being St-Jacques and St-Augustin. Apart from very good shopping the new town, which extends to the west behind the promenade, has little of interest except two museums and a Russian Orthodox cathedral.

✳ *Masséna Museum* A splendid 19th-century palace whose interior is mainly devoted to the Napoleonic period and the memory of Nice's two most famous sons: Masséna and Garibaldi. There are paintings of the 15th- and 16th-century Nice school, the stars being the Bréa family whose works are to be found in churches and chapels all over the Alpes Maritimes and whose limited fame is largely attributable to the deep gloom in which most of the paintings hang.

✳ *Chéret Museum* (Fine Arts) Paintings featuring works by the local artists Fragonard (born in Grasse) and Van Loo, of whom like Bréa there were several.

✳ *Cimiez* The old resort hill behind the centre of Nice is the most interesting part of town for the tourist. Cimiez was the Roman settlement, the Greeks having as usual stuck to the port—which they called Nike after a naval victory won there. Cimiez has its villas and heavy turn-of-the-century hotels (Queen Victoria came to the Grand), and also remains of a Roman arena and interesting museums. One is devoted to Matisse (in the Arena Villa on top of the hill), the other to Chagall (some way down the hill near the station); see page 120. In the abbey church there are three paintings by the Bréas, including a particularly affecting Virgin—an early work of Louis Bréa, and one of his most beautiful.

Excursions from the coast

From Menton and Nice a number of roads lead back into the Maritime Alps, where the enclosed valleys—with cascades and gorges—and numerous perched villages are the main attractions. For the winter (and spring) visitor, ski slopes are only a couple of hours or so from the sea. In the summer there's high mountain hiking in cool thin air, with snowy peaks still visible well into the season. The mountains have little cultivation or pastures and their relatively bare rocky slopes have become progressively depopulated, which adds to the desolate beauty of the half-empty hilltop villages. Such are the difficulties of communication that the main road linking Nice to Grenoble has to climb to well over 2,500 metres to get through—by the Col de la Bonette which boasts the highest road in Europe, although strangely not the highest pass.

✳ **Peillon/Peille** This short excursion behind Nice can be extended round to La Turbie or Ste-Agnès and Menton. Peillon and Peille are two finely set perched villages, both looking down over steep-sided valleys. Peille, set beside a relatively frequented road, is less atmospheric than Peillon whose setting on a high sheer rocky spur above the river far below is beautifully admired from the approach road which zigzags through the olive trees up the side of the valley. The rough stone village itself is nothing much: steep alleyways, an olivewood craft shop and a simple hotel (see Hotels section, page 148) on the terrace outside the village. In the early 19th century the area around Peille and Peillon was terrorised by a notorious band of brigands who eluded all attempts at capture until they set upon the marchioness of Bute and drank the contents of a bottle which she was carrying and which they assumed to be full of alcohol. It was in fact opium and they all collapsed. To everyone's embarrassment they were discovered to be members of the leading families of Nice.

✳ **Roya Valley** This is a busy road into Italy via the Tende tunnel. The Roya cuts through impressively tight gorges below the extraordinarily situated village of **Saorge**, on a horseshoe balcony above the river (access from Fontan). **Tende** is hardly less picturesque in its tiered setting below strange spiky ruins of an old fortress. **La Brigue** has a Romanesque church with the Italianate belfry typical of the old county of Nice, and two Bréa paintings. Beyond it the isolated Chapelle-Notre-Dame-des-Fontaines is decorated with some of the most vivid (and gruesome, in the case of the hanging of Judas) of 15th-century frescoes. The key may have to be obtained from La Brigue. The high mountain areas west of **St-Dalmas** (the Vallée des Merveilles) are excellent hiking country with refuges, lakes and 2,500-metre peaks. Curiously there are thousands of Bronze Age graffiti carved on the rocks. The crossroads resort of **Sospel** has an attractive old arcaded central square and the statutory Bréa in the church, and gives access to the upper Roya valley and to the less frequented, steeply enclosed Bévéra valley, which also has its gorges; there are high mountains and dark forests to be explored from the recent resort of **Peïra-Cava**.

✳ **Vésubie Valley** Just before it joins the Var the Vésubie cuts through a narrow rocky gateway. In its pastoral upper valley **St-Martin-Vésubie** is the centre for many excursions on foot and by car. There are mountain refuges, fishing in the lakes and an Alpine game reserve beyond Le Boréon. Mountain roads link the valley with those of the Tinée and Bévéra. From St-Jean-la-Rivière a narrow road winds up to a 19th-century pilgrimage chapel beyond Utelle.

✳ **Tinée Valley** An important through-route serving the most popular of Nice's mountain resorts. **Auron**, **St-Etienne-de-Tinée** and the recent **Isola 2000**, built high up (at 2,000 metres) by a British property company. The Route de Restefond or de la Bonette over to Barcelonnette and the once very isolated Ubaye valley rises to 2,802 metres at the foot of the Bonette peak, which can be reached from the top of the road by a short but breath-taking climb; the landscape has its own very desolate beauty. At the top of Europe's highest road (usually closed until late June) there is an appropriate shrine to Notre-Dame-du-Très-Haut.

✳ **Cians/Daluis Gorges** Two similar and very impressive sequences of gorges cut by the rivers Cians and Var through fiery red rock. The old Grimaldi stronghold of **Beuil** is now an attractive and peaceful summer and winter resort, sharing its mountainsides with **Valberg** which is more frequented.

Just west of the old national frontier of the Var—whose lower valley is industrial and unattractive—the long **Baie des Anges** is dominated by the sinuous blocks of the modern marina development—also called Baie des Anges—and the resort of **Cros-de-Cagnes**, site of the Nice racecourse. The coastline itself is less worthy of note than the villages set some way back from it, and the fertile hillsides are full of prosperous villas among cypresses, mimosas, oranges, eucalyptus and vines.

Vence is one of the more important of the hill towns; the circular boulevard encloses the old centre where the Place Peyra has great charm and the cathedral amusing choir stalls. More unusual is the Chapelle du Rosaire to the north of town, designed and decorated by Matisse.

St-Paul-de-Vence crowns a ridge which commands excellent views. The village itself is very handsome—golden stone and russet tiles, 16th-century ramparts around which you can walk, narrow pedestrian streets, and an interesting church with a painting by Tintoretto. Not surprisingly, St-Paul teems with day-trippers and its streets are lined with tourist shops. In all these respects it is not exceptional but its style sets it apart from other frequented perched villages. St-Paul has long attracted painters as well as tourists and its houses have been restored and converted with unusual care and restraint. There are as many galleries as knick-knack shops and the Hotel Colombe d'Or beside the shady *boules* pitch is also something of a modern art museum thanks to the enlightened proprietor's willingness to accept distinguished paintings in exchange for his distinguished fare. There is a fine modern art museum (see page 120), and numerous hotels on the surrounding hills, many enjoying marvellous views of the village. Staying in or near St-Paul gives you the chance to wander around when the village is at rest.

Behind Vence roads climb quickly (such as by the Col de Vence) into an area of wild rocky landscapes and steep-sided river valleys (*clues*) which contrast with the more fertile coastal slopes. The **Gorges du Loup** pass beneath **Gourdon**, an example of a splendidly perched village which has become merely trippery.

Grasse is the famous capital of the world scent industry, its factories producing the essence for three out of every four bottles. At the turn of the century it was an important spa and winter resort, but dozens of factories have changed that. The more attractive aspects of the industry are the fields of brilliantly colourful cultivated flowers all along the coast between Nice and Cannes, as well as all the generally more fragrant wild flowers favoured by the industrialists of Grasse. When you learn (as you can by visiting one or two of the factories) how many tons of petals it takes to make a kilo of essence, and how many blooms to make a ton of petals, you will appreciate why the fields are so extensive, and scent so expensive. Much of Grasse is new and it cannot be considered as a whole a very attractive place, but there is an old part in projection from the hillside with an imposing cathedral which contains paintings by Rubens, and a religious painting by Fragonard which is quite out of character with his better-known style. There is a small museum which has a number of examples of his work including the painting of the staircase.

Cagnes stretches down in three separate communities from an old Grimaldi fortress to the sea. The fortress which dominates the enclosed perched village of **Haut-de-Cagnes** is mostly a 17th-century conversion, and is well worth visiting. Some rooms are devoted to the olive, others to modern art.

The attractive hill village of **Biot** should be pronounced to rhyme with pot, which is what the locals have done for centuries. Now Biot is famous for glass making too, and pulls in the crowds, for it is a delightful old village and has an excellent museum of the works of Fernand Léger, painter and ceramic artist inspired by Biot and responsible for its success. On the coast below Biot is France's answer to Florida—called Marineland, with dolphins.

Back on the coast, Antibes and Juan-les-Pins lie close together either side of the base of the **Cap d'Antibes**, and merge into a large built-up area, cutting off the greenery of the Cape which has some quiet unpretentious hotels and a small beach far from the madding crowd. **Antibes** is a port of great antiquity, called Antipolis by the Greeks. The old town, solidly walled on its seaward side in the uncompromising style of Vauban, is full of life (with one of the best and most colourful markets on the coast) and beautiful when admired from the small beach just along the shore towards the Cape. Whether you agree with Augustus Hare that this is the most beautiful seaside view in France in the orange lights and pink shadows of sunset will most likely depend on whether the Alps behind are visible and snowy. In the old town the cathedral, like so many others, has an ill-lit Bréa; of greater interest is the Picasso museum in the old Grimaldi château (see page 120). The rest of Antibes is a modern and bustling resort. **Juan-les-Pins**, also modern, young and very lively at night, had a *raison d'être* untypical of the Riviera—its long beach of pine-backed sand, extending to Golfe-Juan where Napoleon landed in 1815 on his return from Elba.

Picasso and **Vallauris**, another old pottery village on the clay soils behind the Cap d'Antibes, interacted in the same way as Léger and Biot, with an even greater impact on artist and village, now one of the world's most productive centres of artistic, and not so artistic, pottery manufacture.

Cannes is the last extravagant flourish of the true Riviera, and flourish it does thanks in no small measure to the post-war initiative of an annual international film festival, which must be the best advertising for any resort in the world. This was the small fishing port which enchanted Lord Brougham in the 1830s and which became a winter favourite among the rich British, who first covered the hills with villa estates, constructed large harbours, and built up the seafront for five miles. They cared little that Cannes enjoyed few of the climatic advantages of the coast beyond Nice; Cannes depended upon society for its attractions, and it still does. It is the most obviously smart resort of the coast, with a much greater feeling of being a resort than towny Nice. Its face is the gleaming seaside Boulevard de la Croisette which stretches from the winter casino by the port to the summer one on the point. Behind its palms and gardens is a succession of very exclusive jewellers, art galleries, couturiers and hotels. The marinas are full of palatial yachts, but the port and the old town of Le Suquet above it do have some life of their own though not much sightseeing interest. The beach is long and sandy. Boats cross daily to the two wooded **Lérins** islands: on Ste-Marguerite you can visit Vauban's fortress, long used as a prison; on St-Honorat there are the remaining monastic buildings of a community which in the dark days of the collapse of the Roman Empire kept alight the fires of civilisation and Christianity.

The hinterland of Cannes is much less mountainous than further east and there are no fewer than four 18-hole golf courses; one of them is at **Mougins**, an old hill village which has become a prestigious and pricey gastronomic suburb.

Between **La Napoule**, a small beach resort squashed beside the railway and the sea with a heavily restored old fortress, and St-Raphaël the corniche road along the coast is at its most beautiful. It is cut into the rocky hillsides of deep red porphyry which drop into a clear sea from the peaks of the very ancient **Esterel Massif**, now only 500 metres at its highest point, beautiful, wild and desolate and explorable (on foot) by forest tracks with splendid viewpoints. The coast road is not an old one, and the small row of resorts along it have no particular character. From the road you can clamber down to numerous rocky coves and swim among colourful reefs. **Agay** is one of the larger resorts on the sea, and a fine anchorage.

Port-Grimaud

St-Raphaël and Fréjus spread round the mouth of the Argent which divides the Maures Massif from the Esterel. It is the site of the first important port and colony in Roman Gaul. Ancient Forum Julii was four times as big as modern Fréjus which is no Arles or Nîmes, but does have a number of Roman remains (aqueduct, amphitheatre and theatre) and a very interesting cathedral. The 12th-century two-storey cloister is delightful with its well and oleander, the octagonal baptistry survives from the 5th century, and there are interesting works of art within the church. In the museum next to the cloister there are some local archaeological finds; more, found in the sea (scuba diving flourishes around this part of the coast), are displayed in a museum of underwater archaeology in St-Raphaël, a resort which participated in the boom of the late 19th century and which is still very animated, though not very attractive—its looks were spoilt by bombing in 1944. Adjoining Fréjus-Plage is plain and functional, and less lively. Valescure (inland) and Boulouris (by the sea) are more relaxing leafy villa resorts.

Although less immediately striking than the Esterel, the larger and more wooded Maures Massif is hardly less beautiful. Its coastline is indented with splendid bays, of which the finest are those of St-Tropez and Le Lavandou, which attracted artists before tourists. Trees characteristic of the area are chestnuts, cork oaks—whose stripped trunks can be seen all over the hills—and umbrella pines, which look as they should. There are many more good long sandy beaches with shade than there are further east.

Ste-Maxime is an old town and busy resort facing south across the St-Tropez gulf. The palmy prom and port consists not of grandiose late 19th-century façades, but simple ochre-painted houses. Port-Grimaud has been constructed at the head of the gulf between Ste-Maxime and St-Tropez. It is one of the earliest and most successful (at least from the aesthetic point of view) of the new marina resorts with bridged canals and warmly painted houses, the prototype for the Languedoc resorts.

St-Tropez is the old port of the region, and the harbour—where a few fishing boats fight for survival among all the yachts and motor cruisers—is still very picturesque. In the early morning before all the promenaders are out, fish are sold on the quay and the place seems simple and unspoilt. For the rest of the time the port cafés and boutiques are crammed with people; the back streets are full of trend-setting shops and galleries. As well as the people to look at, there is a very fine modern art museum (see page 120) recalling the many painters who followed Paul Signac to St-Tropez in the 1890s. With its studiously relaxed atmosphere, its lively focal port, and its little shingle beaches below open-air restaurant terraces, St-Tropez has something of the atmosphere of a sophisticated Greek island. Little boats ferry tourists around the bay, to the Hyères Islands and to the main beaches which are excellent—spacious, sandy and shady—but further than walking distance from St-Tropez itself.

Set back above the sandy vineyards behind St-Tropez and Port-Grimaud, the old perched village of **Grimaud** is quiet and unspoilt, with arcaded houses and a charming Romanesque church.

The Ramatuelle Peninsula which has all the frequented beaches, and still a few which aren't, is thickly wooded and delightful. Most of the beaches are some way from the main road. The resorts around and beyond it lack the human interest of St-Tropez and few of them are much to look at in themselves, typically with functional blocks of flats behind the beach and villas around the hills. **Le Lavandou**, an old cork industry centre and fishing port, is the most important of them. The centre is old, but the port/marina large and busy, as is the beach. Colourful **Bormes-les-Mimosas** occupies a fine vantage point high above the bay, and has as many flowers as its name suggests.

Hyères was once a popular resort, originally on account of its winter climate; now it's a large town which has its tame resort of Hyères-Plage. "Plage" added on to the name of a town is usually a reliable warning of a rather dreary beach resort outpost and this is no exception. From Hyères-Plage two spits of sandy land, framing salt pans, are very popular though not attractive camping territory. They stretch down to the small resort of **Giens** on the Giens Peninsula, the main departure point (access also to the islands from Toulon, Le Lavandou, and St-Tropez) for the three very beautiful Hyères islands, **Porquerolles**, **Port-Cros**, and the **Ile du Levant**. The last is a naval base and also the South of France's most famous nudist colony (the two halves are kept separate). Porquerolles and Port-Cros both have accommodation; Porquerolles has a small port and good beaches.

Between Hyères and Marseille the coast mainly serves the populations of Marseille and Toulon, the two most important ports of the French Mediterranean. Particularly characteristic are the fjord-like inlets called *calanques* which can be explored by boat from **Cassis**, one of the most picturesquely situated of the resorts. Like St-Tropez, it was a fishing port much favoured by painters early this century; but it is not like St-Tropez in other ways. **Bandol** which like Cassis gives its name to wine of some local distinction is the other unsophisticated, lively resort on this stretch of coast. **Bendor** (a quick boat ride from Bandol) is a popular amusement centre and resort island.

Toulon like Brest in Brittany is a fortified military port with memories of slave labour (in this case galley slaves) which owes its importance to Louis XIV, Vauban, and its magnificent situation on a deep sheltered anchorage. There are fine panoramic drives to be made up in the fortified heights behind the city (the Mont Faron, the Gros Cerveau, and the eerie ruined village of Evenos) but Toulon itself is unattractive—it suffered heavy war damage.

The South

The name of **Marseille** has become associated with pastis, gangs, corruption in high places and the French Connection, that is to say drug running. It is a port of great antiquity—Greeks came in the 6th century BC—but its atmosphere today has little to do with history, except the Second World War, which destroyed much of the most amusing parts of Marseille, and the Algerian War which ended with large numbers of immigrant *pieds-noirs* going no further than this their port of arrival. It has not a great deal to offer the tourist except the colourful human bustle of the old port and a variety of museums which are unlikely to prove adequate reward for the battle with Marseille's traffic. There are regular boats to the formidable prison island of **Château d'If**, which sits prettily in the bay.

Excursions from the coast

* **Ste-Baume Massif** A bare grey theatre of mountains encloses Marseille—hardly less arid than those that surround Athens. Behind it, the massif is surprisingly green and bright, with beech forests and a panoramic peak (St-Pilon). On the northern side of the massif, the sight of **St-Maximim** can be appreciated from all directions. The great Gothic basilica is one of the few of any importance in Provence; it is no lofty greenhouse like the northern cathedrals, but does contain some interesting works of art.

* **Verdon Gorges** Alone among southern French gorges, these have earned the title of Grand Canyon. It is a title not unreasonably bestowed for this is one of the great natural curiosities of Europe. Though their existence was almost unknown until the beginning of this century, the Verdon gorges have recently been made easy to admire from roads engineered along the heights—but they have not been tamed. A good starting point is the village of Moustiers-Ste-Marie—itself an astonishingly set village built on a hillside and on both sides of a rocky crevasse.

Two roads lead south of Moustiers and reveal the incomparable spectacle of the swiftly running Verdon, in some places over 500 metres below. The recently built **Route des Crêtes** along the north side of the river follows more of the canyon than the **Corniche Sublime** to the south, including the deepest section whose walls are twice as high as the Gorges du Tarn. It is possible to walk down into the gorge from the Chalet de la Maline on the northern side, or down a very steep path from the Restaurant des Cavaliers on the Corniche Sublime, to walk along the Martel path for some 15km to the Point Sublime (it takes about 8 hours). Provisions, a torch and some adder repellent should be taken.

The bottom of the gorge is in places no more than 6 metres wide, and the path does not follow it all the way. An attempt to do so should not be undertaken lightly, and requires specialist experience, equipment and guides, and up to three days. Both refuges at the end of the Martel path provide accommodation in summer.

The route south from the Verdon to the coast around St-Raphaël and the Maures crosses peaceful and attractive Provençal countryside with unexceptional market towns. **Bargème**, one of the most atmospheric of perched villages in all the south, is well worth a visit (it lies only a few miles north-east of Comps-sur-Artuby). The almost completely abandoned village is peaceful, and you can clamber around the substantial ruins of its old fortress.

Other attractive hill villages in the region include **Seillans**, **Bargemon**, **Fayence**, **Cotignac** and **Fox-Amphoux**, which all have some accommodation (see also Hotels section).

Modern Art

The South of France is one of the most rewarding areas for anyone with an interest in late 19th- and 20th-century art. In Provence there is the pleasure of seeing landscapes through the eyes of the artists who have made them famous—Van Gogh and Cézanne, sadly not well represented in local museums. Along the fashionable parts of the coast there is a large number of museums housing the collections of wealthy Riviera dwellers and works left behind by the artists who settled among them.

Although surprisingly neglected by the thousands of classically educated 18th-century artists who travelled through Provence on their way to Rome, the South of France was discovered by artists as it was by society in the late 19th century. While intellectuals argued about the nature and role of art in the turmoil of post-1870 Paris, real observations were made in the South. Paul Cézanne was a native of Aix-en-Provence who spent much of his active life contemplating the Mont Ste-Victoire, taking it apart and reassembling it on canvas in his attempt "to revivify Poussin in front of nature". Cézanne was not only interested in form, and in 1876 wrote from the coast near Marseille "the sunlight here is so intense that it seems to me that objects are silhouetted not only in black and white but also in blue, red, brown and violet". The realisation "that sunlight cannot be reproduced but must be represented by something else—by colour" was to be of the greatest importance for the development of art away from Impressionism, the aims of which were essentially naturalistic. It was shared by Monet and Renoir on the coast in the 1880s, by Van Gogh around Arles in 1888/90, and a few years later by the artists (notably Paul Signac) who settled in the old fishing village of St-Tropez and moved from a scientific approach to colour (Pointillism) to a much freer and richer one. Signac's work and ideas, as well as the southern light, were in turn influential on the young Matisse who, working with Derain in Collioure in 1905, made further strides away from naturalism in a manner known as *fauve* (literally, wild). Derain wrote from Collioure of "a new conception of light—negation of shadow. The shadow is a whole world of clarity and luminosity which contrasts with the light of the sun. I am learning . . . to rid myself of the whole business of the division of tones . . . it injures things that derive their expression from deliberate disharmonies". Collioure remained an important artists' colony, and so too did the

Riviera. Some artists drew inspiration from their surroundings, others simply found the coast an agreeable place to live. Fernand Léger, for example, lived at Biot, and his work is better admired there than anywhere else; but apart from a sideline interest in ceramics which was inspired by the local industry at Biot, Léger's artistic contribution as the greatest interpreter of the machine age could hardly be further removed from the Côte d'Azur.

Aix-en-Provence The Vasarély Foundation contains a number of works by this contemporary colourful cubic illusionist. Cézanne's studio (open to visitors) has been left as it was when the artist died in 1906.

Antibes The curator of the castle in the old town complained about the emptiness of the building and Picasso offered to fill it—which he did with his usual astounding facility in paint, pencil and clay. If not specifically related to the south of France, many of the works in the Grimaldi Museum have as their theme the Mediterranean of classical mythology.

Biot The Fernand Léger museum traces the development of the artist with huge and very powerful industrially-inspired paintings, drawings, tapestries and ceramics.

Cagnes Renoir retired here in 1902 but was so old and arthritic that brushes had to be put between his fingers. The château in **Haut-de-Cagnes** houses a varied modern art museum.

Collioure There is a small museum of works by locally-inspired artists in the town hall.

Menton The Salle des Mariages in the town hall is decorated by the artist and poet Jean Cocteau. Nearby there's also a small museum which contains his works in various media.

Nice Matisse lived for many years at Cimiez where there is a varied collection of his works and personal effects in the villa beside the Roman arena. On the slopes of the hill of Cimiez a museum was built especially to house 17 canvases by Marc Chagall, illustrating in his poetic and colourful way the Bible message. There are many other works by the artist in a variety of media in the museum.

St-Paul-de-Vence Just outside the village the Maeght Foundation is an architectural curiosity, and contains a wealth of works by greater and lesser 20th-century painters and a number of sculptures.

St-Tropez The Annonciade Museum is an exceptional collection of mostly early 20th-century paintings, many of them related to St-Tropez.

Vence The Chapelle de la Rosaire is the work of Matisse—architectural design and decoration.

Villefranche The Chapelle St-Pierre is decorated by Cocteau.

Lower Provence

Aix-en-Provence is the old Roman spa and capital, at whose gates 100,000 Teutons were slain in 102 BC by the Roman Marius. Aix was originally a spa (Aquae Sextiae), and remains one. As well as the thermal establishment, there are the moss-covered fountains in the Cours Mirabeau which spout curative water. Aix has also long been an intellectual and cultural centre, particularly brilliant in the 15th century when René d'Anjou—absentee king of Naples and duke of Provence—held his civilised Renaissance court here, and in the 17th and 18th centuries when the local nobility transformed Aix, capital of Provence and seat of the local parliament, into a town of ordered Classical elegance and dignity. In the centre at least, Aix has changed relatively little. It is still relaxing and refined, an important university centre popular with foreign students, and the host every July of an internationally famous music festival. Aix's focus and evening parade-ground for strollers is the Place du Général de Gaulle, formerly de la Libération, and the Cours Mirabeau—a majestic creation of classical *hôtels* and four rows of venerable planes providing an unbroken lofty canopy. Along the Cours there are banks, cafés, and shops selling the local marzipan speciality, *calissons* (Aix is the centre of an important almond-growing area), and along the south side splendid examples of the town architecture where muscular caryatids frame doorways and support balconies. The whole area to the south of the Cours Mirabeau is a model of 17th-century planning, with many beautiful houses around the playful Fontaine des Quatre Dauphins. To the north of the Cours, the old centre of town is a fascinating and endlessly surprising maze of old streets, also with an abundance of beautiful buildings from the 17th and 18th centuries. Highlights are the little 18th-century Place d'Albertas, and the Place de l'Hôtel-de-Ville, where there is a very colourful flower market.

* *St-Sauveur* A composite cathedral resulting from the incorporation of a delightful 12th-century church into a later and larger edifice, of which it now forms most of the south aisle. There is a 5th-century baptistry and hole-in-the-ground font, and a small but beautiful 12th-century cloister. The church's treasures, a painting of the Burning Bush showing king René as donor, and the Renaissance carving on the central doors of the façade, are both shut up but unlocked on request.

* *Tapestry museum* A resplendent collection of 17th- and 18th-century Beauvais tapestries in the old archbishop's palace beside St-Sauveur.

* *Museum of Old Aix* A relatively interesting folklore museum, with local figurines called *santons* (which feature particularly in Provençal Christmas cribs), costumes and pottery.

* *Ste-Marie Madeleine* A 17th-century church containing a very fine 15th-century triptych of the Annunciation and a large painting by Rubens.

* *Granet Museum* Named after the local painter and generous collector, whose fame is assured by the superb portrait of him by his friend Ingres, one of the great treasures of this very rich museum. A collection of antique and local pre-Roman sculpture, and French, Flemish and Italian paintings.

* *Vasarély Foundation* A spacious museum devoted to the modern geometric artist, beside the motorway on the western side of Aix.

* *Cézanne's Studio* Preserved as it was when he died in 1906, but the furniture of the studio does not include paintings by the artist who has done more than most to make Aix famous. Cézanne devotees should explore the land to the east of town, around the long ridge which is the **Mont-Ste-Victoire**, especially around **Le Tholonet** on the D17.

The South

To the north of the Durance, the **Lubéron** range of mountains do not compare with the Mont-Ste-Victoire or the Mont Ventoux, between which they lie, but there is a road along the highest crest (the Mourre Nègre) and there are some attractive perched villages to the north of the mountains. Of these, the most notable are **Ménerbes**, **Oppède-le-Vieux** (carefully restored with arts and crafts activities), **Bonnieux**, **Gordes**, and **Roussillon**. The last two are particularly fine. Roussillon is a village of brilliant red ochre in the middle of a region of red cliffs and ochre quarries of which the largest and most impressive near Rustrel has earned itself the name of Rustrel Colorado. At Gordes, the château in the village houses a small collection of the works of Vasarély. Near Gordes, towards Cavaillon and the Abbaye de Sénanque, there are many interesting primitive dry-stone shepherds' dwellings (*bories*). The **Abbaye de Sénanque** is a beautiful example of Cistercian monastic buildings in a very simple unadorned style, well-preserved and unspoilt in a serene valley setting. In summer there are occasional concerts.

Not far from Sénanque waters well up from enormous natural underground crypts into the great cavernous **Fontaine de Vaucluse**. This, one of the most powerful springs in the world, is a natural curiosity not at its most impressive in the summer, and very trippery. Part of the attraction of the village and spring is its associations with the 14th-century Italian poet Petrarch, who lived at Fontaine de Vaucluse for many years, the fountain of his love for the unknown Laura pouring out lyric poetry.

The small village of **Venasque** is the unlikely capital of the area known to history as the Comtat Venaissin, conceded by the French king to the papacy in the 13th-century, with the important indirect consequence of the popes moving from Rome to Avignon shortly afterwards. In the village is a Merovingian (7th-century) baptistry, and a short distance to the north of it the small chapel (Notre-Dame-de-Vie) which has a richly carved Merovingian tomb.

The most impressive of the gorges of the Vaucluse plateau are carved by the **Nesque**, between Sault and Villes-sur-Auzon. They can be incorporated in a long but worthwhile detour from the road between Carpentras and Vaison-la-Romaine, through the heart of fragrant lavender country, and back over the mighty Mont Ventoux. **Carpentras** is the most important market town of the well-irrigated Comtat; the fertile surrounding plain produces large quantities of grapes, almonds, melons, tomatoes, garlic and herbs, and the commercial streets of the town are colourful and busy. There are no monuments of great importance, but an unusual synagogue in the old Jewish ghetto. You can also visit the 18th-century hospital (Hôtel-Dieu) and the cathedral, a handsome mostly late-Gothic building.

The **Mont Ventoux** is one of the great landmarks of Provence, rising in isolated symmetry to its summit of 1,909 metres. It's appropriately named: the top is often extremely windy, and the expanse of bare rock on the south face makes the Ventoux look snow-capped all the year round. The panorama on the clearest days reaches from the Pyrenees to the northern Alps. The road is not usually difficult, but you are unlikely to beat the record up 22 kilometres from Bédoin which have been covered in nine minutes at an average speed of 90 miles an hour. Walking up takes about four or five hours; the best starting point is Brantes, steeply below the summit on its north-eastern side. The gentlest ascent is from Malaucène, which is the way Petrarch went up on April 26th 1336.

127

Vaison-la-Romaine is a town of great interest and charm built in three parts on both sides of the River Ouvèze, still spanned by a single-arched Roman bridge. The new town is not special, except for the Romanesque cathedral which stands incongruously on its edge. Part of the walls of the building rest on the fragments of old Roman columns and complete ones support the arcade around the inside of the 6th-century apse. There is a small 12th-century cloister with a collection of archaeological fragments. From the cathedral you can get a key and walk northwards to the small chapel of St-Quenin, which also dates mostly from the 12th-century and is decorated in a most unusual style inspired directly by the antique.

✳ *Roman Town* For grandeur, Vaison-la-Romaine cannot compare with the great monuments of southern Provence; its attraction lies in the evocation of the complete layout of an important town. In the two areas which you can visit there are streets, colonnades, gardens, mosaics, courtyards, fountains, and a small museum containing the best fragments.

✳ *Medieval Town* In the troubled times of the Middle Ages, the inhabitants of Vaison deserted the vulnerable right bank of the Ouvèze for the steep hill across the river, where ruins of a 12th-century fortress still stand above the medieval upper town. Its steep and narrow cobbled streets, which climb up from fortified gateways towards the fortress, are exceptionally attractive and have been bypassed by the development of modern Vaison.

The pre-Alpine mountains of the **Baronnies** region east of Vaison are cut by deep valleys full of vines, olives, fruit and herbs. The picturesque arcaded market square of **Buis-les-Baronnies** is the setting every July for a very important herb market. Still further east, **Sisteron** is a busy road junction on the Route Napoléon. Although it suffered heavy damage from bombs in August 1944, there are still narrow and attractive old streets beside the Durance.

✳ *Citadel* Restored to its original massively imposing grandeur on the site of an old fortress high above the town centre (a long staircase climb up), seasoned observers of the frontier lands of France may recognise the hand of Louis XIV's military architect Vauban, but in fact the citadel is mostly the achievement of one of Vauban's unsung predecessors Jean Erard. Very fine vertiginous viewpoints from the citadel walls. Piped commentary from various *points de sonorité*.

✳ *Notre-Dame* The domed former cathedral (12th-century) is a fine example of Provençal Romanesque, dark and powerful and simple in its lines.

Like Sisteron, **Orange** is a gateway to Provence, and there could be no more appropriate gateway than the magnificent Roman triumphal arch which arrests your progress from Montélimar and the north. The third largest such arch in existence, it is also one of the most richly decorated with sculptures despite having been turned into a fortress by the lords of Orange. Orange was an important Roman city of over 80,000 inhabitants in its day and is now a large market town for the surrounding region—though it does not get its name from the fruit. Surrounded by the Comtat Venaissin, Orange was a separate principality in the Middle Ages, and came into the possession of the northern European Nassau dynasty, which provided England with William of Orange. In 1713 Orange was given to the French, but the Nassau family kept the title. The Roman theatre is one of the finest in existence. Here, as nowhere else, there remains the massive façade wall, over 100ft high and 300ft long. Inside there is a stage wall with columns and doorways and a statue of Augustus in a niche, and tiers which originally held 11,000 spectators. The acoustics are renowned. There are also remains of Gaul's largest Roman temple, a gymnasium and the old capitol dominating the town. On the square opposite the theatre, there is a museum of local history, paintings, and very interesting archaeological finds.

Châteauneuf-du-Pape gets its name from the summer residence built there by pope John XXII who was also said to have planted the vines which are now the most prestigious of the Rhône valley. Since 1944 the only remains of the château are a couple of walls and some fragments of vaulting. There is a small wine museum above some cellars in the village and plenty of places to taste.

Avignon owes its unique place in medieval history and its exceptional interest to the modern sightseer to pope Clement V who installed the papal court on the banks of the Rhône in 1308. It was only intended to be a short stay but successive French popes found good reasons not to leave Avignon, best of which was the war-torn state of 14th-century Italy. In 1377 Gregory XI returned to Rome, but a breakaway group of cardinals came back to Avignon the next year with their own anti-pope, thus initiating the great schism of Christendom—a shameful chapter in the history of the Church. The city of Avignon was not French territory but part of Provence, and surrounded by the papal lands of the Comtat Venaissin. In 1348 the pope bought Avignon from the first lady of Provence in exchange for a free pardon for all her sins, which included the murder of her husband. The Avignon popes established themselves in conditions of magnificence unmatched by any royal court in Christendom. The palace they built for themselves was described by the French chronicler Froissart as the strongest and most beautiful house in the world. Popes slept on pillows trimmed with fur, cardinals were described by Petrarch as "satraps mounted on horses decked with gold and champing golden bits whose very hoofs will be shod with gold if God does not restrain their arrogant display of wealth". Papal Avignon became a notorious refuge for the undesirables and outlaws of Europe and the town was summed up by Petrarch "unholy Babylon thou hell on earth, thou sink of iniquity, cess-pool of the world". Avignon today is a busy modern city which extends far beyond the restored medieval ramparts; but because of its riverside situation it has not sprawled in all directions, and seen from across the Rhône it still looks almost as impressive now as when papal and royal fortresses menaced each other in the 14th century. However the ramparts no longer look quite as high as they did, the ditches having all been filled in by the construction of surrounding roads. The famous 12th-century Pont d'Avignon (on which one never used to dance all in a circle—it was *sous le pont* on a grassy island in mid-stream) is now reduced to a few arches which jut out into the Rhône.

✻ *Palais des Papes* Still dominant, strong and severely beautiful. One of the most important and impressive of all Gothic buildings, covering nearly 15 square kilometres. When Stendhal went to Avignon in the early 19th century he noted the ingenuity of the inhabiting soldiers—for the Palais des Papes was long used as a barracks—in chipping off bits of fresco and selling them locally. The interior of the palace has been much restored and there are still a large number of extremely beautiful frescoes, some religious but others in a style more familiar from tapestries whose function they took on the walls—for

Palais des Papes

example in the papal bedchamber. Apart from these there is no impression of a palatial residence but many large and beautiful chambers whose emptiness underlines the fortress-like impression of the exterior. The palace was mainly built in two campaigns in the 1320s and the 1330s but in two completely different styles—one simple and Romanesque, the other Gothic. Guided tours in English.

✳ *Cathedral* The main features of the mostly 12th-century building beside the papal palace are the lamentable 19th-century Virgin who stands on top of the tower and the damaged but splendid tomb of John XXII, greatest of the Avignon popes. Between the cathedral and the river there are some beautiful gardens giving views across the Rhône to Villeneuve.

✳ *Petit Palais Museum* An exceptionally rich collection of Medieval and Renaissance paintings (Italian and Avignonese), and sculptures housed in the old archbishop's palace across the square from the papal fortress.

✳ *Calvet Museum* A beautiful 18th-century *hôtel*, with peacocks in the gardens, housing several different museums including a notable collection of ironwork and post-Renaissance paintings, mostly French. Many big names represented.

✳ *Old Town* Avignon *intra muros* is all old and the *muri* are nearly 3 miles around. The town is split by the main commercial and traffic artery which is the wide plane-lined Cours Jean-Jaurès/Rue de la République which runs from the station towards the Palais des Papes at the other end of town. To the west of it there are a number of beautiful 18th-century *hôtels* in the Rue Vernet, of which the Calvet Museum is one example. On the other side of the Cours the old dyers' quarter—though not as attractive as some other restored old town centres—has many houses dating from the 15th to the 18th centuries, especially on the Rue du Roi René and the Rue des Teinturiers, beside which there are still some mill-wheels in the waters of the little Sorgue.

Villeneuve-lès-Avignon. Newtown-by-Avignon, grew after a clever initiative by the French kings who did a deal with the abbey of St Andrew which stands on a hill opposite Avignon. They built fortifi-

130

cations around the abbey which are in fact no less than a royal fortress, echoing the majesty and might of the papal establishment and reminding the popes of the ever-present reality of French royal pressure on papal policy. The new town itself was established by means of the kind of incentives which are still used today to take people to development areas. Villeneuve became a favoured place for Avignon cardinals to build themselves luxury villas and remains to this day a quiet, peaceful and elegant residential suburb of Avignon with a number of good hotels which make Villeneuve-lès-Avignon a very good base for the surrounding area. Of medieval Villeneuve there remains Philip the Fair's tower which once stood at the end of the bridge and now stands alone on the bank. The powerful fortifications on the top of the hill are worth visiting especially in the evening for the view across the Rhône to the honey-coloured walls and palace of Avignon.

✱ *Chartreuse du Val de Bénédiction* A very large and romantically dilapidated monastery which has only been restored as townsfolk have moved out of its buildings. It was founded in the 14th century but much of it is classical in style. A guided tour reveals the tomb of Innocent VI in the church and 14th-century frescoes in Innocent's chapel. In the church of Notre-Dame there is a beautiful ivory Virgin—you have to enquire to gain access to it.

Only a very few miles west of Villeneuve-lès-Avignon stands one of the wonders of Roman Provence, the **Pont du Gard**, hiding its beauty in the wooded landscape of the Gardon. This is just the bridge part of a long aqueduct which brought water to Nîmes from near Uzès. It consists of three tiers of arches, the upper one over 300 yards long and over 150ft above the river. It is a tremendous engineering feat, achieved without the use of any binding agent for the enormous blocks of stone which were lifted by pulleys powered by men in cages operating a treadwheel. It is also very beautiful and the architect's obvious aesthetic concern in this purely utilitarian construction is extraordinary. Tobias Smollett, the 18th-century traveller, described the bridge as "a piece of architecture so unaffectedly elegant, simple and majestic that I will defy the most phlegmatic and stupid spectator to behold it without admiration". Smollett also considered the bridge an ideal place on a summer's evening for a cold collation under an arch. Large numbers of tourists

Pont du Gard

and the inhabitants of the local towns followed his advice and the Pont du Gard is a beauty spot appreciated by a much wider public than most Roman remains. There are campsites, boats and bathing areas.

The water flowed across the river to Nîmes in a covered channel supported by the small upper register of arches. It is dry now and you can walk along it; the courageous can walk along its roof, and get truly vertiginous and extensive views. It is some 10ft wide, which may sound a comfortable width for a path, but with the sheer 150ft drop to the beckoning waters of the Gardon the effect can be extremely uncomfortable especially when the *mistral* is howling. In the 18th century a carriage road was built beside the top of the lower register of arches and is still used by traffic. The best viewpoint of the bridge is from upstream near the Château St-Privat.

Uzès, supplier of water to Nîmes, is a splendid old town which stands above the *garrigue*—dry scrub and herb-covered limestone plateaux and hills that lie along the southern flank of the Massif Central. Although very close to the great Roman towns of Provence, Uzès is off the beaten track of Provençal tourism and has the atmosphere of a different region. From afar the town looks surprisingly Tuscan, with its three medieval towers dominating the sky-line—one for the king, one for the bishop and one for the ruler of Uzès. All that remains of the cathedral is the cylindrical bell tower called the Tour Fenestrelle because of the Romanesque arched openings in its walls. You can visit the ducal palace which has a fine Renaissance façade; but the main attractions of Uzès are the old streets and restored central square—sleepy and shady with a fountain and substantial arcaded houses. On Saturdays the square comes to life with a busy market.

In complete contrast to Uzès, **Nîmes** is a big and busy city of no particular attraction in itself, but with monuments of the greatest importance. It would be nice to be able to avoid Nîmes and all its traffic, especially in hot weather; but the fact that one cannot advise doing so is a reflection of the quality of its two great Roman buildings, the amphitheatre and the Maison Carrée, unrivalled even by Orange and Arles. Nîmes' Roman monuments can be visited on the same entrance ticket.

✱ *Amphitheatre (Arènes)* Not the largest but by far the best-preserved of all Roman sports grounds. Complete with vaulted galleries and arcades around the outside and accommodation for over 20,000 spectators inside, it has survived because it was transformed into a fortress and later a lodging for over 2,000 people and has never been used, as so many other monuments, as a quarry for later builders. On summer days when it is packed with *aficionados* of Spanish-style bullfighting, the amphitheatre lives again in the true spirit of antiquity. In the old days too, it was the arena for fights between men and beasts.

✱ *Maison Carrée* This small temple is not in fact square, but as its original dedication is unknown no better name for it has been thought of. Built on the purest Greek principles in the 1st century BC, the Maison Carrée is not as well shown off now in the middle of town as it was once on the edge of the Roman forum. But it is remarkably preserved, having been spared the fate of being transported brick by brick to Versailles by Colbert. The interior has served many purposes down the centuries, none more appropriate than its current one which is the display of a small but select collection of local antiquities.

✱ *Jardin de la Fontaine* Around the old magic spring of Nemausus, which was the origin of the city of Nîmes, beautiful gardens and artificial lakes were constructed in the 18th century. The gardens lie at the foot of a tall wooded

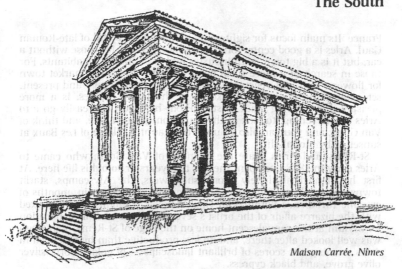

Maison Carrée, Nîmes

hill with a Roman tower (Tour Magne) on top. You can climb up for long views over the surrounding *garrigue*. Within the gardens there are substantial ruins conjecturally called the Temple of Diana.

For modern administrative purposes Nîmes, being on the west of the Rhône, is part of Languedoc. The most impressive point of the watery boundary between Languedoc and Provence—which for a time in the Middle Ages was the boundary between France and Empire—is the point where two mighty medieval fortresses stand facing each other across the river—**Beaucaire** on the Languedoc side, **Tarascon** in Provence. Having effectively deterred any fighting, the Château de Tarascon is exceptionally well preserved; but at Beaucaire, much of the fortress was destroyed by Richelieu in the 17th century. There remain a fine triangular keep and ramparts on the high rock above the river.

Tarascon is no beauty of a small town, but its riverside is dominated by its massive fortress which rises like a monolith from the rocky bank of the Rhône, and by the next door church of Ste-Marthe in memory of the saint who came and tamed the ferocious monster Tarasque which had terrorised the region, specialising in devouring women and children. It had the head of a lion, the bones of its spine broke through its skin like a hundred iron spikes, its six twisted paws had claws of a bear which furrowed the ground and its tail would have resembled an asp had it not been thick as a man's waist and long as the trunk of a cedar. Saint Martha waved a cross and sprinkled some holy water on the Tarasque which dropped the remains of an unlucky individual from its mouth and allowed itself to be led meekly to the Rhône, in which it has remained ever since. The church has a very fine Romanesque south doorway, and a beautiful tomb at the top of the stairs leading down to the crypt, the work of the early Renaissance Italian sculptor, Francesco Laurana. The **Château de Tarascon** is the very model of a late medieval fortress; inside (guided tour) there is a courtyard and an impressive but empty series of Gothic chambers, and fine views from the battlements.

The area to the south and east of Tarascon, Provence by anyone's definition, is one of the most beautiful and interesting in southern

133

France. Its main focus for sightseeing is Arles, the capital of late-Roman Gaul. Arles is a good centre for excursions especially for those without a car, but it is a big town, with industry and over 50,000 inhabitants. For those in search of a more rural base, St-Rémy, the small market town for flowers, fruit and vegetables, the painters' village past and present, set against the impressive backdrop of the rocky Alpilles, is a more pleasant and relaxing place to stay. From here you can easily go into Arles of an evening, to look at the stars from a street café, and think of Van Gogh; and you can also go up to the haunted village of Les Baux at sunset or by moonlight.

St-Rémy and Arles share the memory of Van Gogh, who came to Arles early in 1888 and spent the last two years or so of his life here. At first he painted his lonely room, sunflowers, the Alyscamps, starlit townscapes and Arles women. After the arrival of Gauguin, months of extreme turbulence within Van Gogh's never tranquil mind climaxed with the bizarre affair of the artist's severed left ear and his application for asylum at the convalescent home on the edge of St-Rémy. Van Gogh was well looked after there, and no less productive than he had been in Arles, turning out scores of brilliant landscapes—of golden corn, silver olive grove, and black cypress.

St-Rémy is attractive and popular with artists and British expatriates. There is a small folklore museum in an old 16th-century *hôtel* with courtyard, which includes some items commemorating the 16th-century astrologer and prophet, Nostradamus, who was born in St-Rémy, and whose speculations have not lost their thrall. There is also an archaeological museum, with finds from the very important Roman site of Glanum, which lies a mile or so out of St-Rémy.

On the one side of the road out of St-Rémy into the Alpilles and Les Baux stand two superb Roman monuments, Les Antiques; on the other the only recently excavated remains of the important settlement of Glanum. Les Antiques originally constituted a gateway to Roman Glanum. There is a triumphal arch, by no means intact but well enough preserved to show the influence of Greek art on this the oldest of Roman triumphal arches in Gaul, and beside it a Cenotaph in a quite extraordinary state of preservation. It is an elaborate and elegant memorial to the two grandsons of Augustus, Caius and Lucius. Unlike so many Roman monuments in southern France, Les Antiques stand in an attractive, isolated rural setting. Across the road, Glanum to many people looks like a lot of rubble and a few fragmentary columns, but to the initiated, or those prepared to study the literature, Glanum has remains of three different settlements. There was a town here as early as the 6th century BC, and already excavations have revealed dwellings from the pre-Roman period of the 2nd century BC. There are also Roman remains in two different styles. Just beside Glanum the old monastery of St-Paul-de-Mausole still stands in the attractive vegetation that Van Gogh depicted when he was an inmate here. You may visit it and admire its Romanesque church with a small overgrown tower and a charming cloister.

From Les Antiques and Glanum it is only a short drive up into the completely different world of the desolate heights of the rocky Alpilles. On a natural fortress some half-mile long by a couple of hundred yards wide stand the ruins of the old citadel of Les Baux, which so impressed Louis XIII's destructive minister Richelieu that he demilitarised it, as was his uncompromising wont. Richelieu called Les Baux "the eagle's nest" long before the expression lost power through overuse. It was the right description, for not only does the rocky spur on which the city stood command a birds' eye view, it was also the home of a ruling family who were notoriously proud and rapacious, claiming descent from one of the Three Wise Men, and incorporating the Star of Bethlehem in their emblem. The lords of Les Baux—which means rocks in Provençal—and their ladies held one of the most celebrated and brilliant of troubadour courts of love in the early Middle Ages, and in less poetic mood pushed people off the cliffs of their rocky stronghold for sport. For a time they were among the most powerful lords in the south, and Les Baux numbered several thousands of inhabitants. Now there are only a few hundred, who live on a flank of the outcrop, among elegant ruins of mostly Renaissance town houses. On top of the rocks above them, the heart of the old city is even more ruinous—empty shells which look down sheer cliffs over a colourfully contrasting landscape. It is no surprise that these evocative scrub-covered ruins are overrun with tourists who never seem to feature in the tourist office photographs and who make it very difficult to imagine Les Baux as anything other than a tourist attraction. To savour its atmosphere, you must go out of season or preferably late in the day when the sun sets on the ruins and gives life to this so-called *Ville Morte*. At the foot of the outcrop, a new Les Baux has sprung up, consisting of several good hotels surrounded by spacious and luxuriant gardens. It's a good place to stay for those who seek peace and quiet away from the main towns.

Between Arles and Les Baux, **Fontvieille** is another good place for a base, with several hotels, generally simpler but also peaceful. Just outside the village stands a windmill—the Moulin de Daudet, where the 19th-century novelist did not write his *Lettres de Mon Moulin*, or even stay. It is however the *moulin* about which he wrote, and has been restored and turned into a Daudet museum, probably to the chagrin of the man himself, for what he liked about the mill was its ruined state, "its limbs broken, useless as a poet, while all around mills are prospering".

Standing on the junction of the Rhône and the Aurelian way from Italy to Spain, **Arles** was the capital of late Roman Gaul, and also of the early medieval (9th to 11th centuries) Burgundian kingdom of Arles. Thanks to the exploitation of the surrounding countryside for rice growing, and to tourism, Arles has recently resumed importance after a long period of stagnation. It is a premier example of what the French call an "art town", offering not only Roman monuments—some at its very heart—but also medieval ones and museums of the greatest interest. It is also a very attractive town, in the centre at least. The only disappointment here, as at Aix-en-Provence, is that the artist who has done most to make the town famous—in this case Vincent Van Gogh—is unrepresented. Most of the main monuments listed below can be (but do not have to be) visited on a global entrance ticket which can be acquired at any of them.

✳ *Amphitheatre (Arènes)* By no means as intact as the one at Nîmes, but well preserved nevertheless, thanks to its transformation into a fortress (three medieval towers remain) and later a complete village of 200 houses. Like the Nîmes amphitheatre, it is still a setting for bull-fights.

✳ *Theatre* The remains are incomplete but substantial enough for shows and festivals to be put on.

✳ *St-Trophime* One of the most beautiful and fascinating churches in southern France. The west doorway, slapped on to the otherwise unadorned façade in the late 12th century, contains an abundance of beautiful carving and reveals everywhere the influence of classical architecture and sculpture. The cloister—not accessible through the church—is one of the finest in France, a mixture of Gothic (west and south galleries) and Romanesque (north and east galleries) and like the west doorway has enough carving to absorb you for hours. The cloister also gives the best view of St-Trophime's splendid three-tiered Romanesque tower, again with classical elements incorporated. Inside the church there are fine early Christian sarcophagi.

* *Museon Arlaten* (Arles Museum in Provençal) This is perhaps the most famous ethnographic museum in France, itself something of a monument to Frédéric Mistral, hero of linguistic separatists, and the great champion of Provençal life and culture, who founded the museum and donated the proceeds of his Nobel prize to its enrichment. Set in a beautiful 16th-century *hôtel*, it is particularly rich in furniture and costumes, and also has sections devoted to folklore, local history and Mistral himself. In true separatist spirit, the museum does not participate in the global entry ticket system.

* *Musée Lapidaire Chrétien* A collection of early Christian fragments especially sarcophagi (mostly 4th- and 5th-century) unrivalled outside Rome, and housed in a 17th-century Jesuit chapel.

* *Musée Lapidaire Païen* Also set in a 17th-century church, opposite St-Trophime and curiously built in the Gothic style. Local archaeological finds and mosaics from pre-Christian times. There is a 17th-century cast of the famous Arles Venus which is now in the Louvre.

* *Alyscamps* Even if, as is thought probable, the Alyscamps does not mean the Elysian Fields, it should; for this is the legendary burial ground of the heroes of medieval French epics. Since Gallo-Roman times, the road into Arles from the south-east was lined with funerary monuments, and the fame of the Alyscamps and its legendary inhabitants grew until the townsfolk of Arles took to giving its monuments away as presents. Now only one avenue remains, and that has been truncated by the railway. For those susceptible to the atmosphere of burial grounds, this remains a moody place, overhung and shaded by the foliage of trees weighed down with illustrious memories. The few remaining tombs have been assembled in the Romanesque church of St-Honorat at the end of the avenue.

Just outside Arles on an isolated hill above the paddy fields stands what remains of the important old Benedictine **Abbaye de Montmajour**. It is a building which looks more like a fortress than an abbey, machicolated and unadorned. The 12th-century cloister however is full of fascinating carvings on the capitals, including depictions of Tarasque, the *mistral*, and many animal-related Old Testament stories.

Due south of Arles lies the **Camargue**, an area of about 800 square kilometres, around the two arms of the Rhône delta. The highest point of the Camargue is some four and a half metres above sea level, the lowest point one metre and a half below it. The Camargue is made of deposits from the Rhône, and the coastline is constantly moving. To the east, the land is winning and an 18th-century lighthouse now stands several miles from the sea. Around the Petit Rhône the sea is advancing and Les-Saintes-Maries-de-la-Mer, which used to be an inland town if only by some couple of miles, is now lapped by the waters of the Mediterranean. Until recently much of the Camargue was lagoon, but large tracts in the north have been given over to rice farming and the Camargue supplies the whole of France's needs.

The Camargue has enormous romantic appeal. Its image is of wild horses, stampeding bulls, exotic birdlife, cowboys, cabalistic gypsy

Aigues-Mortes at the edge of the Camargue

pilgrimages and folk music festivals. None of these components are imaginary, but inevitably the Camargue has changed greatly over recent decades, and the unique way of life and wildlife have only survived thanks to careful preservative measures which have themselves subtly changed the character of the area. The Camargue has been a national park for some ten years and the largest lagoon, the Etang de Vaccarès, has been made into a nature reserve to which tourists without naturalist credentials have no access, lest the extremely shy flamingo population be frightened away. The gypsy pilgrimage to Les-Saintes-Maries-de-la-Mer has taken on something of a pop festival atmosphere and the town itself has grown into a commercial and unattractive seaside resort (the closest one to Arles). Times being what they are, the *gardians*—as the Camargue cowboys are called—want money to drive cars instead of horse-drawn caravans, and to get it they guide tourists on horseback. The *gardians* ride their white horses of mysterious descent to control the herds of local bulls which wander around the marshes. They are kept purely to fight, not once in their lives like Spanish bulls, but in the Provençal *courses à la cocarde*. These contests are to be seen all over the area around Arles, in small makeshift arenas, the more dramatic setting of the amphitheatres of Arles and Nîmes being reserved for the altogether more ceremonious Spanish bullfights. The *courses* can be recommended as a tourist attraction without fear of offending taurophiles, for Camargue bulls—which grow small, fast and agile—are not hurt in the sport, where *gardians* compete with one another to snatch a red cockade from between the bull's horns without themselves being punctured. Bulls fight again and again and grow as expert as the nimbly evasive *rasetteurs*.

There are three main roads across the Camargue. The least frequented, and most rewarding for bird-watchers who cannot get into the reserve itself, is the one that runs down to the east of the great Etang de Vaccarès to the wide empty dunes of the Plage de Famarin. There are a number of good viewpoints (binoculars advisable) over the lagoon with its protected birdlife. Apart from the flamingoes, the migrant winged visitors to the Camargue—one of the most important areas of passage in Europe—are to be seen in greatest number and variety in spring and autumn.

The road from Arles to Les-Saintes-Maries-de-la-Mer is the main tourist route. This is where you will find ranches where *gardians* offer accompanied rides through the Camargue, and there are information centres, small local museums and amusement areas. Near Méjanes, you can also get views over the Etang de Vaccarès and follow a dirt-track between the lagoons to **Les-Saintes-Maries**. This is one of the few places in the Camargue which has been allowed to develop into an unattractive resort serving a long beach. Its one interesting building is the extraordinary church—crenellated and almost windowless like a battleship. If, like the Palais des Papes in Avignon, it looks more military than religious in function, this is because it was a fortress: to withstand Saracen besiegers there was even a well inside. In the crypt is the graven image of the venerated patroness of the gypsies: Sara, the black servant girl who landed at Les-Saintes-Maries-de-la-Mer with the Holy Marys themselves (Marie Salomé and Marie Jacobé). The great event which has made Les-Saintes-Maries is the pilgrimage of May 24th–25th when gypsies come from all Europe to pay their respects to the dusky figure in the crypt, and when the little boat containing two figures of the Marys is lowered from the roof and carried down to the sea for a benediction, accompanied by *gardians* on horseback. In the evenings before the pilgrimage day, as the gypsy population builds up, flamenco guitarists lead dancing in the street, and after the ceremony is over there are bullfights.

The eastern route across the Camargue leads to Aigues-Mortes and the Languedoc coast beyond. On the northern edge of the Camargue St-Gilles was once an important pilgrimage monastery on the way to Compostela, and an important port for pilgrims, crusaders and incoming exotic goods. Now its population is only a fraction of what it was, and of the monastery the only noteworthy remnant is the very fine west façade of the church—the most obviously Roman in construction of all Provençal Romanesque works of art, with a wealth of sculpture between the columns, mostly depicting the life of Christ but also with picturesque Old Testament stories and animals. In the crypt, which is really a vast underground church with a groined vault, there is saint Gilles' tomb.

Aigues-Mortes, meaning dead waters, is one of the best-preserved and most evocative of fortified medieval towns in France. Its rectilinear streets of low houses are all still enclosed within the four sides of its ramparts and there are practically no signs of modern growth of the town. The 13th-century king Louis IX (saint Louis), having no Mediterranean port, negotiated the purchase of Aigues-Mortes from a sympathetic religious establishment. He built the splendid Tour Constance (which is the best part of the fortifications to climb up for a view over the Camargue), encouraged the growth of the town and set off from it on two crusades. His heir Philip the Bold completed the fortifications of Aigues-Mortes in the late 13th century, concentrating the points of defence on the one side which could be approached by land, for in those days Aigues-Mortes was, if not exactly on the sea, surrounded by a lot more water than today. Now the landscape is one of salt marshes and is the home of the producers of Listel wines whose cellars you can visit just outside Aigues-Mortes.

The Languedoc–Roussillon Coast

The end of the Petit Rhône today is marked by the first cluster of new resorts, which have grown in four groups over the last twenty years along the barely interrupted sand which stretches from the Camargue to the Pyrenees. In some places the beaches are wafer thin, separating the sea from lagoons where lately oysters and mussels have been farmed. **La Grande Motte** was the first of the series and the most aggressively modern in style, with honeycombed pyramidal blocks which can be seen

La Grande Motte

from miles round the coast. The contrast with Roman Provence and with the Mediterranean coast between Marseille and Menton could hardly be more striking. This, like the other resorts of this part of the coast, is a place for flats and flatlets, water-sports and private boats, for which there is extensive accommodation. Like so many other aspects of French life, La Grande Motte and the resorts of the Languedoc coast have not just grown naturally and gradually but have come into being as a result of a planning decision in Paris. In the early '60s it was decided that the empty sands of the Languedoc coast were to be developed, and the architects who were given a free hand set about their task of building villages from nothing, in a flat and empty landscape, with a positive and uncompromising confidence typical of the decade. The architect at La Grande Motte said of his aims, "to start the resort a hard core (the pyramids) was necessary to mark the countryside with its virile presence". Needless to say the thorough French planners didn't neglect the practicalities of seaside resorts, and summer residents of La Grande Motte and the others are well served with facilities for all sorts of leisure activities, particularly sailing and other water-sports. Since the early days of La Grande Motte a less virile architectural style has been preferred—low-rise villas with more personal access to the marina facilities. The most important of all the modern developments is **Le Cap d'Agde** on a cape near the mouth of the Hérault, between Béziers and Montpellier. It has a large yachting port but is a somewhat bewildering place spreading without apparent focus. There is a large naturist area—Port Nature—and there are plenty of facilities (and people, but only in July and August). The other main new resorts are **Gruissan-Plage**, **Port-Leucate**, and **St-Cyprien**.

One of the few older communities along this stretch of coast is the commercial port of **Sète**. It owes its greatness to the creation by Louis XIV and Colbert of the Canal du Midi which links the waters of the Atlantic to the Mediterranean, ending in the Etang du Thau behind Sète. More recently the Canal du Rhône à Sète has been constructed with the same terminus. The animated centre of the town is the canal which cuts through it from the Etang to the sea, flanked by tall old buildings and the setting on many summer days for the nautical jousts which are so characteristic of the Languedoc coast. The sport, second only in importance to rugby, consists of two crews propelling the two jousters each standing on a raised platform at the back of his boat and bearing a long pole and a shield—the winner is the one who doesn't get his nice white suit wet. Sète has no particular sightseeing interest but a lot of character and very good fish restaurants all along the port. **Agde** is an older port than Sète, standing on the banks of the Hérault a few miles from its mouth. Its origins are Greek (the name is derived from Agatha) and there is a small archaeological museum. Beside the waters of the Hérault the crenellated walls of the cathedral, built of sombre unweathered local volcanic stone, have an even more formidable aspect than most of the fortified churches of this part of the world.

Of the towns which have grown up behind the mosquito-ridden wastelands of the coast, **Montpellier** is the most important. It is one of the oldest and most distinguished university towns of France, whose intellectual excellence as early as the year 1000 stemmed from the town's contact with the Orient through the spice trade. Those who knew their spices and herbs knew medicine too, and this was the discipline of Montpellier when Rabelais came to qualify in the 16th century. Montpellier remains more of a pen-pushing than an industrial town for as well as having an important university, it was from the time of Louis XIV to the Revolution the administrative capital and seat of Parliament of the whole of south-west France. Like so many towns of the south-west, cosmopolitan and intellectual Montpellier welcomed the ideas of religious reform both in the Middle Ages and in the 16th century. Its reward was almost total destruction in the wars of religion; Montpellier's architectural beauty is that of the 17th and 18th centuries. All around the city centre which is animated and attractive with gardens (the oldest botanical gardens in France) and narrow streets, there are large numbers of substantial *hôtels* built by the wealthy lawyers and financiers of Montpellier. Typically Montpellier *hôtels* are simple on the exterior and do not make the streets a joy to walk down, but have richly decorated interior courtyards. The great architectural centrepiece is the Promenade de Peyrou, built at the end of the 17th and early 18th centuries. It is a splendid monumental achievement with a triumphal arch, an equestrian statue of Louis XIV and an elegant hexagonal water tower at the end of the Promenade, where an esplanade gives a marvellous view over the coast and mountains behind, and the aqueduct which brings water to Montpellier. Within the city the most important sightseeing destination is the Musée Fabre which has among many treasures a particular wealth of French 19th-century paintings (Courbet and Delacroix) and sculptures by Houdon.

From Montpellier there are easy excursions into the southern Massif Central with its grottoes and rocky circuses. **St-Guilhem-le-Désert** and **St-Martin-de-Londres** are peaceful and beautiful places to stay, well within range of the coast. Unlike Montpellier, **Pézenas** has lost most of its importance except as a wine market town. Three hundred years ago it was an elegant and aristocratic place where Molière came to entertain the court of the prince de Conti. **Béziers** is a large town of wine industry, rugby mania and Spanish bullfights, which was victimised by the crusaders of 1209 (see page 188). Apart from a long series of locks engineered to allow the Canal du Midi to climb—and considered by Arthur Young to be one of Louis XIV's greatest achievements, a verdict with which it is hard to concur—Béziers has only a fortified cathedral and a wine/local history museum to detain you.

Narbonne, capital of the original Roman Provincia, is another wine town, more rewarding to visit because of the cluster of religious buildings at its heart. These include one of the most beautiful (among few) Gothic cathedrals in the south (which was never completed because it was not allowed to take priority over the town fortifications) and the archaeological (mostly Roman) museum in the Archbishop's Palace which is unusually attractive and informative. Just beside the motorway south of Narbonne, in a landscape of mudflats and shallow hazy lakes, is the **Sigean African Safari Park**. On the road south towards Catalonia and the Pyrenees the small ancient city of **Elne**, once the capital of the Roussillon, is grouped around its 11th-century cathedral. This is a pure example of the Romanesque style with a particularly entertaining wealth of sculpture in the south gallery of the cloister.

The capital of the Roussillon—as the French part of Catalonia is called—is now **Perpignan**, which is proud of the ethnic individuality of its region. In and around Perpignan the people speak Catalan and like to dance the *sardana*, Catalonia's national dance, whose pace quickens like a bolero; even the ambiance late in the day is reminiscent of Spain. For a period in the 13th and 14th centuries Perpignan was the capital of the kingdom of Majorca—a temporary offshoot (which included Montpellier) of the ruling house of Aragon. The kings of Majorca built their palace in Perpignan and it has been restored within the later citadel constructed by Vauban. Other buildings of interest include the Castillet, part of the town fortifications originally built in the 14th century; the late Gothic cathedral, simple in architectural lines, but rich in heavy gilt wooden altar-pieces; and the Loge de Mer which, in the days when Perpignan was a sea port, housed maritime commercial transactions. Appropriately enough it has a rather Venetian look about it. The Place de la Loge is the lively centre of town life.

The Roussillon coast differs from that of the Languedoc in that it is not predominantly the creation of the last two decades. The flat sandy coast finishes at **Argelès-sur-Mer** which is built up without style, and whose buildings are heavily outnumbered by tents; it has become in its own words the camping capital of Europe. To its south the Pyrenees tumble into the Mediterranean producing a completely different coast, without the long beaches but with much greater scenic attraction and fishing ports on the coves which have long brought tourists. **Collioure** is the most picturesque and attracted the artistic avant-garde several decades after St-Tropez (Picasso, Matisse, Juan Gris). Down by the pebble bathing beach stands the church with an Arabic-looking pink domed belfry. Inside there is a very sumptuous collection of carved altarpieces, dating from the end of the 17th century. Like Perpignan, Collioure has its castle, built by the kings of Majorca and later strengthened by Vauban. The last resort in France is **Banyuls**, famous as the home of the finest of the sweet dessert wines of this area.

Collioure

Excursions from the coast

✻ **Abbaye de Fontfroide** A beautiful old Cistercian abbey among the Corbières vineyards, which has been carefully and not too extensively restored by its private owners, and adorned with colourful gardens. More than most places, Fontfroide breathes tranquillity, and makes the attractions of monastic retreat in troubled medieval France thoroughly understandable.

✻ **Carcassonne and Cathar Fortresses** The medieval city of Carcassonne is one of the most popular excursion places in France, and its aspect one of the most famous (see page 193). On the way to Carcassonne there are a number of romantic fortress ruins built in a chain along the old frontier between the Languedoc and the Roussillon, which became refuges for heretics and the object of 13th-century siege. These fortresses are so inaccessibly situated that they could not be attacked, merely reduced to starvation—for which the ascetic Cathars were well prepared. The most accessible of these fortresses is Puylaurens, the most spectacular Peyrepertuse and Quéribus. If you are fit enough to climb over a thousand feet to reach Peyrepertuse, and then the vertical and vertiginous staircase up its keep, you will be rewarded by a marvellous view and an understanding of why this was the one castle that was never taken. Quéribus, which is hardly less impressively set, received some of the last Cathars and only fell through treachery in 1255 (see also page 188).

✻ **Wine Tasting** The drive from the coast to Carcassonne gives the opportunity for a leisurely wine tour. This is not the area for tasting prestigious vintages, but rather for admiring the vineyards and sampling good value wines at small outlets and co-operatives. Lézignan-Corbières, the main centre of the Corbières wine region, stands on the edge of the hilly area on the plain. Between Béziers and Carcassonne the Minervois vineyards produce very drinkable wines and the small village of Minerve enjoys a magnificent setting, its rocky citadel isolated between two rivers. It is no surprise to learn that Minerve was a Cathar stronghold which enjoyed the reputation of being impregnable and to which the crusaders' leader Simon de Montfort duly laid siege in June 1210— he cut off Minerve's water supply with the use of six mighty war engines, and the fortress capitulated. No fewer than 150 heretics preferred the flames to a denial of their faith. At Minerve there are still the remains of the fortifications to see and an attractive Romanesque church. South of Carcassonne, Limoux is another attractive wine growing centre and its product the Blanquette de Limoux is one of the most acceptable of all champagne substitutes. The inhabitants would no doubt object to the term, for Limoux has been making bubbly for much longer than Champagne has.

Agde, 34300 Hérault £££

LA TAMARISSIÈRE   Tel: 67.94.20.87

This hotel is set on a quay at the mouth of the river Hérault, by the little ferry
which links it to Grau d'Agde. There's a terrace overlooking the boats and a
shady garden at the back. Bedrooms have balconies, good bathrooms, well-
planned modern furnishing and colour schemes; public rooms are comfortably
stylish and the overall atmosphere happily relaxed. The standard of cooking is
well above average for this sort of family seaside hotel; fixed-price menus (on
which fish, naturally, features strongly) are good value and interesting.

Closed mid-Dec to mid-Mar (rest Sun dinner and Mon out of season); 35
bedrooms; no lift.

Aix-en-Provence, 13100 Bouches-du-Rhône ££££

DES AUGUSTINS   Tel: 42.27.28.59
3 Rue de la Masse

In a semi-pedestrian side street off the Cours Mirabeau, a 12th-century convent
has been elegantly and expensively converted. Pale stone walls and terra-cotta
tiles set off antiques and modern art in the public areas, which are relatively
small—a salon and breakfast area. Up the graceful staircase (there's also a lift)
spacious bedrooms cleverly combine comfort with the building's medieval
structure: they're lavish, uncluttered and restful, with excellent bathrooms.

30 bedrooms; garage; no rest.

Aix-en-Provence, 13100 Bouches-du-Rhône £££

LE MANOIR   Tel: 42.26.27.20

Converted 14th-century cloister in a quiet residential area close to the historic
centre. Bedrooms are comfortable and traditionally furnished, with good
bathrooms. Breakfast is taken under the cloister ogives; there's a small terrace
and courtyard parking. An excellent peaceful city-centre hotel.

43 bedrooms; no rest.

Aix-en-Provence, 13090 Bouches-du-Rhône ££££

MAS D'ENTREMONT   Tel: 42.23.45.32

A mile out of Aix this peaceful creeper-covered house has a courtyard with a
fountain, and a generous expanse of garden including pool and tennis court. Half
the bedrooms are in bungalows, traditionally furnished and well equipped, with
modern bathrooms. Those in the house are smaller, pretty and equally
comfortable. All have a terrace or a balcony. Public spaces are arched and alcoved
among stout wooden pillars, with clusters of velvet and tapestry chairs. In
summer you eat outside in the shaded courtyard. Good classic food, friendly
service and the relaxed charm of the setting make it a popular place for local
parties.

Closed Nov to mid-Mar (rest Sun dinner and Mon); 16 bedrooms; no lift;
swimming pool.

Hotels

Les Angles (near Villeneuve-lès-Avignon), 30133 Gard   ££
HOSTELLERIE MEISSONNIER; L'ERMITAGE   Tel: 90.25.41.02
(Restaurant): 90.25.41.68

Essentially a restaurant-with-rooms, though that scarcely does the bedrooms justice. The *raison d'être* of the place is undoubtedly the restaurant, where young Michel Meissonnier has gradually been taking the reins from his father Paul-Louis, who still maintains a watchful eye over the proceedings. The excellent-value 180F fixed-price menu is full of interest; Michel's specialities echo those of his father (*loup aromatisé* has taken the place of the renowned *loup en habit vert*), with regional overtones. The bedrooms lack character or charm but are modern, spacious and comfortable, and equipped with minibar.

Closed Jan and Feb (rest Mon, and Sun dinner in winter); 16 bedrooms; no lift.

Arles, 13631 Bouches-du-Rhône   ££££
D'ARLATAN   Tel: 90.93.56.66

Fine, secluded grey stone mansion in the city centre, just off the Place Forum, with terrace and pretty walled garden. Some bedrooms are spacious, others fairly small; all are well furnished in traditional style, with pretty bathrooms. The beamed and tiled salon is elegant, with tall open fireplace and rough-stone walls. There's a separate TV room, and a garage. A splendid city base for Arles sightseeing.

46 bedrooms; no rest; no lift.

Arpaillargues (near Uzès), 30700 Provence   ££££
CHÂTEAU D'ARPAILLARGUES; HÔTEL D'AGOULT   Tel: 66.22.14.48

A dignified 18th-century château in extensive grounds 3 km from Uzès; lawns, trees and terraces near the house, pool and tennis courts across the way. Inside there's a confident style—a blend of antique and well-chosen modern—and the atmosphere is casual and understated elegance, impeccably and invisibly maintained. Some spacious and beautiful individual bedrooms, others smaller and simpler. The food is not overpriced, nor highly imaginative (Black Forest *gâteau* one of three desserts on the more expensive of the two fixed-price menus) but dishes are well prepared.

Closed mid-Oct to mid-Mar (rest Wed out of season); 27 bedrooms; no lift; swimming pool, tennis.

Avignon, 84000 Vaucluse   £££££
D'EUROPE   Tel: 90.82.66.92

Very fine 17th-century mansion, a hotel since Napoleonic times, calmly situated very near to the city centre. Most bedrooms are spacious and elegant; the formal public rooms are comfortable and excellently furnished—antiques, tapestries, marble floors—and there's a delightful terrace for summer meals. A new chef has recently been installed; his "regional" fixed-price menus includes solid country fare (*soupe au pistou, bourride, daube à l'avignonnais*) which is far from heavy, and there are even lighter dishes on the short *carte*.

53 bedrooms; rest closed Sun, and Mon lunch; garage.

Avignon (Le Pontet), 84130 Bouches-du-Rhône   ££££
AUBERGE DE CASSAGNE   Tel: 90.31.04.18

Ten minutes' drive from Avignon, this mellow house in leafy grounds is a surprise in suburban Le Pontet. The interior is attractively Provençal: splendid beams and vast old fireplace in the little salon, traditional furniture and fabrics in the vivid bedrooms. In the single storey annexe, around the terrace of the swimming pool, bedrooms are larger and more airy than those in the house. In summer meals are served in the delightful courtyard, romantically lit at night. The ambience (plus the stiffly-starched linen, heavy silver and vast glasses) may seduce you into being impressed by the food; but the three set menus are over-expensive for the standard of cooking. We've received a report of the proprietor's "surly and unhelpful attitude"; more reports, please.

Les-Baux-de-Provence, 13520 Bouches-du-Rhône   £££££
CABRO D'OR   Tel: 90.97.33.21

One of the hotels below Les Baux (you can pay twice as much higher up the valley), this is a creeper-covered modern *mas* in lovely gardens. Swans, ducks and people have their various pools; tennis and riding are at hand. The bedrooms— separate from the main building—are airily comfortable. Public rooms have rustic tiles and beams, chandeliers and velvet draperies. The one fixed-price menu isn't cheap, but the standard of food is good.

Closed mid-Oct to Mar (rest Mon. and Tues lunch out of season); 22 bedrooms; no lift.

Les-Baux-de-Provence, 13520 Bouches-du-Rhône   ££
LE MAS D'AIGRET   Tel: 90.97.33.54

Just below the ruined fortress of Les Baux, this ancient farmhouse has views over miles of Provence from its terrace with tables among the pines; its pool is floodlit at night like the fortress. Within, the salon is thoughtfully lined with straw matting (floor, walls and ceiling) to contain the sounds of its record collection, classical and jazz. Bedrooms and their bathrooms are simple and pretty. The restaurant is irresistible—its rooms are carved out of the pale rock, half-caves. Food is simple—*omelette aux champignons*, followed by spaghetti *au beurre*, perhaps, on the *pension* menu; the atmosphere is warmly hospitable.

Closed Jan to Mar (rest lunch and Thurs); 17 bedrooms; no lift; swimming pool.

Beaulieu, 06310 Alpes-Maritimes   £££££
METROPOLE   Tel: 93.01.00.08

Not the only luxury hotel in the best sea-front position in Beaulieu, but traditional French formality is less overpowering at the Metropole. Lush gardens and a seawater pool overlook the terrace and rock and shingle beach; public rooms and many of the bedrooms have uninterrupted sea views—and if you settle for the rear, you can contemplate the mountains at a lower tariff. Food is classic (*foie gras*, caviar, smoked salmon, plenty of fish, and straightforward meat dishes) and expensive—only very few dishes are priced in single figures.

Closed mid-Oct to mid-Dec; 50 bedrooms; swimming pool.

Hotels

Biot, 06140 Alpes-Maritimes   ££
CAFÉ DES ARCADES   Tel: 93.65.01.04

Enormously atmospheric 15th-century inn, where tables are set under the
arcades of Biot's most picturesque narrow square. The building is full of modern
art; the cellar is a gallery of Vasarély works, and paintings cover the walls in the
dining room too. Pretty beamed bedrooms are full of splendid antiques and more
paintings—they vary in size, but all have good bathrooms. The cooking is
simple—one fixed-price menu of the day, with three or four choices including a
local speciality or two, such as excellent *soupe au pistou*. This is a cheerfully noisy
local haunt by day, peaceful late at night, and splendid value—if you can get in.

Closed Nov (rest Sun dinner and Mon); 12 bedrooms; no lift.

Bonnieux, 84480 Vaucluse   £££
L'AIGUEBRUN   Tel: 90.74.04.14

This is a grey stone house with a Georgian look, set in a river valley among the
wild wooded hills in the Lubéron National Park, 6 km from Bonnieux, and
reached down a rough driveway. Inside are pleasantly personal rooms with tiled
floors and many paintings; invitingly squashy fireside sofas fill the lounge. Tiled
and beamed bedrooms are comfortable and charming, bathrooms modern. Food is
light and inventive (*petits soufflés de courgettes en sauce*, *turbot à l'émincé
d'artichauts*), and the fixed-price menu good value. It's altogether a civilised,
relaxing retreat, in lovely surroundings.

Closed mid-Nov to mid-Mar (rest Mon lunch); 8 bedrooms; no lift.

Cotignac, 83570 Var   ££
LOU CALEN   Tel: 94.04.60.40

This very Provençal hotel, entered from a corner of the village square, is
immediately welcoming. Tiles and tapestries, plants and paintings, flowers and
bric à brac surround you with unpretentious rustic charm. There's a pretty little
lounge which serves as a breakfast room; log fires blaze cheerfully whenever the
weather is dubious. Interesting old bedrooms and bathrooms continue the
homelike atmosphere—some are split-level family rooms, all are full of attractive
detail. There's a splendid long dining room, red-tiled and raftered; tables on the
terrace overlook a luxuriant garden with a swimming pool among the trees. Food
is regional and simple (*pieds et paquets à la provençale*, *saucisson sec aux aubergines et
à la menthe fraîche*, *daube à l'ancienne*), but very good value, as is the wine list.

Closed Nov to Easter (rest Thurs out of season); 17 bedrooms; no lift; swimming
pool.

Fontvieille, 13990 Bouches-du-Rhône   ££££
REGALIDO   Tel: 90.97.60.22

Splendid and peaceful old oil mill, shuttered and creeper-covered, with pretty
garden, at the edge of the village. Bedrooms range from small and beautiful to
very spacious with terrace; all are extremely well furnished and comfortable, as
are the public rooms—with antiques, log fires, tiles and flowers. There's no fixed-
price menu, and prices on the *carte* might persuade you towards fewer courses
than would otherwise be the norm—a pity, since the standard of cooking is high.

Closed Dec to mid-Jan (rest Mon, and Tues lunch); 13 bedrooms; no lift.

Grimaud, 83360 Var   £££
HOSTELLERIE DU CÔTEAU FLEURI   Tel: 94.43.20.17

This friendly little grey-stone hotel is built into the hillside in a quiet corner of its high village, three miles from the sea. White walls, red-tiled floors, open hearth, traditional furniture and lots of flowers give an impression of welcoming simplicity. The lounge and bar lead to a pretty garden terrace; the restaurant opens onto a delightful countryside view. Bedrooms have this too—they are small and simple, with good bathrooms. Cooking is above average; there's no *carte*, just two reasonably-priced fixed-price menus (on the cheaper you might find *gâteau de foies de volaille au coulis de tomates*, followed by *filet de rascasse à l'oseille* and *poire pochée au vin des Maures*—a more interesting list than on many menus of a similar price).

Rest closed mid-Oct to Easter, lunch except Sun, and Wed except July and Aug; 14 bedrooms; no lift.

Les Issambres, 83380 Var   ££
LA RÉSERVE   Tel: 94.96.90.41

This family-run restaurant-with-rooms has an attractive pine-shaded terrace and a splendid seaview, but is set close to the road; the two rear bedrooms are noisy, the others peaceful. They're simply furnished, modestly comfortable. The restaurant overlooking the sea is big and light, white-walled with colourful tables. The reasonably-priced menus contain plenty of meat dishes, as well as a *marmite du pêcheur*, and a *filet de bar à l'oseille*; a full-blown *bourride* or *bouillabaisse* can only be had à la carte.

Closed Oct to Easter (rest Wed); 8 bedrooms; no lift.

Juan-les-Pins, 06160 Alpes-Maritimes   ££££
DES MIMOSAS   Tel: 93.61.04.16

A hotel since Napoleon III's time, completely renovated a few years ago, this white-painted building with shutters and balconies stands in very pleasant gardens in a quiet residential area. No restaurant; breakfast on your balcony or in the garden. The reception rooms have been combined, and the resulting cool space is spread with chunky modern units, rugs, prints and lamps. Bedrooms vary from similar modern style to the more traditional; all have good bathrooms. An attractive and friendly place.

Closed Oct to Mar; 35 bedrooms; no rest; no lift; swimming pool.

Juan-les-Pins, 06160 Alpes-Maritimes   ££
AUBERGE DE L'ESTEREL   Tel: 93.61.86.55

This modest hotel is a plain cream-washed building in a quiet residential quarter a few minutes from the sea. There's no great charm indoors—a TV-dominated lounge, small bedrooms (with balconies, at the back) and a rustic-style dining room. But in summer you eat under the trees in the pretty rear garden, and the food is the attraction—now better even than before. There's an interesting and good-value fixed-price *menu gastronomique* (including, possibly, *confit de lapereau* with *mesclun*, *fines escalopes de loup de mer gratinées au sabayon*, *jarret de veau cuit à l'ancienne*) and good desserts.

Closed mid-Nov to mid-Dec (rest Sun dinner and Mon); 14 bedrooms; no lift.

Hotels

Monte-Carlo, Monaco   £££££

BEACH PLAZA   Tel: 93.30.98.80

An excellent place for a beach holiday with some style: a tall modern block with its own immaculate stretch of pebbles, strewn with sunbeds and umbrellas. Above is the terrace, with three pools (2 salt, 1 fresh), poolside bar and grill restaurant (fishy). There's also a cheerful indoor "café", and a more formal restaurant. It's one of the Trusthouse Forte chain, and is well maintained; bedrooms have recently been done up in pastel shades. The *carte* is unexciting (*Wienerschnitzel*, grilled chicken, scampi *flambés au pastis*, avocado salad with crab), but dishes are well prepared and the service is good. There are various sports available, and a children's playground (staffed in July and August).

316 bedrooms; 3 swimming pools; children's facilities.

Monte-Carlo, Monaco   £££££

HERMITAGE   Tel: 93.50.67.31

A cream-painted Neo-Baroque palace overlooking the harbour, the renovated Hermitage is as splendid today as when it opened in 1900. The famous Winter Garden foyer under its great glass dome is all green elegance and graceful wrought iron; the Belle Epoque restaurant a most sumptuous extravaganza in pink and gold. Dinner under the chandeliers, or on the broad terrace, to the strains of the orchestra is an experience as rarified as the prices; dishes are classic. Enormous and beautiful bedrooms, faithfully recreated in period style, leave no doubt that this is definitive luxury. Every possible comfort is available; beaches and sporting facilities run by the *Société des Bains de Mer* are at guests' command.

255 bedrooms; swimming pool; fitness centre.

Peillon, 06440 Alpes-Maritimes   £££

AUBERGE DE LA MADONE   Tel: 93.79.91.17

In the middle of nowhere on the edge of a tiny perched village with views down the valley and walks in the hills, this simple modern *auberge* among the trees blends into its setting. There's a sunny terrace, an attractive rustic-style restaurant, and a cosy TV room. The cooking is homely and good value with many regional country dishes. Bedrooms are peaceful and pleasing, with good bathrooms and balconies at the front. An idyllic place to escape from the clamour of the coast (though you might be woken by sheep bells).

Closed mid-Oct to mid-Dec (rest Wed); 19 bedrooms; no lift.

Plan-de-la-Tour, 83120 Var   £££

MAS DES BRUGASSIÈRES   Tel: 94.43.72.42

Built in the style of a Provencal farmhouse with rustic tiles and rosy walls, this little hotel is seven winding miles inland from Ste-Maxime, set among hillside vines in a garden of mimosa. Nothing but the ping of tennis balls or a splash from the pool disturbs its peace. The friendly little lounge gathers comfortable chairs and attractively personal clutter around its big open fireplace; bedrooms are cool and pretty, with tiled floors, pleasant wood and wicker furniture, modern bathrooms.

Closed Jan and Feb; 10 bedrooms; no rest; no lift; swimming pool.

148

Plan-de-la-Tour, 83120 Var ££££

PONTE ROMANO   Tel: 94.43.70.56

Hidden among trees and flowering shrubs, three km south of Plan-de-la-Tour, this is a Provençal-style set of pleasing stone-clad buildings with peaceful gardens and pool beside a little river. There is a rustic-furnished salon with a bar; bedrooms are small but prettily furnished, with modern bathrooms. The restaurant is large and ornamentally traditional, extending (with its piped music) to a leafy outdoor patio. Food is generous and well-served, with some local specialities, but not cheap.

Closed Nov to Feb; 10 bedrooms; no lift; swimming pool.

Poët-Laval (near Dieulefit), 26160 Drôme ££££

LES HOSPITALIERS   Tel: 75.46.22.32

An ancient knights' stronghold of grey-gold stone, occupying much of an uncommercialised perched village, restored but atmospheric with splendid views. No gardens but a fine swimming pool and an attractive terrace outside the cosy lounge. Bedrooms vary: some rooms are very small (those in the annexe generally better), but their unattractive modern furniture has now largely been replaced. The creative *cuisine* will not disappoint, but you will need to be very hungry to attempt the six courses of the third menu.

Closed mid-Nov to Feb; 20 bedrooms; no lift; swimming pool.

Port Camargue, 30240 Gard £££

LE SPINAKER   Tel: 66.51.54.93

As ultra-modern as the whole resort and set right on its marina, the Spinaker spreads bungalow bedrooms round the pool and terrace. Each has a patio between swoops of concrete, and an attractive (newly carpeted) bathroom. You can eat at poolside tables, or in the main building; the first-floor restaurant is air-conditioned and full of greenery and latticework. Atmosphere friendly and relaxed, food—especially fish and *pâtisseries*—very good and not over-priced (with two excellent fixed-price menus).

Closed end Nov, and Jan to mid-Feb (rest Sun dinner and Mon out of season); 20 bedrooms; no lift; swimming pool.

Port Grimaud, 83360 Var £££££

LE GIRAGLIA   Tel: 94.56.31.33

At the edge of the narrow streets and waterways of this picturesquely-planned resort, ten minutes from the centre, Le Giraglia is enviably situated right by the sea. It's an appealing Provençal-style building; the adjoining beach and the terrace with pool are well equipped and cared for. The interior is more anonymously plastic than appears from outside (piped music in the mock 1930's bar-lounge) but the main restaurant is pleasing with a rather nautical flavour and some tables outside. Bedrooms are individual, varying considerably in size, style and quality, but all attractive. Food is well prepared and served, but not very good value (choice of desserts and cheeses limited).

Closed Nov to Easter; 48 bedrooms; swimming pool; parking.

Hotels

Roquefort-les-Pins, 06330 Alpes-Maritimes   ££££

AUBERGE DU COLOMBIER   Tel: 93.77.10.27

Off the busy Grasse road, this low white building is set in lush extensive grounds with pool and tennis court among the trees. Some bedrooms have a fine view over wooded slopes to the sea; all are comfortable, their general style light and spacious. A large dining room, sandy-toned and summery, opens on to a terrace under a striped awning where you eat overlooking the greenery. Food is very good, with an excellent-value fixed-price menu (*buisson de salade au ris de veau poêlé* followed by *mixte du pêcheur gratiné*, cheese and splendid *pâtisseries*, perhaps); on the *carte*, there's fresh pasta, *agneau roulée à la tapénade*, and *bourride de baudroie provençale*.

Closed Jan and Feb (rest Tues out of season); 15 bedrooms; no lift; swimming pool.

Roussillon, 84220 Vaucluse   £££££

LE MAS DE GARRIGON   Tel: 90.05.63.22

Low ochre-coloured pantiled *mas*, set in an oasis of pines about 4 km from the village. All is cool, comfortable and attractive—tiled floors, log fire and classical music in the salon, squashy armchairs and books in the library, rustic furniture in the main restaurant, and flowers and plants everywhere. There's another glassed-in restaurant and bar by the splendid pool, and a terrace; bedrooms are tiled and pretty, with Laura Ashley prints, cane chairs and a terrace. The standard of cooking is good, and the three well-thought-out fixed-price menus good value; there's a short *carte* (*turbot soufflé aux écrevisses, carré d'agneau à la crème de thym*), and a good wine list. A splendid retreat.

Rest closed Sun dinner and Mon lunch, and mid-Nov to end Dec; 8 bedrooms; no lift; swimming pool.

St-Jean-Cap-Ferrat, 06290 Alpes-Maritimes   £££

CLAIR LOGIS   Tel: 93.01.31.01

Up one of the little inner roads of the wooded Cap, this is a 19th-century villa set in its own large garden of tall trees and fragrant flowering shrubs, gravel paths and secluded outdoor tables. Indoor public space is limited to a small TV lounge and the simple high-ceilinged breakfast room. Bedrooms in the main house are attractively old-fashioned and spacious; those in the more modern annexe across the garden are simple and cramped. Bath and shower rooms are adequate. The setting is lovely, the atmosphere relaxed and friendly, and prices low for the area.

Closed mid-Nov to mid-Dec; 16 bedrooms; no rest; no lift.

St-Jean-Cap-Ferrat, 06230 Alpes-Maritimes   £££££

LA VOILE D'OR   Tel: 93.01.13.13

As elegant and luxurious as the palatial Riviera hotels but not as solemnly grandiose, the Voile d'Or—ochre-washed, red-tiled and unobtrusive—is set between yacht harbour and green Cap, with magnificent views. Gardens, terraces, rocky little beach and two seawater swimming pools are casually idyllic. The main restaurant has gaily striped chairs and vast windows which overlook the yachts; there's a poolside restaurant too. Cooking is of a very high standard, and prices are not low. The air-conditioned bedrooms are traditional and utterly peaceful; those facing the garden rather than the port are significantly cheaper.

Closed Nov to Feb; 45 bedrooms; swimming pools.

St-Martin-de-Londres, 34380 Hérault £££

LA CRÈCHE   Tel: 67.55.00.04

Perfectly isolated among undulating hills and *garrigue*, this simple little farmhouse hotel 5 km from the village has spacious grounds with a large pool, tennis court and attractive terrace. Opening onto this, the lounge and bar occupy a veritable barn; bedrooms are simple and rustic. The creative cuisine is splendidly successful; Monsieur Rousset aims for perfection in all things, and a simple-sounding *terrine de légumes au coulis de tomate* becomes a work of art here.

Closed February (rest Tues out of season); 7 bedrooms; no lift; swimming pool.

St-Paul-de-Vence, 06570 Alpes-Maritimes £££

AUBERGE LE HAMEAU   Tel: 93.32.80.24

Le Hameau consists of adjoining villas in the Provençal style, just off the main road at the edge of town. It's set in groves of orange, lemon and apricot trees—home-made products appear at breakfast, on the pretty terrace if it's fine. There's no restaurant or bar, but most of the bedrooms have minibars. Bedrooms do vary in size and some (cheaper) are near enough to the road to suffer traffic noise; all however have charm and character. Run informally by a friendly young couple, this is an unusual and delightful hotel.

Closed mid-Nov to mid-Feb; 16 bedrooms; no rest; no lift.

St-Paul-de-Vence, 06570 Alpes-Maritimes ££££

LES ORANGERS   Tel: 93.32.80.95

In a similar situation to Le Hameau, a fine Provençal house set among orange groves, with a pretty terrace. There's a large, comfortable salon, and traditional bedrooms—with tiled floors and antiques, and good bathrooms. Some rooms have their own terrace.

Closed Jan and Feb; 10 bedrooms; no rest; no lift.

St-Rémy-de-Provence 13210 Bouches-du-Rhône £££££

CHÂTEAU DES ALPILLES   Tel: 90.92.03.33

This distinguished little 19th-century château in extensive wooded grounds just west of St-Rémy is a stylishly modernised hotel, without restaurant (but simple snacks are available, and there's a poolside grill). Ornate public rooms—chandeliers, vast mirrors—assimilate both classic chesterfields and sprightly breakfast furniture; bedrooms and their marble bathrooms are beautifully appointed. Indoors and out, a place of restorative peace and comfort.

Closed mid-Nov to mid-Mar (open Xmas); 16 bedrooms; no rest; swimming pool.

Our price symbols

£	You can expect to find a room for under £15
££	You can expect to find a room for £15 to £25
£££	You can expect to find a room for £25 to £35
££££	You can expect to find a room for £35 to £45
£££££	You should expect to pay over £45 for a room

Hotels

St-Rémy-de-Provence, 13210 Bouches-du-Rhône   ££££
CHATEAU DE ROUSSAN   Tel: 90.92.11.63

Two km from St-Rémy on the Tarascon road, this is a lovely 18th-century house approached by a long avenue of venerable trees and set in gardens just sufficiently wild to be in perfect accord with the untouched building. Inside it's unaltered in its proportions and beautifully kept, full of polished antiques and period décor. Large bedrooms, a fine formal library-salon; no restaurant—guests breakfast on the gravel terrace in fine weather, or in the attractive breakfast room.

Closed mid-Oct to mid-Mar; 12 bedrooms; no rest; no lift.

St-Rémy-de-Provence, 13210 Bouches-du-Rhône   ££
LE MAS DES CARASSINS   Tel: 90.92.15.48

Just out of St-Rémy off the road to Les Baux, this pretty old house among fields and vineyards is utterly peaceful (apart from night-croaking frogs). The large attractive bedrooms are comfortable and imaginatively renovated, with excellent bathrooms; downstairs the tiny salon has a collection of books, and the breakfast-room is beamed and rustic. Better still in summer is a table on the patio, enjoying the garden and the view. Simple snacks are available in the evening—*charcuterie*, cheese, fruit and cakes.

10 bedrooms; no rest; no lift.

St-Tropez, 83990 Var   £££££
LE MAS DE CHASTELAS   Tel: 94.56.09.11

Secluded among vineyards and orchards, this is an old three-storey Provençal *mas*, which has been converted with great charm. It's simple but elegant, with a delightful vine-shaded terrace. Bedrooms are stylish, bathrooms modern; a new annexe houses duplex apartments with their own garden area. There are pretty grounds, tennis courts and the particularly inviting quiet pool area. Whether you eat indoors, on the terrace or beside the pool you are offered a set meal with limited choice, and a single wine – the house Provençal red. The cooking is partly *nouvelle*, unpretentious and good. The English-speaking proprietor and his staff are friendly; the fashionable and famous come here for peace.

Closed Oct to April; 30 bedrooms; no lift; swimming pool.

St-Tropez, 83990 Var   £££
LA PONCHE   Tel: 94.97.02.53

Perfectly tucked away on the edge of St-Trop's most attractive shopping streets with its own restaurant and street-side terrace, La Ponche is inexpensive and welcoming in a typically Trop'ical off-beat way. Bedrooms are individual but mostly spacious and coolly stylish. Not much space in the public rooms, but you're very close to all the quayside action so won't want to idle indoors. There's a splendid little fixed-price menu (including, perhaps, *anchoïade* or *soupe de poissons*, *médaillon de lotte* or *civet de canard*) and a few fine desserts.

Closed Oct to Mar; 23 bedrooms.

St-Tropez, 83990 Var £££££

LE PRÉ DE LA MER   Tel: 94.97.12.23

Almost three km from town, off the Route des Salins, this combines gentle
Provençal appeal with the convenience and privacy of a motel. No pool, but a
beach 100 metres away. Bedrooms (all with a terrace overlooking quiet gardens)
are beautifully cared for, furnished with Provençal antiques and handmade tiles.
No bar or restaurant, but minibars among the mod cons, and light meals (as well
as substantial breakfast) available in your room. The small salon/reception is
attractive; it's a peaceful and welcoming place.

Closed Nov to mid-Mar (except Xmas); 12 bedrooms; no rest; no lift.

Ste-Maxime, 83120 Var ££

MARIE LOUISE   Tel: 94.96.06.05

Peacefully set up a side road just south of Ste-Maxime, surrounded by greenery
and overlooking the sea, this is a modest red-tiled house with a "stable-block"
annexe across the pretty garden. Bedrooms both here and upstairs are small,
pretty and simply furnished in Provençal style. It's a family-run hotel; the
reception lounge with tiny bar is literally lived-in. Beyond it the dining room is an
attractive extension, with a sloping bamboo roof and a mass of foliage beyond its
conservatory windows. The friendly owner serves his wife's tasty home-cooking;
children are welcome.

Closed mid-Oct to mid-Feb; 14 bedrooms; no lift.

Les-Saintes-Maries-de-la-Mer, 13460 Bouches-du-Rhône £££££

PONT DES BANNES   Tel: 90.47.81.09

Between the main road into the resort and the fields and waters of the Camargue,
with well-kept gardens and a stream, this is a low white ranch-style hotel, with
bedrooms in thatched cabins dotted about the scenery. They're small and simple
but well planned and peaceful. Public rooms overlook the pool and terrace. Most
eating and drinking goes on informally outside; good food, local wine, relaxed and
friendly service. Nearby are two sister establishments, the Mas Ste-Hélène (slightly
cheaper, and you can use the pool and restaurant) and Le Boumian.

Closed mid-Oct to April; 20 bedrooms; swimming pool.

Salon-de-Provence, 13300 Bouches-du-Rhône £££££

ABBAYE DE STE-CROIX   Tel: 90.56.24.55

Splendid ensemble of grey stone 12th-century abbey buildings, excellently
restored and converted into a luxury hotel, with sweeping views over the
Provençal countryside. In the fine vaulted public rooms there are log fires, tiled
floors and comfortable sofas; the simply-furnished restaurant looks out onto a
terrace and views. Bedrooms (some exceptionally spacious, others more cell-like)
are simply but beautifully furnished with dark antiques, and rugs on tiles. There's
a beautiful pool, with its own small grill-restaurant. Food (under a new chef) is
good, with a particularly reasonable fixed-price lunch menu (perhaps *gâteau de
moules à la julienne de poireaux*, *gigotin de poulette à la vapeau de menthe*, cheese and
pastries, with wine and coffee included).

Closed Nov to Feb (rest Mon lunch); 24 bedrooms; no lift; swimming pool.

Hotels

Séguret (near Vaison-la-Romaine), 84100 Provence   **££££**

LA TABLE DU COMTAT   Tel: 90.46.91.49

A pretty little old grey stone house perched against the rock face above this tiny hill village, with a shady terrace, lawn and small swimming pool. It's immaculately kept, uncluttered and pleasing. Bedrooms are comfortable with good bathrooms—not all face the view and only two have balconies, but this is reflected in the price. The restaurant takes advantage of the panorama. The food is inventive (*croûte de ris de veau et cervelle d'agneau aux morilles, brésolles de lotte et pétoncles aux pointes d'asperges*), and there's a good-value fixed-price menu, and a fine selection of Rhône wines.

Closed mid- to end-Nov and Feb (rest Tues dinner and Wed out of season); 9 bedrooms; no lift; swimming pool.

Seillans, 933440 Var   **£££**

LES DEUX ROCS   Tel: 94.76.05.33

On one of perched Seillan's tiny squares, with outdoor tables round a fountain, this 18th-century house has been renovated with flair and charm by its *patronne*. Downstairs, an intimate little area of deep-cushioned sofas leads to a peaceful dining room with rough white walls and pretty tables; the menu is not vast, but the cooking is competent. Bedrooms are individual compositions of style and gaiety—unusual fabrics, shapely furniture—and bathrooms modern. A delightful hotel, civilised and personally welcoming.

Closed Nov to 20 Dec (rest Wed. and Thur lunch); 15 bedrooms; no lift.

Tavel, 30126 Gard   **££**

L'AUBERGE DE TAVEL   Tel: 66.50.03.41

In a pleasant wine village—an excellent touring base—this former schoolhouse is a modernised *auberge* with the emphasis on the restaurant, with its bustling and friendly atmosphere. There are interesting good-value menus and the food is very good, especially the desserts; the long wine list contains many Tavels, and there's a special "tasting offer" of five different ones. There are reasonably spacious bedrooms, a lounge and a garden with a small pool.

Closed Feb to mid-Mar (rest Mon out of season, and Sun dinner Nov to Jan); 11 bedrooms; no lift; swimming pool.

Trigance, 83840 Var   **£££**

CHÂTEAU DE TRIGANCE   Tel: 94.76.91.18

An 11th-century fortress, impregnable on its rock above the tiny village; no grounds, but wonderful views from the terrace among the crenellations—even the countryside looks medieval. The building is much restored and rebuilt but feels utterly authentic—rough stone steps, rocky interior walls, tapestries and banners and candles. Above a windowless lounge there's a vaulted dining room where the attentive owner enjoys your appreciation of the stately splendour and where the food is interesting and well prepared. Bedrooms differ—the two more expensive have canopied fourposters. It's an extraordinary place, full of atmosphere.

Closed Nov to mid-Mar (rest Wed out of season); 8 bedrooms; no lift (and rather long and rough walk up from the carpark).

Uzès, 30700 Gard £££

D'ENTRAIGUES   Tel: 66.22.32.68

In a quiet street near the Tour Fenestrelle, this is a 15th-century town house
restored with care and charm, its fine pale stonework effectively lit. A vaulted
lounge area is simply furnished with modern wicker and bentwood; the
restaurant is attractively rustic—tiles, beams and just ten colourful tables. There
are two cheap and excellent-value fixed-price menus (*salade du pêcheur aux petits
légumes*, followed by *goujonnettes de truite au jus d'écrevisses*, *fromage blanc à la
crème* and dessert, perhaps). This hotel has the same owner as the Château
d'Arpaillargues, and achieves similar style.

Closed Jan (rest Tues and Wed lunch); 18 bedrooms; no lift.

Vaison-la-Romaine, 84110 Vaucluse ££

LE BEFFROI   Tel: 90.36.04.71

Delightful old town house, up in the heart of the medieval *cité*, with a shady
terrace and an elegant formal salon. In the rather less stylish dining room, the
food is sadly only competent (desserts disappointing). The bedrooms are not
luxurious, but are large and beautifully furnished, with period charm; bathrooms
are not always modern, but fit in well with the style. A peaceful and good-value
base, with a lot of charm.

Closed mid-Nov to mid-Dec (rest Mon and Tues lunch out of season); 21
bedrooms; no lift.

Vence, 06140 Alpes-Maritimes ££

AUBERGE LES SEIGNEURS   Tel: 93.58.04.24

A tall narrow building on a little square near the oldest part of Vence, this
restaurant-with-rooms is full of character—ornate old fireplaces, quarry-tiled
floors, ceiling beams and period furniture. The bedrooms have similar appeal;
shuttered and quiet, they have ample space for solid beds and massive old
wardrobes; each has a large tiled shower room. There's an excellent five-course
fixed-price menu with local specialities (*soupe de poissons et sa rouille*, *croustade au
basilic*) and succulent charcoal grills. Not luxurious, but splendidly atmospheric
and good value.

Closed mid-Oct to Nov (rest Mon, and Sun dinner out of season); 5 bedrooms; no
lift.

Villeneuve-lès-Avignon, 30400 Gard ££££

LA MAGNANERAIE   Tel: 90.25.11.11

Ancient stone house in a quiet residential area on the outskirts of the village, set
among lush gardens and overlooking a fine pool. It's attractively furnished and
comfortable, in rustic style; bedrooms vary—some are modern, others have
traditional floral walls and rather old-fashioned furniture—but are well equipped
and also comfortable. Cooking is classic and good, and the fixed-price menus good
value.

21 bedrooms; no lift; swimming pool.

The Massif Central

Le Pont d'Arc on the Ardèche

"To climb the trackless mountain all unseen,
With the wild flock that never needs a fold;
Alone o'er steeps and foaming falls to lean;
This is not solitude; 'tis but to hold
Converse with Nature's charms" (Byron)

The Massif Central

The most major of France's minor mountain ranges is in fact no single range, but a huge mountainous region covering one sixth of France, separated from the Alps only by the Rhône valley, from the Mediterranean only by a narrow coastal plain, and from the Pyrenees by the vineyard carpets around the Aude. In such a large area it is the diversity and the unspoilt nature of the landscape that accounts for nearly all the appeal to tourists. There are curious isolated volcanic cones, deep limestone canyons, caves with spectacular formations of natural architecture, eerily desolate windswept plateaux. There is also rural French life at its most attractively primitive. The Massif Central— at least in part—is the area for escaping from civilisation. You can walk for days across the Cévennes and come across isolated villages offering a few roofs and simple fare, just as Robert Louis Stevenson did when he travelled with his donkey Modestine a century ago. Since that time the region has become progressively more and more deserted as its population has moved to greener economic pastures elsewhere in France— Paris has been called the biggest town in the Auvergne.

The southern part of the Massif Central is the best for escapism. The landscape of recently reforested mountains and empty windswept plateaux pitted by deep grottoes and split by river canyons has a climate of extremes and has only proved suitable for summer sheep (which produce Roquefort, one of the most notoriously potent of French cheeses) and military manoeuvres (the Larzac Causse has one of the largest military camps in the country). There are isolated communities of dry stone farms with rough stone roofs which do little to soften the bleak impression of the rocky landscape. Resorts have grown up only in the immediate vicinity of that most impressive natural curiosity, the Tarn gorge, one of a series of such canyons in the region. The Tarn is easy to fit into a drive towards the western Mediterranean, just as the spectacular Ardèche canyon (one of the classic canoe adventures in the country) is only a short diversion from the way south to Provence.

By comparison with the south, the Auvergne of the northern Massif Central is almost populous; its landscape is strangely volcanic but not wild, many of its towns and villages are uniformly grey. The most attractive part is the Cantal, where the mountain scenery is beautiful and where rubicund dairy cowherds live up to the Auvergne's rustic image. The rest of the Auvergne has long been discovered: the volcanic waters of the numerous spa resorts have brought their own kind of tourism and the Auvergne has become an outdoor holiday area for the budget holidaymaker. Accommodation is characterised more by value for money than refinement, and gastronomic specialities are limited to dark bread, mountain ham and mountain cheese.

It is easy to dismiss the Auvergne as a holiday area—as many French people do, drawing unfavourable comparisons with the Alps and the Pyrenees. But there are a number of points in its favour. Precisely because it is not fashionable, its resorts are quiet, unpretentious and inexpensive. The landscape is beautiful and unlike any other in France,

The Massif Central

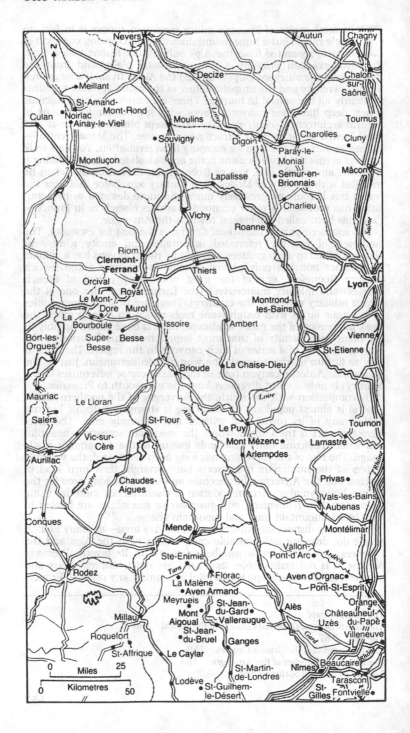

Nevers · Autun · Chagny

Meillant · Decize · Chalon-sur-Saône

St-Amand-Mont-Rond · Moulins · Tournus

Culan · Noirlac · Ainay-le-Vieil · Souvigny · Digoin · Charolles · Cluny

Montluçon · Lapalisse · Paray-le-Monial · Semur-en-Brionnais · Mâcon

Charlieu

Vichy · Roanne

Riom · Clermont-Ferrand · Thiers · Lyon

Orcival · Royat · Montrond-les-Bains

Le Mont-Dore · Murol

La Bourboule · Super-Besse · Besse · Issoire · Ambert · Vienne

Bort-les-Orgues · St-Etienne

Brioude · La Chaise-Dieu

Mauriac · Le Lioran · Loire

Salers · St-Flour · Le Puy · Tournon

Vic-sur-Cère · Mont Mézenc · Lamastre

Aurillac · Arlempdes

Chaudes-Aigues · Privas · Truyère

Vals-les-Bains · Aubenas

Conques · Mende · Montélimar

Vallon-Pont-d'Arc · Ardèche

Rodez · Ste-Enimie · Aven d'Orgnac · Pont-St-Esprit

Tarn · Florac

La Malène · Aven Armand · Alès · Orange · Châteauneuf-du-Pape

Meyrueis · St-Jean-du-Gard · Uzès · Villeneuve

Millau · Mont Aigoual · Valleraugue · Gard

Roquefort · St-Jean-du-Bruel · Ganges

St-Affrique · Le Caylar · Nîmes · Beaucaire

Lodève · St-Martin-de-Londres · Tarascon · Fontvieille · St-Gilles

St-Guilhem-le-Désert

0 — Miles — 25

0 — Kilometres — 50

thanks to its very obvious volcanic origins. Because the mountains are only moderately high (under 2,000 metres at their highest points) nearly all the peaks are easily conquered without equipment or experience. The Auvergne also has much more man-made sightseeing interest than the deserted southern Massif: there are ruined fortresses perched on volcanic outcrops, and an inventive local style of Romanesque church architecture, which uses the volcanic stone to exceptionally colourful and decorative effect.

The Bourbonnais

The Bourbonnais is a fringe area, in appearance less closely related to the Massif Central than to the Berry and Burgundy. At the end of the Middle Ages the dukes of Bourbon were among the most powerful princes in the land and **Moulins** their brilliant capital; now the countryside around is fertile, with gently undulating hillsides and chubby cows—scarcely a part of France to go out of your way to discover. Long after its 16th-century heyday Moulins remained an important market town and staging post, and a notorious snarl-up on the main Paris–Lyon road. But thanks to the motorway, it is now a quiet and pleasant provincial town without much industry. A particular feature is the black stone lozenge patterning in the red brick of the old half-timbered houses.

∗ *Cathedral* The late Gothic flat-ended choir has interesting windows, and the treasury has what is without exaggeration one of the greatest treasures of medieval French art—a triptych of the Virgin in Glory (as the Revelation records, clothed with the sun and crowned with a dozen stars), painted for Pierre and Anne de Beaujeu in about 1500 by the artist who is identified only as the Maître de Moulins.

∗ *Jacquemart* A frequently restored pink stone belfry and clocktower, named after the model family of Jacques (peasants) who hammer the chimes.

∗ *Lycée Banville* The chapel of this former convent contains the magnificent 17th-century marble tomb of the duc de Montmorency (to visit enquire at the tourist office).

To the south of Moulins lies **Vichy**, queen of watering places. It has cinemas, concerts, a casino, plenty of sports facilities, extensive bus tours (they have to be extensive to be interesting), good shopping and dozens of hotels, many of them rather institutional. This advanced infrastructure earned its selection in 1940 as the seat of the government of non-occupied France—a spa resort for the sick nation. Vichy's popularity is attributable to the allegedly beneficial effect on the digestive system of its highly carbonated waters, appreciated since Roman times. In the late 17th century madame de Sévigné wrote that she sweated out over 20 pints in a week and expected to be safe from rheumatism for life, but considered that the most effective part of her stay was a warm bed and the delights of the surrounding countryside with its river, sheep, goats and peasant girls dancing the *bourrée*. Two centuries later, Augustus Hare wrote that Vichy had no attraction but health to offer. Those in pursuit of health do so in an agreeable setting of neo-Muslim thermal establishments, Second Empire casino, and parks and walks beside the Allier. The Parc des Sources itself is the focus of animation with a little crystal palace among the trees and promenades where *curistes* cluster and stand at the troughs, filling their thermos flasks with the spring waters. The atmosphere falls somewhere between campsite wash room, Champs-Elysées street café and pilgrimage basilica.

Excursions from Moulins and Vichy

* **Bourbon l'Archambault** (west of Moulins) A dull spa, despite having been an earlier medieval capital of the dukes of Bourbon. A few fragments remain of the old 14th-century castle destroyed by Revolutionaries.

* **St-Menoux** (west of Moulins) Romanesque church with a choir of splendid proportions and a miraculous tomb with a hole in the side for the mentally afflicted to put their soft heads in and be cured.

* **Souvigny** Attractive small town with the most notable church in the Bourbonnais, built in the late 11th century when it was an important monastery and pilgrimage centre but much altered in the mid-15th century when the dukes of Bourbon made it their necropolis. Urgently in need of repair and damp-proofing, the church is more interesting than beautiful.

* **Besbre Valley** (south-east of Moulins) Very green and pleasant and full of little châteaux, few of them open to tourists. The **Château de Lapalisse**, though not the most beautiful, is the largest and most impressive, set high above the river, dominating the town and its important road junction. Inside there are beautiful tapestries and a deeply coffered gilt ceiling in the Salon Doré, *Son-et-lumière* in summer. The **Château de Toury** is much more endearing, a delicious little pink granite toy fortress, still inhabited, well furnished and well guided by the proprietor. There is a small zoo and some other amusements at **Le Pal**.

* **Château d'Effiat** (south-west of Vichy) A handsome ensemble of farming village and severe 17th-century château at the end of a splendid avenue of limes. Guided tours; beautiful furniture and decoration in period.

The Monts Dômes, the Monts Dore and the Cantal

South of Vichy lie the Monts Dômes volcanoes and the fertile lowlands of the Limagne. Rural life on the plain is more populated and less picturesque, but at Gannat (south-west of Vichy) there is a notable folk festival each July, maintaining the traditional *bourrée* dance and *cabrette* music (a form of bagpipes). The old market towns have considerable charm—like garlic-growing Billom, to the south of Thiers and Clermont.

At the foot of the plateau, the big city of the Massif—and indeed of central France—is a merger of the old rival cities Clermont and Montferrand. **Clermont-Ferrand** gave birth to the rubber industry in the 19th century, and the motor age brought lots of business. It is not a very endearing city, mainly because of the dark grey volcanic stone of its construction. The centre is a maze of old lanes in which the exemplar of the local Romanesque school, the church of Notre-Dame-du-Port (see page 164) is almost hidden. In contrast, the almost black Gothic cathedral stands out supreme, a lonely medieval skyscraper on the 150ft mound on which the old city stands. The view of it from Royat is magnificent, thanks to Viollet-le-Duc who built the twin spires in the 19th century. The interior of the cathedral is as bright as can be expected given the employment of black lava, thanks in part to the strength of the stone which enabled such slender pillars to be used.

Royat was just a picturesque village grouped around its curious fortified Romanesque church until it was rediscovered in the 19th century and became one of the most fashionable of Second Empire spas, sprouting a sudden crop of hotels and other resort establishments. It still has its baths and its hotels beside the steep river gulley which runs down to Clermont from the volcanoes, but is now a moderately stylish suburb of Clermont. You can visit the Grotte du Chien, carpeted (to dog height) with carbonic acid gas which snuffs out candles and anything which inhales it.

Riom grew up like a *bastide* on a regular pattern within circular ramparts, now replaced by tree-lined boulevards. It was for a period the regional capital and has a number of old houses built in dark volcanic stone, a very good local ethnographic and folklore museum and a beautiful Virgin in the church of Notre-Dame-du-Marthuret.

Suburban Riom is not worthy of the once important old abbey church of **Mozac** (see page 164). Another nearby church at **Marsat** has a very splendid and much venerated 12th-century black Virgin, a severely iconic contrast to the sweet human vision of the Virgin in the late Middle Ages, as exemplified in Riom. On a wooded spur high above Riom the ruined 13th-century fortress of **Tournoël** with its crumbling overgrown round tower and empty windows is splendidly romantic—as a local writer has described it "a ruin placed in majesty by a very expert ruin builder on this hillock so obviously destined to receive a ruin". At the southern end of the Monts Dômes, the **Lac d'Aydat** is popular for weekend watersports and there are campsites among the trees.

The older and more eroded volcanic cones of the Monts Dore look more conventionally mountainous than the Monts Dômes; the area has a thriving spa and ski business within easy reach of Clermont.

Le Mont-Dore is the big resort, a spa and more recently ski centre, set in a superb amphitheatre of mountains with the Puy de Sancy, the jagged crown of central France, at its head, easily reached by cable car. The resort is solid and somewhat dour, with a grandly theatrical thermal temple which you can visit. The chalets which have grown up along the valley nearer the winter pistes do not embellish its setting but there are sports facilities and good walking country all round and seasonal evening life. Here the Dordogne springs, and flows in its infancy down through **La Bourboule**, spa for infants and adolescents, whose waters have the highest arsenic content of any in Europe. There are fine driving excursions from Le Mont-Dore, including the beautiful roads to Lake Chambon and Besse. **Orcival** is a deliberately charming little village of cafés and souvenir shops and a couple of hotels clustered in an intimate valley around its noteworthy Romanesque church (see page 164). Nearby you can visit the beautifully restored fortified manor of **Cordès**. **Lake Chambon** is one of the largest and shallowest of Auvergne lakes, with not so much a community as a functional straggle of buildings along the water, as well as campsites, beaches and water-sports facilities. Nearby **Murol** is more of a little resort, with a few hotels tucked beneath the imposing ruins of a medieval fortress.

Lake Chambon is fed by waters which run down from the Puy Ferrand beside the Sancy through the steep-sided wooded and (above the woods) impressively rocky **Chaudefour Valley**—one of the best places hereabouts for walking, botanising and even climbing. Beyond Murol, **St-Nectaire** is well worth a visit to admire one of the finest examples of the local Romanesque style of church (see page 164), although the lower town and spa is dark and gloomy.

Orcival

The most attractive of all the resorts in the Monts Dore is **Besse-en-Chandesse**, harmoniously or at least uniformly grey and medieval. Besse has a number of hotels and lots of animation, especially on market days when the whole village becomes a bazaar. There are lots of walking trails and organised excursions. The nearby **Lake Pavin** is one of the most typical of the crater lakes, small, deep and perfectly circular, surrounded by woods and, usually, by people.

The pastoral Cantal is comparatively unfrequented by tourists and increasingly depopulated. Many inhabitants winter in the towns and valleys; many more leave for good. The mountains are green and beautiful and with their grey villages are reminiscent of North Wales or Scotland. Of the few resorts **Salers** is the most attractive; like Besse it is a grey medieval village with fortifications and a picturesque old main (market) square with beautiful medieval and Renaissance turreted houses. Between Salers and the avoidable town of Aurillac is a very attractive hamlet, with a few convenient auberges, at the foot of the tall and substantially intact 15th-century fortress of **Anjony**. More comfortable living quarters were added later to the round-cornered keep. Inside château and chapel there are some splendid 16th-century wall paintings, including Anjony portraits.

The main (summer) excursion from Salers is the drive up into the heart of the ancient Cantal volcano via the **Puy Mary** (1,787 metres).

The scenery around here is the most pleasing in the Auvergne—you can walk without too much difficulty from the souvenir shops at the Pas de Peyrol up to the Puy Mary itself, and by walking a bit further on escape other people.

For those who want to do the Cantal on foot, the best places to stay are the resorts of **Le Lioran**, just a few hotels thick in the trees beside the main road, and even more modern **Super-Lioran** which enjoys a higher and less claustrophobic setting in a large theatre of mountains. From here you can reach all the peaks that are the remains of the crater; the highest, **Plomb du Cantal** (1,855 metres), is served by a cable car. The Cère valley which runs down past Le Lioran towards Aurillac is one of the most verdant and charming of all the lava paths that radiate from the old crater. **Vic-sur-Cère** is pretty and peaceful—part medieval village and part spa either side of the river. **Thiézac** is a no less attractive resort village, with a trout farm providing the rivers of the Cantal with enough stock to satisfy holiday fishermen—who come in great numbers to the Cère and the Alagnon.

On the eastern edge of the Cantal, the **Truyère** runs down through empty wooded countryside and impressive gorges whose appeal to tourists has been increased by the damming of the river in several places, making reservoirs popular for fishing and watersports. The best place to find out about facilities is at **St-Flour**, a not very charming grey town which enjoys a fine setting on volcanic cliffs (a *planèze*) high above the river; although hardly a place to stay, it is a busy tourist centre and has a grey Gothic cathedral of uncompromising harshness. The drive down the Truyère to Entraygues, which is long and fiddly but in places quite magnificent, begins just south of St-Flour where Gustave Eiffel spanned the river with a prodigious cast-iron bridge. The Grandval reservoir has enhanced the wild setting of the ruined fortress of **Alleuze**, which is now surrounded by water, and looks altogether Scottish. A little further downstream the Truyère passes near **Chaudes-Aigues** of the hot waters (see page 162). For many tourists the main reason for taking this scenic route south-west out of the Auvergne towards the Lot valley will be to join the medieval pilgrimage route from Le Puy to Moissac at **Conques**, an exceedingly picturesque old village on a hillside above the river Dourdou, grouped around its magnificent Romanesque pilgrimage church of Ste-Foy, one of the most important in France. The grey-gold village has some accommodation and abundant craft and souvenir shops. The 11th-century church has been restored to its full splendour, of which the highlight is the vigorously animated representation of the Last Judgement over the main doorway. The treasury, arranged in a museum beside the church, contains the gold reliquary statue of saint Foy, mostly dating from the 10th century, but with later encrustations of jewellery. There are many other veritable treasures of medieval gold-smithery and beautiful tapestries, all very well displayed, so you should not flinch at the relatively heavy entrance charge.

South of Conques, the great pull is the Tarn gorges, (see page 172) on the way to which lies the sleepy market town of the Aveyron, **Rodez**. Its cathedral is imposingly fortified, mostly Gothic but with a curious classical topping on the formidable west end, and a very elegant and delicate 16th-century belfry. North-east of Rodez, **Entraygues, Espalion** and **Estaing** are pleasant old villages beside the Lot; all around this area, the rural domestic architecture is very attractive, with outside stair-cases, and vast, steeply pitched, rough-stone roofs.

Romanesque Churches of the Auvergne

Le Puy cathedral

The Auvergne has a concentration of colourful Romanesque churches of great beauty and a character all their own. The most attractive characteristic of the style is the varied geometric patterning of the exterior stonework exploiting the natural colours of the local volcanic and granite stone (red, black, white and yellow) which in some cases turns the walls into mosaics. Another feature is the raised central section of the transept which supports an octagonal lantern tower. Within many of the churches there are venerated Romanesque statues of the Virgin and Child, awe-inspiring in their stiff majesty, and richly jewelled caskets or reliquaries.

Clermont-Ferrand, Notre-Dame-du-Port One of the most perfect and delightful Romanesque churches in France, in the dark narrow heart of old Clermont. Decorative stonework inside and out, beautifully carved capitals; reproduction black pilgrimage Virgin in the crypt.

Royat, St-Léger A 12th-century church not very typical of the region, fortified in the 13th century and endowed with an octagonal belfry in the 19th. Set beautifully, high above the city of Clermont-Ferrand.

Mozac Once very important, now rather dilapidated abbey church with magnificent carved capitals and very precious reliquaries.

Ennezat The oldest surviving of the Auvergnat Romanesque churches (late 11th century) curiously divided into two ill-fitting parts—Romanesque porch, nave and transept, much larger-scale Gothic choir with vivid 15th-century wall paintings.

Chauriat A typical local church with very colourful stonework.

Orcival, Notre-Dame A grey but charming church with pure and harmonious lines. Prisoners' shackles hang on the walls, given *ex voto* to the beautiful stylised pilgrimage Virgin enthroned against a pillar.

St-Nectaire One of the most attractive and beautifully situated of all the churches of this school, with an elegant and colourful east end, a harmonious interior rich in amusingly carved capitals and two magnificent 12th-century statues of saint Baudime and the Virgin.

Issoire, St-Austremoine Beautiful east end, with geometric patterning and carved signs of the zodiac; splendid interior despite lurid 19th-century re-painting, with beautiful capitals including one of the Last Supper with a tablecloth running all the way round the pillar, a crypt and a 15th-century painting of the Last Judgement in the porch.

Brioude, St-Julien Larger even than Issoire, and magnificent, thanks to the design and colourful decoration of the east end, and the coloured stone of the interior and cobbled floor. Many beautiful works of art including frescoes. Statuary includes a disturbing 14th-century leprous Christ, and a smiling Virgin.

Lavaudieu A vivid pink church in a particularly delightful village. Interior with frescoes under restoration; charming cloister.

Le Puy, St-Michel-l'Aiguille Extraordinarily situated atop a vertiginous 250ft volcanic needle, and a long staircase. Beautiful carvings and coloured stone mosaics around the oriental-looking doorway, and some frescoes within. The even stranger **Cathedral** is one of the great pilgrimage churches of medieval France, built with as much virtuosity as Mont-St-Michel, into the air in projection from the side of the steep hill. Dazzlingly coloured stone exterior, domes, frescoes and a rich treasury within. Long-winded and expensive guided tour around beautiful cloister, and a fascinating maze of vaulted passages.

Volcanoes and Hot Springs

Three of the four volcanic massifs in the Auvergne have recently been cordoned off from random development and declared the Regional Nature Park of Auvergne Volcanoes (between Clermont Ferrand and Aurillac). The fourth volcanic area around the source of the Loire south and east of Le Puy is still so unfrequented that it needs no protection, for the moment at least. In the north the **Monts Dômes** are the youngest volcanoes and the most curious to look at, like boils spoiling the complexion of the landscape; over a hundred little isolated cones burst a few hundred metres above the high plateau in the most populous area of the Massif Central. While Magdalenian man painted caves in the Dordogne, the area was still erupting, some volcanoes throwing up solids which stayed in place leaving a domed mountain, others sending tons of molten lava spilling down their flanks and still shaped just as they were after eruption, with craters. The cones are not inhabited, nor even cultivated; they are simply strange phenomena to look at, best seen from the air or from the top of the highest one—the **Puy de Dôme** (1,465 metres) near Clermont, accessible via a toll road which spirals round it giving marvellous views of the whole chain. On top of the dome, there are remains of a Roman temple, a modern observatory, a Volcano Park Information Centre, a bar/souvenir shop/hotel and week-end hang-gliders. Not many people bother to explore any of the other *puys*. One of the most splendid is the **Puy de Pariou**, with concentric craters—the main one 100 metres deep and a kilometre round. It is a military training zone, and you are only allowed up on certain days of the week. More reliably accessible to walkers is the **Puy de la Vache** which literally split its side when erupting.

The **Monts Dore** and the **Cantal** are two much larger and older volcanic areas. The enormous Cantal volcano, some 80 kilometres across, stood over 3 kilometres high. Extinct for several million years, the Monts Dore and the Cantal have been eroded by glaciers and the passage of time; both now culminate at a similar height—between 1,850 and 1,900 metres—and both present a similar aspect of rural pastures with alpine flowers, famous cheeses and moderate winter sports facilities. In some places the volcanic origins of the landscape are obvious—the **Roches Tuilière** and **Sanadoire** between Orcival and Le Mont-Dore are striking remains of an old crater. There are splendid jagged spikes on the Le Mont-Dore side of the **Puy de Sancy** (summit of central France at 1,885 metres) and in the **Chaudefour valley**, just off the Besse/Mont-Dore road. There are a number of volcanic lakes, some filling old craters, others formed by eruptions closing valleys. The easily accessible **Puy Mary** gives wonderful views along the ruined ramparts of the old volcanic walls, with its lava paths radiating in all directions. St-Flour and Salers are set on one of the fertile lava-based plateaux called *planèzes* which are a feature of all the perimeter of the Cantal volcano.

The **Velay**, the area around Le Puy, is also manifestly volcanic in origin—as Arthur Young noted, "all in its form tempestuous as the billowy ocean". The city of Le Puy itself is extraordinarily situated in a basin like a crater marked by three steep volcanic outcrops of which one is just wide enough at the top to support a small chapel. The volcanic massifs between Le Puy and Vals-les-Bains are among the most remote parts of the Massif Central, between the Rhône and the young Loire which has its source at the splendid volcanic rocky cone which is the

Gerbier de Jonc. The top of the region and the most celebrated viewpoint is the easily climbed **Mont Mézenc**. The region is one of severe beauty, without any developed resorts. The volcanic **Lac d'Issarlès** has been separated from the Loire by an eruption.

All this faulty earth and volcanic activity is not surprisingly accompanied by an abundance of hot springs and mineral-rich cold ones. At **Chaudes-Aigues** south of St-Flour, the waters emerge nearly boiling at 82°C and have been used since Roman times for central heating. In other places the main use of the waters has been curative. **Vichy** has some 200 springs, of which 12 belong to the state. Most of the largest spas in the Massif were known to the Romans, but were not much exploited until the 18th and 19th centuries. The great spring named Eugénie in **Royat**, just outside Clermont, which produces over a quarter of a million gallons a day, was unleashed when the site of the Roman baths were being excavated in the 19th century.

The East

The area south of the Bourbonnais around and between Allier and Loire is a forested one of hills and in places almost mountains. There are few towns of any importance, except along the main rivers, and little of outstanding historical, architectural or scenic distinction. Little, that is, except for Le Puy and the volcanic hills around the source of the Loire, and still further south the magnificent Ardèche gorges, which together are more than enough to justify a visit.

Thiers, whose importance as a centre for cutlery manufacture dates from the Middle Ages, stands on a promontory above the river Durolle and has many well-preserved, substantial old 15th- and 16th-century houses with elaborately patterned and carved timbers. There is a small cutlery and other local crafts/traditions museum. The mountains of the Forez and Livradois are thickly wooded and thinly populated with as many woodcutters as farmers. On the Clermont to Lyon road west of Feurs, the **Château de la Bastie d'Urfé** is well worth a visit. Originally built in the 13th century, it was completely reworked in a very Italian style in the 16th century, with loggias over the courtyard, a curious grotto of shells, and much of its original furniture.

High in the hills, at over 1,000 metres, the imposing village of **La Chaise-Dieu** stands on a crest in a clearing among the forests. It is a modest resort for cross-country skiers in the winter, and a reasonable place to break a journey in the summer in the hope of catching one of the occasional musical evenings in the abbey which towers over the village. The Gothic church of magnificent proportions and sobriety was built in the 14th century to the order of pope Clement VI, an old boy of the abbey. To accomodate all the monks, the church has a larger choir than nave, and the two are separated by an elegant screen. You have to pay to penetrate, and should do so. There are very beautiful works of art within, including Clement's gleaming marble tomb surrounded by a series of marvellous 16th-century tapestries. There are also richly carved choir-stalls and a sketched Dance of Death fresco.

If you are on your way south from La Chaise-Dieu, consider driving three sides of a square, instead of straight south to Le Puy. It is a very pleasant drive through logging country west to Lavaudieu, up the best looking stretch of the Allier, and then back across to Le Puy. **Lavaudieu** means divine valley, and it is indeed a place of irresistible charm—a small rustic village in a quiet vale, its central square always full of cows, hens and farm dogs and its houses stacked with winter logs (see also page 164).

South of **Brioude** (see page 164) the course of the **Allier** is an impressive one, through rocky gorges followed more closely by the railway than by the road. The Allier is favoured by campers and canoeists. One of the most perfectly shapely of all volcanic lakes of the Massif Central is the **Lac du Bouchet**, which fills a crater.

Le Puy is a big commercial and even industrial town, which sprawls between the old *cité* and the Loire. The extraordinary thing about the town is its setting. Three volcanic rocks tower above the agglomeration: the most spindly of them (the chimney of the old volcano), is crowned by a small Romanesque chapel (well worth the climb); the largest part of the cone supports a complete medieval pilgrimage city, beneath a massive 110-ton, bright red 19th-century Virgin. The Holy City, as medieval Le Puy (cathedral and precinct) is called, is best attempted on foot—up the wide staircase street which extends the Rue des Tables, to the dazzlingly colourful west end of the cathedral (see page 164). Down in the modern town by the main road, the Musée Crozatier has among other things a good collection of local lace from different periods. Just north of Le Puy, the **Château de Polignac**—medieval home of a notoriously predatory noble family—stands superbly situated on an isolated volcanic rock.

The area south and east of Le Puy is one of great unspoilt beauty. The young Loire cuts through splendid gorges after it passes Le Puy, and before it passes St-Etienne (you should follow its example and bypass this town of football mania). Further upstream, it runs beneath the magnificent ruins of the **Château d'Arlempdes**, and past the beautifully situated Lac d'Issarlès. Around its source among the rocky volcanic cones, the countryside is superb: pleasing old farming communities with thatched and rough stone buildings of great solidity, fields carpeted with narcissus and volcanic hills with many rare species (see page 166). There are a few simple places to stay in the mountains, or alternatively excursions can be made from the main road south. **Vals-les-Bains** is a long and straggling spa of no particular character or charm, but is a well-situated base on the southern edge of the area of volcanoes, within easy range of the Cévennes and the Ardèche canyon.

From Vals, the **Ardèche** runs down to join the Rhône just before **Pont-St-Esprit**, the northern gateway to Provence. The section of the Ardèche valley which must be seen is between **Vallon-Pont-d'Arc** and **St-Martin-d'Ardèche** where the river runs for some 20 miles at the foot of a superb canyon, in places nearly 1,000ft deep. Until very recently the only way to see the gorge was to take a canoe and brave the white waters of one of the fastest flowing of France's rivers. Now there is a corniche road along the empty scrub-covered hilltops on the north side of the river which does not follow the gorge bend by bend, but gives a number of magnificent views down into it. There being no communities and no road down by the river, the Ardèche presents a less varied sight than the Tarn which has fertile cultivations and villages at the foot of the cliffs; but in many ways the Ardèche is grander. It is also much more exciting for canoeists, with the attraction of escapism as well as the challenge of the rapids. You can hire canoes from a number of places between Vallon-Pont-d'Arc and Pont-d'Arc itself, which is a splendid natural limestone arch over the river. After a day's canoeing you will be picked up at St-Martin and brought back by car. It is not a canoeing trip for beginners; in autumn, the Ardèche becomes a river of violence and danger, its waters capable of rising by over 20ft in a matter of hours, and accelerating like tidal waves. May and June are the best times for a canoe trip. Along the river, rapids and gentle sweeps of water alternate; there are grottoes, and waterside rocks which make perfect picnic tables. The unspoilt natural beauty of the canyon is usually complemented by unclothed campers and there is a naturists' campsite nearby.

The Cévennes and the Grands Causses

The Cévennes and the limestone plateaux which are the Grands Causses offer some of the wildest, emptiest and most grandiose scenery in France. The most extraordinary landscapes, which make the area well worth visiting as part of a sightseeing tour, are those of the Causses: the desolate monotony of the high plateaux is interrupted by deep canyons, slashed like open wounds—the most famous being the Tarn gorges between Florac and Millau. The riverbanks beneath the towering cliffs are green and friendly, and well provided with attractive accommodation, making the Tarn one of the best places to stay in the area, for those who want some comfort.

Many visitors come here for the opposite reason: to escape comforts, and all the trappings of civilised existence. For this purpose it is certainly the best area in France. There is very little in the region in terms of people, buildings, farming, even folklore. The pull of the wildest regions of France attracted the young Robert Louis Stevenson in 1877 to make the journey from Le Monastier, a small town near Le Puy, over the high granite mass of Mont Lozère, across the Tarn and down to Alès. The Scottish novelist set off with a six-foot square sack ("luxurious turning room for one"), a fur cap with hood to fold down over his ears, and in case of heavy rain—the area is subject to the heaviest storms in France—a tentlet (waterproof coat, three stones, and a bent branch); for more immediate needs he had a leg of cold mutton and a bottle of Beaujolais. To carry him and his gear he took a donkey which he named Modestine, and which he only persuaded to accelerate beyond the most agonising funeral march when given a sharp needle by a wily peasant.

169

Stevenson may also have been attracted to the Cévennes by its history as a stronghold of Catholic repression and Protestant resistance. After nearly a century of peaceful co-existence, Louis XIV decided to encourage religious uniformity by ordering dragoons in the area to billet with Protestant families and behave as if they were in conquered territory, that is to say badly. Insincere conversions and inaccurate intelligence having persuaded the king that only handfuls of Protestants remained in his realm, he revoked the Edict of Nantes in 1685. Protestants, no longer guaranteed tolerance and political status, became outlaws. In the Cévennes the de-institutionalised church took to the empty countryside or *désert*. Eventually repressive action provoked guerilla resistance and war (1702–1704); the Protestants took the name of Camisards, after the white shirts they wore to identify each other during night attacks. In two years of war, the Camisards burnt 240 churches, and the royal forces destroyed 41 villages, executed 147 desert pastors, and sent over 7,000 Protestants to the galleys. When one of the guerilla leaders was lured away to fight for the king abroad (he eventually became governor of Jersey) and the other was killed, the war ended; but the desert church continued to exist until the Revolution ensured its freedom.

There is a Camisard memorial museum at **Mas Soubeyran** near St-Jean-du-Gard, at the house of the chief who died—with a Protestant pilgrimage every September. Another reminder is the superb Corniche des Cévennes road, built from Florac to St-Jean-du-Gard by the royal intendant Barville, to dominate the guerilla territory.

Robert Louis Stevenson describes the landscape (specifically the Gévaudan north of the Mont Lozère) as "like the worst of the Scottish Highlands, only worse—cold, naked and ignoble, scant of wood, scant of heather, scant of life". This description conveys something of the bleakness of the Causses, but most of the landscape imprinted by Modestine's hoofs has been thoroughly reforested over the last hundred years, because the increasing nakedness of the mountains, stripped of their vegetation by man and sheep, brought major flood problems to the Cévennes valleys. Now the thickly wooded region has been turned into the huge **Cévennes National Park**, its main area scarcely inhabited by man. Its periphery (which includes the area of the Tarn gorges) is increasingly well organised for excursions on foot or horseback (or in winter on cross-country skis) into the National Park itself, to enjoy its peace and space, and perhaps catch a glimpse of a soaring eagle. The best equipped of these bases on the edge of the Park are **Meyrueis**, **Florac**, **Le Pont de Montvert**, and **Valleraugue**. For drivers the best way to get a fleeting appreciation of the Cévennes is to follow the **Corniche des Cévennes** road above the two Gardon valleys, getting superb views and passing an old medieval hostelry village (L'Hospitalet) for pilgrims and travellers through this wild region. Among the chaos of rocks beside **L'Hospitalet**, there is a plaque in memory of a desert assembly of 1689. You can also drive up to the summit (1,567 metres) of **Mont Aigoual**, which means wet. Here Atlantic and Mediterranean air currents meet over the crest, and more than two metres of rain fall every year, most of it in the autumn. In all directions there are trails for walkers and skiers and there are old sheep paths, rarely used now by the flocks which once made their spring and autumn journeys up and down the mountain on well-worn *drailles*. Now the sheep are shunted around in lorries, and the transhumance paths have been taken over by transient humans.

On the Mediterranean side of the Cévennes, the Gardon rivers drop steeply down to Alès, and the scrub hillsides (*garrigues*) that lie between Montpellier and the mountains. The river Hérault runs south from the Aigoual through the *garrigues*, watering some of the most productive Languedoc vineyards before it flows into the Mediterranean. It drops quickly to Valleraugue, and afterwards has carved gorges in the rock around **Ganges**, a town famous in the past for silk. Silk-worms were a Cévennes speciality from the 17th to 19th centuries—much to the disapproval of the royal minister Sully, who thought that silk would be morally contaminating. Not far downstream from Ganges is the magnificent **Grotte des Demoiselles**, its great underground chamber full of natural pillars and known, inevitably, as the cathedral. It was a hiding place for Camisards and for priests during the Revolution, and is still the setting for a Christmas midnight mass. At the end of another stretch of stark rocky gorges, the **Grotte de Clamouse** was explored for the first time in 1945; it too is very well provided with strange and beautiful rock formations. **St-Guilhem-le-Désert** sounds as if it might be a place of Camisard memory, but in fact it goes back much earlier as a religious refuge: it was to this veritable wilderness that Charlemagne's brother-in-arms William of Orange retired from fighting after a heroic career to take up prayer and fasting, from which he soon died. St-Guilhem is hardly more than a hamlet of very old houses and an inn, grouped around a square with plane tree and fountain, in front of the Romanesque abbey church founded by William in 804 but in its present form dating mostly from the 11th century. The church itself has a particularly beautiful apse, and used to have a beautiful cloister until it was transported to a museum in New York. **St-Martin-de-Londres** is another attractive place (see page 140) to know about in this area, which is conveniently within easy reach of the Mediterranean.

Grottoes, underground rivers and gorges are particular features of the limestone area which makes up most of the southern Massif Central; they are more impressive than those around the Dordogne valley, though without the prehistoric treasures. Another feature is the bizarre rocky chaos, technically known as dolomitic, which looks like ruins. One of the most impressive and enormous of these, with a real village built curiously among the rocks, is the **Cirque de Mourèze** near Clermont-l'Herault. The **Grands Causses**, as the plateaux are called, extend east to the Atlantic flank of the Cèvennes, and are not much lower than the mountains themselves. There are four of these great *causses*, separated by river gorges; starting at the south near St-Guilhem-le-Désert, the **Causse du Larzac** is the largest and the best known. It was a *cause célèbre* of the '70s, when radical youth and local farmers united to save it from assimilation into a huge military zone between Millau and Nant. One excellent reason to save the Larzac is that its pastures nourish innumerable flocks of summer sheep whose milk is made into cheese and sent to the natural cellars (in this sense the French word *caves* is the right one) of **Roquefort-sur-Soulzon**, just southwest of Millau, to evolve into the eponymous cheese known to Pliny and Charlemagne, its structure as labyrinthine as the limestone underground, and its taste as sharp as a winter wind on the *causse*. Like champagne, Roquefort owes its quality to the surroundings of its maturing—a constant temperature of 5°C–7°C with damp draughts issuing from faults in the rock. You can visit the vaults, which smell less frightful than you might expect from a taste of the end product.

From the south the most impressive way to approach the Larzac, or to leave it if you are travelling south, is from **Lodève** and the green and pleasant Lergue Valley with its vines and olives, by means of the Pas de l'Escalette, a hairpin cliff road which has been built to replace ladders attached to the 300 metres of rock face—until a century ago the only way up or down. The Pas de l'Escalette road is the old one across the Causse, used not only by sheep (which had to be carried down the ladders) but also by pilgrims on their way to St-Guilhem-le-Désert and Compostela. The passage of pilgrims was the *raison d'être* of the fortified village of **La Couvertoirade**, built by the Knights Hospitaller in the late Middle Ages. It never outgrew its fortifications, and in this century has lost most of its population. Recently, though, it has attracted some artisans and restorers, and is coming back to a new kind of life.

To the east of La Couvertoirade the Vis runs down from the Cévennes between two minor *causses* before it joins the Hérault at Ganges. Its course is often dry and severely rocky as far as the beautiful Source de Lafoux, which is accessible on foot from the Cirque de Navacelles. There the Vis, no longer dry, has broken through an isthmus of rock which once overlooked a deep meander, leaving a rounded theatre of scrub-covered rock with a green forsaken river-bed and the small village of **Navacelles** itself. The Cirque is one of the most impressive in the *causses*, both sides of it negotiable by a hairpin road.

The river Dourbie separates the Causse du Larzac from the **Causse Noir**, the smallest of the Grands Causses, with the most curious formations of dolomitic rock. To the north it in turn is split from the **Causse Méjean** (the highest and bleakest with an average height of over 1,000 metres) by the river Jonte. These two rivers are tributaries of the Tarn, and their impressive gorges are subsidiary in grandeur to those of the Tarn.

Not only are the **Tarn Gorges** the outstanding sight in a region of outstanding natural phenomena; the valley also has a number of attractive places to stay, which make it a good base for exploring the surrounding area, provided you are prepared for some tiring driving. The Tarn Gorges are some 50 miles long, as the river flows, between Florac and Millau. In places the *causse* walls either side are over 500 metres high, and the width of the canyon at the top varies from just over one kilometre to about two. In stretches the bottom of the gorge is very narrow and dark, in others wide and fertile with cultivations and

Château de la Caze

communities alongside the river. One of the most attractive is the old village of **Ste-Enimie**. All along there is the striking contrast between fertility at the riverside and the barrenness of the *causse* above. The rock walls are beautifully formed and coloured where they are not covered with scrub, and there are a number of very picturesque châteaux, half-hidden among the trees. The prettiest of them, the **Château de la Caze**, has been turned into an hotel of some distinction. The gorges can be seen very well by car, for a road follows the river, except at its narrowest parts, and in a number of places roads have been engineered from the *causse* in hairpins down the canyon walls. But the drive cannot compare with a boat along the river. The classic excursion is to hire what is barely more than a punt (with a punter) from **La Malène**, and sit back beneath the towering walls of the canyon as you are propelled for about an hour down the river, passing some of the narrowest and most impressive parts of the gorge, most not easily viewed from the road. The light is best early in the morning. For canoeists the Tarn is very popular and much less dangerous than the Ardèche. Even so, the current can take you by surprise if you try to swim. By car or by boat, it is best to do the gorges in the same direction as the river flows. For those without a car there are bus excursions from **Millau, Mende** and **Meyrueis**, all busy little towns with plentiful accommodation. Meyrueis has by far the most charm.

Excursions from the Tarn

* **Le Rozier** From this beautifully situated village—between the junction of the Tarn and Jonte—there are some long, spectacular and in a few cases vertiginous walks, high up on the cliffs above the two rivers. Information should be sought before setting off.

* **Gorges de la Jonte** The course of the Jonte, which runs from the **Aigoual** through **Meyrueis** to the Tarn, is only marginally less impressive than that of the Tarn itself and can also be followed by road.

* **Grotte de Dargilan** The best of the many caves on or close to the river, with splendid natural rock forms.

* **Aven Armand** The most exciting and unworldly grotto yet discovered in France, with a petrified forest of 400 of the biggest and best stalagmites.

* **Montpellier-le-Vieux** Named because of its resemblance to a ruined city, an enormous and desolate chaos of weird and fascinating dolomitic rock forms.

173

Hotels

Arlempdes, 43490 Haute-Loire £

DU MANOIR   Tel: 71.57.17.14

The setting is the thing here—in the middle of a tiny, peaceful village nestling at the base of a cauliflower-shaped mound of volcanic stone topped by a ruined castle, and peering down vertiginously at the infant Loire. The hotel, a square three-storey grey building, is very simple, but it's friendly and competently run; there's a rustic, stone-walled dining room, a very plain and simple bar and a small terrace. Bedrooms are small and clean, with two-star views. Food is simple and plentiful, well prepared, and excellent value.

Closed Nov to Feb; 16 bedrooms; no lift.

Besse-en-Chandesse, 63610 Puy-de-Dome ££

LES MOUFLONS   Tel: 73.79.51.31

Few hotels have less atmosphere than Les Mouflons, and there are more attractive (and probably lively) ones in the medieval centre of Besse. This modern chalet block, a few hundred yards on the way out of town, is bright, spacious and clean; and M. Sachapt has won a reputation for one of the best tables in Auvergne—excellent fish specialities, very moderately priced (like the Auvergne wines). Bedrooms are uniformly and irreproachably adequate; many have balconies.

Closed Oct to May; 50 bedrooms; no lift.

Chamalières (near Royat), 63400 Puy-de-Dôme £££

RADIO   Tel: 73.30.87.83

There have been changes at Michel Mioche's hotel. All is newly done up in pure art deco—mirrors, cane, and lace tablecloths in the golden restaurant, black and grey salon with well-chosen *objects*, and bedrooms now stylish and comfortable. The restaurant, however, remains one of the finest in the region; the *carte* still features *suprême de turbot Président Valéry Giscard d'Estaing* (a regular visitor); and the service is still very good. The task of choosing dishes is made difficult by the number of exciting options available.

Closed mid-Nov to Feb (rest Sun dinner and Mon); 27 bedrooms.

Laguiole, 12210 Aveyron £££

LOU MAZUC   Tel: 65.44.32.24

Laguiole is a minor town on a minor road which links the Auvergne to the Lot valley, and lies near the medieval pilgrimage route from Le Puy to Moissac. It's unexceptional in every way except one: in a modest town-centre hotel, young Michel Bras has established one of the best restaurants in France. Perhaps because he is far from modern tourist routes, or perhaps because he is not a household name (at least, not yet), Michel's prices seem ridiculous compared with those of the other great chefs; all the more reason to rush now, to sample his outstanding fixed-price menus, his far-from-humble Rouergue country dishes (*tarte aux cèpes et à la crème de noix, tripous Rouergats, cou de canard farci*), his wonderful light *nouvelle* creations (*filet de lapin rôti aux truffes, ris d'agneau sautés avec crème au parfum de gyromitres et feuilles d'épinards, croustillant de lard au saumon et à l'oignon confit*) and his extraordinary desserts. After this, you probably won't bother with the cosy modern salon, or notice that your bedroom is comfortable. "*Je vous offre le bonheur*" says M. Bras; take up his offer.

Closed mid-Oct to Easter (rest Sun dinner and Mon, except low season); 13 bedrooms.

Meyrueis, 48150 Lozère   ££

LA RENAISSANCE and ST-SAUVEUR   Tel: 66.45.60.19 and 66.45.62.12

A totally charming 16th-century manor house in the village centre which has
been in the Bourguet family since 1720 and has been lovingly furnished and
cared for ever since. There's an elegant restaurant, and a lounge reminiscent of a
Victorian drawing room; some of the bedrooms are similarly atmospheric, others
more modern in style—all are comfortable. Nearby, the Annexe St-Sauveur, an
imposing 18th-century building with terrace over the village square, offers
simpler but hardly less charming accommodation; in summer it operates its own
good-value restaurant. The standard of cooking at the Renaissance is high;
menus offer both local fare (*salmis de pigeon, cèpes à la Cévenole*) and more
extravagant dishes (*fricassée de fruits de mer au coulis d'écrevisses*).

Renaissance closed Jan and Feb; St-Sauveur closed mid-Nov to Feb (rest Oct to
mid-May); 20 and 14 bedrooms; no lift in either hotel.

Montsalvy, 15120 Cantal   £

AUBERGE FLEURIE   Tel: 71.49.20.02

Two hotels compete healthily on the edge of an attractive old village in beautiful
country between the Auvergne and the Dordogne. This one, and its restaurant
Chez Yvonne, is better patronised by locals who drink in the bar (the village *tabac*)
and eat, heartily and very cheaply (*tripoux, potée auvergnate*) in the cheerfully
noisy, attractively rustic restaurant. The ivy-covered hotel is right on the road—
quieter and larger bedrooms are in the cottage annexe.

Closed mid-Nov to mid-Feb; 18 bedrooms; no lift.

Moudeyres, 43480 Haute-Loire   ££

AUBERGE DU PRÉ BOSSU   Tel: 71.00.09.84

Moudeyres is a remote village of beautifully restored thatched houses, set high in
rather unexceptional scenery. A charming Dutch couple have restored this former
farm, and have made no attempt to make the interior too plush; it's simple and
immaculate, with wild flowers, inglenook fireplace and splendid old dressers.
Bedrooms are fairly basic, with good shower rooms. M. Grootaert's cooking is not
confined to local dishes and is far from simple, as guidebook writers have
discovered; his menu prices reflect this (though they're still very good value).

Closed mid-Nov to Easter except Christmas and Feb (rest Tues and Wed out of
season); 12 bedrooms; no lift.

Prades, 43300 Haute-Loire   ££

CHALET DE LA SOURCE   Tel: 71.74.02.39

Exactly 500 km from Paris, but it could be 5,000. This lonely, rather scruffy but
not uncomfortable chalet is on its own beside the upper reaches of the fishy Allier,
looking out over a steep-sided valley lined with crags, boulders and tiny fields
with tumbledown drystone walls. If you stayed long, the ambience could become
oppressively peaceful; you are encouraged through the evening meal as early as
possible, service at the bar rarely lasts beyond a midsummer twilight, the sedate
clientèle (mostly regulars) is hardly talkative, and there is nowhere to go. The
food is unadventurous and inexpensive.

Closed Oct to April; 17 bedrooms; no lift.

The Pyrenees

Roquefixade

"A castle girt about and bound
With sorrow, like a spell" (Swinburne)

The Pyrenees

Rising gently from the Atlantic, falling steeply to the Mediterranean, the Pyrenees form a wall between France and Spain which soars abruptly to peaks of over 3,000 metres from the plains of Gascony in the north and Aragon in the south. Easily crossed at both ends, the wall's height is almost unbroken in the central section, where narrow passes are only a few hundred metres below the summits. Although the Pyrenees are significantly lower than the Alps, and no rival for them for the tourist seeking a picturesque contrast of pastures against summer snows and glaciers—they have only a few square miles of glacier compared with several hundred in the Alps—and although they are much less developed for winter and summer sports, the Pyrenees are much more than just a poor substitute for the higher range.

While there are climbs which demand the highest degree of expertise, it is possible for a tourist who is no more than energetic to make the ascent of one of the majestic of all Pyrenean peaks, the Canigou, which towers over Catalonia from just under 3,000 metres. Alternatively you can follow part at least of the hiking trail No 10 of the *Grandes Randonnées*, which joins the Atlantic to the Mediterranean, traversing the foot and at times the shoulders of the Pyrenean wall. For much of its course it's a magnificent mountain path within the bounds of the Pyrenean National Park, punctuated by inexpensive (and usually very simple) mountain refuges, bases for hikers and climbers alike.

The Pyrenees' lack of development (which is reflected in low prices) adds to their attraction for tourists who want no more than a bed and a roof, or just a campsite and a cheap wholesome meal. The high mountain areas are unspoilt, and in most cases unscarred by the cable-car pylons that go with Alpine development. There are very few high resort villages; though this means that in many places walkers have to climb through wooded hillsides rather than from a cable-car or hotel above the tree line, it does not mean that the mountain range is remote and inhospitable.

Right across their breadth the Pyrenees are characterised by low valleys that cut deep into their heart. The arrangement of parallel steep-sided valleys running north/south from the peaks to the plain makes communication from east to west time-consuming. Where there are roads running laterally, as it were, to link valleys, they are usually slow and narrow, and by comparison with the Alps do not present many dramatic views. The Pyrenees are not ideal mountain territory for those who wish to get their enjoyment from a car or from a cable-car.

The valleys are well watered, except at the eastern end of the range, and fertile. They have always sheltered pastoral communities, which have existed often without much communication from valley to valley, but with more links across the range with the Spanish side. Many of the valley folk lived for centuries unaffected by national politics, and for practical reasons they were granted the right to look after themselves in accordance with their own local laws, and remained exempt from national taxes. They settled territorial disputes amicably with their neighbours, agreed transhumance rights and routes for their migrating flocks which spent the

The Pyrenees

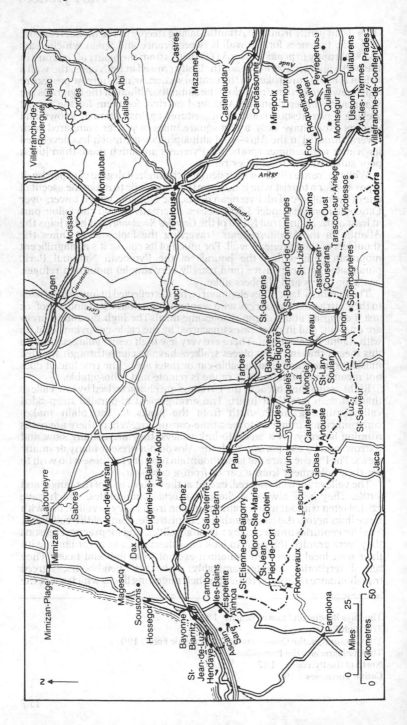

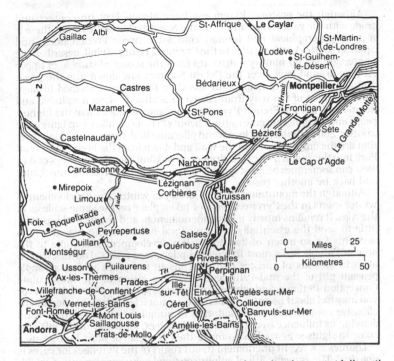

winters in the plains, and generally appear to have lived a rustic idyll until the age of asphalt brought the benefits of civilisation. Andorra survives at least administratively as the last of these independent high mountain areas, with its jealously guarded local laws and its effective autonomy vis-à-vis the two theoretical overlords, Spanish and French. But such has been its success in exploiting its special tax-free status that its character has changed infinitely more than the other valleys, long gobbled up by France.

The relative isolation of all the valleys and the traditions of local independence have led to the development of very pronounced regional differences from valley to valley. The Pyrenees attract lovers of folklore, above all to the two separatist and non-French speaking regions which span the Franco-Spanish border at both Mediterranean and Atlantic ends of the range: the Basque country and Catalonia. Both regions are outstandingly interesting for domestic (Basque) and church (Catalan) architecture, and for language, local dances, sports and food. Like the Pyrenees themselves, both areas occupy more space in Spain and are more concentrated in human, economic and politically activist terms in Spain than they are in France, where Catalans and Basques are just a proud picturesque tourist-drawing fringe.

Regions of the Pyrenees are also sharply differentiated by the effects of the weather. Again, the Basque country—well watered to a fault—and the harsh dry mountain plateaux of Catalonia are the extremes. The Atlantic, which brings all the rain, extends its lush influence more than half way across the range; the eastern area is the driest and sunniest corner of France. The high modern resort of Font-Romeu, with 3,000 sun hours a year, has a solar oven.

Although the pastoral Pyreneans have always kept up contact and trade with the valley inhabitants on the Spanish side of the range, there is a great geographical and human contrast between French north and Spanish south. A recent guide to the Pyrenees, Henry Myhill, described the impression left on him by a drive up from the scorched stubble of Upper Aragon around Jaca, over the Col du Somport and down into the green and damp foothills of Béarn: "in less than fifty miles, I seemed to have travelled most of the way from Africa to Scotland". Less hospitable and populated than the French Pyrenees, the Spanish ones have the highest peaks and areas of supreme natural beauty. The keen hiker can ignore the frontier, and in the steps of locals and pilgrims climb through the high *ports* that are the only breaches in the wall and down from the French National Park into the Spanish one. The driver too will find that the journeys east to west can sometimes be most quickly accomplished by crossing into Spain, and back by another pass.

Although the mountains are very snowy in winter, the development of winter sports in the Pyrenees has not taken place on the same scale as in the Alps. It remains mostly a local phenomenon, and cheap, and has done little to spoil the essentially quiet pastoral nature of the region which accounts for so much of its charm. But development has come to the area of Catholicism's most frequented pilgrimage resort, Lourdes, which attracts millions of *curistes* and pilgrims to the place where a simple peasant girl of the mid-19th century saw a vision of the Immaculate Conception 18 times, and where a miraculous spring appeared. Whatever you may feel about Lourdes – and there are not a few who consider it to be offensive commercialised exploitation of human weakness – there is no denying its influence over the central Pyrenees, for many of the pilgrims come to sightsee as well as to make their requests of saint Bernadette.

Lourdes is a recent phenomenon, but resort to the Pyrenees for cures is not new. The range is full of sulphurous and salty spas, many of which date back to Roman times. Most of these places are cheap and some of them are nasty. But until the development recently of a few modern sports resorts (Font-Romeu, Gourette, La Mongie) they have been the only places to stay in any comfort. Some of the spas are set deep in the mountain valleys and have developed into ski resorts as well; of these the most stylish by far is Luchon. The alternatives to spas or modern resorts are campsites, mountain refuges, and simple mountain villages which put up with tourists, but hardly put themselves out. Pyrenean villages have no more gaily colourful chocolate-box charm than the French Alps. They are simple, often basic, rough-stone communities—except in the Basque country, where the house-proud inhabitants whitewash their walls, and fill their window boxes almost as decoratively as the Tyroleans.

Tourist development is probably too recent to be blamed for the fact that the rare species of Pyrenean wildlife have become so rare that they cannot fairly be claimed as an important reason for the amateur to visit the Pyrenees. There are a lot of izards, the Pyrenean version of the chamois, and there are still large numbers of vultures. But the lynx prefers Spain, and there remain only a few dozen bears and eagles. It is not surprising that the bear has taken to the darkest forests and adopted nocturnal habits. More even than the wolf, it is the great scourge of the shepherd; bears still kill dozens of farm animals every year, and the National Park has to compensate the farmer.

The National Park, which runs in a strip along the high mountains of the border country in the centre of the Pyrenean range, is more reliably rewarding for the botanist, who can climb beyond the woods and cultivations to find gentians, saxifrage and edelweiss; and—more surprisingly perhaps—for the fisherman, who can pursue his sport in nearly all the many hundreds of Pyrenean mountain tarns under no more control than elsewhere in France.

As well as being such a naturally attractive holiday area, the Pyrenees have (for a mountain range) a unique wealth of historical and cultural interest. Prehistoric man painted the limestone caves of the Ariège. In the Middle Ages, Arab domination of much of Spain meant that the Pyrenees were the natural border between Europe and Africa, between Christian and Infidel. The first glorious chapter of the crusading epic of the Middle Ages was written on the basis of what was actually an insignificant ambush of Charlemagne's rearguard by Basque marauders in the Pyrenean valley of Roncevaux in 778. In epic poetry this became a heroic victory for chivalrous Christian prowess and sacrifice over the Saracens, achieved by Charlemagne's legendary nephew Roland. An angel had provided Roland's magic sword Durandal, and with it he had conquered Anjou, Brittany, Poitou, Maine, Normandy, Provence, Aquitaine, Lombardy, Romania, Bavaria, Flanders, Burgundy, Poland, Constantinople, Saxony, Scotland and England. Having resisted the Saracen attack at Roncevaux the invincible Roland split his temples blowing his own trumpet to summon Charlemagne, and to prevent Durandal getting into Infidel hands, he tried to break the sword before he expired, smashing Durandal repeatedly against a rock. He only managed to break the rock—which is why many a cleft in the mountains is called Roland's Breach, however remote from Roncevaux (there is even one in the Massif Central). Throughout the Middle Ages, pilgrims flocked across to Roncevaux, planting crosses on the hill where Charlemagne had done so. The pilgrims were on their way from all over Europe to Santiago (St James) de Compostela in north-west Spain, and the routes converged in the Pyrenees. From all this transit traffic, there is still a wealth of beautiful pilgrimage churches great and small (the most notable are St-Sernin in Toulouse and St-Bertrand-de-Comminges).

The Mediterranean Pyrenees, Spanish and French, are also an exceptional hunting ground for the admirer of Romanesque churches. Even without pilgrims Romanesque art would have flourished in the area, for in the 11th and 12th centuries Toulouse was the capital of a civilisation of great refinement and cultural brilliance, where influences from east and south mingled to fascinating and fruitful effect in poetry and sculpture. Under the influence of the Arabs there was none of the passionate bigotry common in medieval Europe—women had rights of property, the feudal hierarchy was very loose, and many towns governed themselves. The counts of Toulouse welcomed Jews and Arabs and, to their ruin, those Christians whose beliefs deviated from Roman orthodoxy but who were well suited to the social fabric and temperament of the south-west. The beliefs of these Cathars, or Albigensians as they came to be called, implied such fundamental criticism of the church establishment and gained such widespread acceptance in all layers of the Languedoc society (as they did not in other areas of France) that Rome had to launch a crusade, to crush the heretics and bring south-western France into the doubly fortified fold of Roman church and French monarchy. Facing the organised might and greed of feudal France, the pacific sophisticates of Toulouse could not defend themselves; the Cathars retreated to remote rocky strongholds, which today stand ruined and impressive, many of them not easily conquered by the tourist even without defenders. They are dramatically evocative tributes to no less than three-quarters of a million inhabitants of south-western France massacred indiscrimately by their compatriots in the name of God. The crusade eventually crushed the heretics and, thanks to the opportunity it provided, the French monarchy took control of most of south-western France as early as the 13th century.

The Pays Basque and Lower Béarn

The Basque country is one of the most colourful, attractive and fascinating of all France's fringe areas. It is an intimate small-scale landscape, characterised by low-rise Pyrenees which near the coast are hardly more than grassy hills, very green and well watered by the winds that blow in from the Atlantic. The countryside is enhanced by the sparkling whitewash and the rust-red painted timbers and shutters of the solid squat Basque houses, which give the countryside a neatness more characteristic of Switzerland than France or Spain. Like the Pyrenees, most of the Basque country is in Spain. The French part consists of three of the seven provinces: the Labourd, prettiest and most typically Basque; the Basse Navarre, and the Soule. The Basque mountains in the Basse Navarre and Soule are densely forested and relatively deserted. The coastal area is full of small farms and villages, but unlike the Spanish Basque country neither industrialised nor an active political volcano.

Compared with some half-million Spanish Bascophones, there are only about 50,000 in France who speak one of the least comprehensible and least understood languages in the world, one full of recurring combinations of unlikely consonants and of which, it is said, the Devil only mastered three words after seven years' study.

Like so many other proud fringe ethnic groups the Basques are fiercely religious, family orientated and traditionalist, and their ritual of local folklore, arts and crafts is carefully maintained. They have a particular cult of the dead, whom they commemorate with curious little round gravestones, carved with a Basque cross thought to be a Hindu motif. They have their own dances, masquerades, left-over medieval mystery plays or *pastorales*, their own musical instruments (a three-hole flute and a little drum called a *ttun-ttun*), their own costume—the Basque beret and the *espadrille* have spread far beyond the confines of the Basque country in popularity—and their own sport. The famous pelota is not one game, but many different varieties based on the old *jeu de paume*, sometimes played against the characteristic round-topped *fronton* wall which stands next to the church at the heart of so many Basque villages. When played at high standard, it is a marvellous game to watch, even if the subtleties of the rules escape you.

The Béarn isn't such a conspicuously individual area nowadays, but was an important political unit in the Middle Ages, maintaining its independence of the French and Spanish crowns until Henri, king of Navarre and lord of Béarn, became king of France in 1589. He brought as he said France to Béarn, rather than Béarn to France, a distinction which was maintained in law until 1620. Henri turned out to be a far-sighted statesman, and the most beloved of all French kings. On religious issues which had torn the country apart for decades, he was an example of good sense and compromise when all around was intransigence. His Edict of Nantes confirmed the right of the Protestants to freedom of religious practice but could not itself solve the question of religious conflict. In a Paris street in May 1610, Henri IV was stabbed to death by a fanatic. Paris was grief-stricken.

Pelota, played against a fronton

The best place to start a visit to the Basque's south-western corner of France is **Bayonne**, a large town at the meeting of the rivers Nive and Adour. In the Middle Ages it was a port much used by the British for the export of wine, and is still very active—especially at carnival time (a week at the end of July) when there are bull-fights, dancing and folklore displays. The quais and bridges across the Nive are attractive, and so is the animated and arcaded shopping street, the Rue du Port Neuf, which leads up from the river towards the cathedral.

✳ *Cathedral* A handsome building of the 14th and 15th centuries with twin spires added in the 19th. The arms of England are on some of the keys of the vault, and there are some fine Renaissance stained-glass windows. There's an attractive 13th-century cloister, and behind the cathedral some of Vauban's ramparts survive among gardens and trees.
✳ *Musée Basque* One of the most facinating and best-presented regional museums in France, a reason by itself for coming to Bayonne. Varied collections illustrating Basque styles of furniture and interior decoration: local crafts, history and witch-hunts; and a section on pelota with many beautiful old *chisteras* (basketwork rackets).
✳ *Musée Bonnat* Like Granet in Aix-en-Provence, Bonnat was an unexceptional artist, but an exceptional collector who left his extremely high quality collections of paintings and especially drawings to his home town. Drawings by Dürer, Raphael, and Leonardo, paintings by Botticelli, Rubens, El Greco, Rembrandt and Goya. Also some of Bonnat's own works—and those of his more distinguished contemporaries, including Géricault and Delacroix.

The main attraction of the interior of the Labourd is the green and peaceful countryside, and the pretty little typical Basque villages. There is none prettier nor more typical, nor pleasanter as a place to stay, than **Sare**, which has a 17th-century arcaded *mairie*, a *fronton*, and, in the church, wooden galleries for men (a typical Basque feature). Other places with a variety of accommodation are **Aïnhoa**, **Espelette**, and **Ascain**. Between Ascain and Sare there is rack railway up to the top of the main peak of this

183

bumpy landscape, the 900-metre **Rhune. Cambo-les-Bains** is an attractive, very flowery spa resort.

East of Cambo you can visit the caves of **Oxocelhaya** and **Isturits**, interesting by the standards of the Pyrenees, if not those of the Dordogne and the Grands Causses. The upper cave (Isturits) consists of excavations and evidence of the presence of early man, the lower cave is full of concretions and becomes very crowded with visitors.

St-Jean-Pied-de-Port was one of the important through-towns of medieval Europe, the place where several different pilgrimage routes to Santiago de Compostela converged on their way through the narrow low pass to Roncevaux and Spain. The road which goes through now is not the one which Roland and the rear-guard used to go across to Spain, and through which Roland never returned—that was the Ports de Cize route, now only open to walkers. Churches of the area around St-Jean still show the characteristic shell motif which was the emblem of the Compostela pilgrimage (and which gave its name to *coquilles St-Jacques*). St-Jean is an attractive little town beside the Nive, with a citadel and some 15th-century ramparts. It is a busy base for travellers and an attractive place to stay. To the south-east is the dense **Iraty forest** which has some of the finest beeches in the country, but no longer eagles and bears.

St-Etienne-de-Baïgorry is a little village of pinkish-stone houses, several with inscribed door lintels. **Sauveterre-de-Béarn** is more substantial and beautifully set high above the right bank of the Gave d'Oloron. There is a ruined castle, and a 12th- and 14th-century church with a Romanesque door and carved tympanum. Below the village there are remains of a fortified bridge. The nearby spa of **Salies-de-Béarn** is famous for the salt content of its waters, nearly ten times greater than the sea.

Orthez, the capital of Béarn up to the 15th century, is a town of grey houses and brown tiled roofs. It too has an old fortified bridge with four Gothic arches and a single defence tower. In the busy through-town of **Oloron-Ste-Marie** are two churches of distinction: Ste-Marie has a marvellous Romanesque doorway within the porch, and a polished marble carving of the Descent from the Cross surrounded by delightful scenes from everyday life; St-Croix has a fortified tower, and a dome over the crossing which is supported by Compostela shell forms.

To the south and south-west of Oloron, the mountainous **Haute Soule** (also accessible from St-Jean-Pied-de-Port and the Vallée d'Aspe) offers attractive excursions. Much of the area is densely forested. The small village of **Gotein** has a charming church typical of the region with its three-pronged belfry. Up the Saison valley, the great curiosity is the **Kakouetta gorges**, a walk of a couple of hours or so between sheer cliffs covered in greenery, in one place only 15ft apart and over 600ft high.

The **Vallée d'Aspe** is long and narrow, wooded and green, and unfrequented despite the old pilgrimage route through to Spain over the Somport pass. A few miles off the road, the dead-end village of **Lescun** is an attractively rough high village in a beautiful setting of jagged mountains above the pastures. There is some simple accommodation and it is a good base for walks; there are guides for the more severe climbs, and a refuge near the village accessible by car. Those not on foot can go over the **Col du Somport** down into Spain and round back over the **Col du Portalet** into the Vallée d'Ossau—a splendid round trip.

Standing high above the *gave* (the Pyrenean for river) that bears its name, **Pau**, historic capital of Béarn, is a large and handsome town whose charms and those of its surrounding region seduced many of the returning campaigners from the Spanish wars of the early 19th century, who never made it back to England. Pau became a very popular British resort from the 1820s onwards. had the first golf course on the Continent (1856) and lots of other British horsey events and sports—there is still a fox hunt.

Winter is the best time to go to Pau to see its famous view of the Pyrenees, whose snowy peaks are strung out in a chain like a theatrical backdrop, some 30 miles due south of the Place Royale—such a privileged viewpoint that Dornford Yates, the popular novelist of the 20s and 30s who loved the area, termed it the Royal Box of the Pyrenees. The old part of Pau is dominated by its château, partly built in the 14th century, added to and redecorated in the 16th, and restored with rather too much imagination in the 19th. There is a guided tour round the interior, which reveals many splendid 17th- and 18th-century tapestries, and a lot of documentary and anecdotal information about Henri IV. Also in the château (a separate visit) is the local Béarn museum.

To the west of Pau, the suburb of Lescar also has splendid views of the Pyrenees from beside its old Romanesque cathedral, which has 12th-century mosaics in the chancel and beautifully carved Renaissance stalls.

The High Pyrenees

The most mountainous part of the Béarn and the Bigorre is the highest and most impressive part of the French Pyrenees. In the Alps the main massifs rise up in blocks; here there is a wall of almost unbroken altitude running along the Franco–Spanish border, with a few high passes or *ports*, formerly important trading communications but none now crossed by roads. Most of the highest peaks of the Pyrenees are behind this wall of frontier mountains on the Spanish side and can only be seen by climbers and walkers. This is the area for spectacular rocky amphitheatres—of which Gavarnie is the most celebrated.

The **Pyrenean National Park**, a strip of land along some 60 miles of national border between the Vallée d'Aspe and the Vallée d'Aure, is an area of supreme natural beauty, with hundreds of small high mountain lakes reflecting the granite peaks and the few small glaciers clinging to their sides. There are four main gateways with information centres, guides and walking trails; the most important is at Cauterets. The others are in the Vallée d'Aspe, the Vallée d'Ossau (Gabas), and the Vallée d'Aure (St-Lary). Within the park there are a number of mountain refuges, some easily accessible, others more remote and mainly used by climbers. One of the obvious attractions of the park is the very special wild life—animals, birds and flowers. You will almost certainly see the izard, and marmots, which have been reintroduced and flourish. Other interesting species survive in the Pyrenees not because this is their ideal terrain, but because they are simply in retreat; you are most unlikely to see a bear, civet, or lynx, but you may catch a glimpse of one of the few dozen eagles which nest in the Atlantic Pyrenees.

The Béarn's most spectacular valley, the **Vallée d'Ossau**, plunges due south from Pau into the heart of the mountains, where the Pic du Midi d'Ossau rears twin peaks like a mitre to a height of 2,885 metres—one of the most splendid components of the view from Pau. At the head of the valley, the **Col du Pourtalet** leads over into Spain, making it possible to do a magnificent round drive down to Jaca and back up into the Vallée d'Aspe via the **Col du Somport**. The Vallée d'Ossau doesn't start to climb or narrow until after **Laruns**, a busy market village, from which roads branch left over the **Col d'Aubisque** into the Bigorre.

There are good walking excursions in the wooded hills around, and simple accommodation in the small spas and villages, but the tourist should press on up the valley to **Gabas**, a simple base for excursions on foot into the National Park where the narrow valley opens out into green pastures around the *gave*. At the foot of the great granite colossus of the Pic du Midi there is a reservoir and a number of natural lakes, a mountain refuge and a campsite. From the skiing station of **Artouste** you can take a small cable-car excursion to the **Pic de la Sagette**, and from there a train ride to the **Lac d'Artouste**. From here an hour's walk through wild and grandiose scenery takes you to a mountain refuge; sensibly equipped, you can continue for another hour or two and gain the highest Pyrenean ridge accessible to walkers.

The **Col du Pourtalet** itself crosses the border and the mountain range at 1,792 metres and descends to Jaca via Biescas, which gives access to the magnificent **Ordesa National Park**, whose red marble canyon of Arrazas forms the back of the Cirque de Gavarnie. Unusually for the Pyrenees, a road joins the Vallée d'Ossau to the Bigorre.

The **Route du Col d'Aubisque**, up past the ski resort of Gourette, which has some summer acitivity, is a fine one. The Col—high by French Pyrenean standards (1,710 metres)—is impressively engineered to the east; the Tour de France passes here, and even when it doesn't the road is always full of toiling cyclists pushing themselves through the pain barrier. The road descends to the animated valley, resort and spa of **Argelès-Gazoste**, which has a lot of accommodation. Just south of Argelès, **St-Savin** has an interesting fortified early Romanesque church. Beyond lie the high mountains of the seven valleys of the **Lavedan**.

To the north lies **Lourdes**, for many centuries a strategic stronghold on the Gave de Pau, with one of the most powerful fortresses in the Pyrenees, which still stands, restored and impressive and housing an interesting regional Pyrenean museum. But there aren't many other old buildings, for Lourdes' fame dates only from the 19th century, when an uneducated and unhealthy young peasant girl had 18 visions of the Virgin and discovered a miraculous spring. Now over three million pilgrims and tourists come to Lourdes every year. There are 400 hotels, (putting it third after Paris and Nice) and 35 campsites. Its underground basilica is capable of holding over 20,000 people, the whole permanent population of Lourdes. These statistics, and the kind of commercialisation which goes with all pilgrimages places, will suffice to put most non-pilgrims off a casual visit. But whatever one may feel about shops full of plastic Virgins and miraculous water sold by the fluid ounce, there is no denying that Lourdes is a remarkable phenomenon.

The healing powers of the waters of Lourdes had such a profound impact on the humanity of France that it inspired the great observer and analyst of human behaviour, Emile Zola, to go there in 1892 to investigate the phenomenon for himself for a novel called *Lourdes*. He found hard facts about miracles difficult to come by, but he acknowledged that it would be a crime of *lèse-humanité* not to recognise the ray of hope that Lourdes gives to so many unfortunates: "I do not believe in miracles, but I believe in their necessity for mankind". Then as now Lourdes was a great commercial phenomenon; today it is no longer so conspicuously one enormous hospital ward, but an animated resort.

The nearby **Grottes de Bétharram** are extremely busy; chambers with concretions are visited by train and boat and even by a cable car which leads up to the entrance.

Long before Lourdes became popular, the Bigorre had been attracting visitors to the spas at the foot of the highest peaks of the Pyrenees; like Aix-les-Bains in the Alps they rose to fame and high fashion in the early 19th century, when curative travel became chic. **Cauterets**, whose popularity dates back to the 16th century, is the biggest and busiest of the centres. It doesn't seem to have much that is very old now, not even the average age of the visitors—for it is a lively and growing resort on the edge of the National Park, within striking range of the very high peaks and beautiful mountain lakes. In winter it is a busy ski resort.

Beside the road leading south from Cauterets, there are a number of waterfalls, particularly splendid at **Pont d'Espagne**. From here there's a choice of walks and climbs, notably up to the superb Lac de Gaube, beneath the towering Vignemale (3,298 metres) with its glaciers. You can take the puff out of the walk by going up on a chairlift most of the way to the lake. Another route takes you up the charming **Vallée du Marcadau** to a refuge, and to the lakes above. You can continue beyond the Lac de Gaube on the GR10, which leads to more refuges, mountain lakes and eventually, via a tough mountain route, to Gavarnie.

Luz-St-Sauveur is a combined spa resort and old village. It is smaller than Cauterets and altogether more attractive in atmosphere and setting. It stands in a beautiful isolated high mountain valley, which was for centuries a self-administering republic of communes with its own representative government and its own diplomatic relations with the high mountain valleys of Spain. The old village of Luz is animated without being hectic or spoilt, and well-kept, with whitewashed houses with slate roofs and wrought-iron balconies and a number of spruce little hotels. There is a curious 13th-century church, founded by the Knights Hospitaller, with a crenellated curtain wall, and a fine carved doorway.

South of Luz, the **Vallée de Gavarnie** ascends through a famous wilderness of chaotic boulders, described by George Sand as hell. Beyond the chaos is the most celebrated and most visited beauty spot in the Pyrenees, the enormous **Cirque de Gavarnie**, a deep majestic amphitheatre of mountain wall, towering above the valley floor. Waterfalls crash down from the north-facing snows in greater or lesser abundance depending on the season (spring is the most impressive). The five-kilometre donkey ride along the pebble track from the village of Gavarnie up into the pit of the amphitheatre is one of the classic Pyrenean excursions; thanks to the coachloads from Lourdes, the strings of animal transport do very good business. At the end of the track it is well worth walking up to the base of the great waterfall, which at peak periods drops over 420 metres without touching rock, and often brings ice and snow down with it. The *cirque* faces north and is best admired in the light of the end of the day. If the crowds along the track have put you off, you can return from the cirque by the stunning—but easy—high-level track which starts just behind the hotel. You can also get a marvellous view of the top of the cirque by driving up from Gavarnie towards the Port de Gavarnie—formerly a pilgrimage crossing over into Spain, but now the end of the road—and scrambling up the grassy but steep Pic de Tantes.

The **Cirque de Troumouse** is a more spacious amphitheatre than Gavarnie, and if somewhat less grandiose, it has the attraction of being much less frequented and accessible by car (toll road). From the end of the road, there are walks and climbs for all categories of explorer.

East of Luz the **Route du Tourmalet**—one of the most famous sections of the Tour de France—passes through the steeply enclosed old spa and new ski resort of **Barèges**, whose waters are said to be particularly beneficial for bone problems. There are several long and relatively easy walks, including the Montagne Fleurie, which as the name implies is good for botanists. The **Col du Tourmalet** at 2,114 metres is very high by French Pyrenean standards, and is empty and bare. From it there are hikes south to the Col d'Aubert and the Massif de Néouvielle (the GR10 again, which goes on through the lakes down to St-Lary-Soulan) and to the north a rough toll road which leads most of the way up the superb **Pic du Midi de Bigorre** (the last 200 vertical metres can be covered by cable-car in season). The panorama from the top (2,865 metres) is magnificent: they say you can see 1 per cent of the circumference of the earth (400 kilometres).

Beyond the Tourmalet the greener but still wide open and treeless landscape is marred by the ugly modern resort of **La Mongie**, at 1,800 metres the highest of the Pyrenean ski resorts. Things improve below La Mongie, though: the **Vallée de Campan** is wide and lush and full of farmhouses attractively roofed with thatch and stepped stones.

Turning north to Bagnères-de-Bigorre and Lourdes has nothing outstanding to commend it, except the **Grotte de Médous** (exceptional concretions and a boat trip on an underground section of the Adour, within the park of the Château de Médous) near the large and uncharming old spa and industrial townlet of **Bagnères-de-Bigorre**. **Tarbes** is larger still, and similarly avoidable for tourist purposes.

In contrast with the Tourmalet, the **Route du Col d'Aspin** is pretty and gentle, running between wooded hills, with magnificent views of the higher peaks behind. The **Vallée d'Aure** is rural and productive with substantial farms, fruit and maize. The villages are handsome, old and prosperous too, especially Arreau. **St-Lary-Soulan** (*soulan* means a slope exposed to the sun) is the main resort whose recent skiing development hasn't really spoilt the attractive old part and has added a lot of animation, winter and summer. Roads continue past the resort to some magnificent walking territory at the end of the **Vallée du Rioumajou**, and especially up

The Pyrenees

in the Massif de Néouvielle, where a series of 3,000 metre peaks are clustered more like an Alpine massif than the customary Pyrenean wall along the border. The road goes up to a splendid reservoir (**Cap-de-Long**) beneath the Pic de Néouvielle. There are lots of other natural lakes, but fishing is not allowed. Beyond **Fabian** a road tunnel has been cut through the mountains to Bielsa and Spain which gives access to the superb Cirque de Barosa, which forms the back of the Cirque de Troumouse. On the GR10, there are interesting churches at Vieil Aure, and at Bourispe.

From Arreau a pleasant though unspectacular road leads over the **Col de Peyresourde**, past some attractive 11th and 12th century churches at St-Pé, Cazaux and St-Aventin, the last particularly beautiful with twin towers, a carved marble doorway and 12th-century ironwork choir screen.

Luchon is the most lively and fashionable of Pyrenean spas, much the most attractive as a base for excursions and well situated exactly half-way across the range. It is set in a wide flat bowl, surrounded by mountains. Its waters, the most radioactive in France, were well known to the Romans, who considered Illixo, as it was, second in curative quality to Naples. Luchon was never forgotten, but it was not really launched as a fashionable spa until the early 19th century. When Arthur Young went in 1787 he wrote "the present baths are horrible holes, the patients lie up to their chin in hot sulphurous water which with the beastly dens they are placed in one would think sufficient to cause as many distempers as they cure. They are resorted to for cutaneous eruptions".

Nowadays Luchon is a spacious and almost stylish resort, with lively cafés, elegant shops and hotels leading up to the thermal establishment and gardens.

Excursions from Luchon

✳ **Superbagnères** A ski resort on a high grassy plateau. Superbagnères is hardly more than one huge Edwardian hotel, but commands magnificent views over to the highest Pyrenean peaks on the Spanish side of the border, and is very popular for hang-gliding. Well worth visiting just for the drive, a steep and beautiful climb.

✳ **Vallée du Lys** Beautiful mountain views from a flat and pretty valley. From the end, long walks up to wooded *cirques* with waterfalls. Worth the drive even if you don't walk.

✳ **Hospice de France** The classic Luchon excursion, an old pilgrimage route up to an old hostelry among pastures, woods and waterfalls, whence a long walk up a mule track past mountain lakes to the frontier **Port de Venasque** (at 2,448 metres the lowest point of the frontier around here). From the Port, sublime views of the Spanish Pyrenees. The road up to the Hospice de France is not open all the way and the excursion is not worth doing unless you are going on a long walk.

✳ **Lacs d'Oô and d'Espingo** Walk up with many other tourists to the splendid mountain lake of Oô (about 1½ hours from the car park); to escape the crowds continue for another 1½ hours up to the refuge near the Lac d'Espingo, whence paths go on round to Superbagnères. Not an excursion for the car-bound.

Valcabrère

The Comminges, the Couserans and the Pays de Foix

North of Luchon the Pique runs into the Garonne, the great river of south-west France, whose upper valley is the centre of the region of **Comminges**. Its most important settlement in the Roman era and in the Middle Ages was the isolated hill dominating the wide green valley where the Romans built a city called Lugdunum Convenarum, and where a 12th-century bishop of Comminges, soon to be St-Bertrand, built a magnificent cathedral which became a port-of-call for pilgrims on their way to Spain. Much of the church of **St-Bertrand-de-Comminges** was rebuilt in the late 13th and early 14th century. Of the Romanesque cathedral the westernmost part (belfry and carved west doorway) survive, as well as three sides of the cloister, full of relief sculptures and carved capitals of exceptional beauty, and with its south gallery open to the wooded hillsides. The rest of the church (guided tour—well worth while) is Gothic and later, and contains a wealth of beautiful works of art: Renaissance stained glass, 16th-century wooden choir stalls whose carving is full of life and fun, and an organ which sounds as good as it looks (there is an organ festival every July).

The *cité* is picturesquely huddled within old walls around the feet of the great church which dominates miles of the surrounding landscape. At the foot of the hill, the archaeological site of the Roman city has been excavated; beyond it, the Romanesque church of **Valcabrère**, with its golden stone and red tiled roofs, its square belfry standing above the cypress trees, in a landscape of almost Umbrian tranquillity, forms a delightful contrast with the majestic pilgrimage church on the hill.

To the east of the Comminges, the eighteen valleys of the **Couserans** seem relatively gentle, wooded, unfrequented and pretty. Until quite recently, the different valleys were all very isolated and maintained their local traditions, dialects and costumes (including clogs). The most attractive villages are south of Castillon-en-Couserans, in the **Vallée de Biros** and the **Vallée de Bethmale. St-Girons** is the main market town of the Couserans, and nearby run-down **St-Lizier** its traditional religious centre, with a 12th-century former cathedral in the shadow of an ugly and dominant bishop's palace. The church has an octagonal belfry in the style of Toulouse, frescoes and two-storey cloisters of simple beauty.

The most attractive route eastward, unless you are in a hurry, is the Massat road to Biert, then the D18 over the **Col de la Crouzette** and the **Col de Péguère**. From here a short walk takes you to the **Sommet de Portel**, which despite its modest altitude gives marvellous views of the mountains to the south and the seemingly infinite plains extending northwards.

The limestone hills of the Ariège, as the old **Pays de Foix** is now called, are rich in caves and in minerals. The Vicdessos valley was centre of iron production and because of the industry lost most of its forests for burning. The area has a harsh history—its rocky spurs still bear the broken crowns that were the last refuges of the Cathar heretics in the 13th century. **Foix** is the main town of the region, overlooked by the three towers of its castle standing on a rock above the town (to be admired rather than visited). Foix is not an especially attractive place, busy with traffic on the way south to Andorra; but to its south and east lie some of the area's finest caves and Cathar fortresses.

Excursions from Foix

✱ **Grottes de Niaux** (near Tarascon-sur-Ariège) One of the three great painted caves in Europe (the others are Lascaux in the Dordogne, and Altamira in Spain). Unlike Lascaux Niaux is open to visitors, but numbers are strictly limited and you may have to reserve a place several days in advance. You scramble along half a mile of galleries to the huge *salon noir*, a sanctuary whose rounded apse is decorated with a marvellous array of beasts—bison (one known as the Mona Lisa, because his eye follows you everywhere), deer, ibex, horses. Mostly drawn in dark outline with occasional ochre-red highlights, they're not as brilliantly colourful as Lascaux, but viewed by the single light held by the guide, the magical beauty and above all the vitality of the paintings (about 15,000 years old) is irresistible.

✱ **Lombrives** (Tarascon-sur-Ariège) Grottoes connecting with Niaux, but accessible from the spa of Ussat, where information about visiting should be sought. Only one visit a day, which lasts several hours; long and often treacherously slippery galleries and chambers, with concretions including one astonishing mammoth-like mass of stalactites and a chamber called the cathedral, covered in graffiti.

✱ **Underground river of Labouiche** (north-west of Foix) A magnificent underground boat trip (over an hour) past splendid well-lit concretions.

✱ **Mas d'Azil** Speleology for the motorist. The Arize has carved an enormous tunnel through it, and the N119 (from St-Girons to Pamiers) follows the river. You can get out of the car to visit an audio-guided maze of galleries and chambers in which man sought refuge from pre-Magdalenian times to the religious wars. The wall paintings are not on display, but many of the finds from the galleries are, including 21 bear skulls.

Cathar Fortresses

The Albigensian crusade, when northern French Christians slaughtered southern French Christians, is one of the more bloody and dramatic episodes of medieval history. The Cathars (the word, like catharsis, comes from the Greek for pure), or Albigensians as they came to be called, held Christian beliefs irreconcilable with Roman orthodoxy. They rejected the value of the sacraments of baptism and marriage, and did not believe in the concept of grace being dispensed or sold by a chosen priesthood but rather in salvation being earned through a series of reincarnations. The Cathar *parfaits*—priest or "perfect man" as the minority of mystical and ascetic initiates were known—set a shining example of goodness without making excessive demands on the mass of simple believers. By emphasising that life on earth was life in the kingdom of the Devil—in fact, Hell—they removed the fear of punishment in an unknown afterlife.

Cathars were hardworking and did not forbid the lending of money for interest, so the beliefs were well received among the merchant classes. They were also welcomed by the nobility of the traditionally tolerant south-western France, where people of all creeds and nationalities including Jews and Arabs lived harmoniously together, and where women enjoyed a remarkable degree of emancipation by comparison with France of later centuries. There were *parfaites*, many of them noblewomen. By the end of the 12th century there were four Cathar bishops, at Albi, Toulouse, Agen and Carcassonne.

The beliefs of the Cathars implied such fundamental criticism of the church establishment (effectively denying it any role in human salvation) that Rome decided on a crusade to crush the heretics. The crusade became an excuse for the king of France and the nobility of northern France to go land-grabbing in the south. In exchange for 40 days' service, the crusaders were promised the cancellation of all their debts, and the remission of all their sins past and future. On July 22nd 1209 they descended on Béziers to make an example of the city, and when someone asked the abbot of Cîteaux whom to kill he replied in a celebrated formula "kill them all, God will know his own". The indiscriminate massacre of Béziers persuaded most of the nobility of Languedoc not to resist. The formidable fortress of Carcassonne barely lasted a month of siege, affected by a lack of water and by disease. When the 40 days were up many of the crusaders went home; but the job was not done, for the hard-core Cathars refused to abjure their faith.

Pope Innocent III gave Béziers, Carcassonne and charge of the crusade to Simon de Montfort, father of the early British parliamentarian. In one place Simon de Montfort rounded up a hundred inhabitants, cut off their noses and upper lips, and marched them around as propaganda. At Minerve, 140 Cathars walked into the flames rather than recant. At Lavaur, 80 knights were slaughtered, the lady of the place was thrown down a well and buried under stones, and 400 people were burnt. All in all it is estimated that as many as 400 villages were wiped off the map. In the face of blatant territorial acquisitiveness, the count of Toulouse could not but make some resistance: together with the king of Aragon, he mustered an impressive force, but they couldn't agree on tactics and were slaughtered by de Montfort at the battle of Muret in 1213. Resistance continued though, and outside Toulouse Simon de Montfort was eventually killed. In 1224 there was peace, then a second crusade in 1226, and in 1229 the king of France got what he wanted—recognition of his

Montségur

overlordship in Languedoc. In 1233 the Inquisition was sent in for more bonfires. Over the whole period of the first half of the 13th century only one *parfait* is recorded as having abjured his faith. Then, in 1242 came an episode of murdered Inquisitors, and a nine-month siege of the Cathar capital of Montségur, which ended with 200 burnt martyrs. In 1271 Toulouse and Languedoc came under direct royal control in the absence of a male heir, and one of the most brilliant and refined civilisations that Europe had seen was extinguished.

East of Foix, you are in the heart of Cathar country. Because of the nature of the crusades, few of the Cathar castles remain intact for the curious student of military architecture, but they are evocative ruins usually in impressively inaccessible situations. At **Montségur** more than anywhere else the steep and apparently impregnable rocky hill hardly needed fortifications, and all that was built was a single keep and a walled triangular courtyard, which it is hard to imagine as having been the main centre for Cathars from the late 1230s. Even on its easiest side it's a steep half-hour climb to the citadel. There are other beautifully situated fragmentary fortresses at **Roquefixade** and **Usson** (reputed destination of the lost Cathar treasure) and more substantial remains at the former troubadour court of **Puivert**, in a wild romantic landscape.

South of **Vicdessos**, there are a few narrow roads, and climbs south into a very mild and unfrequented mountain area, the desolate valley of Montcalm.

After Foix, the main staging post on the road south to Andorra is **Ax-les-Thermes**, a spa known to the Romans (Ax like Aix being a corruption of Aquae) and also a modest ski resort.

The small feudal relic of **Andorra** is historically interesting as a phenomenon, and its landscape has a severe beauty, away from the main road—the average height of Andorra is over 1,800 metres and there are few trees. But it is no longer a remote place since the road was built over the mountains from France in 1931, and more than anything else Andorra is a duty-free-for-all, its capital lined with modern supermarkets. The road up from France is a four-lane highway, flanked by pylons and busy with tankers and lorries taking petrol and drink to Andorra, and cars going to bring it back. The French make regular journeys from as far as Toulouse to stock up and risk the spot-checks on the N20. In 1278 the Spanish bishop of Urgel and the French count of Foix came to a sharing or *pariage* agreement, to share the overlordship of these remote mountain valleys, and to respect their local laws and customs. Every alternate year Andorra pays a tribute of 1,920 francs to France, and 450 pesetas to Spain, in addition to 12 cheeses, 12 capons, 12 partridges and 6 hams. Andorra has laws based on no written code (capital punishment consisted of being pushed off a cliff on the Spanish side).

If you do choose to spend any time in Andorra, there are hikes up into the bare mountains, and some rough and charming Romanesque churches. In winter, it is a popular ski area for the budget-conscious and thirsty.

The Cerdagne and the Roussillon

French Catalonia is a transitional land, neither French nor Spanish, neither wholly Mediterranean nor wholly Pyrenean. It is in the mixture of influences that the charm of the region lies. The Canigou towers white-headed above the Roussillon long into the heat of the early summer in this the driest and sunniest part of France where cherries ripen before the end of April. The very numerous and very beautiful Romanesque churches reveal all sorts of fascinating influences from Moslem south and Lombard east (the Catalans were great merchant sailors).

The Cathar castle of **Usson** stands high above the river Aude which runs down from the high plateau of the Cerdagne to water the vineyards and fertile plains of the Languedoc. Before dropping down through forests and gorges the Aude crosses two high plateaux: the **Capcir**, sparsely populated and often bleak on the north side of the mountains, and the **Cerdagne**, a great suntrap on the south face or *soulan*. The Cerdagne is artificially and not at all neatly split by the national frontier which was established by the Pyrenean Treaty of 1659. The 33 villages of the Cerdagne were ceded to France but the largest, Llivia, considered itself more than a village and remains a little Spanish enclave a few miles north of the border.

The Cerdagne has become a popular summer and winter sports area thanks to the creation of the modern resort of **Font-Romeu** on the site of an old pilgrimage sanctuary. Around pilgrimage times the statue of the Black Virgin is housed in a beautiful chapel in the hermitage. The rest of Font-Romeu is new and less than beautiful, but lively and by Pyrenean standards very well provided with sports facilities. It was selected as the place for acclimatisation training before the Mexico Olympics, thanks to its altitude and climate—3,000 hours of sun a year. At nearby Odeillo the world's second most powerful solar oven reflects and concentrates the rays. Midsummer is not really the best time to visit the Cerdagne: the light is harsh and the plateau bare of snow and vegetation.

There are plenty of good walking areas around the plateau—around the **Lac des Bouillouses** and south of the attractive old village of Llo; and from the international railway terminus of **Latour-de-Carol** you can catch the narrow-gauge *Petit Train Jaune* which runs through the Cerdagne and steeply down to Vernet-les-Bains in the Conflent.

There is no more striking way of appreciating the height of the Cerdagne than to drive down from **Mont-Louis** to **Villefranche-de-Conflent**, a serpentine descent which demands concentration and patience. Villefranche is the key to the Têt valley, a strategic stronghold since the early Middle Ages. It has kept the walls that the great 17th-century fortifier Vauban gave it, and the towers, barbicans and fortress on a rock some 500ft above the town, reached from it by an underground staircase of 750 steps. Nearby **Corneilla-de-Conflent** has a Romanesque church with a curved white marble façade, and crenellations between a fortress-like belfry. Inside there are several Romanesque wooden Virgins.

Vernet-les-Bains is a spruce new-looking spa which became very popular with the British in the late 19th century. Its main attraction is as a base for visits to the magnificently situated **Abbaye de St-Martin-du-Canigou**, whose typically Catalan square and decorative crenellated belfry so impressively crowns a rocky spur that later Cathar fortress builders must have been jealous. The abbey was founded in the 10th century and after many centuries of dilapidation functions once again as a retreat. The abbey church has been restored to its beautiful rough-stone pre-Romanesque simplicity. The cloister too has been substantially and obviously restored and contains many beautiful carvings. To visit St-Martin, you can catch a jeep up the road from Vernet-les-Bains in the mornings, but for anyone capable of a moderately stiff half-hour climb it is much more satisfying to drive as far as you can (Casteil) and then walk up. A further ten minutes' walk is repaid by a splendid view over the abbey. Going in the morning means fewer crowds at the monastery, and a timely return for lunch in one of the several inviting little cafés in Casteil.

Towering above the rocks and woods of St-Martin is the **Canigou**, eastern bastion of the Pyrenees (2,784 metres) and to many eyes the most majestic peak of the range. Rudyard Kipling thought that the area, with its densely vegetated valleys overlooked by the snowy peak, was like the high valleys of Hindustan. The Canigou is now easily climbed, especially with the help of the Vernet jeeps which take you up along a forest road (practicable to cars in dry weather, but steep, narrow and rutted) to the Chalet Hotel which is about two hours below the summit. If you sleep there you can see the sun rise from the waters of the Mediterranean.

The Têt valley or Conflent is a particularly rich region for Romanesque churches, thanks in part to Villefranche marble, often veined with pink, but thanks also to the influence of the important **Abbaye de St-Michel-de-Cuxa**, founded in the 9th century, not far from **Prades** (an alternative departure point for the ascent of the Canigou and the site of an annual Pablo Casals guitar festival). The abbey church dates in part from the late 10th century and has many fascinating features: horseshoe arches, a pillar like a palm tree supporting the crypt, a tall and beautiful belfry and attractive roofs with red tiles. If you go in be prepared for a lengthy guided tour around what remains of the cloister (much of it is in a museum in

St-Michel-de-Cuxa

New York) which has columns of pink marble and capitals decorated with fantastic rather than religious subjects—an example of Arabic influence. On the sunny side of the Têt the handsome village of **Eus** basks on the hillside beneath a powerfully imposing church.

To the south of the great monolithic massif, the Tech valley or **Vallespir** runs parallel to the Conflent into the fertile Roussillon vineyards. In the severe scrub-covered hills beneath the two valleys stands the lonely, grey, windowless priory of **Serrabonne** (which means good mountain). The contrast between this forbidding exterior and the richly-carved pink marble tribune inside is a wonderful, calculated surprise.

The Vallespir is even drier and sunnier than the Cerdagne. It is full of orange groves and torrential gorges, and like the French Riviera it was patronised at the beginning of this century by artists including Picasso and Braque who divided their time for a while between Collioure and Céret. **Céret** is an attractive town with some accommodation, a modern art museum, magnificent plane trees, and all around an abundance of orchards—mainly cherries, the first to ripen in France. On the edge of town, a restored 14th-century bridge soars in a single span high above the Tech.

Until recently, the Vallespir was a relatively quiet dead-end, but a road now gives a passage over the **Col d'Ares** down into Spain, making it possible to do a round trip from Céret or from Argelès-sur-Mer up the Tech into Spain, to see the superb religious monastery of Ripoll—heavily restored like St-Martin-du-Canigou—and back into the Cerdagne and down the Têt. This is one of the most beautiful possible church crawls for admirers of the wholly admirable Catalan Romanesque. Apart from the churches already mentioned, the enthusiast should also include **St-Martin-de-Fenollar** (visit afternoon only) in the roar of the Costa's motorway, with brilliant and beautiful frescoes, and **St-Genis-des-Fontaines**, whose decorative, lively and very Arabic carved lintel with Christ and the Apostles, inscriptions and horseshoe arches, is France's earliest dated sculpture (1020). Both lie close to the main Céret/Argelès-sur-Mer road. It is also well worth visiting the abbey church at **Arles-sur-Tech**, which faces west—evidence of great age—and has a 9th-century façade, a charming 13th-century Gothic cloister, and a 4th-century sarcophagus, always inexplicably full of pure water. When the Roussillon became French, the old town of **Prats-de-Mollo** (pronounced Moyo) was fortified by Vauban, and the church, which retains its Romanesque belfry, was rebuilt in a curious semi-fortified Gothic style. For a break from churches, you can go for a walk of an hour or so through the impressively narrow and steep **Gorges de la Fou** near Arles-sur-Tech.

North of the Pyrenees

The slopes of the **Corbières** produce large volumes of wine and continue the chain of hilltop fortresses, which mark the heights like beacons eastwards from Foix to the Mediterranean. **Puilaurens**, **Peyrepertuse** and **Quéribus** are the most dizzily impressive of these, and like the ones in the Foix are closely associated with Cathar refuge from the 13th-century crusade—Quéribus was the last Cathar stronghold to fall, in 1255. These fortresses were not originally set up on their soaring perches to shelter heretics but as defences along a traditional frontier land.

The key point in the system and the mother of all these fortresses was **Carcassonne**, the biggest fortress in Europe, defending the invasion route to Toulouse from the sea. Carcassonne was surely a fortress for the Romans, and certainly one for the Visigoths, part of whose walls can still be seen. The fortified city put up a poor showing against the Albigensian crusade, lasting only a month. The fortifications of the upper town or *cité* were rebuilt and when the Black Prince came by and sacked the lower town he gave the *cité* a respectfully wide berth. In the wars of religion, too, the *cité* of Carcassonne, unlike the lower town, remained true to France and resisted all Protestant advances.

Like the other fortresses, Carcassonne's strategic role was played out by the 17th century, and it was used as a quarry until Prosper Merimée sounded the antiquarians' alarm in 1835. Some 15 years later, Viollet-le-Duc started rebuilding; the task continued long after his death. The great restorer himself said of Carcassonne: "I do not know if there exists anywhere in Europe so complete and so formidable a collection of defences from the 5th, 12th and 13th centuries". Thanks to his efforts, Carcassonne, the fortified acropolis, stands again complete as an unrivalled example of medieval fortifications, pointing its multiple warhead turrets skywards from the crenellations of its double system of walls; standing high above the large modern town it presents a tremendous silhouette from afar. For academic visitors, there is the interest of sorting out the works of different periods and the styles of defence which evolved to respond to different styles of attack. For all there is the enchantment of wandering down the grassy *lices* which separate the inner and outer walls and feeling the effect of the time machine. Inside the walls, the old town buzzes with tourist life, with a few attractive leafy little squares and restaurants for those who tire of wandering around. The part-Romanesque part-Gothic former cathedral of St-Nazaire has some marvellous stained glass and statues in the 13th-century choir; in its composite form and general impression the church is comparable with the Merveille of Mont-St-Michel. The guided tour inside the old viscount's castle—the keep of the whole fortress—is of relatively minor interest, but it does get you up onto the walls for splendid views.

The great red-brick city of **Toulouse** stands on a natural crossroads for pilgrims, merchants and waterways half-way between the Mediterranean and the Atlantic. In the early Middle Ages, Toulouse was the brilliant centre of a civilisation of scholarship and lyric poetry, which was crushed under the steamroller of the northern French crusaders. Toulouse is still one of France's big cities, at the centre of spacious, fertile and not particularly interesting plains. It is an exhausting place, horrific to drive around or park in, and lacking a particularly picturesque old town centre. But for the admirer of medieval religious art, Toulouse is not to be missed.

✳ *St-Sernin* The biggest and most splendid Romanesque church in Christendom and one of its great pilgrimage churches, containing relics of over a hundred saints and six apostles. The crossing supports a five-storey octagonal tower, there is a beautiful splay of little round chapels all around the apse and transepts, and marvellous sculpture decorating the doorways on the south side of the church. When Viollet-le-Duc restored St-Sernin, he took down much of the woodwork which framed all the reliquaries in the chapels around the choir and, as was his wont, painted the vaults. The effects of restoration have recently been removed, and the marvellous carved and gilt 17th-century woodwork put back in its place. The church is lit up to magnificent effect at night.

✳ *Église des Jacobins* An unusual Gothic hall church, externally severe, but bright and colourful inside with brick vaults of great complexity, supported by palm-tree pillars; a simple Gothic cloister and octagonal belfry.

✳ *Musée des Augustins* Superlative collections of medieval sculptures, mostly from Toulouse churches, in the words of the museum's guide "witness of a disaster, the fruit of systematic destruction of an inestimable patrimony". This included St-Sernin, whose cloister was destroyed in the 19th century, and the totally demolished church of La Daurade, which were the headquarters of the south-western school of Romanesque sculpture. Also very fine collections of Gothic religious sculpture and painting.

✳ *Musée St-Raymond* Exceptional collection of Roman statues, relief sculptures and mosaics.

✳ *Post-Renaissance Toulouse* Inheritor of Roman traditions. Toulouse was ruled until the Revolution by elected consuls or *capitouls*. The town hall or Capitol is a grand pink-and-white 18th-century building, looking over the busy central market square. To the south are many splendid *hôtels*; the 16th-century Hôtel d'Assézat on the Rue de Metz is the most palatially impressive.

Like the Quercy, the plains of the **Armagnac** to the west of Toulouse lie on the borders between the medieval lands of the kings of England and the kings of France. These green and fertile but not populous areas are characterised by large numbers of *bastides* or planned medieval villages, built by local churchmen, petty nobles or more important distant overlords to establish power bases and potential fortresses in these disputed and strategic regions. After the Albigensian crusade in the early 13th century the count of Toulouse built *bastides* all over his not very extensive remaining lands, and later in the century Alphonse of Poitiers started the arms race with the kings of England which built up to the Hundred Years' War. In 1200 Gascony had about 100 fortresses; by the early 14th century it is thought to have had about 1,000. Of all the *bastides*, one of the most curious and attractive is **Fourcès**, built exceptionally on a circular plan, its low houses with timbers and red-tiled roofs and arcades surrounding a central shady copse. Some of the *bastide* names were merely expressive— Ville Nouvelle or Montréal—others exotically enticing for prospective settlers—Grenade, Valence, Cologne, Plaisance. Many have uncompromisingly fortified churches; there are two fine examples south-east of Auch at **Lombez**, and at **Simorre** which has stalls and windows in the style, if not the brilliant profusion, of Auch, and owes part of its military appearance to the enthusiasm of Viollet-le-Duc.

Auch is the Gascon capital, standing on a hill beside the river Gers, and is the centre of production of Armagnac, France's oldest eau-de-vie, which became an export business when Americans boycotted Scotch during the War of Independence. A monumental staircase climbs up from the river to the central squares around the large pale yellow cathedral, which was built in the Gothic style from the 15th to the 17th centuries. The choir stalls are a masterpiece of oak carving which took over 50 years to complete; and there is a very fine series of Renaissance windows.

Hotels

Aïnhoa, 64250 Pyrénées-Atlantiques £££
ITHURRIA   Tel: 59.29.92.11

A spruce and typical Basque house—a former pilgrims' halt on the Santiago de Compostela route—at the edge of a typical Basque village, all red and green shutters, with a *fronton* by the church, set in lush, green, well-watered fields and low hills. There's an attractive garden, a few small civilised seating areas, and a large and dignified rustic dining room. Bedrooms are pretty, reasonably spacious, and also in rustic style—but modern, not ancient. The food is good: plenty of local dishes including the inevitable *piperade*, *jambon de Bayonne*, and *tripes à la Basquaise*; but there are many more inventive dishes to choose from, both hearty and light, including *pied de cochon en persillade*, a fine *foie gras mi-cuit*, *salade gourmande à la façon de Michel Guérard* and *ragoût de queues de langoustines au pâtes fraîches*.

Closed mid-Nov to mid-Mar (rest Wed dinner except July and Aug); 28 bedrooms; no lift.

Cambo-les-Bains, 64250 Pyrénées-Atlantiques ££
ERROBIA   Tel: 59.29.71.26

This traditionally Basque house is beautifully set in its own grounds (fine old trees, rhododendrons) well away from the town centre. There's no restaurant; breakfast is a pleasure in the garden with its pretty view. The small lounge is a panelled library with armchairs round its marble fireplace; upstairs the bedrooms are light and peaceful, their elegance rather faded but their old-fashioned style very comfortable. An utterly relaxing place to stay.

Closed Nov to Easter; 15 bedrooms; no rest; no lift.

Our price symbols

£	You can expect to find a room for under £15
££	You can expect to find a room for £15 to £25
£££	You can expect to find a room for £25 to £35
££££	You can expect to find a room for £35 to £45
£££££	You should expect to pay over £45 for a room

Hotels

Céret, 66400 Pyrénées-Orientales £££

LA TERRASSE AU SOLEIL   Tel: 68.87.01.94

The terrace is round the neat swimming pool in the garden of this chalet-style
hotel, set in the wooded Pyrenean foothills above Céret, only 7km from the
Spanish border. Indoors, its mixture of rustic chic and modern convenience is
comfortable but rather contrived. The small lounge areas by the bar are pretty,
and the beamed restaurant, with streamlined display-cases, is cool and spacious.
Bedrooms are well equipped, pleasant and impersonal. The cooking is reasonably
good, though not very original or innovative (*saumon à l'oseille, brochette de gigot
d'agneau, melon au Banyuls*); there's no fixed-price menu, and the *carte* is very
short. If you make up your mind early enough, you can order a lunch-platter for
the pool terrace; dinner is served until 9.30, which means that you can take
advantage of the many fine excursion possibilities in the area without feeling
rushed. Service is good, and friendly.

Closed mid-Nov to Mar (rest Mon and Tues lunch, also Mon dinner to non-
residents); 18 bedrooms; no lift; swimming pool.

Eugénie-les-Bains, 40320 Landes £££££

LES PRÉS ET LES SOURCES D'EUGÉNIE   Tel: 58.51.19.01

The world-famous home of Michel Guérard's *cuisine minceur* is an establishment of
many parts—hotel, restaurant, thermal clinic and health farm—all approaching
the ultimate in luxury. Empress Eugénie's 1860 spa hotel is still used and the
splendid new main building, with Scarlett O'Hara décor, is hardly less stylish. All
is set in extensive gardens, dramatically floodlit at night. You can (by prior
arrangement) join the internationally overweight on the various spa regimes and
live delicately "*grand minceur*", or relax and allow yourself "*grand gourmand*". M.
Guérard's food is prepared and presented with artistic perfection; his wife brings
similar taste and talent to her *mise en scène*, from the elegant salons to the smallest
touches in the sumptuous bedrooms. It's all utterly exclusive and correspondingly
expensive, but relaxed and friendly too.

Closed Dec to Feb; 36 bedrooms; 2 swimming pools; tennis; bicycle hire.

Gedre, 65120 Hautes-Pyrénées £

À LA BRÈCHE DE ROLAND   Tel: 62.92.48.54

The location of this hotel is useful for walkers and mere sightseers whose tastes
are simple and expectations not high—near to, but not in, Gavarnie, and within
easy reach of the Cirque de Troumouse. It's in the centre of Gedre village, set back
from the main Luz St-Sauveur road, with fine scenery all around. Renovations are
under way to improve the outside and reception. There's a comfortable lounge
area, and cheerful rustic dining rooms; bedrooms are comfortable and have well-
equipped bathrooms. Food is simple—a cheap fixed-price menu with very little
choice (*potage; civet de mouton* or *côtes de porc*; ice, fruit, cheese or cake) and a
short *carte*. Service is very friendly, even when busy.

Closed Oct to mid-Dec and between Easter and June; 24 bedrooms; no lift.

Llo, 66800 Pyrénées-Orientales £££

AUBERGE ATALAYA   Tel: 68.04.70.04

On the edge of a pretty village, this is a charming stone *auberge* which has been
converted from an almost derelict *mas*, and decorated with a great deal of flair by
the enthusiastic owners. There's a gravel terrace around the building, with views
over the village, a small and pretty bar area with open fire, and a narrow
breakfast room/lounge with upright chairs—rather lacking in comfort. Bedrooms
make up for the limited public areas—spacious, light and pretty, with floral
themes and traditional furniture, and attractive bathrooms. The dining room, too,
is pretty, in rustic style with flowers and piped music. Cooking is well above
average for the area. There's a reasonably-priced set menu with some interesting
dishes for the first two courses, followed by *chèvre chaud* or an excellent *fromage
blanc* with honey, and a rather dull choice of desserts; on the *carte*, there's an
abundance of game, big and small (*sanglier, chevreuil, canard sauvage, caille*) and
rather more tempting desserts.

Closed Nov and Dec, except Christmas (rest Mon, and Tues lunch, out of season);
10 bedrooms; no lift.

Mont-Louis, 66210 Pyrénées-Orientales £

MOULI DEL RIU   Tel: 68.04.20.36

This hotel, which takes its name from the small mill building just in front of it,
nestles in a hollow between the expanding village of St-Pierre-des-Forcats (3km
south of Mont-Louis) and the foothills of the 2,750m Cambre d'Aze. Its setting
isn't a rural idyll—modern ski chalets are now swooping down the hillside behind
the hotel (though the postcard which serves as its brochure is so out-of-date that
these do not appear, but instead there's a large rocky outcrop which has now
mysteriously disappeared). The hotel has been much extended and altered over
the years, in rambling fashion. It's now a large, homely, family guest-house, with
its own smallholding—ducks, chickens and vegetables find their way to the table.
The public rooms (restaurant, breakfast room and rather cramped TV lounge)
have an old-fashioned charm and rather eclectic furniture. Bedrooms are fairly
basic and worn, but at the same time quite stylish—heavy bedsteads, dark-wood
furniture; bathrooms are separated only by partitions and plumbing is quirky,
though some would find the defects endearing. Cooking is well above average for
such a simple place; there are several good-value fixed-price menus with a limited
selection of desserts; the house wine is cheap, quaffable, and forgettable.

Closed Oct to mid-Dec (rest Wed); 15 bedrooms; no lift.

Oust, 09140 Ariège ££

DE LA POSTE   Tel: 61.66.86.33

In the centre of a large village—sleepy except on Saturday (disco) night—in a
verdant valley surrounded by hills, the unassuming exterior of the Poste does not
prepare you for the delights of its little garden and swimming pool, and, more
important, the high standard of its cooking. Jean-Pierre Andrieu, following in the
footsteps of several generations of hoteliers, prepares light and interesting dishes,
some of which appear on the fixed-price menus. Choose a *flan de foie gras au porto*
or *ris de veau au Jurançon doux*, followed by a delicious *papillote de saumon aux cèpes*,
pintadeau au madiran, or a home-potted *confit de canard*, perhaps. For those without
time or inclination, there's a cheap *menu de l'automobiliste pressé*. Bedrooms are
pretty, in rustic style (some with old-fashioned bathrooms) and overlook the
garden.

Closed Nov to April; 27 bedrooms; no lift.

Hotels

Plaisance, 32160 Midi-Pyrénées   ££

RIPA ALTA   Tel: 62.69.30.43

A recently renovated old hotel on the main square of the little town. No grounds,
no lounge; simple clean bedrooms, some with balconies; and the deservedly
popular restaurant. Serious eating here, in an unpretentious room with flowers
but no frills. An impressive collection of old Armagnacs is stored in a vast
cupboard, and the wine list ranges from honest local *crus* to expensive heights.
Service could be better, but the *patron* circulates to supervise and chat, and
everybody has a good time. His food is regional cuisine in inventive hands.
There's a very cheap three-course *"repas rapide"* menu, which includes a glass of
wine; and two other fixed-price menus with no choice but interesting dishes; and
there are permanent and daily specialities (*civet de tripes d'oie, terrine d'aubergine au
fromage de chèvre, mousse de palombe, feuilleté de ris d'agneau aux cèpes*), all good
value.

Closed Nov (rest Sun dinner and Mon out of season); 15 bedrooms; no lift.

St-Étienne-de-Baïgorry, 64330 Pyrénées-Atlantiques   £££

LE TRINQUET-ARCÉ   Tel: 59.37.40.14

A white-painted building with red roof and shutters, Basque-style, most
attractively set on the outskirts of the village beside the river. There is a simple
lounge with brick fireplace and beamed ceiling, groups of chairs and a pile of
magazines. Last year a small but immaculate swimming pool was built, reached
by a new bridge across the river. Some bedrooms have balconies over the river,
others look onto the quiet rear garden; all are modestly comfortable, some more
spacious than others. The apartments are more plush than the bedrooms, with
modern furniture. The spacious dining room is rather plain; in summer the
terrace beside the swift water is a nicer place for meals. There are three fixed-price
menus (the cheapest consisting of *garbure, plat du jour, salade* and *dessert*). There
are local and classic dishes (*pipérade, salmis de pigeonneau aux cèpes,* and *civet de
marcassin à l'Irouléguy*) and son Pascal is trying out some new dishes (*mousse de
poissons aux anguilles de rivière*).

Closed Nov to Feb; 26 bedrooms; no lift; swimming pool.

St-Jean-Pied-de-Port, 64220 Pyrénées-Atlantiques   £££

LES PYRÉNÉES   Tel: 59.37.01.01

The busy tourist centre of St-Jean, one of the important through-towns of
medieval Europe, is hardly a restful place to stay, but it is a convenient and not
unattractive halt between the gentle hills of the Basque country and the higher
peaks to the east, or on the route to Spain (Pamplona is 76km away). Of the many
(mostly unremarkable) hotels in the resort, the Pyrénées is one of the oldest
(1729) and the best—if you are more interested in food than in the
accommodation. Bedrooms are small and distinctly ordinary (four new
apartments are being added); public rooms (small lounge and dark breakfast
room) dull. The restaurant, naturally, is the focal point. Young Firmin Arrambide
is the latest in the family line of distinguished chefs; while he remains loyal to the
regional cuisine of his predecessors, providing two little menus with all the old
favourites (*confit de porc, truite aux amandes* or *braisée au Jurançon*), he is the best
proponent of *nouvelle cuisine* in the area, and his skills are best demonstrated in
the two higher-priced, but not unreasonable, fixed-priced menus and on the *carte*.
*Les raviolis de langoustines au caviar, petits poivrons farcis à la morue, foie gras frais de
canard grillé sur un lit d'artichauts, chaud-froid de pêche blanche à la pistache* and a

renowned *grand dessert au chocolat* are a few of the tempting dishes. Provided you don't make the mistake of expecting *nouvelle* flourishes on his cheap menus, or a low bill at the end of your meal, you will not be disappointed.

Closed mid-Nov to mid-Dec and two weeks in Jan (rest Tues except high season, and Mon dinner Nov to Mar); 25 bedrooms.

Sare, 64310 Pyrénées-Atlantiques £££
ARRAYA   Tel: 59.54.20.46

A lovely old inn in a very pretty village, with a covered pavement terrace near the square and its *fronton*, and a secluded grassy garden at the back. The rooms have dark wooden beams, and shapely solid old furniture; everything gleams with polish and care. Lounge and bar are comfortably welcoming; bedrooms not large, but attractively planned and with excellent bathrooms. In the relaxed and rustic dining room you can order until an agreeably late hour. Cooking is very good: innovative, using local produce, game and wine (*suprêmes de pigeon sauvage, pipérade aux pluches de jambon de canard*), with more interesting vegetable accompaniments than average, and a few good desserts. There are two three-course fixed-price menus, the cheaper one very good value, and some very reasonably-priced local wines—including a house Rioja.

Closed Nov to mid-May; 20 bedrooms; no lift.

Ségos, 32400 Gers £££request
DOMAINE DE BASSIBÉ   Tel: 62.09.46.71

Beautifully renovated old farmhouse set in quiet countryside near the village of Ségos. Jean-Pierre Capelle is a talented chef, his wife Mayi has a flair for interior design; together, they've made a splendid retreat, decorated and furnished with great care and taste—uncluttered, blending stylish modern furniture and fine pastel fabrics with open fires and tiled floors. There are only a few bedrooms, spacious and pretty, which means that there's ample space on the shady terrace, in the large garden or by the attractive pool. The food is very good, but not cheap; there are two three-course menus, both with deceptively simple-sounding dishes (*un potage* was an extraordinarily tasty vegetable soup, *le poisson du jour* a turbot with creamy butter sauce, cooked to perfection); the *carte* is short. Service in the attractive restaurant (with Albinoni played in the background, perhaps) is very good. This is a superbly relaxing place to stay.

Closed Nov to mid-Apr; 9 bedrooms; no lift; swimming pool.

Sévignacq-Meyracq, 64260 Pyrénées-Atlantiques £
LES BAINS DE SECOURS   Tel: 59.05.62.11

A couple of kilometres off the main Laruns to Pau road, amid rolling hills and pastureland just north of the Pyrenees proper, this is a group of ancient farm buildings—neither modernised nor smart, but mellow and obviously well-loved. The focus of the place is the restaurant, simple and genuinely rustic (rare, indeed) with a vine-draped covered terrace for summer eating. Bedrooms are simple too, beamed and pleasant enough. The food is well above average for this area; it's basically good country cooking (excellent *garbure béarnaise* and *jambonette de volaille farcie*) with some lighter and inventive touches; there's just one fixed-price menu—very cheap, and excellent value—but here it's worth straying onto the *carte* which will hardly break the bank.

Closed Mar (rest Sun dinner, and Mon out of season); 9 bedrooms; no lift.

Hotels

Toulouse, 31000 Haute-Garonne   **£££££**

GRAND HOTEL DE L'OPÉRA   Tel: 61.21.82.66

A delightful hotel, right on the central square—Place du Capitole—with a
charming courtyard garden and tiny swimming pool. All except four bedrooms
face away from the street and are calm, well equipped (air-conditioning, TV and
mini-bar) and attractively decorated (fine quilted fabrics, painted bamboo
furniture, well-chosen lamps). There's a very comfortable lounge, a tented bar,
and a very pretty and intimate restaurant—lots of alcoves and small rooms. Food
isn't cheap; there are two small fixed-price menus, and an interesting *carte* which
features the hearty *cassoulet toulousain au confit de canard* as well as rather lighter
dishes. Lunch and dinner are served outside when it's fine.

Rest closed Sun, and mid-Aug; 49 bedrooms; swimming pool; no car-park.

Unac, 09250 Ariège   **£**

L'OUSTAL   Tel: 61.64.48.44

A simple and pretty *auberge*, in a quiet and attractive setting on the upper edge of
the village, with views over rooftops and the wooded valley. There's little in the
way of public rooms—the bar is actually the reception desk (which closes when
the staff have their meal), the TV lounge just a small room with an open fire and
very simple bench seating. None of the bedrooms has a private bath- or shower-
room—though the communal ones are spruce and spacious—but they're
reasonably sized and pretty. The food is good: dishes are interesting, generous and
flavoursome, if rather lacking in subtlety. Menu and *carte* are one and the same:
cost depends on how many courses you opt for (the more you have, the better
value you get). An appealing place to stay, in an area rather devoid of good
hotels.

Closed mid-Nov to Christmas and mid-Jan to mid-Feb (rest Mon from Oct to Feb);
6 bedrooms; no lift.

Villeneuve-de-Marsan, 40190 Landes   **£££**

DARROZE   Tel: 58.45.20.07

Villeneuve-de-Marsan is in the no-man's-land of the south-west, east of the
Landes, north of the foothills of the Pyrenees, and well south of the Dordogne. Just
to its east lie the fertile plains of the Armagnac region and the wine-producing
area around Madiran, distinguished chiefly by the preponderance of highly-rated
restaurateurs. In the centre of town, at the junction of several roads (traffic isn't
heavy as there's a bypass), this is an old and renovated hotel whose bedrooms
face onto a courtyard. The style is cool and sophisticated throughout—bedrooms,
restaurant and lounge. The Darroze in question are now Claude and Francis; the
late Jean established its reputation as one of the area's gastronomic highlights,
and his two sons are carrying on the tradition. There are two fairly expensive
fixed-price menus, four courses (plus *mignardises*) without choice but with
interesting dishes, and a tempting *carte* featuring several duck dishes (a *filet de
boeuf en chevreuil aux griottes* is the only representative of the four-legged
fraternity).

Closed last two weeks in Jan (rest Mon out of high season); 30 bedrooms; no lift.

The Dordogne

Castelnaud

"Meadows trim with daisies pied,
Shallow brooks and rivers wide.
Towers and battlements it sees,
Bosom'd high in tufted trees" (Milton)

The Dordogne

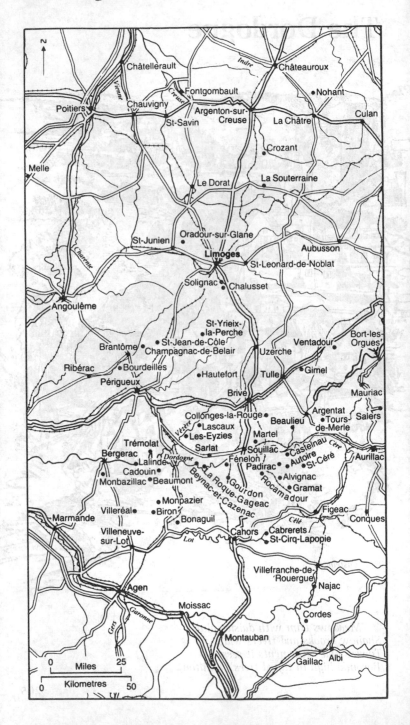

The Dordogne

Sandwiched between the plains of the Atlantic seaboard and the mountains of the Massif Central, a long slice of territory (the Massif's doorstep) is crossed by dozens of rivers—some large, many small—bearing the waters down from the mountains to the ocean. The only north/south communication which unites the area is the N20 from Orléans to Toulouse, one of France's most notorious trunkroads which winds tortuously through the hills of the Limousin and the Périgord and delays impatient travellers drawn southwards in the magnetic field of the Spanish sun. The greatest and most beautiful of the rivers crossed by the N20 is the Dordogne, which rises at Le Mont-Dore and runs into the Gironde near Bordeaux.

The Dordogne is a name often taken in vain; as well as the name of the river, it is a *département*, and it is the name given by British holidaymakers to a vaguely defined rural area around the river valley. The area covered by this chapter is much greater than even the most generous use of the term Dordogne should cover: it follows the N20 southwards from just below the Loire to the Garonne.

On the way, the northern areas of the Marche, the Limousin and the Creuse are rural and unspoilt but will probably not detain a southbound traveller for long. Instead, he may be tempted to tarry for a while on the banks of the Dordogne, to admire the beauty of France's best loved river; but he should not underestimate the dangers of so doing. About half a century ago a British man of the soil Philip Oyler set off southwards from Paris, not knowing exactly where he was going, following the sun. When he came over a hill and looked down over the wide Dordogne valley, suddenly "the desire to go south, farther south, was no longer there. I had seen the Midi and Mediterranean seaboard—its sunshine and its aridity, its lack of comforting greenery in the summer months— it compared ill with the panorama before me. I felt at peace, more than that, I felt at home. All was bounty and beauty, God-given, and man had not desecrated it. He had substituted his crops and his fruit trees for wild flowers and bushes; he had utilised the river to drive his water mills; he had felled trees from time immemorial as he needed them and filled up the gaps with seedlings. He had been wise enough to make return for aught he had taken. If anyone should desire earnestly to know how this earth of ours can be used to serve all the needs of man without being spoilt, he can go and see for himself."

The title of Philip Oyler's book about the Dordogne *The Generous Earth* captures the appeal of an area which has won a large and faithful following of British visitors and *emigrés* in the decades which have followed his writing so fervently of its great goodness. It is not an area where nature impresses itself with breath-taking spectaculars, as in the Alps or in the gorges of the Massif Central; nor has man forced nature to bow to his designs, as at Versailles; here man and nature have achieved an enviable relationship of mutual advantage. In few areas has man contributed so much to the beauty of the landscape. It is not just the warm golden stone and russet tiles of the old villages whose reflections sway on the languid waters of the river, which itself adopts the deep green of the surrounding hills; nor is it the abundance of old fortresses standing high above the river's course in memory of a far-off time when the Dordogne stood on the disputed edge of two kingdoms and when the fruits of its earth were easy pickings for under-employed soldiery. There is also beauty in the cultivation of the land which is of great variety; the small parcels of mixed vegetation give the landscape intimacy and the decorative charm of a patchwork.

The secret of success of the Dordogne rural economy, at least in the eyes of Philip Oyler, was that the peasants who have so much in their own back gardens have never tried to maximise their yield by concentrating on one crop, but have preferred the wealth and satisfaction of self-sufficiency to financial gain. The fertile valleys of the Périgord and the Quercy to its south produce great quantities of fruit, vegetables, cereals and nuts. Pigs are fed on sweet chestnuts which cloak the hills, geese are fattened to yield lusciously rich livers and the fat which, along with walnut oil, forms the basis of Périgord cuisine. There are vines all along the river, mostly for home consumption. Around Bergerac, where the Dordogne approaches Bordeaux country, the vine gains the ascendant and yields a noble red wine and the famous dessert white of Monbazillac. Bergerac is also the centre of French tobacco production and every Dordogne farmer grows and rolls his own. The self-sufficiency and independence of the Dordogne farmer extends even beyond the provision of his daily needs; produce is often sold not by an entreprenurial shopkeeper, but directly by the producer who takes the cash home and stores it under a mattress.

There are similarities between the landscape of the Dordogne and some of the most greenly attractive places in rural England. Philip Oyler remarked that the visitor "will look upon faces nearly all of which could be English; he will look upon a landscape that might remind him of the Wye valley around Tintern; he will also see all his familiar trees and also a few added, and he will find a similar temperament". He wrote of a time a few decades ago when the Dordogne peasantry was riddled with English surnames and Christian names, and when English words like cat, dog and country cropped up in the local patois. The French were 'they' who collaborated in the War and who tried to make 'us' pay to fish in our own rivers and to shoot on our land (and very often tasted the river or felt the buckshot if they came to try to enforce the law); the English were the old ancestors from the 13th and 14th centuries, and the people who flew in help for the wartime resistance which was at its most vigorous, and most vigorously punished, in the Dordogne. The people of the Dordogne were British, down to their very unfrench habits of getting drunk on Saturday nights and telling dirty jokes and neglecting the formalities of Gallic social life. Whatever the truth of these ethnological observations it is indisputable that English people have felt themselves, as Oyler predicted, at home in this area as nowhere else in France, and whereas for the French the Périgord is a region to enjoy for its many domed churches, its prehistoric cave paintings and its *foie gras*, for the English it is a place to inhabit, if only for a few weeks a year.

The Dordogne has, of course, been changed by its sudden use as a tourist and second home area. Houses and whole villages are being carefully restored and property prices have shot up. Crafts have flourished, both those which are associated with renovation of houses and furniture, and others such as pottery and carved wood, examples of which are sold directly (along with farm produce) from stalls by the roadside. You see large numbers of clearly British bicyclists, pottering along through the orchards on their heavy 3-speed machines, skirts billowing in the breeze; the area is nowhere near steep enough for the serious-minded French who take their many-geared racing cycles, their drip-feed water bottles, their salt tablets and their Peugeot T-shirts to more challenging regions.

Because of its charm the area around the river valley is relatively frequented, but not unduly so even in July and August, for the French do not come here *en masse*. In general the impact of tourism on the area is less profound than the density of GB and NL stickers in July (at Les-Eyzies or Domme for example) would suggest, for Dordogne tourism is not of the sun sand and sea variety; rather it is the tourism of those who follow in the footsteps of Philip Oyler, consciously or not, coming south to recharge the batteries by resting, seeking spiritual nourishment from the atmosphere of the Dordogne.

Because of its pulling power the name is often applied to places which are a long way from the river valley, where you may well have a relaxing and satisfactory holiday in a country cottage—as you may almost anywhere in rural France—but where you will not without a long commute see what the Dordogne has to offer. The popularity of the small area around the river valley is no reason to choose to go for a holiday to the "Dordogne" somewhere 50 miles from the river.

For the sightseer the Dordogne has more to offer than its picturesque crop of fortresses, built in most cases for defence rather than gracious living and adequately admired from without. Much rarer is the abundant evidence that early man appreciated these eminently hospitable river valleys, especially the Vézère, whose limestone cliffs are full of caves which offered shelter from the weather, the bears and the mammoths. Since the famous and momentous discovery of the skeletons of Cro-Magnon man in a rock shelter at Les-Eyzies in 1868, sepulchres, stone tools and ornaments have been found in dozens of sites and have yielded many, yet still only a few, of the secrets of early man's progress. The importance of the area is such that Dordogne excavations, like La Madeleine and Le Moustier, have given their names to different prehistoric eras. There are good prehistoric museums in Les-Eyzies and Périgueux to illuminate the darkness of most of our ignorance of Magdalenian or Aurignacian man of the Upper Palaeolithic (Old Stone) Age, about 40,000 to 10,000 BC. But probably of more interest are the cave paintings, drawings and engravings that have survived from this extraordinary period, when man did not merely refine his standard of living by making better tools to defend and clothe himself, he also left evidence of a developed spiritual and artistic sense. Cro-Magnon man crawled into the remotest networks of underground grottoes and by the light of a primitive oil lamp decorated nature's sanctuaries with images of the animals which threatened his life but on whose healthy abundant survival he depended as a hunting carnivore. The survival of these works of art is one marvel—thanks to a stability of natural conditions underground, which is so fragile that in many cases only a few tourists (and in one case none at all) can be allowed in to pollute the air; the other marvel is the quality of the paintings and engravings. It is easy to be sceptical of what in some caves looks at first glance like a mass of scribbles—successive artists often went over the same piece of wall several times—but when your eye becomes accustomed to the handwriting and the tricks of exploiting natural forms, you will be more amazed by the subtlety and life of the art than by its antiquity. The greatest find and the most regrettably inaccessible is Lascaux, discovered by some local lads who followed their dog down a hole in September 1940 and found not a rabbit but herds of bison, bulls, ibex, deer and horses in a multitude of brilliant colours. When they led the great prehistorian abbé Breuil to the place a few days later, he could only gasp in astonishment "It's the Sistine Chapel of prehistory". In less than 20 years the paintings which had survived in all their vividness for over 30,000 years showed such signs of irrecoverable decay that the cave was closed.

The sanctuaries which later man built for himself have not the power to surprise that the cave paintings have, but they are nonetheless fascinating. The Romanesque schools of architecture and sculpture of south-west France are the finest in Europe. Different regions of France have their own very distinctive variations of the Romanesque, and regional influences are swapped. The Auvergne and Poitou variations come outside the boundaries of this chapter but many of their features are shared in the Limousin, which is particularly noted for its elegant, octagonally crowned belfries and orientally scalloped doorways. Sculptors seemed to have travelled more widely than architects, and supremely decorative, stylised and similar carvings crop up all over the place, from Moissac in the south to Souillac on the Dordogne and St-Junien in the Limousin. The great speciality of the Périgord is churches with domes, not just over the main crossing but over every bay of the nave. Of some sixty of these churches which survive from the Romanesque age fully a half are in the Périgord.

Another curiosity of the region is the number of *bastide* towns between the rivers Dordogne and Lot, in the border country between the lands of the late 13th- and 14th-century French and English kings. Where the countryside to be defended was empty of fortresses or of villages on whose loyalty the kings could rely, Edward III and Philip the Bold built village fortresses on strictly geometric lines, not usually characteristic of towns surviving from this period. At the centre of the grid is an arcaded square and nearby a fortified church which served as the keep of the fortress. To encourage their loyalty the new settlers in the *bastides* were given enviable privileges and freedom—Villefranche is a typical name. Some of the most important *bastides* (such as Libourne) have had their particular character dwarfed by the later growth of towns, others have hardly grown at all (Monpazier, Domme). *Bastides* are not a phenomenon unique to this region—saint Louis' port of Aigues-Mortes in the Camargue was founded for much the same reasons and has the same unspoilt geometric medieval plan—but the scale of the dispute in south-west France which gave rise to the Hundred Years' War and the lack of natural fortresses along the border lands means that *bastides* are here in greater number than anywhere else.

Of all the delights of the Périgordian table the mysterious truffle is king. Not so much a crop as a precious stone which is mined, the truffle is an edible fungus which enjoys a symbiotic relationship not far below the surface of the soil with the roots of oak trees. The conditions of its healthy growth are not really known for sure, or if they are the wily Périgordians do not publicise them. Truffles are sniffed out by discriminating pigs and dogs (who are less inclined to devour what they unearth) weaned on truffles from birth. Occasionally gnats with a gourmet's appreciation for good smells can be seen hovering in thin columns above the location of a truffle, thereby helping a keen-eyed farmer to find it—an economical but unreliable method. Once unearthed, the truffles, like garlic, are or should be less noticeable when they are present than when they are not. Not a few visitors decide that the truffle is no better than a cunning peasant's trap for the gullible consumer eager to praise everything that is expensive for that reason alone—something of a Périgordian ginseng. But truffles are not cracked up to do you good, merely to delight your palate, and you will not find anyone who knows his food casting irreverent aspersions.

To the south of the Dordogne, the Quercy has caves, cave paintings, most of the region's *bastides*, and most of the truffles. At Cahors, there is what is considered to be the prototype for the domed churches of Périgord; at Moissac one of the most beautiful Romanesque churches in France; and at Bonaguil a medieval fortress finer than any of the ones that smile down like Narcissus into the Dordogne. But however impressive the list of points in its favour, the Quercy simply does not have the atmosphere of the Dordogne. In the south of the Quercy, between the rivers Lot and Garonne, the fruits of the earth are the best fruit in France, but the countryside is rather uninteresting. In the north the landscape is harsher: the limestone plateaux are in places barely covered by soil, and announce the bleak Grands Causses of the southern Massif Central where the porous rock is carved into enormous subterranean caverns. Even the river valleys are steeper and darker, less of a pastoral delight. The balance between man and nature is tilted just a little against man.

The Limousin

On its way down from Orléans through the Sologne and the Berry, the N20 is straight and monotonous. Travellers with more inclination to visit as they go may head south from the Loire to Loches and then join the Creuse valley to pursue the course of this very attractive river up some of the way to its source in the high Millevaches Plateau, east of Limoges.

West of Châteauroux lies the marshy **Brenne** region which is considered a hunter's paradise. Apart from game on the wing there isn't much to see, but on the north-western perimeter of the Brenne you can visit the **Château d'Azay-le-Ferron**, whose fortified tower dominating the village dates from the 15th century but most of which is the work of later periods in a more gracious style; it contains an opulent collection of 19th-century Empire furniture and varied *objets d'art*.

The Creuse valley is at its handsome best near Fontgombault—with cliffs of white stone to match the *tufa* along the banks of the Loire. The Benedictine **Abbaye de Fontgombault** was founded here on the river's left bank near the hermit Gombault's fountain. Although heavily restored, the originally 11th- and 12th-century abbey church is a splendid building with a majestic tall choir of great harmony and purity of line. After a long period of disuse the monastery was inhabited in the 19th century by Trappists who rebuilt the nave, and more recently by some Benedictines. You can go to services in the church and buy fresh local goats' cheese from the farms which occupy some of the old abbey buildings.

Argenton-sur-Creuse is pierced by the N20 which gives the town something of a roadside quality; there are however some old houses attractively lining the banks of the Creuse. Upstream of Argenton the Creuse runs down through a landscape of green pastures and lanes overhung with walnuts and vines. The area was a particular favourite of the novelist George Sand who came here with her friends, many of them artists, and wrote in her book *Promenade autour d'un village* that from the attractive town of Gargilesse there is an "*embarras de choix pour les promenades intéressantes et délicieuses*".

The ruins of the medieval fortress at **Crozant** are some of the most impressively situated in all France, high above the cliffs of a promontory at the meeting of the rivers Creuse and Sédelle. The Creuse has been dammed downstream from Crozant and you can take boat trips on the reservoir. From Crozant the tourist with a preference for mountainous scenery, perhaps on the way to the Massif Central, will follow the Creuse up towards its source passing the former abbey church at **Moutier d'Ahun**, which dates mostly from the 12th century and has marvellous 17th-century wood carvings in the chancel.

The small town of **Aubusson** is tightly enclosed along the river between steep hills. Its weavers grew famous in the late Middle Ages, and Henri IV exempted Aubusson tapestries from customs duties. A further boost to the business was given by Colbert's designation of the town as *manufacture royale*, but in 1685—on the revocation of the Edict of Nantes—many of the Protestant workers upped and left for safer lands elsewhere in Europe. The tapestry business still exists and has become known for the marvellous tapestries done after the designs of Jean Lurçat. There are tapestry weaving demonstrations and exhibitions in the town hall and an old workshop which you can visit. Although Aubusson's high Protestant population attracted wreckers during the religious wars and Richelieu's destruction of the château in 1623, there are still some old narrow shopping streets of no little charm.

Charm is not the conspicuous quality of the granite **Millevaches Plateau**, named not after its cow population but because of the number of springs, of which the Creuse is one. It is a flat and bleak high plateau where winter temperatures descend below $-20°C$ for long periods and where fewer and fewer people choose to spend their lives. It has been extensively reforested to try and start up a logging industry, but remains largely undiscovered by tourists—a state of affairs which cannot be expected to change in the near future.

If you follow the course of the N20 from Crozant, you will not have to divert far to **La Souterraine** or **Le Dorat**, which both have large and severely impressive granite churches, many of whose features—especially the west façade with its little flanking bell towers and oriental-looking doorways—are characteristic of the Limousin style. Of the two, Le Dorat, which is named after the golden angel on top of the spire, is the more impressive church and also the more attractive, partly medieval, town. Its church was built in the 12th century and hardly seems to have weathered at all (it has been extensively restored). The overall view of the interior from the head of the steps just inside the west door beneath one of the church's two domes is particularly striking.

The drive down through the Limousin is not an especially beautiful one, but it is green and hilly and full of the sweet chestnut trees which have for many centuries played the key role in the local economy. The area is also particularly popular for fishing. In the featureless and unmemorable charm of this rural environment it is a surprise to come across the small village of **Oradour-sur-Glane** which keeps alive the memory of a particularly unpleasant episode in the Second World War, when a company of SS troops swept through south-western France on their way up to Normandy just after D-Day with a brief to exact

retribution for the response of the French Resistance to the news of the Allied Invasion. On 10th June 1944 all the inhabitants of Oradour-sur-Glane were rounded up and, with very few exceptions, killed. Before leaving, the SS burnt the village, whose ruins have been left just as they were, in memorial.

The **Abbaye de St-Junien** was founded around the memory and the tomb of a 6th-century hermit. Only the church remains, very much in the style of Le Dorat and La Souterraine with the additional very great distinction of the tomb of saint Junien—a masterpiece of early 12th-century carving.

Not far upstream from St-Junien, **Limoges** straddles the Vienne. It is one of the big cities of Central France and does not enjoy a reputation for great beauty or liveliness; like our Coventry, Limoges is where people are sent—in this case when they are sacked from high office. Limoges was the most famous centre for the making of enamels during the Renaissance and later of porcelain, the clay for which was discovered just south of Limoges in the 18th century. This industry has been responsible for the town's considerable modern expansion.

* *Cathedral* Of the old Romanesque building only a small part of the entrance tower and porch beneath it remain. The rest is a construction of the Gothic period, so similar to the cathedrals of Narbonne and Clermont-Ferrand that they have been attributed to the same architect. The effect is one of great height and lightness and the interior notable for the delicately carved screen which has been moved to the inside of the west end of the church. The north doorway has a wealth of delicate carving from the early 16th century.

✳ *Municipal Museum* An elegant setting of 18th-century archbishop's palace and gardens, distinguished by a superb collection of Limousin enamels.

✳ *Adrien-Dubouché Museum* Very fine collections of porcelain illustrating the development of the industry not only in Limoges but all over the world.

To the east of Limoges, **St-Léonard-de-Noblat** is an attractive small town with a Romanesque church whose octagonal belfry is one of the most famous and beautiful examples of the Limousin style. There are some amusing carvings on the capitals in the porch and especially on the wooden choir stalls in a distinctly satirical vein. The area around the church is full of old houses of interest, some of them dating from the 13th century.

To the south of Limoges, on the banks of the Briance just off the N20, **Solignac** has a beautiful 12th-century church with elegant arcading around the exterior of the apse and a single aisleless domed nave. **Chalusset** has some very picturesque and romantic old ruins of two fortresses, partly 12th-century, on a promontory at the meeting place of two rivers. It is a steep walk up from the river bank.

The great feature of the drive down to the fruit and vegetable growing basin of Brive-la-Gaillarde is the small town of **Uzerche**, splendidly situated on a promontory in a meander of the Vézère. The town houses are so well provided with turrets that they are referred to as Limousin châteaux. The N20 goes through the middle of town but it's worth getting out of the car for a short wander through the old streets, from the Place Marie-Colein up through the only surviving 14th-century gate to the 12th-century church of St-Pierre, whose typically Limousin belltower (square lower registers and an octagonal top) completes the picturesque scene. Instead of going on down to Brive you can head west from Uzerche to **Pompadour**—not much of a château (which Louis XV gave to his most famous mistress), but a famous stud farm established by Louis in 1761, which specialises in Anglo-Arab horses (closed to visitors from March to mid-July).

St-Yrieix-la-Perche lies at the heart of good fishing country and is the origin of the kaolin or clay for hard-paste porcelain, which was discovered in the 18th century. Like so many other places around here St-Yrieix possesses a splendid 12th-century church with its porch and octagonal belfry. The nearby **Château de Jumilhac** is notable for its astonishing spiky roofscape of machicolations, pepperpot towers and lead statuette weather-vanes.

North and West Périgord

In the north of *Périgord blanc*—called white because it was once less forested than *Périgord noir* to the south-east—lies **Brantôme**, a peaceful and attractive place to stay, with several good hotels and restaurants. Its surrounding area (with the village of Ribérac at its heart) is very popular for the country cottage holidays with which the Dordogne has become synonymous. It is not however convenient for exploration of the Dordogne valley itself. The river Dronne has great charm as it goes through the town beneath weeping willows and limes and elegant 18th-century abbey buildings. Behind the abbey is a beautiful Romanesque belfry which stands apart from the church. An elbow bridge crosses the Dronne by a noisy weir and millwheel; and in the evening fishermen wade out in their thigh boots into the gathering gloom and stand like herons in mid-stream casting for trout until it is completely dark.

Excursions from Brantôme

✳ **Bourdeilles** Only a few miles downstream from Brantôme, Bourdeilles' situation is no less attractive with a handsome mill beside the river and an impressive château above. The sister-in-law of the indiscreet chronicler Brantôme designed the château in a hurry to receive Catherine de' Medici. When she didn't arrive the building was left unfinished; it gives a perhaps unfair impression that the lady of the house would have done well to seek professional architectural advice. A guided tour round the interior of the château is very rewarding, for Bourdeilles was owned not long ago by a couple of Burgundian art collectors who had selected it as the ideal place for the display of their beautiful and varied collections of furniture, paintings and tapestries. Many of the finest items are Spanish.

✳ **Chancelade and Merlande** Near Périgueux, the monastic ruins at Chancelade include a small religious art museum; the abbey church at Merlande has been damaged greatly over the centuries but still displays some splendid carving on the capitals around the arcades of the apse.

✳ **St-Jean-de-Côle** A delightfully picturesque village which has won a national "best roof award" in its time and which clusters around an ensemble of market buildings, château and 11th-century church. The nearby **Villars** caves are not by any means the Périgord's most important subterranean tourist attraction, but the narrow corridors take you to some splendid concretions and a few paintings (very old even by the standards of the Périgord) which are thought to date back to the early days of the Upper Palaeolithic Period.

✳ **Château de Hautefort** The small town and the countryside for miles around is dominated by this magnificent 16th- and 17th-century château whose round towers are crowned by elegant domes and lanterns. All around the castle there are immaculately kept gardens and you can go on a guided tour of the interior, but since a devastating fire in 1968 only a few rooms have been restored for the visitor. Hautefort was the home of one of the most celebrated 12th-century troubadour poets, Bertrand de Born, whose political machinations earned him a place in Dante's *Inferno*. Only the foundations of the château date from Bertrand's time.

Brantôme

Visiting Caves

Lascaux

The porous limestone plateaux of the Périgord and Quercy have been hollowed out by the drainage of rain water into vast networks of underground caverns, lakes and rivers. You can visit a large number of these and admire the natural curiosities therein—not just waterways, but also concretions (stalagmites which grow up and stalactites which grow down) formed by the dripping of mineral-rich water from ceiling to floor, leaving deposits whither and whence it falls. Eventually mites and tites, which grow currently at a rate of about 1 centimetre a century, meet to form pillars. The action of the rivers has also produced an astonishing variety of different forms, including perfect spheres like ballbearings, and rounded discs which look as if they have been carefully formed on a potter's wheel. Caves, for obvious reasons, are visited with guided tours and in many cases numbers and cramped space make it difficult to hear what the guides are saying and difficult to see what they're saying it about, unless you push. Most of the time the guides help you to play the great grotto game, which consists of identifying familiar shapes among the natural forms, which are mostly illuminating about the preoccupations of the French mind—mushrooms everywhere, oven-ready trussed chickens, bunches of carrots and, to quote several guides, "the classical natural form which imitates the statue of the Virgin and Child" . . .

Of all the grottoes in the region, few can rival for splendour those in the Massif Central; those in the Dordogne are much more crowded and you may have to queue for a long time to get in. What you cannot see better in any other area are the caves decorated with wall paintings, nearly always of animals. There are other painted caves in Europe, notably in the Pyrenees and in north-western Spain, but nowhere was there such a concentration of activity as around the Dordogne—and especially around the Vézère, near Les-Eyzies. Cave art flourished during the relatively restricted period of 15–8,000 BC with the peak of achievement and artistic refinement coming in the period known as the Magdalenian era. The beginning of the period marks the end of the last Ice Age, when most of the European landscape was bare tundra, full of wild life but not hospitable to man who clustered during the winters in a few sheltered valleys like the Dordogne, returning again and again to the same caves to paint sacred animal images. Only occasionally are

human forms represented—usually women, as symbols of fertility. As the millennia went by the climate warmed up, more and more of Europe became forest, the mammoths and bison and reindeer all went north and their hunters followed them.

In a few caves the two sorts of interest, natural and artistic, are combined; but in many cases man chose extremely remote or narrow corridors to decorate—some were only a few feet high and have had to be enlarged to admit visitors. Although the paintings have in many places been preserved in astonishing clarity and brilliance of colour, thanks to their being fixed in the rock face (rather like the drying of a fresco), the advent of modern man in large numbers after the discovery of the cave paintings has had severely damaging effects. The greatest paintings of all, at Lascaux, had to be closed after only 20 years (120,000 people breathed carbon dioxide at the bestiary in 1962). Elsewhere, numbers of visitors are strictly limited (and they have to be cleansed) and the air in the cave periodically flushed. The colours of Lascaux, obtained by the use of red ochre, are not to be found in many caves—black outline often reinforced by engraving is more frequent. Artists repeatedly came back to reuse the same pieces of wall and did not hesitate to draw and engrave over existing drawings and paintings, often reusing the forms to depict different images. The result can be that the maze of lines is difficult to untangle for the uninitiated eye. Before going to look at the cave paintings it is well worth visiting the prehistorical museum in Les-Eyzies to find out about the men who produced the works of art. The following list of caves, painted and unpainted, is not exhaustive.

Lascaux (Near Montignac) The most important group of cave paintings known to man cannot now be visited; but a realistic facsimile has recently been opened near the site. Well worth visiting.

Rouffignac An electric train ride through extensive caves which have been known to modern man for centuries, but whose Magdalenian paintings were only recently discovered among fakes and multitudes of graffiti. There are over a hundred mammoths, dozens of rhinosceri and bison, horses, ibex and even a few humanoids.

Abri du Cap-Blanc Subtly signed, a short walk down through the woods from the road beside the river Beune, a small rock shelter rather than a grotto with a single superb relief sculpture of 15,000-year old horses and a skeleton of what is said to be a 23 year-old female.

Combarelles Two long passages originally only a few feet high, and a wealth of engravings and outlines in many places difficult to decipher but very well explained. In high season, tickets may have to be reserved in the morning.

Font-de-Gaume The most beautiful decorated cave you can visit around Les-Eyzies, with some coloured as well as outlined beasts, including a magnificent frieze of bison and some concretions. Very popular, so go before breakfast to reserve tickets.

Grand-Roc Colourfully lit and colourfully guided concretions in a grotto high above the river beside Les-Eyzies. Interesting formations, but extremely popular and can be claustrophobic inside; frequent long queues outside.

La Madeleine Important (Magdalenian) excavation area. Variety of cave dwellings visible, good display area with photos, models and explanations.

La Roque-St-Christophe A series of galleries in the cliffs over the Vézère, where troglodyte man lived from prehistoric times until the 18th century. Heavily marketed in Les-Eyzies and frequented but not particularly exciting. Some elements of defences remain and a laughable model of an ape man fighting a bear.

Proumeyssac Man-made tunnel into a large domed chasm with river and fine concretions.

Le Thot (near Montignac) An interesting alternative to the prehistory museum with an audio-visual presentation of generalities about cave painting in its historical context. In the neighbouring park there are prehistoric-style animals including bison.

Cougnac (near Gourdon) An interesting mixture of concretions great and small and animal paintings. Not usually too crowded.

Lafage (near Turenne) Colourful concretions.

Lacave (near Souillac) Concretions and underground waters. Long queues.

Padirac (near Rocamadour) The great natural curiosity of the region seems to attract more tourists than you would imagine fitted in the whole of the Dordogne valley. If you want to see it go very early. The gaping hole in the ground was for centuries thought to be one of the gates of Hell, but late 19th-century exploration revealed marvellous underground rivers and lakes and huge caverns, one nearly 300ft high. You visit partly by boat and partly on foot.

Pech-Merle (near Cabrerets) An enormous and magnificent grotto, decorated with paintings second in splendour only to inaccessible Lascaux. If you only want to visit one grotto in the area this is the one to choose. The tour is fairly long in distance and time, and in addition there is a good audio-visual presentation in the museum at the entrance. Not being on or particularly near the Dordogne river, the grotto is usually not too crowded. As well as the splendid animal paintings there are signatures with hands outlined by ochre blown on to the rock through blow pipes, and fossilised footprints of a prehistoric man and child.

Villars (north-east of Brantôme) A few paintings and some fine concretions.

The Dordogne

Périgueux is the big market town of the whole Dordogne region. It is not a particularly enticing base for a holiday, but well worth visiting *en passant* because of the great curiosity value of its cathedral and because it is a very good place to shop for all the fruits of the earth that have made Périgord a gourmet's paradise and—unless he has an iron constitution—a glutton's purgatory. In the Middle Ages the once-important Roman city languished while an independent commercial town prospered around the tomb of saint Front. The two towns merged but have kept their separate characters, with the area around the cathedral old and attractive and commercial; the rest is rather dull despite the survival of some fragmentary Roman ruins.

✳ *Cathedral* Seen from afar and at its best from across the river, St-Front with its roofscape of lanterns and domes beneath a tall belfry rising some 200ft above the market square cannot fail to make you think of the Orient. The plan of the church—that of a Greek cross—is in fact very close to St Mark's in Venice and the church of the Apostles in Constantinople, and its building clearly has something to do with the experience of crusaders. Part of the 11th-century church remains (the austere west façade and fragments inside it) but the rest of the church was restored in the 19th century and in the words of Augustus Hare "under the name of restoration one of the most remarkable churches in France has been almost entirely destroyed . . . . white and unsympathetic, the modern church is utterly without beauty and has nothing of interest but its architectural features". Thanks to all the domes the interior is impressively spacious but cold, grey and soulless.

✳ *St-Etienne-de-la-Cité* The old cathedral is very mutilated but still has two of its 12th-century domes and a finely wrought 17th-century wooden altarpiece.

✳ *Périgord Museum* Prehistoric collections from the surrounding area, in many ways more interesting than the museum at Les-Eyzies. There is a complete skeleton of Chancelade man, a mammoth's tusk and fragments from the Gallo-Roman settlement, including mosaics.

✳ *Roman Remains* An 80ft high round tower (the Tour de Vésone) is all that remains of a Roman temple. Near St-Etienne-de-la-Cité there are some fragments of the old amphitheatre.

The road south-west from Périgueux meets the Dordogne river itself at **Bergerac**, the area's second town in importance and approximately the western limit of the part of the Dordogne river which is in the Dordogne *département*. Bergerac has many affinities with the Bordeaux region in that it is more of a wine town than anything else, except perhaps tobacco—of which it is the French capital, thanks to the favourable combination of very fertile soil and summer warmth. Bergerac like Aubusson was a centre of Protestantism, and not much of the old town survives except a small area by the river which has been restored. There is a tobacco museum which is fascinating whatever you think of the habit, which reached France in 1560 when an ambassador sent some tobacco from Lisbon as a cure for Catherine de' Medici's migraines. In the 17th century Louis XIII outlawed the use of tobacco. Pope Urban XVIII excommunicated smokers; but soon the authorities realised that what they couldn't defeat they could exploit. The museum is full of details of the industry and a splendid collection of old smoking-related items from pipes to snuff boxes and 19th-century cartoons making fun of the shocking adoption of the smoking habit by women. The Maison du Vin is nearby and has details of the local wine-producing châteaux which receive tourists. The most handsome and the most famous is the 16th-century **Château de Monbazillac** which contains a museum which has less to do with the luscious wine than with the very bloody religious history of the region.

The western stretch of the Dordogne valley, between Bergerac and the Vézère river, is not its most attractive, apart from the wide *cingle* or loop of **Trémolat**, of which there are fine views from the road on the north bank. Trémolat itself is a small town that will interest those who remember Claude Chabrol's film *Le Boucher*, where the lush rural atmosphere of the area is brilliantly evoked to contrast with the less than idyllic events making up the plot. The church in Trémolat is an almost windowless, decaying fortress of a building. On the sluggish loop of the river there is a watersports centre.

The **Vézère** is an attractive river with many of the qualities of the Dordogne in its lower reaches. Its overwhelming attraction is not its landscape, but its status as the capital of prehistory. The centre of modern tourist congregation—as it was the centre of habitation by Upper Paleolithic man—is **Les Eyzies-de-Tayac**, not a particularly attractive little town and very commercialised, but functional enough and a good place to stay while exploring the area, with a choice of good accommodation. Les Eyzies has an interesting museum of prehistory in the old château, telling the story of excavation, which was something of a gold rush at the turn of the century. The museum gives the uninitiated an idea of the time scale of prehistory, and photographs of the major excavations which are probably as close as most people will be interested to go. It is a good preparation for visits to the caves in the surrounding area (see page 216).

Monpazier

On the edge of Les Eyzies there is reserve of animals which have been chosen for their close relationship to those represented on the caves of the surrounding region. Of the few places of later than prehistoric interest around the valley, the most attractive is **St-Amand-de-Coly**, a small village of houses with rough stone (*lauze*) roofs, clustered around an impressively fortified and beautiful Romanesque church.

Excursions from Bergerac and the western Dordogne

✱ **Bastide Towns** A good selection of the many *bastides* built in the area between the Dordogne and the Lot—not the most important necessarily but some of the least affected by subsequent urban development—can be incorporated in a round trip south of Bergerac and back up to the Abbaye de Cadouin. Some are French (in the south), others nearer the Dordogne river are English; there is no noticeable difference in style of construction. At **Beaumont** there is a good example of the fortified church which served as a keep. Castillonès is another typical *bastide* with a central arcaded square; **Villeréal** has market buildings on the square; **Monflanquin** is an attractive hilltop *bastide*; and **Monpazier** is the most complete of them all, with much of its ramparts and very beautiful low pointed-arch arcading around the square.

✱ **Château de Biron** This is a superb mostly 15th-century fortress in a dominant position surveying vast tracts of open countryside, and larger than the small village that kneels at its feet. The most curious feature is the chapel with two storeys, one opening on the courtyard of the château, the lower serving as the parish church for the village which knows its place.

✱ **Abbaye de Cadouin** An old abbey which for many centuries flourished on pilgrimage business, thanks to its bogus holy shroud which was finally discredited in 1934 when it was discovered to be an extremely precious oriental fabric dating from not much earlier than the time it was brought back from crusade. Cadouin's main distinction is the Flamboyant Gothic cloisters, full of intricate carving of great beauty. The guided tour is excessively long-winded.

The Central Dordogne Valley

The Dordogne between the Vézère and Souillac is at its most beautiful. It winds between cliffs of gold, overlooked but hardly dominated by the turreted crowns of fortresses and châteaux which coyly hide themselves in the vegetation of the hillsides. The valley is a succession of beauty spots, and they are enjoyed by large numbers of tourists—campers, cyclists and canoeists among them. One of the most charming places (which does not neglect to exploit its attractions) is the village of **Beynac-et-Cazenac**, with old houses along the riverside beneath a 450ft cliff, and others on top of it beside the truly dominant 13th- to 15th-century fortress, one of the greatest Périgord strongholds in the Middle Ages. It is now restored inside and informatively guided, but there is not much furniture. From the ramparts there is a splendid view up and down the river and across to the rival ruined fortress of **Castelnaud**, hardly less impressively set. For much of the Hundred Years' War, Castelnaud was in the hands of the English, Beynac was French. Castelnaud is still in the process of being restored, and you can wander around the ruins.

La Roque-Gageac is the other archetypal reflected village, squashed between a golden cliff and the river, many of its houses carved out of the rock. To accentuate the stage-set atmosphere there is a mock 15th-century château built a century or so ago. Unlike Beynac or La Roque-

Goosefair at Sarlat

Gageac, the nearby village of **Domme** stands high above the river on a cliff. It can only be reached (or so it was thought, until some Protestants climbed in along the cliffs in 1588) from the gentler hills behind—on which side Domme is defended by some splendid fortified gateways and ramparts. Once inside the walls the martial frown of Domme changes to a charmingly inviting smile. Its houses are old and golden and beautifully restored, decorated with geraniums and roses and vines, as if the charming streets needed prettifying. At the top of the *bastide*, there is an old market hall which gives access to some caves with concretions, and a shady esplanade which gives a superlative view over the valley. Domme is one of the most picturesque places of the Dordogne and one of the most popular. There are scores of restaurants and shops selling paté, potted goose, and other local delicacies. During the day it teems with campers who come up from the riverside in nothing but their bathing shorts. But it quietens down in the evening, and is a very pleasant place to stay.

Sarlat, the market town of this arcadian stretch of the river, is appropriately handsome apart from the very busy main shopping street. The area to the east of the main street has a number of beautiful and well restored old houses—the Place du Peyrou is a particularly fine ensemble. Sarlat's old cathedral was rebuilt in the 16th and 17th centuries with the exception of its 12th-century belfry and porch. In the gardens behind there is a curious round, conically-roofed Romanesque funerary chapel, the Lanterne des Morts. Sarlat is the most animated town of the region, with pavement entertainers and evening bustle; there is an open-air drama festival at the end of July and the beginning of August.

Souillac is the through-town where the mighty N20 crosses the Dordogne. It is full of amenities for the traveller—shops and banks and hotels and restaurants—but in general lacks charm apart from its one glorious redeeming feature, a domed church, the beautiful rounded forms of whose east end are admirably disencumbered (by a carpark) for your admiration. The interior is a warm and spacious harmony of rounded forms as well, without much decoration except for the astonishingly rich carving on the old west doorway which has been re-installed inside the church. Beneath a three-tier relief illustration of the legend of Theophilus—who like Faust made a pact with the devil but unlike him earned forgiveness—the pillars are carved with a densely decorative tangle of weird beasts of fantasy, and the dancing figure of the prophet Isaiah.

Upstream from Souillac the beauty spots along the river are fewer and further between, but the river itself winds beautifully on, flanked by yet more fortresses. One of the few of the riverside castles which repays a visit to the interior is the **Château de la Treyne**, which has varied and beautiful contents and attractive gardens. It has recently been turned into a hotel. There are caves to visit at **Lacave**, with well-lit concretions, but being by the river they attract more crowds than they deserve. The grey medieval town of **Martel** stands some distance north of the river and is very little affected by tourists. It was named after an abbey founded by Charles Martel to commemorate his victory over the infidel in the 8th century. It has many beautiful old houses, some dating from the 15th century, as does the massive church, built more like a castle than a place of worship, except for the splendid carving of the Last Judgement over the main doorway. Martel has an attractive old covered market, and is an important centre for the truffle business.

Carennac, where François de Salignac de La Mothe-Fénelon was prior for many years and where he is said to have written *Télémaque*—the romantic moral tale of the adventures of the son of Ulysses, which was the most popular work of the French 18th century—is a delightful and peaceful village which slumbers changeless beside the waters of the Dordogne. Its church has a very beautiful 12th-century doorway whose tympanum with Christ in Majesty in a mandorla (almond frame), is closely related to that at Beaulieu among others. Inside there is a moving 16th-century group sculpture of the Entombment. The partially Romanesque cloister is often used for the sale of local craft and food produce.

Just north of Carennac, the large plateau of **Puy d'Issolud** may be the site of the battle of Uxellodunum. The Gauls finally yielded before the might and cunning of Caesar, who triumphed by diverting their water supply—the battle has been described as the death-rattle of Gallic freedom. There is more to see from the high plateau than on it.

Perhaps the most impressive château of the whole valley is the **Château de Castelnau**, which surveys the confluence of Dordogne and Céré from the isolated rocky end of a promontory between the river valleys. Its outer walls could enclose a town, so great is the area they surround. The buildings within are magnificent, and despite having been burnt down in the 19th century—arson for insurance it is said—the interior was restored by a tasteful tenor who left his varied art collection and the château to the nation on his death. The guided tour is more interesting than most, and from the fortifications of this red-stone stronghold (described by Pierre Loti as a blood-red cockscomb) there are magnificent views.

Beaulieu-sur-Dordogne is a small township beside the river, where the Dordogne ceases to be a river of the hills, and starts out on its most beautiful middle section. Beaulieu is a pleasant place with its busy market and plenty of facilities by the river for camping, swimming and hiring canoes. Its fame rests not on any of these, but on the deeply recessed south portal of its former abbey church. This is a magnificent work of Romanesque carving, very much in the style of Moissac as are the less monumental doorways at Carennac, Martel, Collonges and others. Above the door the Last Judgement is represented with great vigour around the central figure of Christ. On the pillars below there are some wonderful demonic figures given an unintended gruesome aspect by the weathering of the stone. The scenes represented in these nether regions are the Temptation of Christ, Daniel with lions and some figures symbolising the punishment of avarice and luxury.

Upstream, the small town of **Argentat** enjoys a picturesque setting, its steep grey *lauze*-roofed houses mirrored in the river. Above Argentat the Dordogne descends through wooded gorges—or used to until it was dammed in no less than five places between Argentat and Bort-les-Orgues, making a succession of long-stepped narrow reservoirs flanked by hills. This landscape has its beauty although it lacks the variety and colours of the valley lower down. For most of the way you can drive along the side of the river and reservoirs and there are a number of good viewpoints, especially from the hills behind **Bort-les-Orgues**, a small industrial town named after the basalt pillars which stand in a row like organ pipes—in some places 200ft high. The damming of the Dordogne has improved the setting of the delightful 15th-century **Château de Val**, whose round towers are now lapped by the waters of the reservoir.

Excursions from the eastern Dordogne

* **Rocamadour** One of the most important pilgrimage destinations in Europe in the early Middle Ages. The origin of the pilgrimage was the discovery in the 12th century of an uncorrupted body, that of the hermit Amadour, identified as none other than the Zaccheus of the New Testament. The incorruptible Amadour was chopped to pieces by the Huguenots and cannot be carbon-dated. Everyone who was anyone in medieval Christendom came to Rocamadour (Henry II came twice) but it was sacked repeatedly and fell into decline before being revived in the 19th century as a tourist attraction and a pilgrimage destination once more. Today it is still both, but predominantly a place for tourists thanks to its very remarkable setting.

The village is built along a couple of very narrow ledges on an apparently sheer cliff-face which is one side of the almost empty Alzou canyon—a cleft in the stony arid *causse*. The main street is very trippery but has a number of restored medieval gateways and houses. From it a staircase of over 200 steps—penitent pilgrims used originally to go up on hands and knees with chains

Dry-stone shepherds' huts

around their neck and limbs—climbs the rock face to a number of restored sanctuaries built into the rock, to an also restored château on the top of the cliff. The ascent can also be made by lift. Although the extensive restoration and rebuilding of Rocamadour gives it a less than authentic look, the overall atmosphere is probably not very different from what it was 700 years ago. The sanctuaries themselves are of no particular distinction as buildings, but the guided tour does get you to see the famous Black Virgin, spindly and mysterious, and for once not clothed in the usual lace and jewellery. Rocamadour being what it is, many people will find the best thing to do is to appreciate the overall view of the setting—from the road down from L'Hospitalet—and go no further.

✵ Causse de Gramat The road between L'Hospitalet and Calès is a good one to take to see some of the bleak but beautiful rocky scenery of the limestone plateau, with its dry stone walls and shepherds' huts.

✵ Around Autoire The attractive and harmonious perched village of Loubressac is clustered around a small 15th-century château. It is something of a British expatriate stronghold, enjoying beautiful views of Castelnau and the Dordogne valley. Above the no less beautiful village of Autoire there is an impressive amphitheatre of rocks and waterfalls. The **Château de Montal** is a small Renaissance château whose exquisite grace is tinged with sadness. The three-sided courtyard is decorated with a marvellous series of portrait busts depicting among others the château's creator, Jeanne de Balzac, who intended Montal for her son Robert de Montal, also represented. When he died young in battle, she inscribed the sombre message "Plus d'espoir" (no more hope) around the beautiful gabled windows of the château. The guided tour around the interior is unnecessarily long-winded, for only a few rooms are on show, but there are some splendid works of art, including a tapestry depicting a Renaissance game of croquet; the staircase is a masterpiece of 16th-century decoration. Montal is a tribute to the energy and devotion of the man who bought it at the beginning of this century, after its contents and the decorative elements of its exterior had been dispersed for easy money at the end of the 19th century. The new owner bought back all the pieces he could from the museums and private collectors who had snapped them up and there is nothing in the interior which is not in period.

✵ St Céré A small old market town with considerable charm but not much specific interest except the brilliantly colourful Aubusson tapestries on display in the old casino. Their designer was the modern artist Jean Lurçat who lived at St-Céré.

✳ **Collonges-la-Rouge and Aubazines** Well-named **Collonges-la-Rouge** is an enchanting village of extraordinary deep purple-red sandstone; like Pérouges near Lyon and Cordes near Albi it has been saved, restored and preserved from change thanks to a society of friends who got together at the beginning of the century. It is bypassed by the modest D38 and seems to have been bypassed by the 20th century. All the houses are built of the same red stone, with slate pepper-pot roofs; many of them are very old and beautiful, overrun by vines and other creepers. The large red Romanesque church has a handsome Limousin belfry—one of the oldest of the genre—and a beautifully carved west doorway. Some of the fortifications which were added to the church in the 15th century are still visible. Despite its very obviously scrupulous state of preservation and picturesque charm, Collonges is far enough from the Dordogne to have escaped the degree of crowding which afflicts Domme for example. It has two appropriately not-too-sophisticated hotels, and is a delightful place to stay. The small village of **Aubazines** near the Corrèze upstream from Brive was the site of a Cistercian abbey in the 12th century, and its church typical of the order in the sobriety of its style. It is a 12th-century building with a typical Limousin belfry, but with the unusual feature that the bays of the nave climb in steps towards the choir. Contents of particular interest include amusing choir stalls carved in the 18th century, a very old oak cupboard in the south transept which dates from the 12th century, and a masterpiece of delicate Gothic stone tracery enclosing the recumbent statue of saint Stephen.

✳ **Turenne** This village lacks the glorious technicolour appeal of nearby Collonges, but is an attractive old village all the same, built at the foot of two impressive windowless towers—one round, one square—which are all that remains on the top of a hill of a fortress which was the power base of a mighty lordship, independent of the crown until 1738. The most famous of its rulers was the great Turenne himself, the 17th-century general whom Napoleon rated more highly as a soldier than any other, except perhaps one.

✳ **Tulle, Gimel and Ventadour** The large town of Tulle is enclosed by hills and has had to grow for a long way along the banks of the fast-flowing Corrèze. It has given its name to a kind of lace work, which has long deserted the town and since the 19th century has been established mainly in Calais. The cathedral has an elegant belfry; there are 13th-century cloisters, and a local museum and some old houses nearby. The small village of **Gimel** enjoys a wild setting beside a series of waterfalls whose total drop is nearly 500ft, and at the foot of which the waters run through gorges called The Inferno. To get to the best viewpoint to admire all this you have to pay. In Gimel church you have to pay as well to see the treasury whose glory is a 12th-century reliquary of saint Stephen (the same one as at Aubazines), decorated with jewel-studded enamels. Above the gorges of the Luzège, north-east of Gimel, are the impressive ruins of **Ventadour** castle, best seen from the narrow approach roads from Moustier-Ventadour.

✳ **Tours de Merle** Ruined feudal fortress which comprised seven individual castles, vulnerably situated surrounded by hills.

The Lot Valley

The Lot charts an unbelievably tortuous course of endless meanders through the *département* that bears its name. One of the most tedious loops, at Luzech—where the river travels for some 3½ miles to cover less than 200 yards of ground—was canalised; but it has since been filled in and nowadays those who canoe or boat down the Lot (and it is one of the safest and most beautiful waterways in France for this purpose) will have to do the full course. Not unlike the Dordogne in many ways, this part of the Lot valley is flanked by the limestone cliffs of the Causse. High on the rocks there are a few splendidly perched villages and a few fortresses; down below, small cultivations of tobacco, maize and rows of poplars.

The swift Célé is hardly less attractive, as it runs down through narrow limestone gorges with old mills and little waterfalls from **Figeac**—a town with many old houses of character and charm but no individual monuments of great distinction—to Conduché where its waters are absorbed by the Lot. Apart from the look of the valley the main reason to follow its course is to visit the **Pech-Merle Cave** near Cabrerets—the most interesting of all the prehistoric, painted caves currently open to the public, and beautiful as a grotto as well (see page 216). **St-Cirq-Lapopie** is a carefully restored old village of beautiful houses which would be worth visiting anywhere and which has the added attraction of a truly magnificent setting on a spur high above the left bank of the Lot. The narrow streets climb up towards a ruined château and a Gothic church—if you wander around the back the view is positively dizzy. In the past St-Cirq has been a traditional centre for wood craftsmen and today it is still very much a place for arts and crafts. The powers that be, it would seem, not only prevent the inhabitants of the village from replacing their impractical but pictures-que old roofs, but also make sure that the tourist shops are *de style*.

Cahors is the capital of the Quercy which in the Middle Ages produced the greatest if not the most likeable of French popes (John XXII), and a blood-red wine which enjoyed a greater reputation then, in the days before phylloxera, than it does today. John XXII may have had something to do with the tradition that the popes had the robust Cahors wine for communion; he also founded a university in his native town and had the bishop of Cahors flayed and torn apart by wild horses for alleged sorcery. The town, which still shows some remnants of the old fortifications, stands on a peninsula in the Lot—whose neck is only half a mile wide, but whose meandering river moat is more than four miles around. Until as recently as 1850 there were three magnificent fortified bridges; only one survives today but it is enough to ensure Cahors an illustrated place in most guide books. Strangely the old town did not fill the peninsula; today the N20, which goes straight through the middle of town, divides the old town on the east from the new and anonymous one to the west.

✳ **Cathedral** The two enormous rough domes of the nave are some of the earliest of the style which was to spread all over the Périgord. The effect of the interior is warm and imposing. Some 14th-century paintings on one of the domes have survived and depict the stoning of saint Stephen, to whom the church is dedicated. The glory of the cathedral is its north doorway—a work of the first half of the 12th century, of the same period and style as Moissac and others. Unfortunately the portal at Cahors is not really shown off to advantage and standing on the narrow street in front of it involves considerable risk from passing traffic. It is worth braving most dangers to see it though, for the central figure of Christ in the mandorla—less awesome than Moissac, but more human—is one of the noblest creations of Romanesque sculpture.

✳ **Pont Valentré** France's most beautiful bridge (early 14th-century) spans the western side of the loop of the Lot, and was not originally part of the town and its defences but an isolated self-sufficient fortress. Three 140ft towers dominate

Pont Valentré, Cahors

the bridge of six pointed Gothic arches, with gates at either end, and protruding machicolations which enabled the inmates to drop unpleasant missiles on anybody who dared approach. The English, who spent a long time outside Cahors in the Hundred Years' War, never even tried.

The fortress of **Bonaguil** is one of the finest survivals of late medieval military architecture set somewhat eccentrically: not commanding the Lot or a vast expanse of fertile countryside, but in a remote and unproductive glen a few miles north of Fumel. Curiously, much of what remains was built in the early 16th century when most other people were erecting pleasure palaces. The fierce and reactionary lord Bérenger de Rocquefeuil preferred the style of an earlier more warlike age, and rebuilt the fortress at Bonaguil to repel the most determined attackers who in the event never came. The defensive buildings of the previous century were adapted to cope with new advances in artillery, and the long and learned guided tour around the impressive but empty buildings concentrates at length on these weighty technicalities of military architecture. In midsummer some musical evenings are held at Bonaguil.

South of the river Lot the countryside is increasingly fertile as it approaches the Garonne, but it has no great variety or beauty. **Agen** is the centre of a great fruit-growing area famous for prunes, plums and fruit liqueurs. Its art museum has Spanish works of art collected by a French ambassador, with a number of works by Goya.

Moissac is another unprepossessing town in the fruit belt which suffered much from a great flood in 1930, none of which dims the beauty of the cloister and main doorway of its great abbey church. Together they make Moissac a high point of 12th-century artistic achievement. The church itself, changed in the 15th century, is not spectacularly beautiful. Below the solid squat belfry tower the south doorway is deeply recessed, which may have helped to preserve from weathering the majestic and awe-inspiring carving on the tympanum which represents the Last Vision of the Apocalypse, as seen and written by saint John the Divine. The surrounding bands of ornamental sculpture are wonderfully decorative, and on the central pillar supporting the whole edifice the figures of Jeremiah and saint Paul flank a pride of interlaced lions. The carvings around the doorway are more damaged— on the left various sins of avarice and luxury are punished and on the right a number of scenes from the New Testament are depicted. The large cloister is architecturally uncomplicated, the vault of each gallery being simply pitched and supported by wooden beams, so there is nothing to distract the eye from the endlessly fascinating wealth of carving on the capitals which support alternately twinned and single columns all around the cloister, earning its reputation as the most beautiful in France. Some of the capitals are ornamental and reveal classical influence; others depict imaginary monsters of oriental inspiration; others detail biblical and apochryphal scenes. To do these carvings justice, a detailed guide is essential.

Montauban is yet another large unattractive town, whose suburbs spread far and wide across the plains. It was a Protestant stronghold and most of its medieval buildings have been destroyed. But the only compelling reason to go to Montauban is to see the museum named after and mainly devoted to Montauban's greatest son, the painter Ingres, born here in 1780. The museum has a superb collection of works of the artist, who set himself up as the champion of classical orthodoxy at a time when France was troubled by romantic (in the form of Delacroix) as well as political subversion.

East of Montauban, the Aveyron, which carves almost as intricate a path as the Lot, has a few places that are worth seeing. The old village of **Penne** and its ruined fortress are dizzily set on a promontory above the river. **Bruniquel**, named because this is where the Visigoth princess Brunhilda is thought to have built a castle, has links with Penne in being an old fortified town with a fortress perched on its perpendicular precipice above the river, and also in the frustrated inscription which can be seen in the château "*Rien sans peine*", a pun on the name of the neighbouring fortress which the lords of Bruniquel wished to possess but never did.

Of all the ruined medieval fortresses in France **Najac** perhaps enjoys the most romantic setting, and conforms best to our ideal. It stands on a conical rocky promontory which plummets 450ft down to a meander of the river Aveyron. As you walk down its single street of picturesque grey medieval houses which leads along the narrow promontory up to the fortress the massive cylindrical keep of the great castle looms majestically to monopolise your field of vision. The fortress is mostly the work of the great local fortifier Alphonse de Poitiers, brother of saint Louis, who as a royal representative in the days following the Albigensian crusade had reason to fortify himself. The church was also built in his time by the local inhabitants, who thereby earned absolution for their heretical leanings.

Villefranche-de-Rouergue is a 13th-century *bastide*, which has out-grown its old grid; its central square is a splendid example of the style and unusually has an impressively massive church tower built into the square. Inside the church there is some fine 15th-century woodcarving.

South of Najac, the beautiful medieval village of **Cordes** sits on top of an isolated symmetrical hill and, thanks to the Society of Friends of Cordes, has been admirably preserved and restored. Some of the old fortifications remain—it was built in the 13th century as a *bastide* by the count of Toulouse—but its great distinction is the number of large and handsome Gothic houses with arched windows which line the main street through the town. Cordes was in the 14th century a prosperous centre for weaving and leather working. Recently artists and craftsmen have returned to the town, adding to its charm and prosperity.

The large red town of **Albi** is not as a whole a place of beauty. After the murderous crusade against the Cathar (Albigensian) heresy, the 14th-century bishops still had to face popular uprisings; their awe-inspiring red-brick warship of a cathedral and adjacent bishop's palace were fortresses from a time when faith meant war and bloodshed rather than contemplation and joy. The cathedral's dedication to the saint Cecilia—patroness of music—who smiles so sweetly from Renaissance paintings is not inappropriate: this early Christian martyr took three days to die in agony after three blows of the axe on her neck.

Najac

230

∗ *Cathedral* For all its severity, this is a magnificent building with a huge keep of a tower and a single vessel of a nave without choir or transept; its buttresses are like round towers, its windows like arrow slits. Within these forbidding walls there is a wealth of decorative interest. The early 16th-century porch on the south side of the church contrasts with the rest of the exterior, in colour and in its dense sculptural richness. Dating from much the same period is the enclosure built inside to make up for the lack of a choir in the architectural scheme of the building. This stone screen invites comparison with lacework and was described by Viollet-le-Duc as the last limits of delicacy and complication of Gothic forms. Amid the delicate tracery there is a very fine series of statues of apostles and sibyls, coloured and depicted with the realism of a portrait and in many cases with a sensuous materialism typical of decadent late Gothic art. The inside of the west end of the cathedral is decorated with an enormous 15th-century fresco of the Last Judgement where—as is usual in the period—the damned in their punishment are depicted with relish. The middle of the fresco, where Christ in Judgement used to be, was spoilt by the later piercing of a doorway. In the early 16th century the entire vault was painted by Italian artists with scenes of apostles and angels.

∗ *Palais de la Berbie* Inside the old bishop's palace there is a varied museum, of which the highlight is the unique collection of works by the artist Toulouse-Lautrec, who was born of noble parentage in 1864 in Albi, was crippled as a youth and grew up the obsessional and merciless observer of seedy and theatrical Montmartre life.

The admirer of Toulouse-Lautrec's harsh social observation will be rewarded by a stop at **Castres**, between Albi and Carcassonne. In the former bishop's palace there is a Musée Goya which contains some of the 18th-century portrait painter's works including a complete series of his etchings.

Hotels

Beynac-et-Cazenac, 24220 Dordogne £££

BONNET   Tel: 53.29.50.01

A perennial British favourite enjoying a beautiful setting on a riverbend beloved by fishermen at the edge of a postcard village. Lunch-time fair-weather eaters are installed on a first-floor terrace, under vines. Menus are good value, and cooking is traditional and above average; the bedrooms are attractively furnished and comfortable. Above all, a friendly, welcoming atmosphere.

Closed mid-Oct to Easter; 22 bedrooms; no lift.

Brantôme, 24310 Dordogne £££££

MOULIN DE L'ABBAYE   Tel: 53.05.80.22

Whether you're charmed or deafened by the roar of the waters cascading below Brantôme's famous bridge, the beauty of this mill's setting is irresistible; swallows dip, and mosquitoes like it here too. From the terrace you can gaze on less fortunate mortals in the public gardens across the water, and on the illuminated abbey belfry; the restaurant is bright and spacious, the few bedrooms very attractively furnished (including reading material) and comfortable. The three fixed-price daily menus have little or no choice, and err on the side of over-indulgence; the wine list includes much that is excellent and expensive, but also a few well-chosen lesser names and halves.

Closed Nov to May (rest Mon); 12 bedrooms; no lift.

Hotels

Brantôme, 24310 Dordogne   **££££**

LE CHÂTENET   Tel: 53.05.81.08

A fine 17th-century yellow stone farmhouse, 2 km outside Brantôme, with a courtyard, and small swimming pool in a pretty garden. No expense has been spared in this delightful and comfortable hotel—salon, breakfast room and bedrooms have antiques and attractive furnishings. The atmosphere is friendly, the owners preferring to consider it a "paying guest" establishment, with much repeat business.

7 bedrooms; no rest; no lift; swimming pool.

Cabrerets, 46330 Lot   **££££**

LA PESCALERIE   Tel: 65.31.22.55

Set in extensive grounds, this 18th-century manor has been since 1980 an idyllic hotel. The interior is designed with taste and expertise in a richly personal style; stone and beams, soft white rugs and sofas in the little salon; antiques and quarry tiles in the luxurious bedrooms. There's one fixed-price menu of the day (without choice) and a small but interesting *carte* on which duck, goose and trout feature strongly; the standard of cooking is well above average for this area.

Closed Nov to Mar; 10 bedrooms; no lift.

Calès, 46350 Lot   **££**

PAGÈS   Tel: 65.37.95.87

In a tiny village lost on the Causse de Gramat near Gourdon, the Pagès family runs a simple hotel without frills. Fixed-price menus include local specialities—*confit d'oie* and *omelette aux perles noires* (truffles); those at the cheaper end are very good value. Simple traditionally-furnished bedrooms; cheaper ones in the annexe. Small salon with TV.

Closed Oct and Jan; 16 bedrooms; no lift.

Champagne-de-Belair (near Brantôme), 24530   **£££££**

MOULIN DU ROC   Tel: 53.54.80.36

A difficult but after all enviable choice between this mill and the one at Brantôme. This is more rural and more of an hotel, with a splendid salon where you sit round the old nut-oil mill machinery, and gardens beside the waters. Furniture throughout (including in the bedrooms) includes many antiques, but the comfort is modern (colour TV, minibar). The food is magnificent, and not as overwrought as the exuberant decoration, nor overpriced.

Closed mid-Nov to mid-Dec and mid-Jan to mid-Feb (rest Tues. and Wed lunch); 12 bedrooms; no lift.

Our price symbols

£	You can expect to find a room for under £15
££	You can expect to find a room for £15 to £25
£££	You can expect to find a room for £25 to £35
££££	You can expect to find a room for £35 to £45
£££££	You should expect to pay over £45 for a room

Collonges-la-Rouge, 19500 Corrèze £
LE RELAIS ST-JACQUES DE COMPOSTELLE   Tel: 55.25.41.02

It's well worth a pilgrimage to this modest red-stone hostelry at the edge of the suspension of disbelief that is Collonges-la-Rouge. There's a terrace for leisurely lunches, an attractive dining room, and bedrooms are airy and comfortable (some with superb views). Fixed-price menus are generous and good value; one includes an excellent *carré de boeuf* which you are left to grill at your table. There are plenty of regional wines.

Closed Dec to Jan (rest Mon out of season); 12 bedrooms; no lift.

Cordes, 81170 Tarn ££££
LE GRAND ÉCUYER   Tel: 63.56.01.03

A superb medieval mansion, centrally situated with fine views. Spacious bedrooms, some with four-posters, and suitably heavy antiques and furnishings contribute to an authentic atmosphere, which manages to avoid being stuffy. Yves Thuries runs the hotel and cooks skilfully, making it clear that his first love is sweetmeats (one menu has no less than four dessert courses).

Closed Nov to Mar (rest Mon out of season); 15 bedrooms; no lift.

Domme, 24250 Dordogne £££
ESPLANADE   Tel: 53.28.31.41

Superbly situated on a cliff at the edge of this tourist-ridden village, which resumes its more natural identity in the evening when the day trips are over, this traditional hotel has its devotees and its critics. Bedrooms and public rooms are attractive and comfortable, many with fine views; cooking is traditional, too, with fixed-price menus offering copious courses which are rather less exciting than dishes à la carte. A small town house down in the village centre serves as a bedroom annexe.

Closed Nov and Feb (rest Mon); 20 bedrooms; no lift

Les Eyzies-de-Tayac, 24620 Dordogne ££££
CENTENAIRE   Tel: 53.06.97.18

Of the competing hostelleries in the Dordogne's main tourist centre, this modern hotel is arguably the most comfortable and offers by far the best food—light *nouvelle cuisine*, which may come as some relief after too many Dordogne *confits*. Public rooms are civilised and stylish, bedrooms traditional and very comfortable indeed; there's a shady garden and attractive new swimming pool. It's worth working up an appetite for one of the fixed-price menus, which are vastly better value than eating à la carte (if not exactly cheap).

Closed Nov to Easter (rest Tues lunch); 29 bedrooms; no lift; swimming pool.

Hotels

Les Eyzies-de-Tayac, 24620 Dordogne   ££
CENTRE   Tel: 53.06.97.13

This relatively modest hotel suffers from being in the limelight of its more illustrious neighbours. Yet its riverside setting, garden and shady terrace, sophisticated rustic charm and above average standard of cooking should please all but the most discerning visitors. Bedrooms are simply furnished, traditional and comfortable; menus are good value.

Closed mid-Nov to Feb; 18 bedrooms; no lift.

Les Eyzies-de-Tayac   ££
MOULIN DE LA BEUNE   Tel: 53.06.04.33

Well-converted 19th-century mill house, centrally situated near the National Museum of Prehistory yet lying away from the main road. It's tastefully decorated and furnished, with a large open fireplace in the salon, and a light and pretty breakfast room overlooking the river and small garden terrace. Bedrooms are uncluttered and stylish, with good bath or shower rooms.

Closed Nov to Mar; 20 bedrooms; no rest; no lift.

Gourdon, 46300 Lot   ££
HOSTELLERIE DE LA BOURIANE   Tel: 65.41.16.37

A solid, traditional small hotel away from the centre of a small hilltop town. There's a garden, bar, breakfast room and rustic restaurant; bedrooms are simple and adequate (those on the second floor somewhat prettier than those on the first), most with shower rather than bath. Fixed-price menus are very good value, and the standard of cooking is high.

Closed Jan to mid-Mar (rest Mon); 22 bedrooms.

Lacave, 46200 Lot   ££
LE PONT DE L'OUYSSE   Tel: 65.37.87.04

In a stunning position on the leafy bank of the river Ouysse, near the village of Lacave, this quiet little hotel offers traditional comfort and several plus points—a shady terrace for summer eating, small garden with swings, and pretty bedrooms. The menu features all the usual local specialities—*cèpes*, truffles, *foie de canard* (the last two even with the *suprême de saumon*).

Closed mid-Nov to Feb (rest Mon Mar to June); 12 bedrooms; no lift.

Montignac, 24290 Dordogne   £££££
CHÂTEAU DE PUY ROBERT   Tel: 53.51.92.13

Two kilometres from the caves of Lascaux, this golden stone Napoleon III château (with its brand new annexe built *en style*) was about to open when we visited in 1986. Bedrooms (including some duplex) and public rooms are sumptuously decorated; there are large grounds and a pool. The owner, Albert Parveaux, is not new to the luxury hotel trade (another local château and a modern hotel in Courchevel have been his successes to date). Reports please.

Closed Nov to April; 40 bedrooms.

St-Cirq-Lapopie, 46330 Lot £££

LA PELISSARIA   Tel: 65.31.25.14

Delightful medieval town house, clinging to the hill in this spectacularly sited
perched village, which has recently been skilfully and very tastefully converted
into a tiny hotel. The comfortable salon has an open fireplace, grand piano, and
fine views; bedrooms have tiled floors and very good bath or shower rooms.
Dishes on the fairly short *carte* are good value; *andouillette en croûte et sa salade
vigneronne* or *truite au gingembre* offer a change from the more usual local fare of
confits and *foie gras*. The owner, Francois Matuchet, is a musician, his wife cooks;
they have together created a friendly and very civilised atmosphere in this
enchanting little hotel.

Closed Nov to Mar; 6 bedrooms; no lift; parking at some distance from hotel; rest
not open lunch.

Tamniès, 24620 Lot £££

LABORDERIE   Tel: 53.29.68.59

The Laborderies must be doing well: they've now added two spanking new
annexes and a swimming pool to their domaine. However, the old village-centre
hotel is still the centre of activity, the hill-top hamlet (near Sarlat) is still quiet,
and the cooking remains resolutely traditional and local—*confit, pâté truffé,
omelette aux cèpes* and trout are hard to avoid on the good-value fixed-price
menus. Bedrooms (some family rooms) and bathrooms are better in the annexes,
which have fine views; all are adequate and prettily decorated. A firm favourite
with many British visitors.

Closed mid-Nov to mid-Mar; 32 bedrooms; no lift; swimming pool.

Trémolat, 244510 Dordogne £££££

LE VIEUX LOGIS   Tel: 53.22.80.06

Le Vieux Logis is not cheap, but it is a real treat and good value; rambling old
buildings beside a sleepy village, with beautiful gardens. Profoundly silent
bedrooms have been lovingly furnished in a variety of styles which combine rustic
charm with great comfort and elegance. The dining room is an equally splendid
chamber with antique-strewn galleries above for after-dinner chess; breakfast is
served in individual *petits salons* or in the garden. The new chef, Pierre-Jean
Duribreux, learnt much of his trade under the Roux brothers; *pot-au-feu de
langoustines aux paillettes de safran, éminé de blancs de poulet mariné au thym et son
ragoût d'artichauts* or *vinaigrette de cervelles d'agneau* have been added to the classic
Perigord repertoire; the fixed-price menus (including two relatively cheap ones)
are good value.

22 bedrooms (some ground floor); no lift.

Our price symbols

£	You can expect to find a room for under £15
££	You can expect to find a room for £15 to £25
£££	You can expect to find a room for £25 to £35
££££	You can expect to find a room for £35 to £45
£££££	You should expect to pay over £45 for a room

The Atlantic Coast

Talmont

"Give me my scallop-shell of quiet . . .
And thus I'll take my pilgrimage" (Walter Raleigh)

The Atlantic Coast

If the Côte d'Azur sounds or has proved too expensive, too polluted, too noisy, too hot, too built up, too *mondain*; if its beaches are too few, too stony, too small, and too crowded; if, in short, your taste in beach holidays is for tides and waves, sands and dunes, not too many people and not too many trappings of sophistication, then the Atlantic coast of France, from the mouth of the Loire to the Spanish border, may be more to your liking. On the Côte d'Argent (south of the Gironde), a silver tongue of incoming and outgoing waves constantly refines the sands of exactly 288 kilometres of arrow-straight beach, interrupted only once by the oyster-rich bay of Arcachon. There are few resorts of any size, and nowhere is it so easy to have miles of beach to yourself.

There is so much sand that before the dunes were stabilised by the planting of pine forests, villages near the sea were buried and it was feared that the mighty mercantile port of Bordeaux would in its turn disappear beneath hundreds of feet of shifting dune. So dangerous are the currents in the ocean that many of the modest bathing resorts have grown up inland, on the lakes that have formed in a row behind the dunes which deny marshy streams access to the sea. Because the area was a wilderness until the last century, the coast has no ports or towns of any age or picturesque charm. Where resorts have grown up, shanty villages are squashed between an infinity of pines and huge dunes which block all sea views. The beachscape is abstract—no crescent sands, no background hills, no rocks, no offshore islands, no promenades, no wedding-cake casinos—just Second World War blockhouses and litter not washed away by the tides but piled up at the high water mark beneath the dunes. Yet the peace and quiet and the pine forests behind the Landes coast do have their appeal, and the Bordeaux bourgeoisie has had its villas at Arcachon since the 19th century. Children love the sand, and most of the small resorts—particularly those on the lakesides—are family orientated. Recently the emptiness has attracted large numbers of impecunious travellers, who settle among the pines and live out their ideal of noble savagery, ignoring families and resorts. For those who like their naturism institutionalised, there is at Montalivet the biggest reserve in Europe, and such is its success that its area is to be doubled in size. Still more recent, and by no means complete, is the very planned development of modern resort complexes along much of the Landes coast (*Mission Aquitaine*), a similar project in a similar style to the development of the Languedoc coast. These modern resorts, designed for convenience, have multiple facilities—campsites, self-catering flats, supermarkets, beach clubs and sports—but few hotels.

The interior of the Landes is the biggest pine forest in western Europe. One hundred and fifty years ago it was a desolate region of extreme summer aridity and winter floods. Its immense plains—as Dumas wrote, "mottled with wild heather, like the skin of a huge tiger"—were the realm of skylarks, partridges, quails, bees and flocks of sheep led by shepherds walking on stilts through the mosquito-ridden marshland. Irrigation dried out the Landes, making it healthier; and the planting of pine trees started a resin industry. Now the area is becoming increas-

The Atlantic Coast

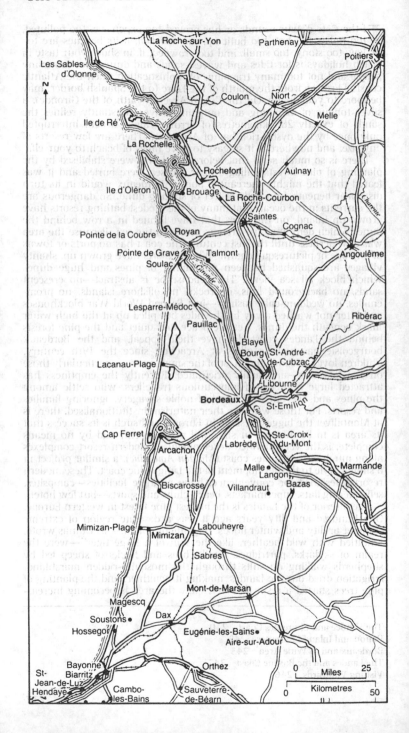

ingly prosperous from tourism and the discovery of oil. But the land-scape of the Landes today, its endless pines never changing in colour and never shedding their leaves, has an oppressive monotony all its own, with the piercing smell of pine and insistent grating of the stridulant cicada.

To the south of the Landes, the brief stretch of Basque coast is much more attractively varied; grassy Pyrenean foothills, adorned with col-ourful Basque villages, roll down to splendid beaches between rocky headlands where surfers enjoy the best waves in France. Biarritz had class and style once, and still has a little. St-Jean-de-Luz pulls in amateur artists and has an excellent, safe beach. The Basque resorts have more to offer than just the seaside; there are excursions into the mountains and to Spain, and there is the fascinating Basque country itself (see the chapter on the Pyrenees).

North of the Gironde, the Charentes and Vendée coast is less desolate and less straight than the Côte d'Argent, but almost as flat and almost as sandy. Resorts such as Royan and Les Sables-d'Olonne have a firm bucket-and-spade emphasis and not much chic. So gently do the beaches of much of this part of the coast shelve that reaching the sea at low tide means walking for miles across mud flats. It is oyster and mussel and salt-pan territory, and these traditional aspects of the maritime economy add some interest to a landscape which the writer and painter Fromentin described as "a doubly flat horizon of land and waters, which takes on striking grandeur because of its emptiness".

Like the coast, the inland region of Poitou and Charentes is flat, its horizons are huge and it has few of the obvious visual attractions and the variegated prettiness of rural France. For most tourists it is a through route with very straight roads to the south-west and Spain—as it was for medieval pilgrims on their way from the Ile-de-France to Compostela. There is at least no chance of boredom for the tourist interested in medieval (and especially Romanesque) churches, frescoes and sculpture, with which Poitou is as well endowed as any region in France. Most of the towns in this traditional Protestant region present an austere, grey face to the passing visitor. Two exceptions are the ports of La Rochelle, a very attractive yachting and fishing port, and Bor-deaux, an elegant, somewhat formal city of 18th-century bourgeois wealth, a mixture, in Victor Hugo's words, of Versailles and Antwerp.

The wealth of Bordeaux, without equal in 18th-century provincial France, came from trade, primarily in wine. The surrounding region—the two banks of the Gironde, and the four banks of the Garonne and Dordogne which flow into it—is the largest area of quality vineyards in the world; over a hundred million bottles of Bordeaux are exported every year to over a hundred countries. It is the area of Rothschilds (Lafite and Mouton), of Margaux, Latour and Yquem, of the *grands crus classés*, and of the noble rot which concentrates the sweetness of a very few Sauternes grapes to produce the world's greatest sweet white wines.

The wine trade has traditionally been dominated by the British, who adopted the Old French word *clairet* and applied it to Bordeaux red wine. The English controlled Bordeaux and Aquitaine for three centuries after 1154, when Henry Plantagenet (who had shortly before married Eleanor of Aquitaine) came to the throne of England. They developed a taste for claret, and gave Bordeaux privileged status which it was reluctant to sacrifice even when the English cause was lost. After the English departure, the claret connection remained; when the philosophical writer Montesquieu, proprietor of a château near Bordeaux, learnt that his books were selling well in London, his greatest joy was that it might help the marketing of his wine there. Wine labels still tell of the British involvement—Palmer, Talbot, Barton, Lynch; and in village restaurants, you hear buyers and proprietors business-lunching in English.

Wine buffs will need no encouragement to visit the Bordelais, especially the Médoc region on the south bank of the Gironde, which comes close to the ideal of grand châteaux surrounded by vineyards with wines maturing in the cask in secular cellars beneath sumptuous reception rooms. Although the châteaux are well worth admiring, and in many cases visiting, it is not a place for the amateur to interrupt a seaside holiday for the odd free tasting—you may not be offered any.

When you are eating in an Atlantic coast restaurant, and the sea breeze turns your appetite to oysters or a *mouclade* (mussels in a white wine sauce), you may wonder why a region of sea food should be blessed with such distinguished red wines, which always heavily outweigh the few humbler whites on the local wine lists. Practical Bordelais will tell you that you can drink claret with fish, and if you are not open to this kind of *nouvelle dégustation*, there is always the magnificent game from the Landes to do justice to the finest of clarets. Your gastronomic experience of the Bordelais may be preceded and crowned by yet more alcoholic specialities: the local aperitif, *pineau des Charentes*, a mixture of cognac and grape juice, and cognac itself. The publicity-conscious brandy firms (many of them also British in origin) are pleased to show tourists around their production lines.

The Vendée and Charentes Coast

The Vendée is a land of granite rocky hills south of the Loire estuary. Its only claim to historical fame is the war of repression which followed a royalist peasants' revolt a few weeks after the execution of Louis XVI. On March 13th 1793 news of national conscription reached the well-respected "saint of Anjou", Chatelineau, who put down the dough he was kneading and marched off with a few peasants wielding pitch forks. A couple of days later they took the town of Cholet, and by June were in charge of Saumur. Here Chatelineau was formally sworn in as *Général-issime* of the Royal and Catholic Army, in the first year of the reign of Louis XVII. Not long afterwards he met his death, but brutal repression and resistance went on for years in the unruly *bocage* of hedgerows and low trees and fourteen rivers, not one navigable.

On the coast, the main resort is **Les Sables-d'Olonne**, a simple family resort, large and busy with an excellent beach. **Pornic**, to the north, is a pretty fishing port and rocky creek, without any good beaches.

A short way north of Les Sables lies the **Ile de Noirmoutier**; it is not always an island—there is a road across the mud at low tide, which is much more fun than the modern toll bridge from Fromentine, but only practicable for a few hours a day. If your car breaks down, or if you set out when the tide is coming in fast, you may have to climb one of the refuge poles, and watch the development of a major rust problem. The only village on the island is old and attractive, with a fortress, and a fishing port linked by canal to the sea. Nearby, there are woods and some very good beaches, but most of the island is wide open with salt-pans and oyster beds, and fertile farmland. Though by no means empty in summer, Noirmoutier is quiet.

From Fromentine, there are boats to the smaller, impressively rocky

Ile d'Yeu, which is thoroughly Breton in character, with its rocky Côte Sauvage and its small sandy beaches on the sheltered north around **Port-Joinville**. From 1946 until his death in 1951, marshal Pétain, premier of Vichy France, was imprisoned at Port-Joinville.

Between **Niort** and the sea, the Sèvre Niortaise is flanked by the **Marais Poitevin**, a network of waterways, mostly the work of medieval monks. The area is at its most picturesque inland; lush woodlands surround and overhang the mossy waters, and locals travel in large punts, if need be taking their cattle with them. The best (indeed the only) way to sample the beauty of this enchanted world is to take a boat trip, most easily done from **Coulon**, where there is also a small museum.

In the Renaissance age, **La Rochelle** was one of the greatest maritime powers in France, and the most proudly Protestant. It starved for 15 months waiting for English relief from cardinal Richelieu's blockade. When mayor Guiton opened the gates on October 28th 1628 there were only 64 French and 90 English soldiers left in the town, and they were too weak to lift their weapons. During the seige the population of La Rochelle had declined from 28,000 to 5,000, and of those, 1,000 died almost immediately afterwards. When asked by Richelieu about his loyalties, Guiton remarked that he preferred to deal with a king who had conquered La Rochelle than with one who failed to defend it. Most of the defences of town were pulled down, but the old port today is still guarded by three medieval towers. It is reserved for yachts and fishing boats; there are artists, smart quayside cafés, and severely handsome buildings around the domed clock-tower and archway. There are more sleepily charming ports in France, but none which has a more appealing combination of beauty and vitality. The main streets are full of attractively decorated and individually arcaded Renaissance houses, and offer good shopping. There are spacious gardens but only a small town beach. Of the several museums the most unusual is the Musée Lafaille, devoted to 18th-century oceanography, with many beautiful and interesting old exhibits. The coast around La Rochelle is particularly popular with the sailing fraternity, which contributes to the well-to-do cheerful atmosphere. There are boat trips from the old port, but if you want to take your car across the water to the Ile de Ré, you must catch a boat from La Rochelle's industrial port La Pallice. In summer, and especially at weekends, there are very long queues.

Just as La Rochelle stands out in terms of charm and style from other towns on the west coast, so wasp-waisted **Ile de Ré** stands out among the islands. Like the others, it is flat, and has an attractively mixed economy of salt, oysters and mussels, a little fishing, but also wine and farming. Compared with the other islands, its villages seem more brightly whitewashed, their shutters more brightly painted; and the Ile de Ré has history. In centuries past it had its own militia and fleet, and being exempt from national customs duties it became an important trading port. The old houses of its miniature but proud capital, the fortified port of **St-Martin-de-Ré**, tell of past prosperity. **La Flotte** is another attractive little port, and there are good long sands on the other side of the small island. In season, Ré is attractively and colourfully lively, and you can take boat trips and learn the local fishing techniques. Out of season, it is no less charming in a very different way—fishermen mind their tackle and their own business, and discuss life over a *pineau* in cafés around the port. All the year round, wealthy villa owners come to enjoy week-end seclusion among the pines.

The larger **Ile d'Oléron** has no ports of any age, but its sandy coast between La Cotinière and St-Trojan has very good beaches and is popular with campers. There is a toll bridge joining it to the mainland.

The east coast of Oléron is muddy and full of oyster beds; so too is the mainland coast between the two islands, although the resort of **Fouras** does have some sandy and sheltered beaches. **Rochefort** is a large and architecturally severe 17th-century military port, some way inland from the Charente estuary. There is little here for the tourist, except the house of novelist Pierre Loti, its interior a strange world of exotic oriental fantasy. Nearby **Brouage** is a lonely spot of melancholy beauty. Its compact 17th-century fortifications, intact but overgrown, look out over miles of flat country which was ocean when Brouage was the busiest salt port in Europe, and the rival of La Rochelle. Now there are not enough houses to fill the walls and many are empty.

Many of the salt pans of the muddy half-land of this part of the coast have been turned to oyster farming. **Marennes** and **La Tremblade** (joined by a toll bridge) are the local capitals, with the characteristic oyster farmers' huts built on stilts in the mud. The coast between La Tremblade and Royan, at the mouth of the Gironde, is one of the major tourist areas of the Atlantic coast. The big resort of **Royan** was totally reconstructed after two short air raids in 1945 reduced it to rubble; it has a variety of very good beaches, and in season is very lively. Ferries cross the Gironde to the **Pointe de Grave** at the top of the Côte d'Argent. Among the trees on the edge of Royan, the sedate villa resort of **St-Palais** escaped the bombs. To the north, where the Gironde becomes the Atlantic, the coast becomes grandiose, with rocks and spray; at **La Grande Côte**, bathing is dangerous even in calm weather. Around the cape, where you can visit the lighthouse of La Coubre, there are enormous beaches with very few tourists (they have to walk some distance from the forest road). At **Ronce-les-Bains**, a popular resort for camping families, beaches are muddier but more sheltered.

Poitou and Inland Charentes

Although the landscape is no great enticement to venture inland from the coast, there are plenty of sightseeing opportunities for a rainy day, particularly attractive to those with a taste for Romanesque architecture. **Poitiers**, not as a whole a town of conspicuous charm, has a number of very interesting churches, and is at the centre of a region of France's best goats' cheese; it is also an important town in the history of France. In 732, Charles Martel reversed the tide of Saracen invasion near Poitiers; in 1356, the Black Prince routed the flower of French chivalry in a few hours before lunch, taking twice as many prisoners as he had English troops.

✳ *Baptistery* Isolated on a main street roundabout, this is one of the oldest Christian buildings in France, dating partly from the 4th century. Despite alterations in later centuries, there are many classical elements in the architecture and beautiful medieval frescoes inside.

✳ *Notre-Dame-la-Grande* On the market square, one of the most famous churches in France, thanks to the blackened and damaged but richly decorated façade—the finest example of the great feature of Poitevin Romanesque. A rather gloomy interior, with 19th-century repainting, but a beautiful choir and vault fresco.

The Atlantic Coast

✷ *St-Hilaire-le-Grand* Surprising, eccentrically planned Romanesque church with a row of domes, seven aisles and some delightfully carved capitals.
✷ *Cathedral* Bright, spacious, 13th-century Gothic cathedral, which seems conventional by comparison with the other churches; 13th-century choir stalls.
✷ *Palais de Justice* 19th-century buildings enclose a medieval tower of the Ducal Palace, and the magnificent 13th-century Gothic Salle des Pas Perdus. It was here that Joan of Arc was grilled for hours by the learned doctors of the University of Paris, who could find no fault with her.

Within a thirty mile radius of Poitiers, there is a high concentration of very old and beautiful churches, of which the following selection is not exhaustive. To the north-west, **St-Jouin-de-Marnes** is outstanding; others are at **Parthenay-le-Vieux** (just outside the attractively situated small market town of Parthenay), and the exceptionally well preserved pre-Romanesque church of **St-Généroux**. To the east of Poitiers, **Chauvigny** on the Vienne has an impressive fortress and church grouped on a hilltop above the town—the church is excruciatingly restored, but has marvellous capitals around the choir; quietly set beside the river on the southern edge of town, the church of **St-Pierre-les-Eglises** has 9th-century frescoes. Of all the Romanesque churches in the region, **St-Savin-sur-Gartempe** (east of Chauvigny) is the one whose beauty will most surely endure in the memory; it is a large and graceful old abbey church with tall belfry, between the river and a wide market square. The narthex is decorated with vivid frescoes of the Apocalypse, a foretaste of the magnificent series of paintings all along the high barrel vault, which have earned St-Savin its title "the Sistine chapel of medieval France". There are binoculars for rent outside, and detailed explanatory leaflets, both advisable for appreciation of the Old Testament scenes, depicted in harmonious tones of red and yellow ochre and green. The crypt also has marvellous frescoes, much closer to the eye.

On the pilgrimage route south of Poitiers, **Melle** has three Romanesque churches worth admiring, but not one to compare with **Aulnay**, which stands in isolation beside the road among cypresses. It is the very image of a pilgrimage-road church, and has one of the most beautiful of all Poitevin doorways, without a tympanum, but with decorated arches.

Saintes does not make much of its interesting monuments, apart from a Roman archway which used to stand on a bridge across the Charente, but now graces one of its banks. The town has long tree-lined avenues, and whitewashed houses giving a foretaste of the coastal style. River cruises up and down the indolently meandering Charente can be taken from Saintes and Cognac.

✷ *St-Eutrope* Once an important pilgrimage church, with a very beautiful Romanesque underground sanctuary.
✷ *Roman amphitheatre* Well preserved, and attractively set near St-Eutrope.
✷ *Abbaye aux Dames* One of the many abbeys famous for the education of noble females under the *Ancien Régime*, subsequently used as a barracks. The Romanesque church has been restored, and houses a photographic display illustrating local architectural features.

Perched photogenically on a rock above the waters of the Gironde south-west of Saintes, the church of **Talmont** is one of the most charming examples of Saintonge Romanesque.
Saintes is on the edge of the region of highest quality cognac

Amphitheatre, Saintes

production, to the south of the Charente around Cognac itself. The *appellation* of Cognac covers a large area including the Charentes coast and islands. The white grape vines of the region are not in themselves especially distinguished, and the hierarchy from modest Bois Ordinaire to Grande Champagne has less to do with the grapes than the alchemy of the distillation process in the alembic, and the ageing of the spirit in the wood (split, not sawn) of Limousin or Berrichon oaks, which gives different brandies their particular characteristics. The history of cognac goes back to the Renaissance when Dutch wine shippers (who had moved in to take the place of the expelled English) thought of distilling the wine to reduce its volume and ensure its long conservation. They called it *brandewijn* (burnt wine), whence brandy. In the 17th century, as Bordeaux produced better and better wines, it became clear to the Charentais that their wine was only good for distilling. Like champagne, the cognac business is dominated by big firms (mostly concentrated in Cognac). They blend their brews to ensure that the taste is the same year in and year out, and they produce a range of brandies which differ in quality according to the age of the various ingredients of each blend, from three star to VSOP. Cognac can mature for up to fifty years in the cask; once in the bottle it does not improve.

The town of **Cognac**, blackened by microscopic mushrooms which thrive on the alcoholic atmosphere, has little sightseeing apart from the cognac houses. The tourist office has information about visits, which reveal the blending and production lines, but not the distilling: this is carried out by thousands of *vignerons* throughout the region.

At the eastern edge of cognac country, **Angoulême** is a thriving and unattractive large town whose commercial centre is situated high above the Charente. The only reason for a visit is to shop or look at the domed cathedral, restored by Abadie in the 19th century almost as hideously as St-Front at Périgueux; the future architect of the Sacré-Coeur in Paris added to the exotic silhouette, but could not spoil the marvellous carvings all over the main façade, which include splendid battle scenes.

Bordeaux and its Wine Area

Of all the great wine growing areas of the world, few can match the Bordelais for quality and none for quantity of quality. **Bordeaux** is an ideal base for the viticulture vulture. There are small hotels in the centre, or, if you prefer, large modern business hotels on the edge of town; there are plenty of good restaurants, and in the centre of town, the Vinothèque is an excellent wine shop to fill your picnic hampers with the clarets you cannot afford in restaurants. Central Bordeaux is a splendid mixture; there is grand 18th-century monumental architecture, appropriately in this trading port at its finest along the *quais* around the magnificent Place de la Bourse (commercial exchange). Later in the century, the prosperous bourgeoisie demanded entertainment; the Grand Théâtre is classically restrained outside, sumptuously decorated inside—its domed staircase was the inspiration for the Paris Opéra a century later.

✳ *Old town* Between the theatre and the cathedral, elegant pedestrian shopping areas and narrow old streets and squares being beautifully restored. Lively restaurants and bars, many open late. Medieval fortress gateway (Porte Cailhau), turned into a triumphal arch; and a 15th-century belfry (Grosse Cloche).

✳ *Cathedral* Large and imposing 11th- to 15th-century mostly Gothic church, with very beautiful carvings on the exterior doorways.

✳ *Musée des Beaux-Arts* A well-endowed and varied museum of paintings (including Titian, Van Dyck and Delacroix), etchings (Goya), and sculpture, in part of the 18th-century Archbishop's Palace.

✳ *Musée des Arts Décoratifs* Excellent silver, porcelain, locks and regional furniture.

In general, the Bordeaux vineyards lack the charming country villages, simple accommodation and even the restaurants that are such an attractive component of wine touring elsewhere in France. The notable exception is **St-Emilion**, a beautifully situated small town, old and confined within well preserved ramparts on a horseshoe hill surveying its own subsection of the Bordeaux vineyards. St-Emilion has a good range of accommodation, a monolithic church carved out of the hillside, a medieval fortress, and beautiful houses of golden stone under roseate tiles.

Most of the vineyard country is flat and dull, none more so than the **Médoc**, but this is the area of the greatest wines (with a few honourable exceptions) and the most impressive châteaux, which makes it well worth while driving through even if you have no intention of paying any visits. Some of the finest châteaux to be seen from the road are Issan, Margaux, Palmer, and Cos d'Estournel. On the banks of the Gironde stands Vauban's eerily desolate **Fort-Médoc** citadel, which defended the Gironde with the help of the fortified port of **Blaye** opposite. Blaye's citadel is not empty but encloses a campsite and hotel. Inland vineyards are more attractively hilly and rural, especially the **Sauternes** between the Garonne and the Landes. Even if, as is to be feared, you are denied access to Château d'Yquem, home of the world's finest sweet white wine, the medieval château is well worth admiring and you can contemplate the vines which each produce no more than a single glass of wine a year. Just across the river, attractive **Ste-Croix-du-Mont** has a picturesque group of church and château on a cliff-top terrace; below there are grottoes walled, strange though it may seem, with fossilised oysters.

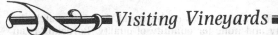

Visiting Vineyards

If you want to do more than admire châteaux from the outside, advance organisation is necessary for the majority of Bordeaux vineyards. Either make an appointment through a wine merchant at home, or contact one of the wine information bureaux below for details of châteaux which receive visitors and offer tastings.

In Bordeaux, the Office de Tourisme arranges vineyard coach tours from May to October. The Maison du Vin, 1 Cours du 30 Juillet, Bordeaux, 33000, tel: 56.52.82.82 can give information on vineyards all around the Bordeaux area and has touring maps showing the châteaux. Centres in the individual wine producing areas have their own *maisons du vin* which offer more detailed local information, and some sell wines; these include the Maison de Vin de Pauillac, 33250 Pauillac; Maison du Vin de Margaux, 33640 Margaux; Maison du Vin de St-Estèphe, 33250 Pauillac; and the Maison du Vin de St-Emilion, 33330 St-Emilion. For information about the *crus bourgeois*, contact the Syndicat des Crus Bourgeois du Médoc, 24 Cours de Verdun, 33000 Bordeaux, tel: 56.44.90.84.

Instead of or in addition to *maisons du vin*, some areas (including Pomerol, Barsac, Ste-Croix-du-Mont, Côtes de Bourg) have informative *syndicats viticoles*. There are also many local co-operatives producing good value blended wines; at most of them you are able to taste and buy (including a particularly good one in St-Emilion which sells a large range of vintage wines).

The following is a selection of vineyards to visit, not for their wines alone, but for a variety of other reasons. Make an appointment.

Château Loudenne (Bas Médoc) Attractive, pink, British-owned 18th-century château; interesting guided tour in English. Tel: 56.09.05.03.

Château Mouton-Rothschild (Médoc) Elegant and immaculate property; no wine for sale, but a very fine museum of wine-related art treasures. Closed August. Tel 56.59.22.22.

Château Lafite (Médoc) Regular guided tours in English, including an explanatory film. Appointments made in Paris. Tel: (1) 42.56.33.50.

Château Margaux (Médoc) The only architectural *monument historique* of the Médoc, with impeccable *chais* where the oak barrels are lined up; the guided tour includes a visit to the cooper's workshop. Closed August. Tel: 56.88.70.28.

Château la Rivière (Fronsac) One example of a lesser known vineyard whose proprietor welcomes individual visitors. Tel: 57.24.78.01. Fairy-tale château, with beautiful old dovecote. Tel: 57.24.78.01.

Château de Malle (at Preignac, in the Sauternes) Beautiful 17th-century château, worth visiting in itself. The guided tour includes a tasting of the fine second-growth sweet dessert wine.

The Landes and the Basque Coast

Judged from the N10, which streaks through the Landes from Bordeaux to Biarritz, the pine forests which have replaced the sandy wilderness are not much of an improvement: Pyrenean views have been obscured, sheep and shepherds have disappeared. But the forest is not all pine, and in clearings among the trees—like pioneers' impressions on a new world—there are small rural communities with low farmhouses of painted timbers and patterned bricks, surrounded by fields of maize and tobacco and gaggles of geese. The most convenient way to find out about traditional life in the Landes it is to take the small train from **Sabres** in the heart of the **Landes Regional Park** to the **Marquèze Ecomuseum**, which is indeed a preserved and reconstituted total ecosystem. There are explanatory displays about the sheep and the bees which formed the basis of the Landes economy, and beautiful old farmhouses traditionally furnished.

In the Landes the great sports are rugby, *pelote*, and the *course landaise*, a bull-fight where, as in Provence, the bulls are not in danger: the *écartant* thrills the assembled crowd with virtuoso leaps at the very last second to avoid the bull's charge. Spanish-style *corridas* are also staged, notably at **Mont-de-Marsan**.

To the north of the forest, **Bazas** has a very attractive town centre, with old arcaded houses beside the cathedral looking down over an expanse of cobbles; nearby **Uzeste** has a surprisingly large and impressive Gothic church. The medieval **Château de Roquetaillade**, in a fine setting, is an entertaining example of 19th-century Gothic restoration, and the beautiful moated **Château de Labrède** preserves the enormous library of the 18th-century philospher Montesquieu. To the south, sedate **Dax** is a famous hot-water spa, with a hot spring right in the middle of town.

Along the Landes coast the beaches vary little, except within the large **Bassin d'Arcachon**, emptied almost completely twice a day by the tide. If you stay around the basin, expect at best muddy bathing. It is an area of oyster farms, and stalls by the road sell oysters very cheaply. There is also a bird reserve, **Le Teich**, open to visitors (signposted walk and explanations). **Arcachon** is large, and by the standards of the Atlantic coast lively and smart: there is a promenade, shaded with small pines, and a spanking white casino, looking out over the pier to Bird Island.

Arcachon's beaches are less good than the ones to the south, around the peaceful and prosperous resort suburbs of **Pyla-sur-Mer**, and **Pilat-Plage** which nestles among the pines beneath the elephantine bulk of Europe's biggest dune (114 metres). You can climb the sand at the expense of considerable energy, or use a staircase. From the top there are magnificent views across the mouth of the basin to Cap-Ferret, its waters usually flecked with sails, and over the pine forests behind.

Cap-Ferret, set on the sheltered side of the point which almost encloses the Arcachon basin, is a quiet, small but sprawling resort, whose beaches—on the Atlantic and Arcachon sides—are linked by a miniature train service. An oil rig fenced off from the curiosity of tourists nods up and down in perpetual motion in the middle of the sands.

North of Arcachon, the **Côte d'Argent** is within afternoon sunbathing range of Bordeaux. The main resorts, old (turn of the century) and new, are situated around the two large lakes of Carcans and Lacanau, and on the ocean beyond the dunes. The most attractive village resort is **Le Montant/Maubuisson**, a quiet leafy little lake port with a large beach. At **Bombannes** there is a new forest and lake recreation centre for campers, sailors and self-caterers. Further north, **Montalivet-les-Bains** is one of the oldest and most traditional of the Landes coast resorts, with a large naturist centre in the forest nearby. At **Soulac-sur-Mer** a Romanesque pilgrimage basilica (Notre-Dame-de-la-Fin-des-Terres) which disappeared under the accumulating sand dunes in the 18th century, has been partly disinterred.

To the south of Arcachon are more lakes between forest and dunes, with watersports and camping; the **Lac de Parentis** is distinguished by oil rigs and a military zone. **Port de Maguide** is the most lively tourist complex. **Gastes** is more of a real village resort. The towns **Biscarosse** and **Mimizan** are useful service areas for campers, and both have their substantial seaside resorts nearby. South of Mimizan, the Landes coast is at its emptiest, with an occasional track from the forest road down to a few shacks beneath the dunes. At **Léon**, there is a small lake with some amenities, including a naturist colony; you can take a boat trip down the **Courant d'Huchet**, which has almost sub-tropical vegetation, and a wealth of noisy birdlife. At the southern end of the Côte d'Argent there is a concentration of resorts of which the most important is **Hossegor**, with a canal linking lake and beach. Lakeside Hossegor has the more style, a safer beach, and an attractive Basque influence.

The **Basque coast** combines long sweeping curves of sandy beach with the beauty of cliffs and rocks which, with the Biscay gales, make surf. To veterans of the Riviera the Basque Corniche road is a disappointment, the summer weather is less reliable, and the pace of life in the resorts strung from Biarritz to the Spanish border is also considerably less hot. **Biarritz**, queen of the coast, has a beautiful setting on tamarisk covered rocky headlands, three beaches (the surfing one should be treated with respect), and two casinos. But it has kept little of its style, except empress Eugénie's villa—now the sumptuous Hotel Palais, which stands above the ocean, imperially aloof from the march of time; the old villas and the Russian Orthodox church are peeling, and summer visitors are an ill-assorted mixture of self-sufficient self-caterers, surfers, and a nostalgic older generation. There is a lack of middle range and inexpensive accommodation and restaurants.

Although Biarritz does not look Basque, it is, and its sea-faring inhabitants used to be whalers when whales abounded in Biscay Bay; now there is only a token fishing port beneath the rocks. **St-Jean-de-Luz** has maintained its traditional fishing activity, and remains an important and colourful tunny port. It is an exceptionally attractive resort—old, picturesque of setting and architectural style (painted Basque timbers), smart and lively. Artists, art galleries and cafés surround the port, and the beach (exceptionally for this part of the coast) is as safe as it is sandy, for St-Jean-de-Luz is on a deep and sheltered bay. You can visit the old house beside the port where Louis XIV waited a month in 1660 for his Infanta to be delivered; the marriage took place in the church of St-Jean-Baptiste, which is a splendid example of the Basque style, with a massive gilt altar-piece covering the east end, wooden galleries around the walls, and a painted wooden vault. The adjacent fishing village of Ciboure, with its handsome Basque houses reflected in the water, is unaffected by tourists.

Hendaye, railway station border town beside the Bidassoa, on whose bridge many historic encounters between French and Spanish rulers took place, has two parts. The town, set back from the ocean, is bustling but without particular appeal; the resort—which sprawls along the whole length of an enormous sand beach—is well-kept, pleasantly old-fashioned and spacious, but suffers from a lack of focus for its seasonal animation.

Hotels

Bordeaux, 33000 Gironde££

ETCHE-ONA
14 rue MautrecTel: 56.44.36.49

In a very central street—so narrow that it almost escapes traffic—close to the Grand Theatre and main shops. There's no bar or restaurant, just a friendly small lounge-reception area, with ongoing television as part of the décor, and a small indoor terrace with plants. Bedrooms vary—none very big or very light but all clean and cared for: quieter at the back. This is, and aims to be, nothing more than a modest and congenial base in a town catering principally for businessmen; as such it is excellently situated and good value.

Closed Christmas to New Year; 33 bedrooms; no rest.

La Rochelle, 17000 Charente-Maritime£££

LES BRISESTel: 46.34.89.37

About a mile from the town centre, Les Brises is a five-storey modern block (much more attractive inside than its exterior suggests) set directly on the sea, looking across (from the rooftop terrace at least) to the Iles de Ré, d'Aix and d'Oléron. The pebble beach is uninviting, but there's a broad paved terrace just above. Most bedrooms have a view and are bright and peaceful, with luxurious bathrooms. Public rooms (no restaurant) are cool and airy. The whole place is stylish, co-ordinated and harmoniously efficient.

Closed mid-Dec to mid-Jan; 46 bedrooms; no rest.

Hotels

St-Emilion, 33330 Gironde   £££

HOSTELLERIE PLAISANCE   Tel: 57.24.72.32

On the central square, next to the medieval bell-tower, with fine views over the small town, this fine old building has been well renovated and offers comfortable accommodation. Six bedrooms, recently done up, are more stylish than the others, which are due to follow. There's a small garden and terrace, lounge, and an attractive restaurant, where you can opt for an astonishingly cheap (considering the area) three-course fixed-price menu, or a larger and more expensive "gastronomic" one. Money saved can, of course, be put towards a bottle of local wine, of which there is a large list at prices which are less generous.

12 bedrooms; no lift.

St-Jean-de-Luz, 64500 Pyrénées-Atlantiques   ££

LA FAYETTE   Tel: 59.26.17.74

Pretty little hotel in the heart of St-Jean's main restaurant street, just moments from the beach and not much further from the port. Bedrooms are fairly small, but comfortable; the restaurant is large and lively, with a terrace on the street. Food is plentiful and good value, with the emphasis on Basque specialities and fish (including tuna, from which St-Jean fishermen still make a living). The whole place has a busy atmosphere, very much in keeping with St-Jean itself.

18 bedrooms; no lift.

St-Jean-de-Luz, 64500 Pyrénées-Atlantiques   ££

POSTE   Tel: 59.26.04.53
83 rue Gambetta

In the heart of town, this traditional 16th-century post house retains a dignified charm, with comfortable public rooms and large bedrooms. There is no garden or restaurant: parking is in the adjacent municipal car park.

Closed Jan to mid-Mar; 34 bedrooms; no lift; no rest.

Our price symbols

£	You can expect to find a room for under £15
££	You can expect to find a room for £15 to £25
£££	You can expect to find a room for £25 to £35
££££	You can expect to find a room for £35 to £45
£££££	You should expect to pay over £45 for a room

The Loire Valley

Château de
Montsoreau

"I love thin slate more than hard marble, my Gallic Loire more
than the Latin Tiber . . . and more than the sea air the sweetness of
Anjou" (Du Bellay)

The Loire Valley

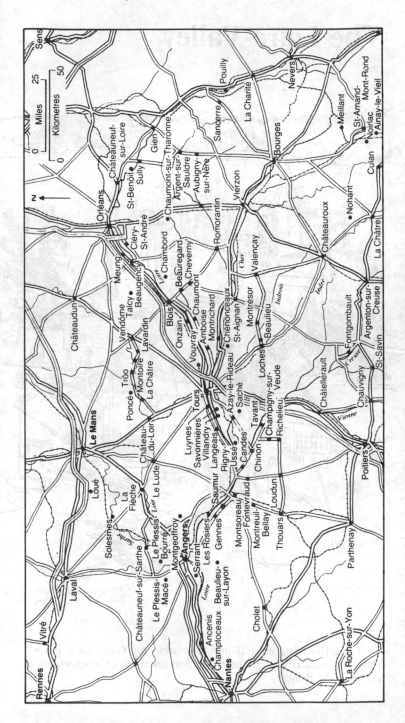

The Loire Valley

The Loire is France's longest river, running more than 600 miles from its high volcanic source in the south-east of the Massif Central to the Atlantic coast. But the area called the Loire Valley or *Val de Loire* is only a part of the course of this great river, which changes character many times as it descends, slows down and fattens. It is a section of the Loire in its maturity, after the definitive change of direction westwards (the Orléans loop) and before the seaward stretch, and it is also the area of tributary river valleys north and south.

The *départements* making up the Loire Valley are many, and significantly all named after rivers—such as Cher, Eure-et-Loire, Indre-et-Loire, and Loire-et-Cher, but not 'Loire' which is in the Massif Central, a long way upstream. These divisions mean less than the provinces familiar from all our history books: Anjou, land of mighty medieval warlords and home of the Plantagenet kings of England; Touraine, bountiful heart of Loire châteaux country, so-called garden of France and the only French region that has never borne the yoke of a foreigner; the Orléanais, where the tide of the Hundred Years' War was dramatically turned; and the wooded and agricultural Berry, rich in treasures from the Middle Ages and Renaissance.

This part of the Loire Valley is one of the most popular tourist areas of France, the simple reason being its unique endowment of Renaissance châteaux. Without them the area's historical associations, its convenience to Paris and even England for week-end visits, its good wine and food and its pleasantly fertile landscapes would attract no more visitors than other areas. The Loire's peculiar richness in châteaux is not just luck: from the time of the Hundred Years' War (when the English and Burgundians kicked the kings of France out of Paris and the north), until the end of the 16th century (when Paris and the Ile-de-France became an irresistibly powerful magnet for the court), the monarchs and their retinue spent more time in the Loire than anywhere else—hunting, playing, and building châteaux.

At first the royal court reflected, in its lack of splendour, straitened royal circumstances. Charles VII, mockingly referred to by his enemies as the king of Bourges because his home town was the only one in France on whose loyalty he could depend, held court at Chinon—an unluxurious fortress even before it fell into ruin. Joan of Arc found him here in 1429, despite his attempts at disguise, and stirred him into action with the result of the almost immediate relief of Orléans and the expulsion of the English from nearly all of France within 25 years. The end of this morally and financially sapping conflict coincided with developments both in the art of war and in the extent of royal power which made the fortification of houses and castles redundant. The fortress gave way to the château.

The end of the 15th century was a period of transition: the château at Langeais, built as a stronghold by Charles' son and successor Louis XI, looks like a medieval fortress on one side with its great barbican and drawbridge, but like a Renaissance dwelling on the garden side. Louis himself was a calculating political operator who had little time or taste for gracious living and preferred to spend his time in the modest château he had built at Plessis-lès-Tours (near Tours). His son Charles, whom Louis had installed with his mother at Amboise, was quite different, and his reign (1483–98) marks the beginning of the glorious century of courtly magnificence and gracious châteaux-building in the Loire. The spirit of the area seems to have changed very suddenly. A very important reason was the French awakening to Renaissance Italy brought about by Charles VIII's otherwise fruitless military campaigns there. The French fell not for Brunelleschi's Florence but the extravagant ornamentation of decadent Gothic buildings around Milan (the Certosa at Pavia is the accepted model for the architectural style of the Loire) and set about building their own Italianate Renaissance châteaux in the Loire Valley.

The typical Loire château is not, as châteaux in other areas are, a vast palace designed and situated to impress a sense of awe, but is rather a private dwelling for gracious and comfortable living, built by people bursting with new ideas and enthusiasm for embellishing rather than dominating the landscape. Loire châteaux seem to express not variations on a theme but personalities; Chenonceau's proprietor Thomas Bohier had as his motto "s'il vient à point me souviendra"—roughly, "if it (the planned château) is achieved they will remember me".

Scenically the Loire Valley disappoints many visitors. The river itself, at least in this section, is not one of France's prettiest, and does not compare with the Dordogne, the Tarn, the Doubs or even the rivers of the Ile-de-France—so much more appreciated by painters. Between Orléans and Tours the Loire is wide and shallow, very often with unsightly mud banks divided only by a few thin streams of water. This makes the river unsuitable for the activities which attract active tourists—canoeing, boat trips, swimming. Its wide bed cuts little into the landscape: there are no steep riverbanks, and in many places the road along the Loire offers views across spacious fields on one side, while on the other an anti-flood bank obscures the river itself from view. So the Loire is a difficult river to admire, especially from any height. Its secretive tributaries are even more so, having made equally little impression on the soil and being flanked more often by woods than roads. The traveller arrives, having seen French Railway posters of Loire châteaux, and assumes that everything about the region will have the same picturesque qualities—Mosel-like vineyard-covered riverbanks, Dordogne-like golden villages reflected in the sluggish water. To his dismay he finds that the Loire proclaims itself "Fleuve Nucléaire", and that great power stations loom over the landscape beside the historic ruins of Chinon castle and the elegantly prominent belfry of St-Benoît-sur-Loire. Many of the villages seem disappointingly grey and anonymous, and many of the finest châteaux do not make majestic river compositions, but are hidden away in the woods beyond.

Disappointment has a good pedigree; the traveller Arthur Young wrote of his impressions from a visit in 1787: "The Loire for so considerable a river and for being boasted the most beautiful in Europe, exhibits such a breadth of shoals and sands as to be almost subversive of beauty". Between Tours and Amboise he found the country "more uninteresting than I could have thought possible for the vicinity of a great river". But Young was intrigued by the cliff dwellings beside the river, inhabited then as now: "Where the chalk hills advance perpendicularly towards the river they present a most singular spectacle of human habitations: for a great number of houses are cut out of the rock, fronted with masonry, and holes cut above the chimneys, so you sometimes know not where the house is from which the smoke is issuing. The people seemed satisfied . . . a proof of the dryness of the climate. In England the rheumatism would be the chief inhabitant".

These reservations are not the whole truth, and if you have time and inclination to explore minor roads along the river you may acquire a taste for the subtle beauty of parts of the valley. They will not quench a thirst for the spectacular, but if the time, the weather and the light are right as you drive along the grassy south bank of the Loire downstream and across from Langeais, the farmworkers will be pedalling idly home, the poplars swaying melodically and shimmering like olive trees, the swallows skimming along the surface of the silvery water, and you will never again say without qualification that the Loire is scenically dull.

Considering the amount of tourism and the importance of the river it is surprising that the area isn't more commercial and industrial. One reason has been the river's impracticability, over the last two centuries, for heavy traffic. Another has to do with the quality of the tourism: people come to visit châteaux and to eat and drink well, not to pass the time of day in bars and tourist shops, and the time of night in discos. Relatively few local people seem to be involved in or affected by tourism.

One aspect of tourism which does thrive is the hotel business. The people of the Loire, and of Touraine in particular, have long enjoyed other people's enjoyment of it. Elizabeth Strutt wrote of her stay at the Hotel du Faisan in Tours in 1832: ". . . we sat down to a *table d'hôte* served with all the variety and profusion which renders travelling on the direct roads in France a luxury rather than a privation to those who may make a gratification of their appetite a primary consideration: sixteen or eighteen dishes including soup, fish, ragout, roast meats and winged fowl of all descriptions, with creams, fruits and dessert was the bill of fare, for 2 francs and a half, including excellent wine and the attendance of the best humoured and most civil servants I ever saw". The coachloads of affluent culture-cravers spending two days of their French week in the Loire have of course had their effect on prices and quality in some establishments, but these are usually easily identified (if only by the coaches) and avoided.

The Loire from Sancerre to Orléans

This region, bounded to the north and east by the Loire as it describes its slow westward bend, is not châteaux country, nor scenically typical. Extremely attractive exceptions to the general flatness of the lower Loire Valley are the hills of the Sancerrois, which give extensive and beautiful views and which produce the most prestigious and delicate of Loire white wines. **Sancerre** and **Pouilly-sur-Loire** (centre of Pouilly-Fumé production) are the best places to taste and buy, with lots of direct growers' outlets in the two villages. Sancerre is the more attractive of the two, finely situated on a round hill topped by a 14th-century round tower with views over the river and the vineyards; it's a pleasant place to stay or pause for a wander around the old streets. To admire the remarkable setting of Sancerre at its best, take the little road through the hills to Vailly (towards Bourges), and look back.

Gien is a much larger town on the water's edge, carefully restored after heavy war damage. The view across the river is imposing: the vast château with its turrets and patterned red brick walls (more like nearby Burgundy than the Loire in this respect) looks down over the town and its very handsome, squatly buttressed old bridge. The main road along the river is the most animated focus of town life.

* *Château* The 15th-century building houses an impressive hunting museum, which justifies its adopted title of "international" by having a lion's head as well as fauna more plausibly of local provenance. There are boars, bears, antlers, fine hunting paintings, prints and tapestries, weapons, horns and falconry-related items, all very well displayed.

* *Ste-Jeanne-d'Arc* Next door to the château and fitting well into its setting, this modern church is remarkable for having attracted nothing but praise. It may seem an unadventurous attempt to recreate a Romanesque church, with the added height and slenderness of pillar that modern techniques allow, but undoubtedly leaves a warm and harmonious impression. Terracotta capitals tell the story of Joan's life.

Sully-sur-Loire is a large riverside village dominated by the splendid, mostly 14th-century **Château de Sully**, which since the 17th century has been surrounded by its own moat separated from the river by an embankment and more recently a large campsite. It is one of those châteaux which looks magnificent and is rich in historical associations, but, like most of the Loire châteaux, has little inside. Swans glide along the still waters at the feet of massive round corner towers topped by swelling crenellations and conical roofs. Inside you are shown chilly medieval halls where Charles VII had two of his interviews with Joan of Arc, and where the young Voltaire, an exile from Paris, entertained with his plays the broad-minded duke of Sully of the time. A modern (17th-century) wing was added by Sully's most distinguished duke, Maximilien de Béthune, one of France's most energetic and omnicompetent servants, about whose working habits and financial acumen the guide will tell you much. The tour would be of minority interest were it not for the remarkable chestnut vault spanning the upper hall. The trees had their tops tied together as saplings so they grew to the required shape, and the beams arch unbroken from the floor to meet 30 feet above like an inverted boat hull and have done so without restoration for over 600 years.

The unspectacular course of the Loire from Sully to Orléans is made memorable by two of the most interesting churches of the whole region. The **Abbaye de St-Benoît-sur-Loire** was a Benedictine abbey called Fleury until its monks rescued their founding father's remains from pillaged Monte Cassino at the end of the 7th century and earned St-Benoît its rechristening. The saint's relics made St Benoît an important shrine, and by the 11th century the abbey could afford to erect the magnificent Romanesque church which still stands, with the relics still in the crypt. The most remarkable feature of the building is the vaulted porch supporting the belfry at the west end. One of the richly decorated capitals is signed by a justifiably proud Umbertus. Inside, the nave is tall and light; you can admire a sweetly sentimental alabaster Virgin, but not go into the elegant chancel without a guide, for whom you apply to the bookshop next to the church where monks sell souvenirs and home-made sweets. Daily services in the basilica, with Gregorian chant, are open to the public.

At the end of the 8th century the abbot of St-Benoît and bishop of Orléans found his abbey too noisy for fruitful contemplation, and built himself a country place with its own small church a few miles downstream at **Germigny-des-Prés**. The church still stands in the centre of a small village, with a nave added later to the original Greek cross plan. The whole was restored so thoroughly in the last century that it's hard to believe it is one of France's oldest churches, but it contains a fine Byzantine mosaic which was executed, along with many others now disappeared, by a 9th-century artist from Ravenna.

Châteauneuf-sur-Loire promises much but yields little. What's left of the 17th-century château is the town hall, with a little museum devoted to the maritime history of the Loire and its tributaries.

Orléans is a large town spreading over both sides of the Loire at its northernmost point. The town centre is on the north bank, severe, grey and treeless. There are some good shopping streets with attractive arcades, but the general impression is of a stark, unadorned, unwelcoming place, although not without things of some interest to see.

✻ *Cathedral* The most curious thing about this building is that it represents an attempt (rare before the end of the 19th century) to restore in the Gothic style of the original cathedral, partially destroyed in the 16th century. The attempt worked well enough for the architecture, but the sculptors working on the façade were clearly unable or unwilling to do their bit in the old-fashioned way. Inside, beautiful 18th-century carved panels surround the choir, open with the crypt and treasury to those prepared to undertake a guided tour.

✻ *Museums* Two of Orléans' finest medieval *hôtels* house the fine arts and local history museums. A small museum in the so-called Maison de Jeanne d'Arc is devoted to the exploits of the Maid of Orléans, with documents and model battles.

✻ *Olivet* An attractive garden suburb of Orléans on the banks of the Loiret, with restaurants, and boat hire; popular at weekends.

✻ *Orléans-la-Source* A very fine array of labelled flowers, shrubs and trees in the park surrounding the bubbling spring which is the source of the Loiret, a resurgence of Loire water which takes an underwater shortcut from near St Benoît, and runs only a few miles above ground before it rejoins the main river.

The Sologne and the Berry

The large area between Orléans and Bourges is quite different from other parts of the Loire valley—an infertile marshland of ponds and woods. Until it became the beneficiary of improvement schemes, the **Sologne** was suitable for neither healthy habitation nor profitable cultivation, so it has a small population and few buildings of note. Important exceptions are the châteaux of Chambord and Cheverny on its northern fringe (see page 272).

The Sologne landscape has a somewhat desolate beauty, with isolated low red-brick and timber-framed buildings, and thatched hides and boathouses beside the ponds; the area is excellent for fishing and shooting. The signed tourist route between Romorantin and La Ferté takes you through some of the most characteristic Solognescapes, but almost any by-road will do, even if it's only for a short detour from the road between Chambord and Cheverny. Anyone who has succumbed to the charm of Alain-Fournier's supremely atmospheric novel *Le Grand*

Meaulnes, set in the southern Sologne, will see the area through his eyes as a melancholy, misty and mysterious land; but nobody seems to feel that way about the Brenne, a very similar region south-west of Bourges.

The main town in the Sologne is **Romorantin-Lanthenay**, childhood home of the future François I. The old centre of town seems to have changed little since his day—a few streets of picturesque brick-and-timber houses with a wealth of interesting carving on their pillars and beams. There are also attractive gardens beside the Sauldre, and an interesting local museum.

Other places of interest in the region include Montevran Zoo near the handsome village of **Chaumont-sur-Tharonne**; the charming miniature **Château du Moulin**, beautifully furnished in Renaissance style; and **Aubigny-sur-Nère**, an attractive small town with old gabled houses, which became associated with the Stuart clan after Charles VII made one member a gift of the town in 1423. Nearby is the very pretty **Château de la Verrerie**, where you can go on a guided tour to see an elegant Renaissance gallery and 16th-century frescoes in the chapel. Near **Argent-sur-Sauldre** the Etang du Puits is a large lake with lots of facilities for watersports, fishing and swimming.

Stendhal's description of the prosperous, rolling agricultural region of the **Berry** as one of "bitterly ugly plains" is unkind and inaccurate, but all the same there would be little to attract the Loire Valley tourist south through the Sologne were it not for the Berry's fascinating old capital, Bourges.

Bourges is a large town with unsightly industrial outskirts, but an unspoilt historic heart, to borrow the favourite pun of Bourges' most famous bourgeois son Jacques Cœur; he was a wizard trader who amassed vast fortunes from the East, and financed the French recovery in the Hundred Years' War single-handed, to be rewarded with jealousy, disgrace and exile before he could enjoy the palace he had built for himself in his home town.

Jacques Coeur's Palace

✳ *Jacques Cœur's Palace* This, as your guide will repeat at every conceivable opportunity, is one of the finest secular Gothic buildings to come down to us intact, albeit cold and unfurnished. Over the entrance, carved figures lean out of *trompe l'oeil* windows to greet you, setting a tone of witty decorative exuberance which is sustained inside on the carved fireplaces and in details all over the palace including Jacques Cœur's ubiquitous motto "nothing impossible to valiant heart". There are also very fine wooden vaults, and a beautifully preserved ceiling painting by Fouquet in the chapel.

✳ *Cathedral* This mostly 12th- and 13th-century building, which dominates the town and the "bitterly ugly plains", is one of France's great cathedrals, with marvellous Gothic and Romanesque carvings outside and beautiful, easily decipherable stained glass. The tall five-aisled interior is of grand proportions, and in the crypt lies the recumbent statue of Jean duc de Berry who commissioned the famous book of *Très Riches Heures*, now at Chantilly.

✳ *Museums* Two fine Renaissance town houses are the Hôtel Lallemant (history of decorative art) and the Hôtel Cujas (Berry Museum: local history, archaeology, folklore).

Excursions from Bourges

Three interesting châteaux lie due south of Bourges on the so-called Route Jacques Cœur.

✳ **Château de Meillant** This is the finest of them, an early Renaissance château completed, like Chaumont, by the ex-Governor of Milan, Charles II of Amboise. Its exterior decoration rivals the exuberance of the Loire châteaux, and it has the added attraction of being inhabited and beautifully furnished.

✳ **Château d'Ainay-le-Vieil** A charming and surprising mixture of medieval fortress and Renaissance dwelling.

✳ **Château de Culan** A mighty medieval stronghold dominating the river Arnan, well-furnished with chests and precious tapestries, although not in period.

✳ **Abbaye de Noirlac** An old abbey on the banks of the Cher between Meillant and Ainay-le-Vieil, this is a typical and well-restored example of the simple Cistercian style of building; some of the monks' quarters are furnished.

✳ **George Sand country** For literary tourists. The area around **La Châtre** is the thickly wooded "Black Valley" where Aurore Dupin de Francueil, later George Sand, grew up. She herself was much more interesting than her output, and her château at **Nohant** is full of souvenirs of her and her circle, the intellectual and artistic élite of mid-19th-century France. The château at La Châtre also contains a museum devoted to the "good woman of Nohant".

The Loire from Orléans to Tours

This stretch of the river is the heart of châteaux country, the royal Loire of the Renaissance kings. On the left or south bank the first place of interest west of Orléans is **Cléry-St-André**, distinguished only by its basilica—pilgrimage destination and burial place of one of its most devoted pilgrims, Louis XI. Inside the unadorned church, a 17th-century statue of the monarch kneels facing the miracle-working Virgin, as Young supposed "praying forgiveness, which doubtless was promised him by his priests, for his baseness and his murders". If you find the right house behind the church you can visit the vault where Louis' and other bones lie, and a beautifully ornate chapel with Renaissance decoration.

Meung-sur-Loire is a small town of medieval literary associations: Jean de Meung was the author of the greater if not better part of that allegorical compendium of medieval thought, the *Roman de la Rose*, and the more accessible poet Villon was imprisoned in the château. Church and château make a handsome picture at the centre of the well preserved old town. One of the most important bridgeheads on the river, much fought over and still preserving its military aspects and a fine, mostly old bridge, is **Beaugency**. The centre of town is dominated by a romantically ruined 11th-century keep, complete with circling rooks and overgrowth; it adjoins a later castle, now housing a regional museum. Old cobbled streets run down to the river from the central square where an isolated church tower stands, like a Californian redwood, with a road going through its trunk. In the Renaissance town hall you can admire a series of beautiful 17th-century embroidered panels.

Downstream it's no great wrench to tear yourself away from the Loire, disfigured as it is by the nuclear power station of St-Laurent-des-Eaux. A few miles north of Mer is the charming **Château de Talcy**, flatly situated on the southern edge of the Beauce plain. A fortified medieval keep hides a beautifully furnished Renaissance dwelling where Ronsard was fruitfully entranced by the owner's daughter, the Cassandra of his poems which allude to the large dovecot which is still there, but not to the even older wine press.

On the wooded fringe of the Sologne south of the Loire, François I chose to transform a hunting lodge of the counts of Blois into the enormous **Château de Chambord** (see page 272). Its fanciful roofscape of lanterns, chimneys, dormers and turrets looks out over nearly 20 square miles of forest, mostly a hunting reserve closed to the public, but crossed by magnificent straight avenues leading up to the château. There can be few more exciting drives in France than this, as the château, at first all but hidden behind the trees, slowly unveils the full majesty of its façade to your advances.

Further south still are the two villages of **Cheverny**, one (Cour-Cheverny) a popular place to stay, the other (Cheverny) famous for the most beautiful classical château in the Loire (see page 272). If you are deterred by the crowds, or even if you aren't, the nearby **Château de Beauregard** is almost sure to be unfrequented. It is another of François' hunting lodges, but unlike Chambord is still inhabited, and full of character. You tug on a bell rope on the side of the house to summon a guide who shows a surprising and varied collection of things—caricature portraits in medallions over the porch, a gallery of fame with 363 portraits and a Delft tile floor, a small but choice art collection, and an exquisite little room decorated in the densely allegorical style of the 16th-century Fontainebleau School.

The road north takes you back to the river, the beaten track, and **Blois**, capital of the Renaissance Loire Valley. The lively and touristy town is impressively dominated by its great royal château (see page 272) on the flat top of a cliff, set back from the north bank of the river. It's an interesting (but hilly) place to explore, with pedestrian shopping streets and more picturesque old quarters down by the river. A few miles upstream, on the south bank, is the large and largely self-explanatory "Camping Sports Centre Lac de la Loire".

Downstream, the **Château de Chaumont** (see page 272) enjoys one of the most perfect settings of all, its round towers half hidden among the trees of a gracious park on a hill above the river, giving splendid views. Not far south-east of Chaumont the **Château de Fougères** is almost contemporary but looks like something from a different age. It stands feudally at the heart of a small village and shows no sign of the passing of the Middle Ages. It is none the less impressive for that and must have been even more so before the moat was filled in, the drawbridge thrown away, and windows installed in the thick curtain walls.

Back on the Loire's south bank **Amboise** bears comparison with Blois, in most ways favourably; the town is smaller and prettier, the situation of the château (best admired from across the river) more picturesque and a tour around it of more varied interest (see page 272). There are other things to see too—a museum devoted to the postal service, and the attractive manor house (Le Clos-Lucé) where Leonardo da Vinci lived and died, and in which are displayed working models constructed from his mechanical drawings. Two miles south of the town an isolated pagoda stands on a hill, all that remains of the magnificent 18th-century **Château de Chanteloup**. You can climb up inside for an extensive panorama.

The road along the north bank to Tours passes the village of **Vouvray**, home of both still and sparkling white wines (with lots of buying and tasting opportunities), and numerous cave-dwellers.

Tours is today's large and thriving capital of the châteaux country, conveniently situated (between the converging Loire and Cher) for exploration of the region, but hardly the most pleasant place to stay unless you like big towns or have no car (there are lots of coach excursions from here). Dominant features of the town plan are two long straight boulevards which intersect at right angles near the station and tourist office. The main shopping street (Rue Nationale) had just been built when Arthur Young arrived, and duly impressed him: "the entrance of Tours is truly magnificent, by a new street of large houses built of hewn white stone with regular fronts. This fine street which is wide and with foot pavements on each side is cut in straight line through the whole city from the new bridge of fifteen flat arches each of 75-foot span. Altogether a noble exertion for the decoration of a provincial town". Fortunately Tours wasn't completely redecorated in the eighteenth century.

✻ *Old Town* The very picturesque medieval quarter around the Place Plumereau has only recently been restored after heavy war damage. The narrow streets are full of interesting old houses, new shops and lively bars and restaurants (Tours teems with students, French and foreign). There are two museums, one with archaeological finds and medieval art, the other devoted to modern stained glass (*gemmail*). Two isolated towers are about all that remain of an enormous Romanesque pilgrimage basilica.

✻ *St-Julien* In the cloisters beside the imposing Romanesque tower a local wine museum has been installed in the old wine cellar.

✻ *Cathedral* Remarkably ornate façade crowned by twin Renaissance lanterns. Extensive view from tower. Earlier and conventionally Gothic interior.

✻ *Fine Arts Museum* Housed in the elegant Archbishop's Palace and full of treasures, mainly thanks to appropriation from demolished châteaux.

The Indre, Cher and Indrois

The Loire's prolific man of letters Honoré de Balzac was a more distinguished observer of man than nature but did leave some word paintings of the Touraine he loved best—the Indre Valley around his residence at Saché. The Indre is considered the most beautiful of the southern tributaries, meandering through woods and chalky escarpments; the Cher is bigger but, like the Indre, lined with interesting villages and châteaux. By far the most interesting of the châteaux is Chenonceau (see page 272), one of the highlights of any visit to the

Loire. The village, curiously spelt **Chenonceaux**, does no more and no less than cater, very well, for tourists. One of the joys of staying there is being able to wander down to the château first thing to see it before the crowds arrive. The château that sits weightless on the Cher like a mirage is familiar from photographs, but somehow never fails to delight the eye when seen afresh.

Montrichard is a lively little market town beside the river, with its own beach and an old bridge that gives a fine view of the old houses overlooked by ruined keep and ramparts. The hillsides on the edge of town house troglodytes, and wine cellars where you can sample sparkling Vouvray.

Quietly hidden away at the end of an enclosed valley the **Château du Gué-Péan** is a splendid late Renaissance building, tumbledown but being done up by the energetic owners. The guided tour is most informative about the scale of the task they have taken on, and includes repeated appeals to your generosity over and above the not inconsiderable entrance charge. The rooms shown contain a remarkable mixture of antique jumble—from Sicilian puppets to Talleyrand's gigantic waistcoat and photocopies of de Gaulle's will. More attractive than all this is the friendly, rather chaotic family atmosphere. There's a riding school in the outbuildings.

St-Aignan is another small town attractively situated by the river, climbing up wooded slopes at the foot of a Renaissance château. The solid late 11th-century church is more interesting, with lively capitals in the chancel and frescoes in the crypt.

Valençay is quite a drive from the normal Loire Valley tourist area, but worth the trouble. The village is well provided with accommodation and the château a magnificent example of the classical Renaissance, its great round towers domed and decorated with classical pilasters. Valençay's associations are mostly with the 19th century when it came into the possession of one of history's greatest diplomats, manipulators and political survivors, Charles Maurice de Talleyrand. The furnishings are luxurious, mostly in Louis XVI and Empire styles, and there are many beautiful *objets d'art*. Peacocks, cranes, black swans, sheep and deer wander around the surrounding park and gardens.

Montrésor is impressively situated beside the little Indrois. Its château was one of the many built in Anjou and Touraine in the late 10th century by the mighty count of Anjou Fulk Nerra; within the well-preserved medieval walls is a late 15th-century manor, beautifully restored and furnished by its Polish owners. Originally the castle was built for the Basternay family who are commemorated by a splendid tomb in the elegant Renaissance church. The road on to Loches passes fragmentary remains of the Carthusian monastery of **Le Liget** founded by Henry II in expiation of the murder of Thomas à Becket. The most interesting fragment is the round chapel with remarkable frescoes—you will probably have to ask locally for the key.

The fortified medieval city of **Loches** is preserved intact on a rocky hill high above the modern town and the Indre. You walk up through a fascinating Renaissance quarter of ornately decorated houses with a fine gateway and belfry beside the town hall, to the old city, entered by the 13th-century Porte Royale. Inside there are some elegant private houses and a number of historical monuments.

✷ *St-Ours* Romanesque church with a domed nave—unusual so far North. The outside, with octagonal pyramids covering the domes, is even more unusual.

✶ *Château and Keep* Separate buildings at either end of the city walls, full of history, but little else. Agnès Sorel, first public royal mistress (of Charles VII) lived here; Joan of Arc came to see Charles VII here; Louis XI kept prisoners in cages here, and Loches remained one of France's fearsome prisons for long afterwards. A walk around all or part of the walls may be more rewarding than the guided tours which demand good French and an interest in history and architecture. The guides are learned and long-winded.

The road back to the Loire along the Indre is a pretty one, but without imperative stops until you reach **Azay-le-Rideau**, a pleasant village full of tourists on their way to and from the most seductive of all the châteaux (see page 272). Literary tourists may choose to pay their respects to Balzac whose rooms at **Saché** have been arranged as a museum. At nearby **Villaines-les-Rochers** wickerwork is a cottage industry; you can watch the industrialists at work and buy their produce from co-operatives.

The Loire from Tours to Saumur, and the Vienne

The road downstream along the north bank of the Loire misses **Luynes** but offers a fine view of its severe medieval fortress. The château isn't open to the public but the village is old and pretty enough to justify a diversion. A few miles further on two medieval towers survive from the old château of **Cinq-Mars-la-Pile** (and are open to the public); on top of the hill is the mysterious monument which has earned the village its name—a solid tower nearly 100ft tall, built to what end and by whom nobody knows.

Langeais is an unprepossessing, noisy town on the main road but it has a remarkably well preserved and furnished fortress (see page 272). An impressive suspension bridge crosses to the south bank of the Loire where beautifully peaceful countryside stretches up and downstream, with a tiny road along the river which contrasts pleasantly with the north-bank highway. On the way back to Tours, **Savonnières** has some large caves with concretions, rivers and waterfalls. A more typical Loire attraction is the nearby **Château de Villandry**, a fine, classical-looking building added on to the old keep at the end of the 16th century. Villandry's great pride is its Renaissance garden (flowers and vegetables), faithfully reconstructed from old drawings, with a complex symbolic design and a wealth of colour at the right time of year (midsummer). You pay only a couple of francs extra to do the guided tour of the château interior as well, and although there isn't much of interest (mostly Spanish paintings and furniture, and a mosque ceiling transported intact for the Spanish owners) you do get an explanation of some of the significance of the garden layout—hedges shaped into billets-doux or hearts swollen with illicit passion or starved by rejection.

Villandry

Following the south bank downstream to the junction of Loire and Indre brings you to **Rigny-Ussé** where the creamy 15th-century **Château d'Ussé**, bristling with dormers, turrets and chimneys, peers out from a wooded hillside over the fertile farmland. This really looks like a fairy-tale castle, and in a sense it is—Perrault is said to have used Ussé as the setting for his Sleeping Beauty. To appreciate the château's superb setting, look back from the little bridge over the river or even further towards the Loire. The privately-owned château isn't as special inside as out, but is not without interest. The delightful Renaissance chapel has lost its fine tapestries, but not its della Robbia terracotta. Inside the main building the *chambre du roi* retains its unrestored 18th-century furniture; and you can do a partial tour of the sentry-walk.

The wooded slopes from which Ussé surveys the valley form the northern edge of the splendid oak forest of Chinon which joins up with the forest of Villandry and stretches all the way from Chinon to Tours. The main road between the two cuts impressively through it, straight as an arrow but up and down like a big dipper. The riverside road passes **Avoine-Chinon** nuclear power station, gilt-domed like a cathedral. Though the countryside between Loire and Vienne is fertile it is not strikingly beautiful, but the confluence of the two rivers is grand—so open and spacious that you suddenly think of the approaching Atlantic; it marks the divide between Touraine and Anjou. The scene is made by the setting of **Candes** on the Angevin side of the junction. Appropriately enough the impressive fortified church (St-Martin) at the centre of the village is an exemplary place to study the Angevin style of Gothic vaulting (the keys of the main ogive arches are higher than those of the other arches). The village is rather spoilt by main road traffic in the narrow high street, but you can escape by climbing up the hill behind the church for a splendid view.

The Anjou Loire, fed by the Vienne, at last seems to have enough water to fill its bed and becomes a river of stature. At **Montsoreau** a tall white 15th-century château rises powerfully from the river bank. The interior has been restored to its original style and houses a museum devoted to Goums (Moroccan Cavalry). From Montsoreau the road south leads to the **Abbaye de Fontevraud** founded by an itinerant 11th-century preacher to cater for all elements of his substantial following—male, female, sick and sinful. The Fontevraud order enjoyed great success and social cachet—Louis XIV's daughters were educated there and the list of abbesses (a female always presided) reads like a who-was-who of the French nobility. The abbey was turned into a prison in 1804 but has been extensively restored by forced labour and offers a great deal of beauty and interest to the guided tourist—especially the British since the abbey is something of a Plantagenet necropolis. The most remarkable feature is the Romanesque kitchen, an almost free-standing building where a style usually associated with churches is ingeniously applied to domestic purposes, with a rare and very successful concern for architectural beauty. Round the central space fireplaces are set in towers like apsidal chapels with a complex arrangement of little domes, arches and chimneys. The abbey church, stripped bare, can be admired in its architectural purity; recumbent figures of Henry II, the formidable Eleanor of Aquitaine, Richard Coeur de Lion and his sister-in-law Isabelle of Angoulême lie in the south transept. The elegant Gothic chapter house has lively 16th-century murals full of costume and portrait interest, and vaulting which fans out like palm leaves from slender columns.

South of Candes the Chinon road starts off following a particularly handsome stretch of the Vienne bordered by massive shady plane trees which makes you realise what the Loire lacks. You can turn off for a pilgrimage to the manor (La Devinière) where the 16th-century human-ist writer Rabelais was born; the area around Chinon and the Vienne was the setting for much of his work. **Chinon** itself is a fine old town attractively situated on the banks of the river and crowned by the imposing ruins of its medieval castle, of interest to imaginative students of military architecture and for its wealth of historical associations. But many tourists will find a guided tour less rewarding than a walk around the streets of old Chinon, especially around the one-time focus of Chinon life, the Grand Carroi. It isn't hard to imagine the town teeming with Rabelaisian life; the author lived in the Rue Jean-Jacques Rousseau.

For church lovers the small village of **Tavant** on the south bank of the Vienne has a treat in store: the little Romanesque church is a building of great charm with remarkable frescoes in its low crypt (you must ask around for a key, inseparable from an admirably explanatory guide). The four aisles of the crypt are no more than head high and well lit, so you can see perfectly the lively biblical and symbolic figures decorating the vault.

South of Chinon on the way to Richelieu, **Champigny-sur-Veude** is a shadow of its former self, but a fine one. Its palatial Renaissance château excited the jealousy of cardinal Richelieu who did not want to be outshone so close to home and had it demolished, except for a few outbuildings (now beautifully restored as a private home) and the chapel, a marvel of Renaissance ornament clothing a skeleton of Gothic architecture. The interior, empty except for the kneeling figure of Henri de Bourbon de Montpensier, rejoices in a superb series of windows which seem more like canvasses than stained glass; there are family portraits and scenes from the life and death of the crusading Louis IX (saint Louis).

Appropriately enough Richelieu's own palace suffered at the hands of the Revolutionaries much the same fate as Champigny—but they did a more thorough job. All that remains is a large park and a few domed pavilions on the edge of town. But **Richelieu** is still worth a visit as a remarkably unspoilt (although sadly ill-maintained) example of a classically planned town, walled and gated, with geometrically straight streets of noble town houses. There is a Richelieu museum in the town hall which gives some idea through old prints of the splendour of the place in the 17th century. On summer weekends a steam train runs between Richelieu and Chinon.

Westwards, the spacious Poitou plains are interrupted by the abrupt hill town of **Loudun**, famous for the 17th-century witch-hunt which enabled Richelieu to get rid of the subversive priest Urbain Grandier. At the time Loudun was commercially as well as intellectually a vigorous town of over 20,000 inhabitants. Today's Loudun (twinned with Ouagadougou in the Upper Volta) is less than half as populous—which accounts for a somewhat depressing atmosphere of urban neglect. The town is topped by a tall windowless square keep which is admirably expressive of the modest aesthetic aspirations and attainments of its builder, the rugged Fulk Nerra. The return to the Loire can embrace the impressively situated château and subsidiary village of **Montreuil-Bellay**. Beneath the old walls the river Thouet lingers in a wide pool, before running on northwards to the Loire. Inside the mostly 15th-century château you can see some heavy furniture, tapestries, and a fine old kitchen.

Saumur is a busy town spreading along both banks of the Loire and across an island in midstream. For many miles around you can distinguish the pinnacles of its massive castle, which stands alone on a rocky hill above the town. Saumur is the home of the celebrated Cadre Noir crack cavalry squad, 2,200 of whose cadets staged a heroic three-day defence of the town against 25,000 Germans in 1940, and which gives an annual display of cavalier virtuosity in July. At other times they can be seen practising (information from the local tourist office). Saumur is also the centre for the production of sparkling wine made by the champagne method, and over half of France's total output of mushrooms which flourish in the local tufa caves. But, apart from the small old town area below the château and the ornately decorated town hall by the river, modern Saumur lacks charm.

✴ *Château* Since the time the Brothers Limbourg portrayed it looking gaily down on the labourers in the vineyards, for the duc de Berry's book of *Très Riches Heures*, the 14th-century fortress has been much altered; but it is still an impressively fortified square-looking building with octagonal corner towers pointing skywards like rockets. Inside there are two museums, one devoted to the decorative arts with a particularly fine porcelain collection, the other to horses with skeletons, harnesses, spurs, engravings and historical documentation. There are fine views from the watch-tower.

✴ *Notre-Dame-de-Nantilly* A grey, mostly Romanesque church near the château with a very fine collection of 15th- to 17th-century tapestries.

✴ *Dolmen de Bagneux* Anjou's most important megalithic monument is somewhat out of context in the thick of modern suburban sprawl. Stones form a long, covered burial chamber; the nearby Café du Dolmen keeps the key to the enclosure.

✳ *Wine tasting* A number of wine houses open their doors to the public in Saumur and in the suburb of St-Hilaire-St-Florent. Ackerman-Laurence is the best-known house for Saumur sparkling wines.

The Loire from Saumur to Angers

As is the case for most of the Loire Valley, the road along the south or left bank is less frequented and prettier than the northern route. But it is worth making the excursion a few miles north from Saumur to the **Château de Boumois**. Built at the end of the 15th century it looks—with its solid round towers and machicolations—like a defensive castle, but hides like so many of the architectural hedgehogs of the same period a delicate Renaissance courtyard façade and interior.

The south bank road passes through **Chênehutte-les-Tuffeaux**, an attractive village in the heart of troglodyte and mushroom country whose 13th-century priory has been turned into a peaceful and distinguished hotel with very beautiful river views. **Cunault's** greatest distinction is one of France's noblest Romanesque churches—tall, white and slim (there is no transept). The view as you pass through the fortified west end to the head of a tall stairway down to the floor of the nave is one of great beauty, the sort they often have on postcards but which you usually can't enjoy without a ladder. The carving on the capitals is marvellous but they are hard to appreciate without binoculars and a stiff neck.

At **Gennes** you face the choice of taking the suspension bridge across the Loire to Les Rosiers (of primarily gastronomic interest) and going to Angers via Montgeoffroy, or staying south for the **Château de Brissac** and the wine villages of the Layon Valley. Brissac is a château of contrasts: 15th-century round towers which no one could pull down flank a mostly restored 17th-century building which is sumptuously decorated inside and out. As time and building went on and the flow of funds slowed to a trickle, the decorative exuberance of the Renaissance gave way to the sobriety of the Louis XIII style. Inside there is a gallery of family portraits (the Cossé-Brissac family have been here since 1502), rich tapestries and carved and gilt ceiling beams. To the considerable interest of the visit is added the pleasure of sampling the proprietary wines brought up from the château's 11th-century cellars.

The **Layon Valley** which runs north into the Loire just downstream from Angers is attractive and its slopes produce fine dessert wines. **Beaulieu-sur-Layon** is a good place to get a flavour of the scenery and its produce. There is a small wine museum and wine tasting, and there are fine views. The road back up to Angers crosses the Loire at **Béhuard**, a very picturesque old village on an island with an interesting church built in the rock to the order of the timorous Louis XI who nearly drowned there.

Accessible from the northern route to Angers, the **Château de Montgeoffroy** is a severely handsome, harmonious 18th-century building, which was only just completed before the Revolution. You are shown a small but beautiful series of rooms remarkable for the unrestored original Louis XVI furniture. One wing houses some splendid old carriages and an interesting saddle room.

Château d'Angers

Angers is a big and busy town on the banks of the short-lived Maine, in the land of black schist stone which contrasts grimly with soft white Touraine tufa. The old town centre around the cathedral has some admirable houses, none finer than the richly carved, seven-storey Maison d'Adam on the Place Ste-Croix.

✻ *Château* The massive 13th-century fortress walls are half a mile round and punctuated by seven 150ft round towers. The fierce black stone exterior is brightened by decorative veins of white, and by the formal gardens which now occupy the deep moat. The 15th-century chapel and inner buildings would hardly pull in the crowds, but the collection of tapestries more than justifies a visit. Angers' great treasure, and one of the Middle Ages' most valuable legacies, is the incomplete series of 70 14th-century tapestries illustrating the Apocalypse of Saint John the Divine, originally woven for Angers cathedral and saved from dispersal by the bishop of Angers who bought them at auction for 300 francs in 1843. The tapestries provide a supremely decorative, lively, and graphically literal illustration of Saint John's writings, complete with plagues of locusts, horses with lions' heads and snakes' tails, rivers of blood, and whores of Babylon. Unless you know the Apocalypse verbatim the audio guide is essential and a model of its kind, spoken in English by an admirably solemn and sonorous Englishman who allows the words to speak for themselves but does not omit to point out the topicality of the Apocalypse in the intensely anxious moral climate of the 14th century.

✳ *Cathedral* A fine church dating from the period of transition between Gothic and Romanesque styles, with a splendid Christ in Majesty carved over the west door. The interior has fine stained glass, mainly high up and hard to decipher.
✳ *Former Hospital of St John* The late 12th-century triple-aisled hall is an excellent setting for the display of Jean Lurçat's dazzling modern tapestries called the Song of the World, inspired by the Apocalypse.
✳ *Fine Arts Museum* In the Logis Barrault near the cathedral, a varied collection of paintings and sculptures, with a number of more interesting items than the complete works (mostly in cast) of the 19th-century sculptor David d'Angers.

Excursions from Angers
✳ **Château de Serrant** An imposing and very beautifully furnished Renaissance-style château. A magnificent staircase and tapestries, and Coysevox's very baroque tomb of the marquis de Vaubrun.
✳ **Château du Plessis-Macé** A charming medieval fortified manor with moat and keep, updated for more gracious living in the 15th century. Little furniture.
✳ **Château du Plessis-Bourré** A moated 15th-century fortress built, like Langeais, by Louis XI's factotum Jean Bourré. The highlight of the interior is the ceiling of the guardroom painted with allegorical and comic figures.

The Northern Tributaries

The **Sarthe** runs from Le Mans to its junction with the Loire just north of Angers through a fertile valley of apple orchards, and piggeries which produce excellent potted pork (*rillettes*). On the way up to Le Mans there isn't a lot to see except the Benedictine **Abbaye de Solesmes**, less distinguished architecturally than chorally; you can attend mass to hear some of the finest singers of Gregorian plainchant. In the abbey church there are some beautiful 15th- and 16th-century sculptural groups. Not far away up the Vègre valley, **Asnières** enjoys an attractive setting and has several fine old buildings including a church with extensive wall paintings.

The old Gallo-Roman (and earlier) city of **Le Mans** is of great interest even if you aren't tempted to join the thousands of pilgrims who flock every June to witness the 24-hour race, when competing cars travel over 3,000 miles round a track (partly public roads) south of Le Mans. Near the track a large motor museum is open through the year. The city itself has an extremely attractive medieval centre surrounded by the partially surviving Gallo-Roman ramparts, and a number of interesting monuments both in the town and in the suburbs.

✳ *Cathedral* A bizarre building of discordant but beautiful parts: a long low Romanesque nave with a soaring Gothic transept. The beauty of Laurana's recumbent Charles of Anjou is hard to appreciate without a bit of climbing; on the other side of the chapel Guillaume du Bellay, dressed as a Roman soldier, reclines nonchalantly propped on one elbow, his hand draped elegantly around a sword. There are lively elongated sculptures round the Romanesque south door.
✳ *Eglise de la Couture* Interesting old abbey church with fine but damaged sculptures round the west door, elegant vaulting in the Angevin style, a squat Romanesque arcade round the choir, and a very sweet white marble Virgin and Child by Pilon (16th-century).

✳ *Ste-Jeanne-d'Arc* A hall church (originally a hospital) with three rows of slender pillars supporting fans of Angevin vaulting.

✳ *Tessé Museum* The old bishop's palace houses a rich collection of paintings, pre- and post-Renaissance.

✳ *Abbaye de Notre-Dame-de-l'Epau* An attractive Cistercian monastery founded by Richard Coeur de Lion's widow Berengaria shortly before her death here in 1230. Most of the standard features of the architectural style of the order can be admired in the remaining buildings which date from after the abbey was burnt down in 1365.

✳ *Museum of History and Ethnography* The setting—the elegant 15th-century *hôtel* near the cathedral anachronistically called the House of Queen Berengaria—is of as much interest as the contents: local pottery, old prints.

The **Loir Valley** is hardly shorter than the section of the Loire covered in this chapter; the confusingly named tributary runs over 200 miles from just south of Chartres to Angers. *Le* Loir cannot match *La* Loire for architectural magnificence; but there is no lack of sightseeing and the river itself is to most eyes more attractive than its bigger sister, meandering slowly through a green and fertile, lightly wooded landscape, with little bridges across the river at every village, and very few tourists. It is at its most attractive, and most interesting from the sightseeing point of view, between Vendôme and Château-du-Loir, which was the homeland of the Renaissance poet Pierre de Ronsard who delighted in the charms of his native surroundings. For much of its course the Loir runs parallel to the Loire within easy reach of any of the big towns on the main river—Saumur, Tours, Blois, Orléans. Particular features of the villages along its banks are churches with medieval wall paintings, and some of the most interesting examples of cave dwellings.

Châteaudun is a busy market town on the Paris/Chartres/Tours road; its massive château, rising dramatically from the banks of the Loir, deserves more than an admiring glance as you speed by. Joan of Arc's brother-in-arms Dunois had much to do with its building. There are two wings—one Renaissance, the other (the Dunois wing) Gothic—which have some fine architectural features but little furniture. The late Gothic Sainte-Chapelle contains 15 colourful and expressive statues of female saints and portrait alleged to be of Dunois himself.

The drive south from Châteaudun is a pretty one provided you follow the minor roads along the Loir, not the N10. **Vendôme** is a fascinating and picturesque town built on islands in the river, with leafy waterside mills and weirs and gardens. On the wooded southern bank there stand enough remains of the old castle to look well, but not enough to make a very interesting visit.

The naturally moated centre of town is reached by the splendid bridge and richly decorated gateway of St-Georges. The busy market square (Place St-Martin) is graced by an elegant Renaissance bell and clock tower which lost its church long ago and now houses the tourist office. The Rue de l'Abbaye takes you into the precincts of the old abbey of La Trinité, once an important place of pilgrimage thanks to Geoffrey Martel's bringing back as an unlikely souvenir from the East the Holy Tear which Christ shed on the tomb of Lazarus. The handsome abbey buildings have been requisitioned for the army and local museum (which has an interesting section on local mural painting); their simplicity contrasts with the extravagance of the 16th-century west end of the church. The elaborate tracery of the window curls like flames and explains better than most places the use of the term *flamboyant*. The interior is relatively simple, tall and light with a gallery all round the triforium, some fine stained glass and 15th-century choir stalls.

On a particularly charming wooded stretch of the Loir, **Lavardin** is a small village of carefully restored old houses at the foot of romantic overgrown castle ruins. The castle is gradually being restored, and the working parties give guided tours round the various ruined buildings in summer. Lavardin's church (St-Genest) is no less in need of attention, damp and decaying inside, but has a variety of interesting wall paintings, with a particularly vivid representation of Hell in the gruesome taste of the late Middle Ages. A few miles away the bigger town of **Montoire**, where Hitler and Pétain negotiated in October 1940, has a less interesting ruined castle and more interesting frescoes, tucked away in the little chapel of St-Gilles where Ronsard was prior (the key is kept in one of the shops on the main street leading from the château to the bridge over the Loir, from which an alley leads to the chapel itself). The river is overhung with weeping willows and old houses, the chapel diminutive and cruciform, and the frescoes dazzling, especially the stylised red and white Christ (early 12th-century) over the main vault.

There are some more very fine frescoes in the small church of St-Jacques-des-Guérets which is attractively set beside a watermill across the Loir from the steep hill village of **Trôo**. There are scores of troglodyte houses in the hillside, a fine view from the top of the hill beside the mostly Romanesque church of St-Martin, and a cave which you can visit at the bottom of the hill to see stalactites and usually get soaked. A speaking well (*Puits qui parle*) is widely advertised; it turns out to be no more supernatural than a deep well shaft with a remarkable echo.

La Possonnière is the Renaissance manor where Ronsard was born. You have to arrange an appointment in advance if you want to go inside; if not the house can be seen from the road, with its decorative windows surrounded by Latin and French inscriptions. Nearby **Poncé** has more to offer: a mostly wooden Romanesque church with very interesting wall paintings (12th-century) and a Renaissance château with an exceptionally richly decorated six-flight staircase, and a local history/folklore museum.

From Poncé or nearby Château-du-Loir you can head back to Tours and the Loire, or carry on down the Loir for the only moderately interesting towns of Le Lude and La Flèche. The Renaissance **Château du Lude** is externally impressive and set in a fine park where the most spectacular *son et lumière* show in the Loire region is performed by a huge cast on some summer evenings. The château consists of three wings from different periods (Louis XII, François I, Louis XVI) with massive round corner towers; the inside (guided tour) is richly furnished and has Italian frescoes in the oratory of the François I wing. At **La Flèche** you can visit a famous military training school founded by Henri IV in 1604 and run by Jesuits until shortly before the Revolution. A few miles south of La Flèche is a large zoo (La Tertre Rouge), and to the east the gracious 15th-century **Château de Gallerande**, visible in beautiful gardens from the road, but not open to the public.

See next page for section on Visiting Châteaux, and page 276 for our selection of hotels.

Visiting Châteaux

The great châteaux, built of the local tufa stone which whitens with age, live up to all expectations from the outside, but their interiors may come as a disappointment. Most of the châteaux, the most famous ones at least, have been uninhabited for centuries and lack furniture. Compared with a typical stately home in Britain you will, in almost all cases, find less in the way of beautiful *objets d'art* to admire, and none of the curiosity interest of seeing family photos and everyday clutter to prove that the house is lived in. Most châteaux force you to troop around with a guide (rarely English speaking), even if notes in English are available. Occasionally this will enhance your enjoyment, but not often. Going around in groups exaggerates the serious problem of overcrowding, especially in small and popular châteaux like Azay-le-Rideau; even if you can understand the guide you probably won't be able to hear, and you almost certainly won't be able to see, what he's talking about. The guides are often bored, a problem which isn't new; when Arthur Young visited Blois nearly 200 years ago he wrote: "the guide tells many horrible stories in the same tone (from having told them so often) in which the fellow in Westminster Abbey gives his monotonous history of the tombs . . . the character of the period and of the men that figured in it are alike disgusting. Bigotry and ambition equally dark, invidious and bloody allow no feelings of regret. The parties could hardly be better employed than in cutting each other's throats".

A final warning hardly needs to be spelt out. Much of the interest of the Loire and its châteaux is historical—you stand in rooms where important things happened. If you are not familiar with or interested in learning about the history of France from 1420 to 1590 you will soon get bored in châteaux such as Blois, Amboise and Loches. If you do want to learn there can be no more fascinatingly illustrated way of doing so, but do not go unprepared. Unless you get your kings, queens and mistresses sorted out visits can be confusing and meaningless, and naturally French guides assume a greater knowledge of French history than most of us foreigners carry around as intellectual baggage. Unless you want a history lesson, an unspectacular private château like Beauregard may make a more amusing visit than a great showpiece like Blois. It will also be less crowded.

These magnificently beautiful, historically rich but empty châteaux are ideally suited to the *son et lumière* treatment—there are dozens of these spectacles throughout the summer, but very few in English. The tourist office near the station in Tours is one of the best places for information about them, and about organised coach tours.

Below we've listed the greatest of the Loire châteaux, by whose architects the valley's image in the railway stations and the travel agencies of the world has been fashioned. No tourist in the area should pass through without seeing the outside of all or most of them, and visiting at least one or two. To try to do more is to risk indigestion, boredom (at the historical repetition), and the muddling in the memory of buildings whose greatest quality is their individuality. Rather than try to sample everything on the long menu, choose a few of the *spécialités de la région*; to enhance your appreciation of them take your time and separate the courses with sorbet-like visits to smaller châteaux off the beaten track—with less of an onslaught of historical information and jostling crowds to satiate your appetite for château visiting.

The following comments on the eight greats are intended to help you choose, not to describe contents or historical associations extensively.

Château d'Amboise Fragmentary but still substantial remains of one of the great royal châteaux, with something of the empty magnificence associated with them. It has a superb setting above town and river, with excellent views from the terrace and roof. The visit is distinguished by the remarkable Tour des Minimes, within which a ramp spirals up 69 feet from river level to the château and which was the main entrance for horses and carts. On the ramparts, the small chapel of St-Hubert has exceptionally beautiful stone carving over the entrance. The interior of the château is a curious mixture of medieval and 19th-century decoration and works of art, and Louis-Philippe's ocean-going-liner of a bed.

Château d'Azay-le-Rideau A perennial favourite, incomparably gracious and decorative and built on a scale that fits snugly into a camera frame, with the repertoire of military architecture irresistibly translated into the ornamental Renaissance language. Beautifully set among trees on the edge of a small village, moated by the Indre, Azay is hard to admire from outside the perimeter and deserves at least a wander around the gardens. The inside boasts a beautifully decorated and pioneering straight (as opposed to the previously conventional spiral) staircase, but apart from some very fine and very old tapestries and beds, little furniture of interest. Being a small and exceptionally popular place, it also gets extremely crowded. Stay in the village and go early.

Château de Blois A vast royal château, architecturally interesting for its great variety and the beauty of some of its parts—notably the spiral staircase, acknowledged masterpiece of the Renaissance Loire, and François I's loggia which looks out over the town. A guided tour of the interior (English text available) reveals richly painted ceilings and walls which owe as much to 19th-century restorers as to the original

decorators. It's light on furniture, but heavy on history, of which the most famous episode was the bloody assassination in 1588 of the enormous duc de Guise, who despite being carved up by eight daggers took as long to fall and die as a bull. There are *son et lumière* performances in English.

Château de Chambord Externally the most breathtaking of the châteaux, built on an enormous scale in the thick of an enormous forest following a fairly conventional ground plan (keep and outer wings in the corner towers round a courtyard) but with a dream topping of a Renaissance roofscape like a crown heavy with jewels. Chambord is the sort of château you might expect to find inhabiting a fanciful architect's portfolio of daydream designs, but not the French countryside. Inside (there's no guided tour) recent refurnishing efforts have done a little to fill the enormous vacuum (there are 440 rooms). A few rooms are devoted to the comte de Chambord, a 19th-century pretender to the throne for whom Chambord was bought by public subscription; others have tapestries and paintings from earlier periods and a hunting museum. There are coffered and carved ceilings, and a remarkable double spiral staircase which gives access to the roof terrace, designed for hide-and-seek and hunt-observation. Access to the mostly forested park, once again a hunting reserve, is strictly regulated. Picnicking, and parking outside the paying car park, are discouraged.

Château de Chaumont Often undeservedly missed out, but, for those who do persevere, all the more pleasant for that. Beautifully situated in a park high above the Loire, Chaumont presents an imposing fortified exterior, beautifully creamy and decorated with proprietary emblems. The guided tour of the interior gives an excellent flavour of a less-than-luxurious château life-style. There are very fine tapestries, a majolica floor and, near the château, superb stables.

Château de Chenonceau Thanks to the 200ft gallery built across the Cher by one of Chenonceau's six great female inhabitants, Catherine de' Medici, this is everyone's choice for the top of the Loire pops, the chocolate-box château now appropriately owned by the Chocolat Menier family. A visit is essential for the view from formal gardens; there's no guided tour, but you receive a free explanatory leaflet. The interior contains very fine paintings, tapestries and some furniture, adequately explained by notes in each room. You can go on a train ride round the gardens and visit an outbuilding containing an amusing if crudely executed wax museum with scenes from Chenonceau's distinguished past. Chenonceau gets very crowded so it's best to stay in the village and go early.

Château de Cheverny Like several of the great châteaux of the region, Cheverny was built by a lady proprietress. Untypical for the region though, it's a severe, symmetrical classical château, small, private, and unaltered since its original completion, a stately home still stylishly inhabited and sumptuously furnished with its original 17th-century décor. Unfortunately this is one of the very worst of the châteaux for crowds, with queues at the entrance to each room. But if you avoid rush-hour and the season, it's a richly rewarding visit—paintings, tapestries, furniture, leatherwork are all of rare quality. The château has a famous hunt; the kennels and trophy room are open to visitors.

Château de Langeais Apart from an unspectacular town-centre setting, a remarkably impressive late medieval fortress. And it is much more interesting than most to visit, thanks to the lack of subsequent alterations to the original disposition and decoration of the rooms, and the exceptionally rich collection of medieval furniture and works of art accumulated by Langeais' last private owner in the late 19th century. Escorted visit, but commentary broadcast by loudspeakers in each room. You may have to wait some time for the English recording to come round; if impatient you can go on the French, or any other, tour with an English translation in your hand, which has the advantage that you can study individual items out of sequence while the crowd is straining to look at something else.

Hotels

Amboise, 37400 Indre-et-Loire £££

LE LION D'OR   Tel: 47.57.00.23

A simple town-centre hotel beside the road at the foot of the château; just behind
the hotel is the lower gateway to the famous Minimes Tower. Bedrooms are
simple (some rather small) but generally bright and traditionally furnished;
however, we've received a report this year of very uncomfortable beds. Bar and
breakfast room are dull, restaurant atmospheric—with painted fireplace, stag's
head, vivid panelling, and views over the Loire. Cooking is traditional, but light,
using local produce and wines—*pot-au-feu de la Loire, matelote de sandre au Chinon
et aux petits légumes*. Visitors and inspectors agree that the staff are friendly and
helpful. More reports please.

Closed Nov to Mar; 23 bedrooms; no lift; garage.

Azay-le-Rideau, 37190 Indre-et-Loire ££

GRAND MONARQUE   Tel: 47.45.40.08

Sad to say, Azay-le-Rideau is a dull village, but this old village-centre hotel is a
good place for a meal, especially under the chestnut trees on the terrace between
the main building and the adjacent, rather more elegant, annexe. Bedrooms are
varied in standard, but in general the hotel is showing signs of decorative neglect.
The ruling family is friendly, but service is sometimes impatient. Food is good, and
menus good value. There is no news yet of the present parrot's speech prowess,
and there must now be some doubt that he will rival the late bird.

Rest closed mid-Nov to mid-Mar; 30 bedrooms; no lift.

Beaugency, 45190 Loiret ££££

L'ABBAYE   Tel: 38.44.67.35

In the heart of one of the few small townships along the Loire to have any charm
of its own, this dignified converted abbey faces Beaugency's famous bridge. It was
completely renovated fairly recently, and strides are now being made to elevate
the standard of *cuisine*. There's a comfortable salon area, baronial restaurant, and
well decorated uncluttered bedrooms—some with tiled floors, beams or
fireplace—with good bathrooms; there are also some duplex apartments.

18 bedrooms; no lift.

Beaugency, 45190 Loiret £

ÉCU DE BRETAGNE   Tel: 38.44.67.60

A splendid, welcoming and inexpensive hotel, which has become popular with
guide readers. The main building spreads broad and low beside the main square,
with a busy restaurant and a bar—a popular local cafe. Bedrooms are bright and
simple, more attractive in the main building, but more modern in the annexe
across the road, where all the rooms have bath or shower. The patron's pride in
the value for money offered in his restaurant is certainly justified, particularly on
the fixed-price menus.

Closed Feb to mid-Mar; 26 bedrooms; no lift.

The Loire Valley

Brinon-sur-Sauldre, 18410 Cher ££
LA SOLOGNOTE   Tel: 48.58.50.29

On the main street of this small Sologne hamlet, the exterior of this typical old red-brick town house belies its charm. Inside, all is comfortable and stylish, with beams, tiled floors and masses of flowers. Bedrooms all look out over the garden, and are individually decorated and charming. The food is excellent, with good-value 5-course fixed-price menus based on the *carte* dishes (*salade de ris de veau aux lentilles, mérou aux poivrons doux, agneau à l'ail aux pâtes fraîches*).

Closed Feb, 2 weeks May and Sept, and Wed (rest Tues dinner out of season); 10 bedrooms; no lift.

Chambord, 412250 Loir-et-Cher £££
ST-MICHEL   Tel: 54.20.31.31

Things are very simple here: you stay at the St-Michel because it is where it is, and you put up with what it is. Its situation is uniquely privileged, on the edge of the forest clearing occupied by the wondrous château, which looks even better when illuminated artificially than it does by day, but best of all by moonlight. The big grey hotel is comfortable enough and very quiet, but there is nothing positively enjoyable about it apart from the château views from some bedrooms. The food is very unexciting and the tiled dining room floor and ceiling amplify clatter like a cafeteria. There is no evening bar and only a very small sitting area like a waiting room beside the reception desk.

Closed mid-Nov to mid-Dec; 40 bedrooms; no lift; tennis.

La Chartre-sur-le-Loir, 72340 Sarthe £
FRANCE   Tel: 43.44.40.16

Handsome ivy-covered building on the central square of a peaceful country town, with streetside tables and chairs under an awning. It's pleasant, friendly, not at all stylish and used by all the locals as the place to eat and drink—the bar is the village café. It's also appreciated as a base by drivers from Le Mans (50 km away), and the bar is full of racing photographs. The bedrooms (some in an annexe on the other side of a pretty garden) are unremarkable but adequate, and quiet. The heart of the place is its busy restaurant: functional and cheerfully provincial, with homely and reasonably-priced food, enthusiastically served.

Closed mid-Nov to mid-Dec; 30 bedrooms; no lift.

Chenonceaux, 37150 Indre-et-Loire £££
LE BON LABOUREUR ET CHÂTEAU   Tel: 47.23.90.02

To enjoy the château (and there's no other reason to go to Chenonceaux) there's nothing to beat staying overnight, to get in first or last thing. There's a wide choice in what is little more than a village of hotels and restaurants. The Bon Laboureur is a good and workmanlike place—simple and attractively decorated bedrooms around a courtyard and in a neighbouring annexe, and reasonable local cooking (though prices are a little high for the standard of presentation, and quality inconsistent). Apart from the ante-room to the restaurant, for waiting diners, there are no public rooms, but plans are afoot to turn the central courtyard into a terrace and garden.

Closed mid-Dec to mid-Feb; 28 bedrooms; no lift.

277

Hotels

Chinon, 37500 Indre-et-Loire   £££££
CHÂTEAU DE MARÇAY   Tel: 47.93.03.47

About five km south of Chinon, hidden in its extensive grounds, this is a fortress-style château dating in its present form from the 15th century. Bedrooms are varied and very well furnished; bathrooms may surprise you—anything from a small shower to a well-converted bit of timbered history, bigger than its bedroom. The "Pavillion" annexe houses some of the cheaper bedrooms—stylish enough and good value; and there's now a new annexe with large and superb bedrooms and bathrooms, all with terrace. The setting is beautiful, there's a fine secluded swimming pool, a terrace for lunchtime eating and elegant public rooms. Cooking is of a very high standard—light and innovative.

Closed Jan and Feb; 38 bedrooms; swimming pool; tennis.

Cloyes-sur-le-Loir, 28220 Eure-et-Loir   ££
HOSTELLERIE SAINT-JACQUES   Tel: 37.98.50.08

16th-century coaching inn on the main road in the centre of Cloyes. There's a pleasantly shaded terrace for eating out; beyond, grass and trees lead down to the pretty river. The bedrooms (with minibars) are all at the back, overlooking the garden and quiet; they're fairly small and traditionally furnished. The attractive baronial-style restaurant is very popular—not surprisingly, as Simon Le Bras' cooking gets better all the time. His cheapest fixed-price menu (*compôte de lapereau et de carottes fondantes* and *blanquette de morue fraîche aux civettes*, perhaps) is very good value.

Closed mid-Nov to Jan (rest Sun dinner and Mon out of season); 20 bedrooms; no lift; fishing.

Langeais, 37130 Indre-et-Loire   £££
HOSTEN   Tel: 47.96.82.12

Jean-Jacques has settled in well, after having taken over his father Jean's hotel and restaurant. It's an attractive creeper-covered building on a bend off the main road through the village. Bedrooms (quieter to the rear) are reasonable and pretty, though not always totally comfortable; public rooms have either been renovated, or are about to be (particularly the salon, which will be rebuilt this year, after a lorry drove into it). The emphasis, as always, is on the cooking—now far less traditional, and with some light touches. There's now a small, simple and cheap fixed-price menu, as well as an interesting *carte*.

Closed mid-June to mid-July (rest Mon dinner and Tues); 12 bedrooms; no lift.

Loué, 72540 Sarthe   £££££
RICORDEAU   Tel: 43.88.40.03

Centrally situated in a quiet provincial town, the Ricordeau is a long low austerely classical building with the proportions of a distinguished stable-block. *La famille* Ricordeau have departed from their elegant hostelry, but the former renown of the restaurant has been restored by *la famille* Laurent (Gilbert in particular), who offer most of the famous dishes (*pigeon de Loué en ballotine aux lentilles*, and various other *volailles de Loué*) as well as some of their own concoctions (exquisite *marquise de chocolat sauce pistache*). Bedrooms are spacious and stylish. Not cheap, but a peaceful and comfortable place to stay.

Closed Jan; 21 bedrooms; no lift.

Luynes, 37230 Indre-et-Loire   £££££
DOMAINE DE BEAUVOIS   Tel: 47.55.50.11

A real, fairy-tale, Loire château set in 350 acres of parkland with lakes and lawns and woodland paths, luxurious and individually decorated bedrooms and comfortable public rooms. There's been a sharp decline in the number of American visitors recently, and it may not now be necessary to book well ahead. The standard of cooking is high, and the fixed-price menus are not as pricey as one might expect. A splendid retreat.

Closed mid-Jan to mid-Mar; 37 bedrooms; swimming pool; fishing; tennis.

Nançay, 18330 Cher   ££££
LES MEAULNES   Tel: 48.51.81.15

Lovely old place in the centre of a quiet village deep in Fournier country. The restaurant and some of the (smaller) bedrooms are in one building, and larger and more flowery bedrooms are in another across a pretty little garden terrace. The heavy-beamed restaurant glows—dark polished wood, crisp tablecloths, candles and flowers. The food is well prepared, though the fixed-price menu is simple (*terrine*, trout, rabbit, *andouillette*) and the *carte* prices rather steep.

Close mid-Jan to mid-Mar (rest Tues in Nov, Dec and April); 10 bedrooms; no lift.

Onzain, 41150 Loir-et Cher   £££££
DOMAINE DES HAUTS DE LOIRE   Tel: 54.20.83.41

Deep in vineyard countryside two km from Onzain, this 19th-century hunting pavilion has been beautifully restored and converted. It stands by a lake (with swans) in extensive grounds. The salon is very fine and formal, the bedrooms are of extremely high standard—spacious, elegantly furnished and utterly comfortable. Cooking is classic; the *carte* is fairly short, the wine list is more comprehensive than before, and the fixed-price menus are not cheap.

Closed Dec to mid-Mar; 27 bedrooms; no lift; tennis.

Onzain, 41150 Loir-et-Cher   £
PONT D'OUCHET   Tel: 54.20.70.33

Modest little restaurant-with-rooms near the central square of the village, attractive chalet-style with window boxes but no garden. The small restaurant has a homely family atmosphere; the food is simple and tasty (*moules*, *rillettes*, *raie pochée beurre noire*, *andouillette*, *tarte au citron*) and excellent value. Bedrooms (some family sized) are simple but bright and fresh, quiet at the back; only three have shower facilities. A friendly unpretentious place in the "cheap and cheerful" category, popular with British visitors.

Closed Dec to Mar (rest Sun dinner and Mon); 10 bedrooms; no lift.

Hotels

Pouilly-sur-Loire, 58150 Nièvre £££

L'ESPÉRANCE   Tel: 86.39.10.68

A simple, family-run hotel in the village centre, with its own vineyard reaching
down to the river at the back, and fine views from the summer restaurant.
Bedrooms (only 4) are comfortable enough, though with little character. The
cooking is good, if a trifle unexciting.

Closed Dec and Jan (rest Sun dinner and Mon); 4 bedrooms; no lift.

Romorantin-Lanthenay, 41200 Loir-et-Cher ££££

GRAND HÔTEL DU LION D'OR   Tel: 54.76.00.28

Grey stone inn on the town's main shopping street, groomed over recent years to
its present stylish modern comfort. No grounds, but attractive courtyard. The food
is excellent (as is the service) and thoroughly innovative; if prices seem heavy, it's
worth noting that you may choose half portions, and that your meal begins and
ends with delicious morsels not mentioned on the bill. The spacious bedrooms
fully live up to expectation; bathrooms are impeccable. There's an overall sense of
talent well used, and no expense spared.

Closed Jan to mid-Feb; 10 bedrooms.

Les Rosiers-sur-Loire, 49350 Maine-et-Loire £££

JEANNE DE LAVAL   Tel: 41.51.80.17

A serious and expensive restaurant famed for timeless classical excellence and
about the best Loire fish dishes you are likely to encounter anywhere. Augereau
père is lately deceased but after 18 years at his father's side Augereau *fils* has
proved himself fully capable of assuming command of the kitchens without
curdling the *beurre blanc*. Although Les Rosiers isn't a particularly exciting place,
except to the palate, this is a pleasant stopover; there are some simple but quite
comfortable bedrooms in the main building above the restaurant, and others in a
nearby annexe—a pretty manor house. Rooms are reasonably priced and, despite
the hotel's unpromising address ("Route Nationale"), not too noisy.

Closed mid-Nov to Dec (rest Mon); 14 bedrooms; no lift.

St-Dyé-sur-Loire, 41500 Loir-et-Cher ££

MANOIR BEL AIR   Tel: 54.81.60.10

An 18th-century manor house literally covered with creepers, set back from the
road five minutes from the village, this is a quiet comfortable hotel with a rural
air. Décor is traditional—the salon rather full of furniture (and stuffed animals),
the restaurant bright and informal. Fixed-price menus are relatively cheap and
good value, and include house specialities (*rillettes de saumon, mousseline de
rascasse, andouillette braisée au Sauvignon*); portions are large. The delightful river
view is shared by the back bedrooms and those in the new wing; they're all light
and quite spacious.

Closed Jan to mid-Feb; 40 bedrooms; no lift.

Tavers (3 km Beaugency), 45190 Loiret   **££££**

LA TONNELLERIE   Tel: 38.44.68.15

Handsome old grey stone hotel, in the centre of a small peaceful village off the
beaten track, with a lovely leafy garden, and a good-sized swimming pool. The
lounge is formal, the bedrooms refined and country-style (those in the annexe are
not quite as good). Both rooms of the restaurant (one summery with wicker and
luxuriant plants) overlook the garden and terrace, where you can eat on fine
days. Cooking is uncomplicated, using local produce (*paupiette de sandre au beurre
blanc, lapin à l'infusion de sauge, matelote d'eau douce, tarte Tatin*).

Closed Oct to April; 26 bedrooms; swimming pool.

Tours, 37000 Indre-et-Loire   **£££**

CENTRAL   Tel: 47.05.46.44

Well situated on a quiet side street near the old town and the cathedral quarter,
this dignified 19th-century building has a small shady garden and terrace, and
attractive and comfortable public rooms. Bedrooms retain original features and
are well decorated and furnished. This is a good base for those without a car
(though a private garage is available for those who need it).

42 bedrooms; garage; no rest.

Villandry, 37510 Indre-et-Loire   **£££**

LE CHEVAL ROUGE   Tel: 47.50.02.07

Externally this is a rather ordinary and less than enticing hotel, and inside the
décor and furnishings are modern, without much charm or style (despite the
addition of a sparkling new *salon du thé*). However, the Cheval Rouge is
comfortable and well placed, at the foot of the old hamlet of Villandry, a short
walk from the chateau and its celebrated gardens; this hotel is a roadside one, but
the road is minor and noise is not a problem. Bedrooms are without any
particular shortcomings, and reasonably priced, and the food in the almost
elegant dining room is good. There's a small *carte*, and a couple of reasonable
fixed-priced menus; specialities include *truite braisée au Vouvray* and *navarin de la
mer*.

Closed Dec to Feb (rest Mon in Mar, April and May); 20 bedrooms; no lift.

Our price symbols

£	You can expect to find a room for under £15
££	You can expect to find a room for £15 to £25
£££	You can expect to find a room for £25 to £35
££££	You can expect to find a room for £35 to £45
£££££	You should expect to pay over £45 for a room

Brittany

"The sea being smooth,
How many shallow bauble boats dare sail
Upon her patient breast" (Shakespeare)

Brittany

Brittany, meaning little Britain, is France's Celtic fringe— geologically, ethnographically and linguistically closer to Wales and Cornwall than to France. In many ways its holiday appeal is closer to these areas too. For the tourist, Brittany is first and foremost a coastline—in Breton the *Armor* or "land of the sea". From the Loire estuary to Mont-St-Michel it is so jagged and indented that estimates of its length vary from 700 to 2,000 miles (either way that is a lot of beach space). Brittany is France's most frequented holiday region after the Mediterranean coast; but it never gets crowded to the nightmarish degree of the Côte d'Azur in August. You can find seaside resorts that are still little more than quiet villages; you can drive a car along the coast roads; you can find a place to lie down on the beach, and if you go just a few miles inland into the *Argoat*—or "land of the forest", no longer wholly appropriate—you lose people altogether. The south coast of Brittany has sheltered sandy coves and inlets and is a popular area for sailing holidays. The north coast has remarkable stretches of huge pink granite boulders and sections of impressively savage cliffs. But the best area for dramatic coastal scenery is the extreme west of Brittany, the bared teeth of France's transatlantic growl.

Like Wales, Brittany has the added attraction of its regional (Bretons would say national) individuality—distinctive local traditions, costumes, culture and language which all attract interest partly because of their tourist value, and partly because the Bretons have learnt that their provincial identity is something of which to be proud.

For many hundreds of years Brittany was a backwater isolated from the impact of political events and from economic and artistic developments elsewhere in the kingdom. It has its own dense and colourful tissue of history (medieval, and much earlier) and legend—often hard to disentangle from each other. Religious feeling runs deep and strong; even the smallest villages boast large and richly decorated churches, and Bretons persist in the veneration of obscure local saints—mostly early Celtic missionaries from Britain and Ireland, many struck off the official register long ago. All over Brittany tens of thousands of people join in the picturesque local religious processions—called *pardons*—to the shrine of the local saint. Their popular religious fervour, as uncomplicated as it is strong, is reflected in Breton art (mainly the decoration and sculptural ornaments of churches).

Brittany is one of France's under-developed areas which at times in the past seemed to have so little going for it that total depopulation was once seriously proposed as the most sensible economic plan for the region. Its population is concentrated around the coast, in the big modern industrial ports of Brest and Lorient, or in fishing ports such as St-Malo, Audierne and Concarneau. The architecture of coastal villages is practical—once again the obvious comparison is with Wales—with small, unadorned whitewashed or plain grey cottages lying low in the open, wind-swept landscape. There are only a few villages where the severity of the grey stone is relieved by thatch. Inland Brittany, once the

Brittany

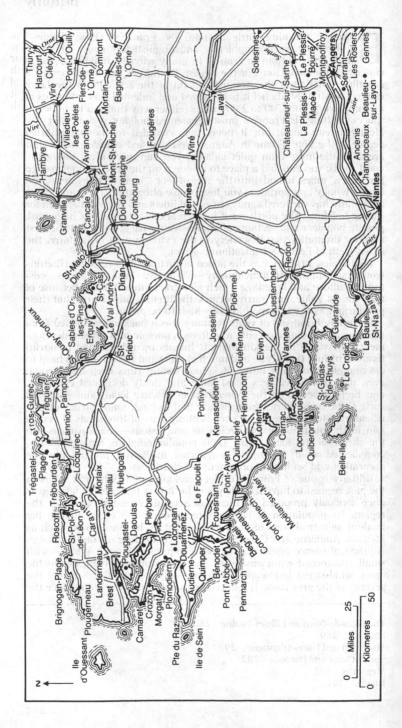

most densely forested of all French regions, is now one of the least so. Although uncultivated heath and waste land has taken its place in some areas (the Black Mountains, for example, originally named after their dark mantle of trees), there is plenty of productive farmland, too, with tasty lamb reared on the coastal salt pastures (*pré salé*) and vegetables of high repute. But the interior of Brittany, increasingly prosperous as it may be, has relatively little to offer the tourist. There are areas which retain the forest beauty of the old Argoat; there are a few impressive castles and some fine churches; and—particularly in Finistère—there are groups of religious monuments around the churches, called parish closes. But in general the countryside lacks the interest of noble country houses, or historic and attractive towns.

Eastern (Upper) Brittany, for all its attractions, is a disappointment to any tourist in search of specifically local colour. Western (Lower) Brittany, called Bretagne Bretonnante because of the survival there of the Breton language, is more rewarding. The language is not easy to understand but its close affinities with Welsh can be seen from any signpost—Aber Ildut, Landéda, Pont-Pol-Ty-Glas, Pen Lan. Local costume is now mostly reserved for special occasions, but in the south-west you can still see some of the many varieties of *coiffe* (head-dress).

Long before the Celts, the Romans and the Gauls, an unknown race specialised in raising megalithic monuments all over Brittany. The stones of these primitive open-air cathedrals and burial grounds whose religious significance, in the absence of any practical utility, is generally accepted (as is their connection with the sun and moon) are thought to have been erected some time between 1,800 and 4,000 BC.

Brittany was one of the theoretical destinations of the Holy Grail, and what remain of the dark forests of the Argoat are thick with the characters of Arthurian legend. The coast is no less rich in more-or-less mythical associations. The old city of Is, once-glorious capital of Cornouaille, was engulfed in the ocean in punishment for the licentious behaviour of the king's daughter who went with the city to the bottom of the ocean and stays there as an irresistible mermaid luring sailors to their doom. Other hazards to shipping were less romantic: islanders made a living out of drawing vessels onto the rocks and looting them. For centuries no merchantman in the Channel was safe from the infamous privateers of St-Malo who wrought havoc as licensed pirates.

The medieval history of Brittany is one of complicated power struggles between Breton nobles and rival claimants to the duchy. During the 14th and 15th centuries Brittany became a zone of proxy war between the French and English. This devastated the province but did produce Bertrand du Guesclin, the great hero of the French cause in the early stages of the Hundred Years' War. This swarthy little Breton was born in 1320 near Dinan, fought a celebrated single combat with an English knight there in 1359 and asked to be buried there. On his death, in 1380 in the South of France, his wishes were partially fulfilled: du Guesclin's last campaign, the funeral journey, swept through Le Puy (entrails buried), Montferrand (flesh buried), Le Mans (skeleton and heart split up), St-Denis (skeleton buried), and finally Dinan (heart buried in St-Sauveur). In spite of du Guesclin's efforts, the English-backed claimants won control and the French crown's eventual success in appropriating Brittany was neither easily achieved nor total. Duchess Anne of Brittany first married Charles VIII and then his successor Louis XII, but was careful to retain separate control of her duchy. On her early death, their daughter Claude was swiftly married off to her father's heir, the future

François I, and was prevailed upon to permit the union of Brittany and France in the person of their son Henry II, who despite being closely related to himself was not disallowed and came to the throne in 1547.

The Côtes-du-Nord and Ille-et-Vilaine

The Bay of Mont-St-Michel is gradually filling up with mud; west of the Couesnon, it has little to offer the traveller except views of the rock, oysters, mussels, and tasty salt-marsh lambs. **Dol-de-Bretagne** used to be a bishopric, beside the sea, and important. It is now none of these things but still an attractive small town with the mainly 13th-century cathedral of St-Samson suitably big, strong and imposing. **Cancale** is an important seafood port, one of the most single-minded shellfish factories in Brittany. The Latin poet Ausone wrote favourably of Cancale's oysters, which were in his day harvested from natural banks in the bay. At low tide you can see the drained beds or parks and the stakes in the sands that mussels grow on, and you will understand why it's called farming not fishing; but the sheer scale of the enterprise is probably best appreciated from the air—in one of the small planes that take tourists around Mont-St-Michel.

North of Cancale the **Pointe de Grouin**, most easterly cape of Brittany's impressive rocky coastline, gives a splendid panorama of the bay and the distant Mont-St-Michel. The inhospitable coastline westward is interrupted by the deep inlet of **Rothéneuf**, where the calm waters are popular for watersports and the granite cliffs along the rocky shore have been remarkably decorated with sculptures and relief carvings by the abbé Fouré, hermit of Rothéneuf.

A virtually uninterrupted built-up area extends round the corner of the Rance inlet from Paramé to St-Servan, and does not do justice to the splendid situation of the granite citadel of **St-Malo**, which is one of the most interesting and attractive of the Channel ports. The city (known as Intra Muros) is packed within medieval ramparts later strengthened by Vauban. It lies on a sandy island, once joined to the mainland only at low tide, flanked on one side by the docks, on the other by beach. The fortifications and stark grey uniformity of the tall houses of Intra Muros make it tremendously impressive as you approach from the sea. As you get closer and go into the town beneath the towers of its cheerless fortress (once a prison, now a waxwork and local history museum) it becomes clear that all, or nearly all, is new. St-Malo was very badly damaged in 1944, and has been rebuilt in a severe style which may approximate to the original but is not welcoming. The city is nevertheless busily commercial and touristy, the walk round the ramparts is very rewarding, and there are other interesting walks at low tide to Vauban's 17th-century fortress and the island of Grand Bé, the chosen tomb of St-Malo's own literary colossus, Châteaubriand. The port's neighbours—Paramé on the sea, and St-Servan on the rocks—are fairly busy resorts with good beaches (Paramé) and rocky cliff walks (St-Servan) but rather urban. From St-Malo there are boat excursions along the coast to the Cap Fréhel, up the Rance to Dinan, across it to Dinard, and hovercraft and ferries to the Channel Islands.

The Rance, like so many Breton rivers, is insignificant by comparison with the size and splendour of its estuary, which stretches nearly 20 miles from Dinan to Dinard and St-Malo at its mouth on the sea. For the harnessing of tidal power the Rance has been dammed: you can visit the installation, the first and one of the most important of its kind, drive across it and sail through it via a lock.

Dinan is a beautifully situated, walled medieval town high above the river where there is a small port for excursion boats and a rebuilt Gothic bridge. At the south of the very complete ramparts is the small castle which houses a local history and folklore museum. In the stylistically very mixed basilica of St-Sauveur is a memorial to Bertrand du Guesclin. More rewarding than any specific visit, though, is a wander around the maze of old streets at the heart of town, with their cobbles and overhanging timbered houses. Dinan had a sizeable expatriate community in the 18th and 19th centuries, and still has its Jardin des Anglais on the east of the old town which gives splendid views out over the Rance. It's a busy and lively town, a very popular place to visit and a very good base for the coast and interior.

Facing St-Malo across the mouth of the Rance, **Dinard** is one of Brittany's two traditionally fashionable resorts (the other being La Baule). Dinard is the older, a British creation of the turn of the century, and shows its age: spacious neo-Gothic villas and a sedate atmosphere. There is plenty to do though—sports, boat excursions, cliff-top walks— and the beaches are sandy and sheltered. There are more good beaches at **St-Lunaire** and **St-Briac**, and a resort of prosperous garden villas with one of France's best golf courses at **Lancieux**. **St-Cast-le-Guildo** is an altogether more popular family resort with a busy fishing and yachting harbour. From the Pointe de St-Cast, as from any number of rocky outcrops along this coast, there are splendid views; most impressive of all is the **Cap Fréhel**, whose 200ft-high grey and reddish cliffs are popular with tourists and no less so with nesting birds. Barely visible along the cliffs is the magnificently situated, mostly medieval **Fort de la Latte** (with guided tours) complete with drawbridge access over clefts in the rocks. Beyond Cap Fréhel the Emerald Coast descends, less savagely rocky, to the big town of **St-Brieuc**, unremarkable except for its fortified 14th-century cathedral (St-Etienne). **Sables-d'Or-les-Pins** speaks for itself—the golden sand beach is enormous, and pines shade a spaciously regular grid of villas and mock-rustic hotels, but there is very little else. Trippery **Le Val-André** also has a long sandy beach. A pleasant contrast with both is **Erquy**, a proper little port well known for its scallops, where there are campsites, good wet sand beaches, and old plain Breton cottages, not the neo-Gothic of so much of this coast.

The west side of the deep V of St-Brieuc Bay has no shortage of sandy beaches but few resorts of any compelling charm. **St-Quay-Portrieux** (port and resort) is the biggest, and best equipped for land and water sports—there is a sailing school and casino. You can make a brief inland detour to two interesting churches. The small pilgrimage chapel of **Kermaria-an-Iskuit** (open in the mornings) has a remarkable mural of the Dance of Death, and typically Breton statues in the porch— sharply characterised to the point of caricature and vividly painted. **Lanleff** has an even more curious temple: a ruined round Romanesque church based on the Holy Sepulchre in Jerusalem. Back on the coast, there are some scanty remains of a Gothic abbey at Beauport just outside **Paimpol**, which was once an important fishing port—made famous by Pierre Loti's novel *Pêcheur d'Islande*, about cod fishing in the Arctic. Now its inhabitants are engaged in less arduous and more profitable oyster farming. North of the town the Pointe de l'Arcouest looks across pinkish rocks and little islands to the nearby **Ile de Bréhat** which is peaceful, lush, sunny and not neglected by tourists.

Tréguier is a small old cathedral and pilgrimage town lying at the heart of an inlet of oyster beds. The former cathedral, dedicated to the 6th-century Welsh missionary Tudwal, dates mostly from the 14th century but of its three towers, one—the Hastings Tower—is Romanesque. The 15th-century cloister is full of flowers and recumbent statues.

North of Tréguier, **Port-Blanc** is a particularly charming little fishing port and resort tucked into a sheltered bay in another inhospitable stretch of coast where isolated rocks and treacherous reefs are exposed at low tide. **St-Gonéry** has a curious little chapel with a crooked spire, painted wooden vaults, an outside pulpit, a Calvary, a very old yew tree, and a 16th-century mausoleum. The stretch of coast from Perros-Guirec to Trébeurden is known as the Corniche Bretonne or, more helpfully, as the Pink Granite Coast. All along the coast the granite, which really does have a dark warm pinkish tint, has been eroded into weird boulders as if fashioned and polished lovingly by an abstract artist. One of the by-products of granite erosion is fine sand, and among the boulders and headlands are some very good beaches and northern Brittany's most frequented family resorts—**Perros-Guirec** (the biggest), **Ploumanach**, **Trégastel-Plage** and **Trébeurden**, without much to choose between them. At Perros-Guirec you can take a boat round the bird sanctuaries of the **Sept Iles**, but can only land on one—the Ile aux Moines, where Vauban built a fortress.

On the banks of the salmon-rich river Léguer, **Lannion** is an expanding modern town, with an unspoilt and very picturesque old centre. There is a pleasant excursion to be made up the Léguer to **Kerfons** chapel which boasts a remarkable carved wooden screen, and to the ruins of the 13th-century Tonquédec castle.

Excursions from Dinan and the coast

The north-east interior of Brittany is the main region for fortifications and castles, built along its frontier with France.

✳ **Combourg** A small old town with an imposing but internally much altered feudal fortress which belonged to the du Guesclin and Châteaubriand families. It was haunted, according to Châteaubriand, by a black cat and a wooden-legged man; even if you aren't afraid of ghosts it is best admired from a distance. Not far from Combourg there are medieval castle remains at **Montmuran**, a church of interesting stained glass at **Les Iffs**, and a zoo in the park of the classical **Château de la Bourbansais**.

✳ **Fougères** A large frontier town, and traditional centre for the manufacture of shoes. Fougères attracts tourists in large numbers to admire its thoroughly admirable and massive 13th-century (and later) fortress which Victor Hugo described as the Carcassonne of the north. The castle is built somewhat eccentrically below the town, beside the river Nançon. However doubtful as defensive strategy this does mean that there are splendid views to be had of the castle as a whole from above (notably from the Place aux Arbres at the end of the town which forms an extension of the curtain wall of the castle). There are guided tours within and around the walls, for a closer and more detailed appreciation of the military architect's achievement. In the lower town outside the castle walls there are some attractive old houses and the interesting Gothic church of St-Sulpice.

✳ **Vitré** Like Fougères, Vitré is a powerful fortified frontier town on the River Vilaine, still enclosed on three sides by its old ramparts and the splendid towers and walls of its late-14th-century castle. The approach to the town, from the direction of Fougères or Rennes, is very picturesque, and the old streets with their carefully timbered and slate-fronted houses are no disappointment. Notre-Dame is an elegant Gothic church with an external pulpit for open-air religious debating, and the castle itself houses a museum of local antiquities and folklore. The nearby **Château des Rochers-Sévigné** is chiefly of interest for its memories of the late 17th-century letter-writing marquise de Sévigné who spent most of her last twenty years here.

✳ **Rennes** Unless the weather is really terrible you're unlikely to be tempted to give much time to the commercially, industrially and administratively important capital of Brittany, most of whose medieval centre was burnt down in 1720. But like most provincial capitals, Rennes has museums of interest: two in the same building, one devoted to Breton history and folklore, the other to fine arts. You can also visit the impressive 17th-century law courts with their ornately decorated parliament chamber, and the 19th-century cathedral which houses an exquisite 15th-century carved wooden altar-piece in a chapel off the south aisle.

Finistère

The three peninsulas of France's end of the earth (Finis Terrae) may look on the map like the snapping jaws of a Celtic dragon breathing the fire of Breton defiance across the Atlantic, but on the spot it is very clear that here land is on the defensive. All the attacking is done by the sea which hurls crashing blows against the rocky capes in spectacular storms. Sometimes the low-lying island of Sein off the Pointe du Raz is totally submerged. In the days before the Entente Cordiale the French historian Michelet wrote: "This whole coast is a cemetery. The sea is English by nature—she does not like France, she breaks our ships". Some of the Finistère coastline—the far-western capes ravaged and scarred by the fight against the sea—is very dramatic. Other parts—the north-west and south-west—are just windswept and bleak. The rest, as it were sheltered behind the front lines of defence against the Atlantic assault, is Brittany at her most attractive and frequented. The sheltered coastline between the estuaries of Quimper and Quimperlé has become the favourite for camping and yachting holidays: its succession of sandy wooded coves and deeper inlets forms a marked contrast with the exposure of the harsher Finistère coastline. The grassy cliff-tops are sparsely scattered with low grey cottages and isolated granite churches, and the villages turn on the charm, with crêperies and coiffed old ladies selling lace at every turn. It is in this part of Brittany that local costumes, customs and languages will be most obvious to the tourist greedy for a diet of folklore, though in other parts of Finistère (inland and in the extreme south-west) the same features of Breton life have a truer ring.

Finistère is not really one area, but two (at least): the north is Léon, unspectacular land of cauliflowers, artichokes and long estuary-like *abers* left muddy and weedy at low tide, shallow and still weedy at high tide; the south is Cornouaille, the Brittany of medieval history and legend and modern picture-books.

Léon's north coast is rocky, indented and pinkish-grey. **Locquirec** is a very popular and lively little fishing and pleasure port (as the French call marinas), with a very attractive church and sandy beach. At the other end of the Armorique Corniche is the enormous Lieue de Grève beach, a league long and almost as wide when the tide is out.

Carantec is a more substantial beach resort at the end of the Morlaix River; hydrangeas and pine trees embellish the colonies of villas at Pen-Lan Point, and there are islands close inshore, one of which is accessible on foot at low tide.

Roscoff is the westernmost and most attractive of Channel ports, with many associations with Britain. Mary Stuart is thought to have landed here in 1548 on her way to meet the Dauphin, and the Young Pretender nearly 200 years later in his flight from Culloden. The elegant Renaissance belfry above the church sports stone cannons to warn off the English, and inside has seven beautiful alabaster reliefs. There are attractive old streets decorated cheerfully with flowers, boat trips to the nearby island of Batz (pronounced Baa) and France's most important marine laboratory (open to visitors). Roscoff itself does not have much of a beach, but there are good sandy ones a few miles to the west. Like all the Léon coast Roscoff specialises in the exploitation of seaweed—there are over 70 varieties here—for health and agricultural efficiency. Vegetable cultivation (artichokes, cauliflowers and onions) and privateering have brought the Roscovites prosperity for many centuries (though in the 1480s they went in for that least profitable of medieval activities, the financing of their sovereign's war against the French).

Just a few miles inland the vegetable market town of **St-Pol-de-Léon** is one of the seven original Breton bishoprics around the coast established by evangelising saintly invaders, in this case saint Paul Aurelian. They made up the once famous pilgrimage, the Tro-Breiz, from Vannes to Dol-de-Bretagne, via Quimper, St-Pol, Tréguier, St-Brieuc and St-Malo. The popularity of the pilgrimage is no doubt attributable to the belief that if not achieved in life the journey had to be made after death, at a rate of a coffin's length every seven years, which would mean a wait of some $1\frac{3}{4}$ million years before even a very tall Breton, of which there are few, could expect to rest in peace. Arriving in the year 530 via the islands of Ouessant (or Ushant) and Batz, saint Paul made his way to an oppidum surrounded by earthworks, which he penetrated to find a garrison of bees in a hollow tree, a bear, a wild bull, and a sow suckling its young. Expelling all but the last family group which he kept as pets, saint Paul established himself in what became his see for 36 years until he went back to Batz where he died at the age of 104, so frail that his hands were translucent. St-Pol-de-Léon's former cathedral is a fine 13th- to 15th-

century building of contrasting Caen limestone and granite, architecturally inspired, it is said, by Coutances. It may not surpass its model, but
the nearby Kreisker chapel—its belfry is one of Brittany's most celebrated landmarks—did until its Norman prototype St-Pierre de Caen was
destroyed in the War.

The amorphous resort of **Brignogan-Plage** straggles round a wide
sandy bay littered with huge boulders. Beyond, the coastline wiggles
round from Channel to Atlantic (a line from the rock on the right of the
Aber-Ildut to the centre of Ushant theoretically divides one from the
other), rocky and unremarkable save for the *abers* themselves; the
northernmost and biggest of them, **Aber-Wrac'h**, is the best looking and
the best provided with tourist amenities. Further south the **Pointe de
Corsen** is the true Finis Terrae, the westernmost point of mainland
France—although most maps, being flat, will fool you into thinking that
the Pointe du Raz sticks out further.

Where the coast turns abruptly back eastwards towards Brest, the
Pointe de St-Mathieu commands splendid views southwards and indeed
all round (especially from the top of the lighthouse) and has evocative
medieval ruins of an old monastery founded in the 6th century.

Brest lies on one of the finest natural harbours in the world, with
nearly sixty square miles of deep anchorage narrowly linked to the
furious Atlantic. The great naval port was relentlessly bombed through
the Second World War but has since grown up again big, clean, logical
and uninteresting. The creation of the naval base and the shipbuilding
colony of forced labourers (which was shifted to Devil's Island off French
Guyana in the mid-19th century) is interestingly remembered in the
Museum of Old Brest in the 16th-century Tour Tanguy.

An impressive new bridge spans the Elorn and links Brest to the
strawberry-growing Plougastel peninsula. Its main town **Plougastel-
Daoulas** is unpleasant, and the church there is very unpleasant, but the
church's Calvary is one of the most elaborate and celebrated in Brittany.
It was built shortly after a great plague in 1598; of its 180 figures the
most vivid is poor Catell-Gollett, a Breton girl who refused her father's
advice to get married because she liked dancing too much and ended up
taking the Devil for a lover and giving him the body of Christ in the form
of a communion wafer. Her punishment, as depicted here, was to be
delivered on the Day of Judgement to the not altogether amorous
treatment of the Devil and his ravenous fiends. Daoulas has a parish
close (see page 292) which is not outstanding in Breton terms, and
Romanesque abbey ruins, which are. Nearby **Dirinon**'s low church is
surprisingly crowned by an elegant Renaissance belfry with twin
balconies below the spire.

Excursions from the coast

* **Huelgoat** A pleasant enough woodland resort which makes an excellent
base for pedestrian and motorised explorers. It's on the edge of the main chunk
of the Armorican Regional Park, established recently to look after and show off
some of the most characteristic areas of islands, coastline and (as here)
woodland or *argoat*, all typical of lower Brittany. All around Huelgoat there are
huge chaotic mossy boulders, and roaring underground rivers and grottos; and
there are interesting walks (maps are available and essential).

* **Monts d'Arrée** Brittany's principal mountain range climbs wild and desolate
or purple and gold according to the state of the heather and the gorse, to a
peak of 384 metres, north of the once darkly-wooded and increasingly
reforested **Montagnes Noires**. Once these heights of Brittany stood ▷ p294

Parish Closes and Pardons

Guimiliau

The parish close, or enclosure, is a churchyard entered by a gateway which often takes the form of a triumphal arch, symbolic as it is of the entry into heaven. Within the enclosure are the graveyard and the church. In Brittany in the 16th and 17th centuries the graveyard became an elaborate work of art as it did nowhere else. One reason was the intensity of religious feeling and a particular preoccupation with death—the skeletal figure of Ankou, death itself, is one of the most important members of the dramatis personae of Breton religious art. Another important contributory factor to the development of the parish close was a fierce local rivalry that forced villages to try to outdo their neighbours by building bigger, better, and more elaborate closes. The parish close is a phenomenon not of the big towns but of the country villages. The art is popular art, and has unambiguous illustrations of the Scriptures for the majority who could not read. The medieval custom of passion plays lasted in Brittany, and the particular liveliness of the parish close sculptures clearly has much to do with this local dramatic tradition.

The church is typically charged with wood carving, much of it brightly painted, all of it vigorous and expressive, but by no means always crude in its execution. A popular feature is a painted Glory Beam across the nave, usually with a Crucifix and often supported by carved pillars or a complete screen. Lively statues decorate the walls of the porch, the meeting place of the notables of the local parish councils. Outside, in the graveyard, the gateway becomes a triumphal arch, and a simple cross in front of the church becomes the Calvary—a complex

free-standing monument in its own right with a Crucifixion scene on a base decorated with a wealth of relief carvings and statuettes telling the stories of the life of Christ and the Passion, with a few local moral tales thrown in for the edification of the masses (these Calvaries were often used as visual aids for sermons). Being carved in granite the Calvaries are mostly preserved in all their detail, if sometimes a little mossy, despite being out of doors; they have also been spared most of the depredations of the religious wars and the Revolution. Beside the church simple charnel houses or ossuaries, built to house the bones exhumed to make room in the graveyard for the newly deceased, became as elaborately designed and decorated as the rest of the ensemble.

The extreme development of the parish close is to be seen in the neighbouring villages of **St-Thégonnec** and **Guimiliau**, south of the Landerneau/Morlaix road. St-Thégonnec is the later of the two and perhaps the more elegant as a whole; Guimiliau boasts Brittany's most crowded Calvary with over 200 figures, and has especially fine wood-carving in the church. There are many other less elaborate, but almost complete parish closes in Léon and northern Cornouaille (and one isolated one in the Morbihan at **Guéhenno** with a splendid Calvary), which may seem more attractive for being less showy. There are also a number of isolated Calvaries all over lower Brittany.

The following tour of religious monuments in the area, not all parish closes, proceeds anti-clockwise from Huelgoat, and does not include places mentioned elsewhere as part of the coastal tour. **St-Herbot**: very fine carved wooden screen in Gothic church; ossuary. **Notre-Dame-du-Crann**: a series of 16th-century stained-glass windows. **Pleyben**: parish close with magnificent Calvary and Renaissance church. **Brasparts**: interesting church and Calvary. **Sizun**: parish close with fine arch and ossuary. **Le Folgoët**: large pilgrimage church, much restored but with very fine granite screen and porch sculptures. **Berven**: parish close with fine arch outside and screen inside the Renaissance church. **Lampaul-Guimiliau**: parish close with exceptional painted carvings inside church. **Guimiliau** and **St-Thégonnec**: parish closes—see above.

Many Breton Calvaries form the object of regular pilgrimage processions called *pardons*, because of the absolution that is their motivation. Like the use of pre-Christian dolmens as crypts and the Christianisation of menhirs by carving a cross on them (the ancestor of the Calvary), Breton *pardons* exemplify the survival of pagan ritual in popular religious observance. The serious procession, like a pilgrimage, makes its way with due solemnity to the given Calvary or chapel, with participants in the costume of the region. Profane celebrations usually follow the ceremony, with drinking, dancing and trials of masculine strength—wrestling and stone-tossing.

The biggest *pardons* are at **Ste-Anne-d'Auray** all through the summer, but with the main event (Ste-Anne's day) on July 26th. There are other important ones at Pentecost and on August 15th.

Other particularly important *pardons* are: **Rumengol** (Trinity Sunday and August 15th); **Tréguier** (May 19th); **Perros-Guirec** (August 15th); **St-Jean-du-Doigt** (June 23/24th); **Ste-Anne-la-Palud** (last Sunday in August; one of the most frequented and spectacular of all from the costume point of view); **Le Folgoët** (first Sunday in September. Several others in May, July and August).

over 4,000 metres tall, and when the Alps are as old—in some 300 million years time—they will be eroded to about this size, say the Bretons to those who scoff at their so-called mountains. After all this time many Breton peaks are rounded (*menez*), others (*roc'h*) are jagged, rocky crests more genuinely mountainous in appearance. Panoramic views are to be had from the Roc'h Trévezel, the **Montagne St-Michel** (both in the Monts d'Arrée), the **Roc'h de Toullaëron** in the Montagnes Noires, and most spectacularly of all from the isolated **Menez-Hom** at the base of the Crozon Peninsula.

For all this the natural beauty of the Finistère interior is a less compelling attraction than its unique richness in religious monuments (see page 292).

Jutting out between Léon and Cornouaille, the **Crozon Peninsula** is blunted by the ocean into a hammerhead and shuts in the bays of Brest and, to a lesser extent, Douarnenez. At the foot of the Menez Hom the estuary of the Aulne River (rich in salmon) has been included in the Regional Park as have sections of the rocky coastline at the end of the peninsula, the Pointe de Penhir and the Pointe des Espagnols. So these are officially typical Breton landscapes. Certainly the two capes are very fine examples of the wild grandeur of Finistère at its best, with dizzy views down on to crashing breakers and rough scrambles for the brave. There is also an impressive alignment of menhirs near the lobster port and resort of **Camaret**, itself shabby and run down. The Pointe des Espagnols, though less impressive than Penhir, does give excellent views towards Brest.

Morgat is the main resort on the peninsula, sheltered from the Atlantic in Douarnenez Bay, with a fine sandy beach and a number of grottoes to explore by boat or on foot.

Past the lonely chapel of **Ste-Anne-la-Palud**—distinguished by its *pardon*, its beach and its hotel, all among the finest of their kind in Brittany—a long empty sand and shingle beach curves round to **Douarnenez**. This was once the capital of Cornouaille and the sardine industry, but is no longer either, though it's still a large and busy fishing port.

Just a few miles inland, **Locronan** is an extremely picturesque village which once grew prosperous from cloth trading and which now stays so from tourism. There are craft shops (they still do a lot of weaving and sell jerseys), tea-shops, organic food shops, and antique shops. None of these should detract from the severe beauty of the monochrome main square with its Renaissance houses and church, all the same dark, damp grey which gives Locronan something of a Scottish look, reinforced by the open moorland hills behind. The church is full of interesting things, including an amusingly naïve carved and painted pulpit, telling the story, or several stories, of saint Ronan whose gleaming, black granite tomb lies nearby. When saint Ronan died in the 5th century, the Bretons, uncertain as to where he should be buried, put his body in an ox-drawn cart to find its own resting-place. The oxen did a circuit of his daily walk and had to squeeze between two rocks, where the passage of the cart left a mark. The steps of saint and oxen are retraced by pilgrims to the Locronan *pardons*. There are small ones in July every year and an extra special bonanza every six (1989, 1995).

From Douarnenez the **Cornouaille Peninsula** stretches out to Brittany's most famous cape, the **Pointe du Raz**, which would be impressively wild but for the complex of tourist shops, a melodramatic museum and diorama, and a car park, where here at the end of nowhere you have to pay to park. Still, the popularity of the place is a measure of its natural grandeur. Beneath a strenuously emotive white statue of Our Lady of the Shipwrecks, a jagged rocky finger points westwards to the horizon, just broken by the almost flat island of Sein. When the spray leaps thundering around these rocks, under the bleak skies of winter storms, no question arises of nature's grand effect being spoilt. There is a path round the point (with a safety rope), which gives some dramatic views.

Between the Pointe du Raz and the less-crowded **Pointe du Van**, the gracefully curving **Baie des Trépassés** is rich in legend, inhabited by the spirits of the drowned, who are to be seen in the crests of the waves on All Souls' Day. The bay is also the site of the legendary city of Is, Brittany's Sodom, submerged in the 5th century in punishment for the licentious and murderous behaviour of king Gradlon's daughter Dahut.

There are more rocky points, mostly deserted and impressive, along the northern coast of the peninsula, and a bird reserve (Cap Sizun). Set in a deep estuary on the south coast, **Audierne** is a handsome old fishing port of some importance and considerable charm, with a quiet beach resort nearby. There are boats from here to the Ile de Sein.

The low-lying **Penmarch Peninsula**, south of Audierne, is the best place in Brittany for the spotting of traditional costume and headgear: the local *coiffe* (the Bigoudène) is one of the most remarkable, perched like a menhir. Centuries ago the peninsula was very prosperous and populous, but the cod deserted its coasts and a rapacious Douarnenez bandit called La Fontenelle laid waste to it. Now the landscape is wide open and unlovely, dotted with little modern cottages. There remain for your admiration the fine, late-Gothic church (St-Nonna) at Penmarch itself (still a sizeable town), and one of the earliest Calvaries of Brittany in a splendid windswept situation by the bleakly impressive coast at **Tronoën**. The spacious, unpretentious fishing port of **St-Guénolé** has a long beach, a tall lighthouse and a museum of pre-history. **Loctudy** is another spread-out, fishy, not very charming little resort, with one of Brittany's finest Romanesque churches. The nearby **Château de Kerazan** has a collection of works of art.

Pont-l'Abbé, the capital of Bigouden, isn't really a place to spend much time, but it does have an interesting local museum in the old castle, with lots of costumes.

The intimacy of the long, narrow wooded estuary of the River Odet contrasts strikingly with the wide, windy openness of the west coast. This is the start of perhaps the most attractive and certainly the most popular stretch of the Breton coast—at least with the camping and yachting fraternity—which extends from Bénodet to Le Pouldu. **Bénodet** is one of the most popular and lively of all the resorts, but extensive recent building and redevelopment has been carried out at the cost of character. There's lots to keep everyone amused—sports facilities, boat trips, and even a certain amount of life after dark (not Brittany's speciality).

Quimper has been the capital of Cornouaille since king Gradlon arrived there in flight from the tidal wave which engulfed Is. The old king still rides on a steed of granite between the twin towers of the cathedral. This is more of an inland than a seafaring town, spanning the junction of the Rivers Odet and Steir where the two become an estuary. In the centre at least it is a very attractive old market town, with timber-framed houses, cobbled streets and costumed old women selling pottery and lace. There are bus and boat excursions, and a folklore festival at the end of July.

*Traditional costume and headgear can
still be seen in the Bigouden, around
Pont-l'Abbé*

∗ *Cathedral* Twin slender spires of this interesting Gothic building dominate
the Quimper skyline. Its most striking feature is the pronounced northward list
of the choir: there is also some fine stained glass and tomb sculpture.
∗ *Breton Museum* In the old Bishop's Palace, worth a visit in itself: cloisters,
ramparts and a spiral staircase. Interesting local costumes, wood and stone
carving, and pottery, the whole not very well presented.
∗ *Fine Arts Museum* Moderately interesting paintings, very well displayed.

Driving down to the west of the Odet gives access to some splendid
wooded gorges (**Les Vire-Court**). Bénodet can be reached by a new toll
bridge.

Beg-Meil is a much frequented, but not particularly lively, resort with
good beaches offering a variety of sand, dunes, rocks and pines. There is
well-situated accommodation behind the beach. **La Forêt-Fouesnant** is
not much of a village but has a little harbour at the head of an
attractive wooded inlet much favoured by campers and sailors. Walks
all round are very pleasant, which is just as well because the beaches
are some way from the village. A few miles inland, **Fouesnant** itself is
known for the best Breton cider and the local headdress; it has an
interesting 12th-century church.

The big tourist attraction, even trap, of this part of the coast is the old
walled town which sits on an island in the waters of one of Brittany's
most important fishing ports, **Concarneau**. The rest of Concarneau is of
moderate interest, as busy ports are, and has a few rather scruffy
beaches. The Ville Close, as the old town is called, is picturesque in the
extreme, with ramparts giving good views over the port and town (they
try to make you pay to walk along them but it isn't necessary). The
single long central street is lined with crêperies and souvenir shops
selling costumed dolls; there is a small fishing museum with old boats

and items illustrating local history. The Ville Close is linked to the mainland by a fortified bridge at one end and a little ferry at the other.

The next estuary along the coast is the famous Aven, less frequented for its seaside facilities than for the artistic associations of Pont-Aven upstream, where the estuary begins to open out. The inlet itself and surrounding countryside are very attractive: hedgerows, curving lanes, woods and rocky river banks. **Kerdruc** is a charming little port, and **Kerascoët** has several of the thatched farm cottages that remain in this area. **Raguenès-Plage** is a small village with a large beach and campsite; **Port-Manech** is a delightful little fishing cove, with a sheltered and not overcrowded beach.

Pont-Aven is intimately tucked below beech- and chestnut-covered hills; the river bounds down to a rocky little port below the village. Once there were as many watermills as houses at Pont-Aven, but only a few are left now. The village teems with people, cars and caravans and is very commercialised—galleries and souvenir shops as well as a museum with temporary exhibitions. You won't see the greatest achievements on canvas of the Pont-Aven School, but you can still follow a signed walk through the Bois de l'Amour up on the hill above the Aven, where many of them were conceived.

Among schools of mostly mediocre artists from all over the world who were attracted by the picturesque Breton life and landscape, the village's most distinguished colonists were Paul Gauguin and Emile Bernard. These two, collaborating fruitfully in the late 1880s, went beyond the merely picturesque to evolve a new style of painting itself—expressive of what Gauguin described as the "great rustic, superstitious simplicity" of the Bretons. Pont-Aven is recorded in a 19th-century guidebook for English art tourists; "The art student who has spent the winter in the Quartier Latin comes when the leaves are green and settles down for the summer to study undisturbed . . . his surroundings are delightful, everything he needs is to be obtained in an easy way . . . the climate is temperate and favourable to outdoor work. At the sunny end of the square the Hotel des Voyageurs gets mostly Americans (some stay all year). Down by the bridge is the Pension Gloanec, the true Bohemian home also decorated with paintings. Board and lodging including two good meals and cider costs 60 Francs a month. Materials for work and opportunities for study are similar to those in Wales with fewer distractions than at Betws-y-Coed. The talk at table is of the Paris Salon, bedrooms and lofts are turned into studios, there is a pervading smell of oil paint. Pont-Aven has one big advantage: its inhabitants in their picturesque costumes have learned that to sit as a model is a pleasant and lucrative profession".

The Belon River, which joins the Aven at the sea, is no less famous than its arty neighbour, because of the local type of oyster that bears its name. *Belons* are the original edible oyster, flat as opposed to hollow (the so-called Portuguese oysters), and are now farmed all over Brittany and beyond; this is a good place to look at the exposure of oyster-beds in the muddy inlet at low tide. **Le Pouldu** was Gauguin's seaside home after he left Pont-Aven in 1889; it's a small port and resort at the mouth of the exotically named and attractively wooded Laita, with a good beach looking south. **Quimperlé** has nothing to do with Quimper except that it too is at the junction of two rivers for which the local word is *kemper*. It has attractive old streets with ramshackle timbered houses, a colourful fish market and a beautiful cruciform Romanesque church, all close together at the heart of the town.

Morbihan and Loire-Atlantique

The south-east corner of Brittany is the land of megalithic monuments and the great lake which is the Gulf of Morbihan (which means little sea). Beyond it the Loire-Atlantique *département* is outside Brittany for administrative purposes, but historically it isn't—Nantes was the capital city of many of Brittany's most prestigious dukes, the Montforts—and for the tourist it is at least as Breton as it is Loire country.

Lorient was a custom-built port for the French East India Company, whence its name; now it's important for fishing. Like Brest it was unattractive even before the second World War reduced it to rubble. The modern church of Notre-Dame-de-Victoire and the Palais des Congrès are, however, of interest. Across the estuary **Port-Louis** still has its own citadel and an interesting naval museum.

Even if you don't approach **Carnac** through its famous alignments (see page 302), there is no mistaking the *raison d'être* of this, the proud capital of prehistory, with its Hotel Megalith and its Hotel Tumulus and many other establishments which it is to be hoped do not carry their prehistoric affiliations further than their names. In no other region of Brittany is there to be found such a variety of megalithic remains— menhirs, cromlechs, dolmens and tumuli—as around the once impressively wild and desolate coast of the Bay of Quiberon and the Gulf of Morbihan. Carnac has an important prehistory museum founded by the archaeologist James Miln, which has changed little since it opened 100 years ago; a facelift is now threatened. There is an interesting 17th-century church and a very good view of the coast and alignments from the top of a tumulus called St-Michel.

Old Carnac almost merges with new **Carnac-Plage**, a pleasantly spacious beach resort in the garden suburb style. It is sheltered from the open sea by the long **Quiberon peninsula**, once an island but now joined by the buildup of a low, sandy strip of land (the same is happening at Mont-St-Michel and Ile de Bréhat). The rocky west coast of this effective breakwater, the Côte Sauvage, seems rather misleadingly named if the weather is good and the sea calm. But bathing accidents do happen and there are warnings against swimming from the enticing sandy coves between the sharp rocks. Round the tip of the peninsula and along its sandy eastern shore, there is a succession of busy, rather unattractive resorts of which **Quiberon** itself is the biggest.

With all its yachts and islands the muddy **Gulf of Morbihan** is very pretty at high tide, and the colour of its water famed for its brilliance. But when the tide is out there are enormous expanses of mud with oyster beds, and its beaches are correspondingly imperfect. At the lower entrance of the gulf, **Locmariaquer** is an attractive little resort as well as the site of very important prehistoric remains (see page 302). The road round the gulf is long and, especially between Auray and Vannes, not very interesting; it is much better to explore by boat.

At the head of its own river estuary, feeding the gulf, **Auray** has a very attractive old quarter (**St-Goustan**) down by the water, across the river from the main town. Nearby is the battlefield where, in 1364, the anglophile Montfort family won control of Brittany from the French. **Ste-Anne-d'Auray** is the most important pilgrimage centre in Brittany; a vast basilica was erected here in the last century.

Vannes is the old regional capital and one of the most favoured residences of the Montfort dukes. It is one of the best-looking old towns in Brittany, with well-preserved town walls, massive fortified gateways, beautiful gardens and the river at their feet. Within the walls cobbled pedestrian streets are overhung by timbered houses, many of them the object of careful restoration. The cathedral is interesting rather than beautiful: there is a round Renaissance chapel with saint Vincent Ferrier's tomb, and remnants of cloisters from the same period. In the old town there is an archaeological museum.

The road south of the gulf along the Rhuys Peninsula gives fine views of its scintillating waters, but neither the landscape nor the waterside villages are of particular interest. **St-Gildas-de-Rhuys** has memories of Abelard, who was miserable here as abbot and whose letters to Heloïse paint a now surprising picture of the desolation of the region, with its population of wolves and bears and scarcely more civilised humanity—the monks repeatedly tried to poison Abelard as they resented his attempts to impose discipline. The old abbey church is partly Romanesque and houses the tomb of the 6th-century Cornish missionary Gildas; it has a rich treasury.

The solid ducal castle of **Suscinio**, built in the 13th-century, is a splendidly impressive empty shell; the sea, which used to fill its moat at high tide, is now half a mile away.

Excursions from the coast

* **Tours d'Elven** (North-east of Vannes) The two imposing granite towers of this château are romantic of aspect and association (Henry not yet the VII of England was imprisoned here); they were made famous in the 19th century by the enormously successful though now not undeservedly neglected novelist Octave Feuillet ("nothing more imposing, proud and sombre than this old *donjon*, impassive in the mists of time and isolated in the thick of these woods. Trees have grown to full stature in the deep moat and their highest branches hardly reach the lowest windows . . . In the solitude, faced with this abrupt mass of bizarre architecture it is impossible not to think of enchanted towers where beauteous princesses sleep away centuries").

* **Château de Josselin** This château stands substantially intact, marvellously situated, rising granite grey from the bank of the reflective River Oust and guarding the old town. Augustus Hare described Josselin as the Warwick Castle of France and the comparison is apt. Behind the forbidding round towers, built in the 14th century, the interior courtyard is over a century younger and

Château de Josselin

beautifully decorated. a marvellous example of the intricate fantasy of late Gothic carving. Josselin's most glorious memory is the Combat of Thirty in 1351, when the English and French captains of Ploërmel and Josselin each led 30 knights into the field for a full day's set-to, to resolve their conflict. The French were victorious under Beaumanoir. whose widow, a Rohan, married Olivier de Clisson. The proud family—Clisson's motto was, roughly translated, "because I feel like it", the Rohan's "king I cannot be, prince I disdain to be, Rohan I am"—still own the château which is open in summer. Most of the interior is the work of 19th-century restorers, but no less interesting for that. The large church—Our Lady of the Brambles—contains the extremely beautiful double tomb of de Clisson and Marguerite de Rohan.

✳ **Ploërmel** This pretty old town has a remarkably ornate 16th-century church with fine stained glass as well as interesting sculptures.

The pleasantly wooded valleys of the interior are worth exploring for churches:

✳ **Le Faouët** Near this attractive old village there are three chapels of interest: St-Fiacre and St-Nicolas have beautifully carved wooden screens full of humour: Ste-Barbe is an important *pardon* chapel.

✳ **Kernascléden** In a tiny village the surprisingly large, mottled grey church has wonderfully decorative architectural features. painted apostles in the porch. and a rare series of frescoes inside, including a gruesome depiction of Hell.

✳ **Guéhenno** This church has a fine Calvary. with an ossuary clearly representing the tomb of Christ. and a splendid statue of a cock crowing.

South of the Vilaine, the Guérande Peninsula, with its saltpans and the enormous beach of La Baule. gives a foretaste of the Atlantic coast. **Guérande** itself is a finely situated and remarkably preserved medieval walled town dominating the salt-pans reclaimed from the sea. There is an interesting local museum in the eastern fortified gateway illustrating. among much else, the how and why of the local salt industry, which originally had much to do with Guérande's status as a tax haven. exempt from the dreaded *gabelle* salt tax. The grey collegiate church of St-Aubin has some interesting features including lively capital carving.

Narrow roads follow the banks between the salt-pans to the Grand Traict lagoon and the attractive old yacht, fish and crustacean port of Le

Brittany

Croisic. It has handsome 17th-century houses around the harbour which is very animated and commercialised, partly because it's so near La Baule. On the quayside there is an exotic aquarium.

The drive round the Pointe back to La Baule follows the Grande Côte (rocky but not particularly impressive) and passes the old salt port of Batz, now unlike Le Croisic a resort with sandy beaches, retaining a late-Gothic church (St-Guénolé) whose belfry gives enormous views.

La Baule is unlike the Breton resorts of north or south coast; it resembles much more the long, modern seafront straggles of the Atlantic coast such as Les Sables d'Olonne and Royan. The essence of the resort is an enormous crescent of fine sand which would probably win a French 'Best Beach' competition. Behind it stand anonymous apartment blocks, palatial hotels and villas with gardens (at the residential Baule-les-Pins end of the beach). It is not much younger as a resort than Dinard but the difference in atmosphere is one of generations. Dinard was fashionable with English and Americans when they were fashionable. La Baule is fashionable and popular with the French now, and is full of young people. There are two 18-hole golf courses, four sailing schools, fifteen beach clubs, tennis clubs, cinemas, discothèques and nightclubs, an aero club, two yacht harbours, equestrian centres, a theatre festival, concerts, a *pardon* and a Breton Week (last week in August). There are 1,500 hotel rooms, 1,000 camping places, 7,000 villas in the pines, 6,000 apartments by the sea and 2,000 hours of sun a year, thanks apparently to the saltpans.

Between the Vilaine and the Loire lies the **Brière Regional Park** established in 1970 in an attempt to prevent the extinction of a unique way of life. The Briérons traditionally punted around the canals and the marshes, shot the abundant wildlife, speared eels, cut peat, thatched cottages, and made their own clogs. Gradually the factories and ship-yards of St-Nazaire claimed more livelihoods and the canals became overgrown. Now a complete old village (Kerhinet) has been restored, canals have been cleared, and cottage industries established. The most interesting and tourist-orientated part of the region is the island of **Fédrun**, which is separated from St-Joachim by a network of canals. You can take boat trips on the canals, and there is a small, marshy animal and bird park nearby.

St-Nazaire is a busy modern shipyard and commercial port created in the 19th century to accommodate shipping which increasingly outgrew the stretch of the Loire up as far as Nantes; like so many other ports it was rebuilt after the Second World War and is without general appeal to the tourist. The maritime stretch of France's greatest river, between Nantes and St-Nazaire, is industrial.

Nantes' prosperity came principally from the sea; but it has histori-cally been more than just a port: the capital of Brittany in the most brilliant years of the duchy (15th century), an important university city and an administrative centre. It is not immediately attractive, having suffered greatly in the Second World War. But if you are stuck in La Baule on a wet day there is no shortage of things to see in the city (except on Tuesdays):

∗ *Ducal castle* Built by Anne of Brittany's father duc François II in the mid-15th century, a splendid combination of military might and decorative richness, not unlike some early Loire châteaux. There are two very interesting museums: one recalling the history of Nantes the port, with mementoes of the slave trade

▷ continued at foot of next page

Megaliths

Alignments at Carnac

There can be few Breton words that have been adopted by other languages. Three that have are menhir, dolmen, and cromlech—different sorts of prehistoric stone monuments or megaliths, the work of unknown inhabitants of the area probably between 4,000 and 1,800 BC. They are to be found all over Europe and beyond but nowhere in such abundance as in Brittany. The area of greatest concentration is in the south-east, around Carnac and the Morbihan gulf, where there are several thousand stones, many of them aligned. The prodigious weight-lifting enthusiasm of the early Bretons (the largest menhir at Loc-mariaquer weighed some 350 tons), and the particular importance of Carnac remain something of a mystery, but the religious and often funerary significance of the megaliths is universally accepted—skeletons, in many cases dating from a much later period than the monuments themselves, have been found under many dolmens (flat-topped, table-like structures previously imagined to have been altars for human sacrifice) and within tumuli (the earth, or stones which used to cover dolmens).

among many other nautical items, the other devoted to Breton art and folklore.
✻ *Cathedral* Although not finished until the 19th century this is basically a soaring late-Gothic church, distinguished above all by Michel Colombe's wonderful double tomb of duke François II and his wife Marguerite de Foix, which was saved from Revolutionary demolition by a brave town architect.
✻ *Museums* The fine arts museum contains a varied collection of paintings, with more than a few masterpieces (including three Georges de la Tours). Just off the Rue Voltaire is a cluster of four varied and interesting museums: natural history; anthropology and ancient sculpture; local archaeology; and in the Palais Dobrée a rich collection of sculptures, *objets d'art*, and paintings.
✻ *Old houses* The former Feydeau Island in the Loire (between the bus station and Place Royale) retains its 18th-century elegance from the time of Nantes' greatest prosperity based on the slave trade.

The following are the most important of Breton megalithic sites:

Carnac Nearly 3,000 menhirs in the fields on the edge of town arranged in three main alignments, two of which (the Menec and Kerlescan alignments) end in semi-circular apse-like rings of menhirs, giving the alignments the look of foundations for enormous cathedrals. Of the numerous theories put forward to explain the significance of the Carnac lines, including the "windbreak for Roman tents" suggestion, the most picturesque is the local legend of Saint Cornelius who was pope in 3rd-century Rome but was expelled and chased by Roman soldiers all the way to Brittany. Here he found the inhabitants of Carnac sowing seeds: "Tomorrow your corn will be ripe," he told them. The next day the Romans arrived and enquired as to Cornelius' whereabouts, and were told that he had passed through when the corn was being sown. Concluding from the advanced state of the crop that Cornelius must be many months ahead of them the Romans struck camp. The saint, hidden nearby, realised himself to be cornered with his back against the sea, and turned all the Romans to stone overnight. More recently it has been concluded from the precise orientation of Breton alignments towards the position of sun and moon at particular times of year (equinoxes and solstices) that these open-air cathedrals were indeed the temples of sun worshippers. A very good view of the lines is to be had from the top of the tumulus St-Michel, whose passages and burial chamber you can visit.

Locmariaquer The so-called Witches' Stone must have been a staggering sight, over 20 metres high and nearly 350 tons in weight, the largest menhir ever raised. Sometime at the end of the 17th or beginning of the 18th century it was shattered, perhaps by lightning, into five pieces of which four remain in situ. Nearby there are splendid tumuli and covered galleries with carvings, and a magnificent dolmen, the Merchant's Table, composed of three granite slabs resting on 17 pointed supports, with some carvings in the stone including one of a primitive plough.

Tumulus de Gavrinis The most impressive covered burial chamber in Brittany, on an island in the Morbihan Gulf easily accessible by boat from Larmor-Baden. There's a long gallery with patterned carvings on the supporting menhirs, and a funeral chamber.

Lagatjar Intersecting alignments of over a hundred stones near Camaret.

Brignogan-Plage Just one of many Christianised menhirs (the Miracle Stone) surmounted by one cross and inscribed with another.

Barnenez Tumulus On the east side of the Morlaix river estuary. Eleven burial chambers with approach galleries.

La Roche-aux-Fées (Fairies' Rock) Between Le Theil and Marcillé-Robert, south-east of Rennes, this is a twenty-yard covered gallery of purple slate stones.

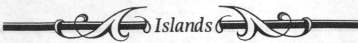

Of the scores of islands around Brittany few are inhabited, easily accessible, or interesting. The two islands that bear the brunt of the Atlantic storms are **Ouessant** (Ushant), and **Sein** just off the Pointe du Raz. These rugged outposts are full of legendary and historical interest, but bleak to visit. Ushant is the westernmost point of France, an important staging post for sailors and migratory birds. (Access from Brest and, in summer, Camaret).

The little island of **Sein** was the last haven of paganism in Brittany, a Druidical burial site, and a renowned residence of wreckers. In 1940 the Germans found a community without any active males, all of whom had responded to General de Gaulle's appeal from London. The island was decorated for its devotion to duty. (Access from Audierne).

Little **Molène** lies between Ushant and the coast and is part of the Armorique Regional Park. There doesn't seem much to preserve except the primitiveness—no trees, no running water. It has an inn, a few creeks and room for some simple camping in summer. (Access from Brest).

The islands off the south coast are more sheltered and clement and are busy in season. Well-named **Belle-Ile** at least merits a visit for reasons other than curiosity. It has excellent beaches (east of Le Palais, and at Port-Donnant), a choice of accommodation (at Port Goulphar), very fine rocky coastal scenery (the south-west coast), and a couple of attractive villages (Le Palais with Vauban fortifications, and Sauzon). The car ferry from Quiberon is in heavy demand in the summer months, and unless you are going for more than a few days it is cheaper to hire a car on the island, which improves your chances of getting off it when you want. The nearby islands of **Houat** and **Hoëdic** are also accessible from Quiberon and have good beaches.

Like Belle-Ile, the island of **Groix** has impressive rocky cliffs at one end, good sandy beaches at the other, and an attractive little port (access from Lorient and nearby coastal resorts).

The **Glénan Islands** have important schools for the instruction of sailing and skin-diving, and large colonies of seabirds (access from resorts between Concarneau and Quimper).

Hotels

Audierne, 29113 Finistère   £££

LE GOYEN   Tel: 98.70.08.88

An old but completely renovated building in the town centre beside the port, recently re-vamped to produce more dining room, and, sadly, no terrace. There's a smart sitting area near reception, and studios and duplex '*grand standing*' suites, with fine port views. Some bedrooms are still on the small side, but they're generally well-equipped; most are peaceful at night, but less so in the morning. The food is of a very high quality: à la carte and wines are expensive but menus are good value and interesting. It's a family-run hotel, with high standards throughout.

Closed mid-Nov to mid-Dec (rest Tues lunch, and Mon in high season); 34 bedrooms.

La Baule, 44500 Loire-Atlantique   ££££

LA CANTELLERIE   Tel: 40.60.26.28
10 Ave de Saumur

Modern balconied building on a quiet tree-lined side street near the beach, with garden and terrace. Inside it's comfortable, with traditional décor—beams, stone fireplace and velvet sofas in the salon, colourful prints and rustic-style furniture in the bedrooms. You can opt for studios with kitchenettes, more modern with bunk beds and pine—all neat and stylish. A good family base in a lively resort.

12 bedrooms, 12 studios; no rest.

La Baule, 44500 Loire-Atlantique   £££

MUSSET   Tel: 40.60.24.08
15 Allée des Cygnes

Steep-roofed turn-of-the-century villa with a small garden, set among pines in a side street in the centre of the resort. It's run by friendly young people, and has been simply and charmingly decorated—wicker, plants and bright colours in the salon and breakfast room, wood and brass in the dining room, painted furniture and Laura Ashley wallpaper in the bedrooms. Food is uncomplicated and wholesome; we enjoyed excellent *moules marinières*, roast beef with *haricots verts*, cheese and a fine *charlotte aux framboises*—a cut above the average fare of many seaside hotels.

Rest closed Oct to April; 11 bedrooms; no lift.

Beg-Meil, 29170 Finistère   ££

THALAMOT   Tel: 98.94.97.38

If you want a simple seaside boarding-house hotel, a stone's throw from one of the best beaches of Brittany's favourite stretch of sheltered, shaded southern coastline, the Thalamot will do you proud. In any other situation, the hotel would seem dowdy and even institutional (though there's a very pleasant shady terrace area), and the cooking is not of the most exciting (but fish is reliably fresh and competently prepared). The setting is everything; 20 yards—across a road, but not a busy one—from the trees behind the beach and much quieter than most proms, for this is not downtown Beg-Meil.

Closed mid-Oct to April; 35 bedrooms; no lift.

Belle-Ile-en-Mer (Port-Goulphar) 56360 Morbihan Castel Clara £££££
Manoir £££

CASTEL CLARA, and MANOIR DE GOULPHAR   Castel Clara Tel: 97.31.84.21
Manoir Tel: 97.31.83.95

A bit irregular perhaps to cover two hotels in one, but they do ask for it; right next door to each other, out on their own, overlooking an alas often scum-filled creek on Belle-Ile's splendid Côte Sauvage. The two establishments look similar—whitewashed and grey-roofed—but have been conceived by the common ownership to be very deliberately distinct. The Manoir is friendly and unpretentious, with functional bedrooms, good honest sea food, and adequate public rooms. Bus tours around the island stop by for lunch. Across the few-feet-wide but nonetheless great divide, the Castel receives beautiful Parisians into a cool modern marbled interior, offers them a tennis court and swimming pool, and seafood more elaborately garnished, if no more purely bred—at correspondingly

Hotels

higher prices. Apart from this social microcosm, there isn't much to Port-Goulphar; no bright lights at night save that of the lighthouse which beams across unshuttered windows with the infuriating regularity of a dripping tap.

Closed mid-Oct to mid-Mar (Castel Clara); Nov to mid-Mar (Manoir); 43 and 52 bedrooms; no lift (Manoir).

Dinan, 22100 Côtes-du-Nord £

CARAVELLE Tel: 96.39.00.11
14 place Duclos

Simple restaurant with rooms in the centre of town—the restaurant by a busy roundabout, the rooms 50 metres away on a quiet cobbled street. Jean-Claude Marmion has acquired a reputation for good innovative cooking, and his fixed-price menus are good value. The few bedrooms (only six with bathroom), with traditional patterned wallpaper, candlewick bedspreads and old dark wood furniture, are simple but more than adequate—and cheap.

Closed Oct and one week in Feb (rest Wed out of season); 11 bedrooms; no lift.

Hennebont, 56700 Morbihan £££££

CHÂTEAU DE LOCGUÉNOLÉ Tel: 97.76.29.04

Four kilometres south of Hennebont, this solid 19th-century château sits in 250 acres of wooded countryside, with meadows stretching down to the River Blavet. There's a pool, tennis and fishing, and lots of space for quiet walks. The castle itself, in the de la Sablière family for centuries and now run by the present Comtesse, is harmoniously decorated with antiques and tapestries; the atmosphere is rather formal. Bedrooms are very spacious and decorated *en style*; there's an isolated cottage annexe in the grounds. The standard of cooking is very high, and prices are not low—but the wine list at least offers the chance of a bottle under £10.

Closed mid-Nov to Feb (rest Mon out of season); 36 bedrooms; swimming pool; no lift.

Moëlan-sur-Mer, 29116 Finistère ££££

LES MOULINS DU DUC Tel: 98.39.60.73

Utterly secluded on its little river deep in the woody countryside, this is an old mill-house, with bedrooms in attractive cottages. Woodland and gardens, duckpond and lawns are a balance of cultivation and wilderness. There's an excellent indoor swimming pool; a bar, but no separate lounge. The cottage bedrooms are lofty and comfortable, with stone walls and old country furniture, and well-appointed bathrooms. The restaurant is intimately candle-lit at night. Alas, the very talented Japanese chef, Shigeo Torigai, whose exquisite cooking attracted devotees from far and wide, left last year, and his successor does not seem to be following in his illustrious footsteps—a daunting task, admittedly. Will he improve? Reports, please.

Closed mid-Jan to Feb (rest Wed); 28 bedrooms; no lift; indoor swimming pool

Pléhédel, 22290 Côtes-du-Nord   £££££

CHÂTEAU DE COATGUÊLEN   Tel: 96.22.31.24

Splendid little 19th-century château near Paimpol, idyllicly set in many acres of grounds. There's a nine-hole golf course, a swimming pool, tennis, riding and fishing. Bedrooms (there are some family rooms) are spacious and elegant but also comfortable; throughout, the formality of the décor belies an atmosphere which is friendly and relaxed, and service which is unobtrusive. The food is good—light and innovative, with very good value fixed-price menus. A wonderfully peaceful place.

Closed Jan to mid-Mar (rest Tues and Wed lunch); 16 bedrooms; no lift; swimming pool and sports.

Raguenès-Plage, 29139 Finistère   £££

CHEZ PIERRE   Tel: 98.06.81.06

An old stone Breton house, in a hamlet two minutes from a fine sandy beach, with a garden and terrace. Chez Pierre isn't quite the simple little family seaside hotel that it used to be: plans are always afoot to add a bit here (new 'luxury' bedrooms), change a bit there (redecorated dining room) and the result is that it is now more comfortable but less charming than many British visitors of old might remember. It's still very popular, and the excellent seafood platters and lobster (not, of course, on the *pensionnaires'* menus) are still better value than almost anywhere—though the cooking has recently fallen out of favour with a French restaurant guide. Bedrooms are neat and comfortable, some well arranged for families. British visitors are made welcome.

Closed Oct to Easter; 21 bedrooms; no lift.

Riec-sur-Belon, 29124 Finistère   ££

CHEZ MELANIE   Tel: 98.06.91.05

Charming old house on the village square, lovingly looked after by Melanie herself, whose generous proportions watch over diners from paintings and illustrated menus. Melanie's reputation has spread far and wide, and transatlantic tones can be heard praising the lobsters, clams, mussels and oysters that form part of the staple fare in the beautiful rustic dining room. There's no hint of *nouvelle cuisine* to lighten the gastronomic burden. Bedrooms are simple and traditional. There's a small pretty garden behind.

Closed Nov to Jan (rest Tues); 7 bedrooms; no lift.

Roscoff, 29211 Finistère   ££

GULF STREAM   Tel: 98.69.73.19

Dull modern hotel built in ubiquitous local style—white with slate roof—well situated at the edge of town (in Roskogoz) with gardens sloping down to the bay. There's nothing to mar the views from many of the bedrooms (plain and very comfortable), or through the large picture windows of the restaurant, though there's no need to be distracted from the prettily presented food. There's an excellent-value small fixed-price menu. A good first or last night stop if you're travelling through Roscoff.

Closed April to mid-Oct; 32 bedrooms.

Hotels

Ste-Anne-la-Palud, 29127 Finistère   £££££

PLAGE   Tel: 98.52.50.12

Even when one of the sexennial *pardons* isn't attracting huge crowds to little Ste-Anne-la-Palud, this hotel packs in small ones. Its comfort (considerable—although it isn't particularly spacious, or the public rooms very stylish), the high standard of the cooking (very good seafood, and much more besides) and even its extra facilities (heated, and carefully groomed, swimming pool with adjacent sauna) count for less than the situation, which must make other hoteliers green-eyed. The Hôtel de la Plage stands isolated on the edge of an empty, wide and splendid sandy beach—facing the west for memorable sunsets.

Closed mid-Oct to Mar; 30 bedrooms; swimming pool.

St-Malo, 35400 Ille-et-Vilaine   ££££

LA KORRIGANE   Tel: 99.81.65.85

Splendid 19th-century mansion in the suburb of St-Servan, just south of St-Malo harbour and about a kilometre from the old walled city. Bedrooms are spacious and very comfortable, luxuriously decorated and furnished with antiques. There are two salons, also very comfortable, and a quiet and pretty garden; there's no restaurant.

Closed mid-Oct to Easter; 10 bedrooms; no rest; no lift.

St-Malo, 35400 Ille-et-Vilaine   ££££

ELIZABETH   Tel: 99.56.24.98

Behind a 16th-century stone façade *intra muros*, that is inside the walled city which was virtually rebuilt after the war, this modern hotel has little space for public rooms—a small TV area, and a small cosy bar in the stone-walled basement—but the traditional-style bedrooms have sufficient space for breakfast. Not cheap, but in an atmospheric setting—particularly at night, when many of the tourists have departed.

17 bedrooms; no rest.

Trébeurden, 22560 Côtes-du-Nord   £££££

MANOIR DE LAN KERELLEC   Tel: 96.23.50.09

In a residential district, this mellow old manor house has sea views, small garden and gravel terrace. Renovated and beautifully decorated throughout, it reflects the charm and style of its young owners who generate a high standard of comfort and pleasure. Bedrooms are pretty and well furnished. The main room of the house is a large and unusual dining hall. Candlelight, tall windows over the sea, comfortable chairs and quiet music all create an atmosphere which makes people linger. Oysters, *foie gras*, home-smoked salmon and interesting fish dishes appear both on fixed-price menus and à la carte; there's a good-value cheap menu (*pension*), but the wine list remains rather top-heavy.

Closed Nov to mid-Mar (rest Mon out of season); 13 bedrooms; no lift.

Trébeurden, 22560 Côtes-du-Nord   ££££

TI AL LANNEC   Tel: 966.23.57.26

Large old granite house on a hill behind the resort, with commanding views over
the sloping garden to the bay, and a private path down to the beach. Inside it's
refined and comfortable; there's a salon and bar, and an attractive light
restaurant with verandah. Bedrooms (some with verandahs, too) are attractively
furnished and decorated—wicker and lace, Laura Ashley prints, handsome old
furniture. The standard of cooking is high; there are three fixed-price menus
(three, four and five courses) and a children's menu, with plenty of choice.

Closed mid-Nov to mid-Mar (rest Mon lunch); 22 bedrooms; no lift.

Vannes (Conleau), 56000 Morbihan   ££

LE ROOF   Tel: 97.63.47.47

A simple, unpretentious and beautifully situated little hotel on the edge of the
island-studded inland sea that is the Golfe du Morbihan, with woods all around
the waters. Yachtsfolk lunch next to solid Vannes professional folk, either in the
bright, jolly restaurant or on the shady terrace; the fare is good honest seafood.
Bedrooms are simple but perfectly adequate; some have balconies.

Closed early Jan to mid-Feb (rest Mon out of season); 11 bedrooms; no lift.

Normandy

"How came the flame-haired Norsemen to these lands of fattest pasture and brightest bloom, fresh-painted daily by a loving dewy brush? Bitter indeed, the north wind that filled their sails" (Fearne d'Arcy)

Normandy is close to England geographically, historically and climatically. Even if the last can hardly be considered a point in its favour where holidays are concerned, it does account for a green and plentiful countryside which many visitors find comfortingly reminiscent of southern England. Of all France's northern coastal regions Normandy has the most varied appeal. The north coast of Brittany has its popular resorts on the rocky and sandy seaside, but relatively little of more than seasonal interest. Artois and Picardy are well worth exploring for individual towns and monuments, but do not leave a visitor with any great sense of regional identity, and the coast is mostly drab. In Normandy the architectural and historical interest is great, the countryside—especially around the Seine Valley—has a prosperous domesticated charm, and there is a wealth of literary and artistic associations. The area has style: colourful manor houses quite different from those in other parts of France, lively and fashionable seaside resorts, and impeccably bred horses which embellish the countryside, and provide the focus of attraction in Deauville, the Monte Carlo of the north.

Scenically Normandy splits into two parts. The more fertile and attractive chalky farmlands of Upper Normandy, north of the Seine and along the coast to the mouth of the Orne, have as their capital the fascinating ancient and modern city of Rouen. This area has more in common with the fertile Ile-de-France than with Lower Normandy which itself belongs geologically to Brittany, land of scrub and harsh granite. Within each part there is great diversity. In the north the spectacular chalky cliffs, shingle beaches and open farmlands of the Caux contrast with the sandy beaches and lush orchards of the Pays d'Auge. In Lower Normandy the bleak rocky north-west coast and flat interior of the Cotentin peninsula are far removed from the rolling hills and steep river valleys of the so-called Norman Switzerland and the Mancelles Alps.

The history of Normandy is a story of invasions, inward and—more characteristically of the bold seafaring race—outward. Adventurous Scandinavians (known as Norsemen, whence Normans) sailed up the Seine in the 9th century. Their right to the area around the lower Seine valley was recognised in 911, and 155 years later the first duke Rollo's great great great great grandson was well enough rooted to press his claim to the English throne. The conquest of England was only one of a glorious series of conquering excursions which brought the systematically structured Norman styles of government and architecture to remote parts of the known world, and at the same time relieved the primogenital system of landless younger sons. For today's tourist there are interesting historical associations between Normandy and Norman Britain, and a style of ecclesiastical architecture which the Normans took across the channel with them.

The D-day invasion which began on June 6th 1944 did as much in a few months as church-building Normans did in generations to change

Normandy

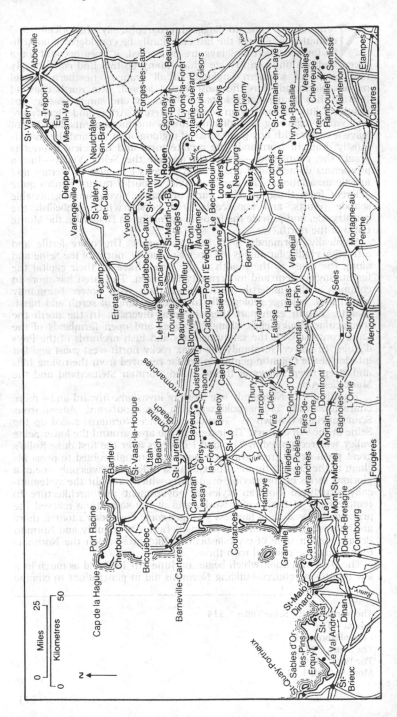

the face of Normandy. The Allied landing on the sandy beaches of the Calvados coast and the east of the Cotentin peninsula was preceded and accompanied by intensive bombing which brought even more widespread devastation to Normandy than the First World War had inflicted on north-eastern France. Many of the 500 rebuilt towns and villages seem as cold and characterless as a Moscow suburb compared with the rambling timbered provincial towns elsewhere in France, but reconstruction has at least ensured that many of the old monuments are shown off to their best advantage. Along the coast there are a number of museums devoted to the history of the Battle of Normandy, and in many places war debris still litters the dunes; as in north-eastern France, there are many war cemeteries, but because the events of the battle are more recent in Normandy there are more tourists who come here specifically to re-visit invasion beaches or pay respects to lost friends and relations. Norman hotels are full of silver-haired Americans determined to tell every other inmate the full story of how they flew in over "Arrowmoosh" (Arromanches) or "Cayenne" (Caen).

Much of the coast cannot pretend to rival Brittany for beach holidays. The most attractive stretch by far is the Côte Fleurie between the rivers Seine and Dives, an almost uninterrupted chain of fashionable resorts built in a characteristic neo-rustic architectural style after the railways brought the Normandy coast suddenly closer to Paris. The wide breezy beachscapes full of human interest provided perfect material for the fresh-air painters of the 1860's, and the pretty village of Honfleur is no less a painters' haunt now than it was in the time of Boudin and Monet. Honfleur—picturesque, old, and situated on the estuary not the sea— is less typical of the coast than fashionable Deauville which made its name by providing summer distractions in the days when the Riviera was considered tolerable only in the winter, and which is now a very horsy resort in season when crowds came to watch the races and to ride along the beach.

If you are susceptible to proud equine beauty—or if you want to take a mare to stud—the stud farms of inland Normandy (most heavily concentrated around L'Aigle and Alençon) will be of great interest and perhaps even fruitful. Those without a business interest should visit the national stud farms—originally for the provision of the army—to learn about breeding for perfection, and to feel the aura of hushed respect which still surrounds the noblest of God's creatures.

Normandy is excellent for a gastronomic tour, with a rich and varied larder. Its pride is dairy produce—France's best butter, milk and cream form the basis of Norman cooking, so you should expect rich creamy sauces and an array of luscious cheeses (of which the most famous is Camembert). Fécamp and Dieppe are important fishing ports for cod and sole respectively, and seafood of all varieties is plentiful.

Of the many aspects of Normandy that make you feel closer to home than in most areas of France, the most striking, after the rain, is the apple. The Normans produce not wine but cider, and although you don't have to drink it with meals many Normans do. Norman cider varies in sweetness and strength and is usually served from bottles corked and wired up like champagne. The apples are also used to produce Calvados (apple brandy) which varies too, not in strength but in quality. Normans drink 'Calva' with or in a morning cup of coffee, between courses in a big meal (*le trou normand* being the hole which a large gulp of Calvados blows in your stomach to create space) and afterwards.

313

The North and the Seine Valley

The **Pays de Caux**, along the channel coast north of the Seine, is a featureless and fertile chalky agricultural region without much to tempt you inland except for the splendid beech forests (especially fine is Eawy forest, south-east of Dieppe). The Alabaster Coast gets its name from the succession of chalk cliffs which are losing their battle against the tide and the weather at the rate of up to six feet a year in some places. The disappearing cliffs tower over narrow shingle beaches (inaccessible for long stretches), and have been eroded into majestic forms of natural architecture. Fishing ports—and, since the 19th century, resorts—have grown up in the gaps between the cliffs. The short distance from Paris has assured the villages a busy summer, but in general they are not particularly attractive places to come for a holiday.

Le Tréport and its neighbour across the mouth of the Bresle, **Mers-les-Bains**, are typical—grey of building and beach, with rows of white changing huts like sentry boxes along the shingle. The beaches here, as elsewhere along this part of the coast, shelve steeply. Le Tréport has an attractive little fishing harbour and a finely situated church looking down over the busy resort centre. The beach is backed by a very ugly block of flats, and the cable car which used to ferry people up to a panoramic Calvary at the top of a cliff is rustily redundant. **Mers** is quieter and nicer, with period boarding houses on the car-free promenade. A few miles inland **Eu**, the marriage site of William-not-yet-the-Conquerer, has a very fine early Gothic church dedicated to the Virgin and St Lawrence O'Toole who died at Eu in 1180. The outside of the choir is ornate in the later Flamboyant style; inside there is a fine 15th-century sculpture of the Entombment.

Dieppe, the resort closest to Paris, is probably France's oldest seaside resort: thalassotherapy goes back to the 3rd century, but only in the 19th when sea bathing became a fashionable pleasure did Dieppe outgrow its long-established role as an important commercial and fishing port. It is now a busy week-end resort with a full panoply of casino, tennis courts and mini-golf stretched along the spacious grassy prom behind the shingle beach; but it's less interesting for all these than for the shabby old area behind the animated and colourful port. Dieppe is no longer a place for English day trippers now that the Brighton hydrofoil is no more, but it's still a popular gateway to and from France with good roads south and to Paris. The busy pedestrian shopping streets are full of tempting goodies for the returning British traveller.

✳ *Château* A characteristic although hardly enchanting feature of the sea front, this imposing 15th-century fortress contains a museum rich in ivories. Their carving was once a flourishing local craft, when ivory was imported from south and east. There is also a collection of Impressionist and other paintings, model ships and old maps.
✳ *St-Jacques* A church of interesting parts from all Gothic periods (13th to 16th centuries).

Excursions from Dieppe
✳ **Arques-la-Bataille** An attractively situated village (south-east of Dieppe) in a hollow beneath the splendid overgrown ruins of an 11th-century fortress which has suffered from being used as a quarry. Across the valley is a monument to Henri IV's remarkable victory, against heavy numerical odds and the forces of the Catholic League, in 1589.
✳ **Manoir d'Ango** West of Dieppe near Varengeville at the end of a splendid beech avenue, this graceful 16th-century manor house boasts, in the middle of

the main courtyard, a remarkably beautiful and ornate dovecote.
✳ **Ailly lighthouse** Just off the coast road between Varengeville and Ste-Marguerite. Enormous views from the top down the coastline of cliffs.

Along the coast south and west of Dieppe there are numerous small and unremarkable resort villages. **Varengeville** and **Ste-Marguerite** are both set back from the sea in very attractive countryside, and have interesting churches.

Fécamp is a big fishing port and resort with very little charm, prospering on cod (its boats go as far as Newfoundland and Greenland) and Benedictine, distilled originally by the monks of the great monastery of which now only the church survives.

✳ *La Trinité* This enormous, mostly early Gothic abbey church is one of the longest in France (some 130 yards). The overall impression of the church is rather less magical than its history. The abbey and its pilgrimages owe their importance to the drops of Precious Blood collected by Joseph of Arimathea, which were pushed out to sea in the trunk of a fig tree only to land here at Fécamp. Some centuries later at the consecration of a new church in 943 an angel pilgrim appeared to officiating bishops and left a footprint which can still be seen beside the beautiful 15th-century sculpture of the Dormition of the Virgin. The nave is impressively severe, the transept and chancel more interesting, with a number of beautiful works of art—tombs, screens and sculptures.
✳ *Distillery* 19th-century buildings house the Benedictine distillery and the museum devoted to the old abbey, both of which you can visit.

Etretat is a small resort in a magnificent setting between spectacularly eroded cliffs, which has attracted artists (notably Corot and Monet) as well as tourists. The village has inevitably lost much of its charm but it is still worth a visit for cliff walks and a boat trip for the best view of the grottoes, soaring arches and the solitary 200ft chalk needle left stranded in the water. The church is mostly Romanesque.

The port and city of **Le Havre** were completely flattened in 1944, and the new town built after the war may be an interesting example of post-war town planning, but it is not what most of us look forward to as a welcome to France: wide straight boulevards and tall featureless blocks all look identical and blankly functional. If you choose to linger there are some interesting modern buildings.

✳ *St-Joseph* Set back from the yachting port this striking modern church has a 325ft tower and is brilliantly colourful inside on a fine day, thanks to the stained glass.
✳ *Fine arts museum* The steel and glass building is architecturally remarkable and well conceived for the display of the paintings. Boudin and Dufy came from Le Havre and they are still well represented here.

On the hill between the Hève lighthouse (where the erosion of the coastline happens faster than anywhere else) and the city centre, Ste-Adresse is a more elegant seaside resort suburb (they call it le Nice Havrais) with some Norman-style villas, and cottages with flowers in the thatch.

The Seine carves deep horse-shoe bends through the Normandy countryside (its name is thought to be derived from the Celtic word for tortuous). The river is commercially important and much ▷ p318

Rouen is more than a museum city: it's a busy industrial river port spreading on both sides of the Seine on the end of one of its meanders, with high-rise modern blocks looking down from the wooded hills which encircle the town. The open-work iron spire of the cathedral (the highest in France) soars gracefully above the old centre of town on the right bank. All the interesting monuments are concentrated nearby, as

are fascinating narrow streets of tall houses whose timber frames survived intensive bomb blast; old Rouen has been and is still being meticulously restored, and is one of the most attractive and interesting city centres to explore in all France. Ruskin, who adored Rouen, described it as "a labyrinth of delight, its grey and fretted towers misty in their magnificence of height".

✳ *Cathedral (Notre-Dame)* One of the country's most beautiful Gothic cathedrals whose stylistic variety betrays construction over many centuries (mostly 13th to 16th): the lofty west end is a mass of intricate detail with ill-matched twin towers—one early and simple, the other (Butter Tower) Flamboyant and sumptuously decorated. Equally fine is the doorway outside the south transept. The inside has some remarkable features—above all the tomb of Normandy's great Renaissance patrons of the arts, the cardinals of Amboise. There is also fine stained glass and a delicate staircase leading up to the libraries.

✳ *St-Maclou* At the centre of a very picturesque square with cobbles and timber-framed houses where a Brasserie Bavaroise hardly looks out of place, this very beautiful late-Gothic church climbs effortlessly to the tip of its see-through spire.

✳ *Aitre St-Maclou* Not immediately obvious down a covered alley off the square behind the church of the same name, the old charnel house has a timbered cloister remarkably decorated with skulls, bones, scythes and other accessories of Father Time. The cloister gives a splendid view of the tower of St-Ouen.

✳ *St-Ouen* This large church, almost as long as the cathedral, is a magnificent achievement of Gothic architecture celebrated for the purity and harmony of its lofty interior proportions. There's very little ornament to detract from the overall impression, but there's fine stained glass and an excellent organ often used for concerts.

✳ *Old town* The famous 14th-century gilt clock, decorated with a wealth of symbolic animals, spans an attractive and animated pedestrian shopping street (the Rue du Gros Horloge) linking the Place du Vieux Marché to the cathedral. The rich decoration of the archway over the street, the nearby law courts, and the Hôtel Bourgtheroulde are the finest of examples of the sumptuously ornate style of Rouen in the times of cardinal Georges d'Amboise who brought the Italian Renaissance to Normandy.

✳ *Museums* The fine arts museum has a large and splendid collection of 16th- to 18th-century Rouen ceramics and many galleries of paintings, with the French 19th century (especially Géricault) particularly well represented. There are many other treasures including an interesting and lively collection of early 20th-century portraits of the social and artistic élite by Jacques Emile Blanche. Other museums are the Le-Secq-des-Tournelles with a well-presented display of iron work; the Musée des Antiquités, whose very varied collection of works of art includes many treasures—among them enamels, icons, and tapestries; the Corneille museum, arranged in the house of the classical dramatist's birth in 1606; and a museum of medical history in the old hospital where the novelist Gustave Flaubert was born and his surgeon father practised. Flaubert's house at Croisset (where he wrote *Madame Bovary*) above the right bank of the Seine, downstream from the town centre, has also been turned into a small museum.

✳ *Saint Joan* The patron saint of France went up in flames on the Place du Vieux Marché on May 30th 1431. There is a commemorative plaque and statue on the spot and a wax museum on the square telling the story of her life.

used for freight; in places it is lined with industrial buildings and refineries. But its winding course is mostly a very attractive one, with sightseeing interest in abundance—the museum city of Rouen, majestic ruined abbeys and castles, and very fine scenery especially on the outside of each loop where the river runs beneath tall white cliffs.

The road upstream from Le Havre passes the impressive modern **Tancarville** suspension bridge, built in 1959 to bridge the Seine between Rouen and the sea for the first time (there are still about a dozen ferries across the river downstream from Rouen). From the terrace of the nearby château there's a fine view down the widening estuary.

Caudebec-en-Caux is the old regional capital, but no longer looks very old after extensive war damage. The church (Notre-Dame) survived; it's a fine Flamboyant Gothic building with many interesting and elegant details including a balustrade running round the roof made of letters forming Salve Regina Magnificat.

A mile or two away from the river the old **Abbaye de St-Wandrille**, a Benedictine monastery founded in the 7th century, still has its community of monks who sing Gregorian chant, sell honey, sweets and wax, and give guided tours. There are a few ruined remains of the Gothic church and handsome cloisters, to which men only are admitted, with a remarkable Renaissance washbasin set in the outside of the refectory wall. The new church is a 15th-century barn which was recently imported stone by stone. It is attractively simple inside, with plain wooden beams supporting a tall pitched wooden roof. A short walk from the abbey entrance leads to the curious and very old chapel of St-Saturnin.

Upstream lie the much more extensive ruins of the **Abbaye de Jumièges**, beautifully set on a promontory almost encircled by a meander of the Seine. Jumièges is one of France's most majestic and atmospheric ruins, often compared to Fountains Abbey and Rievaulx in Yorkshire. Its setting is not as isolated but architecturally Jumièges stands the comparison. The tall 11th-century towers flanking the central door are tremendously imposing and the ruined nave is hardly less fine.

The third great abbey church of the lower Seine is at **St-Martin-de-Boscherville**. The church, St-Georges-de Boscherville, is lesser in dimension than the other two, but intact thanks to its continued use as a parish church; it's beautifully decorated with typically Norman geometric motifs and, less typically, with very entertaining capitals.

Surveying the Seine from on high the castle ruins named after the mythical Robert le Diable now house a Viking museum. Below it La Bouille is an attractive leafy port with a ferry across the Seine and lots of weekenders from Rouen.

Rather than following the Seine upstream directly from Rouen, head due east for the splendid beech forest of **Lyons**, former hunting playground of the Norman dukes. **Lyons-la-Forêt** is a restful and attractive village (with accommodation) at the heart of the forest. Nearby there are two ruined abbeys to visit or admire as you pass: **Mortemer** is pleasantly pastoral, **Fontaine-Guérard** more romantically set beside the river Andelle at the foot of a steep wooded hill.

On the southern edge of the forest, **Ecouis** is grouped around the solid square towers of its collegiate church, whose single-aisled interior of plain red brick and stone is unusual and contains a variety of interesting statuary, and some splendid Renaissance carved panelling behind the choir stalls. The road south from Ecouis rejoins the Seine at **Les Andelys**, twin villages (Petit and Grand Andely) stretching up a narrow valley from a fine bend in the river, which is magnificently commanded by the ruins of Richard Coeur de Lion's **Château-Gaillard**. You can climb the steep hill from attractive riverside Petit Andely, or drive a long way round the back, stopping to admire Grand Andely's interesting church, a mixture of Flamboyant Gothic and classical Renaissance. Château-Gaillard itself was built in only a year, so legend has it, to defend Normandy from the unwelcome advances of the French king. Although considered impregnable, Château-Gaillard was taken from John Lackland by the French king Philippe Auguste in 1204, John having weakened the castle's defences by installing a vulnerably placed lavatory, with window, noticed and exploited by a French soldier called Bogis. In the Hundred Years' War the castle changed hands between French and English a few times, and was finally dismantled in the 17th century as it was proving too useful to the enemies of law and order. The ruins are partly overgrown now, but still imposingly massive (some of the walls are 5 metres thick), and the view down over Petit Andely and the Seine is superb. Château-Gaillard is traditionally thought to have received its name—which means happy or laughing castle—from one of Richard Coeur de Lion's admiring comments when he saw the completed work. A less picturesque explanation is that the castle is named after the town of **Gaillon** on the other side of the Seine. It is not a very attractive town and the remains of Georges d'Amboise's château, once one of the great showpieces of the French Renaissance, are disappointing. Despite heavy war damage in 1940, **Louviers**, situated on the Eure just before its junction with the Seine, retains some attractive old wooden houses and an interesting church built in the 13th century and given a new exceedingly elaborate Flamboyant exterior 200 years later.

South-east towards the Ile-de-France and Paris, **Vernon** occupies a once-important strategic position on the Seine. Two towers remain of the old fortifications, and attractively leafy ruins of a fortified bridge across the river. The Gothic church of Notre-Dame stands over the town, tall and elegant. **Giverny**, where Monet's beloved Epte meets the Seine, preserves the painter's house and garden (of the hallucinatory water-lilies) as a museum. The drive up the Epte valley, the Norman frontier, is a pretty one, with ruined fortresses at **Baudémont** and **Château-sur-Epte**. The Epte and the Seine nearly meet at **La Roche-Guyon** where another hilltop castle was in function, if not in grandeur, the French equivalent of Normandy's Château-Gaillard. **Gisors** was the most important Norman bastion on the Epte, and still has extensive remains of the fortress, with handsome gardens inside the walls. The 13th- to 16th-century church (St-Gervais et St-Protais) is also worth a visit to admire its Renaissance decoration.

Central Normandy

The area between the Seine and the Dives is the most popular part of Normandy. Along its coast lie the most fashionable and interesting resorts, and inland Normandy's most attractive countryside, heavy with blossom or apples and thick with bright green pastures plundered by dairy cattle, which produce the raw material for Camembert, Pont L'Evêque and Livarot. "Even in Switzerland" wrote the delighted Ruskin "the green is blacker and not so soft". To appreciate the intimate charm of the countryside with its colourful manor houses, cottages with flowers planted in the thatch and noisy farmyards, it is essential to branch off the main roads; the most rewarding area for exploration is between the Dives and the Touques valleys, west and south-west of Lisieux.

Honfleur is the most intrinsically attractive village of the Côte Fleurie and perhaps of all Normandy, quite different from the purpose-built 19th-century resorts. Tall slate-fronted houses are tightly packed around the yacht harbour with the 16th-century governor's house (la Lieutenance) guarding its entrance; across the water the church (St-Etienne) has been turned into a local museum. The church of Ste-Catherine on the central square is a great curiosity—built entirely of wood by the Honfleur shipbuilders who are said to have been too eager to give thanks for the English departure after the Hundred Years' War to wait for the stonemasons. Honfleur has attracted painters for over a hundred years: a group of Impressionists (including Boudin and Monet) settled at the Ferme St-Siméon on the hill behind the village (now a hostelry which is nearly as luxurious as it is expensive) and are commemorated in the Boudin museum in Honfleur. Sadly the view across the estuary from the top of the hill (the Côte de Grâce) which they so appreciated is now full of tankers and refineries. Artists still jostle for position round the old port, and Honfleur's charm is enhanced by the numerous art galleries. The wealth of nearby Deauville has clearly overflowed, and there are shops selling furs and expensive carpets as well. But Honfleur is not yet too spoilt and still has its busy fishing fleet.

The rest of the Côte Fleurie, west to Cabourg, is a string of classy resorts on whose long sandy beaches the fashion for sea bathing was born in the mid-19th century. **Deauville** reigns supreme, with its turn-of-the-century neo-rustic villas and the smartest hotels, shops, night life, and people—they come for the yearling sales, racing, roulette, regattas, polo, bridge, golf, tennis and to be seen on the *planches* (a path of

Sunshades on Deauville beach

duckboards all the way along the back of the beach, which is traditionally as close to the water as it is seemly for the blazer and white flannel
brigade to go). There is too much to do to spend time on the beach, at
least in August which is the start and finish of Deauville's butterfly life
of a season. Adjacent **Trouville** has more of a real-life atmosphere;
Blonville and **Villers-sur-Mer** are little more than beach resorts. **Houl-
gate** is a quietly residential resort, as is **Cabourg** with its spacious
promenade, the Boulevard des Anglais, and tree-lined avenues fanning
out from the spacious lawns in front of the overblown casino and the
Grand Hotel which Proust, a frequenter of Cabourg in its heyday,
described as a décor for the third act of a farce.

The social attractions and good beaches of the Côte Fleurie are
complemented by the natural beauty of the green valleys and hills
behind it. Of the hinterland towns **Pont-L'Evêque** suffered greatly in the
last war, as did **Pont-Audemer** which nevertheless has some interesting
old houses, and Renaissance windows in the church (St-Ouen). **Lisieux**
is the biggest industrial centre in the Pays d'Auge, and its biggest
industry is saint Teresa. The short and outwardly unremarkable life of
this Carmelite sister, born in 1873 at Alençon, was an exemplary one of
long-suffering and selfless perfection of the spirit. The main pilgrimage is
in early October, but throughout the year the capacious Romano-
Byzantine Basilica on the edge of town is crowded with pilgrims.
Colourful mosaics illustrate the universal impact of saint Teresa's
autobiography, *The Story of a Soul*. All around town there are souvenir
shops galore and a number of displays, with wax models telling the
story—by definition unspectacular—of saint Teresa's life, and of her
subsequent miraculous achievements. In the middle of all this stands a
fine, uncomplicated early Gothic cathedral.

The delightful manor houses of the **Pays d'Auge** are too numerous to
list; they are all highly individual in design and decoration, many with
moats, pitched roofs of red and coloured tiles, and walls of either timber
frames filled with geometrically patterned tiles or chequerboard brick
and stone squares. Two of the finest, south-west of Lisieux, are **St-
Germain-de-Livet** (open to visitors; Renaissance frescoes and furniture)
and **Coupesarte**, but there are many others to highlight your meander
through the lanes of the Pays d'Auge, which may be given direction by
the established cider and cheese routes—ask at any local tourist office
for a map to lead you to farms which will open their doors for you to
sample and buy their produce.

South-east of Pont-Audemer, in the soft green vale that Ruskin so
admired, little remains (except a proud 15th-century tower) of the
medieval **Abbaye du Bec-Hellouin**, academy of Christendom which
produced a succession of distinguished theologians and church politicians following the example of its two great 11th-century abbots (both
later to be archbishop of Canterbury) Lanfranc and Anselm. Today's
abbey, which you can visit, is mostly a reconstruction of the 17th- and
18th-century buildings. There is also, strangely enough, a display of
racing cars.

To the south and east of Le Bec-Hellouin lie the fertile Neuborg plain
and the more wooded Pays d'Ouche. There are some châteaux to see
and visit (generally week-ends only except in summer)—**Beaumesnil**
and **Champ-de-Bataille** are majestic brick and stone 17th-century buildings, the one tall and imposing, the other low and spread around a
spacious court. The moated medieval fortress of **Harcourt** is hidden in a
vast arboretum of a park.

Château de St-Germain-de-Livet

Evreux is a busy market town, thoroughly rebuilt since the War, but with two interesting churches. The cathedral, repeatedly burnt and restored, displays many styles. Its north and west façades are richly decorated, respectively Flamboyant Gothic and Renaissance. Inside there are fine 15th- and 16th-century windows around the elegant choir whose chapels are all enclosed by remarkable and varied carved wooden screens. The archbishop's palace beside the cathedral houses a local museum, currently being restored. The old Benedictine abbey church of St-Taurin has a few Romanesque elements, and an elaborate silver gilt and enamel reliquary of the saint in the choir.

Conches-en-Ouche is set on a spur rising abruptly from a bend in the river Rouloir. There is a good view from the terrace beside the small church of Ste-Foy whose interior is dominated by a very fine series of 16th-century windows illustrating the lives of Christ and the Virgin.

Once a strategic town on the borders of the Pays d'Ouche and the Normandy Perche, **Verneuil-sur-Avre** has lost its fortifications but retains two churches of interest. La Madeleine, on the spacious central square, is more distinguished outside than in, with splendid sculptures all around the tower and porch. Notre-Dame (follow signs to the Abbaye St-Nicolas) is full of sculptures of saints, varying greatly in date (from the 12th to the 17th centuries) and quality.

The South

The **Normandy Perche** is a very pleasant hilly and wooded area whose main interest lies in its manor houses and its horses (percherons). The manors are quite unlike those of the Pays d'Auge—older, more fortified, and less colourful. Rural itineraries are well signposted from the convenient and attractive bases **Mortagne-au-Perche** and **Longny-au-Perche** to take you past some of the most interesting of them—**La Vove**, **L'Angenardière**, **Courboyer** and **Les Feugerets** (these are places to look at, not visit). Mortagne has some well preserved old houses and a Gothic/Renaissance church with a massive 18th-century carved wooden altar-piece brought from a nearby monastery. On a small hill behind Longny stands the charming little Renaissance chapel of Notre-Dame-de-Pitié, with very delicate stone and wood carving outside.

Horses, and not just the sturdy local percherons which are mainly good for pulling, grace the landscape all over the Perche. The most interesting stud (*haras*) to visit is the national one at **Le Pin**, founded by Louis XIV's minister Colbert for the provision of the army—originally there was a colony of mares as well. The stud farm itself has as good a pedigree as the stallions, for Mansart designed a château of appropriately elegant sobriety, and Le Nôtre put in some terraced gardens which look out over the farm's domain of majestic avenues and fields of brilliantined beasts. A groom guides you for nothing more than a gratuity round the stables and expatiates in tones of due reverence on the technicalities of horse breeding, and the family trees and in many cases multitudinous progeny of France's finest stallions.

A few miles down the road the **Château d'O** could be in the Loire Valley, so delightful is the fantasy and ornament of its architecture. It's not so much moated as built in the middle of a lake.

Sées is a handsome old town with a lofty and bright Gothic cathedral whose twin spires can be seen from the terrace at Le Pin many miles away. As well as the beautiful proportions of the choir and transept, you may admire the 13th-century stained glass and a very sweet statue of the Virgin and Child.

The **Ecouves** forest lies just off the main Sées to Alençon road, and is one of the finest of many in this part of Normandy. There are deer; and an extensive panorama from the Signal d'Ecouves (417 metres). The **Perseigne forest** on the other side of the road is smaller but hardly less attractive, with riding and walking paths and picnic areas.

Alençon is a busy market town on the Sarthe, with an illustrious past; elegant Flamboyant Gothic architecture in the churches of Notre-Dame and St-Léonard and the imposing 15th-century Maison d'Ozé (now a museum of local antiquities) date from the period when Alençon was the brilliant capital of an important duchy. In the 17th century the town became a very important lace-making centre; like so many local crafts, technological progress has reduced it to little more than a curiosity. When you see the price of the handmade lace in the lace-making school you will understand why. In the fine arts museum, there's a good collection of lace, and some paintings of high quality.

South-west of Alençon the so-called **Alpes Mancelles** (Le Mans Alps) rise to a high point of 417 metres. Although not exactly alpine, the landscape is interesting and even impressive, with swiftly running streams, gorges and escarpments and heathery hills. The most attractive villages in the small area, both on the steeply banked Sarthe, are **St-Léonard-des-Bois** and **St-Cénéri-le-Gérei**.

Very similar in its appeal and in the exaggeration of its title is the area to the north called **La Suisse Normande** (Norman Switzerland). Here too the river (in this case the Orne) cuts through steep banks; tourists come for rock climbing and canoeing (the most popular centre for excursions is the resort village of **Clécy**) so perhaps the name is not so inappropriate. For nearly spectacular views the vantage points are the **Roche d'Oëtre** and the **Pain de Sucre**.

These two regions, with their abrupt rocky hills, contrast strikingly with the lush undulations and plains of Upper Normandy. They lie at the eastern edge of the granite Armorican Massif, and thus belong geologically to Brittany. **Bagnoles-de-L'Orne** is a good base between the two areas, provided you enjoy the inimitable atmosphere of spa resorts. It is attractively set in a forest beside a lake, with woodland walks and facilities for riding, boating and gambling, as well as healing waters from a hot spring in the rock, whose fame originated appropriately enough with the miraculous rejuvenation of an old nag. For sightseers there are interesting excursions to the **Châteaux de Lassay** and **Carrouges**. The first is a very impressive 15th-century military fortress, the second a vast brick and granite château of many periods with a fine collection of furniture, styles Louis XIII to XVI. Also within easy reach of Bagnoles-de-l'Orne, **Domfront** is an attractive little town whose old centre is splendidly situated hundreds of feet above the river Varenne. Looking down over the river, the ruins of a once mighty fortress are incorporated in the public gardens. By the side of the river there is a restored Romanesque church (Notre-Dame-sur-l'Eau) of great charm.

At **Falaise**, on the eastern edge of the Suisse Normande, there remains less of an old town than at Domfront but much more of a fortress, where duke Richard II of Normandy's younger son consummated his passion for a tanner's daughter called Arlette. The fruit of the union was William the Bastard, later the Conqueror. The massive 12th-century keep and 15th-century round tower on a rock above the town are tremendously impressive. Two interesting churches (Notre-Dame-de-Guibray and St-Gervais) retain some Romanesque elements. Just off the road north from Falaise to Caen there are two beautiful châteaux to admire from the outside (**Versainville** and **Assy**, both mostly 18th-century) and an impressive limestone gorge formed by the river Laison (La Brèche au Diable).

The West

This area includes most of Lower Normandy, the Cotentin peninsula and its hinterland. The Cotentin juts out north into the Channel, its coastal port **Cherbourg** as convenient a bridgehead for British tourists as it was an important one for the Allied Forces to conquer in 1944. It has little else to recommend it. The peninsula, joined to the mainland by a long strip of low-lying marshland no more than 30ft above sea-level, is not a particularly exciting welcome to France. For the transit traveller there are no spectacular and few interesting landscapes, but rather an only vaguely characterised succession of woods and scrubland. For the explorer there are few treasures (apart from some impressive rocky coastline around the north-west tip not unlike western Brittany) and few exceptions to the drab nature of the resorts which stretch down the west coast looking out to the Channel Islands. In general they have neither the interest of the fashionable Côte Fleurie nor the beauty of the white cliffs of the Côte d'Albâtre. The flat east coast and the north-facing Calvados coast stretching as far east as Caen have even fewer resorts with any charm, but they do have their interest, as this almost uninterrupted stretch of dunes and sandy beaches was the toehold for the Allied invaders in June 1944. The invasion beaches are not only littered with memories, but also with barbed wire, pillbox gun batteries, and all the debris of modern warfare—old mines are uncovered in the dunes from time to time. There are a number of museums along the coast to complement the evocative remains with details of the battle of Normandy.

In this area as in so much of Normandy and Northern France most of the sightseeing interest resides in warfare and the religious buildings, from the great abbeys of the capital of Lower Normandy, Caen, at one end to the mystical acropolis of France, Mont St-Michel, at the other. Caen was one of the worst casualties of 1944, relentlessly softened up by the Allies and then shelled by the retreating ex-occupiers. It has risen again from the rubble, a thriving modern city with industrial zones sprawling without geographical constraint, and clean, broad streets in the city centre. Its great churches and even a few attractive old half-timbered houses survived the bombs. But for the most part Caen is if not ugly, certainly less than picturesque; the bald modern buildings, built of the light local stone which was used in the construction of so many historic monuments in Normandy and England, fit in surprisingly well with the severely undecorative style of Norman architecture. Caen's three great landmarks are tributes to their builders William the Conqueror and his wife Matilda, to whom the town owed its great importance. To win papal approval for their marriage, the cousins founded an abbey each.

✱ *Château* Damaged, but at least unveiled of surrounding later buildings by the last War, the impressive walls of this vast 11th-century fortress house two interesting museums—fine arts and local history.

✱ *Abbaye aux Hommes* William's abbey church (St-Etienne) is remarkable in its severe simplicity and lofty grandeur. Inside there are no side chapels, few capitals, and just a plaque to Guillelmus Conquestor, whose femur alone survived 16th-century Huguenot pillaging, but not the Revolution. The abbey buildings beside the great church date mostly from the 18th century, and their sober classical elegance in no way clashes with the Norman church. Inside you can see some splendid carved wooden panelling, the cloister which gives an excellent view of the church, and a remarkable display of photographs of Caen during the invasion, from June 5th to August 15th 1944, when St-Etienne sheltered thousands of inhabitants.

✱ *Abbaye aux Dames* Matilda's abbey church (La Trinité) is smaller, squatter, more damaged and not spared discordant additions to the original Norman architecture. But apart from them the main façade is handsome, as too are the interior and the crypt, both enlivened by some amusingly primitive carving on the capitals.

✱ *St-Pierre* The mostly Gothic church at the foot of the castle is chiefly remarkable for the exuberant Renaissance decoration of the interior and exterior of the east end. The features of Gothic architecture (hanging keystones and flying buttresses) are transformed into pure ornament, rich in fantasy. It would be hard to imagine a more marked contrast with the spirit of the abbey church of St-Etienne.

✱ *St-Nicolas* An unspoilt Romanesque church with a fine porch.

✱ *Old houses* The finest are to be admired on and off the Rue St-Pierre between St-Pierre and St-Etienne; the tourist office just opposite St-Pierre occupies one of the biggest and best.

Excursion from Caen

* **Fontaine-Henry** North-west of Caen, this 15th- and 16th-century château owes its character to the steep tiled roof over one wing, taller than the body of the building it shelters. The exterior is gracious; short guided tours of the main rooms of the inhabited interior reveal some interesting works of art, and a splendid Renaissance staircase and furniture. Nearby, just off the road and not immediately obvious, is the attractive deconsecrated Romanesque church of Thaon.

Being considerably smaller and much less affected by the Allied blitz than Caen, **Bayeux** is a popular alternative base for Lower Normandy, with picturesque old streets around the cathedral.

* *Bayeux Tapestry* Normandy's greatest historical and artistic treasure—the 70m long series of 58 embroidered episodes illustrating the Norman Conquest is well displayed in the Centre Guillaume le Conquérant, rue de Nesmond. The interest of the tapestry is both documentary—it was almost certainly executed in England to the orders of the bishop of Bayeux not long after the events portrayed—and artistic; the audio guide in English is well worth having. It's also worth taking up the free access which your entrance ticket gives you to the Baron-Gérard Museum, also near the cathedral, which contains a fine collection of paintings, porcelain and lace.
* *Cathedral* Even without the Bayeux Tapestry, destined for the adornment of its chancel, this is a more decorative church than Caen's sober abbeys and characteristic in its mixture of Gothic and Romanesque styles, with some delightful geometric and simple figurative carving on the arches of the nave.

Excursions from Bayeux

* **Abbaye de Mondaye** (ten km south) This abbey still functions and the monks sell their produce; the buildings and church are harmoniously classical, the abbey having been reconstructed in the 18th century.
* **Château de Balleroy** The grandeur of this imposing reddish-grey early 17th-century château is enhanced by the tributary nature of the village which lines the long straight drive down the hill to its gates, where splendid grilles and antler-like spikes discourage intruders. You can go inside to see the rich décor and royal portraits, a hot air balloon museum, and attractive gardens designed by Le Nôtre.
* **Abbaye de Cérisy-la-Forêt** Across the forest from Balleroy, this great Romanesque abbey church stands alone in the fields on the edge of the village. The church has been much damaged (the nave was mostly amputated) but it is nevertheless simple, bright and beautiful. The abbey buildings (partly a farm) can be visited.
* **St-Lô** This large town needed almost total rebuilding after the War, but the mutilated ruins of the façade towers of Notre-Dame were left as an evocative reminder. On the Bayeux road, just outside the town centre, you can visit one of Normandy's biggest stud farms. South of the town the Vire cuts through rocky escarpments. There is good trout fishing and some fine viewpoints—especially Les Roches de Ham near Torigny-sur-Vire, where you can visit the recently restored château of the Breton family from which the princely dynasty of Monaco descends.

The Calvados coast west of Caen, and the east coast of the Cotentin, was the theatre for the D-Day Invasion of June 1944. In the east the British forces met with little resistance (whence the survival of Bayeux) pressing south from Sword, Juno and Gold beaches; so the coastline here, with its succession of busy resorts, shows few signs of desolation. The American forces, landing on Utah and Omaha beaches, had much more trouble establishing a foothold. Of the resorts, **Ouistreham-Riva-Bella** is the most substantial and popular, with a big yachting port. The area is well known for oysters, especially from Courseulles, and seaweed which imparts health-giving fumes to the air when exposed at low tide—which is enormous in many places (over 2 miles at Ouistreham). War memorials are a bigger attraction; the most frequented and interesting of the museums commemorating the Invasion is at **Arromanches-les-Bains**, the small and busy resort where the Allies installed the famous mobile Mulberry Harbour (remains can still be seen out to sea) which for three months (before the port of Cherbourg could be made serviceable) made possible the disembarkation of millions of men and vehicles. The museum at the water's edge, with its models and Royal Navy films, gets extremely crowded. **Port-en-Bessin** is a busy and attractive fishing port tucked between chalk cliffs. The American landing beaches which unlike Gold, Juno and Sword have retained their code names Utah and Omaha, are more exposed, emptier, and in many ways more evocative. There is a huge American war cemetery at St-Laurent-sur-Mer with nearly 10,000 white crosses, and at La Cambe just south of Grandchamp there are twice as many German graves. Utah beach is the most northerly, separated from Omaha, as the Cotentin peninsula is from the Calvados, by the deep and wide Baie des Veys and the rich pastures of the Carentan plain, origin of France's best dairy products. The dunes of Utah beach still yield rusty treasure from time to time, and tanks and amphibians stand as memorials beside a small museum devoted to the American Invasion. Utah beach is hardly more hospitable now than it must have been when tens of thousands of American troops had to advance at dawn through a nightmare of barbed wire and mines on the mudflats exposed by the tide's retreat.

At the end of Utah beach, the rocky Cotentin promontory begins. Dark grey stone contrasts with the chalk of the Upper Normandy coast and gives the Cotentin and its buildings something of a Breton appearance. The north-eastern tip is relatively sheltered, and has two attractive fishing ports and bathing resorts—**Barfleur** (with better beaches) and **St-Vaast-la-Hougue**. The Saire valley inland from St-Vaast is particularly green and pleasant.

The north coast is rocky and bleak; the east-end lighthouses of Gatteville (near Barfleur) and Cap Lévy give panoramic views of the coastline and peninsula. The west (especially the **Cap de la Hague** and the **Nez de Jobourg**) is more windblown and impressively rocky in the style of the Atlantic tip of Brittany. The attractively situated **Port-Racine** is allegedly France's smallest port. In the middle of the north coast, **Cherbourg** is no delight to the eye, having been thoroughly destroyed by the retreating occupiers in 1944, but has two museums of some interest—one devoted to the War and the liberation of Normandy, the other to fine arts.

The west coast of the Cotentin is a succession of sandy beaches with enormous low tidal retreat, and small resorts without much style, but with views of and excursions to nearby Jersey and Guernsey. **Granville** is the busiest with a lively fishing and yachting port and an old (18th-century) upper-town within grey ramparts. **Carteret**, attractively situated on an estuary further north, is the other harbour for Channel Island boats. ▷ p330

Abbey, fortress, village and natural curiosity, Mont-St-Michel proclaims itself France's premier tourist attraction. At its best it is an unforgettable vision of natural and man-made beauty; at its worst, Mont-St-Michel can be a nightmarish experience of suffocation in steep, narrow, overcrowded streets of souvenir shops.

The granite mound, crowned by monastic buildings, rises from the muddy mouth of the Couesnon river, whose main path runs west of the rock thereby placing it in Normandy not Brittany. At high tide sea surrounds the rock, and occasionally floods the car park at its gateway. At low tide the spire of the abbey church soars over miles of mudflats; record tides empty the bay for nearly ten miles. In places the water rushes in and out at over ten miles an hour so wandering around the low tide sands can be very dangerous, especially as there are passages of treacherous quicksand (the Bayeux Tapestry records that Harold saved some Normans from the sands of the Couesnon). Partly because of the causeway built across to the rock 100 years ago, the salt marsh coastline is advancing on the rock, and eventually high tide waves lapping at the gates of Mont-St-Michel will be no more.

The first hermits set themselves up on the so-called Mont-Tombe (thought because of its name to have been a Celtic burial ground) sometime around 500 AD. The monastic community was founded in the 8th century and expanded as miracle stories were put about and pilgrims began to make their way to the rock. From the 10th century the dukes of Normandy patronised the monastery and made possible the remarkably ambitious expansion of the monastic buildings. The stone had to be brought from the Chausey Islands some 25 miles away and the summit had to be surrounded by support buildings; of the church now standing only the crossing itself is founded on rock. A natural stronghold, Mont-St-Michel had fortifications from the earliest times, and still gives the impression of being as much a castle as a monastery. Many of its ramparts which survive today date from the 14th and 15th centuries, when Mont-St-Michael defied all English attempts at conquest, and came for a time under the captaincy of du Guesclin.

Like so many monasteries Mont-St-Michel's post-medieval history is one of disciplinary and architectural decay, here abetted by lightning—which accounted for half the nave. The buildings, including the church itself, were used as a prison and split up into several levels. Restoration was undertaken only just over 100 years ago, and a few monks from St-Wandrille came back to Mont-St-Michel in 1966.

Half a million visitors a year tramp up between the souvenir shops and the restaurants of the Grande Rue to the abbey buildings. The commercialisation of the bottom half of the village, with its souvenir shops, crêperies and the horrific density of people, can be prohibitive at times; but the atmosphere was no doubt not very different 500 years ago. The great surprise that makes toiling up through the tumult worthwhile is that, unlike most pilgrimage places, the fortified monastery of Mont-St-Michel is made up of some of the most beautiful Gothic and Romanesque religious buildings in France. The church, cloister and refectory, the elements of greatest beauty, can now be visited only as a guided tour (some are conducted in English) which takes about an hour.

The church is a triumphant combination of amputated Romanesque nave, and a light, soaring, Flamboyant choir which was added in the

15th century and not completed until 1518. It has been described as the last heavenward rocket launched by the dying Middle Ages. The cloister and refectory form the upper of three layers of the so-called Merveille, built (like a gallery hanging in mid-air from the side of the rock) in the early 13th century. The cloister looks out to sea on two sides and has twin colonnades of great delicacy. The guided tour also covers the Gothic and earlier rooms in the nether parts of the monastery, including the original sanctuary (Notre-Dame-sous-Terre) incorporated in the support system for the enlarged church. There are magnificent views from the terrace in front of the church, from the cloister, and from the so-called lacework staircase built into a flying buttress outside the choir, which rises to 120 metres above the sea.

To see Mont-St-Michel at its best there is nothing to equal an overnight stay on the rock, which will enable you to wander around the deserted citadel by moonlight or at dawn with the abbey buildings looming above you and your own footsteps echoing on the cobbles. You can also do the abbey tour before the crowds arrive. If you do stay overnight, check on the tides before you leave your car unattended on the lower car-park.

Boat trips around the rock are no longer possible, but when the tide is out it is well worth walking all the way around on the sand at its feet. If you are feeling very self-indulgent, consider hiring a small plane from nearby airfields for an exhilarating bird's eye view.

The main points of sightseeing interest on the Cotentin peninsula are churches. The **Abbaye de Lessay**'s large church has been restored to its full beauty, bright, unadorned and harmoniously Romanesque. **Coutances** is an unprepossessing rebuilt town with a soaring slender Gothic cathedral, where very little decoration distracts your eye from the heavenward impulse of the architectural streamlines of the exterior. The interior is as light as it is lofty, thanks to a magnificent octagonal lantern tower over the crossing, which prompted Louis XIV's military architect Vauban to enquire who could be the sublime madman who dared throw such a monument to the skies. Further south, the picturesque ruins of the 12th-century **Abbaye de Hambye**, overgrown and complete with circling rooks, lie in the delightfully secluded Sienne valley. Almost contemporary with Hambye and in a similar setting inland from Granville is the **Abbaye de Lucerne** of which little remains except the church.

South of Granville the coast is lent interest by Mont-St-Michel which stands up across the water, or mudflats, of Avranches Bay. At **Genêts** you can, indeed must, find a guide if you want to walk across to the abbey on foot in the steps of many millions of pilgrims. **Avranches** itself is a busy town with valuable manuscripts from Mont-St-Michel in its museum. Nearby the dammed river Vélune is popular for fishing.

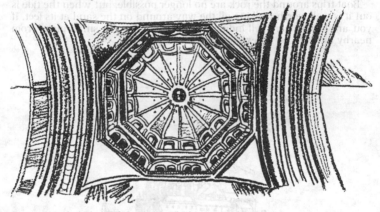

Coutances cathedral— looking up into the lantern tower

Hotels

L'Aigle, 61300 Orne   £££

LE DAUPHIN   Tel: 33.24.43.12

A large rambling old hotel which is part of a large chain, at the centre of a dull town—not perhaps an exciting recipe. Le Dauphin is worth knowing about, though, because the food is very good—the Bernard family have a long-established reputation, and there are two very competent chefs—and because the public rooms have the comfortable leathery warmth of an old London club. L'Aigle is right at the heart of horse country and feels it—sporting prints, and a horsey British clientèle (as well as local businessfolk). The bedrooms are mixed; the cheaper ones still not reached by the redecoration are not recommended.

24 bedrooms; no lift; carpark.

Bagnoles-de-l'Orne, 61140 Orne   £££

BOIS-JOLI   Tel: 33.37.92.77

Several changes have taken place at this ever-popular little hotel. The bar has made way for a full-blown reception area; there's a salon; there's neon lighting in the restaurant, and the gingham tablecloths are no more. But the bedrooms are still as traditional and pretty as ever (though those due for renovation may well join the *nouvelle style* of the public areas); the terrace and garden remain the same; and the cooking is still simple and traditional (but oh dear, why the tinned mandarins and pear on the *assiette gourmande?*). This is a thoroughly friendly and well-run establishment near the centre of the spa, and has many appreciative British visitors.

Closed Nov to Easter; 18 bedrooms.

Bayeux, 14400 Calvados   ££

D'ARGOUGES   Tel: 31.92.88.86

Splendid, peaceful, 18th-century town house, set well back from a bustling square and centrally situated within easy walking distance of Queen Mathilde's tapestry. The elegant salon and breakfast room look out over well-kept gardens and terrace; bedrooms, both in the main house and neighbouring annexe, are pleasant and comfortable, and there are two pretty suites.

25 bedrooms; no rest; no lift.

Le Bec Hellouin, 27800 Brionne   ££

AUBERGE DE L'ABBAYE   Tel: 32.44.86.02

There is something suspiciously pretty about this 18th-century village-centre restaurant, what with olive wood tables outside for mere drinkers, waitresses decked in folklorish Norman costumes, tiled floor, rough-stone walls and timbers, and earthenware mugs, cider for the quaffing of. It is all very charming, and surprisingly the food is very good. *Lapin au cidre* and hot *tarte aux pommes* with thick Normandy cream are menu favourites. The few bedrooms are simple but bright and cheerful.

Closed mid-Jan to Feb (rest Mon dinner and Tues out of season); 8 bedrooms; no lift.

Blonville-Sur-Mer, 14910 Calvados   ££££

GRAND   Tel: 31.87.90.54

Little remains of what once may have been the classic seaside "Grand Hotel", right on the beach in this pleasant, small and relatively quiet resort, which now consists mainly of holiday apartments. It has been modernised, altered and extended, and now offers self-catering studio flats as well as traditional hotel bedrooms. Some classic ingredients are still there: balconies overlooking a fine sweep of golden sand, an indoor sea-water swimming pool, and a broad terrace for evening drinks. The menu features Normandy specialities (tripe, *andouillette, soupe des pêcheurs*) as well as some more exciting concoctions; the cooking is above average for this kind of family seaside hotel. The service is anonymous, and not over-friendly; if you opt for the self-catering formula, this need hardly matter.

Closed part of winter (rest Mon dinner and Tues); 25 bedrooms; 25 studios.

Hotels

Cabourg, 14860 Calvados   ££
MOULIN DU PRÉ   Tel: 31.78.83.68

About five miles south-west of Cabourg, this is a pretty, white-washed farmhouse
set in a delightful garden complete with lake. Bedrooms are in rustic or formal
classic styles, and not very large. There's a small salon, and a gravel terrace for
drinks; the focal point is the large, welcoming, country-style restaurant. The food
is very good; charcoal grills are a speciality, but there are plenty of fishy dishes
too—*escalopes de bar au morgon, bisque de langoustines, rillettes de saumon*.
Charming Monsieur Holtz helps his wife (when he isn't writing poetry), and both
ensure a thoroughly friendly atmosphere.

Closed Oct and first two weeks Mar (rest Sun dinner and Mon out of season); 10
bedrooms; no lift.

Caen, 14000 Calvados   £££
LE RELAIS DES GOURMETS   ·   Tel: 31.86.06.01

The dull modern façade of this hotel, opposite the fortress and its museums, and
near to the church of St-Pierre, belies the charm of its interior. It's a well-run
establishment, welcoming and comfortable; there's a small garden with terrace.
Cooking is well above average for this part of the country—specialities include,
naturally, *tripes à la mode de Caen*, and fine local cheeses; next door, Monsieur
Legras' son runs a fish restaurant, L'Écaille. Parking is sometimes difficult—
there's no garage, and the newly acquired private space is limited.

Rest closed Sun dinner (Écaille Sat dinner and Mon); 32 bedrooms.

Lyons-la-Forêt, 27480 Eure   ££
GRAND CERF   Tel: 32.49.60.44

This is a charming timbered building in the central square of an attractive small
town, surrounded by forest. Bedrooms are simple but more than adequate (some
overlook a small flowery garden); there's a small inviting bar. In the restaurant,
all beams and tiles and hunting trophies, food is well prepared and presented. The
two fixed-price menus are composed of dishes off the short *carte*—including duck
in various forms, and a splendid *charlotte au chocolat et à la menthe*.

Closed mid-Jan to mid-Feb (rest Tues and Wed); 5 bedrooms; no lift.

Mesnil-Val, 76910 Seine-Maritime   ££
LA VIEILLE FERME   Tel: 35.86.72.18

At their long, low, mostly neo-rustic building of which one end is the original
farm—creeper-covered and genuinely old—the Maximes will give you a warm
and friendly welcome. The bar/reception area is dark, woody and cosy, the
country-cottage restaurant often so well-patronised that a second room has to
receive diners. Cooking is solidly classic, and the choice on the two fixed-price
menus (*touristique* and *gastronomique*) unexciting; in fact, it's better, and may not
be more expensive, to opt for à la carte—a rarity, indeed, in France. But dishes are
well prepared, the seafood fresh, and portions large. Bedrooms, which vary in size,
are in cottages in the garden (some have only half-baths). The setting is verdant
and very quiet, some 400m from the beach, with its own tennis court and
childrens' play area.

Closed Jan (rest Sun dinner mid-Nov to mid-Mar); 35 bedrooms; no lift.

Le Mont-St-Michel, 50116 Manche   ££

LA MÈRE POULARD   Tel: 33.60.14.01

At the foot of the living rock (which forms a wall of the dining room), Mère Poulard is an institution, famous for the *vrai de vrai* foaming omelette—whipped up frantically and cooked in long-handled pans over an open fire before your eyes and those of ascending pilgrims. The chef may be new, but the omelette continues—though it is not the highlight of very distinguished cooking which is now even more inventive than previously. The décor leaves much to be desired, but it doesn't matter. This is a unique place for traditional hospitality, quality, and value, unaffected by the exploitative potential of its setting. Bedrooms vary from the simply adequate to the very basic. There is no better way to see and enjoy Mont-St-Michel.

Closed Oct to Mar; 27 bedrooms; no lift.

Pont-Audemer, 27500 Eure   £££

AUBERGE DU VIEUX PUITS   Tel: 32.41.01.48

An absolutely delightful old timbered house, impeccable but not over-restored, furnished with gleaming wood and shining copper, and glowing with loving care. It's the sort of place about which North Atlantic visitors rave—with the simple bedrooms adding to the quaint rustic charm—and where they and we less impressionable Britons are welcomed warmly by the English-speaking host. The house is featured by Flaubert, and the *truite Bovary au Champagne* is but one of the dishes suitable for gross self-indulgence. Aperitifs can be taken in the small and extremely picturesque shady garden; alongside is a new bedroom annexe, suitably built *en style*.

Closed mid-Dec to mid Jan, first week in July and Mon evening and Tues; 14 bedrooms; no lift.

Rouen, 76000 Seine-Maritime   ££

CATHÉDRALE   Tel: 35.71.57.95

A comfortable, quiet and attractive hotel without restaurant, right at the heart of old Rouen, on a pedestrian precinct between the cathedral and St-Maclou, built around an internal courtyard. Bedrooms are rather faded, but comfortable enough. There's no salon or bar; public areas are limited to breakfast rooms.

23 bedrooms; no rest.

St-Pierre-du-Vauvray, 27430 Eure   £££

HOSTELLERIE SAINT-PIERRE   Tel: 32.59.93.29

This large, ugly, '30s building commands a superb position on a broad and non-industrial sweep of the busy Seine, and there's a garden terrace for lazy contemplation. It's an old-fashioned, well-run establishment, with thoroughly comfortable bedrooms (some fairly small), and fine views from the restaurant—designed to look like the deck of a schooner. Appropriately, fish features on each of the three menus (one has three fish courses); the standard of cooking is high. The hotel is popular with British visitors, and is well placed for visits to Rouen (half-an-hour away by car).

Closed Jan to Feb (rest Tues, and Wed lunch); 14 bedrooms.

The North

Grande Place, Arras

"What war could ravish, commerce could bestow,
And he returned a friend, who came a foe" (Pope)

The North

Poor little rich girl. The North, France's unlovely industrial heartland, lays itself open to British advances but gets rough treatment from the tourists who storm impatiently through, their blinkered eyes fixed on the distant charms of other areas, their right feet relentlessly depressed. No more respectful is the behaviour of the rapacious hordes of day-trippers who descend on Calais and Boulogne for a few hours' merciless pillage in the supermarkets, bars and bistros before staggering back, sated and sick, to the white cliffs of perfidious Albion.

Northern France, plain as it is, deserves better than this. Only a small part of it—the strip between the coal-mining belt (Béthune to Valenciennes) and the Belgian border, and the port of Dunkerque—is heavily industrial and unsightly. Artois, Picardy and Champagne remain essentially rural and peaceful. The coast south of Calais has good birdwatching, fine chalk cliff scenery, enormous sandy beaches, and even a couple of fashionable resorts. France north of Paris is the birthplace and spiritual home of the lofty Gothic architectural style, and despite the damage inflicted as everywhere else by anti-religious revolutionaries, and much more than anywhere else in both World Wars, this remains the best area of France for a Gothic cathedral crawl, appropriately crowned by a visit to the coronation city of Reims. In Flanders there are splendid examples of red brick Flemish town architecture, windmills and even modest little northern Venices with canals for streets. The big towns have very good art museums, Lille's being one of the most distinguished in provincial France. The countryside too is a museum in its way—a reminder of man's inhumanity, with countless war cemeteries and memorials to the sacrifice of the lost generation of 1914–1918.

Rough treatment is no novelty to northern France. The nearest part of the country to the old enemy and rival, England, and France's only naturally defenceless border (excluding Alsace which is not historically French and has suffered even more), this has been the great battlefield of Europe, the scene of the most glorious of French victories—at Bouvines (1214) and Fontenoy (1745), both near Lille—and of some of the most inglorious defeats—Crécy (1346), Agincourt (1415) and Sedan (1870). During the First World War an uninterrupted battle front extended from the North Sea to the Swiss border. The World Wars brought total desolation to whole tracts of land, and where villages once stood there are now only simple crosses and the woods which have grown up since the war to cover the scar tissue. In other places imposing monuments stand on strategic positions to commemorate the thousands who fell there in attack or defence. Châteaux, churches, and dwellings were destroyed indiscriminately, countryside laid bare. Earlier campaigns were hardly less devastating, for the general wreaking of havoc was as important a part of military strategy as the winning of set-piece battles. Such was the difficulty of leading a satisfactory life in the now green and peaceful Thiérache region, north of Laon, that the inhabitants fortified their churches, (some fifty of which still stand) for community refuge in all periods from the 12th to the 16th centuries, when the frontier area was continuously plagued by invaders and by the mercenary armies which were often more of a nuisance in peace time than in war.

The North

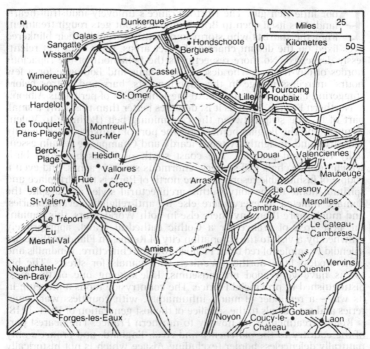

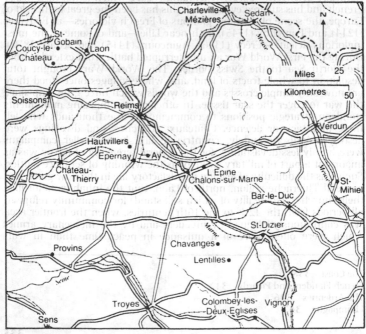

Shakespeare's description of the war-weary France of 1420, when "naked, poor and mangled peace" had for too long been chased from this the best garden of the world, is the story of northern French life down the centuries: "All her husbandry doth lie on heaps . . . her vine, the merry cheerer of the heart, unpruned dies; her hedges even-pleach'd like prisoners wildly overgrown with hair, put forth disorder'd twigs; her fallow leas the darnel, hemlock, and rank fumitory doth root upon, while that the coulter rusts, that should deracinate such savagery. Even our children . . . grow, like savages—as soldiers will that nothing do but meditate on blood—to swearing and stern looks, diffus'd attire, and everything that seems unnatural".

After each war the resilient and industrious northern French people have risen from their knees, their towns prosperous owing to their situation on the edge of the economic nerve centre of Europe, the Low Countries. Long before the discovery of coal in the 19th century the towns of Artois and Flanders had grown rich, famous and coveted thanks to their skill in weaving rich cloth; Arras was the richest of the cloth towns, and today retains the finest architectural monuments of bourgeois pride. As early as the 11th and 12th centuries the northern cloth towns were far in advance of the rest of France, both economically and culturally, developing like north Italian city states until the monarchy extended its power to include them. Powerful merchant-family oligarchies ruled them, fought fiercely for their independence from any outside control, and raised civic buildings symbolic of their non-religious, non-aristocratic power. In the north, town halls and belfries are no less important buildings than cathedrals.

Champagne does not fit comfortably into northern France. It falls south of the great divide between the France of wine and the France of beer and cider, which runs approximately from the mouth of the Loire to the Ardennes. Wine is the great distinction and attraction of Champagne. The chalky hills around Reims and Châlons-sur-Marne are pleasant without being the most beautiful of French vineyard country. Production is centred in the towns, mainly Reims and Epernay, not in vineyard châteaux. Nevertheless, the prestige of champagne, and the history and technicalities of its unique evolutionary process from grape to débutante's dancing slipper, make visiting the cellars in either or both towns extremely interesting and easy to accomplish in a short time. To all this is added the great historical and cultural interest of Reims.

Champagne does share with northern France its bad luck in being on the invasion route to Paris. The First World War front settled just outside Reims, which was largely destroyed like so many other northern towns. Southern Champagne contrasts strikingly in having been spared destruction—beyond the fire of First World War artillery and too rural to be worth bombing in the Second. So Troyes for example, the once brilliant capital of the flourishing court of Champagne, has survived attractively old and wooden.

France claims only a fraction (and not the most interesting fraction) of the almost mountainous Ardennes forests, which are a popular recreation area for campers, Belgian bicyclists, wild boar and its pursuers (one of whom was Charlemagne). The steep and rocky hills which flank the Meuse as it runs north from industrial Charleville-Mézières towards Belgium are interesting as a contrast to the plains of much of northern France, but if you are tempted to stray far from your itinerary by the superlative-ridden landscape descriptions of over-sensitive romantic writers of the 19th century (George Sand was particularly impressed by the Ardennes) you are likely to be disappointed. The area is best combined with the more interesting Belgian Ardennes.

The main reason for a visit to northern France is because it is France: to stock up with wine perhaps, for which you need only go as far as the nearest supermarket in a port, or just to enjoy a week-end break to shorten the distance between holidays and to get a taste of France. And tasting, or more often making unrepentant pigs of ourselves, is what that means. Never mind the cathedrals, the museums and the war memorials; give us week-end break tourists a few good meals and we are content. Northern France's gastronomic links with the Low Countries are hardly less strong than its economic ones, and that is no culinary criticism—the Belgian taste for the best in food and wine goes back for many centuries; like England for claret, and for the same kind of reason, Brussels is the traditional export market for the best burgundies.

In many ways the northern French and especially the Flemings are a race apart. They drink beer, and they play darts. They go in for racing pigeons, archery and cock fighting; instead of *boules* they play skittles and for local folklore nearly every northern town has its giant mascots, brought out in annual festivities and processions.

The Coast

The long coast between Belgium and Normandy is punctuated by three of France's most important ports, all different in nature and aspect—Dunkerque is renowned for industry, Boulogne for fish, and Calais for humanity in transit (three million a year). Being so close to our south coast (only half an hour as the hover flies) Boulogne and Calais have also built up a thriving business in day trips, as well as being the obvious bridgeheads for those of us hardy seafaring Britons whose primary concern it is to rule the waves for the shortest possible time.

The day trip to France used to be a fairly dignified affair involving a flight to Le Touquet-Paris-Plage for a quick gamble and gambol. Now the phenomenon has changed for a number of social and economic reasons including the strength of the pound, the growing popularity of things previously of minority interest (basically French food and wine) and price wars among ferry operators, which have combined to turn Calais and Boulogne (mainly on Saturdays) into spectacles of mass gluttony and acquisitiveness. Small comfort that when the pound was weak the spectacle in our own Channel ports was no more edifying.

The English are no strangers to Calais and Boulogne. After his victory at nearby Crécy in 1346, Edward III took possession of Calais after an eight-month seige marked by the futile heroism of its inhabitants and the reluctant clemency of the English king when the town eventually surrendered. The English held Calais for over 200 years, inscribing on one of the town gates "Then shall the Frenchman Calais win, when iron and lead like corks shall swim". Boulogne was taken by Henry VIII in 1544 and held briefly but profitably—in 1550 Henry sold it back for 400,000 crowns. Napoleon massed troops on the hills beside Boulogne for years in preparation for his invasion of Britain, transformed the harbour to accommodate a fleet of flat-bottomed boats, and even struck medals in 1804 inscribed "Descente en Angleterre, frappé à Londres". Trafalgar and the Austrians made him call off his plans to abolish the monarchy and the House of Lords.

After the outbreak of peace the two ports soon became havens for British people on the run (from creditors and others). In Murray's 1843 Handbook, Boulogne (where 5,000 out of 30,000 inhabitants were British) is described as "one of the chief British colonies abroad. The town is enriched by English money, warmed, lighted and smoked by English coal; English signs and advertisements decorate every other shop door, inn, tavern and lodging house and almost every third person you meet is either a countryman or speaking our language". Things haven't changed much. A traveller in the time of James I described Calais as "a beggarly extorting town, monstrous dear and sluttish". "In the opinion of many," commented Murray "this description holds good . . . a traveller will do well to quit Calais as soon as he has cleared his baggage from the Custom House". In the opinion of many, Murray's advice is still the best. Calais is marginally more convenient than Boulogne for the Paris motorway.

If you do feel like lingering, or if you have to, **Calais** has one of the best sandy beaches along the north coast of France, a reputation for good *croissants*, and Rodin's magnificent memorial to the sacrificial but not sacrificed Burghers of 1347, standing in front of the heavily ornate town-hall and belfry, modern but 15th-century Flemish in style. The town church is the only example of English Perpendicular Gothic architecture in Flamboyant France. There is also a fine arts museum with a section devoted to Calais' important lace industry, introduced in the 19th century by English industrialists. One of them was the father of the great seascape painter Richard Parkes Bonington who studied here and some of whose works can be seen in the museum.

Boulogne was about two-thirds destroyed in 1944 but nevertheless manages to look more interesting than Calais, because the two-thirds did not include the walled old town on a hill above the now rather ugly port and lower town. The walls themselves are impressively solid and enclose handsome 18th-century houses, a fine medieval belfry, and the great landmark of Boulogne—the soaring dome of the Basilica of Notre-Dame, uncharitably but not unreasonably described by the Victorian

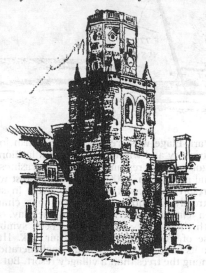

Boulogne's Gothic belfry

traveller Augustus Hare as "pretentious and ill-proportioned with an absurd dome that outrages the older buildings beneath it".

The municipal museum, between upper and lower towns, has a remarkable collection of Greek vases, Egyptian, Gallo-Roman and medieval antiquities, prehistoric finds (including a mammoth's skeleton) and a Napoleonic collection including English cartoons satirising the planned invasion. There is also a collection of paintings. Apart from its sightseeing interest much of the fun of Boulogne derives from its being France's most important fishing port (over 100,000 tons of fish a year). The modern town is always animated and smelly and there are fish restaurants for all pockets. It is also justifiably very popular with Channel-hoppers for day or week-end shopping trips; it has a variety of good shops to suit all tastes, as well as a large and colourful street market (the main one takes place on Saturday mornings).

The Opal Coast, named after its milky waves, is at its most handsome between Calais and Boulogne. At **Sangatte** where the flat Flanders coast ends you can still see remains of the first Channel Tunnel earthworks, planned in Napoleon's day but not dug for some three-quarters of a century. North Sea becomes Channel at Cap Gris Nez, where England and France are closest. Much better views are to be had from the higher Cap Blanc Nez at the other end of **Wissant**'s excellent beach, which is thought to have been Caesar's point of departure for the conquest of Britain. **Wimereux** has a grey pebbly beach and a period atmosphere—like Boulogne it was a fashionable bathing place in the early 19th century.

From Boulogne to the Somme the coast is one of shifting sands blown into dunes and stabilised in places by a forest of pines. The beaches are sandy, windswept and uninterrupted except by the Canche and Authie estuaries; they are therefore very popular for sand yachting—exponents gather for annual regattas at Berck-Plage.

Le Touquet-Paris-Plage was created by the British for the British at the turn of the century and was one of the most fashionable of pre-war resorts. Three golf courses remain, along with casinos, riding centre, luxury hotels and more than 2,000 villas in the forest which surrounds the geometric resort centre; although very lively in summer it's not conspicuously trendy anymore. Le Touquet has changed since the carefree Chelsea élite flew to France for the day, and its special relationship with those across the sea has been symbolically severed with the demise of the Lydd/Le Touquet air link. **Hardelot** is more contemporary in its luxury, and more of an agglomeration of substantial villas hidden among the trees than a villagey resort. But there are hotels and splendid sports facilities, again including golf. The facilities at **Berck-Plage**, which originally attracted visitors because of its curative properties, are augmented by the nearby Parc de Bagatelle where the amusements vary from mini-zoo to riding, go-carting and aeroplane jaunts.

The Somme estuary is wide and muddy (you can walk across at low tide and fish in the pools) and distinguished most of all by the variety of its migratory bird life. There is a reserve on the north side of the bay. The beaches are not ideal, but **St-Valery** and **Le Crotoy** are both attractive old fishing ports facing each other across the bay. Neither of them has the important sea traffic they both did before the estuary silted up and became mostly salt marshes, used for rearing sheep. In 1049 Harold son of Godwin was shipwrecked here and rescued from the local prison by duke William of Normandy who later, on September 27th 1066, set sail from St-Valery to take from Harold the throne which William claimed had been promised him seventeen years before.

South of the Somme the coast takes on a Norman character—cliffs of chalk and beaches of shingle, resorts of little charm. Just up the Somme from St-Valery the big town of **Abbeville** is skirted by most travellers on the Paris–Boulogne road. The town is no beauty now, having been all but obliterated in the Second World War, but from accounts and drawings it was one of the most attractive towns of northern France. "Many of the houses are of wood, with a greater air of antiquity than I remember to have seen," recorded the travelling farmer Arthur Young in May 1787. Abbeville was more to the taste of the Victorian John Ruskin, who wrote: "I have wasted years in mere enjoyment of the Alps, but I never to my knowledge wasted an hour in Abbeville . . . for cheerful unalloyed unwearying pleasure, the getting in sight of Abbeville on a fine summer afternoon . . . rushing down the street to see St-Wulfram again before the sun was off the towers, are things to cherish the past for, to the end". St-Wulfram still stands—dirty, mutilated and under restoration, but with a marvellously carved late 15th- and 16th-century façade well worthy of admiration. There is also a museum (paintings and prehistory) and, on the south side of town, an exquisite pink and white 18th-century folly of a château aptly-named Bagatelle (open to visitors in summer).

A few miles east of Abbeville **St-Riquier** has a squat belfry, and a very fine church (mostly Flamboyant Gothic), the remains of a Benedictine monastery of great antiquity and importance. Typically for Picardy the façade is covered with extremely delicate carving (the chalky stone being easy to work). The interior is clean and bright and pleasing; in the abbey buildings some old photos and farm tools are displayed. North of Abbeville, there isn't much to see at the battlefield of Crécy, except a cross marking the bravery of the blind king of Bohemia who insisted on being led into battle (to be duly hacked up).

Rue is an attractive old village with a 15th-century belfry and a small chapel which presents a wealth of elaborate late Gothic carving inside and out (guided tours in summer). **Valloires** is an old Cistercian abbey which remains preserved as it was rebuilt in the 18th century, sober and elegant in brick and stone, with superb wood carving especially in the church.

Above the attractive green Canche valley a few miles inland from Le Touquet, **Montreuil-sur-Mer** (as it was once) is no Rye, but it is attractive and one of the most pleasant week-end bases in the north. The streets are cobbled, and the hill town is still contained within impressive brick ramparts with a splendid mostly 17th-century citadel at one end. Much of the charm of the place is attributable to the vegetation within and without the walls which makes a walk round them much more pleasant than just any old rampart tramp, especially when there is a rustling autumnal carpet. It's worth pursuing the Canche up to **Hesdin** for the countryside and to wander around the town centre. The town hall has a lavishly decorated 17th-century porch and balcony. The road north from Hesdin to St-Omer passes the site of the battle of Agincourt; but not surprisingly there is little to remind you of this, one of the most idiotic of French military catastrophes.

St-Omer is a sizeable town on the borders of Artois and Flanders but unlike most sizeable northern French towns it is quiet, interesting and good-looking. There are many elegant 17th- and 18th-century town houses. One of the finest is the Hôtel Sandelin which houses a good museum (paintings, sculptures, ceramics and local history). The Gothic basilica of Notre-Dame has the dimensions and air of the cathedral it once was, and contains a number of interesting works of art including a 16th-century astronomical clock and a 13th-century sculptural group which looks disproportionate until you realise that it was intended to be seen from far below. To the north-east of town the marshes between the Aa and the forest of Clairmarais have been canalised into 3,000 kilometres of waterways, and christened the Venice of the North—an overstatement of its beauty perhaps but aptly descriptive of the water-borne life of the communities beside the canals.

French Flanders and Picardy

Waterways, water-mills, windmills and belfries characterise maritime Flanders, reclaimed from the sea in the Middle Ages (much of it is below sea-level). There is little wood and little stone so the Flemings have built houses of brick and tile, low and long because of the wind that meets no natural resistance as it sweeps in from the North Sea. There aren't many windmills left now, but you can visit one, built in 1127, near the Flemish-speaking village of **Hondschoote**. **Bergues** is a more interesting town, with a modern replacement of what was until 1944 the finest belfry in northern France. It has attractive old streets, a good museum (paintings, natural history) and brick fortifications which are mostly the work of Louis XIV's military architect Vauban, who filled the ditches with water and the water with fish (boats for hire). **Cassel** is equally interesting as a typically Flemish little town perched on the isolated Mont Cassel (175 metres) which gives views far and wide of the flat surrounding countryside. Cassel too has its museum of history and folklore and a long central square of 17th- and 18th-century low painted brick houses.

Between the intensively cultivated maritime Flanders and the grimy slag-heaps of the coal-mining belt sprawls the great industrial urban agglomeration of Lille/Roubaix/Tourcoing, over a million strong. Cloth and beer are the traditional foundations of the town, but recently the basis of **Lille**'s considerable prosperity has diversified. The citadel, separated from the old part of Lille by the Deule Canal, is one of Vauban's finest and the best preserved of all the fortresses built along the north-east, France's defenceless frontier. The fine arts museum is generally acknowledged to be one of the best in provincial France (its greatest glory being the local painter Wicar's collection of Renaissance drawings), and there are some good examples of Flemish town architecture of the 17th and 18th centuries. Outstanding among them is the Ancienne Bourse (Exchange), a heavily ornamented brick and stone baroque palace built around an arcaded courtyard. The statue of Napoleon in the middle was made from the bronze of Austerlitz cannon. Other buildings of interest include the modern Palais de Justice and the Flamboyant church of St-Maurice.

Of all the northern towns **Douai** has perhaps the best known (thanks to Corot) and most handsome Gothic belfry, grey and spiky and topped by the proud flag-waving Flanders lion. The town also boasts a very fine museum of old master paintings in an old Carthusian monastery. **Cambrai** also has an art museum which is worth visiting, and two interesting 18th-century churches—there is a large painting by Rubens in the church of St-Géry. Cambrai's central square and belfry is mostly

Windmill at Wormhoudt

the work of restorers. At the nearby town of **Le-Cateau-Cambrésis**, birthplace of Matisse, there is a museum devoted to the artist. **Le Quesnoy** is remarkable as the only example of a Vauban citadel which remains intact as a complete system of town walls. The fortifications, heavily overgrown and surrounded by several lakes, are as attractive to walk around as they are interesting to the student of military architecture. In 1918 New Zealand troops had to take the town by climbing the walls with ladders. Camping, boating and sports facilities and even a small sandy beach are on hand. East of Le Quesnoy is some very attractive countryside, a striking contrast after the coalfields north of it. To the south lies **Maroilles**, origin of northern France's smelliest cheese, and the fascinating **Thiérache** region bristling with fortified churches from hard times when this was the disputed frontier between France and Empire. Many of the red brick buildings are flanked by solid round towers and there are rooms in the space above the nave where the local inhabitants could take refuge. Some of the most interesting are near Vervins, at **Beaurain, Burelles, Prisces**, and **Plomion**.

Undoubtedly the pick of the northern towns, the most prosperous and culturally brilliant in the past, and the most beautiful and interesting today, is **Arras**, capital of Artois. Its splendid cobbled central squares—the Place des Héros and the Grande Place, dominated by Gothic town hall and lofty belfry—are the most complete and harmonious examples of brick and stone Flemish architecture in France. The 17th-century houses are arcaded at ground level, tall, thin and decorated with pilasters and elegant curving gables that could be part of a Dutch skyline. The old abbey of St-Vaast's classical church has become the cathedral, and its 18th-century monastic buildings house the town's art museum, with a fine collection of local, Flemish and Dutch paintings, and sculptures. As well as being the most interesting Arras is also one of the most convenient of the northern towns to visit in transit, situated as it is beside the motorway to Paris and the south. It is also a good base for exploration of First World War battlefields and monuments at the northern end of the front line where most of the English fighting took place. The last hills of Artois looking out over Flanders Fields took on great strategic importance and were bitterly disputed (Notre-Dame-de-la-Lorette and Vimy Ridge; see page 372).

Exploring Flanders in France takes time and is best combined, without hurrying, with Flanders in Belgium (Bruges being the big attraction). It is not on an obvious route south or east of French Channel ports. If you are just passing through, and want to balance progress with interest, and especially if your sightseeing taste embraces Gothic churches, the route through southern Picardy to Reims is clearly the one you should take.

From the interesting churches of **Rue, St-Riquier**, and **Abbeville** you follow the Somme upstream to **Amiens**—a big industrial town very severely damaged in both World Wars and unlikely as a whole to etch an image of enduring beauty on your memory. But its cathedral which survived the bombing is one of the very finest in France, the largest and least composite in architectural style, having been more or less completed in 50 years of the 13th century. The façade is richly adorned with sculptures of great beauty, which inspired Ruskin's Amiens Bible; the nave is France's longest, and impressively lofty; the 15th- and 16th-century carving in wood and stone within and around the choir is endlessly fascinating. Amiens also has a museum of considerable interest, outstanding among its collection of paintings being a series of the altar-pieces presented annually to the cathedral by a local literary and religious guild.

On the edge of Amiens beside the Somme is a network of canals and market gardens (*hortillonnages*) where until very recently punts full of vegetables being poled to market were a common sight on the water. The practice is dying out now but you can still explore the canals by boat.

Eastward roads lead alternatively to Noyon or St-Quentin. **Noyon** is a quiet town whose former importance as a religious centre is suggested by the scale of its cathedral, a very simple and beautiful example of the transition to early Gothic style from the Romanesque, well restored after severe damage in the First World War when Noyon was the closest occupied town to Paris and synonymous with the German threat. **St-Quentin** is much more industrial and its great Gothic basilica less noteworthy. But there is a butterfly and insect museum of rare quality and a large collection of 18th-century pastel portraits by the great flatterer of pre-revolutionary France—Maurice Quentin de la Tour—in the Lécuyer art museum.

Laon is one of the most attractive and interesting towns in northern France. The walled medieval city, capital of Carolingian France, crowns a lonely hill commanding the plains. It's dominated by the openwork towers of its cathedral, like Noyon's a bright and beautiful mixture of the qualities of Romanesque and Gothic styles, dating from the late 12th century, and (unlike Noyon) with some fine stained glass. Most endearing of its features are the stone oxen which stand out from the top of the façade towers, eternal tributes to the heavy task of hauling all the stones uphill. There are a number of other old buildings of interest round the narrow streets of Laon, including a medieval lepers' hospital (the Salle Gothique) next to the Cathedral, a delightful octagonal Templar chapel and another interesting early Gothic church (St-Martin). There are several 14th-century fortified town gates and a path round much of the city ramparts. To the west of Laon **St-Gobain Forest** has some splendid 100ft oaks and three old monasteries—Le Tortoir now a farm, St-Nicolas-aux-Bois part of a private estate, and Prémontré a mental hospital—all worth admiring. On the southern edge of the forest **Coucy-Le-Château** was one of the most formidable citadels in France until the retiring Germans blew it up in 1917; the town walls and gateways are still impressive. In the woods at the feet of Coucy you can see the emplacement of Big Bertha, the gun which shelled Paris in 1918, one of its direct hits being the church of St-Gervais in the middle of mass.

Soissons lies a few miles south of Coucy, on the south bank of the Aisne. Apart from its interesting churches Soissons is an unattractive post-First World War reconstruction. Its cathedral is another very early Gothic one famed for the symmetrical beauty of its nave, something you would never suspect from its lop-sided exterior. A remarkable feature is the earliest part of the church, the south transept—round and arcaded like a second choir. On the edge of town the twin-spired façade of the old abbey of St-Jean-des-Vignes stands in isolation, its rose window a gaping hole, and is the more impressive for its desolate state. The rest of the great abbey church was pulled down at the beginning of the last century; you can still visit the splendid Gothic cellar and refectory and some of the cloister. There are two other ruined abbeys at Soissons—St-Léger, in town, provides an interesting setting for the varied contents of the municipal museum. Of St-Médard to the north of the Aisne there is little left to see except the very old crypt (9th-century).

The Ardennes

The French Ardennes, which are not on the way to anywhere in particular, have no monuments of interest and apart from wild boar pâté not much in the way of gastronomy. Nevertheless this is a frequented tourist area because of its status as an area of natural beauty—which it is, by the less than exalted standards of this part of France. The steep rocky hills which enclose the Meuse as it winds northwards from the twin towns of Charleville-Mézières to Belgium are a convenient recreation area for people from the industrial communities, with woods, rivers and lakes. Apart from the tortuous river valley itself which is in places almost spectacular in its rocky severity the main attraction is the great expanse of forest, not as wild and savagely inhabited as when Charlemagne hunted boar and wild ox here but still extensive—346,000 acres. Some of the rocky crests are good walking goals and give fine views of the wild countryside. North of Charleville, **Monthermé** is well situated on a great loop in the river near its junction with the attractive Semois and a good base for excursions, but has no particular village charm. Finest of the peaks to see nearby are the Rocher des Quatre Fils Aymon, the Roche aux Sept Villages and the Roches de Laifour.

Although the French Ardennes are little more than pleasant, the Belgian part of the Massif is much more interesting, with some châteaux and grottoes and varied countryside and the impressively situated town of Dinant. Taken as a whole the Ardennes area is not so obviously avoidable as a description of its French section makes it sound.

On the southern edge of the Ardennes forests and hills, **Charleville-Mézières** is the capital of the *département*, the result of a merger of the two towns, whose inhabitants now rejoice in the name of Carolomacériens. Set on two tongues of land between deep loops in the Meuse, the towns retain their separate characters.

In the centre of geometrically planned Charleville, the magnificent 17th-century Place Ducale is a fine achievement, despite the later town hall on one side, and is thought to be the work of Clément Métezeau, younger brother of Louis, creator of the Place Royale in Paris (now the Place des Vosges). The two squares are as closely related as the two architects. In an old mill built in the Meuse there is a museum devoted to Ardennes folklore and the memory of Charleville's most famous son, the late 19th-century poet Rimbaud who shot across the literary firmament with all the fleeting brilliance of a comet.

Further upstream, **Sedan** was a rich cloth town in the 16th and 17th centuries, and the site on September 1st 1870 of the battle between the French army of 100,000 men against two German armies totalling 240,000 men which ended in Napoleon III's capitulation. A few months later the Prussians were at the gates of Paris. Apart from the forbidding walls of one of the country's largest fortresses, there is not much to admire in the town.

Champagne   **The North**

Any or all of three things may bring you to Champagne: Reims, bubbly, or a destination such as Alsace, Switzerland or Burgundy beyond its southern or eastern borders. Champagne is the universal *sine qua non* of joyous celebration, "its sparkling foam" in Voltaire's words, "the brilliant image of our French people". The unique manufacturing process, the welcome extended to the tourist by the manufacturers, and the charm of the landscape make a wine stop in Champagne (*le* champagne is the wine, *la* Champagne is the area) as fascinating and informative as it is delicious.

Champagne was famous long before it was fizzy. The Romans found vines when they arrived; popes Urban II and Leo XII, kings François I of France and Henry VIII of England stocked their cellars from the prestigious vineyards of Ay. The elaboration of the complicated double fermentation method to encourage the local wine's natural sparkle came later, and is traditionally attributed to the 17th-century Benedictine abbot of Hautvillers (near Epernay), one Dom Pérignon. Whatever the truth about the great oenophile's contribution, the result today of viticultural evolution in Champagne is an industry and a product quite different from other wines in France.

The vineyard area is called the **Montagne de Reims**. Its gentle slopes of vines crowned by tufty clumps of trees are well worth a leisurely tour, in spite of the fact that there are few places for wine tasting. Not surprisingly the villages are prosperous. Ay lies at the heart of some of the most distinguished vineyards. **Hautvillers** is splendidly situated at the top of a steep hill looking down over the Marne, but of the Abbey where Dom Pérignon had a sparklingly bright idea (now owned by Moët et Chandon who are setting up a museum there) only the church remains to be seen for the time being.

Reims is one of the most important cities in the history of France, the main settlement of the Rémi tribe of Gallo-Belgians, who welcomed Caesar as an ally, and whose descendants saw their city grow in stature to become a major religious centre. On Christmas Day 496 it was the site of the baptism of the previously pagan Clovis, king of the Franks, by saint Rémi himself. In memory of this, the first page in the history of France, coronations at Reims became an essential part of royal legitimacy; in 1359 the pretender Edward III of England headed straight for Reims to be crowned, but was repelled. Joan of Arc's mission was the coronation of Charles VII at Reims, and this she achieved on July 17th 1429. On May 29th 1825 Charles X was crowned in full ceremonial, Reims' last coronation.

Once Reims was no doubt a fine old town, but even before the First World War Augustus Hare complained that wide straight boulevards had been laid down as in Paris. They were not to last long: overrun by the Germans right at the beginning of the First World War, then relieved after a few weeks' pillage, the city was to suffer 49 months of relentless bombardment, for the front line was only a mile or two away. In the old centre of Reims 12,000 of the 15,000 houses were destroyed, leaving the great cathedral miraculously still standing although far from undamaged. The shells did uncover some Gallo-Roman remains. Only in Autumn 1918 was the town evacuated: until then many inhabitants had stayed, living in the 100km of underground galleries of the old chalk quarries, now champagne cellars. A souvenir shop in front of the cathedral sells old postcards of Reims as it looked in 1918. It was quickly rebuilt, without any frills, and escaped the Second World War more or less unscathed.
▷ p350

347

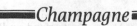

Champagne

Three varieties of grape are grown in an area covering some 50,000 acres (only 2% of French vineyard area), a ribbon of chalky hillside some 100km long by ½ to 2km wide, of which there are three main sections. On the Montagne de Reims, between Reims and Epernay, most of the black *pinot noir* grape is grown; along the Marne valley between Epernay and Château-Thierry the black *pinot meunier* predominates; the delicate white *chardonnay* grape is concentrated south of Epernay along the Côte des Blancs.

After carefully selective harvesting usually in early October, the best grapes are pressed just enough to extract the very best must and taken to the big wine houses for the first fermentation which has taken place by Christmas time. In the New Year each champagne house mixes the different young wines, usually 75% black and 25% white grapes, sometimes adding old ones according to their own individual formulae to produce their range of champagnes. To the blended wine is added a liquor of sugared wine and natural fermenting agents to build the bubbles. In the spring the wine is bottled and when the second fermentation is complete the bottles sit in cellars for two or three years before being placed in racks, necks tilted down, and for six weeks given swift twists of one-eighth of a turn every day by trained *remueurs* (who can manage over 30,000 bottles a day after a long apprenticeship) to settle all the sediment on the bottom of the cork. When this is achieved each bottle's neck is swiftly chilled so that ice forms in it. The ice, sediment and cork are then blown out, the bottle topped up with champagne, sweetened or not depending on whether it is to be a sweet (demi-sec) or a dry (brut) champagne, and recorked. Once it is ready, the wine does not improve with age.

The big champagne houses own relatively few, but choice, vineyards (about 13% of the total), whose yield they augment by buying from co-operatives of small-scale vineyard proprietors. This relieves the little men of the high cost of carrying stocks of three or four years' produce of expensive wines, but it also relieves them of most of the profit, so not surprisingly some of them have tried to by-pass the big firms, making their own champagne and selling it directly. This accounts for some 25% of world champagne sales. The champagne house sells not a variety of wines from different vineyards known by the name of the vineyard or *appellation* and the vintage (for example Duboeuf Morgon 1979), but a standard champagne which is undated and in theory at least unchanging from year to year, thanks to the careful blending. In an especially good year some wine is not blended and is dated (*millésimé*). Many houses produce their own special brews which are of an even higher quality than these vintage champagnes—one example is Moët et Chandon's Dom Pérignon. Some champagne is produced from white grapes only and is called *blanc de blancs*.

Visiting a champagne house is not like visiting a handsome old château in its vineyards, as you do in the Bordeaux region for instance. The big champagne houses are mostly in Reims and Epernay and seem more like production line factories. Nevertheless the Avenue de Champagne in Epernay does have a certain style—wide and straight and flanked on both sides by the most prestigious establishments built in a suitably inflated grand manner. There is also a rather disappointing champagne museum.

   The dozen biggest champagne houses account for some 65% of world sales, and they are the ones that lay on the best organised tours in a variety of languages, and tasting in the universal language of champagne. Mumm and Piper-Heidsieck in Reims and Moët et Chandon in Epernay are the obvious choices, but there are scores of other houses which will welcome you and perhaps make you feel a little less like just another part of the production line. The heart of these places, indeed of Champagne itself, is the enormous extent of chalk galleries in the hillsides where the wine evolves in ideal conditions of constant humidity and temperature (about 10°C) whatever the external weather conditions. Everywhere you will be bombarded with statistics—how many hundreds of thousands of bottles are laid up in the cellars, representing how many tens of millions of francs' worth of stock and so on. One of the most surprising facts is that of world-wide sales of some 190 million bottles a year only one third is for export. You will see the array of different champagne bottles from a dainty quarter (18.7 cl) to the sonorous Jeroboam (4 bottles), Rehoboam (6 bottles), Methuselah (8 bottles), Salmanazar (12 bottles), Balthazar (16 bottles) and mighty Nebuchadnezzar (20 bottles); and you will learn that the best size for the maturing of champagne is the magnum (2 bottles). You will not be forced to buy, and there is no great saving in doing so.

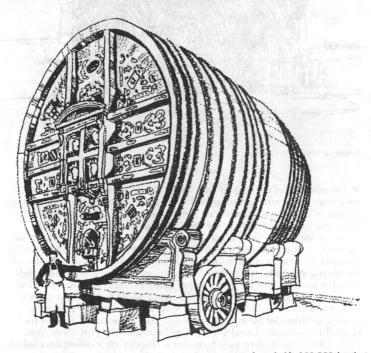

The largest champagne cask (it holds 200,000 bottles)

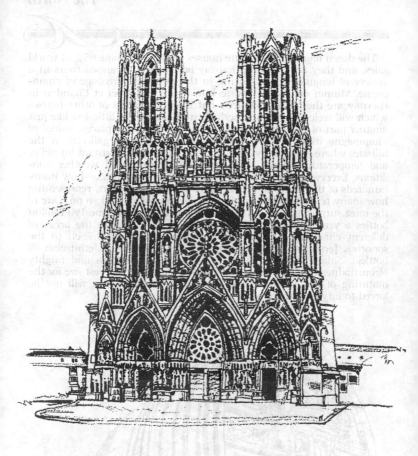

Reims cathedral, west façade

✳ *Cathedral* One of the big four with Paris, Chartres and Amiens, displayed to advantage by the arrangement of rebuilding and a radiant golden colour when the late afternoon sun hits the west façade, the cathedral's greatest glory. To the architectural framework of massive but graceful symmetry is added a wealth of sculpture—a row of sixty-three unidentified kings, each ten feet tall and six tons in weight, and three deep doorways framed by the most beautiful examples of the most charming school of Gothic sculpture. Best loved of all is the smiling angel who stands next to the scalped St-Nicaise, who might well have lost his head over her. More angels flutter in the flying buttresses along the north side of this the "cathedral of angels". Inside too the most striking feature is sculpture—the west end is covered with statues in niches, still marvellously detailed having been sheltered from the weather. Some of the original 13th-century stained glass was restored after the First World War; there is also some modern glass including a chapel with windows designed by Chagall. From April to October a series of seventeen Renaissance tapestries illustrating the life of the Virgin decorates the walls of the side aisles.

* *St-Rémi* An enormous old Benedictine abbey church built in the 11th and 12th centuries; over the long dark Romanesque nave is suspended a gilt crown with 96 lights (once candles) symbolising the lifespan of Saint Rémi. The choir provides an elegant light Gothic contrast. The current version of Saint Rémi's tomb is an enormous 19th-century creation, but incorporates some fine statues from the 16th century.

* *Palais du Tau* The archbishop's palace, dating mostly from the 17th century but retaining a superb vaulted Gothic room, site of post-coronation banquets, which now contains two of the greatest treasures of a very rich museum, 15th-century Arras tapestries telling of the strong king Clovis.

* *St-Denis Museum* A collection of paintings of the very highest quality— Renaissance German (Cranach) to modern French (Matisse, Picasso and Corot).

* *Chapelle Foujita* Neo-Romanesque chapel designed and decorated by a modern Japanese artist.

* *Porte Mars* Damaged and dirty but still very impressive 3rd-century triumphal arch on the edge of the town centre.

Châlons-sur-Marne, not Reims, is the departmental capital. It isn't a very attractive town, despite being crossed by the Marne and some tributary canals, but there are churches of some interest (mainly for their stained glass, of which Châlons was an important centre).

Rather more agreeable as an ecclesiastical pause (and a very good gastronomic one too—see Hotels Section) than a plunge into urban Châlons is **L'Epine**, little more than a string of houses along the straight road from Châlons towards Metz, which makes the basilica of Notre-Dame-de-L'Epine all the more surprising in its isolated domination of the surrounding expanse of corn fields. It is a late Gothic building with extremely intricate decorative tracery all over the golden façade and openwork spires. Although nearly all the statuary is missing, some splendid gargoyles remain. The interior is more simply elegant and contains an emotive sculpture of the Entombment.

Southern Champagne has neither the viticultural nor, quite, the cultural attractions of the north; but this peaceful, spacious landscape escaped devastation in the First World War so its towns, even if they lack monuments of the first order, are more attractive as towns. The plains and woods seem off the beaten track, but in fact Champagne was Europe's most important medieval thoroughfare, and its capital **Troyes** an international trading and artistic centre. Even when merchants stayed put in Antwerp and Florence and Troyes lost its commercial importance, the Trojan school of sculpture and stained glass continued to flourish, particularly in the late 15th and early 16th centuries when local production was distinguished from the mainstream of the Renaissance by its simple realism. Today it is a quiet provincial town tucked into a loop in the young Seine. It still has delightfully picturesque narrow streets of timbered houses leaning over the cobbles, and many interesting churches.

* *St-Urbain* This church is a prodigious achievement for its time (the late 13th century), described by Viollet-le-Duc as "certainly the last limit that construction in stone can reach". It was built to the order of pope Urban IV on the site of his father's shoe shop, much to the annoyance of the nuns who owned the land, and who did all they could to sabotage construction. Elegantly decorated outside with pinnacles, gargoyles, balustrades and flying buttresses, the interior is a dazzling expanse of coloured glass (mostly 13th-century) hardly interrupted by the spindly stone skeleton of the church.

✻ *Cathedral* Although lacking stylistic unity this church is richly decorated outside (especially the Flamboyant west façade and earlier north doorway). There is a wealth of stained glass from 13th-century (choir) to 17th-century, all of the highest quality.

✻ *St-Nizier* Renaissance church containing interesting stained glass and sculptures.

✻ *St-Madeleine* Splendid 16th-century stained glass around the choir and two masterpieces of 16th-century Trojan sculpture—the ornate roodscreen and the statue of saint Martha in the south transept.

✻ *St-Jean* Scene of the marriage of Henry V to the heiress Catherine of France as agreed in the treaty of Troyes in 1420.

✻ *St-Pantaléon* A mostly Renaissance church with a wooden vault, turned into a museum of over 40 statues from deconsecrated and destroyed churches.

✻ *Museums* There are several near the cathedral; fine arts, modern art, archaeology and natural history. More unusual is the local history museum in the fine old Hôtel de Vauluisant near the church of St-Pantaléon; its varied contents include good local sculpture and a separate section devoted to the knitwear industry (*bonneterie*) which has been the mainstay of the town since the 18th century.

✻ *Old Town* The most picturesque old streets with tall overhanging timbered houses are in the area around the church of St-Jean (especially the Rue des Chats and the Rue de Champeaux).

Here in central eastern France the beaches of Atlantic and Mediterranean are remote indeed. But the lucky Trojans and the Bragards—as the inhabitants of St-Dizier style themselves—have their local beaches, on the reservoirs created to regularise the course of the Seine (**Lac d'Orient**) and the Marne (**Lac du Der-Chantecoq**). Both are very extensive, full of week-enders and well provided with facilities for camping, swimming, fishing and water sports. There are some churches of interest in the Der region (sculptures and stained glass at **Chavanges**, unusual timber-framed construction in many village churches but most complete and attractive at **Lentilles**). Most of the forest to the east of the Lac d'Orient has been taken over by tourists (there are walks and rides and picnic areas) but the wild life has been granted its reserves.

The Marne valley upstream from Châlons is not particularly interesting, but improves towards Chaumont. The village of **Vignory** is worth a pause to admire its very fine large church which has been little altered since its construction in the mid-11th century; its arches and pillars are pleasingly round and massive, its vault is still wooden. South-east of Vignory the empty rolling hills bear tributes to two great Frenchmen. A granite double-barred cross of Lorraine, symbol of French resistance and national spirit, crowns a hill on the edge of Colombey-les-Deux-Eglises, adopted home for nearly 40 years of general de Gaulle. Chez de Gaulle (La Boisserie) is a modest place, but you can visit it and see several of the general's rooms preserved as a memorial. Saint Bernard was no less of a colossus in his time, restoring expelled popes to Rome, launching crusades, reforming corrupt practices within the church, combating heresy, and still finding time to look after the Abbaye de Clairvaux which he founded in 1115 beside the Aube. Now this important monastery, once the capital of the Cistercian order, is a prison with more than a thousand inmates. South of Colombey, the market town of **Chaumont** enjoys a fine situation between two rivers, but offers the tourist little more than an impressive railway viaduct and a Gothic basilica with interesting sculptures.

Langres (see map on page 84), at the gates of Burgundy, is an interesting old city of severe classical dignity, which still seems to be a world apart, enclosed within old walls and bypassed by main road and railway. Langres was an important stronghold for the Romans as it had been for the Gauls. Its site at the edge of a high plateau is a magnificent natural fortress, and until the attachment of Lorraine and the Franche-Comté to the Crown it was a major border town; so its fortifications were repeatedly improved from Roman times to the 19th century. From the 3rd century onwards Langres was also a very important episcopal see: the bishop of Langres had the right to strike his own coinage. Walking along or below the ramparts gives enormous views (including the Alps, they say) and reveals a succession of splendid gateways of which the oldest dates from the 2nd century and has been incorporated in the walls. Within the old town the main things to see are:

✻ *Cathedral* A beautiful, severe transitional Romanesque/Gothic building masked by a heavily inappropriate 18th-century façade.

✻ *St-Martin* A much altered Gothic church with a very fine wooden statue of Christ over the altar (16th-century from Troyes).

✻ *St-Didier Museum* Gallo-Roman archaeological finds, and some paintings.

Hotels

Epernay, (Champillon), 51160 Marne   £££££

ROYAL CHAMPAGNE   Tel: 26.51.11.51

Old coaching inn it may be, but this attractive white building on the N51 is nowadays a smart roadhouse, with fine views from the vine-covered hills down over the Marne valley. Accommodation (recently extended) is down the slope well away from the roads in rows of bungalows, each with its terrace and deckchairs; the rooms are peaceful and secluded. Both the interesting *carte* (fairly expensive) and the fixed-price menus (several, with a particularly good-value one for week day lunches) are strong on fish dishes (*grenadin de sandre au champagne et aux fines herbes, rosace de turbot en habit vert*). There's a children's menu, alas not available to merely peckish adults. The restaurant looks out over noble vineyards, and the wine list is impressive, not least in champagnes.

Closed most of Jan; 25 bedrooms; no lift.

L'Epine (Châlons-sur-Marne), 51000 Marne   £££

AUX ARMES DE CHAMPAGNE   Tel: 26.68.10.43

Something of a roadhouse, but one of no little culinary distinction, opposite the gorgeous basilica, on the Châlons-Metz road. Behind is a lovingly contrived garden with lawns and rocks, plastic pools and streams powered by a noisy motor. There are now no bedrooms which face the main road—all (including those in two annexes down the road) are relatively quiet, comfortable and well equipped, with traditional colour schemes. There's a good choice of both food and wine at the lower end of the price-range; in sauces, good use is made of the local red, Bouzy, as well as the more obvious bubbly. Reasonably priced champagnes from lesser-known vineyards can be bought here.

Closed Jan to mid-Feb; 40 bedrooms; no lift.

Hotels

Fère-en-Tardenoise, 02130 Aisne £££££

HOSTELLERIE DU CHÂTEAU   Tel: 23.82.21.13

In the remains of what was formerly a royal palace, restored in the 19th century, and one of the first French châteaux to be transformed into a hotel, the Hostellerie is a splendidly comfortable and relaxing place to stop over near champagne country. Bedrooms and public rooms have solid, traditional décor; service is formal and very attentive. Cooking is of a very high standard, including an extraordinary array of desserts, and very good cheeses, but it doesn't come cheap.

Closed Jan and Feb; 23 bedrooms; no lift.

Montreuil-sur-Mer, 62170 Pas-de-Calais ££££

CHÂTEAU DE MONTREUIL   Tel: 21.81.53.04

Not a château, but a large 1930's house, in the pretty hilltop village that isn't *sur mer* (now about 10 miles away). It's a popular last-night halt for ferry-bound Britons, attracted perhaps by the cooking of young Christian Germain, protégé of the Roux brothers of Waterside Inn. Accommodation is solidly traditional, bedrooms ranging from medieval style with four-posters, to powder-blue classic and now boldly modern (three new annexe rooms). In the attractive restaurant service is good, and Vivaldi may be your musical accompaniment. On fine days, meals are served on the terrace. There are two good-value fixed-price menus, as well as a seven-course "surprise". The quality of the cheeses will come as no surprise to those travellers who have already encountered their supplier, Philippe Olivier.

Closed mid-Dec to early Feb (rest Thurs lunch out of season); 14 bedrooms; no lift.

Reims, 51100 Marne £££££

LES CRAYÈRES   Tel: 26.82.80.80

It is rare indeed for guidebook writers to agree with each other, and rare too for praise to be so fulsome. "One of the finest hotels in France", as well as "one of the finest restaurants in France" is no mean feat; Gérard Boyer and his wife Elyane (generally agreed to be radiant) are no amateurs, and have created a luxury hotel of great style in this beautiful 19th-century château surrounded by the most famous of the champagne *caves* at the edge of the centre of Reims. It doesn't come cheap, of course, but neither is it bad value if you consider, as most people do, that it's a memorable experience.

Closed end-Dec to mid-Jan (rest Mon and Tues lunch); 16 bedrooms; tennis; helipad.

Sept-Saulx, 51400 Marne £££

LE CHEVAL BLANC   Tel: 26.61.60.27

Old coaching inn in the centre of a peaceful farming village, run by the same family since 1830. The current bearer of the chef's hat is the young daughter of the house, Laurence Cuasante, who is acquitting herself creditably, and creating her own repertoire of new dishes (*rouget farci à la mousse de tomate et beurre de safran, tartare de magret de canard aux câpres*), adding these to the tried and tested recipes of *Grand-Mère* Marie (*poulet de Bresse à l'estragon, bisque de homard*). Bedrooms in an annexe (half on ground floor) are solidly traditional and comfortable; there's a very attractive garden with stream and tennis, and a stylish rustic restaurant.

Closed mid-Jan to mid-Feb; 25 bedrooms; no lift.

Alsace, Lorraine and the Vosges

Dambach-La-Ville

"A blending of all beauties—streams and dells,
Fruit, foliage, crag, wood, corn-field, mountain, vine,
And chiefless castles breathing stern farewells" (Byron)

Alsace, Lorraine and the Vosges

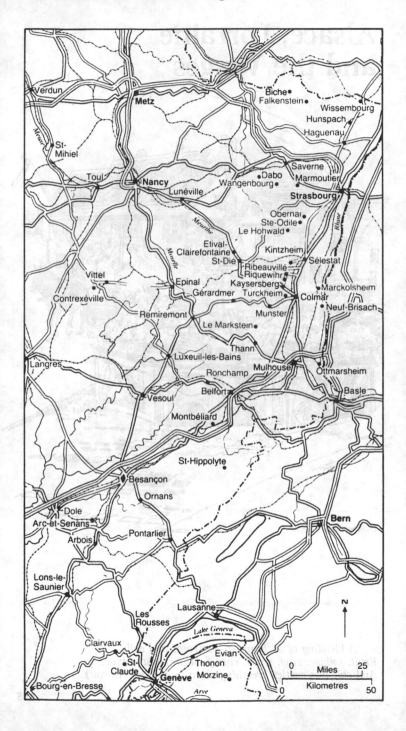

Alsace, Lorraine and the Vosges

Two provinces could hardly be more different one from the other than Alsace and Lorraine, yet modern history has welded them in the collective consciousness. Estranged from France for nearly half a century after the national débâcle of 1870, Alsace-Lorraine or Elsass-Lothringen as it was renamed by the jack-booted Prussian conquerors was an open wound in France's side and a cause of grief to every true patriot. The actress Sarah Bernhardt (not from Alsace despite her Germanic-sounding name) having performed to the same entrancing effect before a German admirer as Salome before Herod, and receiving the same offer, said without a moment of hesitation "Give back Alsace and Lorraine".

The Lorraine of the Alsace-Lorraine issue is not the whole province but the modern *département* of Moselle in the north-east with Metz its principal town. The region is characterised, although less strongly than Alsace, by the widespread use of a Germanic local dialect; there are several of these, spoken regularly by a million and a half people. Apart from this justification of the German territorial claim, and despite being one of the latest of crown acquisitions (the mid-18th century), Lorraine is a thoroughly French region, and encloses within its boundaries many of the most characteristic features of France: the heavy industry of the north (50% of France's iron and 45% of its coal), the supreme elegance of its 18th-century capital Nancy, the quiet spacious rolling farmlands and the seriously relaxing spa towns of its south. So it is not inappropriate that Lorraine should have become for historical reasons synonymous with patriotism. Lorraine is Joan of Arc, saviour of France at the time of her greatest need. The twin-barred cross of Lorraine was the symbol of the Free French Army of General de Gaulle who told the French in 1940 that there was no question of doing a deal with the occupying Nazis. Lorraine is also Verdun, where 300,000 Frenchmen fell in a few months in 1916, the greatest battle in history according to the local propaganda, and certainly the most profligate.

Alsace is the French side of the Rhineland Plain, separated from Lorraine by the natural barrier of the Vosges Mountains which run north-south parallel to the Rhine—the river which has brought the region commercial activity from the earliest times. Local art and architecture display some French and much German influence, but also some from the Low Countries and northern Italy, telling of the region's popularity with travellers between the Mediterranean and the North Sea. The local language is a dialect closely related to Old High German. Names of people and places sound Germanic, faces look Germanic, home-cooking and wines taste Germanic, and the spotlessly clean and colourful villages are reminiscent of parts of Germany too.

From the French point of view the Alsace-Lorraine issue was resolved simply enough, once and for all, by Tacitus who wrote that the Rhine divides Germany from Gaul. After the Roman departure the Germans moved in, and after the disintegration of the Carolingian Empire Alsace remained loosely attached to the anarchy that was the Holy Roman Empire. Towns guarded their freedom and formed a league (the Decapolis) of mutual assistance, and petty local lords in their hilltop strongholds bowed to no one. Only when the religious wars of the early 17th century brought unimaginable devastation to the province, whose population is conservatively estimated to have declined by half in less than half a century, did the Alsatians look to the French monarchy for protection. The French takeover was not complete until 1681 when Strasbourg yielded to the Sun King, but even so reserved its right to freedom of religious practice. Alsace, separated from France by the independent duchy of Lorraine until 1766, was so little affected by being French that when Arthur Young crossed the Vosges five days after the storming of the Bastille, he recorded: "I found myself to all appearance veritably in Germany; here not one person in an hundred has a word of French . . . looking at a map of France and reading histories of Louis XIV never threw his conquest of Alsace into such light as travelling into it did: to cross a great range of mountains to enter a level plain inhabited by a people totally distinct and different from France, with manners, language, ideas, prejudices, and habits all different, made an impression of the injustice and ambition of such a conduct". Even now the visitor will find Young's verdict easy to understand.

For reasons of its own, Alsace espoused the Revolutionary cause with enthusiasm. Mulhouse decided it would rather be French than Swiss in 1798, and the area contributed more than its share of dashing generals to the Napoleonic epic. It started to become much more French, and much more French-speaking, so that when all but Belfort was lost to the Germans again in 1871 some 250,000 Alsatians voted with their feet to stay French and Belfort suddenly became a big town. For many of those who stayed, association with the booming prosperity of Germany grew acceptable with time, and the "liberation" of Alsace in 1918 was not universally welcomed. However the growing and uncomfortably close Nazi threat in the thirties (Alsace has a large Jewish population) and brutal measures of Germanisation during the occupation that followed—names had to be changed (for example from Claude to Klaus), Alsatians were drafted into the German army and deported to Poland, the speaking of French and even the wearing of berets was punishable with prison—all reinforced pro-French feeling. Since 1945 French Alsace and Lorraine have resumed their traditional role of Middle Kingdom between Germany and France. Strasbourg is now the symbol of supra-national politics. Tens of thousands of Alsatians and Lorrains commute to work in the better paid cities of Sarrebrücken, Karlsruhe and Basle. German capital creates new jobs in France.

Of the two provinces, Alsace is by far the more attractive to the tourist. Strasbourg and Colmar are two of the most beautiful and culturally rich towns in France. Crisp, fruity and luscious Alsatian wines are produced on the foothills of the Vosges which rise abruptly from the narrow fertile plain. Delightful old villages break up the carpet of vines and are strung in a chain that makes the most picturesque wine tour in France. The Vosges themselves are mainly wooded with open grassy rounded tops—excellent for breezy picnics and not too arduous walking. There are scores of fortresses to admire and a few simple, relaxing mountain resorts. The climate is dry and in summer hot, especially down on the plain which is sheltered by the Vosges from France and its westerly rain-bearing winds. Not the least of the attractions of Alsace is its compact scale, which enables you to get from museum to vineyard to mountain top and back within a day, and to tour the whole region from no more than two or three bases.

The Towns of Alsace

Capital of the province so often the cause of war in Europe, **Strasbourg**'s choice as the seat of the Council of Europe and one of the capitals of the EEC had a symbolic value of determined hatchet burial. It is a thriving and cosmopolitan, commercial and industrial centre and an important Rhine port. It is also a lively and youthful university town, and in the old centre very picturesque and touristy.

Petite France, Strasbourg

✳ *Cathedral* The characteristic dark greyish-pink façade crowned lopsidedly by a single soaring tower and open-work spire dominates Strasbourg and the Alsatian plain for miles around, and is one of the symbols of Alsace. From the completion of the spire in 1439 until the 19th century this was the tallest building in Christendom (142 metres). Its greatest glory, apart from the spire, is the magnificent sculpture adorning the doorways and on the pillar of angels (13th-century) in the transept which is often hard to see properly because of the crowds of people admiring the gaudy complexity of the 19th-century astronomical clock (guided tours at midday).

✳ *Old Town* The area around the cathedral is very attractive, with cobbled pedestrian streets and timber-framed houses—of which the most decoratively carved is the Maison Kammerzell (a restaurant on the Place de la Cathédrale). There are souvenir shops full of stuffed geese, storks, tins of foie gras and bottles of wine. At night the cathedral is lit up, there are *son et lumière* performances in French and German, and people sit up late outside the cafés entertained by street artists. From the Place du Marché aux Poissons behind the Rohan Palace you can take a boat trip on the River Ill.

✳ *Musée de l'Oeuvre Notre-Dame* This excellent museum, in a partly 14th-century town house, contains (as well as a large collection of local art and furniture) many of the originals of the finest cathedral sculptures which have been taken down in the interest of their own safety and replaced by copies.

✳ *Château des Rohan* Despite war damage this is one of Strasbourg's most beautiful buildings and one of the least Alsatian in character. The stone is white, the style that of the French 18th century, the effect expressive of the grand style of the four Rohan princes, cardinals and bishops who presided from 1704 to 1790. The Palace houses the city's fine arts, decorative arts, and archaeological museums, but the sumptuous and beautifully restored Grands Appartements are more worthy of your attention than any of these.

✳ *Historical Museum* and *Alsatian Museum* These are good examples of their kind and especially interesting because of the turbulent and often bitter history of Strasbourg and the peculiarities of local folklore and popular arts and crafts. The Historical Museum has a painting of one of the proudest moments in Alsatian history—Rouget de l'Isle singing in Strasbourg his patriotic song for the Rhine Army, composed on the moment of declaration of war with Austria in April 1792. Soon the song was to be known as the Marseillaise.

✳ *Ancienne Douane* Modern art collection and exhibitions (and a riverside restaurant) in the old Customs House.

✳ *St-Thomas* Handsome hall church (early 13th-century) with Pigalle's splendidly theatrical tomb of the maréchal de Saxe, victor of Fontenoy.

✳ *Petite France* The most picturesque part of old Strasbourg, where the River Ill divides into four streams or canals spanned by covered bridges with towers and old watermills. It's fascinating to wander around the narrow alleys of this old tanning, fishing and milling quarter, banned to cars.

✳ *European Parliament* This occupies an angular glassy modern building on the banks of the Ill between central Strasbourg and the Rhine. You can visit the building by prior appointment; it stands on the edge of a fine park (Orangerie) with exotic plants, a little zoo and a boating lake.

Colmar is the art-lover's main objective in Alsace. Its old town centre is as unspoilt as the prettiest of Alsatian country villages, with the added interest of richly decorated old town houses and even a "Little Venice" quarter. It is very conveniently situated just a few miles from the heart of the wine road and only a short drive from Strasbourg and the Vosges; not surprisingly it's full of tourists in summer, especially around the time of the wine festival in mid-August. Colmar is a particularly good base for those relying on public transport, but for all its old-world charm not everyone's ideal place to stay: it is an important commercial and industrial town of some 70,000 inhabitants, which sprawls modern and unsightly across the fertile, pylon-scarred plain. Colmar prospered in the Middle Ages and headed the alliance of Alsatian towns known as the Decapolis. In the 15th and 16th centuries its burghers built themselves showy town houses decorated with Renaissance carving. All the arts prospered with the town, and like it benefited from Alsace's position on the great thoroughfares of Europe between Italy and Flanders, France and Germany. Colmar's great master was Martin Schongauer (late 15th-century), who had much to teach the young Dürer, and like his better-known pupil was first a draughtsman and engraver, second a painter. Schongauer's achievement in both media can best be seen in Colmar; indeed, there are hardly any of his paintings of any distinction anywhere else.

* *Old Town* There are beautiful old houses and pedestrian streets around the Dominican church, the cathedral, and the splendid old Customs House, especially the commercial Rue des Marchands. Look out particularly for the Maison Pfister (Rue des Marchands) decorated with delightful medallions and ornamental religious paintings, and the Maison des Têtes (Rue des Têtes), its loggia above the street elaborately carved with heads.

* *Unterlinden Museum* A large, varied and exceptionally rich museum housed in old convent buildings around a shady cloister. The star attraction, and for many tourists the single reason for a journey to Colmar, is the overwhelming Issenheim altar-piece, painted by Grünewald in the first years of the 16th century. The many panels of the work, which were opened and shut according to the religious season, include an anguished and gruesome Crucifixion and a Resurrection of corresponding brilliance. If you can tear yourself away from these hallucinatory images (which were intended to comfort those afflicted with the sickness called St Antony's Fire) there are plenty of other things to admire: Schongauer's paintings and prints; sections devoted to costumes, dolls, furniture, interiors, folklore, crafts; even an interesting modern art collection.

* *Dominican Church* In the summer Schongauer's greatest painting, "The Virgin of the Rose Bush", is usually on show here (there's an entrance charge). It is a bittersweet masterpiece, with a densely symbolic decorative background.

* *St-Martin Cathedral* There are wood carvings all around the choir in the style of the 15th century, interesting sculpture round the west and south doorways and a fine wooden crucifixion group.

Neuf-Brisach is the most interesting remaining example of Vauban's fortification of the Rhine, a complete 17th-century new town geometrically laid out with a double system of walls and canals. The picturesque old town of Breisach (in French Vieux-Brisach) across the river in Germany is well worth a visit to admire its fine setting high above the river, a church with frescoes by Schongauer, and some fortifications. To the south **Ottmarsheim** has an unusual 11th-century octagonal church.

Between Colmar and Strasbourg, **Sélestat** is a partly old town with two large pink churches within the fragmentary old walls, one Romanesque, the other Gothic. You can visit a library, founded in 1542, which contains the precious books of a distinguished Renaissance scholar and friend of Erasmus, Beatus Rhenanus.

Mulhouse (roughly pronounced Moolooze) is Alsace's second city in size and economic importance, and puts money before beauty, perhaps a legacy from its 300-year attachment to the alliance of Swiss Cantons.

* *Town Hall* This is the only old building of interest in town: its walls are decorated with *trompe l'oeil* paintings from the late 17th century. Inside there is an interesting historical museum.

* *Textile Print Museum* (near station) A unique and fascinating museum devoted to the development of the industry which brought wealth and scores of thousands of new inhabitants to 19th-century Mulhouse.

Belfort plugs the wide gap between the Vosges and the Jura—a natural corridor into France from the east. Its strategic importance won it the attentions of Vauban, who did such a good job in building fortifications that the town was able to resist 40,000 German invaders in 1870 for nearly four months, and was awarded to France at the negotiating table, in recognition of its heroism. This separated Belfort from Alsace, and it has remained on its own ever since in charge of its own *département* or *territoire*—an appropriate term since the town's great feature is the monumentally barrel-chested lion carved in blocks of pink Vosges stone beside the walls of the defiant citadel.

A short drive west of Belfort, by the main road at the foot of the Vosges, lies **Ronchamp**. The town is pretty anonymous, in the style of this part of France, but that only adds to the impact of Le Corbusier's architecturally unorthodox chapel of Notre-Dame-du-Haut (1955) which stands as a memorial to soldiers sacrificed here in 1944. There are extensive views from the grassy knoll on which the new chapel stands, across the foothills and the forests of the Jura and Vosges mountains, whose bumps and hollows the architect wished his sanctuary to echo.

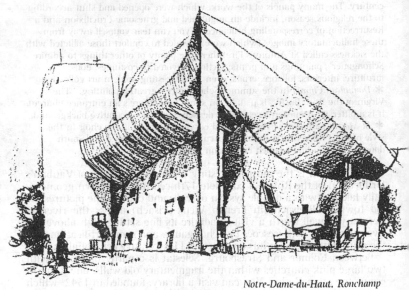

Notre-Dame-du-Haut, Ronchamp

Saverne lies at the foot of the natural gateway into Alsace across the mountains (the Col de Saverne—410 metres). This strategically important fortress town was in the possession of the prince/bishops of Strasbourg for five centuries up to the Revolution; prince Louis-René de Rohan was responsible for the imposing later-18th-century château.

From Saverne a good road leads up into the hills to the south, to the ruins (on three pink rocky outcrops) of the fortress of **Haut-Barr**, first built in 1170 by the bishop of Strasbourg and known as the eye of Alsace. The views from the top justify the name. **Marmoutier**, a few miles on the Strasbourg side of Saverne, is a small town with a large and beautiful partly Romanesque church which survives from the period of the Benedictine monastery's greatest prosperity. The west end is the oldest part, massively solid with tiny windows like elephants' eyes in the greyish-pink façade which is unadorned except for a few isolated panels of decoration, and bands of simple low relief arch patterns (as elsewhere in Alsace, they reveal the Italian influence).

The Wine Road of Alsace

The Wine Road is the most attractive feature of Alsace. It is a signposted route, mostly along minor roads at the foot of the Vosges, from Marlenheim to Thann. Its character doesn't change much from one end to the other; if you want to visit only a bit of it the most picturesque section is at the heart of the vineyard area just north of Colmar (the villages Turckheim, Kaysersberg, Ribeauvillé and Riquewihr).

There is something strangely satisfying about vineyards, a tightly combed corduroy order imposed on nature. Vineyards in Alsace are much like vineyards anywhere else; what makes this wine road so special is their setting: the wooded mountains behind with fortresses in remarkable number surveying the plain, and the villages—pink, walled, cobbled and unspoilt although not undiscovered.

Vines press right up to the village walls and prevent any unsightly expansion of the community. In summer, their brilliant green contrasts richly with the dark pink Vosges stone cobbles. The substantial houses have carved and patterned dark timbers, and balconies decorated with boxes of bright scarlet geraniums. In village centres the little fountains pour forth wine at festival time as if this were some carefree modern-day Canaan. Local inhabitants, viticulturists for the most part, keep their wines in the village cellars, welcome the tourist to taste and buy, and are happy to talk for hours about their wines. Every village has some ingredients of the model wine village; fairy-tale Riquewihr comes closest to the model.

One traditional element of the Alsace wine village is now so rare that to describe it as typical would be an unfair concession to the power of nostalgia and tourist office mythology. Not so long ago the steeply tiled roofscapes and old towers bristled with the distinctive landmarks that are storks' nests, and the birds which returned summer after summer to the same nest were quite rightly considered part of the village population, and bearers of good fortune. But every year fewer and fewer storks return to Alsace, mainly because of massacre in their winter quarters. One of the few villages where your search for a stork may be rewarded is Ostheim, just north of Colmar; a handsome and often occupied nest sits on top of the war memorial in the main square. The Alsatians are now keeping storks cooped up in "reintroduction centres" for a couple of years to discourage their misguided migratory instinct. In these places at least you can see storks, but they don't look the same when they're not on top of a nest on top of a wine village.

Travelling south from Strasbourg, you first come to Molsheim, a sizeable town which has outgrown its old walls, parts of which remain and enclose interesting old streets. The focal point is the central square, with a fountain and the Renaissance Metzig (Butchers' Guild building) which has many interesting architectural features. Rosheim is an attractive small town, built unusually for this part of the world of a yellowish stone, with some impressive gateways, allegedly the oldest

(12th-century) secular building in Alsace, and a very interesting Romanesque church which could almost have been transported from Pisa. Four man-eating lions surmount the façade.

At the foot of the much-frequented pilgrimage mountain of Ste-Odile, **Obernai** is an important and at heart very picturesque town with fine walls and towers, and a typically Alsatian main square with Renaissance public buildings and town houses, and a fountain. The pilgrimage trail from Obernai passes **Ottrott** (Haut- and Bas-), whence forest walks are rewarded by two medieval fortress ruins.

On the wooded summit of **Mont Ste-Odile** there's a popular pilgrimage convent and signed walks through the forest which generally lead you at some point to the massive so-called Pagan Wall whose remains still almost encircle the mountain top. The best section of the wall, which pre-dates the Romans by several centuries, is at the north end near the Dreystein Fortress.

Barr is an attractive and typical walled town with a fountain and a Renaissance town hall. The old village of **Andlau** lies beautifully situated beneath twin fortress-capped peaks. Not much of interest remains of its powerful and exclusive abbey except a Romanesque church with beautiful carvings on the west end, and a stone bear in the crypt, in memory of the real one which inspired the abbey's founder.

Dambach-la-Ville is another very attractive typical old wine village in the vineyards, with fortress ruins high above.

The colourful village of **Kintzheim** has a number of very popular tourist attractions nearby. The **Château de Haut-Koenigsbourg** is real "Where Eagles Dare" stuff, an eyrie 2,000ft above the plain done up like a film set to the orders of Kaiser Bill in the early years of this century, to the disgust of purists and the delight of tourists. In the almost completely reconstructed citadel buildings there are eagles painted on the vaults and skulls of wild beasts hanging from ceiling lamps, a full-blown souvenir shop and an Alsatian tavern with trad-clad barmaids. The owner of the **Château de Kintzheim** itself has got the commercial spirit too: he shows off some fifty birds of prey (including eagles) in free-flying displays several times a day. Nearby there's a monkey park, and a stork reintroduction centre.

For those who deplore the imaginative restoration of old castle ruins, there are literally scores of them on the craggy peaks above the vineyards which stand untouched in all their romantic overgrown raven-circled splendour, making excellent goals for stiff walks up through the vines and woods from the villages below. Two of the finest old ruins are **Franckenbourg** and **Ortenbourg**.

Overlooked by no fewer than three ruined fortresses, and finely set in the pit of a theatre of vineyards, **Ribeauvillé** is an important tourist and wine centre which is busy and commercial but still very typically attractive. The town's most striking monument is the 13th- and 16th-century Metzgerturm which straddles the main street at the head of the square, and its greatest attraction is the Pfiffertag folklore festival in early September, with costumed processions, dancing and free wine. In summer there are numerous local bus tours which include tasting.

The village of **Hunawihr** has a fortified church and a stork reintroduction centre. **Riquewihr** is the most charming and harmoniously unspoilt of all the old wine villages, in the midst of Alsace's highest quality vineyards. It's the home of many prestigious wine firms including Dopff and Hügel. Much of it dates from the 16th century; the town walls are almost complete, with gateways, rampart walk, and torture chamber; there are many interesting buildings and an old Jewish ghetto. **Sigolsheim** has an early Gothic church, and the Blutberg (mountain of blood) memorial, necropolis of the thousands killed in the bitter fighting which preceded the liberation of Colmar in January 1945.

The delightful small town of Kaysersberg is situated between vineyard hills, and overlooked by castle ruins which form part of the town walls. Its Gothic church contains a remarkably carved 16th-century altarpiece. There's a small museum devoted to Albert Schweitzer who was born here. The pretty village of **Turckheim** has many old houses of which the most notable is the splendid olde-worlde inn, the Hotel des Deux Clefs (1620). Alsace's last town crier does an evening turn at dusk with his lantern, his halberd, and his three-cornered hat (he is a fair-weather town crier who only comes out in summer). Fortified **Eguisheim** is the last of the typically pretty wine villages.

High up in the mountains between Turckheim and Kaysersberg **Les Trois Epis** is a summer resort and pilgrimage destination, with substantial hotels. The dull aspect of the place—heavily damaged in 1944—is all the more striking for the contrast it offers with the wine villages. **Munster** lies at the heart of a deep valley and is a convenient, although not very charming, base for walks and drives into the Vosges. The local tourist office can give information about a "cheese route" which takes you to rustic auberges and farms to taste and buy.

The southern section of the wine road lacks the charm of the north but is well worth pursuing to admire some splendid churches from the most individual period of Alsatian church building (the 12th and 13th centuries): at **Rouffach** (Notre-Dame-de-l'Assomption), at dull and industrial **Guebwiller** (St-Léger), and along the beautiful **Lauch Valley** which leads from here into the mountains from **Lautenbach** and **Murbach** both of which have beautiful churches. **Thann**, the terminal point of the wine road, suffers like Guebwiller the influence of industrial Mulhouse; but it too has a richly interesting church, one of the few important ones in Alsace in a fully developed Gothic style (15th-century). Its bell tower is tall and of celebrated beauty, its west doorways are teeming with sculpture, and the choir has lively and in many cases comic carved stalls.

The Vosges and the North

Despite their modest elevation (the Grand Ballon or Ballon de Guebwiller is the highest peak in the range at 1.424 metres) the Vosges have been an important mountain range historically, forming as they do the eastern rim of the wide Paris Basin and France's natural frontier. The mountains rise gently from the west to culminate more in a ridge than in specific peaks, then drop abruptly down to the Rhine plain.

North of the river Bruche which runs from near St-Dié to Strasbourg the Vosges hardly rise above 1.000 metres, or break through the thick covering of forest. Unaffected by the action of glaciers, the northern Vosges have kept their dark-pink sandstone, which characterises the architecture of Alsace from Wissembourg to Belfort. In the south, glaciers have worn away the sandstone leaving grey granite. Above the tree line there are open pastures with rounded mountain tops (called *ballons*). There are many attractive glacial lakes, and valleys which cut deeply into the mountain range. For all these reasons, and because of the panoramic **Route des Crêtes** which runs along the ridge at the very top of the Vosges, the southern part of the range is of greater interest to tourists. As well as being a magnificent evergreen fortress-topped backdrop to the wine road it is excellent walking territory where even the most leisurely stroller can reach the finest viewpoints, which will disappoint only those who hope to see as far as the Alps in summer—Mont Blanc is about 150 miles away and hardly ever visible between April and October. The serious walker can use the exemplary large-scale maps and guidebooks produced by the Club Vosgien. There are a few resorts in the mountains, or which Gérardmer, Le Hohwald and Les Trois Epis are the only three of any size, and Gérardmer the only one of any animation.

The Vosges drop almost as abruptly down to the Belfort Gap which separates them from the Jura as they do to the east. The **Ballons d'Alsace** and **de Servance** are the two southern bastions of the range, easily explored from the attractive Upper Moselle Valley on the Lorraine side, or from the southern end of the wine road in Alsace.

From **Thann** the Thur Valley leads up into the heart of the mountains through some fine scenery, with easy access to the peaks of the **Petit Drumont** beside the source of the Moselle, and the **Grand Ventron**. A more frequented road is the **Route des Crêtes** itself which climbs from **Cernay**, which has a steam train circuit. The Hartmanswillerkopf, or **Vieil-Armand**, was one of the most bitterly disputed strongholds on the Vosges Front in the First World War. There is an appropriately solemn memorial to more than 30,000 men who died here.

Soon after breaking through the tree-line into the high pastures (*chaumes*), the Route des Crêtes passes beside the unremarkable culmination of the Vosges, the **Grand Ballon**. There are long views from the top, and an orientation table with all the names in German from the time of annexation. Beyond **Le Markstein**, a modest ski resort at the junction of the Route des Crêtes with the road up from the Lauch Valley, the Route des Crêtes lives up to its name by following the open ridge at the top of the mountain range with views steeply down to the lakes and valleys below. For much of the way the road is just west of the crest itself, so as to be out of sight of the enemy—it was built to improve communications behind the front in the First World War. Some of the finest excursions in the region are to be made from **Munster** and other points along the Fecht valley (to the **Petit Ballon**, and the lakes of **Schiessrothried** and **Fischboedle**). From Munster a road climbs through the quiet balcony resort of **Hohrodberg** and joins the Route des Crêtes at the Col de la Schlucht (1,339 metres). Nearby there are several lakes and a large botanical garden of mountain plants (Haut-Chitelet).

Five hundred metres below the peaks and some ten miles beyond them into Lorraine. Gérardmer is the main Vosges resort which owes its long established popularity (it has the oldest tourist office in France) to the nearby lakes and forests—strewn with moss-covered boulders known locally as Gérardmer sheep—and to its convenience as a base for exploration of both the Alsace and Lorraine sides of the Vosges. The popularity is certainly not attributable to the town itself, which was systematically burnt and blown up in November 1944 and rebuilt without style. Lake Gérardmer, on the end of which the resort and textile town is built, is the largest in the Vosges, finely surrounded by hillsides of pine, and provided with all manner of amenities, including casino, campsites, boating, bathing, and fishing.

North of the Col du Bonhomme the Vosges are less individually distinctive. Le Hohwald is a tranquil resort (high up in the woods, as its name suggests) and a good walking base. The highest peak in the area is the Donon; from the top the view is extensive and it includes, just across the Bruche Valley, the concentration camp of Le Struthof where over 10,000 prisoners were exterminated between 1941 and 1944. It is a grim and memorable place to visit: there are guided tours around the considerable remains of the camp.

To the north of the Bruche, the Little Vosges, as they're called, present interestingly varied landscapes with the soft sandstone eroded into many impressively weird rocky shapes and cliffs, nowhere better admired than around the small woodland villages of Dabo and Wangenbourg (which have some accommodation). The ruined fortress and cascade of Le Nideck is a short walk from the road south from Wangenbourg to Niederhaslach, which has a large and harmonious Gothic church with splendid Zorn 18th-century choir-stalls. North of Dabo the attractive wooded Zorn valley is the easiest way through the Vosges via the Col de Saverne.

Alsace north of Strasbourg and the Col de Saverne is different. There are no more high mountain pastures, vineyards are outnumbered by hop fields—Haguenau is the great beer production centre—and the traditional old Alsatian villages are spacious and ordered, unlike the wine villages south of Strasbourg, huddled within their fortifications.

The old villages between Haguenau and the border town of Wissembourg are the most interesting feature of the area, as picturesque as the wine villages and considerably less affected by tourism. Local costume is often worn by old village folk, and not just to satisfy the coachloads. Hunspach, Seebach (ex-Oberseebach), and Hoffen are the pick of the villages: Hunspach especially spotless, colourfully best-kept, and ordered with the regularity of a garden suburb.

Wissembourg is a border town much frequented by German shoppers. Its old centre is cobbled and attractive with bridges over the several branches of the Lauter which thread through the town. The building of greatest interest is the Vosges-stone former abbey church of St Peter and St Paul, Gothic except for a single Romanesque tower, and with an enormous 14th-century wall painting of saint Christopher. Just opposite the church beside the river stands the so-called Salt House (15th-century) whose enormous roof is broken up by layers of windows like gills in a fish's scaly side.

The drive west along the German frontier is an attractive one, through vineyards (around Cleebourg) and steep wooded hills with occasional dramatically perched fortresses—**Fleckenstein** and **Falken-stein** are the most impressive. **Lembach** is one of the more attractive villages in the region and **Niederbronn** a substantial spa appreciated by the Romans but altered since, notably during the Second World War. It is a reasonable base for the area and has extensive accommodation. **Bitche** marks the end of the attractive landscape with some sombre Vauban fortifications.

Lorraine

For most tourists Lorraine (excluding its flank of the Vosges already described) is a region to cross with open eyes rather than to explore meticulously. The main points of interest are Nancy, a brilliant high-light of any journey through eastern France, and Verdun with its great battlefields and memorials. The spas of the south also have their appeal. This large and varied province is crossed by three major rivers running northwards—the Meurthe, the Moselle, and the Meuse.

From its source very close to the Col de la Schlucht on the Route des Crêtes, the young **Meurthe** runs down through the Vosges Forest powering sawmills as it goes. **St-Dié** is a substantial town which would be ugly but for its surrounding wooded hills. In 1944 it was burned down like Gérardmer, and is not beautiful to behold in its new form. But there is a trio of religious buildings of considerable interest: the cathedral is a handsome mixture of Romanesque, Gothic and Classical styles; and a mostly 14th-century cloister connects it to the simple and beautiful 12th-century church of Notre-Dame.

Etival-Clairefontaine has a mostly Romanesque and early Gothic former abbey church, and a summer week-end steam railway which covers the short distance to Senones. **Lunéville** lies near the confluence of the Meurthe with the Vézouse, whose course was diverted to enable the 18th-century duke Leopold of Lorraine to embellish the magnificent gardens of his equally magnificent palace, a small-scale Versailles in its day. It now houses a local museum with a fine collection of local 18th-century faïence and an audio-visual tribute to the local artist Georges de la Tour, one of the great masters of the French 17th century. There is a *son et lumière* in the park in summer and drama in the palace chapel. The town retains an 18th-century atmosphere; the church of St-Jacques is a rare and curious example of the Rococo style in France.

As it approaches Nancy the Meurthe becomes heavily and malodorously industrial. Chemical industries predominate to the south-east of town and the magnificent pilgrimage basilica of **St-Nicolas-de-Port**, a masterpiece of late Gothic architecture from the early 16th century, languishes in the dismal surroundings of an industrial suburb.

At the heart of this wide industrial basin, its flanks marked by bucket lifts for the transport of iron ore, lies **Nancy**. This historic capital of Lorraine is chiefly remarkable for the magnificent 18th-century architectural ensemble in the city centre, the Place Stanislas and the Place de la Carrière, one of the great artistic achievements of the period. The Place Stanislas is spacious and harmonious, with gracious palaces, a triumphal arch, leafy baroque fountains worthy of Rome, and wonderfully ornate gilt iron-work gateways and grilles and lanterns adorning the square like jewellery. The effect, especially when the square is lit up at night, is magical. On summer evenings you may visit, with musical accompaniment, the Hôtel de Ville which occupies the finest of all the palaces on the square. Beyond the triumphal arch the Place de la Carrière forms a noble complement to Nancy's brilliant centrepiece, and beyond that the medieval town with an old gateway and the Gothic ducal palace. Apart from these elements, most of Nancy is severe and characterless, having been laid on an ordered grid in the 16th century. It was left unfortified in the 19th century to save it from bombardment. Miraculously it escaped serious damage in both World Wars.

Place de la Carrière, Nancy

✳ *Fine Arts Museum* A good collection of 18th-century French paintings, housed in one of the palaces on the Place Stanislas with some big names from other periods. A sombre canvas by Delacroix depicts the Battle of Nancy (1477) where Charles the Bold, or more accurately Rash, of Burgundy, met his death trying to recapture rebellious Nancy, after attempting a siege of the town in mid-winter with no more than a few thousand ailing troops.

✳ *Museum of Lorraine History* A dauntingly large museum housed in the old ducal palace and covering all aspects of regional geography, prehistory, history, art, costumes and folklore. Items of particular interest include several paintings by Georges de la Tour and his studio, etchings and copper plates of another celebrated local artist Jacques Callot (illustrator of the religious wars in all their horror) and a series of 16th-century Flemish tapestries.

✳ *Church of the Cordeliers* A deconsecrated and dilapidated old church next to the ducal palace, which contains much beautiful funerary sculpture.

✳ *Nancy School Museum* A fascinating presentation of furniture, glasswork and ceramics in the organic style of the turn of the century—called Modern Style by the French—pioneered by Nancy craftsmen, especially the glassmaking family of Daum.

Just north of Nancy the Meurthe runs into the Moselle, setting it off on the least attractive section of its long and mostly pleasant course. The **Moselle**, the most important tributary of the Rhine, springs from the southern peaks of the Vosges and descends north-west through the unremarkably pleasant hillsides and woods of southern Lorraine, passing east of the area of spas. Each of these has its own particular curative speciality, and its own attraction as a quiet and peaceful town with extensive and in most cases comfortable accommodation in pleasant surroundings. **Vittel** is by far the largest and most developed of the spas, and especially restful thanks to the separation of thermal Vittel on one side of the railway line from the town on the other. The spa establishment itself has a casino and extensive sporting facilities (18 holes of golf; tennis; polo) which are set in a beautiful and spacious park. Nearby **Contrexéville**, its waters cold like those of Vittel, shares the pre-eminence and curative properties of its neighbour. **Plombières** and **Bains-les-Bains** are two smaller spas whose hot waters were exploited by appreciative and over-indulgent Romans. **Luxeuil-les-Bains** is larger, and of more varied interest. The waters of Luxeuil were known to Romans too and Gauls before them, but in the Dark Ages the town grew famous because of the great abbey founded there by the Irish missionary Columba among the ruins of the old Roman spa. For centuries it was among the most prestigious establishments in Christendom. The old abbey church is a handsome 14th-century building with a pink stone Gothic cloister, and there are a number of medieval town houses.

The waters of the Moselle itself have none of the mineral richness which have brought the sick and the merely languorous to Vittel and Contrexéville, but the river's course is pleasant enough to follow. **Remiremont** is worth a pause: the main street is lined with arcaded houses, some of them dating from the 13th century. **Epinal** is a large and unattractive town which was very badly damaged in the Second World War. But it has a very interesting museum with a varied and distinguished collection of works of art from Gallo-Roman sculpture to Georges de la Tour paintings.

After Epinal the Moselle is finished with the Vosges, and it is no great sadness to deviate from it to visit the magnificent and sumptuously furnished **Château d'Haroué** built shortly after Lunéville in 1720 by the same architect. A few miles further west an isolated horseshoe ridge, the **Colline Inspirée** rises hundreds of feet above the plateau from Sion to Vaudémont. For thousands of years it has been a place of defence and worship; Notre-Dame-de-Sion still attracts pilgrims in large numbers.

Toul is an important old town, one of the three great eastern bishoprics (the other two are Metz and Verdun), situated between the Moselle and the Marne-to-Rhine Canal. Despite war damage, Toul's tightly packed old centre has many houses of interest, and two splendid Gothic churches both with beautiful cloisters. The glory of the cathedral is its majestic flamboyant façade from the late 15th century, still richly decorated despite the mutilation of its sculptures during the Revolution.

Between Nancy and the Luxembourg frontier the Moselle runs through attractive country which has however become one of France's most important industrial regions, with coalfields to the east and iron ore deposits and steel industry installations to the west. There is not much here for the tourist.

Metz (pronounced Mess) is the very old regional capital of this partly German-speaking area of Lorraine, annexed in 1871. It has always been a crossroads and is one still, with motorway, railway and river junctions. Quite a lot of the town is high-rise from the post-war reconstruction, but all the waterways (the Moselle splits into several branches) give Metz a pleasantly spacious feeling, enhanced by the very attractive gardens beside the river. By the cathedral, the Place d'Armes is an imposing 18th-century ensemble with an arcaded town-hall.

✱ *Cathedral* This splendid cathedral is remarkable for the height of the nave (only surpassed by Beauvais and Amiens), and memorable for its wealth of brilliantly colourful stained glass from the 14th, 15th and 16th centuries.
✱ *Museums* Archaeology, painting, natural history, coin, prehistory, and frequent temporary exhibitions all in the same building near the Place d'Armes. The most important section is the archaeological one, full of beautiful pieces, and imaginatively presented to suggest many aspects of Gallo-Roman life.

The **Meuse** is born in border country between Lorraine, Champagne and Burgundy, not far north of Langres. Leaving the spas of Vittel and Contrexéville to the east it runs down into Joan of Arc territory, where there isn't much to see—a fact which doesn't stop many thousands coming to see it. Joan was born in January 1412, the daughter of a fairly well-to-do Jacques d'Arc of Domrémy (now Domrémy-la-Pucelle). She started hearing the voices of saints Michael, Margaret and Catherine in her father's wood—the Bois-Chenu—during the summer of 1424, and by summer 1428 was convinced of her mission to deliver the kingdom from despondency and the English. By February 1429 she had convinced the locals and the lord of Vaucouleurs who equipped her, and she set off dressed like a man with her hair cut short and with a six-strong escort on the road to Chinon, Reims, Rouen, and very rough treatment at the hands of the English and George Bernard Shaw. You can visit the simple peasant's house, where Joan is said to have been born, beside which there is a small museum.

From the glorious patriotic associations of quiet rolling farmlands which seem hardly to have changed since the days over 500 years ago when the ringing of the church bells, the waters of the fountain, and the rustling of the leaves in the forest all spake the same message to young Joan, the Meuse runs northwards to a land of less romantic if hardly less glorious associations, the battlefields of the Meuse hills where hundreds of thousands of Frenchmen laid down their lives to save their country in a war where heroism was anonymous, and where new limits of human endurance were discovered.

St-Mihiel occupies a key position on the river, tightly enclosed between hills. The German possession of the town from 1914 reduced Verdun's supply lines to one, the road north-east from Bar-le-Duc. As a town St-Mihiel is no beauty spot, but its past is illustrious. The town produced an eminent school of artists, of whom the greatest genius was the sculptor Ligier Richier (1500–1567); two of his works can be seen in the churches of St-Michel and St-Etienne, both featuring a swooning Virgin rendered with great pathos. To see the most celebrated example of Richier's work a short diversion westwards to **Bar-le-Duc** is necessary. In the church of St-Etienne prince René de Châlon is represented, at his own macabre dying suggestion, as a skeleton; the artist's brutal treatment of the decomposition of the body contrasts with its heroic pose, an intriguing mixture of artistic traditions.

The N35 road from Bar-le-Duc to Verdun is the famous Sacred Way, a crucial supply route in 1916 to the beleaguered city of **Verdun**. This road is the appropriate way to approach Verdun whose great interest is almost exclusively related to the battle where the fate of Europe was decided (see below). The cathedral is a strange mixture of Romanesque, Gothic and Classical elements. It has an elegant cloister and a Romanesque crypt, blocked up for centuries but unearthed by bombardment in 1916. Where there were no decorated capitals new ones were carved, with war as their theme.

Considering what it has witnessed, and the grim face of devastation is still worn by the battlefields nearby, the Meuse Valley north of Verdun is surprisingly pretty. It's the sort of spacious and fertile river valley you might describe as smiling if it didn't seem insensitive to do so. Along the river there is an interesting church at **Mont-devant-Sassey**, a large and beautiful one at **Mouzon** in the style of Laon cathedral and Notre-Dame de Paris and a kind of safari park with boars and bears at **Bel-Val** (near Beaumont-en-Argonne). East of the river there are interesting remains of Vauban's old citadel town of **Montmédy** and the pilgrimage church of **Avioth**. This is the most distinguished of the monuments in the area, a delightful building from the 14th and 15th centuries, built of a warm golden stone and set in a secluded valley.

The First World War

In terms of monuments no less than human life Northern France was tragically impoverished by two World Wars, which have given it a reputation for grim, grey and monotonous towns which add no joy to a journey through the region. Among the saddest casualties must be reckoned Coucy-le-Château, by all accounts and from old pictures one of the very finest old fortresses in France. Remarkably, most great buildings have been carefully and successfully restored; the great loss, which no restoration work can recover, is the charm and character of a flattened town. For all their sightseeing interest Amiens, Abbeville, Soissons, even Reims itself are unattractive towns which few tourists are sad to leave.

Yet, from the strictly tourist point of view, the effect of these wars, and especially the First World War, is not all negative. The war itself is the most compelling horror story of our time, and there is no better way to ponder the tragedy of those whom we have sworn never to forget than to visit the monuments nearby that mark the battlefields along the western front. In many places battlefield sightseeing is a matter for those with a particular historical or family interest, and a powerful imagination. The First World War memorials provide more than this, partly because the War itself is thought-provoking beyond the issues of international politics, partly because of the grandeur of the memorials themselves. While there is very little nourishment for French national pride in the story of the Second World War, in the Great War France triumphed at the cost of a whole generation – in 1915 alone France lost more soldiers than Britain was to lose in the whole course of the war, and that was before Verdun – and the national achievement is appropriately commemorated. The most impressive and vividly evocative war memorials are in the areas where the French achievement was greatest, that is to say around Verdun, which now has something of the sacred aura of a national pilgrimage.

Once the front had been established, by the end of 1914, in an unbroken line of entrenchments from the North Sea to the Vosges through Flanders, Picardy, Champagne and Lorraine, the scope for tactical manoeuvres was reduced to suicidal offensives against well-defended positions. The Germans rightly identified Verdun as the symbolic bulwark of France, which the French could not afford to sacrifice, and where her forces would be spent under the weight of German artillery. This opened up, with a bombardment of unprecedented intensity, on February 21st 1916. Throughout the spring and summer the few square miles north and east of Verdun were completely laid waste as the row of concrete forts—which had been built after 1870 to defend the city—and the hills beside the Meuse were lost and retaken at appalling cost and in infernal conditions. By November after a battle of eight months the lines were back almost to where they had been in February, and well over half a million soldiers had died. After Verdun it was the British turn: on the first day of the Somme offensive (July 1st 1916) which took some of the pressure off Verdun, 60,000 British troops were lost.

Verdun In the town there is a memorial to the battle, a solemn knight in armour resting on his sword at the head of a great stairway. Underneath, the monument books containing all the names of the participants of the battle are displayed. In Vauban's old citadel you can visit the underground galleries which were used during the Great War to shelter troops exhausted from the battle. The battlefields around Verdun are well signposted from the town, and there are organised tours. Of the many memorials around the battlefields east of the Meuse and north of Verdun, some of them no more than a small shrine where once there stood a whole village, the most evocative are the memorial museum at the point where the German line came closest to Verdun, in July 1916; the cemetery memorial chapel and ossuary at Douaumont; and two of the forts which were the most important strategic elements of the battle, Douaumont and Vaux.

The corners of French fields which are for ever England, Australia or Canada are in Flanders, Artois and Picardy. The memorials below are listed from north to south.

Notre-Dame-de-Lorette (near Arras) The summit of the Artois battlefields, with an orientation table, a huge cemetery and a museum.

Vimy Ridge (near Arras) An impressive Canadian memorial on a strategic hillside captured at heavy cost by Canadian forces in 1917.

Beaumont-Hamel (between Arras and Amiens) Scene of action of the Newfoundland Division, where many of the elements of the battle landscape are preserved or have been reconstructed.

Thiepval (between Arras and Amiens) British memorial arch of triumph.

Chemin des Dames A ridge, offering a commanding defensive position between Laon and Reims, which the French tried to storm in Spring 1917. The failure and cost of the operation, the exhaustion of the French troops after Verdun and news of the Revolution in Russia combined to provoke a wave of mutinies.

Hotels

Ammerschwihr, 68770 Haut-Rhin ££££

AUX ARMES DE FRANCE   Tel: 89.47.10.12

The unthinkable is happening—the winds of change are blowing at this solid and
heavily traditional establishment in a sombre village almost totally destroyed by
les armes de l'Allemagne. The portrait of the great Point (of Pyramide in Vienne)
still looms over gastronomic proceedings, but he has now been joined by Gaertner
senior, and young Philippe, whose creations are making quite an impression on
the *carte* and fixed-price menus (*canette au miel et aux épices, bar au pinot noir et aux
lentilles vertes*). Regulars, many from across the river, will still be able to eat *la
salade Fernand Point* (*foie gras*, lobster and truffles) and other old faithfuls, but
dishes are now easier on the digestion, if not on the pocket. The bedrooms are just
rooms above the restaurant, but comfortable.

Closed Jan and 10 days July (rest Wed. and Thurs lunch); 10 bedrooms; no lift.

Artzenheim, 68320 Haut-Rhin ££

AUBERGE D'ARTZENHEIM   Tel: 89.71.60.51

A colourfully adorned auberge in the centre of a quiet rural village just a few
miles from Colmar. The garden behind has a drinks terrace, swings and slide, and
lots of flowers. Bedrooms are neat, bright and simply furnished in rustic style.
Cooking is now less Alsatian (or German) and consequently lighter and more
exciting—though there are still plenty of classic dishes; fixed-price menus are
good value. It's altogether a restful and friendly place.

Closed mid-Feb to mid-Mar (rest Mon dinner and Tues); 10 bedrooms; no lift.

Colmar, 68000 Haut-Rhin £££££

TERMINUS BRISTOL   Tel: 89.23.59.59

A substantial hotel close to the station and the town centre, the traditional
location for traditional hotels and excellent cooking. In Colmar, tradition lives on.
Inside it is rather less than stylish, though the lounge is calmly comfortable, the
bar intimate and plush. Bedrooms vary in size, but are newly refurbished and
comfortable, well equipped and double glazed. There are two restaurants: the
simple "Auberge" has reasonably-priced menus and Alsatian specialities available
till a comparatively late hour; in the "Rendez-vous de Chasse", a place of serious
excellence, the food is inventive and good, in menus or à la carte. The wine list
caters for all tastes and pockets.

70 bedrooms.

Colroy-la-Roche, 67420 Bas-Rhin £££££

LA CHENEAUDIERE   Tel: 88.97.61.64

Large, traditional modern chalet, flower-bedecked and pretty, secluded among
pines near the centre of a small village in a quiet valley. It's in huntin-and-fishin
country, and you can either participate actively, or simply enjoy the produce at
table (from humble *pigeon ramier rôti en sabayon aux truffes* to the more noble *selle
de chevreuil à la fondue échalotes*—in season, of course). At the end of your
active, or passive, day you are cossetted in the rather chi-chi luxury of the salon,
or in the fine modern or Louis XV style bedrooms, some with balconies and
peaceful forest views. Dishes à la carte are not cheap, but the three-course simple
menu is more exciting than most in this region, and the execution also compares
favourably; the wine list is daunting, both in extent and price.

Closed Jan and Feb; 28 bedrooms; no lift.

Gérardmer, 88400 Vosges £££££

HOSTELLERIE DES BAS-RUPTS   Tel: 29.63.09.25

An ugly chalet block at the top of a modest pass, 4 km from Gérardmer. A
series of connected public rooms overlook only the road; they're spacious and
comfortable, with modern furniture and plants. Bedrooms in the main building
(some rather small) have balconies; those in the annexe are ground-floor. The
restaurant is plush, with soothing background music and simpering service.
Cooking is excellent—there are solid Alsatian dishes for cold, hungry days (*tripes
au Riesling, civet de joues de marcassin, gratin de munster frais sur salade*), and lighter
creations (*navarin de lotte au Pommard, fricassée de ris et rognons de veau* and
splendid desserts). There are several good-value fixed-price menus, including a
"surprise" five-courser.

14 bedrooms; no lift; tennis.

Kaysersberg, 68240 Haut-Rhin £££

CHAMBARD   Tel: 89.47.10.17

Pierre Irrmann has renovated a fine Alsatian house in this pretty village, to
provide accommodation for the serious eaters in his serious restaurant. The
bedrooms are luxurious; there's a smart breakfast area and bar in the basement,
and a comfortable salon; but the house lacks the feel of a hotel. In the formal
restaurant the atmosphere is relaxed, but the service could be better considering
the standard of the cooking (high) and the prices (not cheap).

Closed 1–15 Dec, and 1–21 Mar (rest Sun dinner and Mon); 20 bedrooms.

Kaysersberg, 68240 Haut-Rhin ££

REMPARTS   Tel: 89.47.12.12

An excellent, quiet, modern base-without-restaurant from which to sample the
serious cooking of Pierre Irrmann (above) at lower cost, provided you don't mind
a stiff walk, or a short drive, to the other end of the village. There's no salon, but a
bright and modern breakfast room and bar area, and pleasant bedrooms.

32 bedrooms; no rest; no lift.

Lapoutroie, 68650 Haut-Rhin ££

DU FAUDÉ   Tel: 89.47.50.35

A polyglot family-run hotel in a bypassed village just below the Col du
Bonhomme. There are two restaurants, one heavily provincial with patterned
wallpaper and stained glass, the other rustic with large fireplace and farm
implements. Bedrooms are plain but comfortable, food honest and reasonably
priced considering the hefty purchasing power of the starved Germans who
invade the area at weekends.

Closed mid- to end-Nov and Christmas; 27 bedrooms; no lift; covered outdoor
swimming pool.

Hotels

Marlenheim, 67520 Bas-Rhin £££
HOSTELLERIE DU CERF   Tel: 88.87.73.73

Marlenheim is a main road village at the top of the wine road and this rambling old (but very renovated) hostelry built around a cobbled flower-filled courtyard is set right beside the road. Most bedrooms are nevertheless quiet, and are more than adequate for comfort and décor. They have been renovated recently, as has the spacious restaurant. The service is still super-smooth, the food inventive and superbly cooked; there's a particularly good-value "businessman's" lunch menu, and a pleasing wine list.

Closed 3 weeks in Feb (rest Mon and Tues); 18 bedrooms; no lift.

Nancy, 54000 Meurthe-et-Moselle £££££
GRAND HOTEL DE LA REINE   Tel: 83.35.03.01

Dignified 18th-century palace on the glorious Place Stanislas, newly renovated and converted into a fine hotel. Most has been decorated and furnished *en style*— sober, refined and formal Louis XV, repro of course. The bedrooms are well-equipped and spacious, some with magic views out over the square, and the atmospheric bar has been decorated by Slavik (much in evidence in Paris). The restaurant is rather coldly formal, but the standard of cooking is high, and the fixed-price menus very good value—particularly the cheapest *menu du marché* which includes coffee and a bottle of wine.

54 bedrooms.

Obernai, 667210 Bas-Rhin £££
PARC   Tel: 88.95.50.08

A substantial new, but not modern, bourgeois establishment on the edge of old Obernai with conference facilities, massage parlour, jacuzzi, solarium, bowling alley, billiards and swimming pool, and lots of eurocratic limos drawn up for lunch. Young and widely praised M. Wucher strides about in pinstripes rather than apron, but the cooking shows no signs of neglect. There's a splendid (though not very cheap) *menu du marché*—5 courses, not including cheese—and a whole range of home-cured hams. Some bedrooms done up in *style Louis XV*, others large and modern in subtle pastel shades; all very comfortable.

Closed Dec (rest Sun dinner and Mon, and last week June); 50 bedrooms; swimming pool.

Ottrott-le-Haut, 67530 Bas-Rhin ££
BEAU SITE   Tel: 88.95.80.61

Picturesque village centre restaurant-with-rooms, a steep-roofed chalet with flowery terrace. Inside, the restaurant is more formal than you might expect, and the food, with many Alsatian specialities, is serious and far from cheap (though there are a couple of short, reasonable fixed-price menus). Bedrooms are simple, traditional and adequate; a couple have neither bath nor shower.

14 bedrooms; no lift.

Ribeauvillé, 68150 Haut-Rhin £££

VOSGES   Tel: 89.73.61.39

Restaurant-with-rooms situated right in the high street of this picturesque wine village, with a sparkling new glass frontage, and newly done-up bedrooms—all pretty and comfortable, with good bath or shower rooms. As for the *raison-d'être* of the place, the restaurant is solidly provincial with a subdued atmosphere, service is expert, and the cooking very good indeed. The *carte* includes few Alsatian dishes, but much that is inventive (*l'étuvée de homard au gingembre et citron vert avec pâtes fraîches, la bouquetière de ris de veau aux langoustines*); there's an excellent three-course cheap fixed-price menu, and a fine wine list.

Closed Feb (rest Mon); 18 bedrooms.

Rouffach, 68250 Haut-Rhin £££££

CHÂTEAU D'ISENBOURG   Tel: 89.49.63.53

Fine 19th-century pale stone château, looking out over the village of Rouffach and distant vineyards. Bedrooms (some huge) are superbly and individually decorated, with fine fabrics and antiques. There's an attractive salon, two dining rooms—one a barrel-vaulted cellar, the other with views and terrace for outdoor eating—and a bar; outside there's a beautiful courtyard garden, tennis and an attractive swimming pool with views. The service is impeccable, the standard of cooking is high, and there's a ruinous *menu dégustation* which includes champagne. Musical evenings are held here, and plans are afoot for helicopter and balloon tours.

Closed mid-Jan to mid-Mar; 40 bedrooms; swimming pool.

Strasbourg, 67000 Bas-Rhin ££££

DES ROHAN   Tel: 88.32.85.11

In the pedestrian precinct at the heart of old Strasbourg, fifty metres from the wonderful cathedral, this delightful hotel has been done up in 17th- and 18th-century styles. Bedrooms, almost all a good size, are individually decorated, attractive and traditional; 12 rooms have air conditioning. Downstairs there's a peaceful formal salon.

36 bedrooms; no rest.

Verdun, 55100 Meuse £££

HOSTELLERIE DU COQ HARDI   Tel: 29.86.00.68

Large, traditional, but far from boring hotel on a relatively quiet street corner, near the river and the brooding war memorial. It's well maintained in a heavy and rather overdone style (much Louis XIII), with choir stalls and galleries, Old Masters in the bedrooms and Neptune and Venus distinguishing Gents from Ladies. In the well-filled restaurant the service is formal and the cooking not confined to Lorraine specialities (*fricassée de crustaces au Sauternes, terrine de ris d'agneau aux pistaches*).

Closed Christmas and Jan (rest Wed); 40 bedrooms.

The Alps

"Mountains are the beginning and the end of all natural scenery" (Ruskin)

Characteristically French, Mont Blanc looks down on all Europe, from a height of 15,770 feet. At its shoulders the French Alps stand guard on the Italian frontier from the waters of Lake Geneva and Evian's Quai de Blonay to the Mediterranean and Nice's Promenade des Anglais, over 200 miles to the south. The area is one of outstanding natural beauty which amply compensates for its relative lack of cultural and historical interest; high mountain roads and cable cars make the spectacular mountain scenery, flora, and wildlife accessible to the least energetic sightseer.

A driving tour around the Alps can be very rewarding (given good weather), but you may be made to feel that there is more to holidaying in the mountains than mere absorption; and you may be stirred by the feeling that mountains exist not simply to be looked at but as a challenge. As you negotiate the steep hairpin bends of some lofty alpine pass your sense of achievement may be dulled by all the toiling cyclists you pass on the way up. For them the climb means much more than a pretty view. And as you stand in a cable car, with sandals on your feet and no more than a single lens reflex slung round your neck, you may find that you are squashed physically and morally by a cabin-load of heavily booted climbers with ice axes poking accusingly out of 40lb packs. They use the dizzy cable car station as a point of departure, the mechanical transport as a way of missing out the tedious part of their trip.

The Alps are also a favourite playground for sports people who are no more than keenly recreational. High up in the mountains the mostly modern and functional ski resorts try to make up for their intrinsic lack of charm by laying on all manner of sports facilities for summer tourists. In a few it is possible to ski all the year round on glaciers. In many more you can ride, swim, play tennis, hang-glide, sail, boardsail, walk on marked paths and of course take mountaineering lessons. At the foot of the range, resorts on the big alpine lakes are no less well equipped.

For many tourists the great outdoors of the Alps does not mean pushing the body to new limits of endurance, nor spending all day every day for two weeks on the polyathletic facilities of highly organised resorts. It means getting away from other people, to enjoy nothing more sophisticated than clean air, beautiful flowers, birds and beasts—and of course the sublime landscape. Two of the highest mountain areas have never been inhabited by man and they are now preserved from all development as national parks; here it is possible to walk for days, staying in refuges, and to appreciate the environment not so much unspoilt as almost unsoiled by the intrusion of humanity. Alternatively you can stay in greater comfort in one of the resorts at the gates of the park and make short forays into nature's kingdom. If you're not such an ecological purist, and actually like the trappings of civilisation—meadows, farms, rustic villages, cowbells—you can more rewardingly and comfortably explore the countryside outside the national parks. Regional parks present a balance of protected environment including traditional architecture and crafts, controlled development for the comfort and pleasure of tourists and, of course, for the prosperity of the locals.

The Alps

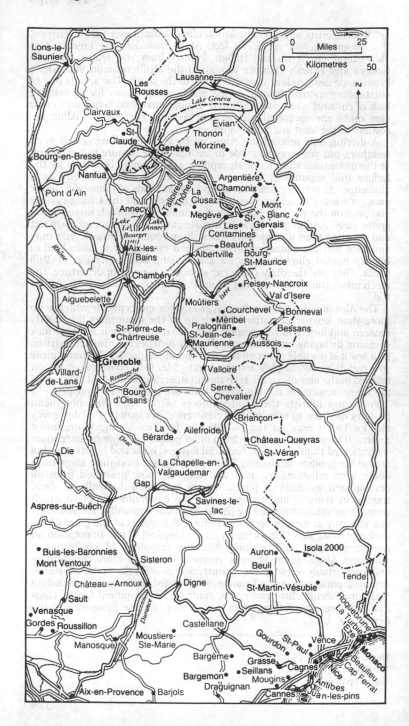

If one side of the alpine coin bears the image of an iron-calved practitioner of the cult of physical and thus moral well-being, the obverse shows a wheezing invalid, gazing at the mountains from afar in the hope that some of their natural strength and vigour might rub off, breathing the pure mountain air and bathing in the richly impure mountain water for the alleviation of all manner of ills. Ironically, perhaps, the Alps have a much longer history as a resort for the sick than for the fit. Spa towns such as Aix-les-Bains, where Romans came to take the waters, and St-Gervais have in the past been as full of the infirm as the ski resorts are now of the emphatically firm. But it is possible to exaggerate the proto-funereal quality of the important Alpine spas; the surrounding area is so full of natural beauty that the abundant tourist facilities in the spas themselves attract large numbers of holidaymakers with no interest in the cure. Evian and Aix-les-Bains in full summer season are fashionable lakeside pleasure grounds—with concerts, theatres, regattas, galas and sporting events—as much as they are spas. St-Gervais is situated on the shoulder of Mont Blanc so the scenery and excursion possibilities are superlative. Even the infernally dull Brides-les-Bains, which specialises in the treatment of obesity and which is a match for any spa in France for cheerless institutional architecture and atmosphere, is not a bad place to stay for exploration of high valleys on the edge of the Vanoise National Park—although it would be unfair to expect too much of its gastronomic resources.

Many people choose to go to the Alps simply to tour around and look. The mountain massifs themselves differ greatly, and the transition from north to south can be remarkably abrupt. The north (the old duchy of Savoie and part of the Dauphiné) has glaciers and eternal snow-fields with brilliant white peaks soaring above the lushest and most colourfully floral of alpine pastures, grazed by plump bell-ringing dairy cows. Communications are good via the main valleys—steeply walled, with fast flowing rivers, main roads and sizeable industrial towns exploiting hydro-electric power. The valleys of the Arve, the Isère, the Arc and the Romanche are all (in parts at least) much more industrial than you might expect of the Alps, and the unpleasant contrast with nature undefiled in the higher mountain areas is often accentuated by the thick smoggy cloud which hangs around in the valleys when the peaks are in brilliant sun. But there are towns of charm and interest—Grenoble, Chambéry and Annecy—and at the feet of the high mountains the deep glacial lakes—Geneva, Annecy and Le Bourget—are beautiful in colour and context.

In contrast the snowless, grey and rocky southern (Dauphiné) Alps seem harsh and forbidding although hardly less impressive. The south is crossed by fewer deep river valleys; communications are less good and development much less advanced. Many of the high valleys remain extremely isolated. The southern Alps may not be the place to go for comfort and the most charming alpine scenery, but it is a fine region for escaping and exploring, and has more reliable weather than the north.

The two areas differ historically, too. In the north, the counts, later dukes, of Savoie established control in the early Middle Ages, and exploited the strategic value of their dominions—which they soon extended into modern Italy—to maintain their independence of French sovereignty until 1860. The Savoyards then voted overwhelmingly to join France, probably because the ruling house of Savoie, from the 15th century onwards, had gradually shifted its power base towards Italy, to the neglect of Savoie proper. Only in 1946 with the abdication of the last king of Italy, called Humbert like the first count of Savoie in the 11th century, did Europe's most durable dynasty yield the reins of power. The Dauphiné was sold to the French crown in 1349 by its profligate rulers the dauphins de Viennois, in a deal whereby the heir to the French throne ruled in Dauphiné with the title of dauphin.

Until the late 18th century nature in its mountainous manifestation was considered unfriendly. Then, in the romantic period, a radical change of taste in landscape in favour of the awe-inspiring coincided with increasing glacier exploration in search of crystals and for reasons of scientific curiosity. The Geneva scientist de Saussure reached the summit of Mont Blanc in 1787 (without a rope and in a long-tailed silk coat) and spent four hours there conducting experiments. Wordsworth was at Chamonix admiring the glaciers in 1790, Shelley in 1816. The race to conquer new peaks and more and more difficult rocky needles gathered speed, with intrepid British Victorians setting the early pace; many peaks still bear their names. Throughout the 19th century thousands of tourists followed royalty to the spas (Queen Victoria went to Aix) and pushed on up into the mountains to see nature's cathedrals. They didn't explore much further than the Mont Blanc massif, with Chamonix and St-Gervais at its feet being easily accessible and offering such spectacular mountain scenery. In de Saussure's words "majestic glaciers, separated by great forests, crowned by granitic rocks to an astonishing elevation, carved into gigantic obelisks and intermixed with snow and ice, offer one of the grandest and most remarkable spectacles that it is possible to imagine. The cool, pure air that one breathes, the high cultivation of the valley and the pretty hamlets one passes, gives the idea of a new world, a sort of earthly paradise". Chamonix and Aix-les-Bains—witnesses to this period of discovery—still have a Victorian style and charm.

Style and especially charm are qualities notable for their absence in the majority of French alpine resorts, in contrast to the abundance of traditional rustic villages and painted wooden chalets in Austria and Switzerland. Houses are more often built of rough stone than timber, and their balconies are more likely to be piled high with winter fuel than with colourful flowers. Old wooden villages high up in the pastures do not exist in many places in France; where they do they have rarely developed into resorts; where they have (for example at Val d'Isère) the development has been neither well thought out nor sightly. More typical has been the creation of new resorts out of nothing (as at Courchevel, Tignes, Les Arcs) situated and planned for the maximum convenience of winter sports people, occasionally with some concern for stylistic uniformity but inevitably with no more charm or soul than a railway station. Self-catering is more popular among holidaymakers in the Alps than in any other French region, particularly in the modern resorts which have more apartment blocks and supermarkets than hotels and restaurants, and tend to be dreary in the evenings. The summer season does not start before July nor extend beyond early September. Having no permanent population they are not so much quiet out of season as boarded up.

Because of the hardy outdoor nature of alpine holidays, accommodation in most places caters for tourists of simple tastes, with the notable exceptions of some hotels in Evian, Talloires, Megève and Chamonix. Sadder and more surprising than this shortage of expensive luxury hotels is the rarity of homely and welcoming chalet-style establishments with cheerful window boxes, chamois heads over the log fire and cow-bells ringing in the background. The region does not rank high for gastronomic tourists, either, though again there are some notable, if expensive, exceptions.

To enjoy the Alps in the summer, good weather is no less essential than it is on the Côte d'Azur. It is also considerably less predictable because of the meteorological effects of abruptly high mountains. In general the northern Alps are colder and wetter than the southern, but there are remarkable local variations of microclimate. It is not unusual for one side of Mont Blanc to be cloudy and wet, the other bathed in sunshine.

The unpredictability of the weather, with not infrequent summer snowfalls at high altitude, can affect the practicalities of driving around the Alps. You can be fairly sure that all roads will be open from late June to late September; but at any other time there's a risk that high passes may be impassable because of snow (and accurate information is to be had only very locally). Remember that even in midsummer melting snow may freeze on the highest roads overnight. But motoring is generally more tiring (for driver and car) than actually dangerous or frightening.

The Savoie Lakes

Banana shaped **Lake Geneva** (Lac Léman) is by far the largest and deepest of the alpine lakes. It is too big to be really attractive (you very often can't see across it except at the thin Geneva end). On the south (French) shore the mountains of the Chablais climb steeply from the waterside behind **Evian**—of which the 19th-century poet Gautier wrote "no decorator ever set a scene with such a marvellous understanding of effect than Evian is set by pure chance".

The town which climbs the wooded hills behind the lake is one of France's most important spas, producing three hundred million bottles of water every year, and one of its most lively. The beneficial properties of the local water supply have been known for centuries, but private ownership of the château and waterside prevented the growth of a resort until the late 19th century. In place of the château they built an exotic domed casino, and spread a handsome spacious promenade (the Quai de Blonay) in front of it. In nearby gardens the thermal spring, particularly noted for its effect on the temperamental imbalances of middle age, is clad in mock-Japanese architecture; behind, a few crowded streets are squashed into the small space between lake and pre-alpine hillsides. A redundant funicular, villas and palatial (in size at least) hotels in spacious gardens climb the slopes in a rather suburban way. To stay full, Evian hotels have had to court conference business which has inevitably detracted from such elegant exclusiveness as the resort may once have had. But at least it's full of active people, there are all kinds of sports facilities including riding, tennis, golf, and sailing (with annual regattas and tournaments), and there is plenty going on in the evenings. Evian is also a very good place for boat trips around and across the lake and coach excursions into the mountains and even as far afield as Venice.

East of Evian towards Switzerland stretches the most interesting section of rocky *corniche* road. **Meillerie** is a particularly attractive unspoilt old fishing village situated below impressive cliffs celebrated by

Byron and Rousseau. On a clear day you can see right across the deepest part of the lake (over 900 feet), where Byron nearly perished in a storm, to the picturesque turrets of the 13th-century Château de Chillon on the Swiss shore, where the dukes of Savoie imprisoned many of their enemies.

From Evian to the Swiss border a few miles east of Geneva the lakeside flattens and the main road, not cramped beside the water's edge, passes through prosperous farmland and vineyards; some of the most prestigious and picturesque of these surround the handsome turrets of the first duke Amadeus' château/monastery of **Ripaille**, which is open to visitors, but is best admired from outside. **Thonon** is another spa familiar to mineral water drinkers. It is the main town of the region, set high on a platform above the lakeside, and has more everyday life than Evian. Of the two adjacent churches in the busy town centre, the basilica of St-François de Sales is the more interesting, for its series of huge canvases illustrating the Passion painted by Maurice Denis in 1943. Nearby in the old château looking out over the lake a local folklore museum has been installed. Below the town is an attractive grassy promenade and port, and a small beach along the road to Ripaille. West of Thonon there are some more bathing resorts, Excenevex and Sciez (which provide as good an opportunity as any to remind you that in the Alps final xs and zs are silent) and the exceptionally pretty and meticulously kept walled and fortified village of **Yvoire**, a very popular destination for Swiss boat trips and usually crawling with admirers. Most of the old chalets are crêperies and souvenir shops.

Annecy

Lake Annecy must be one of the most perfect landscape compositions anywhere. Its colour is a deep milky azure. The twists and turns of its shoreline give constantly changing views as you drive or sail round. Its size is just right too: not big enough to present a monotonous expanse of water, not so small that the variety of rocky cliffs, snowy peaks (usually), and wooded ridges seems oppressive. Elegant residences, classy restaurants and comfortable hotels are strung enviably around the leafy lakeside. Decorative, unconvincingly fortified castles jut out into the water and survey the whole from on high. The lake's water is renewed only very slowly, and a lot of work has been necessary to clean it up; strict controls have been imposed on the use of motorised boats.

At the head of the lake lies **Annecy** itself, one of the most attractive old towns in the Alps, and certainly a showpiece of the French part of the range. It's a busy and prosperous town whose recent rapid growth has luckily not spoilt the look of the lake. Not surprisingly it's a very popular place to live in as well as visit for a holiday. Annecy town has a delightful old (mostly 15th-century) very best-kept centre, with a powerful castle looking down over the waterways, arcaded streets and bridges gaily decorated with flowers. Beside the lake itself there are spacious lawns and gardens and a majestic avenue of venerable plane trees. Swans usually do their bit to complete the scene. From the town you can take boat trips round the lake as well as swim, boardsail and pedalo.

Talloires is the lake's quality resort. Its situation is superb, looking across the narrowest part of the lake (which was originally split into two at this point) at Duingt's castle in the water at the foot of the elegant Taillefer mountain ridge. The village itself is pretty, and celebrated for the cluster of prestigious hotels and restaurants along the waterfront.

Excursions around Lake Annecy

✱ Tour round the lake From **Veyrier** you can take a cable car up the precipitous cliff face of the Mont Veyrier. **Menthon**, overlooked by its splendidly situated castle (open to the public), is mostly residential and peaceful. The climb up behind Talloires to the **Col de la Forclaz** and down the other side to Vesonne just south of the lake is not one of the most spectacular climbs in the Alps but it is certainly one of the most attractive, giving splendid views of the lake (especially if you come from Vesonne to Talloires), and passing through such charming high pastures (alps, to give the word its proper meaning) that you wouldn't be surprised to see Julie Andrews come tripping and trilling over the brow of the hill. Due south of the lake a forest road leads down the dark wooded **Combe d'Ire**. Apart from the **Château de Duingt** the west shore is less interesting, but gives good views of the more spectacular mountains on the other side of the lake. Even better ones are to be had by driving up through the woods which clothe the Semnoz mountain to the **Crêt de Chatillon**. From the top there is a wonderful panorama of the highest peaks of the French Alps, and from further down of the lake itself. There are a number of paths for woodland walks on the mountains.

✱ Aravis Massif The mountains between Annecy and the Mont Blanc massif offer some of the most restful pastoral scenery in the French Alps, with attractive wooden chalets, their balconies brilliant with geraniums. **Thones** is a good base for not too strenuous woody walks, and also the odorous market place for Reblochon (the creamiest of alpine cheeses). Another good base is the long-established winter and summer resort of **La Clusaz**, set among steeper and higher mountains. From the **Col des Aravis** there is an excellent view of the nearby Mont Blanc massif. Some of the most attractive scenery in the area can be enjoyed by taking the indirect route from Thones to La Clusaz via the **Col de la Croix-Fry** and the Manigod valley.

The largest and deepest lake that is entirely French, **Lake Le Bourget** suffers by comparison with Lake Annecy although it was much more celebrated in the 19th century because of the popularity of Aix-les-Bains. The lake is surrounded by less interesting mountains than Lake Annecy but is nonetheless a very pleasant place for a holiday: as well as boat trips on the lake and climbs up into the neighbouring mountains there are beaches and a variety of sports facilities arranged in a number of places around the lake, notably at **Aix-les-Bains**. The great spa, traditional peak of luxury and fashion in the Alps, now seems more traditional than fashionable or even luxurious, but it does not merely live off the memory of its illustrious visitors (two French Empresses and Queen Victoria): in season there are open-air plays and concerts, sporting events including golf, regattas and racing, and even nightlife outside the portals of the inevitable casino. Along the lake spacious gardens are laid out behind the beaches (admission charged) and port. This is the area of play, popular at weekends with the inhabitants of nearby Chambéry. The serious heart of the spa, with its heavily grand casino and hotels and the modern buildings of the thermal establishment (open to the public), is set some way back from the water, and is also pleasantly laid out with gardens at the foot of the Mont Revard. The hill isn't appreciated by all *curistes*, and many hotels lay on special bus shuttles to the baths. For the uninitiated a visit to the baths is of great interest, and there are some Roman remains within. Nearby there is the interesting Dr-Faure museum, with 19th-century paintings of high quality and Lamartine memorabilia.

Excursions from Aix-les-Bains

* **Abbaye de Hautecombe** Splendidly situated on the edge of the lake, this large abbey and necropolis of the Savoyard dynasty is most attractively accessible by boat from Aix-les-Bains (several trips daily). It was extensively re-decorated in the 19th century in an entertainingly extravagant romantic Gothic style with sugary sentimental monuments to the princes and princesses, so it clashes in no way with the atmosphere of Aix. You can attend mass to hear the Gregorian chant.

* **Tour round the lake** The western side is the more interesting. From the quiet waterside resort village of **Le Bourget-du-lac** the route climbs up the side of the Mont du Chat; after you turn off the main road to cross the **Col du Chat** it winds high above the lake through rustic and panoramic farmland.

* **Mont Revard** From Aix to the small resort of **La Féclaz**, there's a delightful drive through wooded mountains with views of the lake on one side and the highest Alps on the other.

* **Chambéry** Animation in this dignified old capital of Savoie is centred on the elegant arcaded main shopping street (Rue de Boigne): an amusing fountain of massive elephants stands at one end and the old ducal château at the other. Guided tours round the château—like visits to the Savoie and Fine Arts Museums—come into the rainy-day category. Of more specialist interest is Les Charmettes, a country house just outside Chambéry, where Jean-Jacques Rousseau spent several years and which has been preserved as a memorial museum to the romantic philosopher.

* **Lac d'Aiguebelette** A popular and relatively small clean lake south-west of Chambéry with good bathing and fishing.

The Savoie Alps

South of Lake Geneva the pre-alpine mountains of the Chablais climb steeply from foothills of vineyards. The highest peaks of this region are modest by alpine standards (under 2,500 metres) and unspectacular. But the region is a pleasant one of green valleys and wooded slopes, fairly characterised by the name of the local breed of dairy cattle, *Abondance*. **Morzine** is the most important winter and summer resort, unexciting but not unattractive and enjoying a very pleasant spacious setting at the meeting place of several high valleys. There are very extensive possibilities for walking and motoring excursions all around, and good sports facilities. The best drive of all from here is over the mountains to Samoëns, splendidly varied with its succession of ever-green woods, high pastures, the sudden appearance of Mont Blanc at the pass, and the steep descent down through orchards. **Samoëns** is an attractive old village and resort in the valley. From here it's only a short drive up the river to its head—the soaring jagged **Cirque du Fer à Cheval** (horseshoe). From the café at the bottom of this spectacular amphitheatre riding excursions are organised.

No less rewarding but certainly not for the faint-hearted is the long walk over the mountains from Sixt to the Arve valley between Sallanches and Chamonix. Most tourists take the road, which leads to the industrial and often smoky section of the Arve at Cluses. A motorway relieves you of the need to spend long down here, but it is worth stopping at **Sallanches** for one of the most celebrated views of Mont Blanc, which towers over 4,000 metres above you at a distance of no more than $13\frac{1}{2}$ miles. From Sallanches there are some very attractive excursions up into the hills which flank the Arve on both sides. The north side is more frequented, with lots of holiday institutions around the **Plâteau d'Assy**, which has an exceptional modern church consecrated in 1950 (Notre-Dame-de-Toute-Grace)—the product of a collaboration between many of the world's leading artists.

Until recently the road up the steep mountainside to the narrow gateway into Europe's most spectacular valley, de Saussure's "earthly paradise", was one of the most tedious in the Alps, a constant nose-to-tail of labouring juggernauts on their way up to the Mont Blanc road tunnel and Italy. Now a motorway, built in dramatic projection from the mountainside, lifts you out of the industrialisation as if your car were suddenly capable of flight. As you approach Chamonix the summit of Mont Blanc is obscured by the nearer peaks which rise so steeply from the widening valley floor that you are not surprised to learn that this is the world capital of *alpinisme*, the parochial French word for climbing even in the Himalayas. It is no longer Mont Blanc itself that brings climbers here. Its ascent, as any alpinist will tell you, is really just a long walk. Chamonix's pre-eminence as a climbing centre is owed rather to the spectacular array of jagged spindly rock needles (*aiguilles*) which line up at the shoulders of the serene, rounded white peak and divide Italy from France like a wall crowned with deterrent spikes. No less spectacular are the glaciers that cascade from on high like frozen waterfalls. Since the last century they have been in retreat but one—the glacier des Bossons—still descends well through the tree line towards the valley floor.

Apart from a few modern buildings **Chamonix** still looks very Victorian, and although the atmosphere is in no way old-fashioned it remains as it has been for over a hundred years—an unpretentious, bustling resort, full (often very full) of climbers and mere tourists.

It is impossible not to be infected in Chamonix by the spirit of

adventure which must have reigned in the town in the last century when mountaineering was pioneering, rather than the search for technical difficulty for its own sake which it has subsequently become. A fascinating and entertaining companion is the guidebook to Chamonix and the range of Mont Blanc, first published in 1896 and recently re-issued, written by the great Victorian mountaineer and explorer Edward Whymper, who died in Chamonix on September 16th 1911 and who lies buried in the English church there. There is also a museum devoted mainly to the history of alpinism and the conquest of local peaks, with old equipment and fascinating photographs—including one of the aged professor Janssen who had an observatory built on the very summit of Mont Blanc (it soon disappeared in the snow and ice) and was carried up to the peak by bearers. In the old days tourists were borne up the hillsides on donkeys to the most famous viewpoints. The favourite viewpoint of one of Chamonix's most enthusiastic devotees, John Ruskin, on the way up the Brévent, is still commemorated. Nowadays there are all sorts of mechanical ways of getting uphill, many of them almost as breath-taking as the panoramas they unveil.

Excursions from Chamonix and nearby resorts

* **Aiguille du Midi** This astonishingly engineered cable car climbs from Chamonix at about 1,000 metres to over 3,860 metres in two stages, the second of which is spectacularly precipitous. From the middle station there are walks down to Chamonix. The top, where you will notice the sudden change of altitude and temperature, is for views across the chain and down to Chamonix, and the sight of climbers setting off further upwards towards Mont Blanc—still over 1,000 metres higher. In good weather the lift will take you across the glaciers of the Vallée Blanche to the Italian side of the chain and thence down to the Aosta valley. Rather than taking all the cable cars twice, which is very expensive, take a bus from Chamonix through the Mont Blanc tunnel in the morning and return by lifts over the mountain range. Don't forget your passport.

* **Brévent** A two-stage cable car from Chamonix's north side giving the most famous view of Mont Blanc itself. The top half is worthwhile for the excitement of the ride alone: the cable car spans an enormous chasm. From the half-way station there are good walks down to Chamonix and along the Balcon de Merlet to La Flégère.

* **Flégère** A two-stage cable car from Les Praz (to the east of Chamonix). There are splendid views from both the half-way station and the snowy top (which has some summer skiing) of the most famous of all the Mont Blanc glaciers, the Mer de Glace, which snakes languorously down from the Vallée

Blanche towards Chamonix. There are good walks from the half-way station.

* Montenvers From the middle of Chamonix a rack railway climbs to the very edge of the Mer de Glace, the classical excursion into glacier territory for over a century. You can wander around on the ice and admire its remarkable colour, visit a grotto (which has to be re-carved every year) within the glacier itself, and see a small zoo where alpine fauna are rather sadly cooped up.

* Nid d'Aigle Accessible by rack railway (Mont Blanc Tramway) from St-Gervais or indirectly from the cable cars which link up with it from Les Houches in the Chamonix valley. This is the beginning of the easy way up Mont Blanc, a mere two days' walk (return) from here. There are shorter walks from the top of the railway to the Glacier de Bionnassay, with extremely impressive high mountain scenery and more gentle walking terrain around the Col de Voza where the St-Gervais and Les Houches lifts meet.

The trouble with Chamonix is that it is always crowded, even in the months when the rest of the Alps are very empty. The Swiss end of the valley is no less beautiful and much more peaceful. **Argentière** and **Le Tour** are attractive old villages and ski resorts with character and a glacier each. **Le Lavancher** is a particularly relaxing hamlet of old chalets with a couple of hotels and superb views. The name, a common one in the Alps, means that this is a place for avalanches. The head of the valley is surprisingly gentle; a road leads over the hills to Switzerland and gives magnificent views back down the Chamonix valley with the towering Aiguille Verte in the foreground above Argentière, and Mont Blanc behind.

Unless you catch the lifts up and over from Les Houches, you have to descend from this "earthly paradise" to reach the old spa resort of **St-Gervais** on Mont Blanc's western shoulder. It is of the same vintage as Chamonix but much less lively. On all sides of St-Gervais there are splendid excursions on foot, by car or cable car or railway. Among the finest is the road up to **Le Bettex** and the cable car onward up the Mont d'Arbois. From St-Gervais the Montjoie valley leads up to the pleasantly spacious resort of **Les Contamines**, steeply overlooked by the glaciated mountains on the Mont Blanc side, but green and pleasant on the west. A track leads on up to the **Col du Bonhomme**, once a frequented route across to Italy. It's a long walk from Les Contamines to the Italian resort of Courmayeur but there are refuges to stay in on the way. This is just one section of the classic walk all the way around the Mont Blanc massif (the *Tour du Mont Blanc*). Whymper describes it and says that a sturdy pedestrian can achieve the walk round the range in no more than four days. Today's *Guide Michelin* says that you should allow between 10 and 12 days, and advises allowing three days to get from Les Contamines to Courmayeur. So much for the evolution of species.

Still benefiting from splendid views of the Mont Blanc range, **Megève** enjoys a much friendlier setting of relatively gentle wooded slopes around the spacious valley. It's one of the earliest and still one of the most fashionable of French ski resorts, and has sprawled far and wide, with substantial chalet-style villas and hotels. The centre is attractive, with its smart shops and fur-coated clientèle, and there are extensive and not too strenuous walking possibilities and sports facilities.

From Megève the river Arly leads down into the cheese country of the **Beaufortin**, through dark wooded gorges. At the bottom of the road, at the junction with the busy commercial and industrial artery of the Isère valley, **Albertville** has a couple of highly reputed restaurants and a rather neglected old walled town on the hillside above it (**Conflans**), which is well worth a wander. It's gradually coming to life again, with craft shops and restoration of the old houses.

The main road along the deep Isère valley gives access to the new generation of French ski resorts high up in the Tarentaise and Vanoise regions south of the river. From each town along its course a road leads steeply up to one of the mountain playgrounds—Méribel, Courchevel, La Plagne, Les Arcs, Val d'Isère. Apart from the extremely attractive rough stone Romanesque basilica beside the road at **Aime**, the road itself reveals little of interest. Of the larger towns which punctuate it, **Moutiers** is the most animated and pleasant, with a large dirty cathedral by the market place. From here roads lead up to the Trois Vallées area of Courchevel, Méribel and Les Menuires/Val Thorens. This, according to its own publicity, is the largest ski domain in the world, but isn't much frequented in summer when the only skiing is at the dismally functional resort of **Val Thorens**. **Méribel** is the least unattractive of the modern resorts, beneath green and open slopes, with lots of sheep enjoying the off-piste grazing.

Much more suitable as a summer base for pedestrian exploration of the **Vanoise National Park** is **Pralognan**, a steeply enclosed climbers' and hikers' resort just on the edge of the park. Guided excursions, from stiff walks to glacier ski tours and rock climbs, are graded and priced according to difficulty so there is something for nearly everyone. The church at nearby **Champagny-en-Vanoise** contains a richly carved and painted altar-piece dating from the early 18th century.

Steeply pitched above the Isère valley and Bourg St-Maurice, **Les Arcs** is a carefully planned new resort catering for all needs unless you require the place to have character. The little old villages of **Peisey** and **Nancroix**, on the other hand, have hardly any facilities but charm and character in abundance and a local costume festival in August.

From **Bourg-St-Maurice** one road winds up to the **Col du Petit St-Bernard** and Italy; buildings of an old hospice founded according to a legend by saint Bernard in the 10th century stand as tribute to the former importance of the pass and still show the damage inflicted when the border was disputed in the Second World War. A long steep and stony scramble gives access to the **Pic de Lancebranlette** and splendid views of the south side of Mont Blanc and its attendant *aiguilles*. An easier way to enjoy the same view, although from a much greater distance, is to explore the mountainsides (with the help of cable cars) above the neighbouring resorts of **Val d'Isère** and **Tignes**, also accessible by road from Bourg St-Maurice. The two villages together constitute one of the world's most famous and extensive ski areas. Val d'Isère is no beauty spot, but at least has the old rough stone houses of the original village, grouped around the handsome belfry of its typically Savoyard church. Since skiers moved in though, Val—as it is known to its habitués—has spread up and down the narrow valley apparently without the expenditure of much planning effort. Tignes has been built from nothing, up in a desolate bowl high above the tree line and a large reservoir (where the old Tignes used to be), at the foot of the graceful Grande Motte, one of the Vanoise's highest and finest peaks (3,656 metres). However unfriendly the skyscraper colonies may seem, Tignes is much frequented in summer as the best place in France for summer skiing, and has an enormous range of sports facilities on land, in the air and on water. It is also a convenient base for access to the Vanoise National Park. One of the few roads within the park itself climbs from Val d'Isère up across increasingly bare mountainsides to Europe's

Ibex, sure-footed on the highest rocks

highest pass, the **Col de l'Iseran** (2,770 metres). There are high banks of
snow by the road in early summer (it usually opens in late June) and
glacier skiing near the top of the pass.

At the foot of the steep and awesome descent to the Arc valley,
Bonneval is one of the most attractive villages in the Alps, whose
primitive charm has been carefully preserved. Rough, rusty-coloured
stone houses huddle close together as if for warmth beneath the
towering treeless mountainsides. Firewood is stacked thick on the
balconies. It is not difficult to imagine the severity of the winters here.
Just outside Bonneval, there is a new village offering accommodation to
climbers and hikers who explore the mountains on the Italian side of the
valley from here. There are several equally attractive villages along the
Avérole valley which joins the Arc near the substantial farming village
of **Bessans**, whose church and nearby chapel contain woodcarvings and
frescoes, both of which are particularly interesting features of this
valley. The decorative richness of the churches of the Arc valley have
much to do with its traditional importance as a route across the Alps via
the Mont Cenis pass to Susa and Turin. Napoleon was responsible for
building the present road in the early 19th century; it replaced a mule
track which had borne so many Grand Tourists towards Italy and the
art treasures of Rome, just as many years earlier it had brought Italian
artists north. The pass was celebrated for the local custom of sending
travellers downhill by sledge, which clearly didn't die out with the
engineering of the road. Murray's Handbook of 1838 describes the
thrilling downhill service which enables travellers to descend 600
vertical metres in less than ten minutes, probably about one-tenth of the
time they would spend going up the same distance.

At the bottom of the Mont Cenis road, the isolated chapel of St-
Sebastien in **Lanslevillard** has remarkably vivid and melodramatic
frescoes depicting the martyrdom of saint Sebastien and Life of Christ.
Further down the valley, **Termignon, Freney** and **Aussois** give access to
the Vanoise National Park, and have some accommodation. Near
Aussois, the narrow steeply walled valley is blocked by the grimly
powerful fortifications built by the Savoyards in the early 19th century
as defence against the French. Other local aggressors included wolves:
near Modane in the late 18th century, one pounced out of the forest,

and carried off Horace Walpole's dog while he was on his way to Italy with the poet Thomas Gray. **Modane** itself is a dull town, and the Arc, as it grows, gets increasingly industrial. Rather than following it down to where it joins the Isère many miles from their adjacent birthplaces, take one of two splendid mountain drives south to the Dauphiné and the Romanche valley

From **St-Michel-de-Maurienne**, it's about 20 miles to the spectacular **Col du Galibier** (2,645 metres) past **Valloire**, a traditional old alpine village, which has managed the transition into a well-equipped summer and winter resort without the sacrifice of too much character. Its church is remarkable for the richness of its decoration. Local costumes are occasionally to be seen, notably for a procession on August 15th. By alpine standards, the cathedral at **St-Jean-de-Maurienne** is of great interest; the decorative carving of the late 15th-century choir stalls and panelling is notable. From St-Jean one of the most varied and attractive drives in the Alps climbs through narrow wooded gorges to emerge into spacious grassy high pastures dotted with old chalets. The adjacent **Col de la Croix de Fer** and the **Col du Glandon** give very fine views respectively south to the peaks of the Ecrins and north to Mont Blanc. There are dramatic gorges (the **Combe d'Olle** and **Défilé de Maupas**) on the way down from the Glandon to Bourg d'Oisans.

The Dauphiné Alps

Grenoble, the most important city within the Alps, owes its development to the space afforded by the confluence of the wide valleys of the Drac and Isère, and also to the boom of alpine industry fuelled by hydro-electric power. Its dynamic period culminated in the 60s with the build-up to the Winter Olympics of 1968, when it was *the* French town for whizz-kid engineers and planners. Grenoble has a rare combination of high-rise modern building and impressive mountain backdrop, perhaps more characteristic of Denver, Colorado, than European Alps; most of the modern building is on the edge of town, bounded by motorways and ring roads. The old centre is tall and severely 18th-century in aspect, and much more busily commercial than Chambéry. Grenoble's big university, and its convenience for winter sports, have assured the town's popularity with foreign students and kept it young and up-to-date. The most interesting monument of avant-garde Grenoble is the fine arts museum, which as well as some old masterpieces contains a varied collection of modern art. The other image of dynamic Grenoble—ancient and modern—is the gondola cable car system which spans the Isère from the old part of town and whisks you up to a rocky citadel built by Vauban. Just outside Grenoble, the **Château de Vizille** is less renowned for its contents (mostly 19th-century) than for the memory of the meeting of the Dauphiné estates which took place here on July 21st 1788. The resolutions passed at the meeting, objecting to Louis XVI's autocratic government, set something of a trend for the rest of France.

South-west of Grenoble the wooded slopes of the Chamrousse massif climb steeply from the green and peaceful spa suburb of **Uriage**. **Chamrousse**, custom-built at the tree line, is Grenoble's ski resort, and has little attraction in summer, except to masochistic weekend cyclists.

The pre-alpine massif of the **Vercors** is fairly tame by high mountain standards but climbs with impressive and forbidding steepness from the Isère Valley. Once you penetrate these outer walls, the Vercors (citadel of the resistance in the last war and theatre of bitter fighting) is green and gentle for the most part, full of cyclists and coffee-coloured cows. **Villard-de-Lans** is the most important resort: sprawling, unsophisticated, perhaps a trifle dull, but pleasant and not too purpose-built, catering for recreational tastes both leisurely and energetic. Cable cars take you up towards fine viewpoints over the whole Vercors range and eastwards to the high Dauphiné Alps. Near Villard-de-Lans there is a particularly fine series of gorges which make a practicable circuit for a day's round-trip in a car. It is a very different kind of scenery from the high Alps, more like the Massif Central, enclosed and dark with views more often down to roaring torrents than up to the open sky. Most spectacular of all are the **Grands Goulets** where river and road squeeze through what seems like a crevasse in the mountain, barely penetrated by the light of day, and the **Combe Laval**, a hair-raising 2,000ft drop to the river Cholet from the **Col de la Machine**, with a road precariously cut into a gallery in the apparently overhanging cliff face. At the western end of the **Gorges de la Bourne**, the houses of **Pont-en-Royans** are built into a rock face dropping down to the water.

Seen from Grenoble, the sharp ridges of the **Chartreuse Massif** rear up like an angry sea. Unlike most of the Alps, the area is one of dense and partly deciduous woodland, which means that the autumn landscape is particularly beautiful. Like the Vercors it is a favourite weekend retreat for the Grenoblois, but there are few resorts or places to stay. **St-Pierre-de-Chartreuse** is attractively situated and has some accommodation. Nearby the crest of the **Charmont Som** rises above the trees to give an extensive panorama. The famous **Grande Chartreuse** monastery was founded in the late 11th century by one Bruno, in what he considered to be safe isolation from the world. The monks comforted themselves in their chilly solitude by brewing up the famous Chartreuse liqueur— using over a hundred herbs. The recipe remains secret and the monks (there are still about 40) maintain their isolation. But you can visit a small museum about monastic life at the entrance to the grounds, and at **Voiron** you can visit the distillery and taste. The circuit round monastic territory (called the Desert), from St-Pierre-de-Chartreuse via St-Laurent-du-Pont and St-Pierre-d'Entremont, passes through some of the finest and most varied scenery in the massif.

Leaving the Vercors southwards by the **Col du Rousset**, you experience an abrupt landscape transition from the lush green domestication north of the tunnel to the comparatively barren hillsides which extend southwards. A long way below lies **Die**, less distinguished by its old ramparts than by the local sparkling wine (*Clairette*). In contrast to the dry and stony mountainsides, the land down in the valleys around Die itself and along the road to Châtillon is pleasantly shady and fruitful, with vineyards and orchards. **Archiane** is a tiny rustic hamlet in the pit of a deep theatre of mountains, excellent for strenuous walks.

One of the most extraordinary peaks in the Dauphiné and one of its traditional seven wonders is the **Mont Aiguille**, admirably seen from the road north to Clelles. In 1492 the ascent of its stubby chimney-like summit was achieved with the aid of ropes and ladders, at the express command of Charles VIII, to discover whether there really were angels on top, as was reported. This remarkable and apparently isolated early rock-climbing feat revealed only chamois and flowers. Eastwards the increasingly austere mountain countryside is relieved by the V-shaped **Sautet reservoir**. Here you encounter the Route Napoléon—a mostly fast main road which commemorates the Emperor's return from Elba in

1815. Although the road is rarely spectacular it is a quick and interesting route from the Mediterranean coast to Grenoble.

The long, steeply enclosed **Valgaudemar** joins the Drac just below the Sautet reservoir, and gives access to the Ecrins National Park and the highest French peaks outside the Mont Blanc massif. The walls of the valley are so steep that from most of its floor you can't see very much (the village of **Les Andrieux** is said to be deprived of sun for a hundred days a year) but it's certainly impressive and a popular base for climbers. **La-Chapelle-en-Valgaudemar** is the place to stay; there are fine walks as well as climbs. To the west of the Drac valley, the **Dévoluy** is a little-frequented area with some fine walking. In the high basin ringed by jagged limestone there's some self-catering development. The valley of the **Drac Blanc** is comparable to the Valgaudemar in steepness and rocky severity. On the more vegetated Drac Noir, **Orcières** has some accommodation and wide open walking territory high above it, if you don't mind the pylons and scarred hillsides of ski resorts in summer. The country over the **Col de Manse** towards Gap is altogether more open and pastoral.

Gap itself is aptly named for any itinerary, but being an important crossroads it is difficult to avoid. The Gap/Briançon (and thence Italy) road, which is busy with lorries and caravans, skirts and crosses the large and impressive **Serre-Ponçon reservoir**. The small resort of **Savines-le-Lac** is charmless but well organised for watersports and camping. A quiet road runs down the west side of the lake, giving good views of it and a curious local phenomenon of *Demoiselles Coiffées* (bonneted maidens)—pillars of soft rock each saved from total erosion by a boulder which still sits on top. South of Savines the splendid forest of Boscodon is rich in elusive chamois; failing a glimpse of these, there's an old abbey to visit and panoramic belvederes. **Embrun**, an important old town long before the damming of the Durance, is impressively situated on a ledge above the river. The 12th-century cathedral of Notre-Dame is interesting and Italianate, with its black and white stone and marble columns supported by lions.

Beneath Vauban's disturbingly empty geometric fortifications at **Guillestre** you must choose whether to pursue the Durance up to the Vallouise and the **Ecrins National Park**, or the Guil into the no less attractive Queyras Regional Park. The **Vallouise** is relatively full of tourists and climbers. **Ailefroide** is a good and attractive place to stay at the foot of the mighty Pelvoux, and gives easy access to the glaciers and lofty peaks of the Ecrins.

The **Queyras Regional Park** is a beautiful dead-end corner of the French Alps, closed off from Italy and Briançon by a wall of 3,000 metre peaks. The attractions of the region are its good sunshine record, exceptional floral richness and peaceful high pastures which make excellent starting points for high-altitude walks. At **St-Véran**, one of the highest villages in Europe (2,000 metres), the air is rarefied and the combination of resort and delightful rustic village of wooden chalets rarer still. The chalets are set in south-facing tiers to maximise their sunlight; the walks and views across the valley and up it to Italy are excellent, with grassy slopes full of horses and cows.

In the Aiguilles valley, **Aiguilles** and **Abriès** are lower and attractively situated winter and summer resorts. A good road up into the bare hills around **L'Echalp** launches walkers towards the Monte Viso. Lower down, the valley is plugged emphatically by the **Château-Queyras**, which despite Vauban's restoration still looks like a medieval fortress on

St-Véran

a hillock complete with turrets, rocky backdrop and village cowering at its feet. The drive over the **Col d'Izoard** to Briançon is one of the most exciting in the Alps—though it's not hair-raising, unless that is how you react to the sudden transition from familiar pine woods to the savage, stripped desolation of the upper slopes of the Queyras side of the Col, the Casse Déserte. The Briançon side of the pass is hardly less fine.

Briançon, sitting on a hill at another strategic river junction, has been an important stronghold since pre-Roman times. Vauban built the impressive walls and gateways which still surround and guard the substantial old town and defy you to attempt to drive round its maze of narrow streets. Vauban was also responsible for the cathedral, which is hardly more decorative than the ramparts.

The road back to Grenoble from Briançon is a major one. The winter and summer resort of **Serre-Chevalier** is a long, barely characterised sprawl beside the road giving access to extensive wooded and higher mountainsides; there is plenty of potential for walkers and for sports (including riding and tennis) down on the valley floor. As you drive up towards the **Col du Lautaret** the hillsides gradually shed their forest clothing and open out into spacious green pastures with magnificent views of the glaciated Ecrins Massif, which now shows its most famous profile, the Meije, towering above the village of **La Grave**. The setting, more than anywhere else in the French Alps, is comparable to Mont Blanc/Chamonix, but La Grave—although an important climbing resort—isn't an endearing place. A new cable car goes up the shoulder of the Meije to over 3,000 metres and the glacier's edge. Ski touring is possible from the top; walking is best from halfway. The classical view of the Meije is from an oratory at Le Chazelet just behind La Grave. A more extensive if less picturesque panorama is revealed from the Col du Galibier (2,645 metres), well worth the detour.

Another favourite base for climbers in the Ecrins is La Bérarde, at the end of the road up the overbearingly enclosed Vénéon valley which takes you deep into the heart of the massif. La Bérarde was the top recommendation of the celebrated American conquistador of alpine peaks, WAB Coolidge, who appreciated the variety of climbs that can be accomplished from it without having to spend the night under the chilly stars. From the valley and from La Bérarde itself there are a number of walks suitable for the merely hearty (notably the Tête de le Maye).

On a high plateau above the Vénéon, reached by road from the Chambon reservoir in the Romanche valley, Les Deux Alpes is one of the Dauphiné's few important custom-built ski resorts, which like those in the Vanoise attracts summer tourists for sports including skiing, riding, tennis, skating, swimming and judo. Another is L'Alpe d'Huez across the Romanche valley, accessible by means of a hairpin road up the almost sheer valley wall from Bourg d'Oisans. There isn't much to choose between the two resorts. From Bourg d'Oisans back to Grenoble the Romanche valley is very industrial.

Hotels

Le Bourget-du-Lac, 73370 Savoie   £££££

OMBREMONT   Tel: 79.25.00.23

About 2 km from Le Bourget, the substantial Ewardian-style house has splendid gardens sloping down to the western side of the lake and a good swimming pool. It's spacious and comfortable, though not consistently stylish; big windows make the most of the view. All the bedrooms are large and quietly luxurious, some with balconies overlooking the lake. The restaurant is elegant, and there's a delightful terrace for outdoor meals. The standard of cooking is well above average for this area, and there's a reasonably cheap four-course (not including cheese) fixed-price menu.

Closed Dec to mid-Feb (rest Mon lunch, and Sat lunch out of season); 20 bedrooms; no lift; swimming pool.

Bresson, (near Grenoble), 38320 Isère   ££££

CHAVANT   Tel: 76.25.15.14

Not an easy place to find, just out of Grenoble (on the D269c), but well worth the trouble. Quiet, genuinely not urban, and very relaxing. Cool, stone-floored, spacious and comfy sitting room round a huge fireplace, a very pleasant leafy terrace for good weather, and panelled dining room with another big open fireplace. The ledger of a wine list is as picturesque as it is unwieldy; many prestigious four-figure bottles, rather short on inexpensive ones. There's a renowned Armagnac collection. Bedrooms mostly very comfortable, but varied in style and some showing signs of wear.

Closed Dec 25 to 31 (rest Sat lunch and Wed); 8 bedrooms; no lift.

Chamonix, 74400 Haute-Savoie   £££££
AUBERGE DU BOIS PRIN   Tel: 50.53.33.51

Much more agreeable (and more expensive) than the established hotels in the town centre, the Bois Prin is a luxury modern chalet, situated aloof from the bustle of the resort in quiet gardens near the Brevent cable car, with fine walking possibilities and a splendid view of Mont Blanc. Bedrooms are very comfortable; guests can use the swimming pool and tennis court of the Albert 1er, under fraternal ownership.

Closed mid-May to mid-June and mid-Oct to mid-Dec (rest Wed out of season); 11 bedrooms.

Faverges-de-la-Tour, 38110 Isère   £££££
CHÂTEAU DE FAVERGES   Tel: 74.97.42.52

A fine château—part medieval, part 19th-century—set in 37 hectares of grounds, with tennis courts, swimming pool, fitness room, and golf course (plans for nine holes this year). It's all very comfortable indeed—salons, barrel-vaulted dining room, shady terrace for eating out on fine days, and a fine marble-columned entrance hall with sweeping staircases. Bedrooms are very spacious, and individually decorated; there's a cottage tucked away in the grounds for those who seek a more rustic style (cheaper, too). The food isn't cheap (though there's a reasonable fixed-price three-course weekday lunch menu:), but the standard of cooking is well above the average in this area and the service is very good.

Closed mid-Oct to April (rest Mon except in July and Aug); 43 bedrooms; swimming pool.

Lanslevillard, 73480 Savoie   ££
LES PRAIS   Tel: 79.05.93.53

A family-run mountain chalet set in the hills just above the village and resort in the Vanoise National Park. There's a comfy salon with open fire, rustic bar and restaurant, a small swimming pool with children's slide and swings, and small but perfectly adequate bedrooms (some with small baths). The cooking is well above average for a mountain area: in addition to classic hearty fare (*fondue, raclette, jambon*) there's a creamy *fricassée de volaille aux herbes et tagliatelles*, a good *magret de canard aux baies de genièvre* and fine *tartes*. Guided walks in the Vanoise are offered twice a week. Studios and apartments are available in a nearby annexe.

Closed mid-Sept to mid-Dec and mid-April to mid-June; 29 bedrooms; no lift; swimming pool.

Manigod, 74230 Haute-Savoie   £££
CHALET CROIX FRY   Tel: 50.02.05.06

High on the Col de la Croix Fry, this is an all too rare example of the sort of chalet that you long to find, managing to combine simple homely atmosphere with comfort and facilities. Accommodation is either in the main chalet, or in smaller and delightful individual ones (with kitchenettes) nearby which range from studio-size to space for nine people. All is spruce and pretty, with log fires and cow bells ringing in the background. Food is simple and homely, owners friendly. The attractive swimming pool is an unexpected bonus, as are the special terms for self-catering chalets which operate out of high season.

Closed spring and autumn; 13 bedrooms; no lift; swimming pool.

Hotels

Nantua, 01130 Ain   £££
FRANCE   Tel: 74.75.00.55

Food is the fame of Nantua and of the Hôtel de France. A meal here is more likely
to broaden your girth than the horizon of your experience, unless your previous
quenelles de brochet sauce Nantua have been the ubiquitous stodgy, tasteless insults
to the fish and the place; there is nowhere better than this for a really pikey one,
and few better for a *poulet de Bresse, aux morilles* if the time is right. The France is
bang in the centre of the small lakeside town, which is a very noisy thoroughfare
for traffic bound for and from Geneva (things should improve greatly when the
new stretch of the A40 motorway opens this year). Bedrooms are spacious,
comfortable and pleasant, and soundproofed up to a point. Apart from the very
dowdy bar and breakfasting area, this is a warmly traditional place.

Closed Nov to mid-Dec (rest Fri, except Feb, July and Aug); 19 bedrooms; no lift.

St-Gervais-les-Bains, 74170 Haute-Savoie   £
LE CHALET RÉMY   Tel: 50.93.11.85

About 3 km and 550 metres above St-Gervais, near the cable-car station of Le
Bettex, this is a totally delightful old chalet, in fine walking country, with superb
views towards the Mont Blanc massif. There's a sun-trap terrace for drinks and
meals, a small bar and a large welcoming dining room; bedrooms, under the
eaves, are small, basic and cosy—none have private bathroom. Classical music is
played from compact discs, about which Madame is only too happy to talk
enthusiastically. Food is very simple and hearty—it's better (and may be cheaper)
not to opt for the pension menu and terms, as you may miss the good *raclette*.

10 bedrooms; no lift.

Valloire, 73450 Savoie   ££
LA SÉTAZ   Tel: 79.59.00.03

Valloire is an old village and modest ski resort, tucked away in a secluded bowl
high up above the Maurienne valley, beside the road up to the very high Col du
Galibier. La Sétaz is in the centre, a modern wood-clad building with a garden,
children's play area and attractive swimming pool. Bedrooms are more than
adequate, some family size with folding-down beds. There's a TV-dominated
salon, and a pretty pink restaurant with a glassed-in terrace. The *carte* and the
reasonable fixed-price menus feature more fish dishes than is usual in the
mountains; the proprietor Jacques Villard is an ambitious chef and a good host.

Closed mid-Sept to 20 Dec and mid- to end-April; 22 bedrooms; no lift.

Villard-de-Lans, 38250 Isère   £££
LE CHRISTIANIA   Tel: 76.95.12.51

Big modern chalet in a quiet residential area outside the town centre, with views
over tennis courts, municipal swimming pool and mountains. There's a pretty
garden, swimming pool, large and comfortable salon and two dining rooms—
each with their own outdoor terrace; all is light, airy and attractive, as are the
bedrooms, in traditional rustic style, with good bathrooms. The cooking is
inventive; we enjoyed an excellent *fricassée de lotte aux pistils de safran*, followed by
a fine *gâteau au chocolat, sauce à la menthe fraîche*.

Closed May, Oct and Nov; 25 bedrooms; swimming pool.

Corsica

Bonifacio

"Nor stones, nor timber, nor the art of building constitute a state; but wherever men are who know how to defend themselves, there is a city and a fortress" (Alcæus)

Corsica

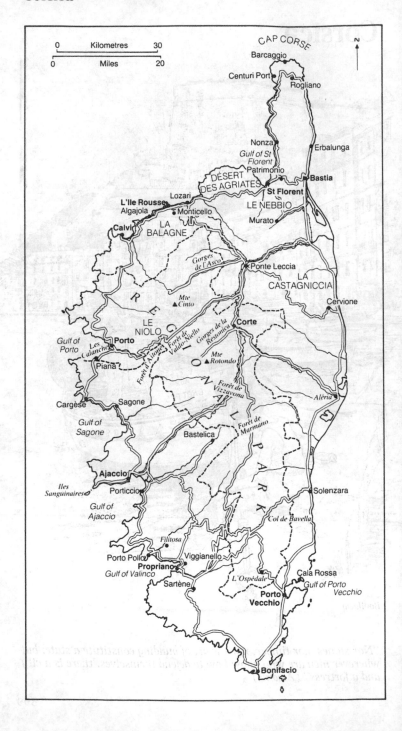

A hundred miles of Mediterranean separate Corsica from mainland France: once or twice a year in certain weather conditions a mirage of its mountains can be glimpsed from high points of the Riviera. Superb mountain scenery rising to great peaks (the highest over 9,000 feet) takes up much of its 3,367 square miles, and its centre is a Regional Park. Geology made its western coast more beautiful than that to the east, and divided it into many distinctive areas. Geography gave it a coveted position in the busiest part of the western Mediterranean, and history brought successive invaders to its coasts, driving its inhabitants inland or abroad in a pattern that formed the extremes of Corsican character.

Greeks, Etruscans, Carthaginians and Romans were followed by Vandals, Byzantines and Saracens before Christian powers disputed possession in the early Middle Ages. The Papacy gave it to Pisan bishops, but after a century or so of gentle rule the naval supremacy of the Genoese took over. They encircled the island with fierce little watchtowers and created citadel towns which were effectively Italian colonies. The Genoese shook off invasions by the king of Aragon (another Papal protégé) and the French (involved in a struggle with Charles V), and had comparatively little trouble with the Corsicans themselves, who suffered (or ignored) a feudal régime of their own. The Corsican seigneurs' idly autocratic habits of aggrandisement and vendetta finally produced a rebellious national consciousness, born of poverty and frustration. If Napoleon Bonaparte had never existed, Corsica's most famous man would be Pascal Paoli, who returned from exile in Italy with plans for a coup, a constitution and a Corsican democracy. He inspired and directed Corsican energies, and for 14 years the island achieved a beleaguered independence. By 1768 the Genoese had had enough; preoccupied elsewhere, they ceded Corsica to France. French troops defeated Paoli, but nationalism was unsuppressed: the English sent a supporting fleet, and the future admiral Nelson learnt a lot of strategy (and lost an eye) in subsequent events. But in 1796, post-Revolutionary France settled Corsica in two *départements* following the old Genoese division of *"en deça des monts"*, ruled from Bastia, and *"au delà des monts"* under Ajaccio. Later, Napoleon made the island a single unit with Ajaccio as its *préfecture*; since 1975 it has been divided back again, into Haute-Corse and Corse-du-Sud.

Nearly half the islanders are corsophone, although few are exclusively so; there are two dialects, the north-eastern one more Latin, and the south-western one closer to the primitive Pyrenean languages. The resident population is far outnumbered by the 400,000 expatriates, many of whom are careful to keep a place on the electoral registers and return regularly to vote. During the last 20 years the Corsicans' strong sense of regional identity has sharpened into angry and frequently violent separatism, as local feeling has in so many places. Whether the increasingly violent modes of expression are signs of increasingly widespread separatist feeling in the population as a whole is doubtful. An opinion poll in 1975, at the height of the troubles, indicated that over half the population was satisfied with Corsica's constitutional status, a large minority wanted a greater degree of autonomy within the Republic, and only 3 per cent wanted independence. The clandestine *Front National pour la Libération de la Corse*, responsible for most of the acts of terrorism, was estimated to have numbered no more than a few score activists and a few hundred supporters. In 1982 Corsica was duly granted a greater degree of autonomy than it had previously enjoyed, and than any other French region, and there are signs of diminishing enthusiasm for acts of violence, at least in the cause of separatism.

Corsica is a collection of landscapes, each with its own characteristics. In the north-east, rugged grey schist rock forms the long spine of Cap Corse and the complex relief of the Castagniccia's ridges and valleys. The larger central mountain mass is many-coloured granite in giant tilted blocks; powerful rivers have gouged out valleys through the parallel ridges, and erosion has produced dramatic distorted configurations. In the west the ridges slope to a coast of bays and promontories; to the east they drop down to a flat plain behind a much straighter shoreline. There are Alpine pastures among the high central peaks, above slopes of magnificent pines; lower down, rich chestnut forests and fertile valleys where vines, olives and orchards can flourish. The famous Corsican *maquis* covers over half the island—an evergreen and often impenetrable mass of low-growing trees, shrubs, climbing plants and fragrant herbs, scented all year and flowering brilliantly in early summer. A less attractive, but now all too frequent, feature of Corsican landscapes is the black stubble and skeletal shapes of lifeless trees produced by forest fires.

For centuries, the Corsicans retreated inland from their invaded coasts. They lived in mountain communes, shepherding huge flocks up and down according to the season, farming land only to provide for minimal needs and building from local materials the villages which vary so attractively from region to region. Poverty, pride and what amounted to imprisonment in their own country produced both lethargy and the high tension of internal vendettas. Those who could went abroad—emigration was the only route to fortune. Despite their resentment at being handed over to the French, Corsicans took full advantage of their new status—Napoleon was among the first to benefit from French education and opportunities for advancement. The island grew ever poorer and more neglected as its younger talent departed to careers in France, particularly in the police, the army and the colonial service. After the Second World War much coastal land was cleared of its malarial mosquitoes, but government grants to develop Corsican agriculture chiefly benefited immigrants from Algeria, able and willing to apply modern methods to farming the fertile eastern plain.

Tourism in Corsica is a comparatively recent phenomenon, concentrated round the tiny fishing villages (*marines*) of the coast and further depopulating the interior—except when expatriate Corsicans return for summer family reunions. Fine beaches and the Mediterranean climate have attracted increasing crowds over the last twenty years, and holiday accommodation is now crammed to capacity each season. French and Italian visitors predominate, but an increasing number of British too are discovering the wild beauty of the island. Development is still low-key; the cost of importing materials and consumer goods is high, and holidays in Corsica not cheap. *Cuisine*, though French, is not *haute*. Food in the resorts is more often basic and international—steak, spaghetti, ice cream. Fish is varied but expensive. Corsican food includes game in season, sheep and goat cheeses, chestnut-flavoured sweetmeats, pâté made from black-birds and a variety of *charcuterie* from the island's small native pigs—hams, smoked fillets, sausages of pigs' liver. Regional cooking tends to be more strongly spiced and herby than that of the Midi. Wines range from fruity

402

whites to powerful reds, and there are local *eaux-de-vie* and liqueurs like *cédratine*, made from Corsica's variant of the lemon. Shops under the name "*Produits Corses*" sell ethnic eatables, while "*Maisons Artisanats*" promote the island's traditional crafts, as distinct from mass-produced souvenirs.

Unless you are content to stay on your idyllic beach, you need a car for exploring. Public transport is limited, and coach trips inadequate for the lure of the magnificent mountain scenery. Roads inland are plentiful, but driving is a test of skill and patience; even the central artery from Ajaccio through Corte to Bastia has its steep hairpin bends, and the lesser narrow roads are tortuous and very tiring. Corsicans seem to drive with the venom once reserved for vendettas, and use signposts for target practice and graffiti. Distances have nothing to do with how the crow flies – the tourist must crawl with caution, and on a long excursion carry spare petrol. The scenery is ample reward.

The West

Corsica's biggest bay, the **Golfe d'Ajaccio**, is the arrival point for many British visitors whether by boat or into the island's biggest airport. The great curve of busy blue water with a backdrop of mountain slopes is best seen from the point at **Porticcio**, a bright little modern beach resort on one of the sandy coves spreading south; the rocky north shore of the Golfe ends at the Pointe de la Parata and its Genoese tower. Out to sea are the little **Iles Sanguinaires**, the largest topped by an old lighthouse: from land or by boat excursion they are especially appealing in the glow of sunset.

Ajaccio is tucked into the north-west corner of the Golfe on its own bay, with a citadel—built by the French when the town was predominantly Genoese—as menacing to landward as over the sea. The high blocks of Ajaccio's modern skyline give it an air of urban sophistication rare in Corsica, and its busy streets are lively and commercial by day, illuminated and conversational at night. The division of Corsica in 1975 into two *départements*, giving Bastia equal status, has not diminished the pride of a town that takes its name from Homer's Ajax and bred the greatest modern Frenchman. Napoleon confronts you everywhere. Near the port in Place Maréchal-Foch his statue, classically robed, is guarded by four lions drooling into the fountain below—the surrounding palm trees and café life are less reminiscent of Trafalgar Square. In the vast Place de Gaulle, Viollet-le-Duc's monument (locally known as The Inkstand) has him on horseback in his toga, above his four (unmounted) brothers; and further west he surveys the town from a long flight of steps, in the familiar cutaway coat and bicorne hat. The main shopping street (the Cours Napoleon) borders Ajaccio's Old Town, a small appealingly shabby area of tall houses below the citadel—which is an army barracks and not open to the public. The 16th-century cathedral is unremarkable; the Buonaparte tombs were moved to their own "Imperial Chapel" near the Palais Fesch.

✳ *Maison Buonaparte* Guided tour (compulsory) of Empire-style rooms with genealogy, busts, photographs of portraits: little of real interest.
✳ *Musée Fesch* Notable collection of Italian paintings from five centuries assembled by one of Napoleon's uncles: includes Bellini, Botticelli, Titian, Canaletto. Closed (prolongedly) for renovation.

From Ajaccio the N193 heads off into the island's interior, the inland route to Bastia on the north-east coast followed also by one of the most scenic railways in the world. For drivers the first 20km up the river Gravona is an untypically fast introduction to Corsican mountain roads; another 10km brings you up to the **Col de Vizzavona** at about 3,500 feet, where there is a ruined Genoese fort and tremendous views. Beyond lies the **Forêt de Vizzavona**, where the steep slopes below the snowline are covered with *laricio* pines. Immensely tall, straight and strong, their trunks were used for ships' masts—and at one time imported by England to be chopped into railway sleepers. Before the watershed of the Col, the spreading hamlets of **Bocognano** among pines and beautiful chestnut trees formed one of the last bandit strongholds. In a domain called "the green palace" the Bonelli dynasty spanned the 19th century. Bonelli *père* had three "wives" and 18 children—a variant on the family name was Bellacoscia, "beautiful thighs"—and controlled miles of valley pasturage. His eldest sons were the blackest of his sheep, with a huge price on their heads for many murders. Unbetrayed, and under official amnesty, they raised a company of musketeers and fought in the war of 1870—only to take to the *maquis* again when it was over. Antoine (the eldest) was caught at the age of 75, but allowed to return to Bocognano where he died in 1912, aged 99, honoured as "royalty in the *maquis*".

A road opened in 1968 runs 20km south from Bocognano to Bastelica over the **Scalella Pass**. It is very narrow, tortuous and steep, but it brings you close to the superb mountain landscape—gorges twisting on all sides, valleys dropping sheer below, cliffs soaring skyward—and about four km from Bocognano it passes Corsica's highest waterfall, a slim torrent spreading into a wide delicate shimmer named the Bridal Veil. From the bleak top of the Col there are views far over the northern peaks; a less hazardous southern descent brings you to the hospitable little community of **Bastelica**, a favourite summer excursion from Ajaccio, surrounded by walks and climbs. Sampiero Corso was born here in 1498: during a melodramatically heroic career he succeeded in briefly liberating Corsica from Genoese rule, but was betrayed and murdered by relatives of his wife. Years before, Sampiero had killed her for suspected treason and infidelity: the family vendetta overruled patriotism. In Bastelica a bronze statue brandishing an urgent sword catches the fiery spirit of the man. From here, the D27 runs down through meadows and vineyards back to the coast: a more spectacular but much more difficult loop through **Tolla** follows the river Prunelli's gorges to its 1950s dam.

North of the Gulf of Ajaccio, the **Golfe de Sagone** has a number of small resorts scattered round it. Near **Calcatoggio** at the mouth of the river Liscia a small development straggles along a rather scruffy beach with few facilities, one or two simple but pleasant quiet hotels and some self-catering. Further north lies **Sagone**. The nearby ruins of a 12th-century cathedral, a menhir, and a Genoese watchtower indicate former settlements, but this little seaside resort is entirely modern: it has a good sandy beach with lots of watersports and several modest hotels. At the northern tip of the gulf lies the pretty red-roofed village of **Cargèse**, its houses rising in neat tiers on the steep hillside. A tiny port lies far below at the foot of the hill. Formerly a Greek colony for refugees from Turkish persecution, Cargèse still has a Greek Orthodox church, which stares gravely across at its Catholic counterpart on the other side of the valley. There are sandy beaches—notably Pero, with hotels—some self-catering, camping and a Club Med village. These resorts are good for very peaceful beach holidays, but there's little to do; a car is essential even for beach-hopping.

The only coastline included in Corsica's Regional Park, the **Golfe de Porto** with its northern bay the **Golfe de Girolata** is varied, beautiful and spectacular. Its most celebrated stretch is to the south, where the corniche road runs along **Les Calanche**: not sea-inlets like the Calanques of the Midi, but red granite cliffs eroded into a chaos of fantastic forms, with twisted needles rising above the pine trees in a glowing backdrop particularly wonderful at sunset. Two small but very popular resorts, Porto and Piana, monopolise this glorious scenery. **Piana** is just a small scattered village, a short but tortuous drive from two pretty beaches. **Arone**, back across Capo Rosso, is an unspoilt crescent of gently shelving pale sand; and the **Anse de Ficajola**, approached by a precipitous series of hair-pin bends and a steep walk, contains an exquisite cove of pink sand with steep red cliffs all around and a stream flowing through it—an idyll discovered by motorists, who crowd there in season. **Porto** is a small modern resort at the bottom of a steep lane. Its buildings are constructed from a version of the local stone, but somehow they lack charm, and have a curiously barrack-like appearance from above. The street leading down to the port is lined with shops, cafés and hotels; more hotels and fast-food restaurants cluster round the harbour area. The beach, divided from the port by a tall rock with a Genoese tower and approached by an arched footbridge, is grey shingle and pebbles, uncomfortable to walk on and shelving steeply at the waterline. Facilities are surprisingly poor for such a popular resort. Further round the gulf are several more sand-and-shingle beaches, but most are difficult to get to. The scenery on the local roads is magnificent—red rocks and eucalyptus trees—but the surface deteriorates further north.

The red granite of Les Calanche continues inland to the savage splendour of the **Gorges de Spelunca**; from Porto, small roads each side of the river run high along the mountainside to meet at the point where the Aitona torrent and its tributary the Lonca form the river Porto. A footpath from the crossroads (many cliff steps) leads down nearer the rushing waters, which are invisible from the roads. Upstream, the D84 continues a winding course to the little town of **Evisa**, set on a high terrace of chestnut trees overlooking the dramatic peaks and cliffs. From this peaceful spot walkers can explore in many directions; one footpath leads to a celebrated viewpoint down into the Spelunca, another descends to follow its bed. Beyond Evisa, chestnuts and red rock give way to immense *laricio* pines in the **Forêt d'Aitone**, climbing to the **Col de Vergio** which is the highest road in Corsica, kept open with snow ploughs in the winter.

Over the ridge, another great forest begins. The towering pines of the **Valdo-Niello** stretch down to the high plateau region called Niello or **Niolo**, enclosed and isolated among the mountain tops. In the range to the north, **Monte-Cinto** (2,710m) rises highest of all Corsica's peaks. The river Golo runs through the plateau, disappearing north-eastward down its own spectacular gorge, the **Scala di Santa Regina**: for centuries this "staircase" was the only way in or out of the region when the Col de Vergio was snowed up. The Niolin shepherds would bring enormous flocks of sheep and goats down to the western coast for the winter, and each summer return to the high mountain pastures dotted with grey stone shepherds' huts. The fertile Golo valley grew chestnuts in abundance and sufficient food for each flock-owning family; the pastoral economy required only a small labour force, and a mere handful of villages lie around the little "capital", **Calacuccia**. The 20th century has brought changes. Flocks are smaller, shepherds fewer; ewes' milk goes to "the Continent" to make Roquefort cheese instead of being processed in the *cave* under each neat stone house. Farming, like forestry, has become more organised. In the 1960s a massive dam, part of a hydroelectric scheme and reservoir system, created a large peaceful lake south of Calacuccia. The Niolo, as well as a paradise for campers, climbers and walkers, could become a summer lakeside playground; for the winter season there is already a small skiing base near the Col de Vergio. But it remains an area strong in Corsican crafts and traditions. The three-day *Fête de la Santa* each September, when the miraculous statue of the Virgin is carried in procession from the church at Calacuccia, keeps alive the chanting songs of the shepherds and the snail-patterned spiral dance called the *Granitola*.

Back on the coast, the D81 twists and climbs north across the western slopes of the Regional Park's mountains, and on behind an inhospitable rocky shoreline. The bay of Galéria is an exception: there's a village with simple accommodation near a couple of good beaches, one naturist. **Calvi** is one of Corsica's historic citadel towns and now its most crowded summer resort. The long sandy beach lies east of the town, gently shelving and safe, well-supplied with cafés and watersports, looking past the harbour to the mighty Citadel on its jutting promontory. The newer part of town stretches along the busy port: Quai Landry is palm-lined and pretty, much congested with traffic and animated (especially at night) with open-air restaurants and cafés. The streets behind hold all the requirements of a modern resort—noisy nightlife is concentrated in the rue Clemenceau—and also considerable charm. Among the red roofs and creamy-grey façades rises the Baroque tower of the lower town's plain white church, begun in 1774 but not completed until 1938; below the Hôtel de Ville are vivid terraced gardens of palms and flowering shrubs. The Citadel on its high rock dominates all. Massive walls of ochre granite blocks slope up to the tall clustered buildings of the enclosed Old Town—another world, of ancient grey houses, twisting cobbled streets and a splendid rampart walk. The Genoese and their financiers fortified it in the 15th century; the town had been completely Genoese in loyalty for 200 years. It stood out against the French in two sieges in the 1550s—the women of Calvi joining their menfolk on the ramparts; it resisted the Corsican patriotism of Pascal Paoli, who in 1758 founded another town up the

Calvi

coast—L'Ile Rousse—as a centre of opposition. In 1794 it finally capitulated to the bombardment of the English fleet. After several weeks of this "siege of 30,000 bullets" the defenders could only throw stones—one of which cost Nelson his right eye. Two years later the English left, and Calvi became as French as the rest of Corsica. Among the houses reduced to rubble was the alleged birthplace of Christopher Columbus in 1441, a time when to be Corsican was not so different from being Genoese; Calvi has as fair a claim as Genoa and marks the spot with a plaque. The Genoese Governor's Palace is today occupied by the Foreign Legion.

✳ *Eglise St-Jean-Baptiste* The old Cathedral's octagonal cupola rises above the jostle of red-tiled roofs and its austere white 16th-century façade dominates the sloping Place d'Armes. The airy interior, a Greek cross, contains various treasures: notably an ebony Christ (credited with the miraculous lifting of one French siege) and a robed Spanish Virgin. Both are carried in festival processions—indeed throughout Corsica the portage of sheer weight seems to earn penitential merit points.

✳ *Oratoire St-Antoine* Elegant 15th-century chapel overlooking the bay, storehouse of religious objects and works of art from the 16th to 19th centuries. There is a very expressive little Florentine crucifix carved in ivory.

To the north **Algajola** is a small, mainly modern resort set on a long sandy beach, with small simple hotels. There's not much to see, apart from some unconvincingly restored Genoan fortifications in what little is left of the old town, but there is easy access to Calvi and L'Ile-Rousse on the little railway line that runs along this part of the coast. Close by, the little **Marine de St-Ambroggio** has self-catering complexes and villas, a Club Med village, watersports and several small sandy beaches.

L'Ile-Rousse is a major resort and sizeable town which takes its name from the reddish rocks of the promontory, La Pietra, that juts out to sea beyond the port. Popular with French visitors, it gets very crowded in high season. There's a lively main square with open-air cafés under shady trees, *pétanque* players, a church at one end and a market place like a Hollywood mockup of a Greek temple to one side. The main beach is of very fine, gently shelving white sand, with plenty of sports and facilities; the town has a number of nightspots. East of L'Ile-Rousse lie more sandy beaches, notably at **Lozari**, a peaceful area with a holiday village at one end. This is the last of Corsica's western holiday coast: the island's north-west corner is the arid, empty **Désert des Agriates**, a region of bare mountain slopes, blistering summer heat and almost no vegetation. A few dry-stone huts, the only signs of habitation, remain from the days when herds of goats were brought here for the winter; now a goat would starve, and even the *maquis* has given up.

The railway services between Calvi and L'Ile-Rousse and inland through the mountains, the plentiful coach and boat excursions, and the interest of Calvi itself make this one area where you might holiday without a car; yet it would be a pity not to explore the region behind the coastal strip. The **Balagne** is a green and fertile area of wooded hills, lush valleys and many charming villages, threaded with little roads and ideal for leisurely touring. Throughout Corsica's history her invaders have enjoyed this region: the Romans first cultivated it, the Moors in the Middle Ages left some flat-roofed cubic villages among the more characteristic red tiles and huddled grey walls, and the Papal forces who expelled the Moors built scores of pretty churches. This "garden of Corsica" flourished like nowhere else in the island, growing olives, oranges, figs and almonds as well as the vines which still produce good wine. As the coast developed, it grew rather neglected and depopulated. But there was a deliberate revival in the 1960s, concentrating also on re-establishing local crafts: woodcarving, pottery, baskets and recently glass. Each village has an individual appeal: sometimes a splendid setting against a mountain forest (**Zilia**, **Speloncato**); sometimes perched with panoramic views (**Lumio**, **Montemaggiore**); many nestle in a valley or cling half-hidden to a sheltered hillside. The churches too have their own individual appeal and a variety of general style: at **Aregno** the green and white chequerboard building with strange little carved figures on the façade is Pisan Romanesque, while at **Corbara** the 18th-century choir is ornamented with splendidly Baroque carved marble columns. One of the tiniest villages, **Pigna**, is a thriving centre both of crafts—in its official *maison d'artisanat*—and of local gastronomic specialities. From the coast to the mountains, the Balagne is a series of delightful surprises.

The North

The **Golfe de St-Florent**, between the Désert des Agriates and Cap Corse's mountain ridge, is deep and sheltered: the little town on a rocky outcrop in its inner curve might be lapped by a lake. **St-Florent** was built by the Genoese in the 1440s below a fine fortress tower (later the Gendarmerie) and kept its strategic value through Corsica's history of conquest. In 1793 when the conquerors were briefly the English, Nelson was moved to declare "Give me the Gulf of St-Florent and two frigates, and not a single ship could leave Marseille or Toulon"—but was never given the chance to prove his point. In the 18th and 19th centuries, the town became neglected and almost depopulated because of the malaria-breeding marshlands round the river Aliso; in the 20th it has new life—tourist development spreads along the road to Bastia and the harbour is enlarged for pleasure craft. Hotels, villas and campsites are overwhelmed by the high-season crowds. A pebble beach stretches east along the bay, and sand west of the reedy rivermouth; but the life of this tiny, pretty resort is concentrated in its shaded central square, the harbour and the oldest streets. Alleys and steps wind between tall houses of faded honey-grey, shuttered and crumbling, along the water's very edge. The port is lined with restaurants and souvenir shops, and in the sandy square open-air eating surrounds the games of *pétanque* and the strolling crowds; it's colourful, animated and very appealing.

✴ *Cathédrale de Nebbio* Half a mile away among the vineyards this 12th-century Pisan church (collect the key from the town tourist office) alone remains of the former Nebbio capital. It is built of pale limestone blocks in a serenely graceful design of tall blind arches; the interior capitals are intricately carved with curious animals, entwined snakes, snail-like motifs. Among the gilded wooden figures, Saint Flor is preserved under glass.

The **Nebbio** is the compact region immediately behind the Golfe de St-Florent, a landscape of fertile hills and valleys encircled by mountains; the Col de Teghime and the more impressive **Défile de Lacone** cross the ridge to Bastia and the east coast. Like the Balagne, the Nebbio has vineyards, orchards, meadows and picturesque villages; local characteristics are houses built of the same thin brownish stone slabs as the many dry-stone walls, and green-tiled roofs. **Oletta** and tiny **San-Pietro-di-Tenda** are the

St-Michel at Murato

most beautifully set. Of many attractive churches, that of **Murato** is outstanding (literally too, on its own ridge half a mile from the village). The Eglise St-Michel is a remarkable concentration of Pisan Romanesque and more barbaric decorative elements. Its simple rectangle has a tall western bell tower, half supported on fat round columns of alternating white and green slabs; the entire church is motley, but not always in regular layers— in places the green and white looks like some haphazard crossword. Around windows and blind arches, and in less likely places, there is a mass of astonishing carving—symbolic beasts, enigmatic figures and Biblical themes. To the north of the Nebbio, at **Patrimonio**, a south-facing amphitheatre of vines produces white, red and particularly rosé wines of some reputation. The local vignerons formed a co-operative in the 1960s, and visitors are welcome to taste.

The long narrow peninsula of **Cap Corse** stretching north of the island is a distinctly different part of Corsica. Its dorsal ridge, dropping steeply to the west and more gradually to the east, is grey schist and slate and sometimes serpentine rock; beaches are mostly grey-green shingle; buildings weathered and grey, roofed with green tiles or heavier stone. Despite the cool colours, the north of the island is hot: the climate here produces good vines, olives, and the Corsican version of the lemon called the *cédrat*. The peninsula is ringed with Genoese watchtowers and old villages. Even before tourism turned each *marine* into a budding resort, the inhabitants of Cap Corse took more interest in the sea than was habitual in the rest of the island: rather than shepherds they were historically fishermen, sailors and (by economic necessity) traders. Their ports still thrive, while the villages up in the interior are inevitably becoming depopulated. The confident corniche road marked on the maps is narrow in the west, but well surfaced, and takes in all but the northernmost tip.

Almost every village seems to have its watchtower: that at **Nonza** is proudly perched on a vertiginous black rock, and lichen-grey houses cluster at the edge of a cliff round the central square and the Eglise Ste-Julie. Far down zig-zagging cliff steps is Ste-Julie's marble shrine and "fountain". Twin jets of water represent the two miraculous springs that rose at her grisly martyrdom, when before strangling her the Roman soldiers cut off her breasts and tossed them away. Nonza's other story concerns the tower: after a noisy siege its Corsican commander relinquished it to the French in 1768 only after demanding that its garrison be allowed to depart with full military honours, banners flying, transport provided ... the French accepted the conditions, but only one man emerged to receive their ceremony. The patriots had prudently abandoned Nonza, and a solitary veteran had put up a splendid bluff.

The dark grey beach beyond the town is vast but deserted. North at **Albo**, asbestos mines were opened after the Second World War and abandoned in 1965; waste matter from the old workings became deposited along the shore. Albo itself has a tiny cluster of shops and houses and a greenish-pebbled beach. Then comes a succession of prettier villages among vines and olives, fruit and flowers. **Pino**, where a road heads east to the other coast, is an attractive little centre with a petrol station as well as pretty houses; tall cypresses shade a cemetery, and the village seems full of chapels. **Centuri-Port** on its small bay has now been thoroughly discovered, and pleasure boats share its pretty harbour with the lobster-fishers. In a setting of utter charm below the *maquis*-covered hills it has old grey houses green-roofed with serpentine, plus hotels, restaurants and a disco.

The D86 swings east from the Col de Serra, but lesser roads lead to the northern extremity of Cap Corse where **Tollare** and **Barcaggio** are tiny clusters of fishermen's houses looking out to the **Ilot de la Giraglia**, a huge rock of serpentine with a lighthouse on top. Winding across the peninsula, the D80 reaches the outskirts of **Rogliano**, a commune of hamlets, churches and a ruined seigneurial château up a short mountain detour – it has a particularly beautiful setting of olives, vines and splendid chestnut trees. The first village on the east coast, **Macinaggio**, is its *marine*; there are watersports in the shingly bay, and a *Produits Corses* shop selling local wine, delicacies and souvenirs. The beach at **Porticciolo** is much more attractive. **Sisco** has its little *marine*, but the hamlets inland up a green windswept valley are more interesting. In the Middle Ages Sisco was a commune of metal-workers, and at Balba the Eglise St-Martin contains a famous hidden treasury including a saint's skull encased in silver-gilt. For a chance of seeing it you must enquire at the house of the *curé*. Further up the valley are more churches, and cypress-shaded cemeteries; but the *maquis* is gaining ground in the meadows, and many of the people have gone.

To reach **Erbalunga** you turn seaward off the corniche road, down to a venerable huddle of picturesque houses lapped by the waves on their tongue of schist rock, protected behind the remains of a massive watchtower. Fishing boats still use the colourful harbour that attracts painters, photographers and—inevitably—crowds of tourists in summer. Behind, there are ranks of terraced houses and appealing little squares. Erbalunga retains both charm and tradition: at Easter, a processional march takes in all the nearby villages and churches, culminating in a torchlit *Granitola*.

South of here the *marines* come into the magnetic field of Bastia, Corsica's big industrial town. **Lavasina** has a celebrated shrine to the Virgin, and **Miomo** a particularly well-preserved Genoese tower complete with machicolations. In the flatter terrain of the cape's east coast, on a road double the width of that in the west, it is easy to speed up, declare the villages dull (which, comparatively, they are) and miss Erbalunga altogether. For a day's tour of Cap Corse it is in fact much better to drive anti-clockwise, saving the west coast for the afternoon sun. The round trip is 180km.

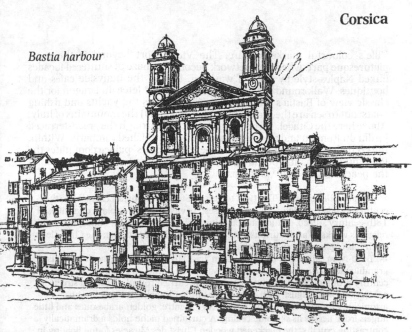

Bastia harbour

The East

At the foot of Cap Corse and the beginning of Corsica's long east-coast plain, **Bastia** faces Italy across the islands (Elba, Capraia) of the Tuscan Strait. Here in 1380 the Genoese built their first *bastiglia* (donjon), to protect the only natural harbour on this coastline exposed to the stormy south-easterly *libeccio*. A century later they set a Governor's Palace inside their Terra-Nova and fortified their stronghold with citadel walls. Non-Genoese residents were mostly kept out: around the harbour, Corsicans lived in the more accessible Terra-Vecchia. As garrison town, commercial port and administrative capital Bastia held almost uninterrupted supremacy until, after Corsica became part of France in 1811, bourgeois Ajaccio was made its capital. Bastia—still the vital centre of commerce and industry—continued to expand as far as the inland mountains allowed, and in separate phases, the most intensive after the Second World War. Now its main industrial zone is to the north, its newest residential development spreading south. Ajacciens (and other Corsicans) still tend to think of it as an Italian city planted on their island, but its vital function in the economy was recognised when in 1975 Bastia regained equal status, as the Préfecture of Haute-Corse.

British tourists arriving here by air or sea can (and do) look with dismay at its teeming charmless sprawl and leave immediately for the island's interior or the west coast. The town is not well endowed with hotels, and the new-sprung resorts along the sandy beaches to the south lack scenic appeal. But Bastia is an agglomeration of distinctive zones: its older quarters, shabby through long neglect, have historic appeal and some lively atmosphere. Behind the modern harbour the vast tree-shaded Place St-Nicolas is the town's social centre, animated day and night and lined with café terraces. From its southern end you reach Terra-Vecchia, a dense network of decaying narrow lanes whose 18th-century houses rise to eight storeys above their street-level commerce and crafts, around the Hôtel de

411

Ville's colourful market square. The Vieux Port beyond is the most picturesque part, where the network becomes a maze of shuttered façades linked Naples-style by lines of washing, behind the quayside cafés and boutiques. Walk round to the harbour's southern Jetée du Dragon for the classic view of Bastia's ancient waterfront across the yachts and fishing boats: out to sea are the islands and (on a clear day) the mountains of Italy. Above here the Citadel, Terra-Nova, is reached through the green-terraced Jardin du Romieu and a postern gate in the refurbished ramparts. Within, the crenellated fort that was the Genoese governors' palace dominates the Place du Donjon, and Bastia's oldest houses fill the twisting alleys round the peaceful little Place Guasco.

＊ *Terra-Vecchia churches* The twin towers of St-Jean-Baptiste's classical 17th-century façade rise high above the houses; its vast interior displays quantities of 18th-century stucco, statues and paintings. The Chapelle de la Conception holds religious works of art luxuriously surrounded by Genoese velvet; the Chapelle St-Roch has copious Florentine carving.

＊ *Terra-Nova churches* A cathedral from 1570 to 1801, the Eglise St-Marie is grandiloquent Genoese Baroque. Its Assumption of the Virgin, a massive 18th-century group of chiselled silver, is somehow carried round all the old streets in procession each August 15th. The modest little Chapelle St-Croix has an astonishing interior resembling a Louis XVI theatre: golden arabesques and little angels frolic across its sky-blue ceiling. A curtained niche holds a dramatically contrasting crucifix, the blackened wooden Christ des Miracles found floating in the sea in 1428.

＊ *Musée d'Ethnographie Corse* Inside the former governors' palace: successive rooms trace Corsica's animal and mineral history, from arsenic ore to Napoleon's death mask. The big showcases and audio-visual displays are a comprehensive introduction to the whole island.

South of Bastia a vast expanse of desolate grey sand stretches for miles between the sea and a huge reed-fringed lake, which dries to a shallow marsh in summer, but is full of bird-life. A number of hotels and resort facilities have grown up along the sand-bar and its hinterland of eucalyptus trees. Beyond the Etang de Biguglia is the Bastia-Poretta airport, and under the flight-paths the site of Roman **Mariana**—the marshes were once cultivated, and the emperor Augustus set a port on the river Golo. Hardly a vestige remains of the Roman settlement but the site was occupied later by others: in the 12th century the Pisans built a cathedral here. **La Canonica** was abandoned in the 14th century when the bishopric was moved inland, and its campanile has gone, but its pure Romanesque style is the prototype of Corsica's Pisan churches—three simple naves and an elegant apse. In shape it resembles the cathedral at Nebbio, but here the walls are warmer shades of stone—amber, gold and grey, their colours cleverly harmonised by the builder. The red tiles of the roof are a modern aberration. Vivid animals form the carved frieze above the tympanum. Among nearby excavations are some 4th-century mosaics carved with Christian symbols, and not far away to the southwest the (restored) cemetery church of San Parteo is a small pretty replica of La Canonica.

The N198 from Bastia down the east coast is the fastest road in Corsica, and local drivers exploit it with zest. As far south as Solenzara it runs mostly through a flat plain, the only extensive one on the whole island. For many years it was ravaged by malaria, but recently its agricultural potential has been realised with the help of government funding. Much of the land is now under maize, vines, orange groves and peach orchards. Long sandy beaches run almost continuously down this part of the coast, and many small resorts have sprung up, but there are few facilities and many of the beaches are rather charmless and dull. The land between the main road and the sea is mostly not cultivatable, because it consists of marshland (lakes in winter) at the mouths of the rivers that flow east from the mountainous interior. The east coast is particularly popular with naturists and there are quite a number of holiday villages and campsites for them, especially near **Bravone**. There isn't much potential for sightseeing on the coast itself, except at **Aléria**, where there are the excavated remains of an important Graeco-Roman town, and a museum.

Inland, however, there is some of Corsica's finest touring countryside. The N193 swings west to Ponte Lecchia, Corte and the high granite mountains: between this route and the coast lies a continuation of Cap Corse's grey schist rock, the large region called the **Castagniccia** after its chestnut forests. Chestnuts have been its livelihood since the Middle Ages—made into flour for the Corsicans' staple diet, and feeding the pigs that wander freely throughout the region, eventually to be rendered into rich and varied *charcuterie*. Vines and olives on the lower slopes, and goats in the *maquis* above, once made up a self-sufficient economy for the scores of villages in this region of rugged hills and valleys. It is a natural fortress, a stronghold of Corsican independence over many centuries, birthplace of several famous men. Still the most characteristically Corsican of all the regions, it is today rather neglected and (except in high summer) depopulated: since the Second World War took its heavy toll of manpower many more inhabitants have moved away—to the plain, the coast, the Continent—returning to their native villages for holidays or for retirement. Only in the north-east corner, in the little area called **La Casinca**, are the villages above the plain as prosperous as in the days when they were a retreat from the malarial marshes. A short but intricately winding loop road from the N198 takes you through **Vescovato**, the "capital" deep in a valley, where the fountain in the shady square bears a black Imperial eagle and the tall grey houses climb to a large Baroque church. Here the bishops of La Canonica spent a century or two before moving their see to Bastia; here in 1557 a Corsican Assembly accepted integration with France, only to be handed back to the Genoese two years later. La Casinca's other villages – from **Loreto**, highest up, to **Castellare**, nearest the plain—are perched on a narrow ridge above their cultivated terraces, looking out over Bastia to the sea.

La Castagniccia too has sea views: from tiny **St-Jean-de-Moriani** they extend to the islands of the Tuscan strait. **San-Nicolao** close by is splendidly set on a sea-facing terrace among chestnut forests, and the elegant campanile of its Pisan church can be seen for miles. At **Cervione** just south, the corniche road ends in a sweeping curve and the church is Baroque. For visitors with spare time, energy and a key from the village, there is a half-hour walk down a rough path to the Romanesque Chapelle Santa-Christina; inside are frescoes, their delicate colours excellently preserved.

The D71 meanders right through the region, under the dappled shade of the chestnuts. Driving is slow (even hazardous on the smaller side roads): the tortuous ups and downs demand concentration, as do the small pigs who rootle unconcernedly all over the place. Animals and provisions traditionally occupy the ground floors of the local houses, built of grey schist stone and roofed with heavy slates (*lauzes*). Many are empty these days, and the *maquis* encroaches on neglected terraces of vines and olives; but the dozens of hamlets recall the region's crowded history. ▷ p416

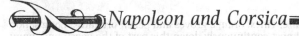

Napoleon's birthday is a matter of no little national importance. Had the future Emperor been born in early 1768, as he registered when he married Josephine de Beauharnais in Paris, he would have been born nominally a Genoese subject but effectively an independent Corsican under the rule of general Pascal Paoli, freedom fighter and enlightened dictator.

It is rather more likely, and much more satisfactory from the French point of view, that Napoleone Buonaparte saw the light of day on the 15th August 1769. Genoa had sold its claim to Corsica to the French in May 1768, and a few months before the birth of her second son, Letizia Buonaparte had fought on the losing side of the decisive confrontation in the French takeover compaign. Paoli had taken flight to sustain the cause of freedom in London, and Carlo Maria Buonaparte, one of his leading supporters, had returned from the mountains to Ajaccio and insinuated himself into the good graces of the new rulers with what must have seemed indecent haste to Letizia, whose staunch Corsican patriotism ran much deeper than Carlo's opportunism. So Napoleon was born French, as national historians have taken pains to emphasise.

Although Napoleone always held his father in contempt and was proud to have inherited all his qualities from his mother, the neatness with which Carlo (now "Charles") trimmed his political sails to catch the prevailing French wind suggests that the inheritance was not entirely one-sided. By befriending one of the French Governors of Corsica and providing evidence of poverty and noble lineage, Charles secured a free military education for Napoleone in France. In 1779, when he was (probably) nearly 10, the boy started at military school in Brienne and from there went on to Paris. He did not return to Corsica for seven years, but far from alienating him from his native land, his education had quite the opposite effect; reading accounts of the curiously dark-skinned youth whose first task was to learn French (the way he pronounced his own name earned him the nickname "paille au nez"), it is easy to understand how he became more rather than less conscious of being a foreigner in France. Rather than make a determined effort to conform, he took pride in his isolation: "I will never forgive my father for having concurred in the reunion of France and Corsica" he said to one of his few friends at Brienne; and "I will make your French people suffer as much as it is within my power to do".

As a serving junior officer in the French army Napoleone lost none of his obsession with Corsican affairs. In July 1786 he ordered from a Genevan bookseller all the books about Corsica the man could obtain, and in June 1789 he wrote to Paoli in London requesting information for a history of Corsica that he planned to write. To Napoleone's grandiloquent words ("slavery the price of our submission . . . island bound by the triple chain of lawyer, soldier and tax collector . . .") the general, who by now nourished no great affection for the Buonaparti and their style of Corsican patriotism, replied dustily that writing history books was no business for young soldiers. The dramatic events in revolutionary France, which might have seemed the natural theatre for an ambitious young soldier with grand ideas of his destiny, seem to have interested Napoleone hardly at all, except as an opportunity to agitate in Corsica where he spent as much time as he could manage. Of the $7\frac{1}{2}$ years up to June 1793, he spent a total of $2\frac{1}{2}$ years in France with his regiment; for nearly all the rest of the time he was in Corsica on extended periods of leave which went unpunished thanks to invented pretexts and the laxity of army discipline.

In Corsica Napoleone looked after his clan (his father died in 1785), and led its political activity, which was too revolutionary in character for the taste of the Paolist majority of Corsicans; they successfully kept him out of office in local elections until 1792 when, by means of intimidatory tactics, he managed to secure himself a position as lieutenant-colonel in charge of the batallion of "*Volontaires de la Garde Nationale*". Shamelessly diverting this body from its intended purpose, he was the acknowledged leader of a mutinous outbreak of fighting at Ajaccio. The failure of this initiative sent him scurrying to Paris to plead a case which at other times would have been heard in court martial. Such was the shortage of officers at the time (thousands had fled the country rather than swear allegiance to the National Assembly) that he got away with it, and was soon promoted. A letter to his brother in August 1792 gave the first hint that he was beginning to sense that things in Corsica were getting too hot for the clan's comfort, and that he would do its prospects no harm by firmly establishing himself in France where, as he had discovered, military advancement was easily won. This concern, which turned out to be well founded, did not prevent Napoleone from returning to Corsica in September 1792 (accompanying his sister). He remained there at a time when the Revolutionary Army was fighting, and losing, an international war, and Paris itself was under threat. Napoleone's contribution to the national struggle was limited to participation in a disastrous attack on the Sardinian island of la Maddalena.

Although both were originally anti-French in their aims, the Buonaparte and Paoli factions had become increasingly antagonistic. Early in 1793, Napoleone's younger brother Lucien saw fit to denounce Paoli to the National Convention which duly gave orders for the general's arrest. If it was intended to strengthen his family's position, Lucien's action was gravely miscalculated. In May a Paolist Assembly at Corte passed a resolution condemning the Buonaparte family "to perpetual execration and infamy", and Napoleone went into hiding. His mother was persuaded by a friendly voice to evacuate her Ajaccio home with the rest of her family, and escaped just before the house was invaded by a furious band of looters and no doubt would-be murderers. Letizia camped rough on the coast until Napoleone appeared in a small vessel with a simple message for his mother: "this country is not for us". They embarked on a stormy crossing to France, and the rest, as the saying goes, is history.

In 1803, when Napoleon Bonaparte (as he now styled himself) assumed absolute power as First Consul for life, it was decreed in Corsica that August 15th, elsewhere the Feast of the Assumption, should be the feast of the little known Saint Napoleon. It is still the occasion of a firework display in Ajaccio, and the town is full of tributes to the glory of its greatest son. In reality, Corsica had little cause to thank the inflammatory subversive who had been chased from the island by the force of popular execration. Napoleon set foot on the island only once again, a fleeting visit on his way back from Egypt, and his style of ruling the island consisted of a measured alternation of neglect and, when necessary, harsh repression of the uprisings against foreign control, which continued much as they had before. So loathsome was French rule that the people of Bastia appealed to the British for help in 1811, and when the emperor abdicated the Ajacciens threw his statue into the sea.

Those round **Valle-d'Alesani**—one of several communities described as "the heart of the Castagniccia"—produced Grosso-Minuto, Corsica's only known humorist. He was a puny but spirited travelling pedlar of the 18th century, who in later life grew fat and famous for his misfortunes and his untranslatably sardonic quips. In this same locality the one and only King of Corsica was crowned Théodore I in 1736, and reigned improbably for eight months. An adventuring German baron, he had some efficient ideas, including proclaiming "liberty of conscience" in Corsica to attract Jewish financiers who might revive the island's economy. He even had his own coinage struck. At the old convent where he was crowned (a mile or two south towards Piazzali) the church holds some vivid paintings, including a pensively charming *Vierge à la Cerise* of the 1450 Sienese school.

Carcheto and **Piedicroce** each have fine Baroque churches, their towers visible from afar above the trees; but the one at **La Porta**, up a series of hairpin bends, outclasses them completely. Free-standing beside the relatively restrained façade and twice its height, the tawny-ochre campanile resembles an extravagantly sculpted candle with five mellow tiers of scrolls and pilasters, arches and pediments. Up another mountain detour north of Piedicroce is **Eaux d'Orezza**, where thermal springs spout the "wine of the rock" to accompany the chestnut-based "bread of the forests". In the 19th century *curistes* found it beneficial to the kidneys, the liver, the nerves and the symptoms of anaemia and malaria; today it is treated to remove its powerful mineral flavours before sparkling on Corsican tables. In the north-west of the region, **Morosaglia** is the home village of the Paoli family—Pascal by far the most famous, but his father and brother also honoured patriots. Pascal Paoli's ashes were retrieved from Westminster Abbey and lie under a flagstone in the family house, whose rooms contain many mementoes. His bronze statue was erected in 1953, financed by Corsicans world-wide.

West of the Castagniccia, in Corsica's central geological division, grey schist rock ends and red crystalline granite begins. The change is not dramatic at **Ponte Leccia**, railway junction and crossroads village in a valley: routes lead off quite gently, later to climb and twist up the mountain passes. A mile up the N197 towards L'Ile-Rousse, the **Vallée d'Asco** heads some 20 miles south-west between the towering ranges of **Monte Padro** and **Monte Cinto**, the island's highest peak. In the fertile lower Asco valley the road runs almost straight through olives and fruit trees, until the *maquis*-covered slopes close in and the little brown village of **Moltifao** comes into sight, perched high on a northern spur. Soon after, the **Gorges d'Asco** begin: the river dashes down its boulder-strewn bed between outcrops of colourful jagged rock and ever more dramatic heights. At the head of the gorge, the solitary village of **Asco** clings to steep terraces, and a Genoese bridge spans the stream below. Further up, the **Forêt de Carrozzica** clothes the mountainsides with great pines, and the peaks above stay under snow for almost all the year. At the end of this Alpine defile, ringed by superb mountain vistas, **Haut-Asco** caters for skiers and summer climbers: mere walkers can scale Monte Cinto, but it takes several hours. The valley is rapidly losing its isolated mystique, but still has its own wildlife. Among the peaks there used to be eagles, and you may still see *gypaètes*, huge bearded vultures with wingspans of over eight feet; and lower down, the *maquis* has its own varieties and fragrance. A rare type of juniper gives Asco honey its special flavour, and is said to account for the "manna" phenomenon—a sweet and sticky white deposit that appears each year for a day or two in midsummer.

From Ponte Leccia the N193 south runs smoothly up the Golo valley for several miles, and then begins a swinging climb round spurs of mountain to arrive at **Corte**, spiritual capital of Corsica, its citadel perched high and proud above a meeting point of mountain routes. This is a logical touring centre, but not a tourists' town. New suburbs spread along the valley roads; the university, founded here during the years (1755 to 1769) when Corte was capital of independent Corsica, was re-established in 1977 and the student population adds youthful energy missing elsewhere inland; but only the Old Town attracts, and its appeal is history rather than charm. Sombre ranks of dark, grey-schist houses heap themselves up the steep slope below the citadel rock. The place looks stern and grim—it was a stronghold emotionally defended, never re-taken by the Genoese, but lost to the French with Corsica's hopes of independence.

From the busy central Place Paoli where traffic surges round the bronze statue of Pascal Paoli, *père de la nation*, a steep lane leads up to the Place Gaffori where the statue of Jean-Pierre Gaffori, *général de la nation*, stands before his bullet-scarred house. Here, at a critical stage of the War of Independence, Gaffori's redoubtable wife held a lighted fuse over a powder barrel, threatening to blow the partisans to hell if they surrendered to the Genoese before her husband's reinforcements could arrive. In a third square, the Place du Poilu, is a house briefly lived in by the Buonaparte family, and the Palais National: originally occupied by Genoese adminis-trators, seat of the parliament of independent Corsica, then successively a prison, a college and a minor museum. The great grey citadel was built under the Aragonese viceroy in the early 15th century; it was large enough to make a vast barracks for the troops of Louis XV, and is today occupied by the Foreign Legion. Visitors can share the view from the terrace on its spur of rock.

Excursions from Corte

✱ **Venaco** South of Corte over the Col de Bellagranajo, this is a favourite destination of Corsicans, half-way between Bastia and Ajaccio by road or rail. It is surrounded by walking, fishing and hunting country—except for an area just south, where moufflons have been reintroduced and are protected in the Parc de Verghetto.

✱ **Gorges de la Restonica** The river descends from the Lac de Melo, among 6,000ft peaks, to join the Tavignano south-west of Corte. A sinuous little road climbs rapidly through chestnut forests to the pine belt: this stretch is dramatic but also very pretty. The road runs close beside the tumbling river full of pools and miniature cascades; conical Corsican pines rise from a landscape of great rounded boulders below the higher rugged outcrops. After crossing the river at Pont de Tragone, the road mounts through much wilder scenery to end near deserted dry-stone shepherds' huts, the *bergeries de Grotelle*, in Alpine terrain. A footpath continues to the head of the valley, and serious walkers can scale Corsica's second highest peak, Monte Rotondo—five hours up and four hours down, ideally with an intervening bivouac, to wake and watch the sunrise from the island's central ridge.

✱ **Gorges de Tavignano** Only a footpath follows this beautiful forested gorge, but a ten-minute walk gives a wonderful view back over the town to the citadel rising against its green mountain backdrop.

✱ **Monte Cecu** The D18 running north-west skirts the summit of Monte Cecu, from whose flat top (with television mast) the view is spectacular all round. To the south, the curious formations called the **Aiguilles Rouges** can be seen more closely by following the same road to Castiglione and Popolasca, the villages perched below them.

✱ **Omessa** North of Corte about ten miles down the N193, a side road winds east up to this delightful village perched above the valley, topped by the tall Baroque campanile of its church. The plane-shaded square is approached through a vaulted alleyway; beyond the fountain, the Chapelle de l'Annonciade has a pretty marble Virgin and Child.

From Corte back to the east coast, the N200 follows the pleasant wooded Tavignano valley to the Plaine d'Aléria, where concentrated government enterprise has replaced the encroaching *maquis* with abundant vineyards, maize, fruit trees and sunflowers. It is the most productive area of Corsica, but not of great scenic interest. **Aléria** itself, on an isolated hill, originated as a Greek colony and was later the capital of a Roman province; there is a vast area of excavations, initiated by Prosper Mérimée, and a museum housed in a 16th-century fort. Exhibits come from hill villages and inland lakes, as well as from the immediate vicinity. The main road south continues inland; there are beaches beyond the coastal lagoons, but they are mostly inaccessible. At the river Solenzara, the border of Corse-du-Sud, another landscape begins.

The South

Between the fast-developing resort of **Solenzara** ribboning along the main coast road, and the lovely seascape of the Golfe de Porto-Vecchio, a rocky stretch of coastline with a few little rivermouth *marines* is christened the Côte des Nacres, after its deep-water shells—huge elaborate shapes called *jambonneaux* and *plumes de mer*. Inland, there is another route: it is longer and infinitely more difficult—often badly surfaced as well as narrow—but one of the most spectacular in Corsica. It winds up to the **Col de Larone**, and on to the **Bavella**—a forest, a gorge, a pass and an extraordinary landscape of towering peaks and rocky chaos, coloured pink and red and ochre under the sun, purple in shadow, all on a heroic scale. Relentless hairpin bends climb to the **Col de Bavella**, between the fantastically twisted and eroded **Aiguilles** and the vast depression, littered with heaps of rock, known as the **Trou de la Bombe**. From the Col, range upon range stretches away into the Regional Park. In this age-old hunting territory there has been much fire damage; chestnuts and cedars have been planted among the soaring pines, and on the high slopes the moufflons are now protected. Tourist traffic explores here all summer; red-roofed little Zonza at a crossroads has cafés. The route south-east to the coast descends more gently through the trees, past spectacular crags around the great Pointe du Diamant, along an unexpected lake and down through the mingled oak and pine of the **Forêt d'Ospédale**.

The sheltered **Golfe de Porto-Vecchio** is fringed by fine sandy beaches and peaceful lagoons. Its hinterland is a gently undulating forest of cork oaks. When the cork is first stripped from the trunks, to a height of about eight feet, the bare wood beneath appears a brilliant russet colour, eventually fading to a softer brown. Holiday developments spread round the Golfe: Sogno, Cala Rossa and St-Cyprien to the north all have excellent beaches. **Sogno** has extensive shallow lagoons in idyllic surroundings—small children can paddle safely, and the horses from the nearby riding school love splashing through. There are a number of sandy beaches, some quiet and secluded, the main one (backed by a large campsite) offering watersports, boat trips, and entertainments. **Cala Rossa** has one of Corsica's most pleasant hotels, some private villas, and a self-catering complex. The beaches are excellent and unspoilt. Watersports, tennis, riding and a nightclub can be found nearby. **St-Cyprien**, further north, has some luxurious villas and a very long beach. There are some shops and nightlife, but the atmosphere is peaceful and relaxed.

Porto-Vecchio itself, set deep in the Golfe, has ancient origins—it was founded by the Greeks, and Roman ships took away cork as a form of tax. The Genoese built fortifications but succumbed to the local malaria. For centuries the town was neglected and largely depopulated, and very little of historic interest remains. Today, it is a major centre of Corsica's tourist trade, rapidly provided with facilities begun in 1965, agreeably planned and still expanding. Streets full of small shops, restaurants and travel agents lead from the small central square with its church and open-air cafés. There are some small hotels in town, but most are some way outside: a car is essential. There is no good beach in the town itself—only a dismal patch of gritty sand near the saltpans by the harbour—but within easy driving distance lie many of the finest beaches in Corsica. The **Plage de Palombaggia**, south of the rocky headland of La Chiappa, is one of the best. In idyllic surroundings, backed by a ridge of pines and dunes, this long beach is split by red rocks into several sheltered shallow coves, and delightfully secluded parts can be reached by walking. Further south lie the sandy beaches of **Santa-Giulia**, with many villas and a Club Med complex; and **Rondinara**, a very peaceful beach, though difficult to get to.

At the southern tip of Corsica, hard crystalline rock gives way to porous limestone, creating an aridly exotic landscape more like parts of Provence. In **Bonifacio**, only a few sea-miles from Sardinia, the Corse dialect is markedly different and the inhabitants speak of "going into Corsica" as other Corsicans say "going to the Continent". An easy drive from Porto Vecchio, this *"petit pays à part"* is unique and unforgettable.

The site is extraordinary. Crumbling creamy bluffs, precipitous and overhung, face the troubled Sardinian strait, but behind them a long inlet enters from the west: the Goulet de Bonifacio, parallel to the sea and completely sheltered. On the narrow promontory the citadel and Haut-Ville rise high, white and seemingly impregnable. A line of steps scores a 45 degree angle up the rockface from the sea: "The King of Aragon's Staircase", cut by Aragonese soldiers in an unsuccessful siege in 1420. From the Ville Basse round the port at the eastern end of the inlet it's a steep walk up; there is a road, but it's not open to high-season tourists. Vantage points with breathtaking views are Capo Pertusato to the east—to which you can drive—or the Col St-Roch up a footpath nearer the encircling ramparts. The cafés and restaurants round the crowded marina can supply energy for a hot but worthwhile climb—through the gates of the old town, you enter another world.

Bonifacio reputedly took its name from a Tuscan marquis of the 9th century. It became a pirate stronghold: the Genoese gained their first foothold in Corsica here only by surprising the pirates drunk at a wedding feast. By the late 12th century, Bonifacio was a Genoese colony. The whole place is built to resist siege: ramparts immensely thick, grain silos below the Place Grandval, houses designed like mini-fortresses with storage chambers on the ground floor and access originally by ladder to the first. The "flying buttresses" crossing the cobbled alleys were part of a system of canals and gutters, carrying water from a communal cistern under the Loggia of the town church. The layout of the promontory town was necessarily compact, a dense little network of streets, shadowed by tall narrow buildings. Today there are trippery souvenir or craft shops and crowded cafés, all with somewhat inflated prices. Half the site is taken up by the citadel, guarding the western point; and the citadel is today occupied by the Legion. But in high season and at fixed hours, visitors are allowed past the guarded gate to visit one of Bonifacio's churches.

✳ *Eglise St-Dominique* Built by the Templars at the end of the 13th century, the citadel church is Provençal Gothic with rare ogive vaulting. The choir, however, was rebuilt in the 18th century. Among many decorative Baroque pieces are two massive religious groups carved in wood, which in true Corsican fashion are manhandled through the streets in the Easter procession.

✳ *Eglise Ste-Marie Majeure* Most interesting is the big arcaded Loggia fronting the Haute-Ville church, where all manner of town business was transacted. The church itself is a medley of styles from the 13th century to the 18th. The bottom tier of the campanile is Romanesque, the three above Gothic.

Corsica's deep south is not well supplied with beaches: around the Golfe de Santa Manza they are strips of gritty sand extensively used for rough camping, and west of the cape a succession of rocky coves, increasingly inaccessible after Tonnara Plage. But at the **Golfe de Valinco** the fine west-coast beaches begin: spacious and sandy along its southern curve, smaller and quieter to the north. This is one of Corsica's developed holiday areas—hotels and self-catering villages have sprung up all round the Golfe. **Porto Pollo** to the north is a peaceful little resort; **Propriano** in the middle is popular with the British. The tourist centre of the bay, it's thoroughly modernised now, the harbour area crowded with restaurants, cafés and souvenir shops. It's not of any great appeal except as a base from which to explore some interesting places inland.

Excursions from Propriano

✳ **Sartène** This thoroughly atmospheric little hill town of narrow streets and gaunt granite houses has a history of fierce resistance to outsiders and savage vendettas among its inhabitants. The strangest Easter rite in Corsica is Sartène's *Procession du Catenacciu*; "the chained one" is both Christ-symbol and town penitent, anonymous, and chosen by the priest from a waiting list of sinners. Hooded and robed in red, he carries a cross (heavy, of course) through the streets while the crowd attempts to unmask him. His stumbles and falls are not all ritual.

✳ **Megaliths and menhirs** South of Sartène the D48 leads through *maquis* landscape to an area of standing stones from the Bronze Age: a race called the Torréens invaded Corsica around 1,500 BC. At **Cauria** there are alignments of 20 and 40 oval granite menhirs, about six feet high, some aslant or toppled completely. The **Dolmen de Fontanaccia** still stands, a chamber composed of six granite slabs supporting a much heavier one some twelve feet by nine. West at **Palaggiu**, over a hundred menhirs form a single mysterious line, facing the sunset.

✳ **Spin' A Cavallu** Corsica is full of medieval bridges built by the Genoese, but they are usually glimpsed far down a ravine. This one is not only well-preserved but accessible, a couple of miles north of Sartène up the D268. The design is a single humped arch of shaped granite blocks, supporting a narrow but secure path in the form of a graduated causeway.

Filitosa

420

✳ **Filitosa** North of the Golfe de Valinco, the biggest prehistoric site in Corsica is still being explored (and somewhat commercialised). A whole Torréen village has been excavated; there are complex mounds of rock constructed for religious ceremony or defence. Most striking are the menhirs carved with faces—stylised, impassive and strange, but each distinct and human.

Hotels

Corsica

Barcaggio, 20275 Haute-Corse   ££

LA GIRAGLIA   Tel: 95.35.60.54

This simple little hotel boasts an enviable position—its small terrace and garden are right on the water's edge (there's rocky bathing) with views over the sea towards the centre of the attractive little port/resort. Barcaggio is in the most northern part of Cap Corse, and reached by a small D road. It has dunes and an excellent beach, thinly populated with cows, rough-campers and windsurfers. La Giraglia's rooms are adequate and cosy, and cooking simple—grills, fish, lobster. Peace and quiet prevail—except for twice-weekly disco evenings in high season.

Closed Oct to Mar; 23 bedrooms; no lift.

Bastia (at Pietranera), 20200 Haute-Corse   £££

PIETRACAP   Tel: 95.31.64.63

It isn't easy to find accommodation in Bastia. The Pietracap, 3km north off the D80 in the direction of St-Martin, is a useful modern lodging house without restaurant: rather unattractive, but quiet and comfortable, with a nice large swimming pool in the garden, and a pleasant breakfast terrace.

Closed Dec to Feb; 22 bedrooms; swimming pool; no rest; no lift.

Calvi, 20260 Haute-Corse   ££££

GRAND   Tel: 95.65.09.74

Smart, stylish though no longer grand hotel in town centre, a couple of blocks away from Calvi's bustling harbour and the citadel (some front rooms can be a little noisy). Ground floor public rooms are traditionally and comfortably furnished, and bedrooms—some spacious—are well decorated with good bathrooms. The large, sky-blue restaurant on the 5th floor, with chandeliers and 30's sailing trophies in cabinets, is now sadly used only for breakfast: magnificent views of Calvi Bay make up for the rather dirty windows.

Closed Oct to Mar; 52 bedrooms.

Our price symbols

£	You can expect to find a room for under £15
££	You can expect to find a room for £15 to £25
£££	You can expect to find a room for £25 to £35
££££	You can expect to find a room for £35 to £45
£££££	You should expect to pay over £45 for a room

Hotels

Centuri Port, 20238 Haute-Corse £

LE VIEUX MOULIN   Tel: 95.35.60.15

A big salmon-coloured house with green shutters (and a pink new annexe in the garden) in the centre of a delightful Cap Corse fishing village, overlooking the harbour and grey stone, green-roofed houses. Public rooms are small and quaint: an attractive sitting room has comfy chairs, old books (de Gaulle and Walter Scott), and views over the port. Bedrooms vary in style. In the main building rooms are very simple and have no bathrooms (and sanitary arrangements are decidedly primitive); in the annexe, rooms are modern and attractively decorated. The food is good, served in the plain little dining room or on the terrace.

Closed Nov to Feb; 12 bedrooms; no lift.

Evisa, 20126 Corse-du-Sud ££

AÏTONE   Tel: 95.26.20.04

A very friendly and inexpensive hotel in a popular walking-base village in the wooded mountains behind Porto. A new section of the hotel has recently been added—bedrooms here are better equipped and altogether preferable to the rather cramped ones in the old part. There are fine views across a steep valley from most of the bedrooms and from the terrace. There's a woody, bright dining room and bar, a TV room next door. Cooking is simple (gamey pâtés and a good *omelette corse*), the *réserve* wine is robust, and prices are low.

Closed mid-Nov to Dec; 32 bedrooms; no lift.

Monticello, 20220 Haute-Corse ££

A PASTORELLA   Tel: 95.60.05.65

In the main square of a charming medieval stone village perched on a steep hill 3km inland from the busy resort of L'Ile-Rousse, this small characterful hotel is the focal point of village life, and has a lively, bustling atmosphere. Traditional rustic furnishings, smallish old-fashioned bedrooms (all with showers, some with stupendous views), and wholesome, generous country cooking. Run by a friendly cheerful family.

Closed Nov and Dec (rest Sun dinner and Mon); 20 bedrooms; no lift.

Porticcio, 20166 Corse-du-Sud ££££

LE MAQUIS   Tel: 95.25.05.55

This stylish hotel consists of a little encampment of white, shuttered, rust-tiled buildings around a central one with a wide terrace and beautiful fresh-water pool. The atmosphere is casual and exclusive; sitting rooms have comfortable modern chairs and sofas, rustic antiques, plants and paintings. Bedrooms are simply furnished—beams, tiled floor and rugs, good bathrooms; some have balconies, ground floor ones are directly on the sandy beach. It's worth putting up with the fairly ordinary cooking—with limited choice on the fixed-price menu—and the relatively high cost, as this is a rather special hotel, and so much better than others in the area.

Closed Jan; 22 bedrooms; swimming pool; no lift.

Porte-Vecchio, 20137 Corse-du-Sud £££

GRAND HOTEL DE CALA ROSSA   Tel: 95.71.61.51

This simple two-storey hotel enjoys a superb position, set in an estate of private villas on an unspoilt sandy beach amid secluded and delightful gardens, where you can eat breakfast. The dining room, bar and sitting room are rather featureless and a bit cramped; bedrooms, too, lack character but are very comfortable. There are fine views from the beach (but, because of the vegetation, not from the gardens, ground floor or many seaside bedrooms). Food is above average, staff friendly and anglophone.

Closed Oct to mid-May; 60 bedrooms; no lift.

Porto-Vecchio, 20137 Corse-du-Sud £££

SAN GIOVANNI   Tel: 95.70.22.25

This small family-run hotel, popular with British visitors, has a peaceful rural position in a forest of cork-oaks, 3km inland from Porto Vecchio. The main house is charmingly decorated with interesting personal touches. Bedrooms are in a bungalow-style block built to one side, with little patios and rockeries; they're comfortable, well-decorated and attractive. Cooking is homely and good. There's tennis and a small swimming pool, and bikes can be hired.

Closed Nov to Mar; 27 bedrooms.

St-Florent, 20217 Haute-Corse £££

DOLCE NOTTE   Tel: 95.37.06.26

An unobtrusive low-rise modern building about 1km from the resort centre, with sea views from all bedrooms over St-Florent's easterly beach of smooth mauve pebbles. Bedrooms are comfortable and quite smart; there are a few cheaper ones in an annexe. Carefully prepared food is served in the restaurant with its attractive terrace overlooking the sea. A civilised and relaxing atmosphere.

Closed mid-Oct to Easter; 20 bedrooms; no lift.

Our price symbols

£	You can expect to find a room for under £15
££	You can expect to find a room for £15 to £25
£££	You can expect to find a room for £25 to £35
££££	You can expect to find a room for £35 to £45
£££££	You should expect to pay over £45 for a room

General Information

Travel

Crossing the Channel

Cross-channel ferries operate most frequently between Dover/Folkestone and Boulogne/Calais. These are the shortest (just over an hour) and cheapest (although not always the most economical) ways of crossing the Channel with a car, except for the speedier hovercraft services from Dover and Ramsgate to Boulogne and Calais. Prices vary significantly between operators and very substantially according to time and season; it pays to shop around. Other services are Dover/Ramsgate to Dunkerque ($2\frac{1}{2}$ hours); Newhaven to Dieppe (4 hours); Portsmouth to Caen ($5\frac{1}{2}$ hours), to Le Havre ($6\frac{1}{2}$ to 9 hours), to Cherbourg (5 hours); Poole to Cherbourg ($4\frac{1}{2}$ hours); Weymouth to Cherbourg (4 hours); Plymouth to Roscoff (6 hours).

Choice of cross-channel route depends on your point of departure in the UK, your destination in France or beyond, and preference for sea or land travel. You rarely save money by taking a longer ferry trip; you may save time spent in the car and an overnight hotel stay; and you may avoid Paris.

Cross-channel operators: Brittany Ferries (Plymouth to Roscoff; Portsmouth to St-Malo and Caen), Hoverspeed (Dover to Boulogne/Calais). Sally Line (Ramsgate to Dunkerque). Sealink-British Ferries (Dover/Folkestone to Boulogne/Calais; Newhaven to Dieppe; Weymouth and Portsmouth to Cherbourg). Townsend Thoresen (Dover to Boulogne/Calais; Portsmouth to Cherbourg/Le Havre). Truckline Ferries (Poole to Cherbourg).

Motoring

Insurance

You will need ordinary travel insurance to cover you for things like loss of your possessions and medical expenses; you will probably want to insure against breakdowns (see below); and you will probably also want to buy special motor insurance to cover you for accidental damage to your car or other cars (or people).

Your ordinary UK motor insurance automatically gives you the legal minimum requirement for France, but this legal minimum is usually much less than the cover you would normally have in the UK.

To extend your normal cover, you need to buy from your insurer a Green Card (motor insurance certificate), which will be accepted in all European countries as evidence that you have satisfactory cover.

Route planning

You can get detailed advice on specific routes from the AA and RAC. The AA Overseas Routes Service also produce a useful *European Through Route Map* for each Channel port, showing recommended routes to places throughout Europe.

Maps showing alternative routes, and how to avoid the worst traffic jams, are produced annually by the French Ministry of Transport. They're called *Bison Futé* (wily buffalo), and are available free at petrol stations, roadside information centres and from the AA. Some roads are labelled *Bison Futé*.

Breakdown insurance

Called "vehicle security" or "vehicle protection" the purpose of this insurance is to protect you from some of the expense and inconvenience which can result from a car breakdown, and also cover other risks. You claim back from the insurer costs which you have had to meet, and most policies also claim to offer practical help and advice at the time of the incident. The scope of the insurance isn't limited to helping you get the car fixed or recovered. If your car is out of action, the

425

policies have provisions for either accommodating you while it's being repaired or continuing your holiday by other means. Some policies cover incidents other than breakdowns—for example the insurance comes into effect if your car is stolen, or if injury or illness strikes the driver.

The four policies used by most respondents to a survey of 3,700 members of the Consumers' Association who had taken their car abroad were AA 5-star, Europ Assistance, RAC Travellers Bond and Caravan Club Red Pennant. The RAC Travellers Bond is available to anyone who takes out temporary membership (if you buy ferry tickets through them you can get a reduced-rate insurance); the Caravan Club Red Pennant service is available only to members of the club.

Breakdown insurance is mainly useful for dealing with major problems when your car is immobilised for several days and required parts are not available. In nearly all cases minor problems can be most conveniently and swiftly solved without recourse to breakdown insurance facilities.

None of the policies covers the cost of parts needed to repair the car, and you may have to pay a labour charge.

It's worth getting hold of a list of dealers for your car: the AA *Travellers' Guide to France* lists garages with breakdown services (with details of which makes of car they deal with and closing days). The red Michelin guide to France also lists garages (a larger number, with details of makes of car, but not of opening times).

Regulations

Seat belts must be worn by driver and front-seat passenger; under-tens may not travel in the front seat unless the car has no back seat.

If your car breaks down, you must place a red warning triangle on the road 30 metres behind it if your car is not fitted with hazard warning lights.

Driving with only side-lights lit is now allowed; it is advisable to have headlight beams adjusted for right-hand drive, or to buy a headlamp converter (the clip-on type also changes the light to amber). You should carry the car's registration document with you (if you've hired it in Britain, you need a certificate from the AA or RAC; if the vehicle is not owned by you, you need a letter authorising you to drive it).

Caravans

Vehicles towing a caravan must be fitted with an adequate rearview mirror. The maximum caravan dimensions are 2.5 metres wide, 11 metres long. On trunk roads and motorways, you must keep a distance of 50 metres between you and the vehicle in front. The *AA Guide to Camping and Caravanning in Europe* gives useful information.

Speed limits

Built-up areas: 60 kph (37 mph); outside built-up areas; 90 kph (56 mph) on normal roads, 110 kph (68 mph) on dual carriageways and toll-free motorways, 130 kph (80 mph) on toll motorways. Speed limits are lower when wet: 110 kph (68 mph) on toll motorways, 80 kph (50 mph) on other roads. The minimum age for driving a car is 18, and for a year after passing their test drivers may not exceed 90 kph (56 mph). Speeding offences may be fined on the spot.

Priority

One of the most perplexing continental regulations for British tourists. The principle is that in the absence of any indication to the contrary, traffic coming from the right has priority. The "indications to the contrary" are either STOP or "give way" signs, where minor roads meet major roads. On a major road, a tilted yellow square means that you have priority; when there's a black bar crossing the diamond, you no longer have priority. Since May 1984, the regulation no longer applies on roundabouts, where traffic entering from approach roads now gives way as it does in Britain.

Roads and road signs
Toutes directions (all directions) in towns means the route for through traffic; *centre ville* indicates the town centre. *Poids lourds* is the route for heavy traffic (lorries); *sens interdit* means no entry; *sens unique* one way.

Pointer signposts can be confusing, as they seem to point across rather than towards the road indicated. A green arrow on its side indicates a route for holiday traffic at busy times, avoiding main roads.

Motorways
Most are toll roads (*autoroutes à péage*); some are expensive, even for relatively short distances. The tolls from Calais to Nice return amount to about £60 for a car, £90 for a car and caravan.

Accidents
Police should be informed, particularly if someone is injured. A *constat à l'amiable* (an accident statement form) must be completed in all cases and signed by both parties (if appropriate); any disputes should be taken to a local bailiff who will prepare a report (*constat d'huissier*).

Emergency telephone numbers
Police and ambulance 17; fire 18.

Car hire
Major car rental companies (including Avis, Godfrey Davis Europcar and Hertz) have offices in almost all towns, and cars can be booked in advance from this country. You can usually arrange to collect the car in one place, and leave it in another at no extra charge (provided the company has an office there). Fly-drive arrangements are available in conjunction with the major airlines.

Motoring vocabulary
Petrol: *essence* (comes in two grades, *ordinaire* equivalent to 2-star—and *super*).
Diesel fuel: *gas-oil, gazole.*
Fill her up: *faites le plein, s'il vous plaît.*
Tyres: *les pneus.*
Check the oil: *vérifiez l'huile, s'il vous plaît.*

The AA publish a useful *Car Components Guide*—a small booklet which lists nearly 500 parts and gives translations and illustrations. It comes free with AA 5-star insurance.

Weights and measures
Distances
8km equals approx. 5 miles
km : miles

3 : 2	10 : 6	80 : 50
4 : 2½	20 : 12	90 : 56
5 : 3	30 : 18	100 : 62
6 : 3½	40 : 25	125 : 78
7 : 4	50 : 31	150 : 94
8 : 5	60 : 37	200 : 125
9 : 5½	70 : 44	

Petrol

The gallon is just over 4½ litres.

Litres	British gallons
5	1.1
10	2.2
15	3.3
20	4.4
30	6.7
40	8.8
50	11.1
100	22.2

Tyre pressures

lbs per sq.in.	kg per sq.cm.
18	1.25
20	1.4
22	1.55
24	1.7
26	1.8
28	2.0
30	2.1
32	2.25
34	2.4

Air

There are many regional airports served from Britain—some of them from small airports in the south of England. Airports with direct flights from the UK (some only seasonal) are: Biarritz, Bordeaux, Caen, Clermont-Ferrand, Deauville, Le Havre, Lille, Lourdes/Tarbes, Lyon, Marseille, Montpellier, Morlaix, Nantes, Nice, Paris, Perpignan, Quimper, Rennes, Strasbourg, and Toulouse.

France is also well served by internal air services, most run by Air Inter.

Rail

French Railways (SNCF) operate a good network of services, with many lines using the comfortable, modern, air-conditioned Corail trains; some major lines have the 1st-class-only Trans Europe Express trains (TEE); and the brand new high-speed train (TGV), with 1st and 2nd class, now operates from Paris to St-Etienne via Lyon, to Besançon via Dijon, and to Geneva via Mâcon (Paris to Lyon takes 2 hours, to Geneva 3¾ hours). SNCF at 179 Piccadilly, London W1V 0BA, tel 01-409 1224, will provide information and make bookings.

Sleeper On the longer routes there are sleeper trains like those in Britain—with single, two berth or three-berth compartments; and also cheaper *couchettes*, compartments for 4 or 6 with bunks.

Tickets When buying a ticket in France you must validate it (*composter*) by using the orange automatic date-stamping machine at the platform entrance. If you fail to do so, you will have to pay a surcharge of 20% of the fare. There are various reduced tickets: rail rover (*France Vacances*); or holiday return (*séjour*) tickets which allow a 25% reduction on fares (with certain conditions); senior citizens can get a 50% reduction by buying a *Carte Vermeil* ticket in advance.

Motorail There are several car-carrying train services which might be useful: from Calais and Boulogne to Biarritz, Avignon and the Mediterranean coast, more services from Paris.

Bus

There are very few long distance bus services in France. Coach tours operated by French Railways (information from 01-409 1224) are organised in the major tourist areas in summer; there are half-day, day and longer excursions. Local buses in rural areas are few and far between—some have only one or two services a week, usually coinciding with local markets. Local tourist offices have timetables.

Cycling

If you want to take your own bike with you, it's probably best to consider a cycling holiday in Normandy. While bicycles are carried free on ferries, further transportation problems are considerable. Unlike British trains, French trains are generally without guard's vans, and those on which it is possible to take your bike with you are very few and far between. French Railways will undertake to carry your bike unaccompanied as luggage; there is no guarantee that the bike travels with you on the same train, and a delay of up to five days is possible in high season. French Railways recommend registering your bike from London Victoria, 12 hours before you travel (you need to be in possession of a rail ticket to the appropriate destination). It's worth packaging your bike carefully to avoid damage.

You can hire a bicycle at 250 railway stations (and at some you can make arrangements to leave it at another station). The Cyclists Touring Club, Cotterell House, 69 Meadrow, Godalming, Surrey GU7 3HS, has a French touring information sheet and touring notes compiled by members, information on recommended routes and advice leaflets. They also organise tours.

Yachting and boating

Inland waterways are extensive, and with a few exceptions, no charge is made for the use of waterways and locks. Yacht holidays are becoming increasingly popular as new marinas spring up. The French Government Tourist Office has information on maps, rules and regulations, organisations that can be of help, and a suggested reading list. For inclusive yachts and boat holidays, consult their list of "special interest" tour operators.

Accommodation

Hotels

Lists of approved hotels (rated on a scale from 1 to 4-star-luxury) are produced by the French Government Tourist Office. Guidebooks (see the section on Recommended Books) list a selection of hotels—usually including simple rural *auberges* (which have few facilities) and restaurants with rooms (which can vary from basic to extremely luxurious—the latter sometimes coinciding with an accolade for food). You need to book well ahead for high season and for popular areas (especially Paris); local tourist offices with an *Accueil de France* service can help with bookings up to a week ahead.

Prices are quoted per room, rather than per person, and do not in theory include breakfast. In many hotels (particularly in resorts or tourist areas) you're expected to eat an evening meal—though French law now says the hotelier cannot refuse you accommodation if you don't. Full-board terms usually apply after three days (but you may find that *pension* menus are different from the other restaurant menus, with less or no choice of dishes).

Camping and caravanning

A very popular way of holidaymaking in France. There are lots of attractive lakeside and riverside sites, although few can match the standard and facilities of similar sites in Austria, Switzerland or Germany. Campsite shops tend to be relatively expensive; but many sites have take-aways which can provide chicken and chips at least. Some of the nicest—although not the least crowded—sites we saw in our inspections were in the Dordogne area, and in the Landes (south-west of Bordeaux). Some of the most attractive sites are members of the *Castels et*

Camping organisation. In popular tourist areas, farms offer *camping à la ferme*; facilities are simple, but numbers restricted—you may get a field to yourself. Local tourist offices have details of these and other campsites.

Self-catering

There are lots of simple rural cottages, and plenty of modern purpose-built apartments in resorts (particularly along the Mediterranean coast and in ski areas). Lots of tour operators organise package holidays combining self-catering accommodation and car ferry, and there are also quite a few packages to the south which include air transport. Some tour operators, and some large letting agencies, rent holiday homes on an "accommodation only" basis. In addition, there are various French organisations which can help you find accommodation.

The *Fédération Nationale des Gîtes Ruraux de France* (or *Gîtes de France* for short) offers thousands of properties all over France. The properties (called *gîtes*) are almost invariably in the countryside and many are renovated farm buildings— some are quite remote, others are in small villages. Properties are all inspected and graded by the organisation but they warn that even a top-rated *gîte* will not compare with a three-star hotel. The minimum standard, however, ensures that all properties at least have running water, a shower, inside lavatory and shuttered or curtained windows. Each *gîte* is privately owned, usually by families living locally, and sometimes the *gîte* may be a self-contained apartment in the owner's house. *Gîtes de France* produces a brochure in English listing 1,600 properties but to get the brochure and use their English booking service you have to pay a fee and join the "*Amis des Gîtes de France*". They operate from Gîtes de France Ltd., 178 Piccadilly, London W1V 0AL.

You can also write directly to the local offices of *Gîtes de France* (called *Relais Départementaux*) or to the agencies run by the tourist authorities in many French *départements* (called *Services Loisirs Accueil*). However, you will probably be sent information in French and have to make your booking direct with the owner.

Another way to book a *gîte* is to get hold of the French Farm and Village Holiday Guide (FHG Publications/Ian Allen) which contains descriptions, photographs, prices and direct booking addresses for 1,500 *gîtes*. *Gîtes* are also increasingly available as part of package holidays, from the French Travel Service and ferry companies.

Special interest holidays

If you want something a little different, there is an enormous variety; some include tuition, with subjects including cooking, painting, art, crafts, archaeology, history or nature studies; some include tickets for music festivals or sporting events, or visits to châteaux or battlefields; some include accommodation on a barge, a cabin cruiser, or a self-sail or skippered yacht; and some are "gastronomic" tours, or include visits to vineyards.

Package holidays

Lots of tour operators offer packages which include travel (by air, coach, rail or car) and stay-put accommodation (in hotels, self-catering cottages, or on campsites); or car, coach, or rail touring holidays with or without booked accommodation.

A list of tour operators offering inclusive hotel, camping, self-catering and special interest holidays can be obtained from the French Government Tourist Office, 178 Piccadilly, London W1V 0AL.

Recommended Books

Accommodation and Restaurants

Most people's starting point when looking for hotels and restaurants is the red Michelin *Guide France*, which appears annually. It is very useful for practical information, with town maps indicating hotels, restaurants and much besides; it selects and gives judgements (in symbol form) on hotels, gives accolades for excellent food and quotes prices. What it does not do is give you much impression of what a place is like. A guide book which does is the *Gault Millau Guide France*, also annual, which is not easily bought in Britain. It is much stronger on food (its authors started the *nouvelle cuisine* fashion) than on hotels; it is written (in French) in an amusingly idiosyncratic and linguistically demanding style. A reliable personal selection of retaurants and hotels is Richard Binns' *French Leave* (Chiltern House). The *Guide des Logis de France* concentrates mainly on one kind of hotel—simple, small, family-run establishments—and has numerous devotees. The annual Michelin guide *Camping Caravaning France* gives a good selection of campsites.

Guidebooks: series

Michelin *Green Guides*, 18, 7 in English; cover all France.
Guides Bleus, 10, French only; cover most of France (Hachette).
Blue Guides to *France; Paris and Environs; Corsica*; (A & C Black).
Berlitz (Pocket) Guides to *The French Riviera; The Loire Valley; Brittany; Paris*.
Companion Guides to *Ile de France; The Loire; Normandy; South of France; Southwest France; Paris*; (Collins).
Mitchell Beazley (Pocket) Guides to *Paris; The South of France*.
France Inconnue series by Georges Pillement, in French only; *Alsace et les Vosges Inconnues; La Bretagne Inconnue; Provence/Côte d'Azur Inconnue*; (all out of print).

Guidebooks: singles in print

Granite Island, Dorothy Carrington (Penguin).
The Loire, Vivian Rowe (Eyre Methuen).
Three Rivers of France, Freda White (Faber & Faber).
Travels with a Donkey in the Cévennes (1879), Robert Louis Stevenson (Everyman's Classics).
Travels Through France and Italy (1766), Tobias Smollett (Everyman's Classics).

. . . . . out of print

Hare, Augustus; *The Rivieras* (1896), and other guidebooks covering all France.
Myhill, Henry; *Brittany* (1969); and *North of the Pyrenees* (1973).
Oyler, Philip; *The Generous Earth* (1950).
Spence, Keith: *Brittany and the Bretons* (1978).
White, Freda; *Ways of Aquitaine*; and *West of the Rhône* (1964).
Whymper, Edward; *Chamonix and the Range of Mont Blanc* (1896).
Young, Arthur; *Travels in France during the years 1787, 1788, 1789* (1792).

Guides to Paris

Michelin *Green Guide*; descriptions of areas and sights, with opening hours, prices, maps; general information (English edition).
Michelin *Paris Atlas*; street atlas and comprehensive municipal index of everything from embassies to swimming pools.
Gault Millau, *Le Guide de Paris* (French only); lists and descriptions of restaurants, bars, nightlife, shops, and services.
Officiel des Spectacles, weekly publication listing events and what's on at theatres, cinemas, nightclubs; *Une Semaine de Paris—Pariscop* is similar.

Food

Charcuterie and French Pork Cookery; and *Vegetable Book*; Jane Grigson (Penguin)
French Provincial Cooking; Elizabeth David (Penguin)
French Regional Cooking; Ann Willan (Hutchinson)
Mediterranean Seafood; Alan Davidson (Penguin)
The New Cuisine; Paul Bocuse (Granada)
The Taste of France; Fay Sharman (Macmillan)

Wine

Guide to Visiting Vineyards; Anthony Hogg (Michael Joseph)
The Wines of Bordeaux; Edmund Penning-Rowsell (Alan Lane)
The Wines of Burgundy; H W Yoxall (International Wine and Food Society)
The World Atlas of Wine; and *Pocket Wine Book*; Hugh Johnson (Mitchell Beazley)

General

Fat Man on a Bicycle; Tom Vernon (Fontana)
France – A Guide for the Independent Traveller; John P. Harris (Papermac)
France in the 1980s; John Ardagh (Secker & Warburg)

Specialist

Access Guides (for disabled travellers) to *Paris*; *Brittany* and *The Loire*; available from G R Crouch, 68B Castlebar Road, Ealing, London W5 200
Inland Waterways of France; Benest (Imray)
Walking in France; Rob Hunter (Oxford Illustrated Press)
Walks and Climbs in the Pyrenees; Kev Reynolds (Cicerone Press)

Historical Background

The Conquest of Gaul; Julius Caesar (Penguin)
Astérix le Gaulois (and many sequels, some translated); Goscinny and Ulderzo (Dargaud)
The Distant Mirror; the Calamitous 14th Century; Barbara Tuchman (Penguin)
The Sun King and *Madame de Pompadour*; Nancy Mitford (out of print)
When the Riviera was Ours; Patrick Howarth (Routledge & Kegan Paul)
A History of Modern France, 1712–1962; Alfred Cobban (Penguin)
The Pelican History of Art; founding editor Nikolaus Pevsner. Relevant titles include *Carolingian and Romanesque Architecture*; *Gothic Architecture*; *Art and Architecture in France, 1500–1700*; *Art and Architecture of the 18th Century in France*; *Painting and Sculpture in Europe, 1780–1880*; *Painting and Sculpture in Europe 1880–1940*; *Architecture; 19th and 20th centuries*.
Pages from the Goncourt Journal; edited Robert Baldick (Penguin).

Literature

Alain-Fournier, Henry; *Le Grand Meaulnes* (Loire/Berry)
Balzac, Honoré de: *Les Chouans* (Brittany); *Le Curé de Tours* and *Le Lys dans la Vallée* (Loire); *Les Illusions Perdues* (Paris)
Fitzgerald, Scott; *Tender is the Night* (South)
Flaubert, Gustave; *Madame Bovary* (Normandy); *Education Sentimentale* (Paris)
Hugo, Victor; *Les Misérables* (Paris)
Hóias, Pierre Jakez; *The Horse of Pride* (Brittany)
Loti, Pierre; *Pêcheur d'Islande* (Brittany)
Miller, Henry; *Tropic of Cancer* (Paris)
Mauriac, François; *Thérèse* (Atlantic Coast)
Orwell, George; *Down and out in Paris and London*
Stendhal; *Mémoires d'un touriste*

Maps

We group the maps available according to the size of the area covered by individual sheets. You've a wide choice of maps covering the whole country on one sheet; for more detailed maps of individual regions the range is much narrower, while all the really detailed maps of the kind you'd need for walking are published by, or based on, the **Institut Géographique National** (IGN)—the French equivalent of our Ordnance Survey. There are also some atlases of France which are now available in the UK.

All of France on one sheet

Most whole-country maps of France are at a scale of 1:1,000,000 (about 16 miles to 1 inch). At this scale, you can't expect much information on sights, scenic routes, villages or minor roads, but you should get enough to follow main-road routes across the country, and maps of this kind are useful for planning. There are four main contenders:

Michelin 1:1,000,000 Clear, detailed, accurate and easy to use. One of the cheapest maps available. The only drawback is the use of solid yellow blobs for big cities, obscuring through routes. You can also buy this map double-sided (though there's little advantage unless you need to save weight) or as two separate sheets—northern and southern France.

Hallwag 1:1,000,000 More expensive than Michelin, but attractive and very well printed, with a useful index booklet.

IGN 1:1,000,000 A very strikingly designed map, with heavily-emphasized mountains; main roads clear and accurate.

Geographia International Recta-Foldex 1:1,000,000 Very accurate, if slightly fussy, with a lot of detail for this scale. Geographia has a helpful (if inaccessible) index on the back of the map—but don't confuse their 1:1,000,000 map with their much less useful pocket map at 1:1,750,000.

Three other national maps worth looking out for are the **IGN Artistic Treasures** and **Long Distance Footpaths** maps, which use the IGN 1:1,000,000 map as a base for overprinted detail of places of artistic and historic interest and long distance footpaths respectively—useful for planning your trip; and the *Bison Futé* (wily bison), a map issued free every year by the French Ministry of Transport. It shows how to avoid the worst summer traffic jams, and you can pick it up at roadside information centres in France—or from the AA before you leave.

Large areas on one sheet

Several publishers produce maps at scales around 1:500,000 (8 miles to one inch). At this scale it generally takes three or four sheets to cover the whole country. But you still won't get enough detail for touring on minor roads—so again, they're useful mainly for main-road motoring or general planning. The main ones to consider are:

Kümmerly & Frey 1:600,000 In two sheets—North and South; also available as a single double-sided sheet covering the whole country (though it's a bit unwieldy). Quite detailed, and very good for touring information—eg clear hill-shading, scenic routes, sights, campsites.

Kümmerly & Frey 1:500,000 Covers France and Benelux in four sheets; design and features similar to 1:600,000 maps.

Geographia/Recta-Foldex 1:550,000 In four sheets—NE, SE, SW and NW. Fairly detailed, but very little touring information and vague-looking minor roads do not inspire confidence.

433

Individual regions on one sheet

There are three map series at scales of 1:200,000 to 1:250,000 (three to four miles to the inch), each of which covers a single region (eg Brittany, Alsace) on each sheet. For local journeys on minor roads detailed regional maps like these are pretty well essential. All three series have their strong points:

Michelin 1:200,000 These familiar yellow-covered maps used to be available only in narrow, strip-shaped sheets covering quite a small area—it took 37 to cover the whole of France. Now they are also available in a much larger (and more convenient) "Regional" format, covering the country in 16 sheets. Both series are admirably clear, easy to follow and comprehensive, with particularly good road detail in villages and small towns.

IGN Red Series 1:250,000 Some detail a bit difficult to read, but a very attractive general purpose map which gives a good idea of the terrain. Covers the country in 16 sheets, with index and lists of major events and festivals.

Recta-Foldex Cart' Index 1:250,000 Very nearly as good as Michelin for navigating, and better for touring information (eg campsites and places of interest). Has an index printed on the back. Covers the country in 15 sheets.

Local maps

There are only two local map series which cover the whole country, both published by IGN:

IGN Green Series 1:100,000 A good choice for really detailed local exploring by car. Shows contours and some footpaths, but not really detailed enough for walking. Covers the country in 74 large sheets.

IGN Orange Series 1:50,000. The equivalent to the British Ordnance Survey Pathfinder Series. The area covered by each sheet is too small for most car touring, but there's enough detail for walking, including contours. Sheets are much smaller than with the British OS equivalent and it takes 1100 of them to cover the whole of France (as opposed to 200 Pathfinder maps for Britain). There are also some large-sheet special editions based on IGN maps, but overprinted with walking and touring information, which can work out cheaper and more convenient than the Orange series if they cover an area you're interested in. These include the *Didier Richard Series* (30 maps of the Alps, the Rhône Valley, the Jura and Corsica at 1:25,000 and 1:50,000); the *Randonnées Pyrénéennes* (11 maps of the Pyrenees at 1:50,000); and the *Club Vosgien series* (17 maps of the Vosges at 1:50,000 and 1:25,000). The more detailed IGN *Blue Series* and *Violet Series* at 1:25,000 cover major parts of the Alps and the Pyrenees. Selected sheets are reproduced as the *Mountain Series* (20 maps of the highest parts of the Alps at 1:25,000).

Atlases

Three very different atlases are available in Britain. None of them gives anything like the detail you'd expect from a road atlas of Britain, and they're in no sense a substitute for the regional 1:200,000 or 1:250,000 maps mentioned above.

AA Illustrated Atlas of France Half devoted to guidebook-style regional descriptions, with colour photographs and small maps, and half to sectional maps of France produced by the Swiss firm, Kümmerly & Frey. The latter are all at 1:1,000,000—ie no more detailed than you get on the single-sheet maps of France, and certainly not good enough for local touring on minor roads.

RAC Navigator France Sectional maps at 1:550,000, based on the same cartography as the Geographia/Recta-Foldex 4-sheet series (see above). Not detailed enough for local touring on minor roads, but better than the AA atlas, and it has some useful tour plans. Gazetteer-style touring information at the back.

Michelin Motorway Atlas Quite different from the two atlases above—a thin booklet of simple strip maps showing motorways in great detail (right down to signs at interchanges) but little else; a central section gives tolls and mileages.

Where to get maps
The following shops have catalogues or lists of maps and will supply to mail order
as well as to personal callers:
Edward Stanford Ltd., 12–14 Long Acre, London WC2E 9LP. Tel: 01-836 1321.
The Map Shop (AT Atkinson and Partner), 15 High St., Upton-on-Severn, Worcs.
WR8 0HJ. Tel: (06 846) 3146.
Heffers Map Shop, 3 Green St., Cambridge CB2 3JA. Tel: (0223) 350701.
McCarta's Map and Guide Shop, 122 King's Cross Road, London WC1X 9DS.
Tel: 01-278 8276.
In addition, you can buy *Recta-Foldex* maps direct from the importer (though it's
unlikely to save you any money):
Roger Lascelles, 47 York Road, Brentford, Middlesex, TW8 0QP. Tel: 01-847
0935.

Weather

The table below compares the temperature and sunshine record of
representative towns on the coasts and inland—the average daily maximum
temperature, and bright sunshine as a percentage of daylight hours.

	APRIL		JULY		OCTOBER	
	temp	sun	temp	sun	temp	sun
	C	%	C	%	C	%
Caen	13	50	22	47	15	39
Nantes	15	49	23	52	16	40
Biarritz*	16	50	23	42	18	38
Montpellier	18	62	29	79	20	54
Nice	17	60	26	77	21	58
Paris	16	47	25	49	16	37
Le Puy	13	47	24	60	15	41
Grenoble	16	48	26	61	16	40
London	13	38	22	39	14	30
Ilfracombe	12	43	19	40	14	30

* Biarritz sunshine figures based on only 2 years' data

There is more to the French climate than the general truth that the further
south you go the hotter and sunnier the weather you can expect to encounter.
The main climatic influences are oceanic (along the Atlantic coast), continental
(the further east the more continental the climate), and Mediterranean. The
oceanic influence is cooling in summer, warming in winter and gently rain-
bearing. The continental influence is more extreme—hotter summers, colder
winters, and storms. The Mediterranean influence is warm and sunny. These
factors account, for example, for harsher winters in Lorraine than Anjou and
much drier and sunnier weather in the eastern than western Pyrenees.

Coasts The Gulf Stream gives the Cap de La Hague on the northern tip of the
Cotentin peninsula (Normandy) the same average temperature in January as

Nice, famous warm winter resort. Brittany too is mild in winter as it is in summer. What the Gulf Stream cannot do is to make the sun shine, in which respect the Côte d'Azur has more than an edge on Normandy. Cherbourg has about 50 hours a month of midwinter sun, Nice about 150 hours. Mountains by the sea mean atmospheric turmoil often in the form of the unpleasant *mistral*, a cold north wind which howls down the Rhône valley into Provence for days on end. Less often there are warm winds, dry or damp, from the south, bringing North African dust and sand with them.

Mountains Mountain ranges are important influences on the weather. The Alps shelter a small section of the Mediterranean coast near the Italian border where the winter is particularly warm and fruit ripens. The annual average temperature in Monaco is 16°C; there is about one frost per decade. Pau, just to the north of the western Pyrenees, is wetter, but also very mild in winter. The formidable natural barrier of the Alps disrupts all normal weather patterns and local variations in climate are remarkable. Mont Blanc in particular is a meteorological law unto itself. The Vosges shelter the Rhineland plain, often resulting in stifling summer weather in Alsace. The Massif Central, the huge mountain area of central southern France, has a variety of climates sharing all influences; as a whole, it is stormy in summer. The southern Massif's climate is one of extremes, the dryness of the summer accentuated by the poor water-retentive power of the limestone sub-soil. The Cévennes region (in the southern Massif) is where all sorts of air currents converge and is more rained on than anywhere else in France (2 metres of rain a year, and on 30/31 October 1963 608 mm in 24 hours, on Mont Aigoual). The northern Massif (Auvergne) is characterised by extreme variations of temperature—an astonishing 41°C minimum/maximum spread was recorded on August 10th 1885—and chilly midsummer days are not rare.

General Information

Medical
Your local Department of Health and Social Security (DHSS) has a leaflet SA28 explaining the formalities you will need to know if you fall ill. You need to complete the form at the end of the leaflet, return it to the DHSS, who will send your form E111 which you should take with you when you go abroad. If you are ill, you should, if possible, take your form E111 to the local sickness insurance office before you seek treatment; if you are unable to go first, show your form to the doctor who is treating you. You may have to pay, but will be partially reimbursed; keep the receipts, including any for medicines.

Not everyone is eligible: check carefully before you go. In any case, it is advisable to take out separate medical insurance.

Money
Hotel Deposits (*arrhes*) Usually demanded especially for high season bookings. An ordinary cheque written out in francs is acceptable; or a Eurocheque, or a banker's draft.

Changing money Before you go, buy some francs in cash from a bank (most ferries have exchange facilities, but they are usually crowded). On top of that, you'll probably need some travellers' cheques. French franc-denominated cheques generally give you slightly better value than sterling ones – despite their greater initial cost—as the exchange rates French banks offer for sterling cheques tend to be rather poor. But you may still find yourself asked to pay commission for changing French franc cheques. If that happens, try another bank. Some hotels accept French franc travellers' cheques at face value, though you can't rely on it; and some exchange cash and sterling travellers' cheques, usually at fairly unfavourable rates.

Eurocheques are very convenient, as you can use them to pay bills in hotels, shops and restaurants, as well as to obtain cash in banks. Apply to your bank at least a fortnight before you go for a supply of cheques and the necessary bank card, which costs £3.50 a year. There is a small handling charge for each cheque.

Credit Cards Major credit cards (Access and Visa—Carte Bleue) are quite widely accepted, though it's unwise to rely on them for buying petrol as you might in Britain. On average, you're likely to lose out on the exchange rate by using them rather than changing money in a bank—but exchange rate fluctuations between the date when you use your card and the date when your bill is calculated can work either way.

Charge cards such as American Express and Diners Club are quite useful for hotels, restaurants and smart shops, though using them will normally work out more expensive than Access or Visa.

Opening hours

Banks Normally open at 9am, close at lunch (12 noon or 12.30pm to about 2pm) and close at about 4.30pm. All close on Sunday; some close on Monday and open for Saturday markets. Crédit Agricole branches sometimes open on Saturday in towns where there is no Saturday market.

Shops Food shops open at about 8am, close at lunch, and open at about 2pm to about 6pm or 7pm. They usually open on Saturday morning, and often on Sunday morning, but may close on Monday. Supermarkets and hypermarkets are usually closed on Sunday, but stay open on Monday.

Restaurants Almost all small town and rural restaurants open for Sunday lunch, but many close on Sunday evening, and on another day in the week. In large towns and cities, many close on Sunday.

Museums and châteaux Many are shut on Tuesday.

Public holidays

Most shops and banks are shut on the following days; if any fall on a Sunday, the holiday is taken on the following day. If they fall on a Tuesday or Friday, the day between it and the nearest Sunday is also taken as a holiday.

New Year's Day; **Easter Monday** (moveable); **Labour Day** 1 May; **VE Day** 8 May; **Ascension Day** 6th Thursday after Easter; **Whit Monday** 2nd Monday after Ascension; **Bastille Day** 14 July; **Assumption** 15 August; **All Saints** (*Toussaint*) 1 November; **Armistice Day** 11 November; **Christmas Day**.

Beaches and bathing

Sea water temperature varies surprisingly little along the length of France's Channel and Atlantic coasts – in midsummer for example the northern French sea is only a couple of degrees cooler than the Basque and Landes coasts (high 'teens C, mid 60s F). The Mediterranean is significantly warmer; and the waters of the Côte d'Azur are warmer than those of the Languedoc coast.

On the Mediterranean coast, public beaches are free (but more generally litter strewn and lacking in facilities); most resorts have a more attractive fee-paying stretch with facilities including sun-loungers, sun-shades, showers, and cafés. On the Atlantic and Channel coasts, beaches are almost always free.

Almost all resort beaches have a lifeguard, or notices and warning signs about dangerous currents and tides. Most resorts have a supervised children's activity area (often called Mickey Club) for which there is a daily charge.

Some parts of the Mediterranean coast are polluted. French consumer organisations monitor bad beaches and improvements: they publish details in the Magazines *Que Choisir* and *50 Million de Consommateurs*, with occasional special issues. Enquire at *Syndicats d'Initiative*.

Metrication
1 kilo (1,000 grams)=2.2 lbs. 1 litre=1¾ pints. 1 gallon=4.54 litres. To convert Centigrade to Fahrenheit, multiply by 9, divide by 5 and add 32.

Telephoning
Since October 1985 French telephone numbers have all been 8-figure, incorporating what used to be the 2-figure *département* code whether or not the call is long distance. The only dialing extra is for calls between Paris (*Région Parisienne*) and the rest of France (*Province*). From Paris to the rest: dial 16, wait for a tone change, then dial the 8-figure number. To Paris from the rest: dial 16, wait for a tone change, then dial 1 followed by the 8-figure number. For calls to the UK, dial 19, wait for a tone change, then dial 44 followed by the UK area code (but omit the first 0—for example, the code for London will simply be 1) followed by the number. For directory enquiries, dial 12; operator 13; telegrams 14; police 17; fire 18.

Tipping
Restaurants Most restaurants include a service charge in their prices; a few exclude it from their prices but mention it in small print on the menu and add it on before the final addition.
Cafés Service is nearly always included in the price of drinks if you sit down, usually excluded if you stand at the bar.
Hotels Porters hover.
Taxis Tip expected.
Public lavatories Very often guarded by fierce women who do not expect tips, simply charge an entrance fee, however agonised your plea.
Cinemas Tip the usherette.
Garages *Pompistes*, even in motorway service stations, very often clean windscreens and check oil. Tips are welcomed, but not expected.

Festivals and Events

January	Monte Carlo Rally
February	Lemon Festival, Menton Nice Carnival
March	Black Pudding Festival, Mortagne-au-Perche, Normandy "Foire à la Ferraille et au Jambons" (Junk Fair), Châtou, near Paris.
April	Daffodil Festival, Gérardmer, Alsace
May	Paris Marathon Monaco Grand Prix Cannes Film Festival Gipsy Festival, Stes-Maries-de-la-Mer, Camargue

May–June	International Tennis Championship, Paris
June	Le Mans 24-hour race
July	Bastille Day Tour de France French Grand Prix Nice Jazz Festival Antibes Jazz Festival Aix-en-Provence International Festival of music and opera Avignon Festival of music and drama
July–August	"Chorégies d'Orange" (opera and recitals in the Théatre Antique)
August	Deauville Grand Prix Cannes Fireworks Festival Blue Fishing Nets Festival, Concarneau Assumption Day celebrations, Brittany
September	Wine and beer festivals in Alsace
October	Grand Prix de l'Arc de Triomphe, Longchamp
November	Dijon Gastronomic Fair "Trois Glorieuses" at Clos de Vougeot, Beaune, Meursault
December	Christmas crib festivities (especially in Provence)

Further information

The French Government Tourist Office, 178 Piccadilly, London W1V 0AL, has a public information service; you can call at their office (open Monday to Friday from 9am to 5pm), or telephone 01-491 7622 (although their lines are very often engaged).

In France, there are local *Offices de Tourisme* and *Syndicats d'Initiative* in almost every town and resort. They can advise on accommodation, restaurants, entertainments and local transport.

Glossary of Food

Agneau lamb; de pré-salé pastured on salt meadows
Aiglefin haddock
Aiguillettes long slices, usually poultry or game
Ail garlic
Aile wing
Aïoli garlic mayonnaise
Alose shad
Alsacienne (à l') usually with sauerkraut, ham and sausages
Armoricaine (à la) with sauce of tomatoes, herbs, white wine, brandy
Amuse-gueule appetizer served with aperitif
Ananas pineapple
Andouille, andouillette pork sausage of chitterlings and tripe
Aneth dill
Anglaise (à l') plain boiled
Anguilles au vert eels with white wine and herbs
Avelines hazelnuts

Ballotine boned, stuffed and bundled
Bar sea-bass
Barbeau barbel (river fish)
Barbue brill
Basilic basil
Baudroie lotte, monkfish
Bavarois custard cream dessert, often flavoured or with fruit
Béarnaise sauce flavoured with tarragon and vinegar
Beignet fritter
Bercy sauce with wine, shallots and bone marrow
Berrichonne (à la) with bacon, cabbage, onions and chestnuts
Betterave beetroot
Beurre blanc butter sauce with shallots and dry wine or vinegar
Beurre noir browned butter with vinegar
Bigarade bitter orange sauce
Bigorneau winkle
Bisque thick cream shellfish soup
Blanchailles whitebait
Blanquette thickened white stew
Boeuf à la mode beef braised in red wine with vegetables
Bonne femme poached in white wine with onions and mushrooms
Bordelaise sauce of red wine and bone marrow

Bouchée tiny filled puff pastry
Boudin large fat sausage
Bouillabaisse Provençal fish soup with wine, garlic, tomato and saffron
Boulangère (à la) braised or baked with onions and potatoes
Bourgeoise (à la) with carrots, onions and bacon
Bourguignonne (à la) cooked with burgundy, onions and mushrooms
Bourride creamy Provençal fish soup with aïoli
Brandade de morue creamed salt cod with oil and garlic
Brème freshwater bream
Bretonne (à la) served with haricot beans, sometimes as a purée
Broche (à la) spit roasted
Brochet pike
Brugnon nectarine
Bruxelloise (à la) served with Brussels sprouts and chicory

Cabillaud cod
Caille quail
Calmar inkfish, squid
Caneton duckling
Capoum rascasse, scorpion fish
Carbonnade de boeuf beef braised in beer, onions and herbs
Cardinal rich, red fish sauce with mushrooms, truffles (usually for lobster)
Cargolade snails cooked in wine
Carré d'agneau rack of lamb
Carrelet plaice
Cassis blackcurrant
Cassoulet casserole of beans and varied meats eg pork and goose
Céleri celery
Céleri-rave celeriac
Cèpes fine, delicate mushrooms
Cerfeuil chervil
Cerise cherry
Cerneau green walnut
Cervelle brains
Chanterelles mushrooms
Chapon capon
Châteaubriand thick centre cut of fillet of beef
Chausson puff pastry turnover
Chemise (en) wrapped, generally in pastry
Chevreuil roe-deer
Chicorée curly endive

Chipirons à l'encre squid, stuffed and stewed in their ink
Choron Béarnaise sauce with tomato purée
Choucroute garni sauerkraut with various sausages and potatoes
Ciboule spring onion
Ciboulettes chives
Citron pressée fresh lemon juice
Citron vert lime
Civet rich game stew
Civet de lièvre jugged hare
Civettes chives
Clafoutis batter cake with fruit
Cocotte small cooking dish
Coing quince
Colin hake
Confit(e) preserved or candied
Confit de canard (d'oie) potted duck (goose) cooked and preserved in its own fat
Contrefilet part of the sirloin
Corbeille de fruits basket of fresh fruit
Coque cockle
Coquillages shellfish
Coquilles St-Jacques scallops
Cornichon gherkin
Côte de/côtelette chop
Cou (d'oie) neck (of goose)
Coulibiac fish cake (usually salmon) in pastry
Coulis thick sauce or purée, of vegetables or fruit
Court-bouillon aromatic poaching liquid
Crécy (à la) with carrots
Crème anglaise light custard
Crémet fresh cream cheese eaten with sugar and cream
Cresson watercress
Crevettes grises shrimps
Crevettes roses prawns
Croque monsieur toasted cheese sandwich with ham
Croustade mould or puff pastry shell with various savoury fillings
Croûte (en) pastry case (in a)
Cru raw
Crudités (pieces of) raw vegetables
Crustacés shellfish

Darne large fish steak
Daube meat slowly braised in wine and herbs
Daurade sea bream

Diable highly seasoned sauce; also type of cooking pot
Dijonnais (à la) with mustard sauce
Dinde (dindon) turkey
Dorade red sea bream
Doux (douce) sweet
Duxelles stuffing or seasoning of cooked minced mushrooms

Ecrevisses freshwater crayfish
Endive chicory
Entremets desserts
Epaule shoulder
Epinards spinach
Epis de maïs sweetcorn
Espadon swordfish
Estouffade as *daube*; meat is first marinated and browned
Estragon tarragon

Faisan pheasant
Farci(e) stuffed
Faux-filet part of the sirloin
Fenouil fennel
Fève broad bean
Flageolets kidney beans; fresh green, dried white
Flétan halibut
Foie liver
Foie gras goose liver
Fonds d'artichauts artichoke hearts
Forestière (à la) with bacon and mushrooms
Four (au) baked
Fourré stuffed
Frais cool
Fraises des bois wild strawberries
Framboise raspberry
Frappé iced or chilled
Fricandeau topside of veal
Fricadelles small balls of minced meat
Fricassée creamy stew of white meat
Friture small fried fish
Fruits de mer seafood

Galantine cold pressed poultry, meat or fish in jelly
Gamba large prawn
Garbure thick vegetable soup
Gardons small roach
Gaufre waffle
Genièvre juniper
Gésier gizzard
Gibier game
Gigot leg of lamb or mutton

Glossary of Food

Gingembre ginger
Girolles/chanterelles mushrooms
Gougère cheese-enriched choux batter
Goujon gudgeon
Goujonnettes small fried fillets
Gourmandise sweetmeat
Grand Veneur sauce for game with wine, redcurrants, pepper
Granité grainy water ice
Gratin/gratiné browned topping, often with breadcrumbs or cheese
Gratin Dauphinois sliced potatoes baked with cream and garlic (eggs and cheese often added)
Grecque (à la) vegetables cooked and marinated in wine, spices and herbs
Grenade pomegranate
Grenouilles (cuisses de) frogs (frogs' legs)
Griotte bitter red cherry
Groseille, groseille à maquereau gooseberry
Groseille rouge redcurrant
Groseille noire blackcurrant

Hareng herring
Hareng fumé kipper
Hareng salé bloater
Haricots blancs dried white beans
Haricots rouges red kidney beans
Haricots verts French (string) beans
Hochepot thick casserole
Hollandaise sauce with butter, egg yolk and lemon juice
Homard lobster
Hongroise (à la) with paprika, tomato, onions and cream
Huile oil
Huître oyster

Ile flottante dessert of poached egg whites in vanilla custard

Jambon Bayonne/à la bayonnaise mild ham cooked partly in wine
Jambon persillé cold pressed ham and parsley in white wine jelly
Jambonneau small ham, knuckle of pork
Jardinière with diced mixed vegetables
Julienne with matchsticks of vegetables

Laitue lettuce
Lamproie river lamprey, eel-like fish
Langouste spiny lobster, crayfish
Langoustine scampi

Langue tongue
Lapin rabbit
Lapereau young rabbit
Lavaret lake fish of salmon type
Lièvre hare
Limande lemon sole
Lotte de mer monkfish, anglerfish
Lotte de rivière burbot, river fish
Loup de mer sea-bass
Lyonnaise (à la) with onions

Macédoine mixture of diced fruit or vegetables
Magret (de canard) fillet, breast (of duck)
Mangetout young peas in the pod, eaten whole
Maquereau mackerel
Marcassin young wild boar
Marchand de vin in a red wine sauce
Marengo (poulet) fried chicken, eggs, and tomatoes with garlic, brandy and crayfish
Marjolaine marjoram
Marmite tall cooking pot
Marron glacé candied chestnut
Matelote (d'anguilles) wine stew of freshwater fish and eel
Merlan whiting (hake in S. France)
Mérou bland Mediterranean fish
Mesclun mixture of salad leaves
Meunière (fish) cooked in butter with lemon juice and parsley
Mirabelle small golden plum
Moelle bone marrow (usually beef)
Montmorency with cherries
Morille type of mushroom
Morue salt cod
Mouclade mussels in creamy sauce with saffron, turmeric and wine
Moules (à la) marinière mussels cooked in white wine with shallots
Mousseline hollandaise sauce with whipped cream
Mulet grey mullet
Mûres mulberries
Myrtilles bilberries

Nage (à la) (shellfish) poached in court bouillon with herbs
Nantua cream sauce for fish with crayfish purée
Navarin mutton or lamb stew with potatoes and onions
Navet turnip

Noisette small round steak
Noix (de veau) topside of leg (veal)
Normande (à la) with cream and any
or all of: calvados, cider, apples
Nouilles flat noodles

Oeufs eggs
    brouillés scrambled
    en cocotte baked in oven
    à la coque soft boiled
    durs hard boiled
    mollets soft boiled
    à la neige see *île flottante*
    sur le plat cooked in butter in a
    shallow dish in the oven
    pochés poached
    poêlés fried
Oie goose
Omble chevalier freshwater char, type
of salmon
Ombre grayling
Omelette Norvégienne meringue-
covered sponge and ice-cream; like
Baked Alaska
Orange (jus d') usually canned or
bottled orange juice
Orange pressée fresh orange juice
Oseille sorrel
Oursin sea-urchin

Palmier (coeurs de) palm hearts
Palourdes farcies cooked stuffed clams
Pamplemousse grapefruit
Panais parsnip
Pan bagnat large bread roll filled with
salad, olive oil, anchovies
Papillote (en) baked in a packet of
grease-proof paper or foil
Parfait (de) creamy iced mousse
Pastèque watermelon
Pâte brisée shortcrust pastry
Paupiette thin slice (of meat or fish)
stuffed, rolled and braised
Pavé (slab) thick slice
Perdreau young partridge
Persil parsley
Petite marmite individual pot of
consommé
Pétoncle small scallop
Pieds de porc pigs' trotters
Pigeonneau young pigeon, squab
Pignons pine kernels
Piment doux sweet pepper
Pintade guinea-fowl

Pipérade scrambled mixture of eggs,
onions, green peppers and tomatoes
Pissaladière dough-based tart of
onions, tomatoes, anchovies, black
olives
Pissenlits dandelion leaves
Pistaches pistachio nuts
Pistou (soupe au) strong vegetable
soup with garlic, basil and thick
vermicelli
Plie franche plaice
Pochouse stew of eel and other
freshwater fish in white wine
Poire pear
Poireau leek
Poivrade peppery sauce served with
game (roebuck)
Poivre pepper
Poivron sweet pepper, pimento
Polonaise (à la) with browned
breadcrumbs, chopped hard-boiled
eggs, parsley and butter
Pommes apples
Pommes de terre potatoes
    à l'anglaise boiled
    à la vapeur steamed
    allumettes matchsticks, fried
    boulangère, rôtie roast
    frites deep fried (chips)
    lyonnaise sautéed with onions
    nature, au naturel boiled
    purée de mashed
Porc (carré de) loin of pork
Porcelet suckling pig
Portugaise (à la) includes tomatoes
Potage thick soup
Pot-au-chocolat chocolate cream
dessert
Pot-au-feu boiled beef, vegetables and
broth
Potée heavy soup of various meats,
cabbage, beans/lentils
Poulet chicken
Poussin small baby chicken
Praires small clams
Printanière (à la) with mixed spring
vegetables
Provençal (à la) with tomatoes, oil
and garlic
Prune plum
Pruneau prune

Quenelle light poached dumpling of
fish, veal or poultry
Quetsche small, purple plum

443

Glossary of Food

Queue de boeuf oxtail

Râble de (lièvre/lapin) saddle of (hare/rabbit)
Ragoût stew, usually meat
Raie skate
Raifort horseradish
Raisin grape
Rascasse scorpion fish
Ratatouille stew of aubergines, courgettes, tomatoes, green and red peppers and onions in oil
Reine-claude greengage
Rémoulade sharp-flavoured mayonnaise
Rillettes potted pork seasoned with herbs or spices
Ris (d'agneau/de veau) sweetbreads (lamb or veal)
Rognon kidney
Romarin rosemary
Rôti roast
Rouget red mullet
Roulade (de) roll (of)
Rouille strongly flavoured creamy sauce served in/with fish soups
Royan large sardine
Rutabaga swede

Sabayon French version of Zabaglione
St-Germain with peas
St-Jacques see *coquilles*
St-Pierre John Dory
Saisons (suivant) depending on season
Salade niçoise substantial salad including eggs, green beans, olives, anchovies, sometimes tuna
Salade panachée mixed salad
Salade verte green salad
Salmis roast joints of game or poultry in a red wine sauce
Sandre river fish; pike-perch
Saucisse fresh raw sausage (sold uncooked)
Saucisson larger sausage for slicing (sold cooked)
Sauge sage
Saumon blanc hake
Scarole endive
Selle saddle
Selon grosseur/grandeur priced according to size (*sg* on menus)
Soissonnaise (à la) with white haricot beans

Sole:
   à Dieppoise fillets with sauce of mussels, shrimps and white wine
   Dugléré with tomatoes, onions, herbs and cream sauce
   Marguéry with mussels, shrimps and rich egg sauce
   Véronique poached in white wine with grapes
Soubise with purée of onions and sometimes rice
Suprême boneless breast or wing of poultry

Tartare (steak) finely minced steak served raw with raw egg yolk, onions and capers
Tarte Tatin substantial upside-down apple tart
Thon tuna fish
Thym thyme
Tiède lukewarm
Topinambour Jerusalem artichoke
Tournedos fillet steak
   chasseur with shallots, mushrooms, tomatoes
   Rossini topped with pâté in a madeira sauce
Tourte covered savoury tart
Tourteau large crab
Truffes truffles
Truite (au bleu) trout poached in vinegar *court bouillon*, giving a blue tinge to skin
Ttoro Basque fish stew

Vacherin meringue ring filled with whipped cream, ice-cream and fruit
Vallée d'Auge with Calvados, apples and cream
Veau veal
   pané breadcrumbed escalope
   à la viennoise escalope with chopped egg, capers and parsley
Volaille poultry
Waterzooi freshwater fish or chicken stew

Hotel Maps

The maps on the following pages show the location
(in **bold** type) of our selected hotels throughout France

A **North-West**
B **North-East**
C **Central**
D **Southern**

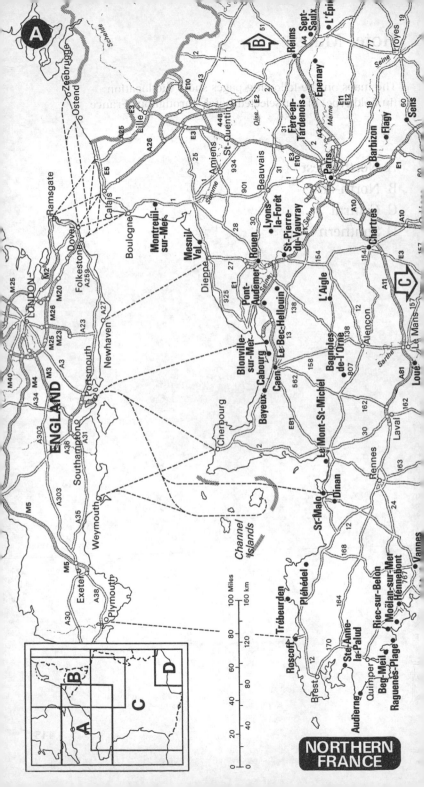

NORTHERN FRANCE

0 20 40 60 80 100 Miles
0 40 80 120 160 km

NETHERLANDS

Ems

Waal

Maas

Ruhr

Zeebrugge
Ostend

E5

Schelde

WEST

A25
E3
Lille
A26

GERMANY

BELGIUM

Rhine

E3
E10

2

Amiens
44B
St-Quentin
934

Oise E2

51

LUXEMBOURG

uvais

31
E3
E10

31

Fère-en-
Tardenois

Reims

18

A31

Sarre

2

A4

Sept-
Saulx

Verdun

A4

Paris

A4

Epernay

Marne

L'Épine

E11
E12

Moselle

A31

E12

Nancy

Marlenheim

A4

Barbizon

19

Seine

77

E1

Flagy

60

Troyes

19

E2

Chaumont

Strasbourg

Ottrott-le-Haut
Colroy-la-Roche

Obernai

E9

Sens

57

Lapoutroie 415
Kaysersberg

Ribeauvillé
Artzenheim

La Celle-
St-Cyr

St-Florentin

Joigny

A31

Gérardmer
Ammerschwihr

Colmar
Rouffach

Auxerre

Mailly-le-Château

71

E17

57

66

19

Vézelay

St-Père-
sous-Vézelay

Val-Suzon

E2

Saône

Belfort

A36

Pouilly-
sur-Loire

151

Bouilland

Dijon

Gevrey-Chambertin

NORTH-EAST
FRANCE

E43
E1

C

h. Collins, Sons & Co. Ltd.

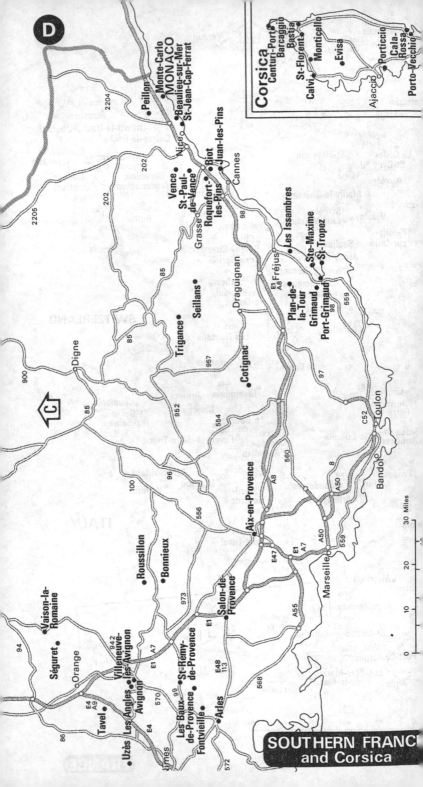

D

**SOUTHERN FRANCE
and Corsica**

Hotels Index

Hotels Index

Town	(Chapter)	Hotel	Page
Agde	(The South)	Tamarissière	143
Aïnhoa	(Pyrenees)	Ithurria	199
L'Aigle	(Normandy)	Dauphin	330
Aix-en-Provence	(The South)	Augustins	143
Aix-en-Provence	(The South)	Manoir	143
Aix-en-Provence	(The South)	Mas d'Entremont	143
Aloxe-Corton	(Burgundy, Rhône)	Clarion	101
Amboise	(Loire Valley)	Lion d'Or	276
Ammerschwihr	(Alsace, Lorraine)	Armes de France	374
Les Angles	(The South)	Hostellerie Meissonnier	144
Arbois	(Burgundy, Rhône)	Paris	101
Arlempdes	(Massif Central)	Manoir	174
Arles	(The South)	Arlatan	144
Arnay-le-Duc	(Burgundy, Rhône)	Chez Camille	101
Arpaillargues	(The South)	Château d'Arpaillargues	144
Artzenheim	(Alsace, Lorraine)	Auberge d'Artzenheim	374
Audierne	(Brittany)	Goyen	304
Avignon	(The South)	Auberge de Cassagne	145
Avignon	(The South)	Europe	144
Azay-le-Rideau	(Loire Valley)	Grand Monarque	276
Bagnoles-de-l'Orne	(Normandy)	Bois-Joli	331
Barbizon	(Ile de France)	Clé d'Or	82
Barcaggio	(Corsica)	Giraglia	421
Bastia	(Corsica)	Pietracap	421
La Baule	(Brittany)	Cantellerie	305
La Baule	(Brittany)	Musset	305
Les Baux-de-Provence	(The South)	Cabro d'Or	145
Les Baux-de-Provence	(The South)	Mas d'Aigret	145
Bayeux	(Normandy)	Argouges	331
Beaugency	(Loire Valley)	Abbaye	276
Beaugency	(Loire Valley)	Ecu de Bretagne	276
Beaulieu	(The South)	Métropole	145
Beaune	(Burgundy, Rhône)	Cep	102
Beaune	(Burgundy, Rhône)	Parc	102
Le Bec Hellouin	(Normandy)	Auberge de l'Abbaye	331
Beg-Meil	(Brittany)	Thalamot	305
Belle-Ile-en-Mer	(Brittany)	Castel Clara	305
Belle-Ile-en-Mer	(Brittany)	Manoir de Goulphar	305
Besse-en-Chandesse	(Massif Central)	Mouflons	174
Beynac-et-Cazenac	(Dordogne)	Bonnet	231
Biot	(The South)	Café des Arcades	146
Blonville-sur-Mer	(Normandy)	Grand	331
Bonnieux	(The South)	Aiguebrun	146
Bordeaux	(Atlantic Coast)	Etche-Ona	249
Bouilland	(Burgundy, Rhône)	Vieux Moulin	102
Le Bourget-du-Lac	(Alps)	Ombremont	396
Brantôme	(Dordogne)	Châtenet	232
Brantôme	(Dordogne)	Moulin de l'Abbaye	231
Bresson	(Alps)	Chavant	396
Brinon-sur-Sauldre	(Loire Valley)	Solognote	277
Cabourg	(Normandy)	Moulin du Pré	332
Cabrerets	(Dordogne)	Pescalerie	232
Caen	(Normandy)	Relais des Gourmets	332
Calès	(Dordogne)	Pagès	232
Calvi	(Corsica)	Grand	421
Cambo-les-Bains	(Pyrenees)	Errobia	199
La Celle-Saint-Cyr	(Burgundy, Rhône)	Fontaine aux Muses	102
Centuri-Port	(Corsica)	Vieux Moulin	422
Céret	(Pyrenees)	Terrace au Soleil	200
Chagny	(Burgundy, Rhône)	Lameloise	103
Chamalières	(Massif Central)	Radio	174
Chambord	(Loire Valley)	St-Michel	277
Chamonix	(Alps)	Auberge du Bois Prin	397
Champagnac-de-Belair	(Dordogne)	Moulin du Roc	232
Charolles	(Burgundy, Rhône)	Poste	103
La Chartre-sur-le-Loir	(Loire Valley)	France	277

Hotels Index

Hotels Index

Hotel	Town	(Chapter)	Page
Deux Rocs	Seillans	(The South)	154
Dolce Notte	St-Florent	(Corsica)	423
Domaine de Bassibé	Ségos	(Pyrenees)	203
Domaine de Beauvois	Luynes	(Loire Valley)	279
Domaine des Hauts de Loire	Onzain	(Loire Valley)	279
Ecu de Bretagne	Beaugency	(Loire Valley)	276
Elizabeth	St-Malo	(Brittany)	308
Entraigues	Uzès	(The South)	155
Errobia	Cambo-les-Bains	(Pyrenees)	199
Espérance	Pouilly-sur-Loire	(Loire Valley)	280
Espérance	St-Père-sous-Vézelay	(Burgundy, Rhône)	106
Esplanade	Domme	(Dordogne)	233
Esterel	Juan-les-Pins	(The South)	147
Etche-Ona	Bordeaux	(Atlantic Coast)	249
Europe	Avignon	(The South)	144
Faudé	Lapoutroie	(Alsace, Lorraine)	375
Fayette	St-Jean-de-Luz	(Atlantic Coast)	250
Fleurie	Montsalvy	(Massif Central)	175
Fontaine aux Muses	La Celle-Saint-Cyr	(Burgundy, Rhône)	102
France	La Chartre-sur-le-Loir	(Loire Valley)	277
France	Nantua	(Alps)	398
France	Les Rousses	(Burgundy, Rhône)	105
Georges Blanc	Vonnas	(Burgundy, Rhône)	107
Giraglia	Barcaggio	(Corsica)	421
Giraglia	Port-Grimaud	(The South)	149
Goyen	Audierne	(Brittany)	304
Grand	Blonville-sur-Mer	(Normandy)	331
Grand	Calvi	(Corsica)	421
Grand Cerf	Lyons-la-Forêt	(Normandy)	332
Grand Ecuyer	Cordes	(Dordogne)	233
Grand Hôtel de L'Opéra	Toulouse	(Pyrenees)	204
Grand Hôtel de la Reine	Nancy	(Alsace, Lorraine)	376
Grand Hôtel du Lion d'Or	Romorantin-Lanthenay	(Loire Valley)	280
Grand Hôtel de Cala Rossa	Porto-Vecchio	(Corsica)	423
Grand Monarque	Azay-le-Rideau	(Loire Valley)	276
Grand Monarque	Chartres	(Ile de France)	82
Grande Chaumière	St-Florentin	(Burgundy, Rhône)	106
Grands Crus	Gevrey-Chambertin	(Burgundy, Rhône)	104
Gulf Stream	Roscoff	(Brittany)	307
Hameau	St-Paul-de-Vence	(The South)	151
Hermitage	Monte-Carlo	(The South)	148
Hospitaliers	Poët-Laval	(The South)	149
Hosten	Langeais	(Loire Valley)	278
Ithurria	Aïnhoa	(Pyrenees)	199
Jeanne de Laval	Les Rosiers-sur-Loire	(Loire Valley)	280
Korrigane	St-Malo	(Brittany)	308
Laborderie	Tamniès	(Dordogne)	235
Lameloise	Chagny	(Burgundy, Rhône)	103
Lion d'Or	Amboise	(Loire Valley)	276
Lou Calen	Cotignac	(The South)	146
Lou Mazuc	Laguiole	(Massif Central)	174
Madone	Peillon	(The South)	148
Magnanerie	Villeneuve-lès-Avignon	(The South)	155
Manoir	Aix-en-Provence	(The South)	143
Manoir	Arlempdes	(Massif Central)	174
Manoir Bel Air	St-Dyé-sur-Loire	(Loire Valley)	280
Manoir de Goulphar	Belle-Ile-en-Mer	(Brittany)	305
Manoir de Lan Kerellec	Trébeurden	(Brittany)	308
Maquis	Porticcio	(Corsica)	422

Hotels Index

Hotel	Town	(Chapter)	Page
Marais Saint-Jean	Chonas-l'Amballan	(Burgundy, Rhône)	103
Marie-Louise	Ste-Maxime	(The South)	153
Mas d'Aigret	Les Baux-de-Provence	(The South)	145
Mas d'Entremont	Aix-en-Provence	(The South)	143
Mas de Chastelas	St-Tropez	(The South)	152
Mas de Garrigon	Roussillon	(The South)	150
Mas des Brugassières	Plan-de-la-Tour	(The South)	148
Mas des Carassins	St-Rémy-de-Provence	(The South)	152
Meaulnes	Nançay	(Loire Valley)	279
Meissonnier, L'Ermitage	Les Angles	(The South)	144
Mère Poularde	Le Mont-St-Michel	(Normandy)	333
Métropole	Beaulieu	(The South)	145
Mimosas	Juan-les-Pins	(The South)	147
Mouflons	Besse-en-Chandesse	(Massif Central)	174
Mouli del Riu	Mont-Louis	(Pyrenees)	201
Moulin	Flagy	(Ile de France)	82
Moulin de l'Abbaye	Brantôme	(Dordogne)	231
Moulin de la Beune	Les Eyzies-de-Tayac	(Dordogne)	234
Moulin du Pré	Cabourg	(Normandy)	332
Moulin du Roc	Champagnac-de-Belair	(Dordogne)	232
Moulins du Duc	Moëlan-sur-Mer	(Brittany)	306
Musset	La Baule	(Brittany)	305
Ombremont	Le Bourget-du-Lac	(Alps)	396
Orangers	St-Paul-de-Vence	(The South)	151
Oustal	Unac	(Pyrenees)	204
Pagès	Calès	(Dordogne)	232
Parc	Beaune	(Burgundy, Rhône)	102
Parc	Obernai	(Alsace, Lorraine)	376
Paris	Arbois	(Burgundy, Rhône)	101
Paris et Poste	Sens	(Burgundy, Rhône)	106
Pastorella	Monticello	(Corsica)	422
Pelissaria	St-Cirq-Lapopie	(Dordogne)	235
Pescalerie	Cabrerets	(Dordogne)	232
Pietracap	Bastia	(Corsica)	421
Plage	Ste-Anne-la-Palud	(Brittany)	308
Plaisance	St-Emilion	(Atlantic Coast)	250
Ponche	St-Tropez	(The South)	152
Pont d'Ouchet	Onzain	(Loire Valley)	279
Pont de l'Ouysse	Lacave	(Dordogne)	234
Pont des Bannes	Les Saintes-Maries-de-la-Mer	(The South)	153
Ponte Romano	Plan-de-la-Tour	(The South)	149
Poste	Charolles	(Burgundy, Rhône)	103
Poste	Oust	(Pyrenees)	201
Poste	St-Jean-de-Luz	(Atlantic Coast)	250
Poste de Lion d'Or	Vézelay	(Burgundy, Rhône)	107
Praies	Lanslevillard	(Alps)	397
Pré Bossu	Moudeyres	(Massif Central)	175
Pré de la Mer	St-Tropez	(The South)	153
Prés d'Eugénie	Eugénie-les-Bains	(Pyrenees)	200
Pyrénées	St-Jean-Pied-de-Port	(Pyrenees)	202
Radio	Chamalières	(Massif Central)	174
Réserve	Les Issambres	(The South)	147
Regalido	Fontvieille	(The South)	146
Relais des Gourmets	Caen	(Normandy)	332
Relais St-Jacques de Compostelle	Collonges-la-Rouge	(Dordogne)	233
Remparts	Kaysersberg	(Alsace, Lorraine)	375
Renaissance/St-Sauveur	Meyrueis	(Massif Central)	175
Ricordeau	Loué	(Loire Valley)	278
Ripa Alta	Plaisance	(Pyrenees)	202
Rohan	Strasbourg	(Alsace, Lorraine)	377
Roof	Vannes	(Brittany)	309
Royal Champagne	Epernay	(The North)	353

Hotels Index Out of Paris

Index

465

Hotel reports

The report forms on the following pages may be used to endorse or criticise an existing entry or to nominate a hotel that you feel deserves inclusion in the next edition of the *Guide*, or in an issue of *Holiday Which?* magazine. There is no need to restrict yourself to the space available. All nominations should include your name and address, the name and location of the hotel, when you stayed there and for how long.

There is no need to give details of prices or number of rooms and facilities, as all nominated hotels will be inspected by the *Holiday Which?* team. We are anxious to find out from readers details of food, service and atmosphere, and should also be grateful for any brochures and menus.

To: *The Holiday Which? Guide to France*
Freepost, London WC2N 6BR

Name of hotel ....

Address ....

....

Date of most recent visit ....

Duration of visit ....

Report:

(Continue overleaf if you wish or use separate sheet)

Signed ....

Name and address (CAPITALS PLEASE) ....

....

To: *The Holiday Which? Guide to France*
Freepost, London WC2N 6BR

NOTE No stamps needed in UK, but letters posted outside the UK should be addressed to 14 Buckingham Street, London WC2N 6DS and stamped normally. It is not our policy to publish names of readers who recommend a new hotel or criticise an existing entry. Unless asked not to, we shall assume that we may publish extracts from any report either in the *Guide* or in the magazine
Holiday Which?

Name of hotel ....

Address ....

....

Date of most recent visit ....

Duration of visit ....

Report:

(Continue overleaf if you wish or use separate sheet)

Signed ....

Name and address (CAPITALS PLEASE) ....

....

To: *The Holiday Which? Guide to France*
Freepost, London WC2N 6BR

NOTE No stamps needed in UK, but letters posted outside the UK should be addressed to 14 Buckingham Street, London WC2N 6DS and stamped normally. It is not our policy to publish names of readers who recommend a new hotel or criticise an existing entry. Unless asked not to, we shall assume that we may publish extracts from any report either in the *Guide* or in the magazine
Holiday Which?

Name of hotel ....

Address ....

....

Date of most recent visit ....

Duration of visit ....

Report:

(Continue overleaf if you wish or use separate sheet)

Signed ....

Name and address (CAPITALS PLEASE) ....

....

To: *The Holiday Which? Guide to France*
Freepost, London WC2N 6BR

NOTE No stamps needed in UK, but letters posted outside the UK should be addressed to 14 Buckingham Street, London WC2N 6DS and stamped normally. It is not our policy to publish names of readers who recommend a new hotel or criticise an existing entry. Unless asked not to, we shall assume that we may publish extracts from any report either in the *Guide* or in the magazine
Holiday Which?

Name of hotel ....

Address ....

....

Date of most recent visit ....

Duration of visit ....

Report:

(Continue overleaf if you wish or use separate sheet)

Signed ....

Name and address (CAPITALS PLEASE) ....

....

To: *The Holiday Which? Guide to France*
Freepost, London WC2N 6BR

NOTE No stamps needed in UK, but letters posted outside the UK should be
addressed to 14 Buckingham Street, London WC2N 6DS and stamped
normally. It is not our policy to publish names of readers who recommend a
new hotel or criticise an existing entry. Unless asked not to, we shall assume
that we may publish extracts from any report either in the *Guide* or in the
magazine
Holiday Which?

Name of hotel ....

Address ....

....

Date of most recent visit ....

Duration of visit ....

Report:

(Continue overleaf if you wish or use separate sheet)

Signed ....

Name and address (CAPITALS PLEASE) ....

....

To: *The Holiday Which? Guide to France*
Freepost, London WC2N 6BR

NOTE No stamps needed in UK, but letters posted outside the UK should be addressed to 14 Buckingham Street, London WC2N 6DS and stamped normally. It is not our policy to publish names of readers who recommend a new hotel or criticise an existing entry. Unless asked not to, we shall assume that we may publish extracts from any report either in the *Guide* or in the magazine
Holiday Which?

Name of hotel ....

Address ....

....

Date of most recent visit ....

Duration of visit ....

Report:

(Continue overleaf if you wish or use separate sheet)

Signed ....

Name and address (CAPITALS PLEASE) ....

....